LAW AND THE INTERNET

Law and the Internet

A Framework for Electronic Commerce

Second Edition

Edited by

LILIAN EDWARDS and CHARLOTTE WAELDE

·HART·
PUBLISHING

OXFORD – PORTLAND OREGON
2000

Hart Publishing
Oxford and Portland, Oregon

Published in North America (US and Canada) by
Hart Publishing c/o
International Specialized Book Services
5804 NE Hassalo Street
Portland, Oregon
97213-3644
USA

Distributed in the Netherlands, Belgium and Luxembourg by
Intersentia, Churchillaan 108
B2900 Schoten
Antwerpen
Belgium

First Edition Published 1997, reprinted 1998 (3 times), 1999 (twice)

Hart Publishing Ltd is a specialist legal publisher based in Oxford, England.
To order further copies of this book or to request a list of other
publications please write to:

Hart Publishing Ltd, Salter's Boatyard,
Folly Bridge, Abingdon Road, Oxford OX1 4LB
Telephone: +44 (0)1865 245533 or Fax: +44 (0)1865 794882
e-mail: mail@hartpub.co.uk
WEBSITE: http//www.hartpub.co.uk

British Library Cataloguing in Publication Data
Data Available
ISBN 1 84113–141–5 (paperback)

Typeset by Hope Services (Abingdon) Ltd.
Printed and bound in Great Britain on acid-free paper by
Biddles Ltd, www.biddles.co.uk

Preface

Internet law, the subject of this volume of essays, emerged in the latter half of the Nineties as a novel and vociferous hybrid of several well established legal domains: intellectual property law, commercial law, contract law, and media law being some of the more obvious candidates. In similar style, this book is also a hybrid production: mainly new, but in small part, a second edition. Four of the essays, on lawyers and the Internet, copyright, trademarks and domain names, and defamation were to be found in, but have been entirely revised from, their predecessors in *Law and the Internet: Regulating Cyberspace* (Hart, 1997); the other ten chapters are entirely new. This in itself provides an index of how fast the speed of change has been in this new and vigorous area. When we began the process of editing this book, our intention was to provide some kind of overview of the development of global e-commerce before addressing the attendant legal issues; in a short space of time however it became apparent how futile an exercise this would be and how short the sell-by date of the result. In the space of a couple of years the dot.com bubble has boomed and bust; Amazon has become a household name and lastminute.com has gone to the wall; immediate legal attention in e-commerce practices has moved from fighting for domain names to fighting for stock options to fighting for the mailing lists of bankrupt e-start-ups. On the other hand in the UK, e-commerce transactions, worth around £2.8 billion in 1999, are still expected to grow by tenfold over the next ten years, according to the Government's *e-commerce@its.best.uk* report, while in the US, e-commerce is now said to be responsible for around 35% of real economic growth.

Net access, previously said to be restricted to an economically favoured, technocratic and mainly young, white and male elite has been widened out, in the developed world at least, to embrace women, children, the old, ethnic minorities and in general many who would previously have been thought to have been socially excluded. In the US, remarkably, it was reported that in May 2000 more than 50% of those surfing the Web were female, while "silver surfers", retired persons taking to the Web, are one of the fastest growing net-active groups. In the UK, in early 2000, 6.5 million households were reported to have Internet access while about one third of a billion people are on-line worldwide. Convergence, the ability to access the Internet from non-PC objects such as mobile phones and digital TVs, is already transforming access to Internet services and e-commerce. In the UK, Tony Blair has famously set the target that the UK is to become the best environment in the world for e-commerce and that by 2002, a higher percentage of both business-to-business (B2B) and business-to-consumers (B2C) transactions will be carried out here over e-commerce networks than in any other G7 country. In Europe, the EU has ambitiously embarked upon the eEurope 2002 initiative which intends to turn Europe into "the most competitive and dynamic economy in the world". In the meantime, in reality the USA continues to set the benchmarks for integration of e-commerce into the economy and the acts of super-corporations such as Microsoft and Time-Warner/AOL arguably have more significance for legal regulated phenomena such as privacy and consumer protection than many acts of the elected governors of nation-states.

Against this kind of background, it becomes plain that the regulation of e-commerce, by law and other means, is more than a moving target: it is one in a sort of constant and frantic Brownian motion, as global communities and their regulators, and the teachers and students of the discipline continue to discover to their fascination and dismay.

In consequence this book is in ambition relatively modest. It is not a book on "How to do business on the Internet." It merely attempts to describe, comment on and critique the legal developments relating to Internet law and e-commerce in what we saw as the key areas when the book was first imagined in early 1999. The book deals firstly with the vital components of entering e-business, such as electronic contracting, authentication of digital transactions, data protection and Internet payment mechanisms; moves on to look at the most important and relevant intellectual property concerns and associated issues of international private law; and finally looks at the issues of Internet content control, telecoms regulation and Internet Service provider liability, the last of which impacts on access to the Net for all. Although the focus is on UK law (with a certain added tartan twang as many of the authors are or were based in Scotland), inevitable and necessarily when talking about a globalised medium, the contributors have considered where appropriate the laws of other states such as the USA, Australia, and the countries of the European Union, as well as "soft law", trade practices and the many unconventional sources which inform Internet regulation including control by software ("code as code" in the famous parlance of Lawrence Lessig) and netiquette. The law is stated as at 31 March 2000; however it has been possible (and in some cases absolutely essential) to take into account later developments. The period of writing of this book has seen the passing of many important and influential pieces of legislation; in the UK, notably, the Electronic Communications Act 2000 and the notorious Regulation of Investigatory Powers Act 2000 (and its Scottish counterpart); in the EU, the Electronic Commerce Directive, which impacts on many of the chapters herein is reproduced in its final form while at the date of writing (October 2000) the ink is almost but not quite dry on the Draft Copyright Directive. Because of their overall importance, we have chosen to include the latter two instruments as Appendices, but not the UK legislation, since it is in any case readily and freely available on the Web.

As always with a book of this kind, more people than can be mentioned are owed thanks. Much of the Australian material within was collected by Lilian

Edwards during her sabbatical period in 1999 in the course of which she was made most welcome both at the Faculty of Law at Sydney University and at the Australasian Law Information Institute (AustLII), itself a joint institute of the University of Technology at Sydney and the University of New South Wales. Grateful thanks are due in particular to Philip Chung and Graham Greenleaf of AustLII, to Patrick Parkinson, Isabel Karpin and Kathryn McMahon at Sydney University, to Kathe Boehringer at Macquarie University, and to John MacPhail and Anne Flahvin at Baker and McKenzies, Solicitors, all of whom gave generously of their precious time and expertise. Charlotte Waelde is especially indebted to the numerous contributors to the discussion groups and information lists with which she is associated. Members of these groups, from all over the world, provide thoughtful and insightful comments and make contributions on a wide variety of e-commerce topics. As such, these communities provide a fertile testing ground for ideas, and in many cases give early warning of international developments which do or may impact on domestic practice. The members of these Internet communities have helped to ensure that the contents of this book reflect current thinking on the topics dealt with within its covers. Both editors must also express their thanks to Shepherd and Wedderburn, Solicitors, for their continuing support for SCRIPT, the Shepherd and Wedderburn Centre for Research into Intellectual Property and Technology established within the Law Faculty at Edinburgh University, and to our colleagues in SCRIPT, Professor Hector MacQueen and Graeme Laurie. Much of this book has been shaped by the need to create teaching materials for the Honours and Masters courses in IP and IT law taught by SCRIPT and has been enriched in return by that teaching experience. Finally of course both editors would like to express their thanks towards all the contributors for the time and effort they have been put into a book whose gestation period was rather more extended than was first proposed by the vagaries of the passing of European legislation.

Lilian Edwards and Charlotte Waelde,
Edinburgh, October 2000.

Contents

Table of Cases   xi

Table of Legislation   xxiii

List of Contributors   xxxv

1. The Internet – An Introduction For Lawyers   1
   Andrew Terrett and Iain Monaghan

Part 1: E-commerce issues

2. Entering Into Contracts Electronically: The Real W.W.W.   17
   Andrew D. Murray

3. Secrecy and Signatures – Turning the Legal Spotlight on   37
   Encryption and Electronic Signatures
   Martin Hogg

4. Payment in an On-Line World   55
   Saul Miller

5. Data Privacy in Cyberspace: Not National vs.   79
   International but Commercial vs. Individual.
   Andrew Charlesworth

Part 2: Intellectual Property

6. The Domain Name System   125
   William Black

7. Trade Marks and Domain Names: There's a Lot in a Name   133
   Charlotte Waelde

8. Trademarks – other Internet issues   171
   Charlotte Waelde

9. Copyright and the Internet   181
   Hector MacQueen

10. Private International Law Aspects of IP – Internet Disputes   225
    Paul Torremans

Part 3: Content Liability

11. Defamation and the Internet   249
    Lilian Edwards

12. Pornography and the Internet   275
     Lilian Edwards

13. Canning the Spam: Is There a Case for Legal Control of Junk   309
     Electronic Mail?
     Lilian Edwards

14. Legal Regulation of Telecommunications: The Impact on   331
     Internet Services
     Paul Carlyle

Appendix I Directive 2000/81EC   343

Appendix II Directive SN/2696/00 (PI)   367

Index   387

Table of Cases

A & M Records Inc. v. Napster Inc., (USDC No Cal., 5 May 2000)............188
ACLU v. Reno II, 31 F Supp 473 (ED Pa. 1999) 289
Adams v. Lindsell (1818) 1 B & Ald. 681 23
AKM v. X [1999] EIPR N-1 (S Ct of Austria) 199
Alcoholics Anonymous World Services Inc. v. Lauren Raymond, WIPO
   Case No. D2000–007 *(alcoholicsanonymous.com)* 163
America Online Inc. v. iDomainNames.com, National Arbitration Forum
   File No. FA0002000093766 *(go2aol.com)* 163
America Online Inc. v. IMS, 48 USPQ 2d 1857 (ED Va 1998)
   3 ECLR 1329..179, 315, 316
America Online inc. v. Prime Data Systems Inc., No. 97–1652–A
   (ED Va. 1998) 312, 316
Anacon Corp. Ltd. v. Environmental Research Technology
   [1994] FSR 659 189
Armitage Hardware v. Weber-Stephen Products, LEXIS 165
Asphaltic Limestone Concrete Co. Ltd. v. Glasgow Corp., 1907 SC 463 72
Atkins v. DPP; Goodland v. DPP [2000] All ER 425 ....285, 291
Att-Gen v. Guardian Newspapers Ltd. (No. 2) [1990] 1 AC 109 208
Audi-Med Trade Mark [1998] RPC 863 ....137, 145, 147
Avnet Inc. v. Isoact Ltd. [1998] FSR 16...................136, 138–40, 141
Avrahami v. US News & World Report Inc., No. 95–7479 (Arlington Co. Gen.
   Dist. Ct. filed Oct. 1995)...94

Baars Kaas and De Vijfheerenlanden BV v. Westland Kaas Export BV,
   Gerechthof Amsterdam, 4 Apr. 1984, [1986] BIE 77................241
Ballard v. Savage, 65 F 3d 1495, 1498 (9th Cir. 1995) 234
Bally Total Fitness Holding Corp. v. Faber, (CD Cal. 1998) No. CV 98 1278
   DDP (MANx) 172
Barr v. Lions Ltd., 1956 SC 59 31
Bata v. Bata [1948] WN 366..259
Baywatch Production Co. Inc. v. The Home Video Channel
   [1997] FSR 22 137
Beloff v. Pressdram [1973] RPC 765
Bensusan Restaurant Corp. v. King, 937 F Supp 295 (SD NY 1996) 234
Berezovsky v. Forbes [2000] 1 WLR 104......................................258
Bernstein v. JC Penney Inc., (CD Cal., 22 Sept. 1999) 186
Beverages and More Inc. v. Glenn Sobel Mgt, eResolution Case No.
   AF-0092 *(beveragesand-more.com)*...163

Blumenthal v. Drudge, 1998 BNA EC&L 561 ....264, 268
Board of Regents v. Roth, 408 US 564, 577 (1972)
Bolger v. Youngs Drug Prods. Corp., 463 US 60, 64–5 (1983) 99, 100
Bravado Merchandising Services Ltd. v. Mainstream Publishing
    (Edinburgh) Ltd., 1996 SLT 597, 1996 SCLR 1 139 ....139, 151
Brinkibon Ltd. v. Stahag Stahl und Stahlwaren handelsgesellschaft mbH
    [1983] 2 AC 34...23, 24
British Leyland v. Armstrong Patents Co. Ltd. [1986] RPC 279 ....203, 209
British Nylon Spinners Ltd. v. Imperial Chemical Industries Ltd.
    [1953] Ch 19..239
British South Africa Co. v. Companhia de Mocambique
    [1893] AC 602 ....231, 236, 237, 240–1
British Sugar Plc. v. James Robertson & Sons
    [1996] RPC 281 ....140, 141, 147, 151
Bruner v. Moore [1904] 1 Ch 305
BT and others v. One in a Million [1998] 4 All ER 476,
    [1999] RPC 1 ....128, 136, 143, 147
Burger King Corp. v. Rudzewicz, 471 US, 105 S Ct. 2174 (1985) 234
Butler v. Michigan, 353 US 380, 97 S Ct. 524 (1957)....................................288

Caesars World, Inc., v. Caesars-Palace.com, et al., Civil Action
    No. 99–550–A (ED Va, 3 Mar. 2000)...168
Campbell v. Ker, 24 Feb. 1810, FC 21
Canon Kabushiki Kaisha v. Green Cartridge Co. (Hong Kong) Ltd.
    [1997] AC 728 210
Canon Kabushiki Kaisha v. Metro-Goldwyn-Mayer Inc. (formerly Pathé
    Communications Corp.) (Case C-39/97)[1998] All ER (EC) 934,
    [1999] RPC 117, [1999] CMLR 77 141–4
Cantiere San Rocco SA v. Clyde Shipbuilding and Engineering Co.,
    1923 SC (HL) 108 69
Car Toys Inc. v. Informa Unlimited Inc., Natioanl Arbitration Forum
    File No. FA 0002000093682 164
Carlill v. The Carbolic Smoke Ball Co. Ltd. [1893] 1 QB 256 21
CBS Inc. v. Ames Records and Tapes Ltd. [1982] Ch 91 200
CBS Songs Ltd. v. Amstrad Consumer Electronics plc [1988] AC 1013.........200
CD Solutions Inc. v. CDS Networks Inc., D Or Civil No. 97–793–HA,
    22 Apr. 1998..155
Chapelton v. Barry UDC [1940] 1 KB 532..30
Chaplin [1971] AC 356...236, 260
Charge Card Services, In re, [1989] Ch 497 71
Chevy (Case C-375–97) 144
Chinon Corp. v. Evans Medical Ltd. and others [1996] FSR 863 230
Christian Dior SA & Parfums Christian Dior BV v. Evora BV (Case C-337/95)
    [1997] ECR I-6013, [1998] RPC 166, [1998] 1 CMLR 737........................152

Church of Spiritual Technology v. Dataweb BV, 9 Jun. 1999 200

Coin Controls Ltd. v. Suzo International (UK) and others
[1997] 3 All ER 45 ....232, 236, 242

Commission v. Germany *(Beer Purity case)* (Case 178/84)
[1987] ECR 1227 86

Commission v. Germany *(Milk Substitutes case)* (Case 76/86)
[1989] ECR 1021 86

Commissioners of Inland Revenue v. Muller & Co.'s Margarine Ltd.
[1901] AC 217 239

Compuserve Inc. v. Cyber Promotions Inc., No. C2–96-1070
(SD Ohio 24 Oct. 1996) 312, 315

Compuserve Inc. v. Patterson, 89 F 3d 1257 (6th Cir. 1996) 234

Crawford v. Royal Bank of Scotland (1749) Mor. 875.............................73

Cubby v. Compuserve, 766 F Supp 135 (SD NY 1991) 262–3

Cumming v. Scottish Daily Record and Sunday Mail and others
[1995] EMLR 538 258

Curtis v. Thompson, 840 F2d 1291 (7th Cir. 1988) 100

Cybersell Inc. v. Cybersell Inc., Webhorizons Inc., Websolvers Inc.
and others, 130 F 3d 414 (9th Cir. 1997) 234, 235

Data Concepts Inc. v. Digital Consulting Inc., No. 97–5802 (6th Cir.
8 May 1998) 142, 155

Debtor, Re a (No. 2021 of 1995) 2 All ER 345 42

Dee Empire v. IFPI, ED HC, Denmark, 8 Dec 1997 [1998] EIPR N-203........186

Dior v. Evora *see* Christian Dior SA & Parfums Christian
Dior BV v. Evora BV

Doe v. America Online Inc., Fla. Cir. Ct., No. CL 97–631 AE,
13 Jun. 1997 264

Dollar Land (Cumberland) Ltd. v. CIN Properties Ltd., 1998 SLT 992 71

DPP v. Bignell [1998] Masons CLR, Rep. 141 317

Duijnstee v. Goderbauer (Case 288/82) [1983] ECR 3663.........................231

Dun & Bradstreet, Inc. v. Greenmoss Builders, Inc., 472 US 749, 762 (1985)......100

Dunlop Pneumatic Tyre Co. v. New Garage and Motor Co.
[1915] AC 79 314

Earthlink Networks v. Cyber Promotions, No. BC 167502
(Cal. Super. Ct., LA Co. 30 Mar 1998) 315

Electronic Techniques (Anglia) Ltd. v. Critchley Components
[1997] FSR 401 189

Elvis Presley Enterprises Inc. v. Sid Shaw Elvisly Yours, *Times*,
22 Mar. 1999...153

Entercolor Technologies Corp. v. Gigantor Software Development Inc.,
National Arbitration Forum File No. FA0002000093635
(gigantor.com) 163

Lion Laboratories Ltd. v. Evans [1985] QB 526 209
Lockheed Martin Corp. v. Network Solutions Inc., 985 F Supp 949,
    956 (CD Cal. 1997) 148
Longworth v. Hope and Cook (1865) 3 M 1049 259
Lonhro plc v. Fayed [1990] QB 490 316
Louisville Joint Stock Land Bank v. Radford, 295 US 555,
    596–602 (1935) 100
Lunney v. Prodigy Services Co., 2000 US LEXIS 3037 262–3
Luttges v. Sherwood (1895) 11 TLR 233 73
Lynch v. United States, 292 US 571, 179 (1934) 100

Macquarie Bank v. Berg [1999] NSWSC 526 ....255, 257
Mai Systems Corp. v. Peak Computer Inc., 991 F 2d 511 (9th Cir. 1993);
    114 S Ct 671 (1994) 196, 229
Marinari v. Lloyds Bank plc and another (Case C-364/93)
    [1996] 2 WLR 159..229
Maritz v. Cybergold Inc. 947 F Supp 1328 (ED Mo. 1996)
    1 ECLR 587..177, 234
Marriott International Inc. v. Café au Lait, File No. FA0002000093670
    (*marriott-hotel.com*) 163
Mars UK Ltd. v. Tecknowledge Ltd. [2000] FSR 138................................210
Mary-Lynn Mondich and American Vintage Wine Biscuits Inc. v. Shane
    Brown, t/a Big Daddy's Antiques, WIPO Case No. D00–0004
    (*americanvintage.com*) 163
Mason v. Benhar Coal Co. (1882) 9 R 883 24
Mattel Inc. v. Jcom Inc., (SD NY 1998) No. 97 Civ 7191 (SS) 172
Matusevitch v. Telnikoff, 877 F Supp; Civil Action no. 94–1151 RMU 260
McDonald v. Dennys Lascelles Ltd. (1933) 48 CLR 457 69
McIntosh v. Alam, 1997 SCLR (Notes) 1171..23
Merrick Homes v. Duff, 1996 GWD 9–508; 1997 SLT 570..............................23
Microsystems and Mattel v. Scandinavia Online et al., Civil Action No.
    00–10488–EFH (USDC Mass.)..299, 306
Miller v. Race (1758) 1 Burr. 452...74
Mölnlycke AB and Another v. Procter & Gamble Ltd. and Others
    [1992] 1 WLR 1112..227, 238
Moorcock, The (1889) 14 PC 64..31, 70
Moorhouse v. University of New South Wales [1976] RPC 151 200
Moser v. Federal Communications Commission, 46 F 3d 970
    (9th Cir. 1995) 324

New Kids on the Block v. News America Publishing, 971 F 2d 302
    (CA 9 1991)..152, 178
New York Times Co. v. Sullivan, 376 US 254, 11 L Ed. 2d 686,
    84 S Ct. 710 (1964)..260

Newspaper Licensing Agency v. Marks & Spencer Plc., *Times*
26 January 1999, *Independent* 28 January 1999 ....151, 207
Niton Corp. v. Radiation Monitoring Devices Inc., D Mass No.
98–11629–REK, 18 Nov. 1998..175
Norbert Steinhardt & Son Ltd. v. Meth (1961) 105 CLR 440...............240, 241
Norman v. Ricketts (1886) 3 TLR 182 73
Novello & Co. Ltd. v. Hinrichsen Edition Ltd. [1951] Ch 595 239

Oasis Stores Ltd. v. Ever Ready Plc [1998] RPC 631......................137, 146, 147
Ohralik v. Ohio State Bar Association, 436 US 447, 456 (1978).....................99
Ontario Inc. v. Nexx Online Inc., 127623, Ct. File No. C20546/99
(Ont. Super. Ct. of Justice, 14 Jun. 1999) 314
Oppedahl & Larson v. Advanced Concepts, Civil Action
No. 97–Z–1592 175
Origins Natural Resources Inc. v. Origin Clothing Ltd.
[1995] FSR 280 139

Panavision International LP v. Dennis Toeppen, 945 F Supp., 1296, 2 ECLR
789 (DC Cal. 1996), 141 F 3d 1316 (9th Cir. 1998) 150, 162, 235
Parker v. South Eastern Railway Co. (1877) 2 CPD 416 29
Partridge v. Crittenden [1868] 2 All ER 421 21
Patmont Motor Works Inc. v. Gateway Marine Inc., (DC N Cal. 1997)
No. C-96–2703 THE 152, 176
Paul v. Davis, 424 US 693 (1976)..91
Pearce v. Ove Arup Partnership and Other [1997] 3 All ER 31,
[1997] 2 WLR 779..226–32, 236, 242
Pharmaceutical Society of Great Britain v. Boots Cash Chemists
(Southern) Ltd. [1953] 1 QB 401 21
Pitman Training Ltd. v. Nominet UK [1997] FSR 797.................................136
Planned Parenthood Federation of America Inc. v. Bucci, 97 CIV-0629
(KMW) 19 Mar. 1997, 2 ECLR 370 150
Playboy Enterprises Inc. v. AsiaFocus International,
(ED Va Apr. 22 1998) 176–7
Playboy Enterprises Inc. v. Calvin Designer Label, Civil Action
No. C-97–3204 (ND Cal. 1997); 985 F Supp 1220 (1997) 175, 176
Playboy Enterprises Inc. v. Chuckleberry Publishing Inc., 939 F Supp 1032
(SD NY); 939 F Supp 1041 (1996) 176
Playboy Enterprises Inc. v. Frena, 839 F Supp 1552 (MD Fla. 1993) 175
Playboy Enterprises Inc. v. Russ Hardenburgh Inc., 982 F Supp 503
(ND Ohio 1997) 175, 229
Playboy Enterprises Inc. v. Universal Tel-A-Talk Inc., (ED Pa 1998)
No. 96–6961...176
Playboy Enterprises Inc. v. Webbworld Inc., 968 F Supp 1171 (ND Tex.);
991 F Supp 543 (1997) 175, 186, 229

Thorey v. Wylie and Lockhead (1890) 6 Sh. Ct. Rep. 201 73
Thornton v. Shoe Lane Parking [1971] 2 QB 163..28
Ticketmaster Corp. et al. v. Tickets.com Inc., US DC, CD Cal.,
    27 Mar. 2000 ....174, 186
Ticketmaster v. Microsoft, CV 97–3055 RAP (CD Cal.
    28 Apr. 1997) 173, 174, 186
Torquay Hotel v. Cousins [1969] 2 Ch 106 316
Trumpet Software Pty. Ltd. v. OzEmail Pty. Ltd. [1996] 18(12)
    EIPR 69..203
Turnbull v. McLean & Co. (1873) 1 R 730 69
Tyburn Productions Ltd. v. Conan Doyle
    [1990] 3 WLR 174 ....237, 238–9, 240, 242

UMG Recordings Inc. and others v. MP3.com Inc., USCD, SDNY
    4 May 2000 ....187, 205, 208
United States v. Miller, 425 US 425 (1976)...91
United States v. General Motors Corp. 323 US 373 (1945) 101
University of London Press Ltd. v. University Tutorial Press Ltd.
    [1916] 2 Ch 601 205

Van Dale v. Romme [1991] Ned Jur 608, [1994] Ned Jur 58 191
Virginia State Board Pharmacy Bd. v. Virginia Citizens Consumer Credit
    Council, Inc., 425 US 748, 771–2 (1976) 99, 320

Walter Latham, Mr, v. Todd Shurn, Mr, National Arbitration Forum
    File No. FA0002000094184 *(kingsofcomedy.com)*....................163
Warlow v. Harrison (1859) 1 E & E 309 21
Webb's Fabulous Pharmacies, Inc. v. Beckwith, 449 US 155,
    161 (1980) 101
WGN Continental Broadcasting Co. v. United Video Inc., 693 F 2d 622
    (7th Cir 1982) 190
Whalen v. Roe, 429 US 589 (1977) 91
William Grant & Sons v. Marie Brizard Espana SA, 19 Jan. 1988..................34
William Morton & Co. v. Muir Bros. & Co., 1907 SC 1211.......................31
World Wrestling Federation Inc. v. Michael Bosman, WIPO Case No.
    D99–0001 162
Wynn Oil Co. v. American Way Serv. Corp., 943 F 2d 595, 600 (
    6th Cir. 1991) 142

Yahoo! Inc. v. World Wide Network Marketing, ND Cal. No. C-99–20234 (14
    Apr. 1999) 4 BNA ECLR 384 317

Zeran v. America OnLine, 1997 US Dist. Lexis (ED Va.
    21 Mar. 1997) 261, 262, 264

Zino Davidoff SA v. A & G Imports [1999] 3 All ER 711 212
Zino Davidoff SA v. M & S Toiletries; Joop! GmbH v. M & S
    Toiletries, 2000 SLT 683 212
Zippo Manufacturing Co. v. Zippo Dot Com Inc., 952 F Supp 1119
    (WD Pa. 14 Feb. 1997) 2 ECLR 202 ....177, 234, 258

Table of Legislation

AUSTRALIA
Copyright Amendment (Digital Agenda) Act 2000 ....210, 215
Electronic Transactions Act 1999 53
    s. 8(1) 45
    s. 10 45
    s. 40(1)(b) 302
    cl. 9 45

FRANCE
Intellectual Property Code, 1 July 1992
L122–5, L211–3, L212–10, L311..204

GERMANY
Copyright Act 1965
    s. 53 207
    ss. 53, 54 & 54 a-h 204
Teleservices Act 1997 201

SINGAPORE
Electronic Transactions Act 1998 53

UNITED KINGDOM
Banking Act 1987
    s. 89 62
Bills of Exchange Act 1882
    s. 3(1) 74
    s. 83(1) 74
Civic Government (Sc) Act 1982
    s. 51 282
    s. 51(8) 282
    s. 52 284
    s. 52A..282, 284
Civil Jurisdiction and Judgments Act 1982 ....226, 256
    Sch. 8, Arts. 1 and 5(3)...256
Coinage Act 1971..66
Companies Act 1985 ....130, 131
Competition Act 1980 333
Competition Act 1998 ....332, 333

s. 1(1)(b)..265, 266
s. 1(1)(c) 266
s. 1(2) 265, 266
s. 1(2)(c) 266
s. 1(2)(e) 266
s. 1(3) 265, 266
s. 1(3)(c) 265
s. 1(5) 266
Electronic Communications Act 2000 ....5, 6, 20, 37–8, 42–4,
                                                        46–9, 53, 201, 341
Pts. I, II & III 38
s. 2(1)..47
s. 2(1)(a)..47
s. 2(4)..48
s. 6(1)(a)..47
s. 6(1)(c)..47
s. 7 47
s. 7(1)..45
s. 7(2)..41
s.8...20
s. 8(1)..46
s. 8(2)..46
s. 9(7)..46
s. 14(1)(a) 48
s. 15(2)(a) 45
s. 15(2)(b)..45
Fair Trading Act 1973 333
Human Rights Act 1998 ....222, 282
Insolvency Act 1986
s. 78(2) 72
s. 178(3) 72
Interception of Communications Act 1985..43
Interpretation Act 1978...19, 43
c. 30, s. 5, Sch. 1. 43
Obscene Publications Act 1959...282, 291
s. 1(1) 282
s. 1(2) 282
s. 2(1) 281
Obscene Publications Act 1964
s. 1(2) 281
Patents Act 1977 237–8
s. 30(1) 237, 239
Police and Criminal Evidence Act (PACE)
ss. 19(4) & 20 43

Private International Law (Miscellaneous Provisions) Act 1995 259
  s. 10 236
Protection of Children Act 1978...282, 283–4
  s. 1(1)...285, 286
  s. 1(1)(b), (c) 294
  s. 1(4) 294
  s. 7(2) 284
Protection of Children Act 1984
  s. 1 282
Regulation of Investigatory Powers Act 2000 ....50–1, 278
  s. 46(1) 50
  s. 46(2)(b)(ii) 50
  s. 49 50
  s. 49(9) 50
  s. 50(1) 50
  s. 50(2) 50
  s. 50(3)(a) 50
  s. 51(4) 51
  s. 54 (2) 51
  s. 55 51
  s. 56 50
Sched. 2 50–1
Requirements of Writing (Scotland) Act 1995 43
  ss.1–3..19
  s. 3 46
  c. 7, s. 1. 43
Sale of Goods Act 1979..21, 49
Sexual Offences (Conspiracy and Incitement) Act 1996.....................283
Telecommunications Act 1984...332
  s. 7 332
  s. 43 319
Theft Act 1968 319
Trade Marks Act 1994...130, 135, 138, 151, 237
  s. 1 ....135, 173
  s. 5(3) 146
  s. 10 133
  s. 10(1) 137, 138–9, 142, 148
  s. 10(2) 137, 138, 140–2, 148
  s. 10(3) 137, 138, 143, 144, 146, 147
  s. 10(6) 152
  s. 11(2) 152
  s. 11(2)(a) 153
  s. 12 153
  s. 22 237

s. 56 ....137, 144
Unfair Contract Terms Act 1977...49, 59, 314
    s. 18 267

Statutory Instruments
Consumer Credit (Exempt Agreements) Order 1989, SI 1989/869
    Art. 3(a)(ii)...61
Copyright and Rights in Databases Regulations 1997 SI 1997/3032..............190
    reg. 12(1) 191
    reg. 13 191
Copyright (Librarians and archivists) (Copying of Copyright Material)
    Regulations 1989 SI 1989/212...207
Dual-Use Items (Export Control) Regs. 2000, SI 2000/2620 52
Export Goods Control Order 1994, SI 1994/1191 52
Insolvency Rules 1986
    r. 13.12(1)(b) 73
Telecommunications (Data Protection and Privacy) (Direct Marketing)
    Regulations 1998 SI 1998/3170..323, 324
Telecommunications (Interconnection) Regulations 1998...........................334
Unfair Contract Terms in Consumer Contracts Regs. 1999,
    SI 1999/2083...49, 314
    reg. 2(1)..314
    reg. 3(1)..314

UNITED STATES
Anticybersquatting Consumer Protection Act 2000 ....154, 166–9
Child Online Protection Act 1998 (COPA) 94, 106, 288
    s. 1403(a)..288
Title XIV..94
Title XXIII 94
Communications Decency Act 1996...............................94, 263, 264, 275, 280,
                                                                                                      268, 287–90
    s. 230(c)...264, 268
Title V..94
Constitution 168
    Art. 1, s. 8 184
First Amendment 99, 100–2, 253
Fifth Amendment...99, 100–2
Copyright Act 1976
    s. 107 ....204, 207
Digital Millennium Copyright Act 1998 ....83, 200, 201, 210, 215, 270–1
Title III...196
Driver's Privacy Protection Act 1994 93
Electronic Communications Privacy Act 1986 103

Electronic Signatures in Global and National Commerce Act 2000
(E-SIGN Act) 45
Fair Credit Reporting Act 1970 (amended 1996) (FCRA) 103, 113, 114
Federal Trade Commission Act 1914 117
  s. 5 117
Federal Trademark Dilution Act 1995 ....143, 145, 167
  s.43 145
  s. 43 c.(4) 152
Financial Modernization Act 1999 113
Internet Consumer Protection Act 1999 (California) 327
Lanham Act 1995 ....143, 145
  s.43 145
  s. 43 c.(4) 152
Omnibus Consolidated and Emergency Supplemental Appropriations
  Act 1999 94
Privacy Protection Act 1974 ....92, 95
Privacy Protection Act 1980 92
Right to Financial Privacy Act 1978 ....92, 100
Sonny Bono Term Extension Act 1998 83
Telecommunications Act 1996 94
Telephone Consumer Protection Act 1991 92
Trademark Act 1946
  s. 43 167
Uniform Computer Information Transactions Act 1999
  (UCITA) 46, 53, 54, 204
  s. 107(a) 45
  ss. 108, 114 & 212 46
Uniform Electronic Transactions Act (UETA) 46, 53
  s. 7(c) 47
  s. 7(d) 45
  s. 9(a) 46
  s. 9(b) 46
US Code, Title 17, chapter 5 270
Video Privacy Protection Act 1988 ....92, 93, 100, 103
Virginia Long Arm Statute, Virginia Code 8.01.328.1(A) 177

TREATIES AND CONVENTIONS

Berne Convention 182–3, 210, 225, 243–4
  Art. 5(2) 244
  Art. 9(1) 211
  Art. 9(2) 216, 219, 222
  Art. 10 211
Brussels Convention on Jurisdiction and
  Judgments 1968 ....226, 236, 256–8, 271

Art. 1 227
Art. 2 228–31
Art. 5(3) 227, 228–9
Art. 16 ....227, 241
Art. 16(1) 227, 230
Art. 16(4) 227
Art. 21 258
Art. 22 258
Council of Europe Convention for the Protection of Individuals
    with Regard to Automated Processing of Personal
    Data 1981 ....85, 86, 96, 320
Art. 8(1) 33
Art. 8(2) 33
Art. 9 32
Council of Europe Draft International Convention on Crime in Cyberspace
    (April 2000) 292
EC Treaty
Arts. 28 and 49 328
Arts. 81 and 82 332
European Convention on Human Rights 289, 320
Art. 8 222
Art. 10 222
OECD Model Tax Convention 6
Paris Convention
Art. 6*bis* 137, 144
Rome Convention on the Law Applicable to Contractual
    Obligations 1980 ....32–4, 60
Art. 1 33
Art. 3 ....33, 34
Art. 3(1) 33
Art. 3(3) 60
Art. 4 ....33, 34
Art. 4(2) 33
Art. 5 ....33, 34
Art. 5(2) 34
Art. 8 33
Trade-Related Aspects of Intellectual Property Rights (TRIPS)
    Agreement 1994 ....144, 183, 235, 245
Art. 13 212
Art. 16.2 144
Art. 16.3 144
UNCITRAL Model Law on Electronic Commerce 6, 20, 27
Wassenaar Arrangement 51–2
category 5, part 2 51

WIPO Treaty 1996 211
  Art. 8 211
  Art. 10..212
  Arts. 11 & 12..212
  Art. 22..212

DIRECTIVES
Dir. 89/104/EC (Trade marks) 144
  Art. 5(2) 144
  Art. 7(2) 152
Dir. 91/250/EC (Legal protection of computer programs) 196
  Art. 1(3) 190
  Art. 4(a) 196
Dir. 92/100/EEC ....(Rental right directive) 197
Dir. 93/83/EC (Satellite broadcasting) 245
Dir. 93/98/EC (Harmonising the term of protection of copyright and
  certain related rights)..83, 84, 268
Dir. 95/46/EC (Data protection) 82, 86–90, 95, 96, 104, 108, 117, 320
  Art. 1(1) 89
  Art. 2(a) 87
  Art. 2(b) 87
  Art. 2(c) 87
  Arts. 3(1)-(2) 87
  Art. 8 87
  Art. 9 88
  Arts 10–12...87
  Art. 14 87
  Art. 15 87
  Arts. 22–24..88
  Art. 25 ....88, 107
  Art. 25(6) 122
  Art. 26 ....88, 107
  Art. 28 88
Dir. 96/9/EC (Database directive) 196
  Art. 3(1) 190
  Art. 5(a) 190
Dir. 97/7/EC (Distance selling of financial products) 9, 59, 322, 324
  Art. 2 323
  Art. 8 59
  Art. 10(1) 323
  Annex 1...323
Dir. 97/13/EC (Common framework for general authorisations and individual
  licences in telecommunications services) 332
Dir. 97/33/EC (Interconnection in telecommunications) 334

Dir. 97/66/EC (Telecommunications data protection) 232
   Art. 12...323
Dir. 99/93/EC (A common framework for electronic signatures) 44, 53
   Art. 5(2) 45
   Art. 6(1) 49
Dir 2000/31/EC (Electronic Commerce)......9, 20, 27, 28, 201, 211, 268, 271, 292
   Art. 2 221
   Art. 3 28
   Art. 5 28
   Art. 6...28, 311, 325, 326
   Art. 7 ....311, 325, 326
   Art. 7(2) 326
   Art. 9 45
   Arts. 9–11 27
   Art. 10(1) 28
   Art. 10(3) 28
   Art. 10(4) 28
   Art. 11 28
   Art. 11(1) 27
   Art. 11(3) 27
   Art. 12 ....201, 268, 269
   Art. 13...202, 214, 221, 268, 269
   Art. 14 ....202, 269, 270, 294
   Art. 14(1)(b) 296
   Art. 14(2) 268
   Art. 15 ....202, 269, 327
   Arts. 12–15 201
   Art. 17..272
   recital 17 221
Draft Dir. on Copyright and the Information Society COM
   (1997) 628 ....210, 211, 212, 223
   Art. 2 213
   Art. 3 213
   Art. 4 212
   Art. 5 ....213, 215, 217, 218, 221, 222
   Art. 5(1) 214
   Art. 5(2)(a) 216
   Art. 5(2)(b) 221
   Art. 5(2)(c) 220
   Art 5(2)(d), (e) 218
   Art. 5(3) 213, 221
   Art. 5(3)(b), (e) 218
   Art. 5(3)(c), (o) 221
   Art. 6 ....212, 217, 218

Art. 6(3) 218
Art. 6(4) 219
Art. 7 ....212, 218
recital 3 212
recitals 8–10, 14bis 212, 213
recitals 10ter, 14bis 212
recital 18 212
recital 22 ....213, 215
recital 24bis...217
recital 29bis...220
Addendum 12...215
Addendum 13...215, 216
Draft Dir. on Electronic Commerce COM (1998) 586;
    COM (1999) 427...27, 268, 271, 326

REGULATIONS

Council Reg. 1334/2000 (control of export of dual -use items and
    technology) 52
Council Reg. 40/1994 (Community Trade Mark) 154

1997). She is Reviews Editor of the *International Journal of Law and Information Science,* a member of the board of the *Journal of Law and Information Science,* and a member of the BILETA executive.

Martin Hogg has lectured at the University of Edinburgh since 1995 and is a qualified solicitor. His main areas of interest lie in obligations law, construction Law, and information technology Law. He has previously published on encryption and electronic contracting, privacy, as well as a range of obligational issues.

Hector MacQueen is Professor of Private Law at the University of Edinburgh and a Director of SCRIPT, the Shepherd and Wedderburn Centre for Research into Intellectual Property and Technology. He has written extensively in the field of intellectual property law and is author of volume 18 of the *Stair Memorial Encyclopaedia* on Intellectual Property (1993) and *Copyright, Competition and Industrial Design* (2nd edn, 1995). He is Editor of the *Edinburgh Law Review.*

Saul Miller is a lecturer at the School of Law, University of Edinburgh. Having previously studied both law and commerce at the University of Cape Town, his primary research interests lie in commercial law and the law of obligations. He is currently pursuing research into payment systems on the Internet, third party unjustified enrichment and the relationship between contract and unjustified enrichment.

Ian Monaghan is a partner with Masons, Solicitors. He has wide experience of IT industry transactions. These include; domestic and international computer and communications projects for public utilities, public companies, government departments and financial and regulatory bodies. He specialises in major project work, outsourcing and e-commerce.

Andrew Murray is a lecturer in the Law Department of London School of Economics and Political Science. He teaches a course in Computers and the Law and carries out research into Internet Regulation. Andrew's recent publications have examined the role of trade marks in relation to domain names and meta tags, the regulation of formal transactions over the Internet and the Anticybersquatting Consumer Protection Act 1999.

Andrew Terrett is a technology consultant with Baker Robbins and Company. Andrew has been involved in legal technology for over ten years. He is a qualified solicitor in England and Wales has a Masters degree in law and technology from the University of British Columbia, Canada and was a IT project manager with Masons for over 3 years. He has spoken and written extensively on legal technology and his first book, *The Internet—Business Strategies for Law Firms* (Law Society Publishing, 2000) was published in December 1999.

Paul Torremans is a Senior Lecturer in Law, at the University of Leicester, having studied law in Leuven (Belgium), Le Havre (France) and Leicester (UK). His publications include *Intellectual Property Law*, with Jon Holyoak, which was shortlisted for the Butterworth Prize (Butterworths, 1995, 2nd edn, 1998) and *Intellectual Property and the Conflict of Laws*, with Prof. J.J. Fawcett, (Clarendon Press (OUP),1998). He was Moderator of the first WIPO/ATRIP Electronic Conference on Strategies for Intellectual Property Teaching in Faculties of Law, Business and Engineering in 1998–1999.

Charlotte Waelde is a Lecturer in the School of Law, University of Edinburgh. She is also a co-director of SCRIPT and assistant director of the Law School's Legal Practice Unit. Her main research interests lie in the field of intellectual property, in particular copyright and trade marks. Her current interests lie in the application of both copyright and trade marks to the Internet, and she has written and spoken extensively on these subjects. She is co-editor, with Lilian Edwards, of the first book in this series, *Law and the Internet: Regulating Cyberspace*, which was published by Hart in 1997.

1

The Internet—An Introduction For Lawyers

ANDREW TERRETT* and IAIN MONAGHAN†

Given the intense media coverage that the Internet has attracted over the past few years, one might reasonably argue that the Internet needs no introduction. It has successfully permeated into our everyday lives in a myriad of ways. Every parent must now feel the obligation to ensure that their child has access to the Internet as part of their overall education. Similarly, no advertising campaign is now complete without reference to a Web site and if you want to know something about an unknown organisation (whether company, university or law firm), the first thing you do is look up its Web site. Over the past few years, most Internet users have ceased worrying about what the Internet is and how it works and have begun to treat it more like the telephone—a convenient appliance for certain tasks. But at the same time, the Internet is becoming an increasingly complex place. There are an ever-increasing number of different terms that are being used in Internet circles—not only do we have e-mail, we now have e-anything e.g. e-commerce, e-business, e-journals, e-solutions, and not just the Internet but intranets and extranets as well. Meanwhile the digirati are dreaming up ever more obscure terms of art—channels, clickstream and enterprise information portals, to name but a few of the current buzzwords.

This chapter is divided into two parts. The first part is designed to explain a little of how the Internet works, both in terms of the technology and the administration. In the second part, the main legal issues relating to the Internet are addressed. This second part of this chapter is intended to set the stage for the remainder of this book.

WHAT IS THE INTERNET?

Although there is no official definition of the Internet, most industry commentators would agree upon a description of the Internet as a public international network of networks. Inevitably, those working in technology introduce the

---

* Technology Consultant, Baker Robbins and Company.
† Partner, Masons Solicitors.

notion of networks into any conversation about the field. Networks sound complicated but the principles are straightforward. On a conceptual level a network is simply a group of computers that are physically linked together with cabling. In addition all of these computers must be running particular software that allows them to recognise that they are all part of the same network. The Internet is simply a public international network of networks. Back in the late 1960s, American military researchers decided to attempt to link up various networks that they had created in order to enhance their abilities to share academic research. The benefits were obvious and the idea quickly spread—in the early 1970s, technologists managed to establish the first trans-Atlantic link-up of computer networks. The Internet is now 30 years old and during that time a huge number of new networks have been attached to the original structure. At the same time, older networks have been retired. In the past five years, we have seen the rapid commercialisation of the Internet (hence the need for a book on the law relating to the Internet), with privately funded networks becoming far more prevalent. It is unclear exactly how many networks are currently attached to the Internet. However, current estimates (or rather, educated guesswork) suggest that about 180 million people have access to the Internet from either home or work, and this number is growing all the time.[1]

INTERNET SERVICES

There are various services available on the Internet, the most important of which are e-mail and the World Wide Web (also referred to as 'the Web'). Other less important services include FTP (File Transfer Protocol), Usenet, Telnet, MUDs, Talk and Internet Relay Chat (IRC). These latter services are not addressed in this chapter because they are of minor importance to most Internet users, particularly lawyers. However, it should be noted that services such as IRC may give rise to significant liabilities for the organisations that host such services.

E-mail should now need little explanation, given its prevalence—it is a simple asynchronous mechanism for text-based one-to-one or one-to-many electronic communication. It is also the most popular Internet service. The Web, on the other hand is more complex. It can be defined as a 'wide-area hypermedia information retrieval initiative aiming to give universal access to a large universe of documents'.[2] More simply stated it is a system of linking together hundreds of millions of electronic documents ('Web pages') on millions of computers[3] ('Web

---

[1] See surveys by the Georgia Institute of Technology http://www.gvu.gatech. edu/user_surveys/ which are widely quoted in the media.

[2] See the WWW FAQ at http://www.boutell.com/faq/.

[3] Five million Web sites were counted as at April 1999—see the Netcraft Web Server Survey at http://www.netcraft.co.uk/survey/.

sites') together across the Internet, each of which are reachable via a unique but changeable name or Universal Resource Locator (URL). Thus a Web site is simply a collection of Web pages. When Web sites first appeared in the early 1990s, all Web sites were publicly available. After all, it was designed as a mechanism by which academic researchers could more easily share information with colleagues. However, it did not take long for human ingenuity to dream up new uses for the same technology. Hence, we now have private Web sites or 'intranets' and semi-private Web sites or 'extranets'. Intranets were perceived as a very useful mechanism by which users within a particular company, university or other organisation could share information relevant to other users. Thus, in a law firm context, an intranet can be used to share information on everything from maternity benefits to precedents. Extranets were a further extension of this idea of sharing information using Web technology. They can be used for a variety of different purposes—the first extranets were used by large corporations such as Boeing—a company that has to deal with thousands of different suppliers. By developing an extranet, they could effectively open up its enterprise to selected suppliers, making its supply chains more efficient and cost effective. It has not taken long for other companies to follow suit.[4]

WHO OWNS THE INTERNET?

The most straightforward answer is that no one does. There is no single body that controls all activities on the Internet. It is simply out there and is virtually impossible to 'switch off'. Governments in countries such as China are attempting to limit access to the Internet but should recognise that they are fighting a losing battle. Networks within different countries are funded and managed according to national policies. Links between countries will be managed by agreements between telecommunications providers. The Internet is the first global 'institution' that has no government. This is both one of the Internet's greatest strengths and one of its main weaknesses. Ownership is distributed between countries and their own governments, corporations, universities and the major telecommunications ('telecoms') utilities. Each individual computer attached to the Internet will be owned by a corporation, firm or individual. Large telecommunications utilities such as BT and MCI WorldCom own a large percentage of the physical wires and routers over which data are transferred. Internet Service Providers (so-called ISPs) will own the majority of servers on which information is hosted. Individuals and companies will own the intellectual property rights in the information that is hosted on such servers. In addition, universities will also own some of the most critical systems without which the Internet would cease to function (reflecting the Internet's academic

---

[4] Ford recently announced that it would be doing precisely this, using Oracle technologies with a system called AutoExchange—'Oracle system joins Ford production line', *Computing*, 11 November, 1999, 8.

against the background of a commercial revolution which leaves a minimum of time for reflection.

But the true complexity of the situation becomes apparent—and the analogy with the seventeenth century breaks down—only when one appreciates that the UK Government is not alone in facing this dilemma. It is being faced to a greater or lesser extent by every developed country in the world, and many of the developing countries. And the legislature in each of these countries is being pressed by influential constituents to do something to make the country a leader in electronic commerce—often in reaction to steps being proposed by a rival nation (such as the UK). At times it appears as if the developed nations will succumb to legislative panic, with each country trying to out-legislate its neighbours and the only cool heads being found in the USA—a situation which will no doubt continue only for so long as the USA believes it has such a commanding hold upon e-commerce that it has more to gain from openness than protection.

TRENDS IN LEGISLATION

There are, however, some developments which give grounds for hope that calmness will prevail and that Internet law will develop in a more harmonious fashion. Fittingly, they arise from the move towards international co-operation in the field of law-making.

First there is the influence of the European Union. While this may be an unpopular view in the UK, the interest which the European Commission has shown in electronic commerce, and the fact that two or three significant new directives are always circulating in draft form, acts as a restraint on those Member States which would otherwise be tempted to go it alone. So, while the UK Government trumpets the Electronic Communications Act as its own invention, the reality is that the sections of the Act which relate to e-commerce (in particular, digital signatures) merely anticipate provisions which the UK will be required to implement in any event when the Electronic Commerce Directive comes into force. The effect of the European Union is to increase harmonisation of e-commerce law within Europe.

Secondly, there are the efforts of various multi-national bodies such as the UN and the OECD. The UN was the first into the field with the UNCITRAL Model Law on Electronic Commerce, a model for legislation which is being followed by countries as far apart as Australia and the Isle of Man. The OECD is particularly prominent in the field of taxation where it seeks, through amendment to the OECD Model Tax Convention, to achieve a degree of unanimity on the treatment of such matters as whether a Web site constitutes a 'permanent establishment' and whether payments made for data are to be treated as payments for goods, payments for services or royalties.

A consideration of the complex international dimension might lead one to the conclusion that electronic commerce is properly the province of directives, treaties and protocols and that national legislators, courts and practising lawyers have little to contribute. But the reality is that electronic commerce is burgeoning in the absence of any such documents and that many of the problems which it throws up are on a fairly mundane level which can be dealt with by minor adaptations to contracts or regulations—for example, the removal or amendment of a requirement that a particular transaction be 'evidenced in writing'. Despite the apparent need for overwhelming change, a programme of incremental improvement might not only be adequate to cope with most problems, but also be preferable to any more rapid or revolutionary solution. As we have seen with early proposals in the field of security and electronic signatures it is only too easy for legislatures to be stampeded into framing legislation around the first plausible technical solution which appears on the market, only to find that market practice moves on and that alternative solutions become more widespread and important.

THE THREE LAYERS OF THE INTERNET

So how does the Internet impact upon the law? It is easiest to explain its impact by analysing it into three layers.

> First, it exists as 'physical' infrastructure—as a data network 'managed' at a high level by the international bodies referred to above and at a day-to-day level by the various public bodies and corporations whose networks it uses. This is the lowest layer.

> Secondly, it exists as a service infrastructure provided by ISPs who offer access to the Internet, e-mail, hosting facilities, etc. using the physical infrastructure.

> Thirdly, it exists at the level of the users where (as regards the Web) it takes the form of a series of individual 'shop-windows' and electronic forms through which commerce can be conducted electronically.

Each of these layers impacts upon, and is impacted on by, different areas of law and the chapters in this book touch on all three.

'PHYSICAL' INFRASTRUCTURE—THE FIRST LAYER

Chapters 6, 7 and 14 on infrastructure and domain names cover the first layer. Domain names, in their relation to the law of trade marks, are also relevant to the third layer and the manner in which rights in the 'shop window' and products appearing in the 'shop window' can be protected (see the chapters on intellectual property rights).

a website which describes a product in a manner which is intended to attract customers will be considered an advertisement for that purpose. That does not trouble SalesCo. It is authorised to conduct investment business in Ruritania so its advertisements (provided that they comply with regulations as to warning notices) are automatically authorised for Ruritanian purposes.

Unfortunately, Narnia has an identical Financial Services Act, and the Narnian FSA takes the view that SalesCo's Web site, being accessible by Narnian investors and clearly intended to attract their custom (there is a screen explaining the advantages of the product as a shelter from Narnian tax), is an advertisement circulating in Narnia. As SalesCo is not an authorised person for Narnian purposes (and has not had the advertisement authorised by someone who is), the Web site is in breach of the Narnian law regulating investment advertisements.

Worse, the Narnian authorities claim that because the Web site is hosted on a server in Narnia, the server is owned by a fellow subsidiary of SalesCo, and SalesCo clearly hopes to do business with Narnians, SalesCo is in practice carrying on an investment business in Narnia. It therefore requires to be authorised by the Narnian FSA. The Narnian FSA talks to the Narnian tax authorities and the tax authorities then claim that the server (and associated activities) constitutes a 'branch or agency' of SalesCo in Narnia and brings it within the Narnian tax net.

This example provides the bleakest view, but it is based on real companies, real laws and real regulatory authorities. In practice, as the UK/Narnian law currently stands, while SalesCo is still concluding contracts on paper in Ruritania, only the Narnian investment advertisement regulations probably apply to SalesCo. But the remaining arguments of the Narnian authorities—both the FSA and the Revenue—have all been deployed in practice and may still turn out to be applicable in the future. And even if SalesCo could come to an understanding with the Narnian authorities—for example, it should not be too difficult for SalesCo to become authorised by the Narnian FSA, as in practice the Narnian FSA will normally authorise any company which is in good standing with the Ruritanian FSA—it might still face exactly the same problems (certainly as to investment advertisements) in every country in which its potential investors are resident.

There are two points to make about the example.

The first is that most of the problems which are described arise from the international nature of the transactions. A lawyer dealing with a company selling financial products to foreign nationals has always had to consider most of the problems referred to above—incorporation of terms, choice of jurisdiction, effect of foreign consumer laws, need for authorisation, regulation of advertisements, whether a permanent establishment is formed. The additional elements added by the Internet are the difference in the manner of concluding contracts (and its relation to national contract law); the 'virtual' nature of the establishment (which is particularly relevant to questions of authorisation and tax); and the multiplicity of jurisdictions in which potential customers may be resident (each of which has its own consumer law). Only the first of these is a 'national' issue. If a supplier restricts his activities to a single country and adopts rigorous measures to ensure that orders from any other country will be rejected, he still has to ensure that his electronic contracts are as enforceable as paper contracts but he is not concerned with any of the other issues.

The second point follows from the first. The risks of trading on the Internet match the benefits of trading on the Internet. Restrict your activities to a single country and the risks are easily manageable. You gain the benefits of electronic trading without an undue addition to your risk. Confine your activities to two or three countries and the risks increase but are still manageable. You have the difficulty of complying with the regulations of those countries, and the major problem of ensuring that you do not contract unawares with residents of other countries, but you can assess and manage those risks. Offer to contract with the whole world and you are dealing with the unknown (or paying prohibitive legal fees). In other words, the larger the market to which you aspire, the greater the risk.

WHERE IS THE INTERNET GOING?

This is an intriguing question. No one, not even Tim Berners-Lee (inventor of the World Wide Web) or Bill Gates has a crystal ball. The Internet is the fastest moving technological innovation ever. Furthermore, the Internet today has so many different aspects. This chapter focuses on just two.

Over the past five years we have seen the introduction of new ways of doing old business—for example online banking, online book-selling, online auctions and so forth. We have also seen new information or technology companies spring up in response to a newly identified need created by the Internet. Yahoo is a very good example of this; a company that gives users a directory by which to navigate around the ever-expanding network. There are now thousands of new small technology companies working on new faster, more intelligent applications designed to work on the Internet. At the same time there are thousands of so-called 'dot.com start-ups'—small companies that see the potential of the Internet in fulfilling a particular need for an Internet audience category. Indeed, every entrepreneur appears to have an Internet-based project plan in his or her back pocket. But where is it all leading?

The future of the Internet is a topic worthy of a book in itself, if not several books. As Bill Gates famously said, 'the Internet changes everything'. One of the key themes over the next five years will be convergence—the bringing together of disparate technologies. Despite its phenomenal growth, current estimates suggest that only around 14 per cent of the UK population have access to the Internet. One of the main problems is that the Internet is only available to those people who have access to a PC, either at home or at work. This will change. It is only a matter of time before the Internet will be available via more common home appliances such as the television or the new generation of mobile phones (via the Wireless Application Protocol). At the same time, the prevalent model of Internet access via the PC will come under attack from smaller hand-held appliances such as the Psion organiser, the PalmPilot or other similar devices. These new appliances will also incorporate voice capabilities. (It is already possible to use the Internet to conduct a telephone conversation but the quality is somewhat lacking—this will improve.) This technology convergence based around Internet technologies will bring the likes of Nokia and Vodaphone (companies that will have to re-create themselves as information appliance companies rather than simply the makes of mobile phones) into competition with the likes of 3com and Casio. In addition, if users can access the Internet using the television (just another information appliance), there is no reason why users cannot access material traditionally available on the television, via a pay-per-view Web site. This type of scenario will bring traditional players in television media such as the BBC, ITV and News International into competition with BT, Cable and Wireless and Worldcom. The Internet provides new possibilities for companies that were traditionally confined into particular markets. It offers intriguing possibilities, and not surprisingly we are witnessing a piranha-like feeding frenzy over the potential market-places that the Internet offers.

Thus while BT and its ilk may be seeking to undermine the stranglehold of traditional media operations in the belief that eventually they will have a unique combination of content ownership and the means to deliver it (because of their ownership of residential and commercial voice and data lines) there are also organisations working to undermine their stranglehold on this access. Internet in the sky is more than a mere fanciful wish—there are a number of global initiatives under way to create global networks to deliver Internet-based information. For example, Teledesic is a $15 billion network, partly financed by Bill Gates, comprising 288 low earth orbit satellites. Its competitor, Skybridge, is a $4.2 billion network of 80 satellites. Both intend to offer forms of data transfer services (probably e-mail initially) as well as voice-based services. It will still be a few years before these companies offer commercial services. But theoretically satellite offers two key advantages over any form of cable-based service. The first is that satellite-based services can reach people in remote locations where it would not be either feasible or economic to lay additional cables. The second is that satellite services allow for organisations that need to deliver the same set of bulk data to multiple clients. Thus organisations will be able to broadcast information to Internet appliances very effectively.

While full convergence and Internet in the sky are still some years away, there are some technological developments that we will see much more quickly. XML stands for eXtensible Markup Language. The World Wide Web consists of approximately 800 million Web pages. All of the pages, hosted on millions of machines across the World are created using a mark-up language called HTML (Hypertext Mark-up Language.) HTML was an invention of Tim Berners-Lee, father of the World Wide Web. It is a document description language and very good for turning pure text documents into a Web-readable format. It is very easy to learn, having a taxonomy of only about 90 tags. However, as technologists have been quick to note, it is also incredibly limited as a document formatting tool. Thus, the Internet community has set about developing a new language that could work on the Web, which allows documents to retain their original look and feel and one that improves the usability of Web documents.

XML is this new language or rather it defines the rules for all future document formatting languages. XML allows different communities of users to establish and define their own mark-up. Thus, chemists can develop a chemistry mark-up language and mathematicians can develop a Maths mark-up language. Similarly in the law, we will be able to develop and define a legal mark-up language. This will allow document creators not only to define certain words as having particular characteristics such as bold, underline and italicise, but also to define certain parts of documents. XML will turn unstructured documents into structured data. For example, in future when legal publishers are producing case reports for publication, they will be able to mark up the headnote, the names of the parties or the names of the solicitors involved, with particular tags. These tags will be recognised by other pieces of software used by lawyers or legal institutions and allow for much better searching, retrieval and re-use of the information. There are already trials of this technology taking place in courts in the USA, allowing for the electronic filing of court documents.

CONCLUSION

This chapter has described the Internet in terms of three levels—physical infrastructure, service infrastructure and e-commerce. The remainder of this book looks at each of these areas in turn. For example at a physical level, there are a number of outstanding legal issues to be resolved in relation to domain names and trade marks, copyright and other intellectual property rights. At a services level, there are legal issues in relation to spam (Internet junk mail) and defamation. In relation to e commerce there are unresolved legal issues and legal concerns in relation to the formation of contracts, data protection, encryption and payment mechanisms. This book does not, indeed cannot, provide the definitive legal position. It does, however, identify the main components and provide a new perspective on that fluid mass of regulation loosely described as 'the law of the Internet'.

PART 1

E-Commerce Issues

2

Entering Into Contracts Electronically: The Real W.W.W.

ANDREW D. MURRAY*

INTRODUCTION[1]

The formation of contracts feature in all areas of our lives. Every day we unconsciously enter into a variety of contracts: we travel by bus or rail, we purchase goods and accept services and we carry out duties regulated by contracts of employment. Contracts are so prevalent that the ordinary man or woman in the street does not realise the legal complexities of the transaction into which they are entering. As lawyers are aware, these transactions are not as legally simple as their everyday nature suggests. We require evidence of a *consensus* in *idem*, or a meeting of the minds, achieved by a clear and unambiguous offer and an unqualified acceptance of that offer. We have developed special rules to allow us to determine what the exact terms of the contract are, when it was formed and where it is governed.

The Internet is the world's fastest growing commercial market place. Estimates of its growth show unprecedented development. Recent figures from the Department of Trade and Industry put the current value of worldwide electronic commerce at US$12bn *per annum* with an estimated value of US$350–500bn by 2002.[2] Even the DTI's most conservative estimate suggests a growth in e-commerce of over 2,900 per cent in four years. At the heart of this development is the ability to contract electronically. The question how, when

* Department of Law, London School of Economics. E mail a.murray@lse/.ac.uk. I am grateful to Mr Scott Wortley and Mr Douglas Vick for their useful and thought-provoking comments on earlier drafts of this chapter. I alone remain responsible for any errors or omissions.

[1] The following introduction is, necessarily, limited in its detail. Much more detailed and erudite discussions of the general rules of contract may be found in McBryde, *The Law of Contract in Scotland* (W.Green/SULI, Edinburgh, 1987); Walker, *The Law of Contracts and Related Obligations in Scotland* (3rd edn., T&T Clark, Edinburgh, 1995); Beale *et al.*, *Chitty on Contracts* (28th edn., Sweet & Maxwell, London, 1999).

[2] Department of Trade & Industry, *Our Competitive Future: Building the Knowledge Driven Economy* (HMSO, London, 1998), para. 4.14. A more recent survey carried by Forrester Research suggests the value of the US e-commerce market could be US$184 billion by 2004. This suggests a more conservative but still substantial growth rate of 870% over 5 years. Source: E-commerce Survey, *The Economist*, 26 Feb. 2000, 6.

and where contracts are formed over the Internet is no longer academic, it is an important commercial consideration. We will find in a few years that we enter into contracts over the Internet as freely, and with as little thought, as we currently do in a bookshop or a café. As lawyers though we must ask the same questions of these new electronic contracts as we currently ask of traditional contracts: when are they formed, where are they governed and what are the terms of the contract? These three questions will be revisited throughout this chapter, as the WWW of When, Where and What will prove to be increasingly important for the development of e-commerce.

MAKING SENSE OF THE TECHNOLOGY[3]

The Internet is merely another tool of communication. The law has, to date, dealt with the advent of the Royal Mail, the telephone, telex and fax machine. There is no reason to suppose the development of e-mail or the World Wide Web will affect in any way the application of the current principles of contract law. The Internet, though, does raise unique technological issues when examining contract formation. It is these technological issues which all too often cloud our analysis of the contract. Before going on, it is therefore necessary to take some time out to examine the practicalities of contract formation on the Internet and to explain some terminology which will be used throughout this chapter.

There are two main methods of electronic contracting, each with their own characteristics, and each requiring to be treated separately. Most people are familiar with the first; electronic mail, or e-mail. E-mail is the digital equivalent of a letter. You type it out, sometimes attach things to it, address it and then send it to your desired recipient. E-mail can do all the things that real mail (sometimes called snail mail) can do. It can be used to make an offer or to communicate acceptance. It can be used for advertisements and circulars and can even be a source of junk mail (spam). E-mail is even sent and received like real mail. The sender puts it in his outbox, the digital equivalent of a post-box, and this is then collected by his mail server, who forwards it to the recipient's mail server, who then deliver it to the recipient's inbox, which may be seen as the equivalent of his letter-box.[4] This process, although usually very quick, is not instantaneous. Just as in actual reality letters can be delayed or even lost in the post.

---

[3] For an excellent, and detailed, discussion of the technology involved in e-mail and the World Wide Web see Davies in L. Edwards and C. Waelde (eds.), *Law & the Internet* (Hart, Oxford, 1997).

[4] This is, of course, a simplification of the process. The mail is split into packets and then each packet is sent individually, perhaps via several servers, before it finally reaches the recipient. More detailed analyses may be found at: Davies *ibid*, 102–3, and Gringras, *The Laws of the Internet* (Butterworths, London, 1997), 17–18.

The second method of contracting is perhaps less familiar. This is the click-wrap method of contracting used on the World Wide Web.[5] These contracts are formed using the link between server and client machines which is in place during data exchanges on the Web. The usual format of such a contract is that the webpage operator places an advert on its page called a webvertisement, offering a product or service for sale. For example, the Web site may carry an advertisement for this book, where the operator offers to supply it in exchange for a certain sum of money. On this webpage will be a hypertext order form which the customer will fill out. At the end of this form will be a button saying '*Submit*', '*I Accept*', or something similar. When the customer clicks this button, they submit their order to the Web site operator. This is like taking the goods to the cash register in a shop, except that the cashier will usually be a computer instead of a person. Like communications between a customer and a cashier in a shop, communications across the Web are instantaneous. This is important for the analysis which follows.

ALLOWING FOR ELECTRONIC CONTRACTS—PERMISSIVE REGULATION

The first question which requires to be addressed, with regard to electronic contracting, is whether such virtual contracts are allowed at all by the current law. Only if that question is resolved in the affirmative can we move on to more complex issues of exactly when a contract is concluded, what its terms are, and where it is regulated.

Many everyday contracts are devoid of formalities, and as such may be concluded in writing or orally, electronically or physically. These informal contracts, which are the vast majority of all contracts including most contracts of sale and lease, can safely be concluded over the Internet. Many contracts, though, require to be in writing, or have some other form of formal requirement such as the attachment of a physical signature or attestation by witnesses to be effective.[6] These formal requirements can cause problems when the principles of e-contracting are applied. A major issue is the application, in Cyberspace, of rules which require the contract to be 'written', or 'in writing'.[7] Can a digital document fulfil the necessary formal requirements of such a contract?

Experts agreed the answer was no.[8] If there is a requirement for a contract to be 'in writing', reference will usually be made to the Interpretation Act 1978

---

[5] Web-based contracts are termed click wrap as they are seen as the modern equivalent of shrink wrap contracts. For more on shrink wrap contracts see Gringras, 'The Validity of Shrink Wrap Licences' (1996) 4(2) *International Journal of Law & Information Technology* 77; Bainbridge, *Introduction to Computer Law* (4th edn., Longman, London, 2000), ch. 18.

[6] See e.g. the effect of ss. 1–3 of the Requirements of Writing (Scotland) Act 1995 (RoW(S)A).

[7] Such as contracts for the sale of land, RoW(S)A s.1.

[8] See Select Committee on Trade & Industry, *Seventh Report* (19 May 1999) <http://www.parliament.the-stationery-office.co.uk/pa/cm199899/cmselect/cmtrdind/187/18702.htm> at para.53; Department of Trade & Industry, *Building Confidence in Electronic Commerce—A Consultation Document* (The Stationary Office, London, 1999) at para.16.

change in status. This is because all communications between clients and servers have an inbuilt self-checking mechanism called a checksum.[46] If the checksum does not arrive, or is not confirmed the client/server will know there has been a breakdown in communications within seconds. The checksum is almost the computer equivalent of, 'someone saying "Okay?" after asking a question over the telephone'.[47] The legal impact of this technical development is that click wrap contracts demonstrate the characteristics of a telephone conversation rather than a mail message. As the sender of the acceptance is in a position to be able to determine whether their message has been successfully received, almost instantaneously, the postal rule will therefore not apply because it does not need to. Click wrap acceptances require to be received to be effective.

The Postal Rule—Conclusion

Given the above analysis, and increased reliance on electronic communications,[48] it is perhaps time the postal rule was restated for the twenty-first century. A possible reformulation would focus on the non-instantaneous nature of communications which benefit from the rule. Perhaps the new rule should state that, 'where an offer contemplates acceptance by a non-immediate form of communication, that acceptance is effective from the time it leaves the acceptor's control'. Such a definition would remove the need for a trusted third party and would encompass all non-instantaneous methods of communication (including those not yet invented). It does, though, require that methods of communication can be split into immediate and non-immediate, a distinction that may become blurred with future technological advances.

WHEN?—CURRENT EUROPEAN PROPOSALS CONCERNING CROSS-BORDER
TRANSACTIONS

As can be seen from the above analysis, contract formation over the Internet is technically complex, and is, to date, legally uncertain. There are several reasons for this uncertainty. There is the debate, discussed above, over whether or not the postal rule applies to electronic communications, and there is the issue of what qualifies as 'receipt' in the digital world: to be received does the commun-

---

[46] The checksum is there for technical rather than legal reasons. All Internet communications are packet switched. This means they are sent as several packets rather than one whole. The client machine reassembles the information and, with the World Wide Web, displays the page on a browser. If any packet were to go missing the information would be corrupted, therefore the client receives with the information packets a checksum, a calculation of exactly how much information there should be. If the checksum does not match the received information, the client knows there is missing/incorrect information and can request it is resent.

[47] Gringras, *supra* n.4, at 26.

[48] E-mails now outnumber, by volume carried daily, traditional (or snail mail) communications.

ication have to reach the offeror or is delivery to his mail or Web server sufficient?[49] Above all, though, contracting over the Internet is legally problematic
due to its disregard for national boundaries. The above discussion addresses the
question of contract formation from a United Kingdom perspective. The rules
discussed, and the application of these rules in the manner discussed, provide a
method of analysing the formation of electronic contracts within the UK. Many
electronic contracts are not domestic contracts. One of the great successes of the
Internet is the creation of a worldwide market place. A trader in Rome can,
through a webpage, reach a customer in New York just as easily as one in
Sorrento. This cross-border impact of the Internet adds a further dimension to
electronic contracting, that of international private law, with questions of jurisdiction and choice of law awaiting settlement.[50]

In an attempt to stimulate electronic commerce, and provide for harmonisation in the process, the European Union has examined the issue of contract
formation in the Electronic Commerce Directive.[51] The Directive had a difficult
formative process. The original draft was finalised by the European
Commission in November 1998 (as Directive COM(1998)586) but following
detailed examination in May 1999 by the European Parliament it became clear
the original proposals regarding contract formation were in urgent need of
review.[52] This review was carried out in the summer of 1999 and the amended
proposals were published in August 1999 (as Directive COM(1999) 427).
Following further detailed analysis by the Council of the European Union the
draft Directive was substantially amended once more. The Directive was finally
enacted on 8 June 2000, with little change made to the Sections regulating contract formation. The following section analyses the potential effect of the new
Directive on the formation of Electronic Contracts.[53]

The Directive requires Member States to amend existing legislation to ensure
that current requirements, including requirements of form, which may restrict
the use of electronic documentation in the formation of contracts, are
removed.[54] The Directive therefore employs a functional equivalent approach
seen previously in the UNCITRAL model law on electronic commerce.[55] The
formation of electronic contracts is to be regulated in accordance with Section
3 (Articles 9–11) of the Directive.

The final version of the Directive differs substantially from the previous
drafts in determining when a contract is concluded electronically. Both the

---

[49] For more discussion on this vexed issue see, Dickie, *supra* n.32, at 333; Gringras, *supra* n.4, at
24. Art. 11(1) of the e-commerce Dir., *supra* n.12, provides that a communication is delivered when
the party to whom it is addressed is able to access it. This should deal with this problematic issue.

[50] Discussed *infra* at pp. 31–34.

[51] *Supra* n.12.

[52] See in particular the report of proccedings of the European Parliament for 6 May 1999, available from <http://www.europarl.eu.int/dg7/cre/mi2/0506.pdf>

[53] See Appendix I to this volume.

[54] See Recital 34.

[55] *Supra* n.12.

November 1998 and the August 1999 proposals specifically provided when a contract was deemed to be concluded.[56] The final Directive has replaced all attempts to define when a contract is concluded with guidelines as to when orders from customers and acknowledgements from service providers are deemed to be received.[57] The revised language is a compromise which has been arrived at following intensive lobbying from consumer groups, members of professional organisations and representatives of the Internet community. Like most compromises it proves to be an unsatisfactory solution. The revised draft was obviously devised to allow its application equally in the Civilian and the Anglo-American models of contract formation, both of which are in use in the European Union. The effect of this compromise is that the Directive says remarkably little on contract formation. It provides duties for those who market their products over the Internet,[58] but makes no attempt to define the legal position of an electronic offer or acceptance. In addition the Directive is of limited effect when dealing with contracts concluded exclusively by e-mail due to several exceptions which apply to e-mail communications.[59]

The Directive proves to be extremely disappointing to those who read it with a hope of obtaining guidance on the formation of contract within the European Union. It will prove a valuable tool in identifying the domicile of service providers and it will assist consumers in seeking redress once a breach of contract has been determined,[60] but it provides no more than equivalence at the point of formation of a contract. Although the Directive may assist in cross-border disputes, it will not alter the current position on formation of electronic contracts previously discussed.

WHAT?—INCORPORATING CONTRACTUAL TERMS

The terms of any contract, whether it is formed in virtual reality, or actual reality will be those agreed upon by the parties at the time the contract is concluded. This was clearly illustrated in the celebrated case of *Thornton* v. *Shoe Lane Parking*,[61] where Lord Denning treated the issue of a ticket by an automated ticket machine as the point at which the contract was concluded, ruling that the

---

[56] In the Nov. 1999 revisal it was provided that: 'where a recipient, in accepting a service provider's offer, is required to give his consent through technological means, such as clicking on an icon, the contract is concluded when the recipient of the service has received from the service provider, electronically, an acknowledgement of receipt of the recipient's acceptance' (Art. 11).

[57] Art. 11(1)

[58] See in particular Arts. 10(1), 10(3) and 11(1).

[59] See Arts. 10(4) and 11(3).

[60] This is achieved through Arts. 3 (Internal Market), 5 and 6 (Information to be Provided) and 16–20 (Implementation).

[61] [1971] 2 QB 163.

terms of issue printed on the ticket could not form part of the contract. This approach may be seen as a development of the rule in the so-called ticket cases, particularly *Parker* v. *South Eastern Railway Co.*[62], where terms printed on tickets or receipts have been held only to be validly incorporated into the contract if the terms have been brought to the other party's attention before the contract is concluded.

Two separate issues determine which terms have been agreed by the parties. The first is, 'when is the contract concluded?' This is because, as seen, extra terms cannot be incorporated into the contract after it has been concluded. At the point the contract is concluded the parties have consensus, and any attempt to introduce further terms after this point creates dissensus unless, of course, all parties agree to the new term.[63] From our previous analysis we have established that all contractual terms to an e-mail contract must be introduced prior to the acceptance being sent, and for click wrap contracts all terms must be introduced before the acceptance is received by the offeror. The second issue is the identification of what terms have been introduced into the contract. Generally, these fall into three categories: Express Terms, Terms Incorporated by Reference and Implied Terms.[64]

Incorporating Express Terms

The incorporation of express terms into either e-mail or click wrap contracts should not pose any difficulties. Such terms will be clearly set out in the transmission of information between parties, and as such should be easily identified. There are, though, two problem issues regarding express terms which parties should always bear in mind when negotiating an electronic contract. The first is that parties must take care to identify the document or documents which are intended to constitute the contract. This will be more common with e-mail contracts than with click wrap contracts due to the potential for prolonged exchanges between the parties at the negotiation stage.[65] The second potential problem of express terms is their interpretation by the courts in the event of a dispute. Contracting parties should attempt to limit as far as possible any inconsistencies or ambiguities in their contractual terms. In the event of any

---

[62] (1877) 2 CPD 416.

[63] In effect agreeing a new contract.

[64] For detail on these categories see Walker, *supra* n.1, chs. 20–22; McBryde, *supra* n.1, chs. 6, 13.

[65] Web site operators making use of click wrap contracts have to ensure that automated response systems only accept terms which they find acceptable. Thus, if I were to operate a site selling steel at £100 per tonne, I would need to ensure that the automated response system on my server was programmed in such a way as to ensure it would not accept a communication saying, 'I wish to order 100 tonnes of steel at $100 per tonne'. The result of such an automated acceptance would be to create a contract on these new terms. This can easily be remedied by giving the response system a checksum against which it checks any offers received.

disagreement between the parties on the terms of the contract the court will apply the established rules of contractual interpretation.[66]

Incorporating Terms by Reference

The structure of the Web, with its interconnected, hyperlinked pages, lends itself to incorporation by reference.[67] Consequently, terms incorporated by reference are common in relation to click wrap and e-mail contracts. The terms that the contracting party wishes to incorporate are set out in a separate document and are incorporated into the final contract by a reference to this separate document somewhere in the contractual documentation. Commonly with click wrap contracts, this separate document is a separate web page held on the same server as the click wrap contract. This is usually known as the terms and conditions page and is accessible via a hypertext link embedded in the main click wrap agreement page. The problem is, though, that to be effectively incorporated the terms must not only be clear and unambiguous, they must also clearly have been intended to form part of the contract. This means that the party relying upon these incorporated terms must take all steps to bring them to the attention of the other party before the contract is concluded and in such a manner as to make it clear these terms are intended to be contractual terms.[68]

What does this mean with regard to click wrap contracts? It is suggested that as webvertisements are *prima facie* advertisements, not contractual documents, customers will not expect to find contractual terms and conditions contained therein. The Web site operator will have to draw these terms clearly to the customer's attention and will have to do so before the contract is concluded.[69] The design of the Web site must be such that any terms to be incorporated by reference are referred to prior to the '*Submit*' or '*I Accept*' button. This is because once the submission button is clicked the transaction will be processed in a matter of seconds with the customer receiving their confirmation (the acceptance) before they have an opportunity to scroll further down the page. Further, the terms and conditions must be clearly signposted; merely giving an opportunity to find the terms on another page would probably be insufficient, as would

[66] See McBryde, *supra* n.1, ch.19; Walker, *supra* n.1, ch.24. The Parole Evidence Rule and the Rule of Prior Communings have been greatly modified by the Contract (Scotland) Act 1997, available at: <http://www.legislation.hmso.gov.uk/acts/acts1997/1997034.htm>.

[67] As do modern e-mail systems which allow for embedded hypertext links.

[68] Thus courts have continually held that where 'contractual' terms are found in places where the customer would not expect to find them they do not form part of the contract. See *Chapelton* v. *Barry UDC* [1940] 1 KB 532, *Taylor* v. *Glasgow Corporation* 1952 SC 440 (both involving tickets/receipts) and *Lightbody's Tr.* v. *Hutchison* (1886) 14 R 4 (advertising leaflet).

[69] Some terms will require a greater degree of highlighting than others. Exclusionary terms for instance will require a significant degree of explicitness. See Denning LJ in *Spurling* v. *Bradshaw* [1956] 2 All ER 121, 125F, 'Some clauses which I have seen would need to be printed in red ink on the face of the document with a red hand pointing to it before the notice could be held to be sufficient'.

putting the terms on a general information page. Effectively to incorporate any external terms and conditions the site operator must offer a clearly marked and prominent link to the specific terms and conditions they wish to incorporate into the contract before the customer can enter into the contract. The site operator can ensure the terms and conditions have been incorporated into the contract by requiring the customer to indicate they have knowledge of, and have accepted, these terms and conditions before processing their order. This is easily done by requiring the customer to check a box on the order form or by placing the order form on a separate page which requires the customer to click an acknowledgement as the link to the order page.[70] If the customer has acknowledged they are aware of the terms then the terms and conditions will be incorporated into the contract even if the customer has not read them.

Implied Terms

As with contracts concluded in actual reality there will be occasions where terms will be implied into contracts concluded in virtual reality. As implied terms usually come about apart from the contract formation process, the fact that a contract has been concluded in Cyberspace will be of no impact to the rules on formation of contract. Implied terms may be implied by fact, such as terms required to give a contract business efficacy,[71] and terms implied on the basis of custom or usage.[72] Additionally terms may be implied by the common law such as the implied term of seaworthiness implied into contracts for the carriage of goods by sea,[73] and the implied rule of non-derogation from grant.[74] As the introduction of these terms is uniform, no matter how the contract was negotiated and concluded, the use of e-mail or click wrap contracts will not affect the established rules and reference should be made to traditional contract texts for further guidance on implied terms.[75]

WHERE?— CHOICE OF LAW AND CROSS BORDER TRANSACTIONS[76]

Having spent most of this chapter discussing the questions *when* the contract is formed and *what* its terms are, we arrive, finally, at the question *where* it is

[70] The author would always advise any webvertiser to take the action described above. Simply offering a link to a terms and conditions page may prove insufficient as people become used to modern technology and begin to ignore parts of pages of no interest to them, scrolling immediately down to the order form/button.

[71] See *The Moorcock* (1889) 14 PD 64.

[72] See *William Morton & Co. v. Muir Bros. & Co.,* 1907 SC 1211.

[73] See *Steel* v. *State Line Steamship Co.* (1877) 3 App. Cas. 72.

[74] See *Barr* v. *Lions Ltd.* 1956 SC 59.

[75] McBryde, *supra* n.1, ch.6; Walker, *supra* n.1, ch.22.

[76] This section deals with choice of law, not jurisdiction. For a discussion of jurisdictional issues in Cyberspace see, Chapter 10 by Paul Torremans.

governed. As has already been discussed, the Internet is a unique market place in terms of market penetration. Any computer, anywhere in the world, connected to the Internet can access a Web site and may conclude, through that site, an electronic contract.[77] The potential for cross-border disputes in web contracts is, obviously, much greater than in actual reality where most consumer contracts, and a high degree of commercial contracts, are domestic in nature. Issues of private international law, and in particular choice of law, are therefore to the fore when disputes arise.

Assuming a Web site operator is based in Scotland, which legal system regulates his contracts with overseas customers? At common law, the proper law of the contract, usually the *lex loci contractus*, governed the contract.[78] In essence, this is still the position today, but now the proper law of the contract will be interpreted in light of the Contracts (Applicable Law) Act 1990 which introduced the Rome Convention[79] into the UK. The convention provides rules to assist in the identification of the proper law of the contract, in effect replacing the common law in most areas.[80] Throughout this section, reference will be made to the convention, and to the report of Professors Giuliano and Lagarde,[81] in an attempt to answer this question.

When dealing with cross-border contracts, choice of law issues are pertinent on three levels. For formal contracts we must determine which law applies in answering the question whether the contract is formally valid. That is to ask, have all necessary formal requirements been complied with? This will include issues such as requirements of writing, witnessing and signatures.[82] As most Internet contracts are currently of an informal nature formality will not be discussed further here, except to say that regulation of this area may be found at Article 9 of the Rome Convention and is discussed at some length in the Giuliano and Lagarde report.[83] Secondly, we must deal with the issue whether the contract is materially valid, that is to ask whether the contract has actually been formed, and is legally valid, according to the laws of the jurisdiction which apply to the contract.[84] If there is the possibility that the contract is materially

---

[77] The most recent Internet Software Consortium survey (Jan. 2000) reveals that 227 countries are currently connected to the Internet and have at least one host computer. <http://www.isc.org/ds/WWW-200001/dist-bynum.html>

[78] See Leslie, 'Private International Law', *The Laws of Scotland: Stair Memorial Encyclopaedia* (Butterworths/Law Society of Scotland, Edinburgh, 1989), vol. 17, para.244ff.

[79] The EEC Convention on the Law Applicable to Contractual Obligations. See Sch.1. of the Contracts (Applicable Law) Act 1990.

[80] Although the common law still regulates some rules of contract formation and validity. The capacity to contract, for example, is still regulated by the common law. See Art.1(2)(a) of the Convention and North and Fawcett, *Cheshire and North's Private International Law* (12th edn., Butterworths, London, 1992), 469–70.

[81] *Report on the Rome Convention* [1980] OJ C282/1. The report may be considered when interpreting the Convention. See s.3(3)(a) of the Contracts (Applicable Law) Act 1990.

[82] All these matters are dealt with as matters of formal (contractual) validity not matters of procedure. See Cheshire and North, *supra* n.80 at 507.

[83] *Supra* n.81. at C282/28–C282/32.

[84] See Cheshire and North, *supra* n.80 at 505–7.

invalid, the courts have to decide whether this is the case, by applying the law of some particular jurisdiction. The question is, though, if the parties have not agreed this, which jurisdiction's laws should apply? This is regulated by Article 8 of the Convention, which states that 'the existence and validity of a contract, or of any term of a contract, shall be determined by the law which *would* govern it under this Convention if the contract or term were valid'.[85] Material validity is established, therefore, using the proper law of the contract, discussed below. This may seem unreasonable if, as one of the parties is obviously claiming, there is in fact no contract. The best explanation for the terms of Article 8(1) is provided by Giuliano and Lagarde who state that, '[t]his is to avoid the circular argument that where there is a choice of the applicable law no law can be said to be applicable until the contract is found to be valid'.[86] Finally, we have the issues covered by the applicable law, for example questions of interpretation, performance and the consequences of breach of contract. These, like the question of material validity, are dealt with by establishing the proper law of the contract in accordance with Articles 3, 4 and 5 of the Convention as follows.

The Convention applies to choice of law issues in contract, and begins by identifying the law applicable to the contract.[87] The general principle is that the parties are free to choose the law applicable to the contract. This choice can be made expressly or can be implied from the circumstances.[88] This means that, generally, a Web site operator may include a choice of law clause in the terms and conditions of the agreement and, according to the Rome Convention, the law of the place identified will govern the contract.[89]

If the parties to the contract choose no applicable law, the issue becomes more complicated. Article 4 of the Convention regulates such occurrences. In such a case, the applicable law is the law of the country which has the closest connection with the contract. Article 4(2) contains a presumption to help identify this country stating, 'the contract is most closely connected with the country where the party who is to effect the performance which is characteristic of the contract has, at the time of conclusion of the contract, his habitual residence, or for traders the country in which their principal place of business is located'. The characteristic performance of a contract is usually the act for which payment is made.[90] This may be the supply of goods or services or the provision of information. The effect of this is that the courts will usually apply the law of the country where the person who has to provide/supply the required goods or

---

[85] Emphasis added. There is an exception to this in Art. 8(2) when a party wishes to establish they did not consent to the contract and it would be unreasonable to apply the terms of Art. 8(1). For more on this see Cheshire and North, *supra* n.80 at 506–7.

[86] Report on the Rome Convention, *supra* n.81 at C282/30.

[87] Art.1.

[88] Art.3(1). An example of circumstances which would allow choice of law to be implied would be where the contract fails to comply with the formalities of one of the possible jurisdictions interpreting the contract. In such a situation, the court may imply the parties' intended for the contract to be governed by the law of another jurisdiction.

[89] *Ibid.*

[90] The Giuliano and Lagarde report, *supra* n.81 at 282/20.

service maintains their principal place of business or is habitually resident. Thus, to give an example, if Company A, which is based in Edinburgh, runs a Web site offering to supply software and that software is bought and downloaded by Company B in Germany, then, in the absence of a specific choice of law clause, the contract will be governed by Scots law, as the company carrying out the characteristic performance (the supply of the software) has its principle place of business in Scotland.[91]

The above analysis alters substantially if we replace company B with consumer B. The Rome Convention ensures that consumers can rely on their usual consumer protection measures when contracting with overseas traders. If the object of the contract is the supply of goods or services to a party who is not buying in the course of trade then Article 5 applies to the agreement.[92] The effect is that if the seller advertises in the consumer's country of residence the contract will be regulated by the law of the consumer's place of residence, not the place of residence of the party carrying out specific performance. Thus, to return to our example, if company B is replaced with consumer B, German law, not Scots law, now regulates the contract. The provisions of Article 5(2), though, qualify this. The buyer's place of habitual residence comes into play only if: (1) conclusion of the contract was preceded by a specific invitation from the seller to the buyer or the seller intended to advertise to consumers such as the buyer,[93] (2) the seller received the buyer's order in the country in which the buyer was habitually resident, or (3) if the contract is for the sale of goods, and the buyer travelled from the country of his habitual residence to another country to give his order, and the seller arranged his journey with the intention of inducing him to enter into the contract. If none of these circumstances arises the proper law of contract as determined by Articles 3 and 4 will govern the contract. Transactions concluded over the World Wide Web raise many issues when dealing with Article 5(2). Is a webvertisment made in the country of the buyer's habitual residence or is it made in the seller's country of residence? Where is the order received?[94] By putting an advertisement on the Web does the webvertiser *intend* it to reach consumers in all 214 wired countries? These questions are causing problems, both for the determination of choice of law and for consumer protection.[95]

---

[91] A similar (non-Internet) case which illustrates this point is *William Grant & Sons v. Marie Brizard Espana SA*, 19 Jan. 1998, available at: <http://scotcourd1-1-http.pipex.net/opinions/HAM0601.html>. This case involved the export of whisky from Scotland to Spain. Lord Hamilton found that the characteristic of a contract of sale of goods was the sale and delivery by the seller of the goods, and that the contract was therefore regulated by Scots law.

[92] See Cheshire and North, *supra* n.80 at 495 and 509.

[93] The invitation or advertisement must be in the country in which the buyer is habitually resident. It would not be enough for the seller to advertise in his own country and for the buyer to reply to an advertisement there.

[94] This is particularly pertinent when the seller is based in one country but operates out of a server based in another country.

[95] See below Chapter 10.

CONCLUSION—ANALYSING ELECTRONIC CONTRACTS

The wired world is coming. Electronic communications will soon become the most common method of contracting. Smart fridges will order groceries directly from the store and interactive televisions will replace high street shops. The way we live our lives will be changed forever by e-commerce, and to drive all this the electronic contract has to be valued and respected in a similar manner as the oral or written contract.

The above is, of course, gross hyperbole.[96] The Internet is a remarkable communications tool, and undoubtedly e-commerce will grow in importance, but the Internet is no more than a tool of communication like the telephone, telex or fax machine. Just as they have been integrated into our rules of contract so will Internet communications. What is undoubtedly true is that electronic contracting is becoming commonplace, and in a few years' time a substantial percentage of both commercial and consumer contracts will be concluded in Cyberspace. This discussion has hopefully emphasised that, although e-contracts do suffer some problems not usually associated with oral or written contracts, these problems are easily surmountable, in most cases by the simple application of current rules. By asking three basic questions, *when* was the contract concluded? *what* are the terms of the contract? and *where* is the contract governed?, we can deal with most questions asked about a contract whether it is formed electronically or by more traditional means. There is nothing different in the eyes of the law about a contract formed in Cyberspace. These questions are equally valid when analysing traditional or electronic contracts. The 'Real W.W.W.' when analysing contractual relationships is not the World Wide Web, but When What Where.

---

[96] At least the author hopes it is.

3

Secrecy and Signatures—Turning the Legal Spotlight on Encryption and Electronic Signatures

MARTIN HOGG*

INTRODUCTION

Of the subjects covered in this book, that which is perhaps the most controversial at the present time is cryptography, the technology underpinning both encryption and electronic signatures.[1] The proposals for legislation in this area have generated interest from a wide variety of bodies. This may be seen from the disparate parties who participated in the British Governmental and parliamentary consultations on electronic commerce.[2] These included the Confederation of British Industry, commercial enterprises (such as British Telecommunications plc), the Internet Service Providers' Association, academics, the National Criminal Intelligence Service, and civil rights groups (such as Cyber-Rights and Cyber-Liberties (UK)).

The interest generated was the result of varying concerns, amongst them human rights, privacy and the prevention and detection of crime. It is principally the phenomenal rise in the use of cryptography for commercial reasons, however, which has prompted the need for a consideration of the legal regulation of electronic signatures and encryption.

The British Government has now enacted an Electronic Communications Act.[3] The Government have managed to stick closely to their timetable for the

---

* Lecturer, The School of Law, University of Edinburgh.

[1] Or 'digital signatures' as they are also referred to.

[2] Notably, in the responses to the DTI's Consultation Paper, *Building Confidence in Electronic Commerce, A Consultation Document* (Mar. 1999), and the witness interviews conducted as part of the House of Commons Trade and Industry Committee's investigation of Electronic Commerce (whose Report was published on 12 May 1999).

[3] The Electronic Communications Act 2000. c.7, available at htp://www.hmso.gov.uk/acts/acts2000/20000007.htm. For the consultation paper issued prior to the Act, see *Promoting Electronic Commerce: Consultation on Draft Legislation* (Cm 4417, The Stationery Office, London, July 1999), available at <http://www.dti.gov.uk/cii/elec/ecbill.pdf>. The Bill was amended by the House of Commons in Committee on 16 Dec. 1999, and subsequently intorudced into the House of Lords on 26 Jan. 2000. The current text of the Bill is available at: <http://www. parliament.the-stationery-office.co.uk/pa/ld199900/ldbills/024/2000024.htm>

promulgation of this Act, despite the view expressed by several parties that matters were proceeding at an unseemly pace merely in order to coincide with the millennial date. The Act is in three parts, and addresses cryptography service providers (Part I), electronic signatures and certificates (Part II), and Telecommunications licences and other matters (Part III). The first two parts are of particular concern in this chapter and the relevant provisions of the Act are discussed below. Provisions concerning law enforcement access to encrypted material are included in separate legislation, the Regulation of Investigatory Powers Bill.[4]

The following discussion is divided into four parts. In the first part, there will be an explanation of the nature of cryptography, and the dependent applications of document encryption and electronic signatures; secondly, the current state of the law regarding these areas will be assessed; thirdly, proposals for law reform will be considered; and lastly, the international dimension, in so far as not already covered, will be considered.

CRYPTOGRAPHY, ENCRYPTION, AND ELECTRONIC SIGNATURES

Cryptography

In the business world, there has been an ever increasing interest in ensuring that electronic communications are afforded the qualities of authenticity, integrity and confidentiality. A handwritten signature has traditionally been the best guarantee of the first two of these qualities in a document: it uniquely verifies the person from whom the document originates,[5] and indicates assent to the contents of the text appearing above it.[6] Confidentiality has had to be assured by, for instance, enclosing the document in a sealed envelope. However, forgery is not unknown and envelopes can be opened and resealed. Technological developments now offer a more ironcast guarantee of achieving all of these qualities, via the use of cryptography.

Cryptography is used to create electronic signatures (which are used to achieve authenticity and integrity) and to encrypt such signatures or other data (such as e-mails or commercial documents, thus achieving the end of confidentiality). Attempts to alter electronic signatures are easily detectable and the document's authenticity would then be doubted; attempts to decrypt an encrypted document should prove impossible if a secure enough encryption program has been used. If company A wishes to send company B a confidential electronic transaction, it can 'sign' it by means of an electronic signature and then encrypt the whole message, secure in the knowledge that it may be deciphered only by the intended recipient, who will be able to identify the sender.

---

[4] <http://www.hmso.gov.uk/acts/acts2000/20000023.htm>.
[5] Although with handwritten signatures forgery is not unknown.
[6] Although changes to documents after signature are normally accompanied by a further signature next to the alteration, it is not impossible to alter a paper document without detection.

Cryptography, simply put, is the 'science of codes and cyphers',[7] and involves the application to electronic data of a mathematical algorithm, the encryption 'key', in order to render the data indecipherable by anyone not having access to the appropriate decryption 'key'. There are two principal types of cryptography in use, *private* or *symmetric* key cryptography, and *public* or *asymmetric* key cryptography. The way in which these differ is discussed below. In both of the examples discussed, the sender of the message is Romeo and the recipient Juliet.[8]

Private key cryptography

Figure 1 depicts a *private* or *symmetric* system of cryptography.

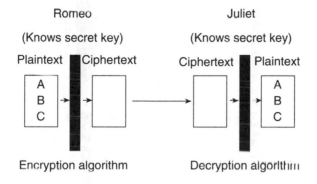

In such a system, both parties have the *same* key, which they keep secret, and this key is used both to encrypt and decrypt any messages sent by the parties. The symmetric system is faster than the asymmetric or public key system, as it uses a smaller number of 'bits' (or digital symbols) in the key (typically 56 to 128).

Various symmetric key algorithms have been in use in recent years, amongst them the Data Encryption Standard (DES), the Fast Encryption Algorithm (FEAL), the International Data Encryption Algorithm (IDEA) and the Secure and Fast Encryption Routine (SAFER). However, some of these may now no longer offer the highest level of security. Philip Zimmermann, the creator of Pretty Good Privacy (PGP),[9] has stated that, with an expensive enough computer system, DES could be cracked in times spanning from 3.5 hours down to two minutes (depending on the size of the computer).[10] Such an enterprise

---

[7] *Ibid.*, 17.

[8] The diagrams are taken from the European Commissions' paper, *Towards a European Framework for Digital Signatures and Encryption* (8 Oct. 1997), which may be found at <http://www.ispo.cec.be/eif/policy/ 97503toc.html>.

[9] See the mention of this in the section on public key cryptography below.

[10] See Philip Zimmermann's testimony before the United States senate: <http://www.nai.com/products/security/phil/phil-quotes.asp>.

would require a computer costing millions of pounds. However, Zimmermann points out that such a figure could be hidden in the budget of a major corporation intent on industrial espionage.

Public Key Cryptography

Figure 2 depicts a *public* or *asymmetric* system of cryptography.

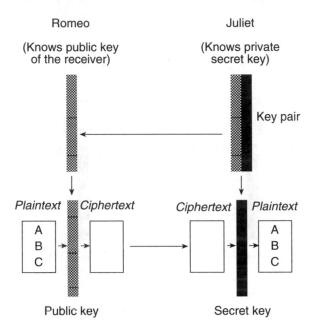

In such a system, there is both a *public* and a *private* key, which are a pair. The public key is published, the private key is known only to the individual who generated the key pair. Only the private key fits together with the public key to form a compatible pair.

If Romeo wishes to send Juliet an encrypted message, he encrypts the message using *her public key*. She alone can decrypt it using *her private key*—thus the communication's contents are secure. This is the process depicted in Figure 2. In addition, though not shown in this figure, Romeo could also have included in the message an electronic signature identifying him as the sender. He would have encrypted this using *his private* key. Once Juliet had decrypted the message contents with her private key, she could have decrypted Romeo's electronic signature using *his public key*, thus verifying that the message came from Romeo. Had Romeo and Juliet used this system of cryptography, rather than entrusting their communications to a senile Friar, Shakespeare's story might have had a happier ending.

The disadvantage of public key systems is that they are slower to operate, using larger keys—typically 1,024 bits.

Examples of asymmetric systems which have been in use in recent times are the RSA public key, and the Diffie-Hellmann algorithm. RSA has been embedded in the USA in Microsoft Windows, Netscape Navigator and Lotus Notes amongst other software packages. New products are coming on to the market all the time.

It is possible to speed up asymmetric systems, by using a technique known as a *digital envelope*. This technique combines both symmetric and asymmetric algorithms. An example is the well-known Pretty Good Privacy (PGP) developed by Philip Zimmermann.

Applications of Cryptography

Electronic Signatures

An electronic signature[11] may be described as a string of electronic data used to identify the sender of a data message, in much the same way as a handwritten signature—a collection of letters scribbled in a particular way—identifies an individual. The effectiveness of an electronic signature requires that it be produceable by the sender alone and that any attempt to alter it be incompatible with the integrity of the signature. These qualities of authenticity and integrity can be achieved using cryptography. An electronic signature created using a unique cryptographic private key can only have emanated from the person having control of that key. This of course means that the private key must be guarded securely, much as a physical seal has to be safeguarded against theft.

Encryption

The explanation of cryptography given above sufficiently explains how data may be rendered encrypted and thus confidential. One may encrypt as much or as little of a message or a document as one wishes. One might wish to encrypt merely the electronic signature at the end of a non-confidential message, so that a specific individual is identified as the sender, or one might wish in addition

---

[11] Defined in the text of the Electronic Communications Act, s. 7(2) as:
   'so much of anything in electronic form as—
   (a) is incorporated into or otherwise logically associated with any electronic communication or electronic data; and
   (c) purports to be so incorporated or associated for the purpose of being used in establishing the authenticity of the communication or data, the integrity of the communication or data, or both.'
In the first draft of the Bill, the definition of electronic signature included the requirement that the signature be 'generated by the signatory or other source of the data'. The final text as passed omits the requirement, and it thus seems that a signature could emanate from a third party and still fall within the definition.

then to encrypt the whole message, if the intention is to keep the message contents secret.

A problem, however, is that anyone can create an encryption key and claim to be a particular individual. Because of this, unless one knows the person with whom one is dealing, one cannot automatically verify the identity of the sender of a message purely from the electronic signature attached to it. One solution is through the use of an electronic certificate attached to the digital signature. Such certificates are normally issued by bodies known as Certification Authorities (CAs). Such bodies provide certification that an encryption key emanates from the person from whom it purports to emanate. The legislative regulation of such bodies is addressed in the Electronic Communications Act.[12]

THE LAW PRIOR TO THE NEW ACT

Electronic Signatures

Two principal questions arise in respect of the legal status of electronic signatures prior to the coming into effect of the new Act:

(i) where the law does not require a signature to be appended to a document, but an electronic signature has been appended to an electronic document, does this sufficiently identify the purported signer of the electronic document in the eyes of the law?

(ii) where the law requires an individual's signature before a legally binding effect can be achieved, will an electronic signature suffice?

As regards the first question, where there is no legal requirement that there be a signature, there appears to be no objection to a court taking into account an electronic signature as evidence helping to establish that a document emanated from a particular person. Such evidence, if held credible by a judge, could, like any other evidence, help to establish the provenance of a document.

As regards the second question, what if a signature is required by law? Thus far, the law has proved flexible in its estimation of what counts as a signature. In English law, the decision in *Goodman* v. *Eban*[13] established that a rubber stamp could act as the equivalent of a handwritten signature on a document. Similarly, a faxed signature has been held acceptable.[14] Such decisions have prompted one academic to comment that 'any form of signature will work under English law'.[15] The same consideration would seem to apply to Scots law.

---

[12] See below for the relevant provisions.

[13] [1954] QB 550.

[14] *In Re a Debtor (No 2021 of 1995)* [1996] 2 All ER 345.

[15] See the Trade and Industry Committee's Report (May 1999), para. 41, quoting the opinion of Chris Reed of Queen Mary and Westfield College, available at <http://www.parliament.the-stationery-office.co.uk/pa/cm199899/cmselect/cmtrdind/187/18702. htm>.

It should be added, however, that the cases thus far have at least involved paper documents, and there must remain a question whether the flexiblity of the law displayed would extend to non-paper signatures.

A further problem exists, namely that there are few legal provisions which require a signature without also requiring some form of 'writing'. What may constitute 'writing'?[16] The principal rules on writing in Scots law are now contained in the Requirements of Writing (Scotland) Act 1995. The Act states that certain things must be constituted in a 'written document' subscribed by the granter in order to be valid, subscription meaning signing by the granter at the foot of the last page (or for wills, the foot of every page).[17] However, the Act does not say what constitutes a 'written document' or 'writing', so one must look to the Interpretation Act 1978 for assistance. This statute says that writing includes 'typing, printing, lithography, photography and other modes of reproducing words in a visible form, and expressions referring to writing are construed accordingly'.[18]

Thus, even if one could interpret 'signing' to include an electronic signature, it does not seem possible to interpret 'writing' as including electronic documents. The British Government shares this view: 'the Interpretation Act, by placing emphasis on visibility, rules out electronic "writing", which is, in essence, a series of electronic impulses.'[19] For this reason, the Electronic Communications Act addresses both the status of electronic signatures *and* the rules on formal writing.[20]

Encryption

There are no explicit controls currently on the use of encryption to secure the confidentiality of a document's contents. A statutory power is already conferred upon the police in England and Wales to seize computerised data in a legible form,[21] which has prompted debate in England about the necessity of any new powers in this area.[22] Unauthorised efforts to decipher an encrypted document might well occur in circumstances where the document has been unlawfully intercepted in the course of transmission,[23] or where a computer is being unlawfully used to access the document.[24]

---

[16] This issue is dealt with further in the specific context of electronic contracts in Murray, *supra* p. 19

[17] See for more details, the Requirements of Writing (Scotland) Act 1995, c.7, s 1.

[18] Interpretation Act 1978, c.30, s 5, Sch. 1.

[19] *Building Confidence*, para. 16.

[20] See below.

[21] In England and Wales under the Police and Criminal Evidence Act 1984 (PACE), ss. 19(4) and 20.

[22] The Law Society of England and Wales appears to be of the opinion that no new powers are needed (see Trade and Industry Committee Report, para. 99 (n. 28 below)) due to existing powers in England and Wales under PACE.

[23] See the Interception of Communications Act 1985.

[24] See the Computer Misuse Act 1990, ss. 1–3.

Domestic Law Reform

Over the past two years, the British Government has published several documents setting out its intention to reform the law affecting electronic signatures and encryption. In April 1998 the British Government issued a *Secure Electronic Commerce Statement* setting out its broad legislative views on reform of these areas,[25] which followed an earlier 1997 paper addressing the more specific issue of Trusted Third Parties.[26] The Government began consulting in this area by issuing the consultation document *Building Confidence in Electronic Commerce*.[27] The consultation period was remarkably short, one of the many criticisms of the process and proposals made by the House of Commons Trade and Industry Committee in its May 1999 Report, *Building Confidence in Electronic Commerce: The Government's Proposals*.[28] The newly formed Performance and Innovation Unit (PIU) of the Cabinet Office also published a report on *Encryption and Law Enforcement*,[29] which essentially mirrored most of the British Government's proposals in its consultation paper. The Government published its draft Electronic Communications Bill[30] in July 1999. This was followed by consultation on the content, before the publication of a new draft of the Bill in December 1999 after the Committee stage, and then the Bill's introduction into the House of Lords in January 2000. The Bill was finally enacted as the Electronic Communications Act 2000 (hereinafter the "ECA") on 25 May 2000. The Government's view is that the provisions in this new legislation for the recognition of electronic signatures will have to conform with the parameters of the European Directive on a Community framework for electronic signatures,[31] and the final text of the draft Directive on electronic commerce.[32]

Electronic Signatures

Validity/Admissibility

The British Government originally proposed creating rebuttable presumptions that would apply to certain electronic signatures.[33] However, they were per-

---

[25] See <http://www.dti.gov.uk/CII/ana27p.html>.

[26] See <http://dtiinfo1.dti.gov.uk/cii/encrypt/>.

[27] See <http://www.dti.gov.uk/cii/elec/elec_com.html>.

[28] See <http://www.parliament.the-stationery-office.co.uk/pa/cm199899/cmselect/cmtrdind/187/18702.htm>.

[29] See <http://www.cabinet-office.gov.uk/innovation/1999/encryption/index.htm>.

[30] See n. 3 above.

[31] Dir. 1999/93/EC, see <http://europa.eu.int/comm/dg15/en/media/sign/Dir99-93-ec%20EN.pdf>.

[32] For the latest text, see document 14263/1/99 REV 1, issued on 28 Feb. 2000.

[33] Namely, that the electronic signature identified the signatory it purported to identify, and secondly, where the signature purported to guarantee that the accompanying data had not been altered since signature, that they had not been so altered.

suaded that this was a bad idea.[34] The current terse proposal on electronic signatures is now contained in section 7 of the ECA:

7.- (1) In any legal proceedings—

(a) an electronic signature incorporated or logically associated with a particular electronic communication or with particular electronic data, and

(c) the certification by any person of such a signature,

shall each be admissible in evidence in relation to any question as to the authenticity[35] of the communication or data or as to the integrity[36] of the communication or data.

The British Government has thus chosen to address the validity of electronic signatures in terms of their evidential admissibility, rather than via a blanket statement that electronic signatures are legally valid. This contrasts with the approach taken in other legislation, such as the US Electronic Signatures in Global and National Commerce Act (the E-SIGN Act)[36a] the Uniform Computer Information Transactions Act (UCITA)[37] and the Uniform Electronic Transactions Act (UETA),[38] the Australian Electronic Transactions Act 1999,[39] and the EC Directive on a common framework for electronic signatures,[40] which do contain a general statement as to the validity of electronic signatures.

The provisions of section 7 apply to all electronic signatures, not simply those issued by approved providers and regardless of the jurisdiction in which the signature was issued. However, because the provision merely says electronic signatures are to be admissible in evidence, and does not provide that they create

[34] This argument was forcefully put by, amongst others, the T&I Committee. The two main points it made were (1) that to create two tiers of signature—those that would qualify for the presumptions and those that would not—was alien to an English law approach, and (2) that it would reverse the burden of proof, thus undermining confidence in electronic commerce.

[35] S.15(2)(a) defines references to the authenticity of any communication or data as references to whether the communication or data come from a particular person or other source, is accurately timed and dated, and/or is intended to have legal effect.

[36] S. 15(2)(b) defines references to the integrity of any communication or data as 'references to whether there has been any tampering with or other modification of the communication or data'.

[36a] This Act was signed by the US President on 30 June 2000 and takes effect on 1 Oct. 2000. An electronic version is available at the http://thomas.loc.gov website.

[37] The UCITA provision (s. 107(a)) states: 'A record or authentication may not be denied legal effect or enforceability solely because it is in electronic form'. For details on UCITA see <http://www.2bguide.com>. The text of the Act is at <http://www.law.upenn.edu/bll/ulc/ucita/cita10st.htm>.

[38] The UETA provision (s. 7(d)) states simply: 'If a law requires a signature, an electronic signature satisfies the law'. For details on UETA see <http://www.webcom.com/legaled/ETAForum/>. The text of the Act is at <http://www.law.upenn.edu/bll/ulc/fnact99/1990s/ueta.htm>.

[39] See http://scale.puls.law.gov.uk/html/cornack/10/6074/rtf/162of99.rtf. Section 8(1) reads: 'For the purposes of a law of the Commonwealth, a transaction is not invalid merely because it took place wholly or partly by means of one or more electronic communications'. Cl. 9 provides for the use of electronic communications to meet writing requirements, and section 10 states the requirements which electronic signatures must meet to be valid.

[40] Art. 5(2) of which states that 'Member states shall ensure that an electronic signature is not denied legal effectiveness and admissibility as evidence in legal proceedings solely on the grounds that it is:—in electronic form . . .'. One may also note the latest draft (from the Parliament and the Council) of the Dir. on electronic commerce, Art. 9 of which reads: 'Member States shall . . . ensure that the legal requirements applicable to the contractual process neither create obstacles for the use of electronic contracts nor result in such contracts being deprived of legal effectiveness and validity on account of their having been made by electronic means'. See http://europa.eu.int/eur-lex/en/tif/dat/1999.en_399L0093.html.

any presumptions as to the provenance, authenticity or date of any data carrying an electronic signature, it will be for parties to lead evidence on these issues.[41] Similarly, the US provisions do not provide for any presumptions, though they provide a little more guidance on the circumstances to be considered. UETA allows the identity of the author of an electronic record or signature to be 'shown in any manner',[42] and provides for the effect of such data or signature to be determined 'from the context and surrounding circumstances',[43] while UCITA provides that the court is to consider the commercial reasonableness of the technology used.[44]

Requirements of Writing

As regards the equivalence of an electronic signature to a handwritten signature for the purposes of requirements of writing, the British Government has chosen to leave this to secondary legislation. The provisions of the ECA allow, the relevant Government Minister,[45] to amend legislation by statutory instrument 'in such manner as he may think fit for the purpose of authorising or facilitating the use of electronic communications or electronic storage (instead of other forms of communication or storage)'[46] for any of various specified purposes.[47] This will leave it to Ministers to decide, for instance, whether one will be able to make an electronic will or to transfer heritable property by electronic disposition. Whether the signatory of, for instance, a will would also require to find an electronic witness in order to render the will probative[48] is an unknown factor. It may be that the Government's view would be to the effect that the certificate of a Certification Authority would suffice. In respect of wills, however, regard will no doubt be had to the provisions of the Directive on electronic commerce, when it is eventually finalised. In Article 9 of the most recent draft,[49] Member States are given power to exclude certain categories of transaction from the general principle upholding electronic contracts. The categories include contracts creating or transferring rights in real estate (excluding leases), and contracts governed by family law or succession (which would include wills).

---

[41] The Westminster Government was stated that '[i]t will be for the court to decide in a particular case whether an electronic signature has been correctly used and what weight it should be given': see Commentary on Cl.s in *Promoting Electronic Commerce* (Cm 4417, The Stationery Office, London), 22.

[42] UETA, s. 9(a).

[43] UETA, s. 9(b).

[44] UCITA, ss. 108, 114 and 212.

[45] As to which see s. 9(7).

[46] S. 8(1).

[47] They are specified in s. 8(2), and include the doing of anything which is required to be done in writing or otherwise using a document, notice or instrument, and the doing of anything which is required to be or may be authorised by a person's signature or seal, or is required to be witnessed.

[48] That is to say, to gain the benefits of certain presumptions specified in s. 3 of The Requirements of Writing (Scotland) Act 1995.

[49] 28 Feb. 2000: Common position of the Council and Parliament (14623/1/99 REV 1).

We must thus wait to see to what extent British or Scottish Government Ministers decide to amend existing statutory requirements relating to the requirements of writing. The US drafters of UETA have taken a bolder step. Their provision simply states: '[i]f the law requires a record to be in writing, an electronic record satisfies the law'.[50]

There is one further crucial aspect to note concerning the power of amendment delegated to Ministers. That is, that any such amendment may include provisions concerning the determination of whether a thing has been 'done' using electronic communication or storage, and, where something has been so done, the time and place at which it was done, the person by whom it was done, and the contents, authenticity and integrity of electronic data.

This means that while the provision of the ECA generally recognising the admissibility of electronic signatures[51] contain no guidance on how a court is to adjudicate on such issues as time and place of signature, authenticity of contents, and so forth, individual pieces of delegated legislation may contain particular rules for particular areas of law. The wisdom of such a scheme, entailing as it does the potential for conflict, is doubtful, and may result in confusing legal differences.

Cryptography

The ECA creates a *voluntary approvals regime* to cover providers of all 'cryptography support services',[52] not just for those providing certificates in respect of electronic signatures. Other services might include the storage of encrypted data, and the provision of key escrow and key recovery. These latter two are variations on a theme, allowing a key which has been lost either to be replaced with a copy held by an agency (key escrow) or to be rebuilt by the agency (key recovery). Such agencies are often referred to as Trusted Third Parties (TTPs).[53]

The purpose of the Register is to build confidence in electronic commerce, by providing a list of agencies which have met approval conditions upon which consumers will be able to rely in purchasing cryptography support services. The ECA permits assessment of compliance with the approval conditions to be

---

[50] UETA, s. 7(c).

[51] That is, s. 7.

[52] S. 2(1)(a). The term is defined in s. 6(1) as meaning:
'any service which is provided to the senders or recipients of electronic communications, or to those storing electronic data, and is designed to facilitate the use of cryptographic techniques for the purpose of—
(a) securing that such communications or data can be accessed, or can be put into an intelligible form, only by certain persons; or
(c) securing that the authenticity or integrity of such communications or data is capable of being ascertained.'

[53] The Government referred in *Building Confidence* to Trusted Service Providers (TSP) as an umbrella term to describe an agency choosing to offer any cryptographic service, whether it be as a CA or TTP.

carried out by a person specified by the Secretary of State,[54] thus allowing him to appoint an expert in cryptography to assist with this function.

In its earlier consultation document, the British Government set out the conditions which it expected agencies to have to meet before they would be certified[55] by the person or body supervising these arrangements.[56] These were strongly criticised by the Trade and Industry Committee as 'not fit to be written into law'.[57] The British Government has, however, rejected this criticism, though the exact criteria which agencies will have to meet have not been specified in the ECA. It has been left to the Secretary of State to ensure that arrangements are in force for granting approvals to those seeking inclusion in the Register of approved providers,[58] and we must await the publication of these requirements in due course.

The British Government's earlier intention to require certified agencies to offer key escrow as part of their services, or at least to promote key escrow,[59] has now been abandoned.[60] This followed heavy criticism of key escrow from many parties, including the Trade and Industry Committee, who commented that '[w]e are disappointed . . . that the Government should still hold a candle for key escrow and key recovery'.[61] The final blow was a distinct lack of enthusiasm for key escrow from the Cabinet Office PIU. However, in the text of the ECA as passed a provision which will enable Ministers to include within subordinate legislation a requirement that a key be deposited with an intended recipient of electronic communications, or, as an alternative, for arrangements to be made to ensure that encrypted data do not become unusable through key loss. It is unlikely that the imposition of such a requirement could assist electronic commerce. The Government may have had in mind here the possibility of utilising this provision in relation to the submission of official forms and documentation, though the requirement to deposit a key seems to be a recipe for slower communication, something which electronic communication with government departments was supposed to improve!

Liability of Providers of Cryptographic Services

A major issue on which the British Government consulted was the liability of Certification Authorities (CAs) and other providers of cryptographic services

---

[54] S. 2(4).

[55] See *Building Confidence*, Annex A.

[56] The conditions for the appointment of such supervising person or body are set out in s. 3. The Government has proposed that these functions will be delegated to OFTEL.

[57] T&I Committee Report, para. 73.

[58] See s. 2(1).

[59] Though the Performance and Innovation Unit concluded in their report (May 1999) that 'widespread adoption of key escrow was unlikely in the current industry and climate' (para. 6.9).

[60] There is a specific prohibition against a requirement for key escrow as a prerequisite for inclusion on the register of approved cryptography service providers: s. 14(1)(a).

[61] T&I Committee Report, para. 90.

for losses caused by them. Such losses may occur, for instance, through the issuing of a certificate to the wrong party. The Trade and Industry Committee recommended that in the current 'nascent market' the Government 'exercise caution'[62] in instituting a statutory liability regime. In drafting the ECA, however, the British Government will have had to bear in mind that Article 6(1) of the EU Directive on electronic signatures requires that 'Member States shall ensure that by issuing a certificate as a qualified certificate to the public or by guaranteeing such a certificate to the public, a certification-service-provider is liable for damage caused to any entity or legal or natural person who reasonably relies on that certificate'.

Given this European background, it might be thought surprising that the British Government has decided that 'the liability of Trust Service Providers (TSPs) both to their customers and to parties relying on their certificates, is best left to existing law and to providers' and customers' contractual arrangements'.[63] Customers will certainly be able to look to their contracts, though these will be subject to exclusion and limitation clauses,[64] but what of the position of third parties? Such parties will have to rely on the law of delict/tort, arguing misrepresentation along *Hedley Byrne* lines,[65] or perhaps (in Scotland) arguing for a *jus quaesitum tertio* (third party right) in their favour, though this is more unlikely. The impression is given that the British Government considers the existing law adequate to meet its European obligations, though whether it has thoroughly considered this issue may be doubted.

There is also the question of the liability of the holder of a private key, should the key's secrecy become compromised, another use it, and loss be caused. This would not constitute misrepresentation, but could arguably be negligent, though if the result were pure economic loss then recovery would be unlikely.[66] The Bill does not address this issue of the liability of private key holders.

Law Enforcement Agency Access

The most thorny issue on encryption is probably that of law enforcement access to encrypted material and keys. A startling change between the first and second

---

[62] T&I Committee Report, para. 79.

[63] *Promoting Electronic Commerce* (Cm 4417, The Stationery Office, London), 2.

[64] Which in turn, however, are subject to the provisions of the Unfair Contract Terms Act 1977 and the Unfair Terms in Consumer Contracts Regs. 1999, S.I. 1999 No. 2083.

[65] That is to say, basing their argument on the principle laid down in *Hedley Byrne & Co Ltd* v. *Heller & Partners Ltd* [1964] AC 465. There appears to be a strong case to support liability based on this principle, as the whole purpose of a certificate is for third party reliance.

[66] There is also a question whether a certificate or a key constitutes goods. This question has relevance with respect to liability under the Sale of Goods Act 1979 and product liability under the Consumer Protection Act 1987. The answer is unclear. It is not certain whether computer software constitutes goods (see MacQueen, Hogg and Hood, *Muddling Through: Legal Responses to E-Commerce from the Perspective of a Mixed System* (Europees Privaatrecht 1998, Molengraaff Instituut). A key is an algorithm and a certificate a statement of the identity of a key-holder. Neither seems to bear much resemblance to a 'good'.

drafts of the Electronic Communications Bill was the removal of the law enforcement provisions contained in the first draft, and their subsequent reinsertion into the Regulation of Investigatory Powers Act 2000 ('the RIP Act').[67] The decision to remove these provisions from the ECA was undoubtedly influenced by criticism from various bodies, including the Trade and Industry Committee, which had commented that it was 'unfortunate that legislation to deal with the recognition of electronic signatures in law, and related measures, should have become entangled with the requirements of law enforcement agencies to tackle criminals' use of encryption'.[68]

The provisions of the RIP Act include a power for law enforcement agencies[69] to require disclosure of a decryption key[70] necessary to access protected information.[71] This power is exercised by serving a notice of disclosure on the person holding the key. Such a notice can be served only after obtaining permission to do so from the appropriate judicial authority[72]. Key disclosure may be required by law enforcement agencies if they reasonably believe that such access is necessary on grounds of national security, the purposes of preventing or detecting crime, or in the interests of the economic well-being of the country. Disclosure may also be compelled if it is necessary for the purpose of securing the effective exercise or proper performance by any public authority of any statutory power or statutory duty',[73] an extremely wide justificatory reason, which seem to cover a whole range of public authority duties and powers, many with little or no connection to the more specific over-riding interests stated.

Section 50 spells out the effect of a disclosure notice being issued. If the person to whom it is addressed has both the encrypted information and the key, that person may use the key to make the information intelligible and is required to disclose *either* the information in an intelligible form[74] or the key.[75] If the addressee has the key, but not the encrypted information, he must disclose the key.[76] It is possible for the law enforcement agencies to ask that only disclosure

---

[67] <http://www.hmso.gov.uk/acts/acts2000/20000023.htm>. The Scottish Parliament has also passed a Regulation of Investigatory Powers (Scotland) Bill. However, this Scottish bill does not include provisions on decryption, as this issue is dealt with for the whole of the United Kingdom in the RIP Act. For the text of the Scottish Bill see http://www.scottish.parliament.uk/ parl_bus/billsb16bsl.pdf.

[68] T&I Report, para. 116.

[69] Amongst others. On the categories of persons who may require access, see s. 46(1) of the RIP Act.

[70] The Act excludes keys which are intended to, and do, only create electronic signatures, rather than encrypted text: see *ibid.*, s. 49(9).

[71] *Ibid.*, s. 49. Protected information is defined in s. 56 as, broadly, encrypted electronic data.

[72] On the appropriate judicial authority, see Sched. 2, *ibid.*

[73] *Ibid.*, cl. 46(2)(b)(ii).

[74] The Government suggested that an example of a situation where this might apply would be to "allow a company—that might have received an encrypted message from the target of a particular enquiry (e.g. a criminal)—to offer up an intelligible copy of the message (e.g. a printed copy) rather than the decryption key" (*Promoting Electronic Commerce*, 24). Could such a decrypted message be proven to be accurate? There are various ways of demonstrating this. For instance, the document as de-encrypted could be re-encrypted with the public key, and this re-encryption could be compared with the original encrypted document. If the two are the same, then the de-encryption was accurate.

[75] S. 50(1),(2).   [76] S. 50(3)(a).

of the key will meet the requirements of a disclosure notice. The relevant judicial authority[77] may only grant such a request if there are special circumstances which would otherwise mean that the purposes for which the request was made would be defeated, and if the direction would be proportionate to the goal sought to be achieved.[78] This caveat will allow a police officer to convince a judge that investigation of a crime would be compromised unless the key itself were obtained. Cautious police officers might well be likely to ask for this direction every time. It remains to be seen whether the judiciary will challenge such a request if it becomes standard practice.

The provisions on access to encryption keys may be seen to be wide, and whilst there is some provision for supervision of the persons who obtain keys under the provisions,[79] the law enforcement access provisions of the Act have come in for stiff criticism from advocates of personal privacy and freedom of e-commerce.[80] The most strident criticism has been reserved for the new criminal offences which the Bill will create, namely an offence of not complying with a disclosure notice (section 53) and an offence of tipping off another person about a disclosure notice (section 54).[81]

THE INTERNATIONAL DIMENSION

Export Controls

The Wassenaar Arrangement

Certain cryptographic products are treated as restricted dual-use technology under the Wassenaar Arrangement.[82] Under this international agreement, signed by 33 nations (including the United Kingdom and the United States of America), the export of certain cryptography is subject to restrictions similar to those applicable to munitions.

The Wassenaar controls apply to the transfer of conventional arms and dual-use goods and technologies, dual-use technologies being those capable of use both for innocent and non-innocent purposes. Participating states are required to control all items set out in the list of dual-use technologies and munitions.[83] Cryptography falls under the dual use list,[84] though not all cryptography is controlled. The list specifies the types of symmetric and asymmetric algorithm that are caught, which includes RSA and Diffie-Hellmann.

---

[77] As to which, see Schedule 2 to the Act.

[78] S. 51(4)

[79] *Ibid.*, s. 55.

[80] The provisions have been criticised by, amongst others, STAND and the Foundation for Information Policy Research. See, also, the interesting scenarios suggested by Lindsey, which he uses to criticise the provisions on law enforcement access, available at <http://www.cs.man.ac.uk/~chl/scenarios.html>.

[81] Not all disclosure notices are affected by an obligation of secrecy: for those that are, see s. 54(2)(3) of the Act.

[82] See <http://www.wassenaar.org/>.

[83] s.III.1.

[84] In category 5, part 2, Information security.

Section I.4 of the Arrangement states that the provisions on cryptography will not impede *bona fide* civil transactions, though this is an assertion challenged by civil libertarian groups.[85] It should be noted, however, that the Arrangement does not say that *possessing* cryptography must attract sanctions, but only the *transfer* of it across national boundaries.

United Kingdom Controls

In the United Kingdom, the current export controls imposed under the Export of Goods Control Order 1994[86] and the Dual-Use Items (Export Control) Regulations 2000[87] mirror the provisions in the Wassenaar Arrangement as regards the types of cryptography caught. The new 2000 Regulations replace previous 1996 regulations, and were introduced to comply with the terms of the EC Regulation for the control of export of dual-use items and technology[88] which took effect on 18 September 2000. Unlike the prior UK regulations, the new regulations cover the export of items in both tangible and intangible form. Thus, whereas previously exports of cryptographic technology on paper (for instance, setting out on paper a cryptographic algorithm) or on computer disc were caught by the regulations, but export via file transfer on the internet was not, the latter will now also be subject to export control.

The USA

The abandoned attempt by US law enforcement agencies to prosecute Philip Zimmermann for breaking export controls with respect to his PGP, testifies to the level of governmental concern about the potential use of cryptography by criminals. However, given that the Wassenaar restrictions apply only to exports across national borders (and it is therefore not illegal to distribute *within* the signatory states those products which it would be illegal to export), and given the ease of evading export controls and transferring software internationally via the Internet, the drafters of Wassenaar appear somewhat like King Canute holding back the waves.[89]

The US Department of Commerce issued new encryption export regulations in January 2000. The status of these regulations may, however, be affected by a US Court of Appeals decision[89a] that computer source code is a form of speech and thus protected by the First Amendment.

[85] See, for instance, the arguments advanced at <http://www.gilc.org/crypto/wassenaar/>.

[86] SI 1994 No. 1191, as amended.

[87] SI 2000 No. 2620.

[88] EC Council Regulation 1334/200, available at <http://europa.eu.int/eur-lex/en/lif/dat/2000/en_300R1334.html>.

[89] The Trade and Industry Committee also expressed its scepticism about the value of export controls, and recommended that 'the Government consider the case for a review of the rationale for the continuation of export controls on cryptographic products, in the light of their widespread availability' (T&I Report, para. 112).

[89a] *Junger* v. *Daley*, US Court of Appeals, 6th Circ., 4 April 2000, see http://pacer.ca6.uscourts.gov./cgi-bingetopn.pl?OPINION=00a0017p.06

International and Supra-national Proposals for Law Reform

As the British Government note in *Building Confidence* '[e]lectronic commerce is essentially a global, rather than a national, issue'.[90] The ECA purports to have been drafted with supranational proposals in mind. Such supranational proposals include the EU Directive on electronic signatures,[91] the proposals from the Organisation for Economic Co-operation and Development[92] and the United Nations Commission on International Trade Law,[93] and the US Computer Information Transactions Act (UCITA)[94] and Uniform Electronic Transactions Act (UETA).[95] The ECA is generally in conformity with the requirements of the Directive on electronic signatures. Indeed, in some ways it goes further. For instance, under the Directive, Member States are not required to set up a voluntary licensing scheme, though the Act does so.

On the international stage, other governments have been producing legislative proposals in this field also. Amongst them, the Australian[96] Parliament has recently promulgated an Electronic Transactions Act; the Singaporean Government has promulgated the Electronic Transactions Act 1998;[97] and the Irish Government is about to publish a Bill dealing with electronic signatures and related e-commerce matters.[98]

CONCLUSIONS

The area of cryptography, like all areas of information technology, is fast moving, and law reform is always at least three steps behind. Commentators in this field find themselves much like on-the-spot television reporters, narrating events as they unfold without much opportunity to sit back and assess the longer-term perspective. Bearing this in mind, what comments are possible on the proposals for law reform in this country?

There is a danger that both the EU Directive and the UK provisions for the recognition of electronic signatures, by tying themselves to a technology based upon public key cryptography, will run the risk of requiring a radical overhaul in a short timescale. There is much to be said for a more technologically neutral

---

[90] Para. 6.

[91] See <http://europa.eu.int/eur-lex/en/lif/dat/1999/en_399L0093.html>.

[92] See their Guidelines on Cryptography Policy at <http://www.oecd.org/dsti/sti/it/secur/prod/e-crypto.htm>.

[93] See their Model Law on Electronic Commerce at <http://www.uncitral.org/english/texts/electcom/ml-ec.htm>.

[94] Previously proposed as new Art. 2B of the Uniform Commercial Code. See <http://www.2bguide.com/>.

[95] For details on UETA see <http://www.vetaonline.com>. The text of the Act is at <http://www.law.upenn.edu/bll/ulc/fnact99/1990s/ueta.htm>.

[96] The Electronic Transactions Act 1999. See <http://scalepuls.law.gov.au/html.comact/10/6074/rtf/162of99.rtf>.

[97] The Electronic Transactions Act 1998. See <http://www.cca.gov.sg/eta/index.html>.

[98] See <http://www.entemp.ie>.

approach, such as that adopted in UCITA.[99] That said, the British Government has committed itself to an approach based on electronic signatures. The old law of signatures and writing was clearly outmoded, and the reforms will provide a somewhat belated legal recognition of the existing use of electronic media in business and consumer transactions.

Then there is the issue of law enforcement access to encryption, now addressed in the Regulation of Investigatory Powers Act. Whilst some steps must no doubt be taken, to show a determination to act, if for no other reason, the ready availability of strong encryption techniques and the ease with which encrypted documents may be transferred will no doubt mean that most intelligent criminals are able to avoid the long arm of the law. In practice, new provisions are unlikely to make more than a minimal impact in crime prevention and detection, and may simply be perceived as rendering the United Kingdom less attractive as a forum for the conduct of e-commerce.

The widespread use of computers and the Internet has made encryption available worldwide for the majority of computer users, as more and more software packages come with built-in encryption technology. This ever increasing availability is certain to provoke continued heated exchanges between those concerned at the prevention of crime and those favouring privacy protection. What is almost as interesting in this area as the legal developments, however, is the extra-legal pressure exerted in the attempt to achieve overt or covert access to encrypted material by law enforcement agencies.[100]

In the field of cryptography, the fluctuating consensus between government, business and private individuals will be formed less often within the parameters of the legal world and more often within those of the online community; it will be driven less by politicians and law reformers, and more by individual computer users. The British Government is aware of the importance of self-regulation in the area of the provision of cryptography support services. This is not surprising, for the spotlight of the law only shines so far into the information technology ether.

---

[99] That is, leaving it to the parties to decide which technology to use, subject to a court's determination of the commercial reasonableness of such technology: see the discussion of this in the main text at p. 45 above.

[100] A classic example of covert, or at least quasi-covert, law enforcement access is a recent well-publicised liaison between certain security agencies of the US Government and software producers. An example of this relates to the National Security Agency in the USA, which managed to ensure that the cryptography bundled with some software systems exported from the USA provided less security than users might have thought. Netscape and Microsoft, for instance, have both altered their net browsers' security systems, SSL, which are used to encrypt Internet credit card transactions amongst other things, so that 88 of the 128 bits of the encryption are broadcast at the start of the transaction. The remaining level of security, 40 bits, means that so-called 'secure' web transactions may be read by signals intelligence computers. The Swedish Government was caught out with a similar problem affecting the Lotus Notes e-mail system they purchased for all government employees. It believed that the 64-bit key provided relative security. In fact, the version it was using extracted 24 bits of each key and passed it to the NSA in America. When questioned, Lotus openly admitted that it had modified the program in this way.

4

Payment in an On-Line World

SAUL MILLER*

INTRODUCTION

Although payment with physical notes and coins is still an ordinary feature of our daily lives, the time when transactions can and will be paid for entirely by electronic means is not far off. One can imagine without difficulty the scenario of a day in the life of Adam and Eve Everyman perhaps five years from now:

> Adam and Eve wake at 8am as usual, kiss, yawn and begin to get ready for their busy day. After washing and dressing, Eve thinks about breakfast, checks the fridge and discovers that supplies are low of milk, cheese, butter, bread, tomatoes and olive oil (Adam has recently embarked on the Mediterranean diet). She presses the fridge smart-pad button for 'essentials, refrigerated—delivery' which sends the pre-formatted order through to the local supermarket, payment being automatically calculated at the supermarket end and extracted from the joint household account with On-Line First Virtual Bank. It's almost 8.30am by now, so Adam runs to catch the new automated Edinburgh light monorail into town, entering his e-cash smart card into the reader on the train before he sits down, and selecting 'Waverley Station' as his destination. On the way to his office he buys *The Scotsman* from a news-vendor, sticking his e-cash card into the vendor's reader; there's still something about a real newspaper that the Web has not quite replaced, he thinks. Meanwhile Eve, who is a programmer specialising in insurance work, begins her day tele-working from her own PC at home. Adam turns on his computer in his small two-partner lawyer's office in Charlotte Square and checks to see what e-mail he has and what Web documents of interest his personalised intelligent software agent has discovered for him over night. Adam browses the list and selects the most interesting dozen or so items (mainly from *Scots Law Times* and *Which Golf Course?*), which are then retrieved for him to read and /or print off, on a pay-per-view and per-print basis; the law office's on-line electronic cash account is debited for the micro-charge made for each payment. At home meanwhile, Eve is making a similar survey, except that she pays via her e-cash smart card which she inserts into the reader attached to her PC.

* B. Bus. Sci., LLB (U.C.T.), Lecturer, The School of Law, University of Edinburgh.

She makes several calls to foreign clients via Internet audio and video telephony and conferencing software, connecting to the best Internet access
supplier for each call based on speed and cost, and paying via her work-
issued smart card this time. Meanwhile Adam is reviewing the firm's client
income arising from on-line purchase of generic and bespoke legal documents. Documents are made available via the firm Web site to clients, again
paid for by e-cash, security being guaranteed by encryption and password
protection. Nowadays these sales generate a fair part of the firm's profits
and clients who actually come in person to the office rather than communicating by e-mail are becoming rare. Eventually the business day ends and
Adam and Eve settle in for a quiet night at home. Adam scans the lists of
TV programmes his smart TV has suggested for evening viewing based on
past preferences, dismisses the free-to-air options as rubbish (he really must
give up *EastEnders* before 2010, he thinks, not for the first time) and down-
loads a lightweight action movie instead, the e-cash pay-per-view being
debited from his account by the chip in the TV via its permanent cable connection to the Internet. Meanwhile Eve is finally getting round to assembling a compilation of electronic bagpipe tunes for a friend in Seattle,
examining the lists of relevant MP3 files her e-music agent has located and
downloading and playing possible selections. Each tune selected is of
course paid for on a per-copy basis, the rates varying from site to site; Eve
feels she has to respect copyright (although she knows some of the stuff is
available free on pirate sites) and anyway some of the tunes (by newer
artists) are freeware anyway. It's late when Adam and Eve finally snuggle
in bed together. Adam laughs. 'Do you remember when I had to get all
those heavy coins out of the pockets of my trousers before I went to bed?'
Eve smiles back. 'I know. Isn't it funny to think that our kids will never
know that hard cash ever existed?'

E-COMMERCE, THE INTERNET AND PAYMENT MECHANISMS

It is already a cliché to say that Internet e-commerce has radically altered the
way trading partners interact with each other, both in the commercial and consumer worlds. What is less noted however is that on the whole this change has
not affected the payment mechanisms used in these transactions.[1] Most business-to-business e-commerce transactions are, and will in future continue to be,

---

[1] In respect of business-to-business non-strategic supplies, trading partners are now able to use
the Internet as a platform for exchanging EDI (Electronic Data Interchange) formatted messages.
Recently, the Ford Motor Company purchased the first non-strategic supplies in the UK using EDI
and the Internet <http://iecsolutions.com/news/pressrels/pressrel21.html>. Furthermore, the
Internet will also be used to exchange dematerialised documents in cross-border transactions.
Although the Bolero scheme is still in the trial phase, it nevertheless provides a useful glimpse of the
future world of electronic international trade. For details on the Bolero scheme see <http://www.
bolero.net> and <http://www.webcom.com/pjones/bolero.html>.

paid for using existing electronic payment mechanisms: corporate credit cards and electronic funds transfers.[2] The nub of legal interest for the foreseeable future lies in business-to-consumer transactions and digital cash. These will be the main focus of this chapter. Currently, business-to-consumer Internet transactions comprise only 20 per cent of European Union e-commerce.[3] The principal reason for this lag is thought to be a lack of consumer confidence in shopping on-line. This is probably caused by two of the main risks which consumers face when they shop on-line, namely:[4]

(1) that someone might use a consumer's payment card information to make fraudulent purchases for which the consumer will be held liable, and

(2) that merchants, having received payment, will not perform their side of the contract or perform it defectively, and consumers fear being left without a remedy or with a remedy that is difficult to enforce.

Clearly, one way to increase consumer confidence in paying on-line is by technological means, principally encryption.[5] On a different tack, there are currently schemes being developed to help give consumers greater confidence in the integrity of the particular merchants from whom they are making purchases. In the UK, for example, the *Which Online* web trader scheme requires merchants displaying their logo to comply with a code of practice for online traders. Furthermore, it provides legal back-up for any complaints made against one of its members.[6]

However, the law also has a role to play in fostering consumer confidence. The aim of this chapter is to explore the legal and commercial consequences of the most important payment mechanisms used in on-line purchases: credit cards, debit cards and electronic or digital cash.

---

[2] For an overview of the law on electronic funds transfers see Arora, *Electronic Banking and the Law* (2nd edn., 1993), Reed, *Electronic Finance Law* (1991) 2 and 14; and Brindle and Cox (eds.), *Law of Bank Payments* (2nd edn., 1999) 41 ff.

[3] <E-commerce@its.best.uk>. A Performance and Innovation Unit Report 11 at <http://cabinet-office.gov.uk/innovation/1999/ecommerce/index.htm>.

[4] Recent surveys have highlighted lack of trust as a major obstacle to e-commerce. <E-com merce@its.best.uk>, *supra* n.3, 70.

[5] For credit cards, the two leading payment card schemes, Mastercard and Visa, have developed the SET (Secure Electronic Transaction) protocol which is the technical standard for safeguarding payment card details transmitted over the Internet. With the use of digital certificates and strong encryption it greatly reduces the risks of card information being abused. In fact merchants do not actually get to see a consumer's card details. For a description of the numerous steps involved in a SET transaction see Caplehorn, 'Payment Systems on the Internet' in *A Practitioner's Guide to the Regulation of the Internet* (1999/2000) 159 at 166. However, there has been relatively slow uptake of the SET technology. For a discussion of SET see generally Chissick and Kelman, *Electronic Commerce: Law and Practice* (1999) 130–1. Currently, the lower-level SSL encryption technology is most widely used for transmitting credit card information securely over the Internet. Encryption is discussed in Hogg, Ch. 3 of this vol.

[6] <http://www.which.net/webtrader/consumer_guide.html>.

TRADTIONAL ELECTRONIC PAYMENT MECHANISMS[7]

Credit Cards

Payment cards, particularly credit cards, have long been used to make payment for purchases made at a distance.[8] Given that the Internet is simply another means of facilitating communication over a distance, it is hardly surprising that credit cards have proved to be the most common method of paying for on-line purchases.[9] Although the content of the law on credit card payments is identical in the real and virtual worlds, it is worth examining how the law operates when applied to on-line purchases. The three relevant statutory provisions are sections 83, 84 and 75 of the Consumer Credit Act 1974.

Consumer Protection under the Consumer Credit Act 1974
(hereafter CCA)

Sections 83 and 84 and Credit Card Fraud

It is undoubtedly true that Internet e-commerce has, in expanding the commercial market place, also increased the opportunities for credit card fraud. Visa stated in April 1999 that 47 per cent of Visa credit card fraud in the European Union was Internet-related. This figure is significant (perhaps even remarkable) given that only 1 per cent of Visa's European Union turnover is Internet-related.[10] How is such fraud addressed by UK law? As Brownsford and Howells have observed, if the government, financial institutions and merchants want consumers to have the confidence necessary for business-to-consumer e-commerce to flourish, then it is axiomatic that consumers need to be protected from card fraud.[11]

Example 1
A, a consumer, uses his credit card to buy a book over the Internet from B. C, a crook, intercepts A's card information and uses it to buy goods from

---

[7] A payment mechanism can be defined as 'any machinery facilitating the transmission of money which bypasses, in whole or in part, the transportation of money and its physical delivery from the payer to the payee, thereby eliminating or at least reducing the cost of storage and transportation as well as the ensuing risk of loss or theft': Geva, 'International Funds Transfers: Mechanism and Laws' in Norton, Reed and Walden (eds.), *Cross-Border Electronic Banking: Challenges and Opportunities* (1991) 1.

[8] Traditionally in MOTO (mail order or telephone order) purchases.

[9] *Electronic Commerce*, Tenth Report by the Select Committee on Trade and Industry, para. 67, <http://www.parliament.the-stationery-office.co.uk/pa/cm199899/cmselect/cmtrdind/648/64802.htm>.

[10] National Criminal Intelligence Service, 'Project Trawler: Crime on the Information Highways' para. 49. See <http://www.ncis.co.uk/newspage1.htm>.

[11] Brownsford and Howells, 'When Surfers Start to Shop: Internet Commerce and Contract Law' (1999) 19 *Legal Studies* 307.

another merchant, D. The example would raise the same legal issues if B were operating a sham site, i.e. one that pretends to be legitimate but is merely a front for luring consumers to enter their credit card details.[12] These sham sites offer non-existent goods and services and are thought to be the major source of credit card fraud over the Internet.

A will discover the fraud only when his bank (the card issuer) issues his monthly statement reflecting the unauthorised purchases from D. The question is whether A can be made liable for these fraudulent transactions?

Section 83(1) of the CCA 1974 safeguards consumers from liability for fraudulent use of their credit cards. The section states in effect that a credit card holder (the consumer) is not liable to the his bank (the card issuer) for 'any loss' arising as a result of unauthorised use of the card.[13] This protection, however, is subject to section 84(1) which provides that card holders can be made liable for the first £50 of such loss if the credit card was misused while out of their possession.[14] There are two reasons why section 84(1) will generally not be triggered in situations like example 1. First, consumers generally remain in possession of their credit cards when shopping on-line. Secondly, card issuing banks will usually not suffer 'any loss' in these circumstances as charge-back clauses effectively place the risk of such fraudulent transactions on merchants.[15] These charge-back clauses, which operate in all transactions where the merchant does not actually see the consumer's credit card (so-called 'card not present' transactions), allow the merchant's bank to debit the merchant's account for the amount of a disputed transaction and return this amount to the card holder's bank.[16]

In any event most merchants provide their customers with a contractual shield against liability for the £50. For example, Amazon.co.uk says that:

[i]f your bank or card issuer holds you liable, Amazon.co.uk will cover your liability up to £50.00 provided that the unauthorised use of your credit or debit card resulted through no fault of your own from purchases made at Amazon.co.uk while using the secure server.[17]

---

[12] This method avoids the expense and effort of hacking into genuine transactions.

[13] Strictly, s.83(1) applies only to regulated consumer credit agreements as defined in s.8 of the Consumer Credit Act 1974. Essentially these are agreements whereby a creditor (card issuer) provides a debtor (card holder) with credit not exceeding £25,000. Most bank-issued credit cards will qualify as regulated consumer credit agreements.

[14] These statutory provisions impose a ceiling on the liability which banks can impose on a card holder for fraud. It may well be that the Distance Selling Dir. (Dir. 97/7/EC) further restricts consumers' potential liability for fraud as Art. 8 effectively states that consumers must be recredited in full for fraudulent use of their payment cards.

[15] Where, however, the merchant has gone insolvent in the interim, the loss will fall on the merchant's bank.

[16] For a discussion of the validity of charge-back clauses see Brownsford and Howells, *supra* n.11, 308–12. The authors conclude that these clauses are unlikely to be defeated by challenge under the Unfair Contract Terms Act 1977.

[17] <http://www.amazon.co.uk>.

So from a legal point of view consumers in fact have little to fear from giving their credit card details over the Internet. Of course, someone is absorbing the loss caused by on-line fraud and here by virtue of the charge-back clause, it is in general the merchant. It might be asked if it is appropriate for the ordinary 'card not present' rules to embrace all on-line transactions. Banks undoubtedly benefit from credit card purchases, so perhaps they should also bear some of the risk of credit card fraud ? This may become an interesting issue for EU law reformers, given the current drive to expand the uptake on European e-commerce.

Section 75 and the Non-performing or Defectively Performing Merchant

Example 2

A, a consumer, orders an expensive lamp from a merchant, B. The lamp never arrives. Where B is operating a sham site, section 83 of the CCA 1974 protects A from being held liable for any subsequent purchases made by B. However, what happens if B is legitimate but does not deliver the lamp or delivers a defective lamp. Or worse still, what if the defective lamp explodes after delivery and causes considerable physical injury to A?

Naturally A will have a contractual claim against B in all these circumstances. The problem is that these claims may be difficult to enforce because the merchant is no longer traceable, has gone bankrupt or is simply too far away.[18] Fortunately for A, section 75 of the CCA 1974 provides him with a powerful alternative to pursuing his remedies against B. Effectively, this section allows A to sue his bank (the card issuer) for any misrepresentation or breach of contract by B. The bank's liability under section 75 is entirely dependent on and contemporaneous with A's claim against B.[19] Thus A first has to establish that he has a claim against B before the bank's liability arises.[20] This means that the law governing the contract between A and B determines not only the requirements for establishing a cause of action against the bank but also the extent of any ensuing liability.[21] It is worth emphasising that A's claim is not limited to the

---

[18] Although the Internet has created a global market place that allows parties to enter into contracts at a distance, it has not created a global courtroom in which remote parties can settle disputes. The EU is however currently investigating the possibility of extra-judicial determination of inter-EU consumer disputes, which might include on-line ADR: see Council Resolution 7220/1/00 on a Community wide network of national bodies for the extra-judicial settlement of consumer disputes, 25 Apr. 2000.

[19] S.75 uses the term 'like claim'.

[20] A does not, however, have to institute an action against B. Basically, s.75 provides the card holder with another person to sue for a claim that he has against the merchant. Another consequence of the dependent nature of the bank's liability is that it can raise any defence *vis-à-vis* the card holder that the merchant could have raised against the card holder: Jones, *The Law Relating to Credit Cards* (1989) 210 and Howells and Weatherill, *Consumer Protection Law* (1995) 268.

[21] The applicable law, of course, is a matter which falls to be determined according to the rules of private international law. For contracts falling within the scope of the Rome Convention on the Law Applicable to Contractual Obligations 1980 as implemented in the UK by the Contracts (Applicable Law) Act 1990, merchants cannot deprive consumers of 'mandatory rules' which are defined by Art. 3(3) as rules of law in the consumer's country which cannot be derogated from by

purchase price of the goods but can include consequential losses caused by B's breach subject to the rules of the applicable law. In effect therefore, section 75 means that a credit card holder's bank acts as the guarantor for any misrepresentation or breach of contract claim that the card holder might have against a merchant in question.

Not all transactions, however, fall within the ambit of section 75. Three requirements must be satisfied to trigger the section:

(a) the purchase price of the goods is greater than £100 and less than £30,000,[22] and

(b) the credit card agreement is used to finance a particular transaction between a debtor (card holder) and a supplier (merchant),[23] and

(c) the credit card purchase is made under pre-existing arrangements, or in contemplation of future arrangements, between the card issuer and the merchant.[24]

There is one particularly controversial aspect of section 75, at least in the context of transnational e-commerce. The card-issuing banks in the UK have argued in the past that a credit card holder cannot use section 75 to make a claim against his bank where the goods/services were purchased from a merchant recruited to the card network by a bank other than the card holder's bank (particularly where the merchant is located overseas). In example 2, this would occur, for instance, where A holds a Bank of Scotland Visa credit card and purchased the lamp from B in America who was recruited to the Visa network by an American bank. The UK banks' argument is that in these circumstances the credit card transaction has not taken place under 'pre-existing arrangements', or in 'contemplation of future arrangements' between themselves and the merchant as required by section 75.[25]

The thrust of the bank's argument (which originated before the Internet had significantly impacted) is that allowing consumers to sue the bank for a merchant's misrepresentation or breach of contract (including consequential losses) reflects neither the extent of the bank's involvement with the remote merchant

---

contract. For a discussion of aspects relating to private international law in respect of contracts concluded over the Internet see Murray, Ch. 2 of this vol.

[22] S. 75(3)(b).

[23] S. 12(b) read with s. 11(1)(b). These are known in the Act's parlance as 'restricted use agreements'. For a discussion of the difference between restricted use and unrestricted use agreements see Harvey and Parry, *The Law of Consumer Protection and Fair Trading* (London, Butterworths, 1992) 266.

[24] Of course the credit card agreement must be subject to the CCA 1974. Thus s.75 will not apply where the credit granted exceeds the maximum limit (currently £25,000) or the agreement stipulates the full amount of credit granted for each specified period to be paid in full (Art. 3(a)(ii) of the Consumer Credit (Exempt Agreements) Order, SI No 869 of 1989 made under s.16 of the CCA 1974.) Charge cards are an example of the latter.

[25] For a full discussion of this dispute see Brindle and Cox (eds.), *Law of Bank Payments, supra* n.2, 242–6.

nor the profit made from the transaction.[26] However, the matter is probably now academic as the Department of Trade and Industry has stated that if section 75 is interpreted by the courts as not applying to contracts entered into with overseas merchants, then it will 'speedily bring forward legislation to fill the gap'.[27] This stance is clearly understandable from the point of view of fostering e-commerce. On balance, it seems far more important to bolster consumer confidence required for the growth of e-commerce than to worry about card-issuing banks which already earn significant profits from very high interest charges. In any event, the bank has the right to claim the extent of its loss (including the cost of defending any legal action) from the merchant in question.[28]

It is worth noting that section 75 can operate either as a sword or a shield. Consumers can use section 75 either to raise an action against the card issuer or as a defence to a card issuer's claim for payment of the purchase price. A consumer will generally have to raise an action if he has already paid the card issuer or wants to claim for consequential losses.[29]

Debit Cards

A debit card is simply a plastic card used to effect an electronic funds transfer at a point of sale (EFTPOS). By using a debit card to make payment, a cardholder grants authority to his bank to debit his account with the amount of the transaction.[30]

As debit cards generally do not involve extending credit to a card holder, the consumer using a debit card does not gain the protection of the CCA 1974. Even where the agreement does allow a card holder credit (i.e. an overdraft), section 187(3A) of the CCA 1974 (as amended by section 89 of the Banking Act 1987) specifically precludes electronic funds transfers from qualifying as 'arrangements' for the purposes of section 75. This means that debit card holders have to proceed directly against merchants for any misrepresentation or breach of contract as the alternative remedy against the card issuer is blocked. Although section 75 of the CCA does not apply to debit cards, where a debit card *does* allow the consumer a credit facility, section 83 of the CCA 1974 protects overdraft-bearing debit card holders from liability for unauthorised purchases made with their cards.[31]

---

[26]   *Connected Lender Liability: A Second Report by the Director General of Fair Trading of section 75 of the Consumer Credit Act 1974*, May 1995, 6.

[27]   *Electronic Commerce*, Tenth Report by the Select Committee on Trade and Industry, *supra* n.9, para. 123.

[28]   S.75(2) of the CCA 1974. This may, of course be difficult to enforce where the merchant is geographically far away. The bank also runs the risk of the merchant's insolvency.

[29]   Jones, *supra* n.20, 211.

[30]   The most common examples in the United Kingdom are SWITCH and VISA Delta.

[31]   Because the protection in s.83 is from misuse of a consumer's *credit facility*, this section will not apply where a debit card holder's account is in credit. For a useful discussion see Stephenson,

However, even if the CCA 1974 does not apply, a similar result is achieved via the voluntary code of practice (The Banking Code) to which most leading banks have subscribed. The code sets out the minimum standards of good banking practice for all subscribing banks in their dealings with personal customers. In respect of debit cards, the code contains provisions almost identical to sections 83 and 84 of the CCA 1974. The code states that a debit card holder will not be liable for any loss resulting from unauthorised misuse of the debit card *after* a consumer has reported the card lost, stolen or that someone else knows the PIN, password or selected personal information. However, where the loss resulted from misuse *before* such information was reported, a cardholder's loss is limited to a maximum of £50 provided that he has not been fraudulent or grossly negligent.[32] It is clear from the wording of these provisions that they are primarily intended to cover situations where debit cards have been misused after being lost or stolen. However, where debit card information is obtained while being used to shop on-line, the card will usually not have left the card holder's possession. Technically, therefore, banks could argue that the section does not protect consumers from liability for fraudulent transactions made after shopping on-line. However, as a matter of practice, banks do not hold consumers liable for unauthorised purchases even where their actual cards have not been lost or stolen.[33] It is unlikely that card holders would fall foul of the gross negligence proviso where card details are sent securely over the Internet using one of the encryption technologies. Thus while debit cards are on a par with credit cards in respect of protection from liability for unauthorised purchases, credit card users have the benefit, if the requirements of section 75 are met, of being able to sue the card issuing bank for a merchant's misrepresentation or breach of contract.

DIGITAL CASH PAYMENT MECHANISMS

What constitutes 'electronic' or 'digital' cash? These types of payment systems are not easy to pin down in an all-encompassing definition. Basically, they involve a system whereby digitally represented units of value, denominated in a particular currency and stored on an electronic device (integrated circuit chip embedded in a smart card or a computer's hard drive) are transferred from a buyer to a seller.[34] These digital cash systems, in which actual units of digital

---

Credit, Debit and Cheque Cards: Law and Practice (1993) 104. For a commentary on whether debit card agreements with overdraft facilities should be covered by the CCA 1974 see Brindle and Cox (eds.), *supra* n.2, 208–9.

[32] 4.12 and 4.14 of *The Banking Code* (1998 edn). Where the consumer has been fraudulent there will not in fact be a 'misuse' of the card.

[33] APACS has stated that subsequent banking codes will be changed to reflect this current banking practice.

[34] Reed and Davies, *Digital Cash—the Legal Implications* (1995), A Report of the Internet Law Research Project, Centre for Commercial Law Studies, Queen Mary & Westfield College, University of London, 1.

value are transferred, are different from traditional EFTs where all that is transferred are *instructions* to a bank to make payment through one of the existing
banking networks.[35]

There is currently a wide variety of digital cash products competing in the
Internet payment market. Some are specifically aimed at the low value or
'micro-payments' market, i.e. payments ranging from a fraction of a pence up
to a few pounds.[36] None of these systems has as yet proved to be particularly
popular. Others are designed specifically for use over the Internet—e.g.
Digicash's eCash, which is based on a digital coin system. Each digital coin is
assigned a particular currency value and, with the aid of cryptography, is capable of being verified as authentic.[37] Only certain banks are granted the licence to
issue eCash to their customers. These customers can then can purchase eCash,
store it on their hard drives and spend it at participating merchants or transfer
it to other customers. Merchants, who must also hold an account at a participating bank, can then redeem their digital coins for real value at their bank.
Although highly innovative, eCash has not been as successful as was initially
predicted. There are no banks licensed to issue eCash in the UK and in America,
Digicash Inc. had to file for Chapter 11 bankruptcy protection. At this juncture,
it appears that the most promising type of digital cash products are those which
have the flexibility not only to deal with the transfers of any payment value, but
also to operate equally both in the real and virtual worlds. The most prominent
example is Mondex digital cash, and it will be used in this chapter as an example to focus discussion of the legal issues raised by digital cash payment mechanisms.[38]

Mondex Digital Cash

The Mondex scheme operates under the umbrella of Mondex International
Limited. Mondex International concludes shareholder franchise agreements
with selected banks in a particular region. In terms of these agreements, these
banks are obliged to develop and implement the Mondex scheme in that area.[39]

Mondex digital cash is not based on digital coins (like eCash) but is rather a
stored value system based on smart cards. These smart cards are capable not
only of storing the computer-readable code in which the stored value is

---

[35] Brindle and Cox (eds.), *Law of Bank Payments* (2nd edn., 1999) 250–1.

[36] See e.g. Millicent at <http://Millicent.digital.com>. For a comprehensive overview of
Millicent see O'Mahony, Peirce and Tewari, *Electronic Payment Systems* (1997) 192–208. For a brief
overview see Brindle and Cox (eds.), *supra* n.2, 253.

[37] For an extensive description of eCash see O'Mahony, Peirce and Tewari, *supra* n.36, 146–58.

[38] Another is Visacash: see <http://www.visa.com/pd/cash/main.html>.

[39] Mastercard International owns 51% of the shares in Mondex International Limited. The
remaining shares are owned by the shareholder franchisee banks in each region. In addition to the
UK, Mondex currently operates in the United States, Canada, New Zealand, Hong Kong and South
Africa. In the UK, HSBC Bank Plc and National Westminster Bank have entered into shareholder
franchise agreements with Mondex International Limited.

expressed as units of a particular currency, but also of carrying out sophisticated mathematical computations necessary for a secure electronic cash payment system.[40] Although the structure of the Mondex scheme varies slightly from country to country, the following figure depicts its core features.

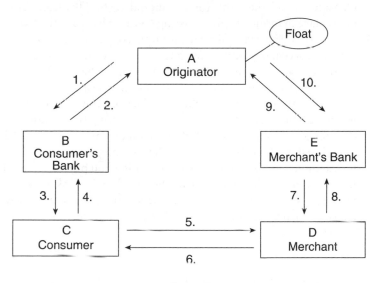

FIGURE 1

1. The issuer of digital cash is known as the originator.[41] Origination is the process of creation and original transfer of computer-readable code in which stored value is expressed.[42] A bank participating in the scheme then purchases digital cash from the originator.[43] This digital cash is transferred from the originator's master chip to the bank's purse (a rack of in-house Mondex chips).
2. The bank then makes payment to the originator for the digital cash it receives using one of the traditional methods e.g. a CHAPS transfer. The originator holds this payment in a float. This transaction takes place in terms of a pre-existing contract between the two parties.

---

[40] It is highly likely that the traditional magnetic strip credit cards and debit cards will be replaced by multi-function smart cards. These cards have multi-application operating systems which allows them to perform numerous financial and non-financial functions ranging from credit/debit card and digital cash facilities to loyalty schemes and access to buildings. For the advantages of multi-function smart cards see *E-commerce@its. best.uk, supra* n.3, 79–80.

[41] In the UK, the originator is a company called Stirling Origination Plc. The banks which hold shareholder franchises are obliged to create an originator for their region.

[42] Loubser and Swart, 'Electronic Money in South African Law' (1999) 10 *Stellenbosch Law Review* 359.

[43] The three participating banks in the UK are HSBC Bank Plc, National Westminster Bank and the Bank of Scotland.

3. Consumers, in turn, purchase digital cash from the bank. This digital cash is transferred from the bank's purse to individual chips embedded in consumers' smart cards. Consumers can 'load' up their cards in this way from an Automatic Teller Machine (ATM), a payphone or a computer (if fitted with a smart card reader).

4. Consumers pay the bank for the digital cash. This transaction also takes place in terms of a pre-existing contract between the two parties.

5. Consumers then use this digital cash to make purchases from merchants willing to accept payment by Mondex value. In order to make payment, a consumer transfers stored value from his chip to the merchant's chip.

6. Thereafter, the merchant delivers the goods/services to the consumer.

7. The merchant then deposits the digital cash received at his participating bank. Once again this is done by transferring stored value from his chip onto the bank's chips. Although a merchant will usually deposit digital cash with his bank, he is under no obligation to do so. He can, for example, purchase goods from a supplier and pay with digital cash.

8. In exchange for the digital cash, the merchant's bank will credit the merchant's account with an equivalent amount less any transaction charges. Again this transaction takes place in terms of a pre-existing contract between the two parties.

9. The merchant's bank then deposits digital cash held on its chips with the originator.

10. The originator will make payment to the merchant's bank for all digital cash received. This transaction too takes place in terms of a pre-existing contract between the two parties.[44]

Ironically, although Mondex digital cash has been the subject of many real world pilot schemes, the smart card readers and requisite software required to send Mondex value over the Internet have only very recently been developed.[45]

Legal Issues relating to Digital Cash

If digital cash were legal tender, holders of such digital cash would, as a matter of law, have the right to exchange it for goods/services or to deposit it in a bank account.[46] Legal tender is defined by statute and is essentially limited to UK coins and Bank of England notes.[47] Mondex digital cash, therefore, does not

[44] For a detailed and informative outline of the contractual relationships which underlie the Mondex scheme as depicted in Fig. 1 see Finlayson-Brown, '*Mondex: Structure of a New Payment System*' (1997) 12 (9) *Journal of International Banking Law* 362.

[45] See e.g. the software developed by the Scottish company Intertrader at <http://www.intertrader.com>.

[46] For an argument why digital cash should not be recognised as legal tender see Hooley, '*Payment in Cashless Society*' in Rider (ed.) *Realm of Company Law* (1998) 259.

[47] Coinage Act 1971 as amended by s. 1(3) of the Currency Act 1983 and s. 1(2) of the Currency and Bank Notes Act 1954. Scottish banknotes are not legal tender. They are merely promises by the individual note-issuing banks to pay legal tender to the bearers of such notes.

qualify as legal tender in the UK and as a consequence has to rely exclusively on a contractual basis for its operation.[48]

There are four noteworthy features about the contractual basis of the Mondex scheme. First, merchants (D) are not legally obliged to accept digital cash from consumers and do so only by consent.[49] Secondly, merchants (D) are *only* in a direct contractual relationship with the participating bank (E) that recruited them to the scheme. Thirdly, a merchant's right to real value (bank debt) only arises once digital cash has actually been presented to his participating bank. The merchant's right to insist that the participating bank redeem digital cash for real value is found in the express provisions of the contract between the two parties. The relationship between a participating bank and the originator (A) is identical to the relationship between a merchant and his participating bank.[50] Finally, the contract between a participating bank (B) and a consumer (C) does not appear expressly to give the consumer the right to compel his bank to redeem digital cash for real value.[51]

While the scheme is fully operational, contractual arrangements ensure that consumers can spend their digital cash at participating merchants, merchants can exchange digital cash for real value at their participating bank and the participating banks can likewise exchange digital cash for real value at the originator. Nevertheless, there are a number of risks inherent in digital cash payment systems that need to be considered. They are (a) the planned withdrawal of the scheme; (b) the insolvency of the originator; (c) the insolvency of a participating bank; (d) digital cash getting lost *en route* to the merchant; and (e) digital cash being stolen or fraudulently obtained and subsequently transferred to an innocent third party acting in good faith and for value.

Withdrawal of the Scheme

It is not inconceivable that Mondex International Limited might, in certain circumstances, decide to discontinue the Mondex digital cash scheme. This could be for a number of reasons: it could turn out to be commercially unviable[52] or the security of the scheme might become irrevocably compromised.

The question that arises is what happens to all the digital cash in circulation held respectively by consumers, merchants and participating banks. First, unless merchants have a continuing right to exchange digital cash for real value, they will no longer be prepared to accept digital cash from consumers. From the

---

[48] I am grateful to Christine Pearce at the Bank of Scotland for making the contracts involved in the Mondex scheme available to me. Any views expressed about Mondex digital cash are, of course, my own.

[49] The letters in this description (D, etc) refer back to Fig. 1.

[50] Naturally, the consumer's participating bank can also be the participating bank for merchants.

[51] See e.g. the Bank of Scotland's *Mondex Terms and Conditions*. Since the time of initial writing, the Bank of Scotland has terminated its real world pilot scheme at the University of Edinburgh.

[52] E.g. the payment product offered by First Virtual Holdings, Inc. has disappeared from the market.

operating regulations[53] and supporting documentation,[54] it appears that the intention in the event of withdrawal is to grant consumers, merchants and participating banks the right to present any digital cash they still hold to the originator for redemption. It is not, however, entirely clear that the actual contracts in the UK are set up to reflect this intention. One major difficulty is that the originator is only apparently in a direct contractual relationship with each participating bank and *not* with either merchants or consumers.[55] This means in principle that the originator cannot be directly sued in contract if the scheme is withdrawn, even though it is the originator who has the power to withdraw the scheme. Accordingly, what strategies do merchants and consumers have to demand that their digital cash be redeemed in the event of withdrawal? There are three possibilities worth considering:

(i)   a claim in contract against the originator based on *third party rights*;
(ii) a claim in contract against the *participating bank* that recruited them to the scheme and
(iii) a claim in *unjustified enrichment* against the originator.

If a merchant does not succeed with any of the above, then, as a final last-ditch effort, he could (iv) try to raise an action against the *consumer* on the basis that the consumer has not discharged his payment obligation.

(i) Contractual Claims against the Originator

In the absence of a contract between the originator and a merchant or consumer, one way for a merchant/consumer to establish a contractual claim against the originator is with a clearly worded clause in the agreement between the originator and a participating bank which grants the merchant or consumer a *third party right* to insist that the originator redeem their digital cash in the event of withdrawal. In both English and Scots law, this clause, broadly speaking, needs clearly to identify the third party either by name or by class and must expressly provide that such a third party is to benefit from the contractual provision.[56] If such a clause were established, then merchants and consumers would have a

---

[53]   There are two sets of operating regs.: the International Operating Regs. and the UK Operating Regs.

[54]   Mondex UK Limited's *Submission to the Bank of England: Sterling Origination Plc*, Mar. 1998. See also *Encyclopaedia of Banking Law* vol 1 D1 315.

[55]   If this contract does not contain an express term which allows a participating bank real value from the originator after termination, then similar considerations apply as discussed in (ii) and (iii) below.

[56]   Scots common law has long recognised that third parties can be granted rights (a *jus quaesitum tertio*) under a contract to which they are not directly parties. For a useful overview of the law see *The Laws of Scotland: Stair Memorial Encyclopaedia*, xv, paras. 824–37. Recently, English law has also allowed third parties to acquire rights under a contract to which they are not party. The law is found in the recently enacted Contracts (Rights of Third Parties) Act 1999 c.31. The requirements for establishing a third party right are broadly the same as in Scots law (see s. 1 of the Act). For a comparison between English law and Scots law see MacQueen, 'Third Party Rights in Contract: English Reform and Scottish Concerns' (1997) 1 *ELR* 488.

contractual right to present their digital cash to the originator for redemption after withdrawal. Another possibility for consumers is to try to argue that the participating bank, when selling digital cash to consumers, is acting as the originator's agent.

Finally, it has been suggested that the originator (and participating banks) could be taken to have made an offer to the public to redeem digital cash, capable of being accepted by any merchant or consumer.[57] The problem with this argument is that when the scheme is withdrawn, it is likely that the offer to the public will be taken to have been withdrawn. Accordingly, there will be no offer for merchants/consumers to accept when they present digital cash to the originator. A similar argument can be made under Scots law that a unilateral enforceable promise might have been made by the originator that they would redeem any digital cash presented. However, the same problem intervenes, namely that the promise is likely to be conditional on the scheme not having been withdrawn.

(ii) Contractual Claims against a Participating Bank

The second option for merchants and consumers is to proceed in contract against the *participating bank* that recruited them to the scheme. In a merchant's contract with a participating bank, the merchant has the right to compel his participating bank to redeem digital cash for real value. But what happens to this contractual right if the contract is terminated when the scheme is withdrawn? In accordance with the general principles of contract in both Scots and English law, unless a right to a contractual performance has accrued prior to termination, termination of the contract puts an end to both parties' primary obligations to perform in the future.[58] Accordingly, merchants would have to argue that their right to compel their bank to redeem digital cash has accrued and thereby survives termination. In general, rights accrue when a performance on one side has been met by the anticipated counter-performance on the other side.[59] This becomes a question of working out which performance obligations are reciprocal to each other. From the bank's perspective, it is clear that they are obliged to redeem digital cash presented to them by the merchant. But merchants are not required to render any direct reciprocal contractual performance to secure the bank's performance. Rather, the merchant has the *right*

---

[57] Reed and Davies, *supra* n.34, 14–15.

[58] In Scots law see *Turnbull* v. *McLean & Co* (1873) 1 R 730 at 738, *per* Lord-Justice Clerk Montcreiff. For a discussion of accrued rights in Scots law see MacQueen, 'Unjustified Enrichment and Breach of Contract' [1994] *Juridical Review* 137 at 144–6 and 'Contract, Unjustified Enrichment and Concurrent Liability: A Scots Perspective' in Rose (ed.), *Failure of Contracts* (Oxford, Hart, 1997) 199 at 217–22. For the English law on accrued rights see *Bank of Boston Connecticut* v. *European Grain and Shipping Ltd* [1989] AC 156 at 1098–9 and *McDonald* v. *Dennys Lascelles Ltd* (1933) 48 CLR 457 at 476–7. For a commentary on accrued rights in English law see *Chitty on Contracts* (28th edn., London, Sweet & Maxwell, 1999) i, para. 25–050.

[59] *Cantiere San Rocco SA* v. *Clyde Shipbuilding and Engineering Co*, 1923 SC (HL) 108.

to present digital cash to the bank for redemption. On this analysis, it seems that merchants will be hard pressed to argue that their right to present digital cash has accrued prior to termination. It seems much more likely that a court would take the view that termination of the contract extinguishes the bank's future obligation to redeem digital cash from merchants.

Perhaps a better alternative for merchants is to claim that their contracts with their participating banks contain an implied term which obliges the bank to redeem digital cash even after the termination of their contract with the merchant. In order to succeed, merchants would have to establish that the term was required to give business efficacy to the contract,[60] was an obvious inference from the contract (the officious bystander test)[61] or was in line with custom or usage.[62] It is difficult to predict in the abstract whether the courts would consider any of these tests to have been satisfied.

A consumer's position is even more precarious than a merchant's because his contract with the bank does not appear even to contain an *express* provision requiring the bank to redeem digital cash.[63] As a result, the question of accrued rights does not arise. A consumer's only chance of establishing a contractual right to compel his bank to redeem digital cash after withdrawal would be on the basis of an implied term along the lines suggested for merchants above.

(iii)   Unjustified Enrichment Claims against the Originator

If a merchant and/or a consumer does not have a claim in contract against the originator or participating bank, then another possibility is to proceed against the originator in *unjustified enrichment*.[64] When the originator issues digital cash to the participating banks, it receives real value in return and holds this value in a float.[65] This float is later used to pay the participating banks for returned digital cash. In a sense the float can be seen as representing the sum total of all potential claims that might be made against the originator for the redemption of digital cash. If consumers and merchants are left without a contractual claim against the originator or a participating bank, then the originator might be left with a portion of the float against which no claim will be made. The question arises whether consumers and merchants can use this to make an unjustified enrichment claim against the originator. This is not easily answered. On the one hand, there is the extremely complex problem of allowing enrichment claims in situations regulated by express contracts. If the parties have chosen to allocate the risk of losses by contract, then allowing an unjustified

---

[60]   *The Moorcock* (1899) 14 PD 64.

[61]   *Shirlaw* v. *Southern Foundries (1926) Ltd* [1939] 2 KB 206 (affd. [1940[AC 701).

[62]   *Strathmore Steamship Co. Ltd* v. *Hugh Baird & Sons Ltd*, 1916 SC (HL) 134.

[63]   See e.g. the Bank of Scotland's *Mondex Terms and Conditions*.

[64]   There is no question of a participating bank being enriched in the Mondex scheme as they will always have paid either the originator or merchants for any digital cash they hold.

[65]   This float is of major commercial value to the originator as it can be invested while the issued digital cash is in circulation.

enrichment claim might undermine this risk allocation. If so, then the originator's enrichment will probably be justified.[66] On the other hand, it might be considered unfair that the originator can secure a windfall by its own act of withdrawing the scheme.

(iv) Action by Merchant against Consumer?

If a merchant is unable to compel either the originator or his participating bank to redeem his digital cash for real value, then the only person left to attack is the consumer who paid him in digital cash. Can the merchant insist on being 'paid' again? Legally, a creditor has the right to insist on payment in legal tender. However, parties commonly agree that alternative modes of payment will discharge the debtor's payment obligation. The test is the parties' intentions.[67] In order to determine these intentions, the following factors are crucial: the workings of the particular payment mechanism, the parties' conduct and any surrounding circumstances.[68] The leading case of *In re Charge Card Services*[69] held that payment by charge card discharged a consumer's payment obligation even in circumstances where the merchant did not actually receive payment from the card company. Two of the most important reasons for this decision were, first, that consumers should not be liable to pay twice for goods received and, secondly, that merchants had no record of consumers' addresses and thus no ready means of tracing them. Both these reasons seem particularly relevant to digital cash systems. It is apparent from the description of Mondex digital cash that a consumer has to pay in advance for digital cash that he subsequently spends at the merchant. Thus, if payment by digital cash were not taken to discharge a consumer's obligation unconditionally, then this could result in double payment. Furthermore, merchants have no effective way of tracing consumers who transferred digital cash to them. Even if a merchant does have a record of who has transferred digital cash to him, this will only be of the consumer's name and card number and will not include his address. Both these factors point to payment by digital cash being absolute, and thereby discharging a consumer's payment obligation to the merchant.[70] Merchants who cannot exchange digital cash for real value accordingly have no 'second bite at the cherry' as against the consumer who transferred it to them.

---

[66] In *Dollar Land (Cumberland) Ltd* v. *CIN Properties Ltd*, 1998 SLT 992 it was held that a clause in a contract of lease which provided for certain forfeitures in the event of breach by a tenant was sufficient to block a claim against the innocent party in unjustified enrichment. The enrichment in this instance was held to be justified as a result of the clause in the contract.

[67] *In re Charge Card Services Ltd* [1989[Ch. 497 at 513.

[68] *Ibid.*, at 512–13.

[69] *Ibid.*

[70] See also Caplehorn, 'Payment Systems on the Internet' in *A Practitioner's Guide to the Regulation of the Internet* (1999/2000) 159 at 168; Brindle and Cox (eds.), *supra* n.2, 254 and *Encyclopaedia of Banking Law*, i, D1 315 who all favour the view that payment by Mondex digital cash discharges a consumer's payment obligation.

In summary, the position seems to be that if consumers and merchants can establish claims against the originator either in contract or in unjustified enrichment, then subject to considerations of insolvency dealt with immediately below, neither will suffer loss as a result of the scheme being withdrawn. If no claim can be established on either basis, then both merchants and consumers may well be left stranded with worthless digital cash. We shall consider below what this says about the overall pros and cons of digital cash over the traditional payment mechanisms.

Insolvency of the Originator

As digital cash in circulation represents the sum total of potential claims against the originator, if the float held by the originator falls below the value of digital cash in circulation, then there is a real risk of the originator becoming insolvent. There are at least two factors that could lead to this result: forgery of digital cash or the dissipation of the float.[71]

In many ways the originator's role combines features of both a note-issuing and a deposit-taking institution. Furthermore, as digital cash has the potential to replace actual cash it could have a direct bearing on the money supply in the UK. Both these factors show why digital cash raises crucial regulatory issues. However, given the novelty of digital cash, it is hardly surprising that there are problems applying the United Kingdom's existing regulatory regime to digital cash issuers.[72] These complex issues are beyond the remit of the present study and the following paragraph will focus merely on unravelling the consequences of the originator's insolvency for the participating banks, merchants and consumers.

It goes without saying that only parties who actually have claims against the originator will be affected by the originator's insolvency. In both Scots and English law, although for different reasons, the liquidator has the option of not continuing with certain contracts[73] in which the insolvent company in question is involved.[74] As the originator's liability to holders of digital cash only arises

---

[71] The float could be eroded, for instance, due to mismanagement or simply poor investment decisions.

[72] For a discussion of the regulatory issues see Tether, 'Electronic Cash—The Regulatory Issues' [1997] *Butterworths Journal of International Banking & Financial Law* 202; Reed, *Legal Regulation of Internet Banking—A European Perspective* (1996), A Report of the Internet Law Research Project, Centre for Commercial Law Studies, Queen Mary & Westfield College, University of London. For a commentary on the early stages of regulation at EU level see Dickie, *Internet and Electronic Commerce Law in the EU* (Oxford, Hart, 1999) 14–15.

[73] Contracts of employment are treated differently.

[74] In Scots law this right is based on the common law. See *Grays Trustees* v. *Behar Coal Co (Limited)* (1881) 9 R 225 and *Asphaltic Limestone Concrete Co Ltd* v. *Glasgow Corporation*, 1907 SC 463. In English law it is regulated by statute, s.78(2) of the Insolvency Act 1986, which grants a liquidator the power to disclaim any onerous property. Onerous property is broadly defined and according to s.178(3) Insolvency Act 1986 includes 'any unprofitable contract'. Once exercised, the disclaimer operates to terminate the contract in respect of liabilities accruing after the disclaimer. See Goode, *Principles of Corporate Insolvency law* (1997) 128–9.

after such digital cash has been presented, it seems that the liquidator can avoid exchanging digital cash for real value after liquidation.[75] Holders of such digital cash technically of course still have a claim for breach of contract against the originator, but it is unlikely to be worth much, given that each holder will rank behind preferred creditors in the insolvency.

Insolvency of a Participating Bank

Where one particular participating bank becomes insolvent for reasons unrelated to the Mondex scheme, consumers will be unaffected as they will simply continue to spend their digital cash with participating merchants. Unless merchants can construe the Mondex scheme as creating a series of offers to the public by the originator and participating banks displaying the Mondex logo,[76] then they may have to rank in the insolvency in order to have their digital value redeemed.[77] However, in order to maintain confidence in the scheme, it is not inconceivable that another participating bank will undertake to redeem that merchant's digital cash and act as his bank for future purposes.

Missing in Action: Digital Cash Lost in the 'Post'

As digital cash is nothing more than encrypted information, it is not inconceivable that it could be lost or intercepted *en route* to a merchant. Who bears the loss in these cases? On the one hand, sending a banknote in the post will not constitute payment if it is lost or stolen.[78] On the other, there is also authority for the view that a transferee, who impliedly or expressly authorises transmission of payment in a certain way, takes the risk of the payment not arriving if the transferor complies with the guidelines of the transmission.[79] Gringras concludes from these authorities that a web merchant who allows payment by digital cash takes the risk of its non-arrival. However, he suggests that merchants can shield themselves by a properly worded contract clause indicating that the merchant's obligation to perform is subject to the digital cash actually arriving.[80]

Reclaiming Digital Cash

Finally, what happens to the ownership of digital cash which has been fraudulently obtained or stolen from a consumer and subsequently transferred to an

---

[75] In English law this is known as proving a debt and is regulated by the Insolvency Rules 1986 rule 13.12(1)(b) which defines a 'debt' as including any debt or liability *to which the company may become subject* after the date it goes into liquidation by reason of any obligation incurred before that date. (emphasis added).

[76] Or in Scotland, as a unilateral promise.

[77] See text to n. 56 above.

[78] *Luttges* v. *Sherwood* (1895) 11 TLR 233.

[79] *Norman* v. *Ricketts* (1886) 3 TLR 182; *Thorey* v. *Wylie and Lockhead* (1890) 6 Sh. Ct. Rep. 201.

[80] C. Gringras, *The Law of the Internet* (1997) 31–2.

innocent third party acting in good faith and giving value? If such digital cash could be identified as belonging to a particular consumer and tracked down, can it be retrieved? For digital cash to function properly as a payment mechanism the answer must clearly be in the negative. The essence of 'cash' is its free and unburdened transferability. But does the existing law achieve this desired result? In respect of physical coins and banknotes any *bona fide* purchaser for value acquires good title *vis-à-vis* the original transferor irrespective of whether his predecessor's title was tainted by fraud or theft. In other words these coins or bank-notes cannot be vindicated from a *bona fide* possessor.[81] The obstacle in applying this rule to digital cash is that it is premised on currency being in corporeal form and digital cash is nothing more than incorporeal encrypted information. One solution might be to treat digital cash as a negotiable instrument. However, there are numerous technical difficulties with this, one of which is that the Bills of Exchange Act 1882 requires bills of exchange and promissory notes to be in *writing* and *signed*.[82] Although digital cash falls outside the scope of the Bills of Exchange Act 1882, new forms of negotiable instruments can be recognised by mercantile usage.[83] Given the novelty of these digital cash systems, it seems unlikely at this early stage that the courts will recognise that digital cash is negotiable by mercantile usage. If the rationale behind the rule applying to physical cash cannot be extended to non-corporeal digital cash, it will probably be necessary to introduce new legislation (or change existing legislation) to fill this gap.

Digital Cash and Credit/Debit Cards Compared

There are important consequences which flow from digital cash not being reclaimable. A consumer who transfers digital cash to a merchant operating a sham site will almost invariably suffer an immediate loss as a merchant will easily be able to spend his fraudulently obtained digital cash before he can be traced. This is in stark contrast to the result achieved when paying by credit or debit card in similar circumstances. Here, a consumer will not suffer any loss because he is protected from any fraudulent purchases subsequently made with his card information.[84]

So using digital cash is clearly disadvantageous to consumers. The flip side of the coin is that it is manifestly *advantageous* to merchants to receive payment by digital cash. The big risk for a merchant receiving payment by credit or debit card is that the buyer is fraudulently using another person's credit/debit card

---

[81] *Crawford* v. *Royal Bank of Scotland* (1749) Mor. 875 in Scots law and *Miller* v. *Race* (1758) 1 Burr. 452 in English law.

[82] S. 3(1) and s.83(1) of the Bills of Exchange Act 1882. For a fuller analysis of why this is problematic see Hooley, *supra* n.46, 249–51.

[83] *Goodwin* v. *Robarts* (1875) LR 10 Exch. 337 (affd (1876) 1 App. Cas. 476, HL).

[84] See ss. 83 and 84 of the CCA, discussed *supra*.

details. In these circumstances, the merchant will not receive payment from his bank as a result of a charge-back clause, and will carry the burden of fraud. On the other hand, when a merchant receives digital cash, he can immediately deposit it at his bank and thereby avoid being charged back.

Given the fact that digital cash does not afford consumers any of the legal protection offered to credit and debit card users, one might well ask why digital cash was invented. The answer seems to lie largely in the commercial advantages that it offers merchants and banks, although there also benefits to consumers in terms of expanded shopping opportunities.

Advantages of Digital Cash

These are:

(a) The Internet has created new markets for goods and services such as the sale of small amounts of on-line information e.g. access to pay-per-view computer games; access to information databases;[85] downloading individual songs as MP3 files; or access to the Internet itself.[86] If the purchase price is sufficiently high, then payment can easily be made by credit or debit card. However, both carry relatively high processing costs which make it uneconomical for merchants to offer goods requiring 'micro-payments'.[87] Digital cash, however, is a relatively cheap payment mechanism which enables merchants to overcome this above hurdle.

(b) Digital cash systems can hold multiple currencies simultaneously which lets consumers buy goods/services in different countries. This will be particularly important in the global micro-payments market.

(c) Digital cash may increase consumer confidence to shop on-line as credit or debit card details do not need to be sent over the Internet. Even if this risk is illusory, given the legal protection afforded to consumers, it clearly affects consumer confidence to shop on-line.[88] Furthermore, consumers will avoid potentially protracted disputes with card issuing banks over unauthorised transactions.

(d) Because digital cash systems involve advance payment, banks should be much more willing to issue consumers with smart cards holding digital cash than credit cards. There is no risk of consumers becoming

---

[85] *The Economist* e.g. currently only offers subscribers who pay an annual fee access to their online archive. Digital cash will enable such companies to offer non-subscribers the opportunity to purchase, e.g., a few pages from the archive. See <http://economist.com>.

[86] The Scottish company, Intertrader, recently launched the technology which enabled Bank of Scotland employees to buy Internet access using their Mondex cards.

[87] The cost of a credit card payment can be up to 7.5% of the value of a transaction for a small business and subject to a minimum charge: Chissick and Kelman, *supra* n.5, at 125.

[88] A recent survey showed that only 7% of general UK consumers felt secure in submitting their credit card details over the Internet. *E-commerce@its.best.uk*, *supra* n.3, 70.

5

Data Privacy in Cyberspace: Not National vs. International but Commercial vs. Individual

ANDREW CHARLESWORTH*

There is a growing consensus that if the jumble of . . . statutes, consumer pressure, and self-help is to be unified into meaningful privacy protection in the digital age, then we will have to do more than pass a law. The law in general, and each of us in particular, will have to make some fundamental adjustments in the way we think of personal information and electronic communication. In doing so, we will ultimately have to change our idea of what we can reasonably expect to keep private.

Ellen Alderman and Caroline Kennedy.[1]

'You have zero privacy anyway. Get over it.'

Scott McNealy, Sun Microsystems CEO.[2]

INTRODUCTION

The discussion of the approaches which differing political systems and ideologies have taken with regard to the collection, sorting and dissemination of personal information, whether by public or private bodies, is by no means a new one. Privacy, as a broad concept, is a topic that has long exercised some of the

---

* Andrew Charlesworth, Senior Lecturer in IT Law and Director, Information Law and Technology Unit, University of Hull Law School, Hull, UK, HU6 7RX <A.J.Charlesworth@ law.hull.ac.uk>. I would like to thank Professor Joel Reidenberg of Fordham University School of Law, and Professors Patrick Birkinshaw and Gary Edles at the University of Hull Law School for their helpful comments on versions of this chapter. All errors and infelicities of style are, of course, my own.

[1] Alderman and Kennedy, *The Right to Privacy* (Random House, New York, 1997) at 332.

[2] Comment to a group of reporters, reported in Sprenger, 'Sun on Privacy: "Get Over It" ' *Wired News*, 26 Jan. 1999, <http://www.wired.com/news/print_version/politics/story/17538. html>.

finest jurisprudential and political scholars;[3] and the concepts of 'informational privacy', 'personal data privacy' and 'personal data protection' appeared as a topic of academic discussion well before the arrival of the personal computer, the wide area network, and the commercial development of the Internet.[4] However, as the myriad of books, articles and conference papers (and, when the mood strikes, the media, the editorial columns, colour supplements, and TV documentaries) over the last 25 years constantly remind us, it is the processing power of the computer, the distributive speed of the network, the global nature of the Internet, that have sprung the topic from the fusty realms of jurisprudential and political discourse and into the lower reaches of the public consciousness.[5]

This chapter will focus primarily upon the regulation of personal data privacy practices in the private sector. This is not to imply that the public sector is not worthy of consideration, as it is clear that national governments remain major collectors and processors of personal data, and that, as a result, ensuring public control and oversight of that collection and processing remain a vital part of any meaningful data privacy regime. Indeed, the attitudes of national governments towards proposed restrictions on their own uses of personal data, and the enforcement in practice of existing laws demonstrate some interesting public sector interpretations of personal data protection.[6] However, it is arguable that, over the last 25 years, the combination of several key political, commercial and technological issues has resulted in the elevation of private enterprise above

---

[3] See e.g. Warren and Brandeis, 'The Right to Privacy: the Implicit made Explicit' (1890) 4 *Harvard Law Review* 193; Winfield, 'Privacy' (1931) 47 *Law Quarterly Review* 23; Prosser, 'Privacy' (1960) 48 *California Law Review* 383; MacCormick, 'Right of Privacy' (1972) 89 *Law Quarterly Review* 23; Posner, 'The Right of Privacy' (1978) 12 *Ga. Law Review* 393; Schoeman (ed.), *Philosophical Dimensions of Privacy: An Anthology* (CUP, Cambridge, 1984).

[4] See further: Westin, *Privacy and Freedom* (Athenium, New York, 1967); Long, *The Intruders: The Invasion of Privacy By Government and Industry* (Praeger, New York, 1967); Ernst, *Privacy: The Right to be Let Alone* (MacGibbon & Kee, London, 1968); Rosenberg, *The Death of Privacy* (Random House, New York, 1969); Warner and Stone, *The Data Bank Society: Organizations, Computers and Social Freedom* (Allen & Unwin, London, 1970); Miller, *The Assault on Privacy: Computers, Data Banks, and Dossiers*, (UMP, Ann Arbor, 1971).

[5] I use the term 'lower reaches' advisedly, for while the public may be aware of the personal data privacy debate, it remains debatable whether the average person is fully aware about the extent of the use of data collected about them. In the UK, the apparent popularity of supermarket loyalty cards, the main purpose of which is to collect data on consumers, the relatively low number of requests made by individuals under the DPA 1984 for access to their personal data held by third parties, and the phlegmatic attitude to the rising tide of junk mail all seem to suggest that personal data privacy remains low on the list of citizens' day-to-day concerns. In Canada, despite the evidence of an Angus Reid survey taken in July 1998, which suggested that 80% of Canadians thought personal data should be kept strictly confidential; 65% thought it was 'not at all acceptable' for companies to sell, trade or share detailed lists of personal information with other organizations; and 90% strongly disapproved of companies trafficking in information about their private lives without their consent, the situation in practice is strikingly similar. Survey cited in *Consumer Quarterly*, Mar. 1999, Vol.4, No. 1 at <http://strategis.ic.gc.ca/SSG/ca01128e.html>.

[6] See further Charlesworth, 'Implementing the European Data Protection Directive 1995 in UK Law: The Data Protection Act 1998' (1999) 16(3) *Government Information Quarterly* 203 at 230–1.

national government, at least in the West, as the largest potential threat to personal data privacy. These include that:

- *Private enterprises are better at data processing.* As computer technologies have become cheaper and widespread, private enterprises have caught up with, and in many cases surpassed, the ability of public authorities to collect, and make meaningful use of, personal data.[7]
- *Private enterprises have more motivation to push the envelope of acceptable personal data use.* While national governments are not averse to profiting from personal data when the opportunity arises, even in this politically fiscally conservative age their need to generate profit from such sources is less than that of private enterprises.
- *Private enterprises are subject to limited public control.* While governments are responsible to their general electorates and thus susceptible to some degree to democratic oversight and control, corporations are, subject to their legal obligations, beholden only to their owners, or to their shareholders.
- *Private enterprises have benefited from the free market and deregulation ethos of recent years.* Many Western governments have begun to roll back the extent to which they 'interfere with', or regulate (depending on one's political slant), the 'free market'. This has led to an emphasis upon seeking methods of sectoral self-regulation for private enterprises and in turn a reduced role for both government agencies, and the courts, in intervening in disputes between private enterprises and individuals.
- *Private enterprises have been given a larger role to play in international organisations.* The corollary to the reduction in government regulation at a national level has been an increase in the influence of private enterprise at an international level. This inevitably reduces the influence of the ordinary citizen as democratically elected government representation is replaced by unelected and unaccountable private interest groupings.[8]
- *Private enterprises are often able to relocate internationally.* Modern technology, and in particular computer networking, has facilitated the growth in the number of multinational corporations. Such corporations are able to alter the legal obligations placed on them by their choice of business location.
- *Private enterprises dealing primarily in data can relocate internationally more easily.* Multinational corporations that deal primarily in intangibles are able to relocate their business operations more easily than those dealing

---

[7] e.g., in the USA, Equifax Corporation carries personal information on nearly every US citizen, including consumer credit and motor vehicle records. See Brin, *The Transparent Society* (Perseus, New York, 1999).

[8] Most recently demonstrated in the handing over of the various responsibilities for DNS administration that were performed by, or on behalf of, the US Government to ICANN, a new, not-for-profit corporation formed by the private sector. <http://www.icann.org/>.

in tangibles. In that sense, they are the 'true' multinationals in that they have limited ties to any particular jurisdiction.[9]

As such, parts of the private sector are now better equipped than most governments to make use of personal data, have significant financial reasons for doing so, have limited reason to respect individual personal data privacy in the absence of data privacy laws, increasingly have control over the types of dispute resolution between commerce and citizen which are emerging from governmental free market and deregulatory policies, and where regulation is mooted are able to relocate, or threaten to relocate, to unregulated jurisdictions. This inevitably has a significant impact upon the nature of the data privacy debate.

In academic terms, the dominant discourse in data privacy regulation has been that of 'convergence and divergence'; that is, how the pressures for a harmonised transnational or international approach to such regulation are offset by resistance from national ideologies and influences.[10] Yet, whilst it remains centre-stage, the convergence and divergence discourse now has to be reformulated outside the boundaries of transnational vs. national interaction to take account of: the non-geographical nature of networked computer communications; the decline of the desire of nation states in the West to engage in certain types of regulation, either at home or in multinational fora; and the development of truly multinational corporations.

The debate surrounding the European Data Protection Directive,[11] and the reaction of the US government, commercial enterprises, and legal and political commentators to its implications appear, on its face, to be a demonstration of classic convergence and divergence activities in action. In fact, the key aspect of convergence has little to do with either the Directive and its transnational effect, or the US government's response to that effect—instead, it has everything to do with the struggle between a multinational-oriented commercial convergence and the weakening forces for a differently focused rights-based convergence, at both transnational and national levels. To put it another way, the modern model for personal data privacy, especially in relation to cyberspace and e-commerce, is increasingly being manipulated into an economic and commercial con-

---

[9] An example of this and the preceding point can be seen in the developments in the UK bookmaking market. In the past, UK bookmakers, while operating offshore betting centres, were constrained by a voluntary code that they would not accept bets from the UK. However, in May 1999, Gibraltar-based Victor Chandler International began breaching the code and actively seeking to attract UK customers. Chandler charges a 3% levy on these UK bets, against the UK Betting Duty rates of 6.75%. In response, the big UK bookmakers have threatened an expansion of their own offshore centres to take UK bets. The loss of duty revenue, and the potential damage to the UK horseracing industry has led to the UK government strengthening a ban on advertising by offshore bookmakers on teletext services and other media in the UK. It is obvious, however, that this action will have little effect on such advertising on the Internet.

[10] See, in particular, Bennett, *Regulating Privacy: Data Protection and Public Policy in Europe and the United States* (Cornell University Press, New York, 1992).

[11] Council Dir. 95/46/EC on the protection of individuals with regard to the processing of personal data and on the free movement of such data [1995] OJ L281/31, <http://europa.eu.int/eur-lex/en/lif/dat/1995/en_395L0046.html>.

struct, rather than a human rights construct. In the United States this appears to be succeeding, largely due to the acquiescence of the US government and its agencies, but, ironically, also as a result of the credence provided to it by some of the more outspoken cyberspace activists and libertarians.[12]

The US government is unwilling to act, in part, because there are legal difficulties inherent in providing a coherent framework for personal data privacy, but also because of the lobbyist-inspired concern that any such regulation would harm the development of e-commerce. The libertarians, on the other hand, are chanting the same tired mantra—'the Internet should be free of government regulation because national regulations cannot work in Cyberspace'. Yet this is exactly the same argument used to predict the imminent demise of intellectual property rights on the Internet in recent years, a period during which, both in the EU and USA, the rights granted to rights holders have instead become more extensive than ever before—at the expense of society and the individual.[13] If intellectual property rights can survive, and seemingly prosper, in cyberspace, why not personal data privacy? A quick consideration of the vested interests provides a clue. Who will benefit the most from increased intellectual property rights? Primarily commercial interests able to provide extensive financing for lobbying.[14] Who will lose out? The individual. Who will benefit from increased personal data privacy? The individual. Who may lose out? Primarily commercial interests able to provide extensive financing for lobbying.[15] Dress the matter as one may[16] and, while the result is not inevitable, it is predictable. Unless governments are prepared to legislate to protect the data privacy rights of the individual, that privacy will continue to be eroded by commercial interests.

The remaining divergence is thus no longer centred on protecting national ideologies or preferences, but rather on an increasingly one-sided struggle between two competing models of international data protection regulation. The first model is based on the theory that government has a role to play in ensuring that individuals retain some degree of control over the use of their personal data, by balancing the interest that society has in protecting the privacy of the individual against the weight of commercial concerns; the other is based on the

---

[12] The Electronic Frontier Foundation, for example, is a founding member of TRUSTe, the Internet industry privacy organisation, which has been heavily criticised for its toothlessness in the face of privacy breaches by its members.

[13] See, e.g., the Council Dir. 93/98/EEC of 29 Oct. 1993 harmonising the term of protection of copyright and certain related rights [1993] OJ L290/9 and its corresponding US legislation, the Sonny Bono Term Extension Act 1998; also The Digital Millennium Copyright Act of 1998. Extending copyright terms delays the entry of copyrighted material into the public domain, thus increasing the rights holders' economic gain, at the expense of the wider public benefit of the material's free distribution.

[14] The US term extension legislation was extensively lobbied for by Disney and other large entertainment companies. Without the 20-year extension, Mickey Mouse would potentially have entered the public domain in 2004.

[15] See The Center for Public Integrity, *Nothing Sacred: The Politics of Privacy* (The Center for Public Integrity, Washington, DC, 1998) 55–61, http://www.publicintegrity.org/nothing_sacred.pdf>.

[16] And writers such as David Brin do provide eloquent, if flawed, arguments for reducing data privacy rather than increasing it; see Brin, *supra* n.7.

theory that government intervention is unnecessary, undesirable and ultimately unworkable. The first model, as exemplified by the EU Directive, provides the individual with legislated rights with regard to the collection and use of their personal data by third parties, with a precise mechanism for the enforcement of those rights, and with the powers to obtain the necessary information effectively to exercise those rights. Such rights are broadly enforceable against both public and private sectors. The second model provides few legislated rights beyond, perhaps, limiting the secondary use of personal data by government entities, and relies upon industry self-regulation and the 'invisible hand' of market forces to ensure that private enterprises adopt data privacy practices that are broadly acceptable to the general public.

THE CONVERGENCE AND DIVERGENCE DISCOURSE: US V EU?

The Parameters of the Problem

What then are the variables that have to be considered when one analyses the problem of establishing a data privacy regime in cyberspace? How does one provide a workable solution to the competing demands between individual personal privacy and the wider societal interest in the free flow of information? The first issue to be faced lies in the varying social, political and legal understandings of, and societal status accorded to, the concept of 'personal privacy'. The second issue arises from the fact that in order to operate efficiently, both Western society and the 'free market' require that some types of information, including certain personal data, be made publicly available. The third issue is whether it is necessary for governments actively to intercede in commercial activity, by way of legal regulation, to protect the individual. The fourth and final issue, which existed before the Internet, but whose importance has been exponentially increased by it, is whether national governments should, or indeed can, attempt to exert control over the content of cross border data flows.

The EU Approach

The EU's approach to the issues above is, first and foremost, a pragmatic one. The attainment of the Single Market requires that the governments of the Member States should refrain from engaging in activities that impede the free movement of persons, goods, services and money within the EU. However, Member States often have particular policies that they are unwilling to sacrifice outright to the free movement principle, or they are bound by international commitments which place restrictions on their freedom to engage in particular forms of activity.

In the case of data privacy, the 'ideal' position, that of the unrestricted and unregulated movement of all personal data within the Single Market was effectively prevented by the fact that all the EU Member States were signatories to the Council of Europe's Convention on the Automated Processing of Personal Data of 1981.[17] This required ratifying nations to:

- Protect the privacy rights of individuals in circumstances where information about them was to be processed automatically; and
- Facilitate a common international standard of protection for individuals, with the aim that the free flow of information across international boundaries could proceed without disruption.

This need not have been a significant problem, for if all the Member States had adopted similar data privacy legislation, there would still be a level economic playing field within the EU with no distortion of markets. However, the Member States had considerably different views upon the nature of personal data privacy. Some, like Germany, France and the Nordic countries, saw the issue as having a significant human rights element. Others, such as the UK, were concerned primarily with ensuring that the minimum standards of protection required by the Convention were achieved in order that international trade not be disrupted. Greece, which ratified the Convention only in 1995, had no data privacy laws at all.[18] Thus, even where Member States actually had data privacy laws, the nature and scope of that national legislation was extremely varied.

By the early 1990s this lack of consistency was beginning to be viewed by the EU Commission as constituting a potentially serious impediment to the attainment of the Single Market. Two key factors behind this assessment were the rising use of information technologies throughout European industry, and the rapid development of the heavily IT-dependant service sector industries. Faced with serious competition in the primary and secondary industries,[19] the economies of the Western European nations had reduced their economic dependence on those industries as the motors of their economies and were placing increasing importance on the tertiary and quaternary industries.[20] Within the EU, it was feared that as competition in the tertiary and quaternary industries increased, Member States with strict data privacy laws might be inclined to use

---

[17] Convention for the Protection of Individuals with Regard to Automatic Processing of Personal Data, ETS No. 108 (Strasbourg: Council of Europe, 1981), <http://www.coe.fr/eng/legaltxt/108e.htm>. This Convention appears to have been developed from the OECD's *Guidelines on the Protection of Privacy and Transborder Data Flows of Personal Data* (Organization for Economic Co-operation and Development, Paris, 1980).

[18] Bainbridge, *EC Data Protection Directive* (Butterworths, London, 1996) at 17.

[19] Primary industries are associated with resource extraction and agriculture and include mining, fishing, farming, lumbering and oil drilling. Secondary industries are associated with the transformation of primary resources and include the steel industry, food processing and refineries.

[20] Tertiary industries are associated with service provision and include wholesaling and retailing functions, transportation and government services, and personal and professional services. Quaternary industries may be seen as a sub-set of tertiary industries, or as a distinct category in their own right, and include research, information processing and dissemination, and administration.

those laws to inhibit the free movement of persons, goods, services from Member States with laxer or no data privacy laws, in order to protect developing national industries and interests. The main purpose of the Directive was thus to harmonise the level of protection afforded to personal data by the different Member States, in part to prevent the erection of protectionist trading barriers nominally based on concern over personal data privacy.[21]

The harmonisation of laws process in the EU can be a long and drawn-out process, and this was particularly true in the area of personal data privacy. As noted above, the attitude of the Member States to the concept ranged from indifference, through pragmatic acceptance, to its elevation as a quasi-human right. It is not surprising, therefore, that there was significant disagreement between Member States over the early drafts of a directive, with Germany reluctant to accept any measure which might reduce the high level of protection afforded its citizens, and the UK, Netherlands, Ireland and Denmark convinced that Member State ratification of the Council of Europe Convention was all that should be required. Adding to the complexity of the negotiations was the heavy lobbying against strong data privacy rules by influential business interests, in particular, the banking, direct mail and medical research sectors which were concerned about the degree of restriction that would be placed on their use of personal data, and about the potential costs of compliance.

Given these factors, it is not surprising that the gestation of what was eventually to become the European Data Protection Directive was a protracted one.[22] In addition when the Commission introduced the initial draft in 1990,[23] it caused yet further difficulties by doing so with little warning, or prior consultation, an approach viewed with suspicion by some Member States.[24] After discussions with the Member States and the European Parliament the Commission then produced a considerably restructured proposal in October 1992.[25] Despite this fairly radical overhaul, the amended proposal remained unpopular, and agreement on the text proved unusually difficult to reach. In the event, a

---

[21] While there appears to be little evidence of any overtly protectionist activity having arisen from discrepancies between national data protection laws, the activities of the Member States in other areas, notably the free movement of goods, where 'public health' and 'consumer protection' have frequently been invoked to attempt to justify laws that discriminate against goods from other EU states (see e.g. Case 178/84, *Commission* v. *Germany (Beer Purity case)* [1987] ECR 1227 and Case 76/86, *Commission* v. *Germany (Milk Substitutes case)* [1989] ECR 1021), suggests that such fears were not entirely unjustified.

[22] For a detailed history see Platten, 'Background to and History of the Directive' in Bainbridge, *supra* n.18 at 13–32 and Pearce and Platten, 'Achieving Personal Data Protection in the European Union' (1998) 36 *Journal of Common Market Studies* 529.

[23] COM(90)314 final.

[24] While the European Parliament's Legal Affairs Committee had discussed data privacy as early as 1979 (PE 56.386/fin Doc 100/79), and the Commission had adopted a Recommendation addressed to the Member States in 1981 suggesting that they sign and ratify the Council of Europe Convention ([1981] OJ L246/31), until the draft Dir. there had been little concerted effort on the part of the EU to act in this area. There had been no consultative document in the form of a Green Paper, and several Member States seem to have been caught entirely off guard by the initiative as a result.

[25] [1992] OJ C311.

Common Position was eventually hammered out in the Council of Ministers on 20 February 1995, and the Directive was finally adopted in October 1995, five years after its initial introduction.

The Directive contains elements drawn from several of the national data privacy regimes of the time, but does not appear to draw unduly from any particular one—there are certainly concepts common to the previous German, UK, Dutch and French regimes.[26] It applies to situations where data are processed wholly or partly by automatic means, where the relevant processing activities are within the scope of Union law. As a result, personal data processed for the purposes of law enforcement and national security are not included. The only major exception to this rule is data processed by natural persons in the course of private and personal activity.[27] 'Personal data' are defined in broad terms and potentially cover a wide range of types of information, including but not limited to, text, photographs, audiovisual images, and sound recordings of identifiable individuals.[28]

'Processing' is equally widely defined, and is designed to ensure that the regime applies to every aspect of personal data processing from collection to destruction.[29] The regime is not confined to computerised information as it also applies to manual systems where data are held as part of a 'structured filing system'.[30] Processing of data is legitimate only in certain specified situations, and must comply with a list of data protection principles, although there are a number of exceptions. Certain data such as indications of 'racial or ethnic origin, political opinions, religious or philosophical beliefs, trade union membership and health or sex life' are regarded as particularly sensitive, and may only be processed with the 'explicit consent' of the data subject.[31]

Individuals whose data are processed are given the right to be provided with certain information, for example, about the purpose of processing; the right of access to their personal data; and the right to have inaccurate data amended, erased or destroyed.[32] Individuals are also provided with rights to object to lawful processing of their data and to their data being used for direct marketing purposes.[33] Additionally, information about processing operations must be publicly available. Limits are placed on the use of data processing equipment to make decisions that may adversely affect a data subject. Automatic processing is not permitted as the sole basis for making such a decision, although this is also subject to certain exceptions.[34] Specific exemptions are provided for the

---

[26] For fuller analysis of the Dir. see Bainbridge, *supra* n.18 and Cate, *Privacy in the Information Age* (Brookings Institution Press, Washington, DC, 1997) at 32–48.

[27] Art. 3(1)–(2), DPD, (1995).

[28] Art. 2(a), DPD, (1995).

[29] Art. 2(b), DPD, (1995).

[30] Art. 2(c), DPD, (1995).

[31] Art. 8, DPD, (1995).

[32] Arts. 10–12, DPD, (1995).

[33] Art. 14, DPD, (1995).

[34] Art. 15, DPD, (1995).

purposes of journalism, literature, and artistic purposes, to attempt to ensure that data privacy is not used as a reason to suppress freedom of expression.[35] With regard to the enforcement of the rights granted, the Directive requires the Member States to provide: a national independent supervisory agency to oversee the operation of data protection legislation,[36] a publicly accessible register, and remedies for breach of the Directive.[37]

As far as cyberspace is concerned, however, the key Articles of the Directive concern the transfer of data outside the EU and EEA, as the Directive sets detailed conditions for transfer of personal data to third party countries, forbidding transfers where, subject to limited exceptions, non-Member States fail to ensure an 'adequate level of protection'.[38] The main exception is when the transfer of data is 'necessary for the performance of a contract between the data subject and the controller' and the data subject has been informed of both this and the fact that the country receiving the export does not provide 'an adequate level of protection'.[39]

This has clear implications for existing on-line data transfers, and, more importantly, for the widening variety of data transfers and data uses envisaged by international e-commerce companies, including the amalgamation of existing marketing data with those collected during on-line transactions.[40] It might, for example, make personalization of e-commerce sites, an increasingly common phenomenon, more difficult where EU consumers are dealing with non-EEA based companies, or hinder the use of devices such as individually targeted advertisements on webpages.[41]

Consideration of the adequacy of protection of data privacy in a non-EU/EEA country to which personal data are to be transferred must encompass two criteria. First, the substantive rules that will apply to the data; and secondly, the methods of enforcement available to ensure that compliance with those substantive rules is enforced. The first of those criteria will be fulfilled if the substantive rules that apply to the transferee will achieve the same, or a similar, effect to those contained in the Directive. There are a number of ways that this might be achieved: national legislation in the jurisdiction to which the data are transferred; codes of conduct at an industry or sectoral level; or specific contractual provisions between the EU/EEA-based transferor and the non-EU/EEA transferee; or elements of all three. However, the second criterion may be somewhat more difficult to achieve, particularly if Member States or the EU Commission insist on complete concordance with the provisions in the Directive. It is difficult to see, for instance, how data subjects might be provided with similar private rights of action against non-EU/EEA data transferees to

---

[35] Art. 9, DPD, (1995).
[36] Art. 28, DPD, (1995).
[37] Arts. 22–24, DPD, (1995).
[38] Art. 25, DPD, (1995).
[39] Art. 26, DPD, (1995).
[40] See *infra* n.96.
[41] Not, of course, that every consumer would necessarily regard this as a wholly bad thing.

those that they have available against EU/EEA-based transferees under the Act without some national legislative regime.

How, then, does the EU approach address the four issues outlined above? There is certainly a clear attempt in the Directive not just to create an EU-wide legal framework for the protection of personal data privacy, but also to elevate the concept of personal data privacy into an understood and enforceable privacy right. Article 1 of the Directive states that 'Member States shall protect the fundamental rights and freedoms of natural persons, and in particular their right to privacy with respect to the processing of personal data'. This is a very stark and unambiguous assertion of the human rights-based approach envisaged by the European Union legislators. How successful that approach will be remains to be seen. In the UK, at least, where neither Parliament nor the judiciary has been minded to provide more than minimal sectoral privacy protections for the individual, either against third parties or the State, there remains a significant conceptual gap between the Directive and the national implementing legislation. The UK Data Protection Registrar's suggestion that the Data Protection Act 1998 should include a direct reference to Article 1(1) of the Directive 'to draw attention to the context in which the new UK data protection legislation is placed and to the general approach which should be adopted when the legislation is implemented'[42] was not taken up, and the idea that personal data privacy should be considered part of a wider 'right of privacy' or part of an individual's 'fundamental rights and freedoms' is not reflected anywhere in the language of the Act. The success or failure of the rather bold attempt in the Directive to establish the concept of a right of personal data privacy may thus in the end come to rest on the interplay of ideas between the EU and its institutions, notably the European Court of Justice, and the European Court of Human Rights in Strasbourg. It is certainly too early to state with any certainty that there is a definite consensus either as to what 'personal data privacy' entails, or the rationale for protecting it, agreed between the Member States of the EU.

It is equally clear that, whatever the nature of the 'fundamental right' envisaged by those drafting the Directive, it will remain very much a conditional, rather than absolute, right for the individual. The Directive can only cover activities within the scope of the Union's competence to act, leaving the extent to which Member States' law enforcement and national security agencies are regulated entirely to the discretion of the Member States.[43] Where the activities of government agencies and related bodies are subject to the Directive, there are also wide exemptions. Even where data are processed by third parties, the rights of the individual are hedged around with exceptions and exemptions, and much of the onus of pursuing those rights is left to the individual, with limited support

---

[42] Office of the Data Protection Registrar, *Comments of the Data Protection Registrar on 'Data Protection: The Government's Proposals'* (Aug. 1997) para.3, <http://www.dataprotection. gov.uk/whiteres.htm>.

[43] It should be noted that the ECHR mechanism is also at its weakest when it comes to addressing the activities of the Contracting Parties in these areas.

from the State or from the data privacy agencies established under the Directive.

Yet, despite its economic background, the way in which the Directive is drafted demonstrates that the EU retains the desire, not always readily apparent on the part of individual Member States, actively to intercede in commercial activity by way of legal regulation, and to make clear that it is doing so to protect rights of the individual. The drafters of the Directive are also clearly aware that, where sufficient international consensus exists, whether on human rights grounds, or for pragmatic economic reasons, it is possible, despite the rhetoric of ungovernability surrounding the Internet, to exert control over the content of cross-border data flows, and to subject multinational entities to national and international regulation.

However, in any examination of the EU's current position, the length and complexity of the struggle that took place between the Member States before they reached a common position on the Data Protection Directive, as well as the strenuous and well-funded opposition of several important tertiary and quaternary industries during the process should not be overlooked. In the debate over data privacy laws, United States-based commentators often portray the EU as a monolithic entity with one fixed and inflexible approach to the issue of data privacy. A more nuanced analysis shows that this is far from the case. While it is true that, from the start, the European Commission adopted, and has indicated on numerous occasions its intent to maintain, a tough stance with regard to the EU/US negotiations on data privacy (discussed below), it is far from clear that the Directive enjoys unanimous support within the European Union. Although the implementation date for the Directive was October 1998, by October 1999 only six of the 15 Member States had fully implemented it.[44] Even where compliance with the Directive has been achieved, Member States were given the discretion to phase in elements of the full implementation over a further 12 years, still further reducing the immediate impact of the regime on government and business alike.

The US Approach

In the United States, the approach taken to the concept of personal data privacy is a rather more complex one. Despite the lack of an explicit Constitutional

---

[44] The UK, e.g., did not achieve full compliance with the Dir. until Mar. 2000. On 29 July 1999 the European Commission sent reasoned opinions to France, Luxembourg, the Netherlands, Germany, the UK, Ireland, Denmark, Spain and Austria for failure to notify all the measures necessary to implement the Dir.—the second stage of formal infringement proceedings under Art. 226 of the EU Treaty, <http://europa.eu.int/comm/internal_market/en/media/dataprot/news/99-592.htm>. On 11 Jan. 2000, the Commission announced it was to take action against France, Luxembourg, the Netherlands, Germany and Ireland before the ECJ due to continuing failure—the third stage of formal infringement proceedings under Art. 226 EC, <http://europa.eu.int/comm/internal_market/en/media/dataprot/news/2k-10.htm>.

basis for a right to privacy, the concept of privacy in the sense of 'the right to be let alone'[45] has long been accepted in principle by the US legal system as a constitutional right, if rarely enthusiastically supported in practice with regard to informational privacy.[46] For example, in *Whalen* v. *Roe*[47] the Supreme Court was asked to consider whether a New York statute, requiring physicians to submit copies of prescriptions for abused drugs to the state for inclusion in a centralized computer file, invaded patients' privacy. The Court reaffirmed the right of an individual to have his personal information kept private, holding:

> We are not unaware of the threat to privacy implicit in the accumulation of vast amounts of personal information in computerized data banks or other massive government files. The collection of taxes, the distribution of welfare and social security benefits, the supervision of public health, the direction of our Armed Forces, and the enforcement of the criminal laws all require the orderly preservation of great quantities of information, much of which is personal in character and potentially embarrassing or harmful if disclosed. The right to collect and use such data for public purposes is typically accompanied by a concomitant statutory or regulatory duty to avoid unwarranted disclosures.[48]

but still upheld the statute, finding that an experiment designed to control the distribution of abused drugs was a legitimate exercise of the state's police power.[49]

In fact, of the Bill of Rights, the First, Third, Fourth, Fifth, Ninth, and Fourteenth Amendments all contain elements attributable to a right to privacy.[50] Yet the types of privacy issues addressed by federal and state legislators

---

[45] The phrase drawn from the seminal article by Brandeis, and Warren, *supra* n.3.

[46] For an excellent discussion of the historical and philosophical development of privacy theory in US law, see further Scoglio, *Transforming Privacy: A Transpersonal Philosophy of Rights* (Praeger, New York, 1998). See also Schwartz and Reidenberg, *Data Privacy Law* (Michie, Charlottesville, 1996).

[47] 429 US 589 (1977). See also *Laird* v. *Tatum*, 408 US 1 (1972) (unsuccessful challenge to surveillance by the United States Army of civilian political activities during peacetime); *Paul* v. *Davis*, 424 US 693 (1976) (no constitutional protection against the public disclosure by police of individual's arrest on a shoplifting charge, even though he had never been convicted); *United States* v. *Miller*, 425 US 435 (1976) (no protectable fourth amendment interest in bank records relating to bank depositor's account maintained pursuant to the Bank Secrecy Act).

[48] *Ibid.*, at 605.

[49] Cited in Gindin, 'Lost and Found in Cyberspace: Informational Privacy in the Age of the Internet' (1997) 34 *San Diego Law Review* 1153, also published with some changes at <http://www.info-law.com/lost.html> and Petersen, 'Your Life as an Open Book: Has Technology Rendered Personal Privacy Virtually Obsolete?' (1995) 48(1) *Federal Communications Law Journal* <http://www.law.indiana.edu/fclj/pubs/v48/no1/petersen.html>.

[50] Scoglio, *supra* n. 46 at 226 and *Griswold* v. *Connecticut*, 381 US 479, 484 (1985) (Connecticut's birth control law ruled unconstitutional under Fourth and Fifth amendments), where Justice Douglas, in writing the majority opinion, stated:

'The right of association contained in the penumbra of the First Amendment is [a zone of privacy]. The Third Amendment in its prohibition against the quartering of soldiers 'in any house' in time of peace without the consent of the owner is another facet of that privacy. The Fourth Amendment explicitly affirms the 'right of the people to be secure in their persons, houses, papers, and effects, against unreasonable searches and seizures.'

The Fifth Amendment in its Self-Incrimination Clause enables the citizen to create a zone of privacy which government may not force him to surrender to his detriment. The Ninth Amendment

and courts have tended to revolve around physical privacy (e.g. from government surveillance in those circumstances where a person has a 'reasonable expectation of privacy')[51] and decisional privacy (e.g. a woman's right to decide whether or not to have an abortion).[52] Of course, where the Constitution has been held to support determinable positive privacy rights, those rights are always exercised against either federal, or state government. Constitutional rights prevent the government from encroaching upon an individual's rights; they do not require the government to protect those rights against third parties.[53] Thus, records held by third parties, such as financial records, rental records or telephone records, are usually not protected unless a legislature has enacted a specific law, and even then that law may be subject to challenge for infringing the First Amendment rights of those wishing to hold or use those records, such as junk mailers, unsolicited telephone callers and unsolicited faxers.[54]

This is not to say that the USA lacks personal data privacy laws outside the constitutional sphere. Little could be further from the truth. It would perhaps be more accurate to say that the USA lacks *meaningful* personal data privacy laws. One of the main problems cited about US data privacy laws is that there are simply too many of them. A scan through *The Privacy Law Sourcebook 1999*[55] provides the reader with a list of 14 federal laws with some personal data privacy element, and the addition of state laws and regulations would create a list running into the hundreds.[56] Yet as Rotenberg notes,[57] the US federal privacy statutes have tended to arise less out of a concerted attempt to provide US citizens with a coherent personal data privacy regime, than out of a series of attempts either to fill legal lacuna that the courts had specifically refused to address,[58] or to assuage public concern arising from the use and abuse of new technologies.[59] The same is largely true of the efforts of the state legislatures. As Alderman and Kennedy so aptly put it:

provides: 'The enumeration in the Constitution of certain rights shall not be construed to deny or disparage others retained by the people'. Cited as above in Blackman, 'A Proposal for Federal Legislation Protecting Informational Privacy Across the Private Sector' (1993) 9 *Santa Clara Computer & High Tech. LJ* 431 at 439.

   [51]   See *Katz* v. *US*, 386 US 954 (1967).
   [52]   See *Roe* v. *Wade*, 410 US 113 (1973).
   [53]   Cate, *supra* n.26 at 99.
   [54]   See e.g. *Rowan* v. *United States Post Office*, 397 US 728 (1970); also Carroll, 'Garbage in: Emerging Media and Regulation of Unsolicited Commercial Solicitations' (1996) 11 *Berkeley Technology Law Journal* <http://www.256.com/~gray/spam/law.html>.
   [55]   Rotenberg, *The Privacy Law Sourcebook 1999* (EPIC, Washington, DC, 1999).
   [56]   Consider, e.g., the bewildering array of health privacy laws at contained in Pritts, Goldman, Hudson, Berenson, and Hadley, 'The State of Health Privacy: An Uneven Terrain/A Comprehensive Survey of State Health Privacy Statutes', July 1999 <htp://www.healthprivacy.org/resources/statereports/contents.html>. See also Smith (ed.), *Compilation of State and Federal Privacy Laws* (Privacy Journal, 1997) and EPIC's *Privacy Laws by State* at <http://www.epic.org/privacy/consumer/states.html>.
   [57]   Rotenberg, *supra* n.55 at i–ii.
   [58]   E.g. Right to Financial Privacy Act 1978; 12 USC § 3401; Privacy Protection Act 1980 42 USC § 2000aa.
   [59]   e.g. Privacy Act of 1974, 5 USC § 552a; Video Privacy Protection Act 1988, 18 USC § 2710; Telephone Consumer Protection Act 1991, 47 USC § 227.

the biggest problem with the statutory scheme is that there is no overall privacy policy behind it. As even a partial list of privacy laws indicates, they address a hodge-podge of individual concerns. The federal statutory scheme most resembles a jigsaw puzzle in which the pieces do not fit. That is because the scheme was put together backwards. Rather than coming up with an overall picture and then breaking it up into smaller pieces that mesh together, Congress has been sporadically creating individual pieces of legislation that not only do not mesh neatly but also leave gaping holes.[60]

An examination of just two of the lesser federal data privacy laws will give some idea of the problem. The Video Privacy Protection Act 1988[61] came about very largely as a result of the public outcry that arose when a journalist was able to obtain, and publish, the video rental records of a Supreme Court nominee, Robert Bork, listing the 146 videotapes Bork and his wife had rented over a two-year period. As the name suggests, the Act regulates solely the disclosure to third parties, and the destruction after use, of specific video sales and rentals information. However, it should be noted that that limited protection is more than is granted by federal law to medical records.[62] Interestingly, a similar measure to protect library lending records was dropped, apparently at the behest of the FBI, which wanted to continue to monitor the reading materials borrowed by foreign nationals.[63] Equally, the Driver's Privacy Protection Act 1994[64] was enacted following public disquiet after the 1989 murder of actress Rebecca Schaeffer by a deranged fan. The fan had obtained her address from a private investigator who had, in turn, received it from the California Department of Motor Vehicles. The Act forbids the states' DMVs from releasing personal information from a driver's records, unless the request fits one of 14 exemptions. As Cate drily notes, one of the range of 14 exempted requests is 'use by any licensed private investigator'![65]

In fact, the most heavily regulated sector in the USA with regard to data privacy remains the government. Not only are there important constitutional controls on its ability to collect and use personal data in the law enforcement sector, but with regard to government collection and use of personal data for other purposes, most aspects of federal agency collection, maintenance, use and disclosure of personal information are regulated by the Privacy Act 1974,[66] and subsequent amendments.[67]

---

[60] Alderman and Kennedy, *supra* n. 1 at 330–1.

[61] *Supra* n. 59.

[62] Schwartz and Reidenberg, *supra* n.46 at 11.

[63] Interview with Evan Hendricks, *Privacy Times*, 8 June 1988, cited in The Center for Public Integrity, *supra* n.15.

[64] 18 USC § 2721–5.

[65] Cate, *supra* n.26 at 79.

[66] 5 USC § 552(a) <http://www.usdoj.gov/foia/privstat.htm>. See further, *Overview of the Privacy Act of 1974* (Sept. 1998) at <http://www.usdoj.gov/04foia/04_7_1.html>.

[67] The Computer Matching and Privacy Protection Act 1988 (Pub. L. 100–503) amended it to establish procedural safeguards affecting agencies' use of Privacy Act records in performing certain types of computerised matching programs. The Computer Matching and Privacy Protection Amendments 1990 (Pub. L. 101–508) further clarified the due process provisions.

How then does the US approach address the four issues outlined above? The US legal system certainly recognises a fundamental right of personal privacy, but it is clear that this right becomes rather nebulous in the area of informational privacy. The federal legislation fails to provide anything like a comprehensive regime for data privacy, and the state coverage is, at best, patchy. Even where there is federal legislation covering either the public or private sector, it is often so liberally festooned with exemptions as virtually to negate its purpose. This is due largely to the fact that much of the legislation appears to have been designed primarily to send a message from the legislature, either of reassurance to the voters, or of rebuke to the courts, without the measure actually impinging unduly on the ability of either government or commerce to carry on with their personal data use much as before. The current willingness of the US government actively to intercede in the commercial use of personal data appears all but non-existent, particularly in the sphere of electronic commerce, where it has shown a great reluctance (not necessarily shared by the states) to involve itself in any form of regulatory behaviour, up to, and including, taxation. This *laissez faire* approach appears likely to continue in the near future. While the US government is occasionally prone to enacting laws with significant extraterritorial application, at present, with the exception of the Communications Decency Act 1996[68] the Child Online Protection Act 1998,[69] and the Children's On-line Privacy Protection Act 1998,[70] it has done little to attempt to exert control over the content of cross border data flows.

A Clash of Approaches?

Is there then a tenable middle ground between the two approaches, or are they simply inimical? In theory at least, there certainly appears to be a not inconsiderable degree of common ground. Only the more extreme protagonists to the data privacy debate would assert that individuals could manage with no data privacy protection,[71] or alternatively that individuals should have complete control over their personal data, perhaps via some kind of property right.[72] Both EU

[68] Communications Decency Act 1996, Title V, Telecommunications Act of 1996, Pub. L. 104–104, much of which was struck down in *Reno* v. *American Civil Liberties Union*, 117 SCt. 2329, 138 LEd.2d 874 (1997).

[69] Child Online Protection Act 1998, Title XIV, Omnibus Consolidated and Emergency Supplemental Appropriations Act of 1999 Pub. L. 105–277, 47 USC 231, suspended by TRO pending a ruling on its constitutionality.

[70] Children's Online Privacy Protection Aft 1998, Title XIII, Omnibus Consolidated and Emergency Supplemental Appropriations Act, 1999, Pub. L. 105–277; 15 USC 6501–6505.

[71] See Brin, *supra* n. 7 and, with regard to the private sector, Singleton, 'Privacy as Censorship: A Skeptical View of Proposals to Regulate Privacy in the Private Sector' *Cato Policy Analysis No. 295*, 22 Jan. 1998. <http://www.cato.org/pubs/pas/pa-295.html>.

[72] See *Avrahami* v. *US News & World Report, Inc.*, No. 95–7479 (Arlington County Gen. Dist. Ct. filed Oct. 1995) cited in Kirsh, 'Recommendations for the Evolution of Netlaw: Protecting Privacy in a Digital Age,' *Journal of Computer-Mediated Communication*, <http://www.ascusc.org/jcmc/vol2/issue2/kirsh.html>; and Alderman and Kennedy, *supra* n.1 at 329.

and US approaches are concerned not to stifle commerce unnecessarily, to interfere with the freedom of the media and arts, or to block the workings of government regulatory agencies and law enforcement. Both clearly consider certain
data more sensitive and deserving of protection than others, although on the US
side that list appears to have been somewhat more randomly selected. In both
approaches it is deemed necessary to require certain minimum standards of
personal data privacy from both the commercial and private sectors. In fact, the
more one examines the issue, the more apparent it becomes that the key differences between the EU and US approaches are more in the mechanics of achieving data privacy than with the concept itself.

In practice then, the key difference between the two approaches comes down
to the fact that the EU Directive provides for a legislatively backed data privacy
regime in its Member States, which applies to both public and private sector, is
overseen by national regulatory authorities and provides remedies to individuals whose data privacy rights are breached. Even then, there are striking similarities in the US approach, in as much as the Privacy Act 1974 provides a similar
regime for the US government and its agencies,[73] although it does not have a regulatory body to monitor compliance and enforcement and has been accused of
suffering from overgenerous administrative interpretation, and a lack of a credible oversight.[74] That notwithstanding, the basic criteria for personal data use
by the US government differ surprisingly little from the EU model. This appears
to leave the US treatment of the private sector as being the main obstacle to a
convergence in data privacy laws between the EU and USA. That being the case,
it is interesting to consider the reasons the prevailing mood in the USA appears
to weigh against the introduction of a regulatory regime similar to that of the
EU.

When studying the plethora of reading material produced about the extraterritorial effect of the EU Directive, and its potential consequences for the USA,
the arguments by (primarily) US commentators against the USA adopting a similar regime are many and varied, ranging from constitutional analysis to somewhat petulant rhetoric, they include suggestions that:

- the US should not comply with the extraterritorial application of another
  jurisdiction's laws;
- the trade in personal data in the USA is so far advanced that it is too late to
  provide a data privacy regime;
- a centralised government privacy regulator cannot be trusted to have US
  citizens' best interests at heart, and centralisation of data and knowledge
  about data protection are a greater threat to personal privacy than diverse
  commercial activity;

---

[73] 'The principles of transparency and finality are represented in the Act as are requirements for
access security, data quality and limits on data collection. The Act also provides remedies, including both civil and criminal penalties': Gellman, *DM News* (16 Feb. 1998) 14, 45, cited in
Charlesworth, *supra* n.6 at 230.

[74] Cate, *supra* n. 26 at 78.

consumer data marketer with five-year buying profiles on 88 million American households, and DoubleClick, a Net advertising firm.[96]

The cost of compliance with a legislative data privacy regime is extremely difficult to quantify. The UK government estimated the initial compliance costs for central and local government of conformity with the national legislation implementing the Data Protection Directive at £194 million and the recurring costs at £75 million. For business the figures were £836 million and £630 million respectively.[97] However, the UK has had specific data privacy legislation in place for 15 years, and the implementation costs would thus be lower than in a situation where businesses were effectively starting from scratch. On the other hand, it is possible that those estimates are themselves too high. It should be noted that when the Data Protection Act 1984 came into force the Department of Health and Social Security in the UK planned to have to deal with 200,000 requests in the first six months of the operation of the access provisions, whilst the Home Office expected 50,000, in the event they received 270 and 16 respectively.[98] The cost of compliance argument does, however, highlight an important point, that in the USA the right to personal data privacy is perceived as a sufficiently nebulous right that it can legitimately and openly be attacked on cost grounds—one cannot imagine the right to free speech, or the right to bear arms, being treated in quite such a fashion, although the financial cost of both must be impressive.[99]

It has been suggested that US information-intensive industries, like the credit card industry, which were considering expanding into global markets were dissuaded from rapid expansion into Europe because of the impending European Directive.[100] With respect, this argument fails to take account of the fact that, prior to the discussion of the Directive, let alone its implementation, two of the major European players, Germany and France, already had relatively strict data privacy regimes in place, and while the regimes of the other Member States might have been weaker, they too would already have had an influence upon the behaviour of the credit card companies.[101] A more likely problem for the credit card companies was not the slowing of expansion into Europe due to difficulties

---

[96] Macavinta, 'Privacy Advocates Rally against DoubleClick-Abacus Merger' *CNET News.com*, 22 Nov. 1999, <http://news.cnet.com/news/0-1005-200-1461826.html?tag=st.ne.1002. bgif.1005– 200–1461826>.

[97] The Data Protection Bill, (25 Mar. 1998) (Stationery Office, London, 1998). Explanatory Memorandum at p. v.

[98] Tapper, *Computer Law* (4th edn., Longman, London, 1989) at 330.

[99] 'The cost of firearm injuries in the US in 1990 was an estimated $20.4 billion. This includes $1.4 billion for direct expenditures for health care and related goods, $1.6 billion in lost productivity resulting from injury-related disability, and $17.4 billion in lost productivity from premature death': Max and Rice, 'Shooting in the Dark: Estimating the Cost of Firearm Injuries' (1993) 12(4) *Health Affairs* 171–85.

[100] See Regan, 'American Business and the European Data Protection Directive: Lobbying Strategies and Tactics' in Bennett, and Grant, (eds.), *Visions of Privacy: Policy Choices for the Digital Age*, (University of Toronto Press, Toronto, 1999).at 199–216.

[101] In 1996, Citibank agreed to observe German privacy standards in processing credit card transactions in the United States for German citizens. Gumbel, 'High Tech Zaps German Privacy Laws', *Wall Street Journal*, 5 Jan. 1996, at A6.

in compliance, but the avoidance of having to explain why their European customers were being granted more control over the use of their personal data than their American counterparts. This differential treatment issue remains a key issue in the current negotiations between the EU and USA over the development of a 'safe harbor' for US companies (see below).[102]

Cate suggests that in the EU it is socially and politically acceptable to place privacy rights alongside, or even above, rights such as freedom of expression, the acquisition and use of property, and the right not to have the government interfere in daily life.[103] He adds that this approach may be untenable in the United States because societal values militate against the elevation of a right that is not explicitly guaranteed in the Constitution to equal or greater status than those rights which are explicitly guaranteed.[104] Certainly both First and Fifth Amendment issues have been raised as possible barriers to a European style regime.

The First Amendment argument is often raised by critics of any attempt to assert a right to information privacy. Such critics are, unsurprisingly, often affiliated with businesses that sell personal information, or use it to promote and sell their products.[105] The argument goes that the guarantee of free speech in the First Amendment is an explicit constitutional right and must therefore be a superior right to an implicit constitutional right to privacy, and any legislative information privacy rights granted to individuals. However, to claim that the commercial holding and use of *all* personal information are subject to protection under the First Amendment is somewhat disingenuous, as it is clear from the case law of the Supreme Court that this is not so.

While for-profit dissemination of personal information does seem to have a legitimate claim for protection under the First Amendment,[106] the Supreme Court's position has been that speech that only proposes a commercial transaction has a lower value and can be regulated,[107] not least because commercial speech is less likely to be deterred by regulation than political speech.[108] There

---

[102] See Response of the Center for Democracy and Technology to the Draft International Safe Harbor Principles, 15 Nov 1999, for the clearest expression of this issue. <http://www.ita.doc.gov/td/ecom/cd&t1299.htm>.

[103] Cate, *supra* n.26 at 100.

[104] *Ibid.*

[105] See, e.g., the submission of the Magazine Publishers of America to the National Telecommunications and Information Administration commenting on the Department of Commerce staff discussion paper 'Elements of Effective Self-Regulation for the Protection of Privacy' at <http://www.ntia.doc.gov/ntiahome/privacy/mail/disk/MPA.html>. US Direct Marketing Association President & CEO H. Robert Wientzen is quoted as stating 'The DMA opposes, as we have historically, a blanket government prohibition on unsolicited commercial e-mail. Really, this is a First Amendment freedom of commercial speech issue'. <http://www.the-dma.org/texis/scripts/news/newspaper/+_wwBmWeyBhlwwwn/displayArticle.html#3>. (No longer functional).

[106] See further the discussion in Volokh, 'Freedom of Speech, Information Privacy, and the Troubling Implications of a Right to Stop People from Speaking About You', The Independent Institute Working Paper 14, Dec. 1999.

[107] *Bolger* v. *Youngs Drug Prods. Corp.*, 463 US 60, 64–5 (1983); *Ohralik* v. *Ohio State Bar Ass'n*, 436 US 447, 456 (1978).

[108] *Virginia Pharmacy Bd.* v. *Virginia Citizens Consumer Credit Council, Inc.*, 425 US 748, 771–2 (1976).

have been, for instance, a number of cases concerning junk mail where statutes, which forbade the mailing of commercial solicitations to individuals who had stated they did not want to receive them, have been upheld on the ground that such regulation is a constitutionally permissible protection of individual privacy.[109] The Court's interpretation, however, requires the individual to decide what types of advertising they wish to reject, and subsequently act to stop the advertising from reaching them. The government may not simply ban unsolicited commercial solicitations outright, or on the ground that they are offensive, for then the government does violate the First Amendment.[110] Also, with regard to credit reports, in *Dun & Bradstreet, Inc* v. *Greenmoss Builders, Inc*[111] it was held that if commercial speech was to be afforded full protection under the First Amendment, it must address a matter of public concern, and that credit reports concerned no public issue.[112] Indeed, the very fact that federal legislation like the Right to Financial Privacy Act 1978, the Video Privacy Protection Act of 1988 and the Telephone Consumer Protection Act 1991 exists also demonstrates that restrictions may be placed on the collection and use of personal data without breaching the First Amendment.

Cate raises a rather speculative Fifth Amendment argument suggesting that, in order to implement a European-style data privacy regime, the US government would breach the principle that 'government cannot take private property, whether by physical occupation or extensive regulation without according due process and paying just compensation to the owner'.[113] It is clear that the Supreme Court considers a variety of intangible interests to be property for the purposes of the Fifth Amendment.[114] Cate cites *Ruckelshaus* v. *Monsanto*[115] as suggesting 'privacy regulations that substantially interfere with a private party's use of data that have been collected or processed, may require compensation under the Fifth Amendment'. The *Monsanto* case involved the Federal Insecticide, Fungicide, and Rodenticide Act (FIFRA) which authorised the Environmental Protection Agency (EPA) to use data submitted by an applicant for registration of a covered product (hereinafter pesticide) in evaluating the application of a subsequent applicant, and to disclose publicly some of the submitted data. Monsanto claimed that that the data-consideration and data-disclosure provisions of FIFRA were a 'taking' of property without just com-

---

[109]   *Rowan* v. *United States Post Office*, *supra* n.54 where Chief Justice Berger, writing for the Court, explicitly noted that the right to communicate must be balanced against every person's right 'to be let alone'; *South-Suburban Hous. Ctr.* v. *Greater S. Suburban Bd. of Realtors*, 935 F2d 868 (7th Cir. 1991); *Curtis* v. *Thompson*, 840 F2d 1291 (7th Cir. 1988).

[110]   *Bolger* v. *Youngs Drug Prods. Corp.*, *supra* n.107. See Carroll, *supra* n.54 and Amaditz, 'Canning "Spam" in Virginia: Model Legislation to Control Junk E-mail' (1999) 4 *Va. J.L. & Tech.* 4 <http://vjolt.student.virginia.edu/graphics/vol4/home_art4.html>.

[111]   472 US 749, 762 (1985).

[112]   See further Petersen, *supra* at n.49.

[113]   Cate, *supra* n.26 at 72–5 and 99.

[114]   *Louisville Joint Stock Land Bank* v. *Radford*, 295 US 555, 596–602 (1935); (real estate lien); *Lynch* v. *United States*, 292 US 571, 579 (1934) (valid contracts)

[115]   467 US 986 (1984).

pensation, in violation of the Fifth Amendment. The Supreme Court held that Monsanto's health, safety, and environmental data were a trade-secret property right and were thus protected by the Taking Clause of the Fifth Amendment. A successful invocation of the Taking Clause does not require governmental acquisition or destruction of the property of an individual. The fact that the former owner is deprived of a right or interest is the key, not whether or not the State then obtains that right. In fact, any action by the government which falls short of acquisition of title or occupancy will still be a taking if its effect is to deprive the owner of all or most of his interest in the subject matter.[116]

However, the Supreme Court has had difficulties in determining when 'justice and fairness' require that economic injuries caused by public action must be deemed a compensatable taking. It has, however, identified several factors that should be taken into account when determining whether a governmental action has gone beyond mere 'regulation' and effected a 'taking'. Among those factors are 'the character of the governmental action, its economic impact, and its interference with reasonable investment-backed expectations'.[117] Cate argues that '[a] data processor exercises property rights in his data because of his investment in collecting and aggregating them with other useful data', and adds that, because the USA has not to this point imposed significant regulation on such activities, an information processor might reasonably invest in them, with the expectation of being able to use the data for commercial purposes.[118]

While this argument would undoubtedly be music to the ears of US data processors, there are several potential problems with it. First, it appears to be a significant stretch to extrapolate from cases which relate to trade secrets, real estate liens and valid contracts that the Supreme Court would necessarily consider collections of personal data as property protected by the Taking Clause of the Fifth Amendment. Trade secrets, real estate liens and valid contracts are all intangible property rights whose existence is already acknowledged by law. As the Court in *Monsanto* noted:

> we are mindful of the basic axiom that '[p]roperty interests . . . are not created by the Constitution. Rather, they are created and their dimensions are defined by existing rules or understandings that stem from an independent source such as state law.[119]

It is certainly arguable that the fact of adding value to personal data by collecting and collating it does not automatically determine the future ownership of that personal data.[120]

---

[116] *United States* v. *General Motors Corp.*, 323 US 373 (1945), at 378.

[117] *Prune Yard Shopping Center* v. *Robins*, 447 US 74 (1980), at 83.

[118] Cate, *supra* n.26 at 74.

[119] Quoting from *Webb's Fabulous Pharmacies, Inc.* v. *Beckwith*, 449 US 155, 161 (1980), in turn quoting *Board of Regents* v. *Roth*, 408 US 564, 577 (1972).

[120] Laudon, 'Extensions to the Theory of Markets and Privacy: Mechanics of Pricing Information' in *Privacy and Self- Regulation in the Information Age supra* at n.80. The difficulty of ascribing ownership to personal data is discussed at length in Branscomb, *Who Owns Information* (Basic Books, New York, 1994).

Secondly, data privacy laws generally do not forbid data processors to hold and process data, they rather place obligations upon data processors to ensure that:

- their activities meet certain standards of accuracy and completeness;
- the data processing does not cause harm to individuals;
- certain categories of sensitive data are given particular protection;
- citizens retain some degree of control over their personal data.

As such data privacy laws are unlikely to deprive the data processors of all or most of their interest in existing or future collections of personal data, although they may deprive them of some potentially lucrative avenues. That would not seem to meet the criteria for the Taking Clause of the Fifth Amendment.

Finally, as has already been noted, both US federal government and the states have, over the last 25 years, imposed piecemeal, but increasingly stringent controls on the collection and use of various types of data. This, combined with the increasing trend world-wide towards the development of data privacy regimes, must surely tend to militate against any expectation on the part of US data processors that they will be permitted to continue unfettered processing of personal data indefinitely, especially in circumstances where such processing may result in significant public disquiet. In short, the Fifth Amendment data privacy argument that Cate proffers is based on an extremely imaginative interpretation of the scope of the ruling in Monsanto, and it seems unlikely therefore that it would in fact provide much succour to US data processors, other than as a further 'Constitutional' ploy to use in their campaign against federal privacy legislation.

The final and most popular argument at present is that voluntary self-regulation of data privacy in the commercial sector is preferable to government interference. Indeed, this issue currently dominates the debate over personal data privacy in the USA, with the commercial sector scrambling to put into place self-regulatory systems, in order to forestall the imposition of data privacy regimes via legislation. The US government, however, remains racked by indecision, as it receives conflicting reports from its agencies as to the efficacy of those self-regulatory efforts, and constant lobbying from the direct marketing, banking and Internet businesses claiming regulation will kill the golden goose of e-commerce. Overall, despite mounting public pressure, there appears to be sparse support for a privacy approach based on the lines of the European model, or for the establishment of a centralised governmental privacy agency, amongst US government agencies,[121] and commercial enterprises.[122] US academic and

---

[121] See, e.g., The Information Infrastructure Task Force, Privacy Working Group, Privacy and the National Information Infrastructure, *Principles for Providing and Using Personal Information* (Washington, DC, June 1995); US Dept. of Commerce, National Telecommunications and Information Industry Administration, *Privacy and the NII, Safeguarding Telecommunications-Related Personal Information* (Washington, DC, Oct. 1995).

[122] See Regan, *supra* n.100.

political opinion remains divided, with what appears to be the weight of academic commentators in favour of the development of a more effective US approach towards the protection of personal information privacy, but, perhaps unsurprisingly, with much of the media and business attention going to those opposed.[123]

Interestingly, Mulligan and Goldman suggest that US commercial interests have not always been opposed to legislative attempts to provide informational privacy.[124] In the past, it is claimed, they often have been quite fervent supporters of privacy legislation, although this is usually legislation that limits government access to information about individuals, such as The Electronic Communications Privacy Act of 1986. However, in some cases, such as the Video Privacy Protection Act of 1988, commercial interests and interest groups actively lobbied for legislation to limit both government and private sector access to personal data. It is suggested that, in both those types of circumstance, the motive of the relevant industries was primarily to obtain a base level of consumer trust and confidence in new products and technologies, and to ensure a level playing field for competition, as self-regulated businesses sought to legally bind unregulated businesses to a minimum standard of protection. With other legislation, such as the Fair Credit Reporting Act of 1970, it is supposed that the bad publicity arising from incidents has led industries to support legislation on the basis that it was inevitable, and in supporting it they could influence its nature.[125] However, it can be argued that this attitude towards the role of commercial interests in past legislation is in fact a revisionist view of events, showing commercial attitudes to be much more accommodating to privacy measures than was the actual case at the time.

Assuming for the moment that Mulligan and Goldman's perceptions are accurate, either of the two scenarios (achieving minimum standards, or engaging in 'damage limitation') could be seen to mirror the type of developments

---

[123] Cate, *supra* n. 26; Swire and Litan, *supra* n.75; and Brin, *supra* n.7, all oppose that approach. Similar sentiments can be found in BeVier, 'Information about Individuals in the Hands of Government: Some Reflections on Mechanisms for Privacy Protection' (1995) 4 *William and Mary Bill of Rights Journal* 506, and Kirsh, Phillips and McIntyre, *supra* n.72. Swire's opposition is particularly important as the Clinton administration recently appointed him as its Chief Counsellor for Privacy.

For contrast, see Smith, *Managing Privacy: Information Technology and Corporate America* (UNCP, 1994); Kang, 'Information Privacy in Cyberspace Transactions' (1998) 50 *Stan. L. Rev.* 1193–1294; Reidenberg, 'Restoring Americans' Privacy in Electronic Commerce' (1999) 14(2) *Berkeley Technology Law Journal* 771; Schwartz, 'Privacy in Cyberspace' (1999) 52 *Vanderbilt Law Review* 1609; Petersen, *supra* at n.49; and Gindin, *supra* at n.49.

[124] Mulligan and Goldman, 'The Limits and the Necessity of Self-Regulation: The Case for Both' in *Privacy and Self- Regulation in the Information Age, supra* at n.80.

[125] In the case of the Fair Credit Report Act 1970, the influence of the credit bureau, banking and financial services industries in both Senate and Congress was such that the original Act seen by privacy advocates as being 'more loophole than law'. The subsequent amendment to it made in 1996, while providing some minor privacy gains, failed to deal with the most pressing problems with the original Act such as the ability of credit bureaus to sell credit headers, and additionally had the effect of actually reducing consumer privacy in other areas. See The Center for Public Integrity, *Nothing Sacred: The Politics of Privacy, supra* n.15 at 17–24.

currently occurring on the Internet. So why then the opposition to the type of privacy regime required by the EU Data Protection Directive? Surely this would improve the low public perception of privacy on the Internet, and ensure a level privacy playing field for Internet e-commerce? There are in essence two fundamental reasons why US commercial enterprises remain so dogmatically opposed: the Directive offers credible oversight and enforcement mechanisms, and legal redress for the individual. These are two things that are noticeably lacking from either existing US federal legislation or the privacy policies currently being promoted by the new on-line industry self-regulatory bodies such as TRUSTe,[126] the Online Privacy Alliance[127] or BBBonline.[128]

While TRUSTe, the Online Privacy Alliance and BBBonline aggressively promote and publicise their model policies, their rhetoric ignores the fact that, even if they have the inclination to do so, they are ultimately incapable of enforcing their members' adherence to any of the promises and guarantees contained in those policies. TRUSTe, whose stated aim is to provide an 'industry-regulated, cost-effective privacy program' based on a branded online seal, and whose activities are funded by amongst others America Online, CyberCash, Excite, IBM, MatchLogic, Microsoft, Netcom, Netscape, and Compaq, has already been faced with major privacy breaches on the part of three of its 'licencees', Microsoft, Real, and GeoCities.[129] TRUSTE claims that it is:

> the only organization that provides established, comprehensive oversight and consumer resolution mechanisms to assure that stated privacy policies are being enforced and that users' online privacy is protected.[130]

Yet, in the most egregious of the breaches, that committed by Geocities, TRUSTe failed to take any action, neglecting even to withdraw Geocities' TRUSTe privacy seal. The issue might, in fact, simply have been ignored if the Federal Trade Commission (FTC) had not stepped in, announcing in August 1998 that it and GeoCities had agreed on a consent order to settle the first FTC case of privacy violation. The FTC charged GeoCities with misrepresenting to users its reasons for collecting the personal information it required to establish a user's home page, and with deceptive practices relating to its collection of information from children. The Director of the FTC's Bureau of Consumer Protection stated that 'GeoCities misled its customers, both children and adults, by not telling the truth about how it was using their personal information'.[131] GeoCities denied to the media that it had in fact done anything wrong, but

---

[126] <http://www.Truste.org/>.

[127] <http://www.privacyalliance.org/>.

[128] <http://www.BBBonline.org/>.

[129] There have also been allegations against Sun Microsystems, a member of the Online Privacy Alliance: see Glave, 'Sun Violated My Privacy', *Wired News*, 18 Dec. 1998, <http://www.wired.com/news/news/politics/story/16929.html>.

[130] See TRUSTe: Frequently Asked Questions <http://www.etrust.com/about/about_faqs.html>.

[131] See n.83 for details of the consent order. Interestingly neither GeoCities nor TRUSTe refer to the matter on their respective home pages.

tellingly did not fight the order. Given the widely expressed antipathy by US commercial concerns to the government's role in protecting personal information privacy, it seems odd that the FTC, a US government agency, should need to reprimand a member of the foremost self-regulatory privacy scheme on the Internet for lying about its use of personal data.

In March 1999, Microsoft, a 'Premier Corporate Sponsor' of TRUSTe, admitted to collecting special identification numbers from users' PCs during the Windows registration process regardless of whether users chose to send this information or not. After investigation, TRUSTe reported that Microsoft did 'compromise consumer trust and privacy', but did not breach TRUSTe's licensing agreement, as that covered only data collected specifically by Microsoft's website.[132] Thus, TRUSTe did not require a third-party audit, nor did it impose any penalty beyond a mild verbal rebuke. If that was not embarrassing enough, then in August 1999 it was revealed that major flaws in Microsoft's free e-mail service Hotmail could allow access to any user's account without a password. In this case TRUSTe made a 'strong recommendation'[133] that Microsoft have a third-party firm validate that the Hotmail security breach was resolved. While Microsoft agreed to that recommendation, on the conclusion of the audit, Microsoft refused to reveal the name of the firm that carried it out, or to release the results of the investigation, stating simply that the auditing firm had confirmed that the security problem had been resolved and that the service conformed to the privacy standards set by TRUSTe. Privacy advocates understandably met this announcement with some cynicism. On this evidence, there appears to be little true public accountability within TRUSTe's current self-regulatory regime, and little or no incentive for companies to pay more than lip service to the notion of credible personal data privacy.

Given these recent developments, it seems increasingly unlikely that industry funded oversight agencies will be able, or willing, to ensure properly accountable compliance with their privacy policies. The fact that there are now several bodies claiming to provide self-regulatory privacy functions merely muddies the issue further. A credible independent oversight enforcement agency will be required if current privacy policies are to be more than simply words on a website. Certainly self-regulation is likely to work effectively only where it will cost businesses more, either in financial terms or in terms of competitiveness, to breach the policies than to comply with them. Public pressure for companies to operate in compliance with sectoral codes of conduct, while much touted as a valuable mechanism for facilitating effective sectoral self-regulation, is simply insufficient by itself to ensure that this will occur on a consistent basis. Although the idea that the free market will deal with commercial privacy abusers is

---

[132] <http://www.truste.com/users/users_w1723.html>. This was much the same line as it took with the Real incident, where after an initial investigation TRUSTe decided the privacy breach lay (just) outside its remit.: Oakes, 'TRUSTe Declines Real Probe', *Wired News*, 9 Nov. 1999, <http://www.wired.com/news/technology/0,1282,32388,00.html>.

[133] <http://www.truste.com/users/users_adv.html>.

another favourite argument of those favouring self-regulation, there is little, if any, historical evidence to support this conjecture. US credit reports are notoriously inaccurate, yet consumer concern has led to little improvement in business practices in the past 30 years.[134] Firms like Real, Microsoft and GeoCities have all been clearly and publicly in breach of their stated privacy policies, yet have suffered little, if any, financial damage. The very lack of transparency in business privacy practices militates against any meaningful public pressure being exerted, consumers cannot make informed decisions about competing ventures on the basis of their privacy protection if no useful information is available about that protection, or if businesses are able to lie to, or mislead, consumers about their business practices with impunity.

It is also noticeable that none of the policies generated by the commercial sector provide individuals whose privacy has been breached with any meaningful relief; certainly there is no mention of legal redress. As a result, given the lacklustre performance of the self-regulatory bodies, US citizens at present find themselves find themselves without meaningful opportunity to have their legitimate data privacy grievances addressed, or to be compensated for breaches of policy.

The Safe Harbor Proposals: An Acceptable Compromise?

Thus far, despite its obvious shortcomings, the self-regulatory argument seems to be holding sway, and perhaps even gaining ground.[135] In June 1998, in a report to Congress, the FTC noted that while the majority of Web sites collected personal data from visitors, only a handful had any kind of visible privacy policy available on their sites.[136] The FTC Chairman, in his testimony to Congress, stated that, given the failure of the business community to implement a system of self-regulation for online privacy, and the fact that trade association guidelines failed to reflect industry acceptance of the basic fair information practice principles, the FTC was recommending that federal legislation be produced to protect the online privacy of children, and that further recommendations would be forthcoming. That statement was followed, in fairly short order, by the passage of The Children's Online Privacy Protection Act of 1998, but since that time the FTC has appeared to be backing away from the federal regulation option. In July 1999, in its further recommendations,[137] the FTC decided by a three to one vote not to propose further legislation on the ground that the online industry was now making substantial progress attributable to industry self-

---

[134] See The Center for Public Integrity, *supra* n.15 at 18–19.

[135] See Belgum, 'Who Leads at Half-time?: Three Conflicting Visions of Internet Privacy Policy', 6 *Rich. J.L. & Tech.* 1, (Symposium 1999), <http://www.richmond.edu/jolt/v6i1/belgum.html>.

[136] Federal Trade Commission, *Privacy Online: A Report to Congress*, June 1998 available in 1998 WL 299974 FTC, and at <http://www.ftc.gov/reports/privacy3/toc.htm>.

[137] *Self Regulation and Privacy On-line: A Report to Congress*, July 1999 available at <http://www.ftc.gov/os/1999/9907/privacy99.pdf >.

regulation. It quoted approvingly from two industry-funded surveys carried out at Georgetown University that suggested that matters on-line were improving.[138] Interestingly enough, none of the consumer organisations consulted during the first of those surveys reached the same rose-tinted conclusion as either the FTC or the commercial interest groups.[139] The data in the report seem to demonstrate little other than an increase in the number of sites posting privacy policies, which without credible enforcement and oversight, remain, as noted above, of little real consequence to business, or to the rights of the individual. More alarmingly, given the weight apparently ascribed to the reports by the FTC, the GIPPS report suggested that less than 10 per cent of Web sites surveyed had a privacy policy which met the very basic privacy policy suggested by the FTC in its 1995 white paper 'Privacy and the NII'.[140] In this respect, it is regrettable that the FTC appears to have allowed itself to be swayed by what was little more than effective public relations material, at the expense of any meaningful action.

None of this, however, addresses the issue of the EU Data Protection Directive, except to continue to demonstrate that, at present, the USA does not have a data privacy regime that would meet the requirements of the EU for the transfer of data to non-EEA countries.[141] However, whilst the negotiations with US trade officials have continued, the EU has not made any determination under Articles 25–26 of the Directive concerning data transfers to non-EEA countries, with regard to the USA. This may be due to a desire to avoid unnecessary trade disruption, but may also be related to the fact that while the General Agreement on Trade in Services recognises the protection of personal data as a legitimate reason for restricting the free movement of services,[142] the fact that several of

---

[138] *The Georgetown Internet Privacy Policy Survey* (GIPPS) and a report commissioned by the Online Privacy Alliance (OPA) on the Top 100 Web sites, <http://www.msb.edu/faculty/culnanm/gippshome.html>.

[139] The Center for Democracy and Technology, the National Consumers League, the Consumer Federation of America & Consumer Action and the Privacy Rights Clearinghouse.

[140] Privacy and the NII: Safeguarding Telecommunications-Related Personal Information, <http://www.ntia.doc.gov/ntiahome/privwhitepaper.html>.

[141] Data Protection Working Party, Working Document: Judging industry self-regulation: when does it make a meaningful contribution to the level of data protection in a third country? 14 Jan. 1998, DG XV D/5057/97, <http://www.europa.eu.int/comm/internal_market/en/media/dataprot/wpdocs/wp7en.htm>; Data Protection Working Party, Working Document: Transfers of personal data to third countries: Applying Articles 25 and 26 of the EU data protection directive, 24 July 1998, DG XV D/5025/98, <http://www.europa.eu.int/comm/internal_market/en/media/dataprot/wpdocs/wp12en.htm>.

[142] GATS, Article XIV—General Exceptions

'Subject to the requirement that such measures are not applied in a manner which countries where like conditions prevail, or a disguised restriction on trade in services, nothing in this Agreement shall be construed to prevent the adoption or enforcement by any Member of measures:

. . .

(c) necessary to secure compliance with laws or regulations which are not inconsistent with the provisions of this Agreement including those relating to:

. . .

(ii) the protection of the privacy of individuals in relation to the processing and dissemination of personal data and the protection of confidentiality of individual records and accounts;

the Member States have thus far failed to implement the Directive would tend to weaken the EU's case should the USA take the matter to the World Trade Organisation.[143]

Two possibilities have been put forward as potentially meeting the EU's requirements. The first, and least likely, is that a technical solution may be possible, at least for Internet transactions. The World Wide Web Consortium (W3C)[144] has produced a privacy specification via the Platform for Privacy Preference Project (P3P),[145] designed to allow Web sites to broadcast their privacy practices and allow users to decide whether those practices are acceptable to them. A P3P enabled Web browser would allow users to determine their own information release settings, to interrogate Web sites about their privacy practices, and to automate most privacy related decisions, thus delimiting their relationship to specific sites. Sites with practices that meet a user's preset preference could be accessed 'seamlessly', sites outside those parameters could be referred to the user for a determination of suitability. However, while developments like P3P may make an automated system of personal data privacy on the Internet possible, at present neither the technology, nor its methodology, meets the standards required by the EU, nor is the proposed technology able to prevent secondary abuses of data collected.[146]

The second solution is that put forward by the US Department of Commerce, which involves the creation of a 'Safe Harbor' for US companies. The concept behind the 'Safe Harbor' is that a set of data privacy principles would be agreed between the USA and the EU, and self-certified compliance with these principles would entitle a company to shelter within the 'Safe Harbor'. A company entitled to 'Safe Harbor' status would automatically be granted a presumption of adequate compliance with the Directive, and thus data transfers from within the European Union to it would be allowed. The theory is relatively simple, unfortunately the devil, as always, is in the details. The US Department of Commerce wanted principles that would provide 'adequate' privacy protection for European citizens, but which would also 'reflect U.S. views on privacy, allow for relevant U.S. legislation, regulation, and other public interest requirements, and provide a predictable and cost effective framework for the private sector'.[147] As may be gathered from the foregoing analysis, this was never going to be an easy task.

---

[143] See the World Trade Organisation at <http://www.wto.org/>.

[144] See <http://www.w3.org/>.

[145] For a more comprehensive examination of the project, see the following publications: Reagle, *P3P and Privacy on the Web FAQ*, Version: 2.0.1 <http://www.w3.org/P3P/P3FAQ.html>; Reagle and Cranor, *The Platform for Privacy Preferences* P3P Note Draft, (31 July 1998) <http://www.w3.org/TR/1998/NOTE-P3P-CACM-19980731/>.

[146] See Data Protection Working Party, Opinion 1/98, *Platform for Privacy Preferences (P3P) and the Open Profiling Standard (OPS)* (16 June 1998), <http://europa.eu.int/comm/internal_market/en/media/dataprot/wpdocs/wp11en.htm>.

[147] Letter from Ambassador Aaron and Safe Harbor Principles as of Nov. 1998, <http://www.ita.doc.gov/ecom/aaron114.html>.

The initial 'Safe Harbor Principles'

These are:

an organization qualifies for the safe harbor if it is subject to a statutory, regulatory, administrative, or other body of law that effectively protects personal information privacy. An organization may also qualify for the safe harbor through membership in private sector developed privacy programs that adhere to these principles. In addition, adherence to these principles is subject to national security, risk management, information security, public interest, regulatory compliance and supervision, and law enforcement requirements as well as to other legal and regulatory proprietary or manually processed information.

1. NOTICE: An organization must inform individuals about what types of personal information it collects about them, how it collects that information, the purposes for which it collects such information, the types of organizations to which it discloses the information, and the choices and means the organization offers individuals for limiting its use and disclosure. This notice must be provided in clear and conspicuous language that is readily understood and made available when individuals are first asked to provide personal information to the organization.

2. CHOICE: An organization must give individuals the opportunity to choose (opt out choice) whether and how personal information they provide is used (where such use is unrelated to the use(s) for which they originally disclosed it). They must be provided with clear and conspicuous, readily available, and affordable mechanisms to exercise this option. For certain kinds of sensitive information, such as medical information, they must be given affirmative or explicit (opt in) choice.

3. ONWARD TRANSFER: Individuals must be given the opportunity to choose whether and the manner in which a third party uses the personal information they provide (when such use is unrelated to the use(s) for which the individual originally disclosed it). When transferring personal information to third parties, an organization must require that third parties provide at least the same level of privacy protection as originally chosen by the individual. For certain kinds of sensitive information, such as medical information, individuals must be given opt in choice.

4. SECURITY: Organizations creating, maintaining, using or disseminating records of personal information must take reasonable measures to assure its reliability for its intended use and must take reasonable precautions to protect it from loss, misuse, unauthorized access or disclosure, alteration, or destruction.

5. DATA INTEGRITY: An organization must keep personal data relevant for the purposes for which it has been gathered only, consistent with the principles of notice and choice. To the extent necessary for those purposes, the data should be accurate, complete, and current.

6. ACCESS: Individuals must have reasonable access to information about them derived from non public records that an organization holds and be able to correct or amend that information where it is inaccurate. Reasonableness of access depends on the nature and sensitivity of the information collected and its intended uses. For instance, access must be provided to an individual where the information in question

is sensitive or used for substantive decision-making purposes that affect that individual.

7. ENFORCEMENT: Effective privacy protection must include mechanisms for assuring compliance with the principles, recourse for individuals, and consequences for the organization when the principles are not followed. At a minimum, such mechanisms must include (a) readily available and affordable independent recourse mechanisms by which individuals' complaints and disputes can be resolved; (b) systems for verifying that the attestations and assertions businesses make about their privacy practices are true and privacy practices have been implemented as presented; and (c) obligations to remedy problems arising out of and consequences for organizations announcing adoption of these principles and failing to comply with the principles. Sanctions must be sufficient to ensure compliance by organizations and must provide individuals the means for enforcement.

Certainly the first draft of the 'Safe Harbor Principles' appeared to satisfy almost no-one, being criticised by the European Commission's Data Protection Working Party,[148] US business,[149] and US legal commentators.[150] The Working Party felt that it was unclear which companies would be covered by the 'safe harbor' principles, and that the lack of independent compliance monitoring combined with company self-certification was a serious weakness. Additionally, they wanted an independent body to deal with and adjudicate upon complaints from individuals whose data had been transferred from the EU. They had particular problems with the fact that the 'safe harbor' principles differed from the OECD Privacy Guidelines in that they:

- Limited an individual's right of access to that which is 'reasonable', rather than stating it must be exercised 'in a reasonable manner';
- Allowed data collected for one purpose to be used for another provided individuals had the possibility of opting out;
- Excluded proprietary data and any manually processed data from their scope;
- Were drafted so the 'choice' principle provided no protection to data collected from third parties;
- Were drafted so the 'access' principle excluded public record-derived information;
- Contained a number of vague and open-ended exceptions from adherence to the principles including 'risk management' and 'information security'.

---

[148] Data Protection Working Party, Opinion 1/99 concerning the level of data protection in the United States and the ongoing discussions between the European Commission and the United States Government, 26 Jan. 1999, DG XV 5092/98, <http://www.europa.eu.int/comm/internal_market/en/media/dataprot/wpdocs/wp15en.htm>.

[149] See the responses of the Direct Marketing Association <http://www.ita.doc.gov/ecom/com2abc.htm#dma>; and the Online Privacy Alliance <http://www.ita.doc.gov/ecom/com2abc.htm#opa> to Ambassador David Aaron's 4 Nov. 1998 letter requesting comments on the 'draft international safe harbor principles'.

[150] See <http://www.ita.doc.gov/ecom/comabc.htm#cate>.

US business interests were concerned that the 'safe harbor' approach might inadvertently change both international and domestic privacy policies, and that the Principles might impose burdens on US business greater than those imposed on European business. The issue of certainty was raised in the context of US businesses needing to know with certainty that companies adhering to approved sectoral codes of privacy protection would be granted expeditiously authorisation to transfer data without an additional approval process. Both the DMA and OPA wanted a specific provision creating a safe harbor for companies that complied with industry-based codes claiming that the guidelines developed by the DMA and the Online Privacy Alliance would fit into the category of codes of conduct that adequately protect privacy. As far as sanctions for breach of the principles were concerned, the DMA remained vehemently opposed to monetary penalties or private rights of action, suggesting instead that a loss of privileges and benefits associated with an endorsement by a private sector privacy programme, including censure, suspension, or expulsion, would be sufficient to ensure compliance. Given the past history of both the direct marketing and the online industries in achieving effective self-regulation, this suggestion has to be admired for its *chutzpah*.[151]

The US Department of Commerce also received a heavyweight academic response from five influential US data privacy researchers and authors.[152] They criticised the principles as:

- being too imprecise, with an attempt to mix potentially incompatible methods of determining adequacy such as sectoral regulation, collective action, industry self-regulatory schemes and other independent mechanisms
- unable to cater adequately for companies that might use personal data in a number of different activities, such as online transactions, personnel records etc.
- exempting proprietary information from the principles without defining it.
- failing to provide adequate transparency, in terms of disclosure of the identity of an organisation collecting personal information, ambiguity about the ability of individuals to access their personal data, the complete exclusion of public record information from the access right, and the public disclosure of companies promising to adhere to the safe harbour.
- relying too heavily on consent as an absolute basis for any treatment of personal information.

---

[151] 'The [direct marketing] industry ardently promotes self-regulation, through its trade group, the Direct Marketing Association. The DMA has issued 'Guidelines for Personal Information Protection' and has established a 'Privacy Task Force'. . . . However, polls suggest that less than 25 per cent of the industry is willing to initiate self-regulatory practices, and a chairman of the Privacy Task Force even recognized that the founding members ignore them. Members of the Privacy Task Force even ignore the DMA guidelines': Schwartz and Reidenberg, *supra* n.46 at 309. Schwartz and Reidenberg's analysis of the US direct marketing industry (307–48) provides ample evidence of the lack of veracity in the DMA's claims for its self regulatory mechanisms.

[152] Cate, Reidenberg, Schwartz, Swire and Litan. Part of the document collection at <http://www.ita.doc.gov/td/ecom/comabc.htm>.

- failing to provide a clear framework for enforcement and thus offering unclear protection for individuals and uncertainty for US business.
- being inconsistent with the content of the EU Working Party's opinions and thus unlikely to be accepted by the EU.

The Principles were redrafted by the Department of Commerce in the light of the feedback received, and were resubmitted in April 1999.[153] However, the resubmitted Principles remained controversial, with the EU still unhappy about various aspects, including the fact that the Principles effectively exempted manual data from their scope, did not require explicit notice and choice when personal data were transferred to a third party not adhering to the safe harbor requirements, and still placed too many conditions on individuals' access to their personal information.[154] In June 1999, the European Commission and the US Department of Commerce published a short joint report detailing the progress of the negotiations, and stating that only a limited number of points were still at issue. Those issues appeared largely to centre on the thorny issues of enforcement and implementation.[155]

A further draft of the Principles appeared on 15 November 1999 requesting comments by 3 December 1999.[156] This draft appeared initially designed to satisfy some of the EU's outstanding difficulties,[157] although there was still clearly disagreement about the extent to which an individual should be given the choice to opt out of having their data transferred to parties outside the scope of the safe harbor, the Directive, or a written agreement. The European Commission's Data Protection Working Party, however, was unimpressed, not least by the fact that, as previously pointed out by Cate *et al.*,[158] the redrafted Principles appeared simply to ignore the majority of the comments made in the Working Party's previous reports.[159] Their position was thus that the proposed 'Safe

[153] See <http://www.ita.doc.gov/ecom/shprin.html>.

[154] Opinion 2/99 on the Adequacy of the 'International Safe Harbor Principles' issued by the US Department of Commerce on 19 Apr. 1999, 3 May 1999, DG XV 5047/99, <http://www.europa.eu. int/comm/internal_market/en/media/dataprot/wpdocs/wp19en.htm>. Opinion 4/99 on the Frequently Asked Questions to be issued by the US Department of Commerce in relation to the proposed 'Safe Harbor Principles' on the Adequacy of the 'International Safe Harbor Principles', 7 June 1999, DGXV 5066/99 <http://www.europa.eu.int/comm/internal_market/en/media/dataprot/wpdocs/wp21en.htm>.

[155] Joint Report on Data Protection Dialogue to the EU/US Summit, 21 June 1999, <http://www.ita.doc.gov/ecom/jointreport2617.htm>.

[156] <http://www.ita.doc.gov/ecom/Principles1199.htm>.

[157] As outlined in the working document on the current state of play of the ongoing discussions between the European Commission and the United States Government concerning the 'International Safe Harbor Principles' 7 July 1999, DG XV 5075/99, <http://www.europa.eu.int/ comm/internal_market/en/media/dataprot/wpdocs/wp23en.htm>.

[158] See *supra* n. 152.

[159] Opinion 7/99 on the Level of Data Protection provided by the 'Safe Harbor' Principles as published together with the Frequently Asked Questions (FAQs) and other related documents on 15 and 16 Nov. 1999 by the US Department of Commerce, DG XV 5146/99, 3 Dec. 1999. 'The Working Party notes that some progress has been made but deplores that most of the comments made in its previous position papers do not seem to be addressed in the latest version of the US documents. The Working Party therefore confirms its general concerns'. <http://www.europa.eu.int/comm/ internal_market/en/media/dataprot/wpdocs/wp27en.htm>.

Harbor' arrangements as reflected in the 15–16 November documentation remained inadequate and that the US Government should take steps:

- to clarify the scope of the 'Safe Harbor' and in particular to remove any possible misunderstanding that US organisations can choose to rely on the 'Safe Harbor' principles in circumstances when the Directive itself applies;
- to provide more reliable arrangements allowing 'Safe Harbor' participants to be identified with certainty and avoiding the risk that 'Safe Harbor' benefits will continue to be accorded after 'Safe Harbor' status has, for one reason or another, been lost;
- to make it absolutely clear that enforcement by an appropriately empowered public body is in place for all participants in the 'Safe Harbor';
- to make it the rule that private sector dispute resolution bodies must refer unresolved complaints to such a public body;
- to make the allowed exceptions and exemptions less sweeping and less open-ended, so that exceptions are precisely that—that is, they apply only where and to the extent necessary, and are not general invitations to override the principles; this is particularly important as regards the right of access;
- to strengthen the Choice principle, which is the lynchpin of the US approach.[160]

They further refused to accept the US suggestion that compliance with the Fair Credit Reporting Act 1970[161] or the Financial Modernization Act 1999[162] would be considered to ensure an adequate level of protection, as regards an organisations' activities falling within the scope of those Acts stating that insufficient time had been allowed for analysis of those Acts by the Working Group. As it appears that even the briefest analysis of the FCRA would demonstrate significant flaws and loopholes relating to individual data privacy,[163] it is unlikely that the Working Group will accept this statement as satisfactory in the future, unless it is prepared to allow a significant undermining of the EU data privacy principles.

On the consumer front, the recently formed TransAtlantic Consumer Dialogue (TACD), representing consumer organisations from the United States, Canada and Europe[164] were of the opinion that the November version of the

---

[160] *Ibid.*

[161] 15 USC § 1681 ff.

[162] Otherwise referred to as the Gramm-Leach-Bliley Act, the Financial Modernisation Act 1990 (Pub. L.106–102) shares several of the FCRA's privacy loopholes, and as with the recent amendments to the FCRA, its more effective privacy measures, such as the establishment of a consumer grievance process to deal with privacy violations, were quietly lost during the legislative process. Senator Gramm was heavily involved in the passage of both the FCRA amendments and the FMA. His 1993–8 campaign contributions data (notably the sectoral data) at the Center for Responsive Politics website thus makes interesting reading, <http://www.opensecrets.org/politicians/index/N00005709.htm>. See also campaign contributions data for Senator Leach, <http://www.opensecrets.org/politicians/index/N00004280.htm>, and Senator Bliley, <http://www.opensecrets.org/politicians/index/N00002126.htm>.

[163] See *supra* n.125.

[164] Including the European Consumer Association (BEUC), Consumer Federation of America, Center for Media Education, Consumer Project on Technology, Electronic Privacy Information Center, and the National Consumers League.

Guidelines remained unsatisfactory properly to protect consumers from improper use of their personal data and should simply be rejected.[165]

The US business response also remained, at best, resistant to even the limited regime proposed by the Guidelines. For example, in a letter dated 3 December 1999, the Associated Credit Bureaus were concerned to emphasise that '[i]t remains essential that the European Union agree to acknowledge as adequate the privacy protections found in and fairness provided by the FCRA (Fair Credit Reporting Act)'.[166] The DMA too, continued to lobby for safe harbor principles that 'do not include language that would require explicit notice and choice when personal data is transferred to a third party that does not adhere to the safe harbor requirements'.[167] Both these positions and the continuing resistance to any meaningful form of enforcement appear inimical to a meaningful data privacy regime.

It thus appeared that, despite frequently expressed optimism about a pending agreement between the EU and USA on the part of the negotiators,[168] a wide conceptual gulf remained between the position of the EU Commission and its Working Party, and that maintained by the key US commercial players, with significant attempts to water down the requirements for access to the 'safe harbor' still underway. This meant that the announcement, in early March 2000, that European and US negotiators had in fact finalised a data privacy agreement, based on the safe harbor principles,[169] appeared to provide a somewhat abrupt, not to say unexpected, resolution to the situation.[170] There had been relatively little sign, prior to that point, that certain issues, especially the US provision for meaningful enforcement of the safe harbor principles, a key requirement of the EU's negotiating position, were remotely close to resolution.

---

[165] See the (apparently truncated) document at <http://www.ita.doc.gov/td/ecom/TACD1299. htm>.

[166] Response of the Associated Credit Bureaus to the Draft International Safe Harbor Principles, 15 Nov. 1999, <http://www.ita.doc.gov/td/ecom/assoccredit1299.htm>, a refrain echoed individually by the credit reference agency Experian <http://www.ita.doc.gov/td/ecom/experian 1299.htm>, itself no stranger to unfortunate accidents with credit references: see James, 'Internet Service Goes Haywire With Credit Reports', *Chicago Tribune,* 19 Aug. 1997, cited in Swire & Litan, *supra* n.75.

[167] Response of the Direct Marketing Association to the Draft International Safe Harbor Principles, 15 Nov. 1999, <http://www.ita.doc.gov/td/ecom/dma1299.htm>.

[168] See draft letters between Ambassador David Aaron and John Mogg, representing the Commission, posted on the ITA website on 15 Nov. 1999, <http://www.ita.doc.gov/td/ecom/ USletter1199.html>, <http://www.ita.doc.gov/td/ecom/EULetter1199.html>.

[169] Cover letter from Ambassador David L. Aaron to U.S. organisations requesting comments on the newly-posted draft documents, 17 Mar. 2000, <http://www.ita.doc.gov/td/ecom/aaron317let ter.htm>; EU press release, Data protection: draft package agreed for protection of data transferred from EU to US, 15 Mar. 2000, <http://europa.eu.int/comm/internal_market/en/media/data prot/news/harbor3.htm>; de Bony, 'EU and US reach data privacy accord', IDG News Service\ Brussels Bureau, 14 Mar. 2000, <http://www.idg.net/go.cgi?id=238013>.

[170] Although the fact that Ambassador David L. Aaron, the chief US negotiator, was to leave his post on 31 Mar. 2000 to return to the private sector, may have played some part in accelerating the process. <http://www.ita.doc.gov/media/Aaronleaves.htm>.

The final 'Safe Harbor Principles'

[Preambulatory material omitted]

. . .

NOTICE: An organization must inform individuals about the purposes for which it collects and uses information about them, how to contact the organization with any inquiries or complaints, the types of third parties to which it discloses the information, and the choices and means the organization offers individuals for limiting its use and disclosure. This notice must be provided in clear and conspicuous language when individuals are first asked to provide personal information to the organization or as soon thereafter as is practicable, but in any event before the organization uses or discloses such information for a purpose other than that for which it was originally collected or processed by the transferring organization or discloses it for the first time to a third party(1).

CHOICE: An organization must offer individuals the opportunity to choose (opt out) whether and how their personal information is:

(a) to be disclosed to third parties, where disclosure is for a purpose other than the purpose for which it was originally collected or subsequently authorized by the individual, or

(b) to be used where such use is for a purpose that is incompatible with the purpose(s) for which it was originally collected, or subsequently authorized by the individual. Individuals must be provided with clear and conspicuous, readily available, and affordable mechanisms to exercise choice.

For sensitive information, (i.e. personal information specifying medical or health conditions, racial or ethnic origin, political opinions, religious or philosophical beliefs, trade union membership or information specifying the sex life of the individual) they must be given affirmative or explicit (opt in) choice if the information is to be disclosed to a third party or used for a purpose other than those for which it was originally collected or subsequently authorized by the individual through the exercise of opt in choice. In any case, an organization should treat as sensitive any information received from a third party where the third party identifies it as sensitive.

ONWARD TRANSFER: An organization may only disclose personal information to third parties consistent with the principles of notice and choice. Where an organization has not provided choice and the organization wishes to transfer the data to a third party, it may do so if it first either ascertains that the third party subscribes to the principles or is subject to the Directive or another adequacy finding or enters into a written agreement with such third party requiring that the third party provide at least the same level of privacy protection as is required by the relevant principles. If the organization complies with these requirements, it shall not be held responsible (unless the organization agrees otherwise) when a third party to which it transfers such information processes it in a way contrary to any restrictions or representations, unless the organization knew or should have known the third party would process it in such a contrary way and the organization has not taken reasonable steps to prevent or stop such processing.

SECURITY: Organizations creating, maintaining, using or disseminating personal information must take reasonable precautions to protect it from loss, misuse and unauthorized access, disclosure, alteration and destruction.

DATA INTEGRITY: Consistent with the principles, personal information must be relevant for the purposes for which it is to be used. An organization may not process personal information in a way that is incompatible with the purposes for which it has been collected or subsequently authorized by the individual. To the extent necessary for those purposes, an organization should take reasonable steps to ensure that data is reliable for its intended use, accurate, complete, and current.

ACCESS: Individuals must have access to personal information about them that an organization holds and be able to correct, amend, or delete that information where it is inaccurate, except where the burden or expense of providing access would be disproportionate to the risks to the individual's privacy in the case in question, or where the rights of persons other than the individual would be violated.

ENFORCEMENT: Effective privacy protection must include mechanisms for assuring compliance with the principles, recourse for individuals to whom the data relate affected by non—compliance with the principles, and consequences for the organization when the principles are not followed. At a minimum, such mechanisms must include (a) readily available and affordable independent recourse mechanisms by which each individual's complaints and disputes are investigated and resolved by reference to the principles and damages awarded where the applicable law or private sector initiatives so provide; (b) follow up procedures for verifying that the attestations and assertions businesses make about their privacy practices are true and that privacy practices have been implemented as presented; and (c) obligations to remedy problems arising out of failure to comply with the principles by organizations announcing their adherence to them and consequences for such organizations. Sanctions must be sufficiently rigorous to ensure compliance by organizations.

Yet, on closer analysis, the agreement hailed in the negotiators' press releases looks a much less impressive solution than initially suggested, not least because it does not include the financial services sector. The agreement also sets no deadline for compliance with the safe harbor principles, stating instead that US and EU officials will meet in mid-2001 to review the situation. The EU press release stated that a key point that EU negotiators had 'clarified successfully is the way in which the principles of data protection will be enforced in the US, and in particular the accuracy and reliability of the list of companies adhering to the "Safe Harbor" and the possible sanctions for non-compliance'. However, a detailed examination of how this might in practice be achieved has not been immediately forthcoming.

The 'final' draft of the Safe Harbor Principles[171] appears to remain flawed from a European perspective, not least with regard to the linked issues of industry self-regulation and enforcement. For example, the Principles state that:

---

[171] Draft Safe Harbor Principles, 17 Mar. 2000, <http://www.ita.doc.gov/td/ecom/Redlined Principles31600.htm>.

Organizations that decide to adhere to the principles must comply with the principles in order to obtain and retain the benefits of the safe harbor and publicly declare that they do so. . . . if an organization joins a self-regulatory privacy program that adheres to the principles, it qualifies for the safe harbor. Organizations may also qualify by developing their own self-regulatory privacy policies provided that they conform with the principles. Where in complying with the principles, an organization relies in whole or in part on self regulation, its failure to comply with such self regulation must also be actionable under Section 5 of the Federal Trade Commission Act prohibiting unfair and deceptive acts or another law or regulation prohibiting such acts.

This statement should be considered in the light of the fact that some of the self-regulatory bodies, such as the DMA and OPA, already claim to be broadly in conformity with the Principles, when they clearly are not. With regard to enforcement, the enforcement principle provides a list of required enforcement mechanisms, but no concrete suggestions as to how they are to be achieved in practice. Additionally, enforcement of self-regulation is being given to the FTA, not under specific privacy legislation, but under the 'consumer protection' leg of the Federal Trade Commission Act 1914. Roscoe B. Starek, III, a Commissioner of the Federal Trade Commission has described the FTC's role under Section 5 FTCA thus:

> In determining whether to prosecute a case under . . . Section 5, the Commission generally must satisfy itself that two legal thresholds have been met. First, the Commission must have 'reason to believe' that the law has been or is being violated. And second, it must find that an enforcement action against the violation would be in the public interest. . . . The 'public interest' standard demands more explanation. The agency has no duty to prosecute a case simply because precedent exists that would support a finding of illegality. Nor is the agency required to prosecute a case for which plausible arguments of illegality can be made, unless prosecution would be in the public interest.[172]

This interpretation does not appear, on its face, to provide the level of individual data privacy for EU citizens that the Directive requires, as it appears to leave that protection to the administrative discretion of an agency that has already shown itself, in the online sphere at least, to be often incapable of distinguishing between meaningful privacy self-regulation and industry-funded public relations exercises.[173] To quote Starek further:

> For a government agency to carry out a coherent and conscientious program of law enforcement, it must exercise its prosecutorial powers with care and with the

---

[172] Starek, 'Prosecutorial Discretion: A View From the Federal Trade Commission' *Regulation: The Cato Institute of Business and Government.* <http://www.cato.org/pubs/regulation/reg20n4d.html>.

[173] One might also consider the fact that FTC enforcement decisions are largely beyond judicial scrutiny. See *Heckler* v. *Chaney*, 470 US 821 (1985) (agency failure to initiate enforcement proceedings presumptively unreviewable) and *Lieberman* v. *FTC*, 771 F 2d 32 (2d Cir. 1985) at 37 (agency action whether to disclose information may be unreviewable).

paramount objective—furtherance of the public interest—uppermost in its institutional mind. . . . At the Federal Trade Commission, the role of prosecutorial discretion means that many law violations will be investigated and challenged but some—although infractions of the law in a technical sense—should not be targeted.

Bearing in mind the FTC's last approving report with regard to US on-line privacy developments,[174] one might reasonably wonder about the extent to which 'technical infractions' of privacy in US commerce might be tolerated or permitted, and indeed the extent to which the FTC might take the interests of a European citizen, as opposed to a US citizen or commercial interest, into account when determining what the 'public interest' might be. The FTC has 'indicated its readiness to investigate complaints irrespective of the nationality or country of residence of the complainant'[175] but 'investigation' is hardly synonymous with 'enforcement'.[176]

Thus, while the US negotiators might be said to have given way to a degree on some key sticking points, for example in the areas of notice and choice, and over the extent of the allowed exceptions and exemptions, it is arguable that given the proposed enforcement mechanisms for the Principles, conceding those points will, in essence, have little real bearing on the usefulness of the safe harbor as a method of protecting EU citizens' personal data in the USA. Thus, leaving the EU's semantic gains aside, and despite the worries of US commercial concerns, the US negotiators have hardly 'given away the farm' with this agreement. Acceptance of the agreement will still, however, depend heavily upon the acquiescence of the Beltway lobbyists, notably the Direct Marketing Association, for as with so many US data privacy related measures in the past, their supporters in Congress will be in a prime position to kill the agreement.

The EU negotiators, on the other hand, may face a rather more difficult task in selling the proposed agreement to the EU institutions and Member States by the late June or July 2000 date suggested for its formalisation. While the European Commission has granted its initial approval to the agreement,[177] the Commission will have to obtain an opinion on it from the Member States' data protection commissioners,[178] submit it to the scrutiny of the European Parliament which will check that the Commission is using its powers under the directive correctly, and obtain approval from a qualified majority of Member

---

[174] *Self Regulation and Privacy On-line: A Report to Congress, supra* n. 137.

[175] Draft Commission Decision on the adequacy of the US Safe Harbor Principles, <http://europa.eu.int/comm/internal_market/en/media/dataprot/news/harbor5.pdf>.

[176] Although, to be fair, it seems that the FTC is engaging in a low-key Section 5 based investigation of on-line privacy practices amongst some of the higher profile US e-commerce players, including Double-click, Amazon and Yahoo. See further: Mercury News Staff and Wire Reports, 'FTC probe targets Amazon, Yahoo', 30 Mar. 2000; Richtel, 'Yahoo Says It Is Discussing Internet Privacy With the F.T.C.', *New York Times on the Web*, 31 Mar. 2000, <http://www.nytimes.com/library/tech/00/03/biztech/articles/31yahoo.html>.

[177] Data protection: Commission endorses 'safe harbor' arrangement with USA <http://europa.eu.int/comm/internal_market/en/media/dataprot/news/harbor4.htm>.

[178] Via the EU Dir.'s Art.29. Working Party.

States.[179] It is likely that the Article 29 Working Party's response will be the key to acceptance of the agreement in the EU. The European Parliament has, for example, previously expressed a desire for the Working Party to present a final report to it before it makes any final decision. It is no secret that the Working Party has been largely unimpressed by the previous drafts of the 'safe harbor' agreement,[180] and it can be safely assumed that they will pull no punches in their criticism of the final agreement, should they find it deficient in any regard.[181]

Other Developments

In the interim, at least one other international approach has surfaced. In March 1999, the Global Business Dialogue for Electronic Commerce (GBD), an international consortium of companies including America Online, Barclays, Deutsche Bank, Deutsche Telekom, DaimlerChrysler, Disney, EDS, Fujitsu, Microsoft, NEC and Toshiba with the stated aim of strengthening international co-ordination of e-commerce rules and laws, released a First Draft Statement on Personal Data Protection.[182] This endorsed a privacy seal approach that combines principles drawn from the OECD 'Guidelines for the Protection of Privacy and Transborder Data Flows of Personal Data' with a compliance programme. It argued that protection of personal data would be most effectively achieved through private-sector leadership, and that establishment of effective self-regulation enforcement programmes was key to this objective. It also raised issues to be discussed at a later date by GBD members. Of the companies named, AOL, Disney and Microsoft have played a large part in the push for self-regulation in the USA, supporting TRUSTe, OPA and BBBonline. It appears that, as some form of agreement begins to emerge from the EU/US negotiations, the multinational companies may be attempting to renegotiate the issue on their terms on the international stage. Certainly the list of issues tabled for future discussion seems to suggest that those companies disagree with a number of the decisions already taken both in the USA and EU.[183] It is perhaps a matter for slight

---

[179] Via the EU Dir.'s Art. 31 Committee (composed of representatives from each of the Member States) which must approve any text. It is not at all clear that the strong opposition from some of the Member States can be overcome in the Art. 31 Committee where voting is on a weighted basis.

[180] *Supra* at n.154.

[181] See the guarded warning in the Working Party's Opinion 3/2000 on the EU/US dialogue concerning the 'Safe harbor' arrangement (WP 31 (5019/00)) at <http://europa.eu.int/comm/internal_market/en/media/dataprot/wpdocs/wp31en.htm>.

[182] <http://www.toshiba.co.jp/gbde-prv/draft1d0.htm>.

[183] e.g., question 2: To what degree (contents and number of countries/regions) should harmonisation be attained for it to be substantially effective? Is the OECD an appropriate forum from such a perspective? If not, which organisation would be suitable?; question 3: Who will evaluate seal providers? Is it enough for the market to serve as judge? Is any surveillance or supervisory body required? Is any qualification to be a seal provider required?; and question 8: Is privacy for a child to be protected more rigidly in a special way? If so, how and to what degree? What is the minimum age for a child concerning privacy protection in EC? How is a collector of personal data able to confirm a declared age?

concern, given past US Internet privacy breach disclosures, that that the GBD contact point for the Working Group on Privacy in the Americas is a Microsoft representative.[184]

A DIFFERENT HYPOTHESIS: INDIVIDUAL RIGHTS VS. COMMERCIAL MIGHT

It is argued here that the barrier to the adoption of an effective transnational personal data privacy regime does not arise from the differences between the legal system of the EU and the legal system of the United States. It is not grounded in the mistrust of the American people for their government, the potential harm to e-commerce, or constitutional law. Where it is grounded is firmly in the steadfast opposition of the commercial sector to personal data privacy laws that would make their activities more accountable to ordinary citizens, whether of Europe or the United States, and which would impact on their ability to intrude ever more effectively and profitably into those citizens' right 'to be left alone'. They are aided ably in their opposition by the neo-libertarians, those individuals who would see the 'tyranny of government' replaced by the lighter touch of industry self-regulation, or the free-for-all of *laissez faire* market discipline.

Yet despite the unenthusiastic analysis of the US self-regulatory approach above, it would be unfair to suggest that all industry self-regulatory schemes are simply conspiracies to deter effective oversight. Self-regulation is not inherently a bad thing and, if it is carried out scrupulously, significant advantages can accrue both to society and to the self-regulated businesses.[185] However, it is clear that self-regulation in the data privacy sphere can have some very significant downsides, as amply demonstrated by both the direct-marketing and Internet industries in the USA:

- *voluntary standards are often set in an unaccountable and non-democratic manner by business alone or in combination with NGOs.*
  Thus 'inconvenient' standards such as rights of access to personal data, credible oversight and enforcement mechanisms, and legal redress for the individual can be omitted, or weakened by exceptions to the point where they are meaningless.
- *voluntary standards are unevenly adopted within and across industries and because they are by definition voluntary, self-regulation can mean no regulation.*

---

[184] GBDe 2000 Working Group on Privacy, <http://www.gbd.org/structure/working/privacy.html>.

[185] For instance the development of codes of business ethics in the areas of child labour and 'sweatshops'. See Bureau of International Labor Affairs, 'The Apparel Industry and Codes of Conduct: A Solution to the International Child Labor Problem?' at <http://www.dol.gov/dol/ilab/public/media/reports/iclp/apparel/main.htm>, and Compa and Hinchliffe-Darricarrere, 'Enforcing International Labor Rights Through Corporate Codes of Conduct' (1995) 33 *Columbia Journal of Transnational Law* 663–8.

If charter members of industry self-regulatory bodies feel free to ignore standards, it bodes ill for compliance by the rest of the industry. The standards are then simply misleading public relations material designed to soothe public concerns without actually addressing the problems.

- *voluntary standards can be used by industry to co-opt critics, minimise justifiable litigation, and avoid government regulation even when it is needed.* Highly hyped but legally unenforceable privacy policies backed by high profile lobby groups like the EFF are no substitute for rights of access to personal data, credible oversight and enforcement mechanisms, and legal redress for the individual.
- *the multiplicity of self-regulatory initiatives may be overwhelming, allowing companies to pick and choose the standards they like best, and self-regulatory certification systems can be confusing for consumers and buyers, so their usefulness may prove negligible.* Confusion is the enemy of transparency, and transparency about personal data processing activities on the part of data users is an essential part of meaningful data privacy rules.
- *'Self-regulation depends for its very life on the presence of governmental threats or very strong private pressures. Without such threats or pressures, it is likely to resolve itself into a minor part of a public relations program.'*[186]

In terms of government intervention, while the current trend is very much for 'smaller government' and for less governmental involvement in regulation, national governments should not be permitted to use this as an excuse to avoid their obligations to their citizens. If there is an imbalance between the desires of the citizens and the desires of commerce with regard to the use of personal data, the State has an obligation to intervene to establish a reasonable balance between the two, and to ensure that commercial might does not simply override individuals' rights. The difficulty in the data privacy sphere is that the likelihood of meaningful government action is being undermined by the insidious expansion of commercial influence into State processes, with well funded lobbyists dominating and manipulating the political agenda.

In the final analysis, the term 'data protection' is a misnomer, data protection or data privacy regimes do not seek to protect data themselves, they seek to protect the individual from unwanted or harmful uses of their personal data. As such data privacy regimes do not seek to cut off the flow of data, merely to see that they are collected and used in a responsible and accountable fashion. With regard to cyberspace, the activities of many Internet-related companies, the attitudes of their management, and the effectiveness of self-regulatory bodies that

---

[186] Randall, *Censorship of the Movies* (University of Wisconsin Press, Madison, Wisc., 1968) at 10, cited in Jacobs, 'Comparing Regulatory Models—Self-Regulation vs. Government Regulation: The Contrast Between the Regulation of Motion Pictures and Broadcasting May Have Implications for Internet Regulation' (1996) 1 *J Tech. L & Pol'y* 4, <http://journal.law.ufl.edu/~techlaw/1/jacobs.html>.

purport to supervise them demonstrate neither responsible personal data management, nor a belief in the accountability of their actions. Instead the current activities of bodies such as TRUSTe, BBBOnline and the Direct Marketing Association would seem to represent a cynical spin on an old joke 'the secret of a privacy policy is accountability. Once you can fake that, you've got it made.'

ADDENDUM

Since this chapter was written, some important developments have occurred. To the surprise of some, the EU Directive Article 31 Committee unanimously approved the "safe harbor" proposals, apparently on the grounds that a finding of adequacy with regard to the US could still be revoked at a later date if significant non-compliance with those self-regulatory rules was to occur. Then despite the fact that the European Parliament, in a Resolution based on the Article 29 Working Party reports, expressed the view that the "safe harbor" arrangements need to be improved before the Commission found it offered adequate protection,[187] the Commission decided, on 13 July 2000, to push ahead with a Decision determining that the "safe harbor" arrangements provided adequate protection for personal data transferred from the EU to the US.[188] The European Commissioner for Internal Market, Frits Bolkestein, noted that despite its negative view of the "safe harbor" agreement, the European Parliament's Resolution did not state that, in making that Decision, the Commission would be acting beyond the powers granted to it by Art. 25(6) of the Data Protection Directive in assessing the adequacy of protection afforded by non-EU countries to personal data from the EU. He stated that in the event of non-compliance by US organisations the EU would seek to repoen negotiations with the US on the adequacy of its measures.[189] Regardless of the possibility of future renegotiations, the Commission's decision appears to be a significant surrender of position by the EU, and is likely to signal to US opponents of data privacy regulation that they may yet be able to treat the EU's measures with the cavalier contempt with which they have thus far greeted US legislative measures and self-regulatory bodies.

Interestingly, the mood in the US has also changed slightly. In its most recent report, the Federal Trade Commission (FTC) has apparently decided that, after all, the efforts of the self-regulatory bodies have been less than wholly satisfactory. In *Privacy Online: Fair Information Practices in the Electronic Marketplace* (May 2000) the five Commissioners decided by 3-2 that self-regulation alone had not adequately protected consumer online privacy, and as a result, legislation was needed to supplement self-regulatory efforts and guarantee basic consumer protections.[190] Needless to say, this report has met with rather more industry opprobrium than its predecessors which recommended either limited or no federal action.

[187] Committee on Citizen's Freedoms and Rights, Justice and Home Affairs A5-0177/2000, Report on the Draft Commission Decision on the adequacy of the protection provided by the Safe Harbor Privacy Principles Committee on Citizens' Freedoms and Rights, Justice and Home Affairs, PE 285.929/DEF. Voted on and passed with minor amendments by the Parliament on 5 July 2000.

[188] Data protection: Commission adopts decisions recognising adequacy of regimes in US, Switzerland and Hungary. <http://europa.eu.int.comm.internal_market/en/media/dataprot/news/safeharbor.htm>

[189] Frits Bolkestein tells Parliament Committee he intends to formally approve "safe harbor" arrangement with US on data protection.

[190] FTC, *Privacy Online: Fair Information Practices in the Electronic Marketplace* <http://www.ftc.gov.reports/privacy2000/privacy2000.pdf>.

PART 2
Intellectual Property

6

The Domain Name System

WILLIAM BLACK*

MECHANICS OF THE DOMAIN NAME SYSTEM

In the press, Domain Names are often confused with electronic mail addresses or address references on the World Wide Web, which are known as Universal Resource Locators (URLs). A Domain Name is a key part of both of these. For example, in the e-mail address: John.Smith@nominet.org.uk, only nominet.org.uk is the Domain Name. In the URL: http://www.bbc.co.uk/sports.html, only bbc.co.uk is the Domain Name. The remaining pieces are determined by the specific Internet application being used.

As far as the computers are concerned, Internet services are actually identified by Internet Protocol addresses, which comprise four numbers in the range 0–255 separated by dots, for example, 123.45.67.89. E-mail and web pages can in fact be referenced by using Internet Protocol addresses alone. The Domain Name System (DNS) was introduced to associate easily remembered and convenient names with the numeric addresses, thereby making the system more user-friendly. As a whole, the DNS simply provides mapping between a given name and the corresponding Internet Protocol address (and vice versa).

Domain Names are registered in a hierarchical system with a limited number of *country code* and *generic Top Level Domains*. Examples of country code TLDs are:

.uk   United Kingdom
.fr   France
.jp   Japan
.sg   Singapore

Examples of generic TLDs are:

.com   commercial entities
.org   non-commercial organisations
.net   network operators

These Top Level Domains are then divided into Second Level Domains and so on. At each level of the tree, a computer called a *name server* is operated to

---

* Dr William Black, Managing Director, Nominet UK.

maintain a table of all the names registered under that level. The responsibility of the name server operator at each level is to maintain the table of names and to point all enquirers to the name server registered for that name.

Nominet UK operates the primary .uk name server containing the dozen or so Second Level Domains (SLDs) under .uk, for example:

.co.uk   UK commercial entities
.org.uk   UK non-commercial organisations
.net.uk   UK network operators
.sch.uk   UK schools

In turn, each of these SLDs requires a name server to maintain the table of Third Level Domains (3LDs) and so on.

A succession of enquiries and responses is performed by the computer's networking software behind the scenes when the user types an e-mail address or URL. There are a dozen *world root servers*, whose fixed Internet Protocol Addresses are built into most networking packages.

A user on the Internet making a call to www.bbc.co.uk, for example, first enquires of the World Root to establish the address of the *.uk* TLD server (see Figure 1). A subsequent query to the .uk server reveals the address of the .co.uk server. Next this returns the address of the bbc.co.uk server and so on. . . .

In this example the server is probably operated by the BBC's internal IT support department, although in most cases it will be operated by an Internet Service Provider.

NOMINET UK: THE UK TOP LEVEL DOMAIN MANAGER

In the early days of the Internet, and indeed for many years before that, name servers were managed and operated by volunteers. However, the exponential

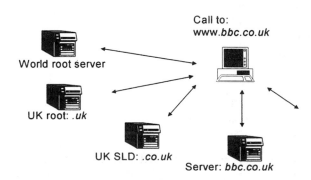

FIGURE 1. How a domain name is resolved on the internet

growth of the Internet over the last decade led to the requirement to establish professionally managed organisations to operate the TLDs and these organisations would be funded by registration fees. At the time of writing, Nominet UK has over 600,000 Domain Names registered in .co.uk (25,000 three years previously) and is registering in the region of 100,000 new Domain Names per month (2,000 three years previously) for illustration see the figures below.

Nominet was established as a not-for-profit company limited by guarantee, and subject only to a small fee its membership is open to all those with an interest in the policy and development of the .uk Top Level Domain. There are at the time of writing over 1,500 members who are mostly, but not exclusively, drawn from the Internet industry.

Since Nominet is a natural monopoly, it is very careful not to abuse its position. It operates only to recover its costs of operation from the fees levied, and takes care to promote competition external to itself where possible. For example, Nominet avoids attracting end-customers directly (direct registrations), since most customers really require a variety of value added services: their own name server, connectivity, web hosting or e-mail boxes. These services are best provided by the open competition of the members of Nominet, which act as agents for potential Registrants of Domain Names in a similar fashion to company formation agents in dealings with Companies House. Nominet also restricts its activities to the minimum required to give business efficacy to the registration process and operation of the DNS (see Figure 2).

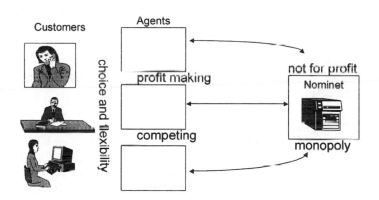

FIGURE 2. Nominet UK's competitive model for domain name registration

NOMINET'S ROLE

There are four core functions carried out by a Registry such as Nominet UK.

Maintaining the Integrity of the Database

Nominet takes legal responsibility for the integrity of the Register Database and the processes supporting it. It is responsible for maintaining the accuracy of the details that are contained in the database, but Nominet does not take legal responsibility for the intellectual property rights in the names used as Domain Names.

Nominet does not have a large 'warehouse' of Domain Names for sale; a fee is levied for making and maintaining the registration of Domain Names that have been chosen by registrants. Nominet works within the established English legal system and believes that any liability for infringing rights by registering a Domain Name rests solely with the registrant and does not include the registry itself.

The ruling in the *One In A Million* court case has provided authoritative guidance for the legal position of the registration of well-known Domain Names. In 1996 and 1997, a company called One in a Million Ltd (OIAM) and others, registered a number of Domain Names which included prestigious or well known names. These registrations included: britishtelecom.co.uk, ladbrokes.com, marksandspencers.co.uk, sainsburys.com and virgin.org. The registrations took place without the consent of the companies owning the goodwill in the well-known names (the companies).

At the High Court in November 1997 the companies were granted injunctions ordering OIAM to transfer the registrations to the companies. Substantial costs were also awarded. The judge in the case said: '[a]ny person who deliberately registers a Domain Name on account of its similarity to the name, brand name or trademark of an unconnected commercial organisation must expect to find himself on the receiving end of an injunction to restrain the threat of passing off, and the injunction will be in terms which will make the name commercially useless to the deale'.[1]

Ensuring Consistency and Fairness

Domain Name registration is not simply a technical operation on the Internet (a very small part of the registry's business and costs) but more importantly a rigorous management process. Businesses both large and small need to rely on their registrations being kept intact and not wantonly moved, as result of a bullying attempt by a challenger. Therefore, the registration process is carried out in accordance with clear rules—see http://www.nic.uk/ref/terms.html—and the subsequent transfer, suspension and cancellation of a Domain Name has strict operational procedures.

---

[1] For full details of the case see Waelde Ch. 7.

Nominet's second core function is therefore to ensure equitable processes for:

initial registration
transfer of a registration from one registrant to another
surrender of a registration
temporary suspension or full cancellation of a registration.

Once a Domain Name has been fully paid for and the details have been entered into the register database, Nominet issues a registration certificate for the Domain Name. Certificates are important documents that can be used as legal proof of the registrant of a Domain Name. Certificates contain all the registration details that are held on the national database, and these details must be checked thoroughly and the registry kept informed of any subsequent changes to the contact details throughout the registration period.

Cancelling or 'surrendering' a Domain Name requires the completion of a surrender form that is found on the reverse of the registration certificate. This must be sent to Nominet, along with a letter of authorisation on the headed paper of the registrant. Only on receipt of these documents is the cancellation of a Domain Name implemented.

In a similar way, if a registrant wishes to transfer a Domain Name to a third party, a transfer form must be submitted to Nominet. The existing registrant must also submit a letter of authorisation on headed paper, and the new registrant is also required to sign the form and/or prepare a similar confirmatory letter on its own headed paper. The two signatories (transferor and transferee) of the letters must be different people. In the case of a company name change, the Domain Name registration certificate, a confirmatory letter and a copy of the Certificate on Incorporation on Change of Name issued by Companies House must be included.

Making the Relevant Data Available Publicly

One of the most important functions of a registry is to provide an on-line look-up facility for people to find out whether a Domain Name has been registered and, if so, the details of whom it is registered to. The search facility managed by Nominet is called the *whois* service and covers *.uk* registered Domain Names only.

Anyone can access the complete list of .uk registered Domain Names in a matter of seconds by simply dialing-up http//www.nominet.org.uk/whois. html. This service is vital for potential registrants and businesses that sell .uk Domain Names. Nominet also provides the data in a compressed form to established name watching services: this is called the Public Register Subscription Service (PRSS).

Not all the information on a registrant can be made publicly available, as the Registry must operate under the provisions of Data Protection legislation.[2]

---

[2] For a discussion on Data Protection see Charlesworth Ch. 5.

Although detailed personal information stored in the register database is not normally made public, it is nevertheless important that no registrant can hide anonymously behind a Domain Name. This is similar to the requirement for company directors' names to be on public record.

Offering a Dispute Resolution Service Based on Mediation

Occasionally (less than 1 per cent of all registrations) there may be a clash between two people wanting to use the same Domain Name. In this instance, Nominet does not judge the legality of such claims, but instead offers a dispute resolution service that is based on mediation. The last core function of Nominet UK is therefore to manage, but not solve, disputes arising from Domain Name registrations.

Nominet tries to encourage the two parties in dispute to reach a mutually agreeable solution. If it unsuccessful in bringing about a resolved outcome, Nominet will take a decision under its rules—see http//www.nominet.org.uk/rules/rup2.html—to suspend or cancel the Domain Name. If dissatisfied with the decision, either party can refer the case and a member of a panel of legal experts will seek to make a further recommendation.

THE LEGAL SIGNIFICANCE OF REGISTRATION

It is helpful to consider the legal significance of a Domain Name registration. For trade marks we have the Trade Mark Act 1994. Similarly, for the creation and registration of companies, we have Companies Acts. However, there are no statutes specifically governing Domain Name registration, and there is no statutory power over or significance *per se* in a Domain Name registration. Therefore the legal significance of a registration has to be based in the contract between the registrant and registry. Nominet has standard terms and conditions for Domain Name registration that can be found at http://www.nominet.org.uk/terms.html.

This contract is complicated because the majority of registrants register Domain Names through an ISP, in which case the ISP acts as a registration 'agent' for the customer and not as an agent of Nominet. ISPs offer a range of services—including web site design, hosting and Domain Name registration—and their customers will enter into an additional contract with their ISP when buying these services. It is particularly important for the agents to be scrupulous in explaining the terms and conditions of their own contract to the customer. Registrants should be aware of what ongoing powers they give to their agents, for example, the power to retain control (lien) of the Domain Name registration until payment for other services has been fully rendered (see Figure 2).

As part of the contractual obligations with the registry, the registrant warrants that the registration and use of the Domain Name does not and will not infringe the rights of any third party. They also indemnify Nominet against any costs in challenges arising from the registration. Applications are accepted on a first-come first-served basis. When payment has been made, the registration certificate is issued so that the registrant confirms his or her acceptance of the terms and conditions in writing.

It has been stated above that Nominet, and other TLD registries, take no legal responsibility for any intellectual property rights associated with the Domain Name or its use, and no statute *per se* endows such rights in a registration. However, it appears that *the market* is treating registrations as having intellectual property rights. In the UK we have had a few cases where Domain Names were registered for companies which were subsequently dissolved from the Companies House register. The Companies Act 1985 defines assets of such companies to be *bona vacantia* and they are deemed to be Crown property. In most cases, the Treasury Solicitor has thus far agreed to disclaim these registrations, allowing their transfer to new registrants.

DISPUTE RESOLUTION SERVICE

As with trade mark infringements and cases of passing off in traditional business, Domain Names, regrettably, are also abused by a minority of registrants. Disputes can also arise because businesses have similar names or trade marks. Some 0.1 per cent of Domain Names registered give rise to a dispute: a small number absolutely, but of great importance to a party whose rights may have been infringed. These disputes take up a lot of Nominet staff time. Their resolution cannot be automated. Sometimes they are pursued by parties beyond economic reason, when one of several alternative names or an agreement to operate jointly on a common name would suffice without undue loss of trade. By appropriate use of a web home page, confusion to callers can generally be easily resolved with cross-links and references.

Nevertheless, Nominet offers a meditative dispute resolution service. Nominet will talk to both parties and keep a careful record of correspondence, web pages and so on. Without giving legal advice, Nominet will explain the processes involved and can summarise previous similar examples of disputes and how they were resolved. Nominet, however, although encouraged to on many occasions, cannot and will not make intellectual property judgments. This is the proper function of the courts of law.

SUMMARY

Perhaps the most important message is that it is the use made of Domain Names, and the content of Web sites which can lead to more significant infringements, not the registration *per se*. After all, once content is established and referenced by Internet search engines, customers will usually arrive at the Web site without even noticing the Domain Name.

Nominet's web site is at *http://www.nominet.org.uk*.

7

Trade Marks and Domain Names. There's a Lot in a Name

CHARLOTTE WAELDE[*]

Over two years ago, it was predicted that the end of the Internet was nigh unless there were concerted efforts put into place to solve the problems associated with domain names and trade mark clashes.[1] Certainly, the person who predicted the demise of the Internet had an interest. It was Sally Tate, the managing director of Prince plc, the UK company which had at the time just won the UK round of its case against Prince Sports Group Inc. over the domain name www.prince. com.[2] Happily, Tate's prediction has not come true, and the Internet continues to survive. The domain name problems, however, continue.

The purpose of this chapter is twofold: first to discuss the nature of the problems concerning trade mark and domain name disputes. The focus will be on the UK with relevant comparisons being made in particular with the USA where most of the reported litigation has taken place. The second aim is to provide support to what might be called minority interest groups which participate on the Internet, whether they be small businesses or individuals. Much emphasis is often placed on the 'rights' of the party with superior bargaining power (or clout), the big business in the trade mark domain name disputes. Too often the legitimate interests of the minority are lost in practices of 'reverse domain name hijacking', as will be explained below. This chapter seeks to redress that balance by highlighting a number of the legitimate practices that individuals and small business can indulge in that are legally acceptable.

The first part of this chapter will focus on UK law, looking at the arguments that have been used under Trade Marks Act 1994, section 10. We will move to look at defences that may be available to the return of a domain name primarily in terms of US law where a number of arguments have been considered. We will consider how disputes were dealt with under the Network Solutions Inc. (NSI) dispute resolution policy, and move to look at the ways in which disputes are now dealt with under the rules promulgated by the Internet Corporation for Assigned Names and Numbers (ICANN).

[*] Lecturer, The School of Law, University of Edinburgh. E-mail Charlotte.Waelde@ed. ac.uk.

[1] *Scotsman*, 6 Aug. 1997.
[2] *Prince Plc* v. *Prince Sports Group Inc* [1998] FSR 21.

TRADE MARKS AND DOMAIN NAMES

There have been many articles written on this subject both in the UK and the USA.[3] These articles give an overview of the problems with the domain name system.

What is a Domain Name?

A domain name is part of the address of the location of a site on the Internet. For instance harrods.com is the domain name of the London department store, Harrods.[4] The portion of the address taken by 'harrods' is sometimes the part of the address that equates to the registered (or unregistered) trade mark of the person seeking to use the domain name: for instance, virgin or caesars-palace. The next part is the top level domain (TLD). .com, .net and .org are all generic Top Level Domains (gTLDs). .uk, .de and .fr are Country Code Top Level Domains (ccTLDs). It is important to note that there are three 'open' gTLDs in which any business or individual can make an application to register a domain name. As will be seen, it used to be that only one registry could register domain names in these gTLDs—Network Solutions Inc (NSI) based in the USA.[5] Competition has now been opened up in these gTLDs and there are many competing registrars.[6] The policy of registrars is broadly to register on a first-come first-served basis. However, most operate dispute resolution policies in the event of a conflict between the holder of a trade mark, and the holder of a domain name. Those who register in the .com .org and .net gTLDs all operate the same dispute resolution policy.[7] The dispute policy operated by NSI before these changes came about was, as will be alluded to, the subject of fierce criticism.

---

[3] Waelde 'Trade Marks and Domain Names. What's in a Name' in Edwards and Waelde (eds.), *Law and the Internet: Regulating Cyberspace* (Hart Publishing, Oxford, 1997); Murray 'Internet Domain Names: The Trade Mark Challenge' [1998] *IJLIT* 285; Thorne and Bennett, 'Domain Names—Internet Warehousing: Has Protection of Well-known Names on the Internet Gone Too Far?' (1998) 20 *EIPR* 468–70; Haftke, 'One In A Million—Domain Names Reconsidered' (1998) 9 *Ent. LR* 241–4; Haydoutoya, 'Trade Marks: Infringement on the Internet—Distinction Between Domain Name and Uniform Resource Locator Address' (1998) 20 *EIPR* N76; Stoodley, 'Internet Domain Names and Trade Marks' (1997) 19 *EIPR* 509–14; Morton, 'Opinion.com' (1997) 19 *EIPR* 496–8.

[4] For further information on the way in which domain names are made up see Black, chap. 6 in this vol.

[5] Network Solutions Inc. was sold for $17b in stock to VeriSign Inc. in Feb. 2000. For an account of the history of NSI see <http://www.lawnewsnetwork.com/practice/techlaw/news/A20216-2000Mar31.html>.

[6] For information see <http://www.icann.org>.

[7] *Ibid.*

What is a Trade Mark?

A trade mark is a sign or symbol that is used in the course of trade by a trader and is defined in the Trade Marks Act 1994 (TMA) as 'any sign capable of being represented graphically which is capable of distinguishing goods or services of one undertaking from those of other undertakings'.[8]

A registered trade mark does not give an absolute monopoly to a trader; rather the monopoly is limited to the particular goods and services for which the mark is registered. There is nothing to stop a competing trader entering the same market with the same goods and services so long as she does not use an identical or similar trade mark, or cause some sort of dilution to an existing mark. Similarly, subject to notions of confusion or dilution, there is nothing to stop a trader in a different market from using the same trade mark in connection with different goods and services. In addition, trade mark law is territorial. Therefore, there is nothing to stop a trader in a different jurisdiction from using the same trade mark for the same goods and services in another country.

Trade Mark and Domain Name Disputes: Why have They Arisen?

The disputes have arisen first because trade mark law is territorial and the Internet is global, and, secondly, because no two domain names can be identical. Therefore there can only be one microsoft.com; one avnet.co.uk; one marksandspencer.com; one prince.com, or one harrods.com. There may, however, be two or more business in the same country or in different countries equally entitled to the use of a name, but only one name of a particular variation is permitted on the Internet. prince.com is a good example, in that it was the subject of a dispute between Prince plc in the UK and Prince Sports Inc. in the USA. Prince plc registered the domain name first and was challenged by Prince Sports Inc.[9] The name remains with Prince plc. This type of dispute might be viewed as 'domain name envy'.

Then there are the cases where Internet participants, with a degree of entrepreneurial spirit, have registered domain names where very often the name is the same as or very similar to the trading name or registered trade mark of a company that is well known or famous, or which has a reputation. Generally the intent has been to do one of two things. One option might be to offer it to the owner of the registered trade mark or trading company in return for some payment. Alternatively, if it is a name that is similar to the well known name, such as porschegirls.com, the intention might be to use the domain name in an effort, not necessarily to confuse, but to draw people to the site. In other words to draw on the magnetism that attaches to the mark. The name that has been given to

[8]   Trade Marks Act 1994 s. 1.
[9]   *Prince plc* v. *Prince Sports Group Inc* [1998] FSR 21.

this type of activity is 'domain name hijacking' or more commonly 'Cybersquatting'.

And finally, there are the cases where the owners of well known or famous marks have aggressively pursued policies to prevent other Internet participants from using any rendition of a name that includes or alludes to their registered trade mark, in some cases quite unjustifiably. These cases are sometimes termed 'reverse domain name hijacking'.

Two main legal weapons have been used in these battles; the first is the law of registered trade marks, and the second is passing off. We will focus mainly on the law of registered trade marks.

THE UK: THE CURRENT SCENE

There have been surprisingly few cases that have, as yet, reached the courts in the UK, although one suspects that there is a great deal of activity that never reaches the stage of litigation.[10] The first case concerned Harrods (the London department store) and Michael Laurie. Michael Laurie registered the name 'harrods.com' This was handed back, after a brief (and unreported) judgment to the department store.[11] This was followed by *Pitman*[12] where the dispute arose because the domain name pitman.co.uk was in the first instance allocated to one party and then to another. The first party to register was given the domain name. Then there was *Prince plc* v. *Prince Sports Group Inc.*[13] which, as mentioned, concerned the domain name Prince.com which was registered by the UK company and fought over by the US company which argued that it was 'rightfully theirs'. The UK court decided that there had been unlawful threats by the US company but did not discuss in detail the trade mark issue. Prince plc still has the coveted domain name, and although the litigation did at one time return to the USA it has now settled. There have however been a number of more recent UK cases which have given us a little more detailed insight into the trade mark issues surrounding these controversies. We shall focus on two. The first is *Avnet Inc.* v. *Isoact Limited*[14] and the second *BT and others* v. *One in a Million and others*.[15]

---

[10]   *Courier*, 26 Jan. 2000 has reported that a company based in Sussex, Webhound Ltd has registered over 15,000 domain names in the co.uk TLD consisting of the names of villages in Scotland, England, Wales and Northern Ireland. Offers have been made to sell these to interested parties at prices starting at £500. A number of commentators have called this 'cyberpiracy'.

[11]   For comment see *Harrods Ltd* v. *UK Network Services Ltd* (Ch.D, unreported, 1996) (1997) 19 *EIPR* D106–7.

[12]   *Pitman Training Ltd* v. *Nominet UK* [1997] FSR 797.

[13]   *Prince plc* v. *Prince Sports Group Inc* [1998] FSR 21.

[14]   [1998] FSR 16. See also Montagon, 'Strong Marks Make More Goods Similar' [1998] EIPR 401.

[15]   [1998] 4 All ER 476, [1999] RPC 1. Two other cases in Scotland, one concerning Scottish Widows and the other Haggis Backpackers seem to have been concerned with much the same issues as *BT* v. *One in a Million* and in both cases the court ordered that the domain name be handed over

Perhaps one point worth emphasising at the outset is that there is a distinction between a trade mark and a domain name. In most cases a domain name is not a trade mark and does not function as one. A domain name is rather part of the address that points to the location of a computer on the Internet and allows one 'to locate and communicate with a place or a person'. However, it does not 'without more, function as a trademark'.[16] A trade mark is generally viewed as a badge of origin, and must be used in the consumer market place to signify the source of goods or services. A trade mark cannot exist in a vacuum (a registered trade mark can be removed from the register for non-use) and does not function as a trade mark if it is used purely as an address of a particular trader. As we will see, there has been an unfortunate tendency in disputes to treat the two as synonymous with little discussion and potentially far reaching consequences.

First, a brief reminder of the ways in which a registered trade mark can be infringed under the TMA:

(1) *Section 10(1) of the TMA* provides that that if a sign that is identical to a registered trade mark is used in the course of trade in connection with identical goods and services for which the mark is registered then there is infringement. There is no need to show any likelihood of public confusion.

(2) *Section 10(2) of the TMA* provides that if an identical or similar sign is used in conjunction with identical or similar goods for which a mark is registered then there is infringement if there is a likelihood of public confusion.

(3) *Section 10(3) of the TMA*[17] provides that a registered trade mark is infringed in the UK if a similar or identical mark is used in relation to goods or services which are not similar to those for which it is registered, where the trade mark has a reputation, and the use of the sign without due cause takes unfair advantage of or is detrimental to the distinctive character or repute of the trade mark.[18]

---

to the pursuer. However, in neither case was an opinion issued. In England, one slightly odd case concerned the trade mark FCUK and the domain name fcuk.com. *French Connection Ltd* v. *Anthony Toolseeram*, Ch.D, Dec. 1999. The domain name was registered by Antony Toolseeram trading as First Consultants UK and claimed by French Connection plc the owners of the registered trade mark. The case was distinguished from *BT* v. *One in a Million*. It would appear from reading the case that the judge may have been somewhat coloured in his judgment due to a dislike of the word 'fcuk'.

[16] McCarthy, *Trademarks and Unfair Competition* (4th edn. 1998), § 7:17.1.

[17] Note that there is no explicit requirement for confusion under this section despite the judgment of the court in *Baywatch Production Co Inc* v. *The Home Video Channel* [1997] FSR 22. Two other cases exist concerning registration under s. 5(3) which might throw doubt on the view expressed in *Baywatch*. These are *Audi-Med Trade Mark* [1988] RPC 863 and *Oasis Stores Ltd* v. *Ever Ready Plc* [1998] RPC 631.

[18] This s. can be contrasted with s. 56 of the Trade Marks Act 1994 which is designed to implement obligations under the Paris Convention Art. 6*bis*. This s. provides protection for well known marks belonging to nationals of Convention countries. A number of points are important. First the goods or services must be similar; secondly there must be a likelihood of confusion; and thirdly, although the mark must be well-known in the UK, there is no requirement for the proprietor of the mark to have traded in the UK using the mark.

TMA 1994 Requirements for Infringement	Identical mark Identical goods and services	Identical or similar mark identical or similar goods and services	Similar/ Identical Mark Dissimilar Goods and services Reputation	Public Confusion	Takes unfair advantage detrimental to distinctive character
Section					
10(1)	Yes			No	No
10(2)		Yes		Yes	No
10(3)			Yes	No	Yes

Avnet Inc. v. *Isoact Limited (Avnet)*[19]

Trade Marks Act 1994 section 10(1)

This case can be seen as one of domain name envy. The owner of a registered trade mark tried to use trade mark law to obtain the coveted name 'avnet.co.uk'. The case is atypical of many others, in that a famous or well known mark was not in question.

Avnet Inc., a US company, runs a business selling goods by catalogue and in so doing it carries advertisements for different manufacturers.[20] It registered the trade mark 'Avnet' in the UK in class 35 for advertising and promotional services. Isoact Limited, by contrast is an Internet Service Provider with a particular interest in aviation. It uses the words Aviation Network and Avnet in connection with its interests. Isoact Limited registered the domain name avnet.co.uk and allowed customers to display their own advertisements on its site.

Avnet argued that Isoact infringed its registered trade mark by using the word 'avnet' in its domain name. Section 10(1) of the TMA was relied upon as the ground of infringement. So Avnet Inc. was arguing that the sign used by Isoact was identical to its registered mark and used in connection with identical goods and services. Therefore, looking to the specification of the goods and services, its registered trade mark had been infringed. Jacob J disagreed with Avnet. Judgment was given purely by looking to the terms of what was covered by the registration of the mark 'Avnet'. Jacob J decided that in substance Isoact was not providing advertising and promotional services within class 35 of the Trade Mark Register, but rather provided the services of an Internet Service provider. These activities would (if registered) probably fall within class 42. In other words, the services provided were different. Therefore there was no infringe-

---

[19] [1998] FSR 16.
[20] Jacob J doubted that this activity actually fell within class 35 of the Trade Mark Register and thought the activity was more akin to retail sales, but did not decide the point.

ment under section 10(1). Therefore Isoact had a perfect right to keep and use the domain name.

This judgment is interesting for a number of reasons. First, Jacob J is well known for his crusade to keep intellectual property within reasonable limits, in particular that the monopoly conferred by each of the rights should not extend too far. This is a good example of setting just such limits. Secondly, Jacob J looked to the underlying registration of the goods and services and indicated that those who registered trade marks were going to have to be careful to keep these specifications within tight control if the monopoly claimed was not to be seen as too wide. And if too wide, the implication is that it will be struck from the register for non use. Thus, for anyone who infringes under section 10(1) of the TMA, the infringing use is going to have to fall squarely within the registration—or there will be no infringement. Thirdly, although Avnet already had a prior registered trade mark, there was no question of that right taking precedence over an unregistered right where there was no overlap between the services provided by the respective right holders. The domain name itself was not treated as a trade mark, which, as mentioned, has been a tendency in other cases particularly where a well-known mark is in issue.[21] So the specification of goods and services in the trade mark register is still highly relevant when it comes to disputes in cyberspace.

But what if the argument was over the identity or otherwise of the registered mark? For instance, many trade marks are registered in a highly stylised form, or with a particular font, or in conjunction with a logo. It has already been accepted that identical does not mean absolutely identical[22] and that external matter should be discounted in comparing a mark with a sign,[23] and indeed it must be remembered that domain names come (at least at present) only in plain type; stylised letters are not possible. It would therefore be reasonable to assume that for words that are registered trade marks, it is the word or words that should be considered, rather than the way in which it is presented.[24] Thus, if the address 'wetwetwet.com' were registered as an address by a publisher for the purpose of selling covers for books with the words 'wet wet wet' incorporated, then that would infringe the rights of Bravado Merchandising (Services) Ltd which has a registration of the stylised words for just that purpose.

The matter of identity of a domain name with a registered trade mark has been considered in the USA in the case *Jews for Jesus* v. *Brodsky*.[25] The organisation Jews for Jesus had a registration[26] for the phrase 'Jews for Jesus' but

---

[21] See the discussion below on *BT* v. *One in a Million*

[21] See the discussion below on *BT* v. *One in a Million*.

[22] *Bravado Merchandising Services Ltd* v. *Mainstream Publishing (Edinburgh Ltd)*, 1996 SLT 597, 1996 SCLR 1.

[23] *Origins Natural Resources Inc* v. *Origin Clothing Ltd* [1995] FSR 280.

[24] Under the NSI dispute resolution policy note was only taken of registered trade marks where they were identical to the domain name. http://www.internic.net/faq/dispute.html.

[25] *Jews for Jesus* v. *Brodsky*, DC NJ Civil Action No. 98–274 (AJL) 3/6/98.

[26] In class 16 of the Trade Mark Register for *inter alia* pamphlets.

with a stylised 'O' in the form of the star of David. The court found that it had rights to the phrase on the Internet without the stylised 'O' because such was the nature of the Internet that it was impossible to have a stylised letter in a domain name.[27] It is possible that our courts would take a similar view in the event that the argument was over the identity of a trade mark.

So from the *Avnet* case we can conclude that if you hold a registered trade mark and covet the domain name that someone else holds which incorporates an identical mark, then you are going to have to be sure that the goods and services covered in your registration are identical to the goods or services being traded on the site—or you will not win your case nor indeed the domain name using section 10(1) of the TMA. Also, and importantly, it is clear that a registered trade mark does not give a 'right' to a domain name; hence the need to secure domain name registration as soon as possible.

Trade Marks Act 1994, section 10(2)

In *Avnet* Jacob J makes observations which are more pertinent to the issue of confusion than to identity between trade marks, and so are rather more relevant to an infringement that might take place under section 10(2) of the TMA. Indeed, he may well have had in mind cases which might arise under this section in making those comments.

So how might a trade mark domain name case brought under this section proceed? First a little background on how this section has been interpreted. We were not long with the 1994 Act before section 10(2) fell to be interpreted in *British Sugar plc* v. *James Robertson & Sons*.[28] Very broadly it was argued that the word Treat used by James Robertson in connection with a toffee flavoured spread, infringed the trade mark 'Treat' which had been registered by British Sugar in connection with dessert sauces and syrups. The test to see whether there was infringement was in three parts. First it was necessary to consider the identity/similarity of the mark with the sign; secondly to analyse the concept of similarity between the respective goods and services; and, thirdly, to determine whether there was a likelihood of confusion because of that similarity. In the instant case the court decided that although the marks were identical, the goods were *not* similar, taking into account *inter alia* the uses of the products, their locations in supermarkets and the respective food sectors into which they fell. As there was no infringement at this stage, the third part of the test was not discussed in detail.

Had matters rested here, then the implications for a trade mark and domain name infringement actions brought under this section would have been reason-

---

[27] Brodsky had registered the domain name JewsforJesus.com. The court found that there was a likelihood of confusion between the two sites. It is also important to note that the court found the actions of Brodsky, in disseminating information about the organisation to be in bad faith.

[28] [1996] RPC 281.

ably clear. If the domain name was the same as or similar to the registered trade mark, the next question would have been are the underlying goods and services similar, and the focus would be on the underlying goods and services covered by the registration, and that within the fairly tight guidelines drawn in *British Sugar*. If not, then there would be no question of infringement. If there was similarity, then the question is over whether there is a likelihood of public confusion, and this is where the comments by Jacob J in *Avnet* should perhaps be borne in mind. In *Avnet* Jacob J argued that the real concern was not that Isoact would compete with Avnet—it is clearly in a different business—but that there will be confusion when a search engine returns a hit on a particular site, over which "Avnet" has actually been found. Jacob J then went on to say that it is actually difficult to see how such confusion could occur. Once a surfer arrived at a site, she would soon see that she was not where she actually wanted to be. In this case at aviation products rather than electronic products. The implication is that the surfer then simply presses the back button and surfs to where she want to go after a bit of a muddle as a result of the hits returned by the search engine. In other words, there is no confusion about the origin of the goods and services (the indication of origin function of the trade mark being the most basic one). The confusion is rather over the hits the search engine returns. That is not a matter for trade mark law.

By way of illustration, on 3 March 1999, I typed the word Avnet into Yahoo! The search engine returned 74 hits. The first five were for the domain name avnet.com and clearly were the plaintiff's sites; the sixth was for avnet.co.uk and was the defendant's site—quite clearly from the explanatory text. At about hit 15 there was an avnet.irl which was concerned with security systems and appeared to have no connection to either Avnet Inc. or Isoact Ltd. This writer was personally not confused, and certainly not as to the origin of the underlying goods and services. Potential customers of either Avnet or Isoact will find what they are looking for.

However, as always, things are not that simple. The European Court of Justice (ECJ) has ruled in *Canon Kabushiki Kaisha* v. *Metro-Goldwyn-Mayer Inc.*[29] that the first important factor to decide on when determining liability under section 10(2) is the distinctive character of the mark, and in particular its reputation. The more distinctive the mark and the greater its reputation, the wider the ambit of goods and services which should be considered similar to those represented by the mark, and which are therefore more likely to give rise to a likelihood of confusion. Thus, a mark which is distinctive and has a reputation will have protection over a wide range of goods; a weak mark will have protection over a narrow range of goods. The question of similarity of goods and services, therefore, depends on the distinctiveness and reputation of the mark.[30]

---

[29] Case C–39/97, *Canon Kabushiki Kaisha* v. *Metro-Goldwyn-Mayer Inc (formerly Pathé Communications Corp)* [1998] All ER (EC) 934, [1999] RPC 117, [1999] 1 CMLR 77.

[30] It would appear that currently the ECJ is vacillating over the monopoly that is to be conferred to a registered trade mark, particularly where infringement concerns the likelihood of confusion. In

This of course begs a whole number of questions such as how do you determine how distinctive a mark is? What does reputation mean? How dissimilar must goods and services be before they fall out of the ambit of this protection? Leaving aside these questions for a minute, it is clear from this ruling that the monopoly conferred on a registered mark is expanding.

What are the implications for trade mark and domain name disputes in the UK? It appears that it would be much easier to claim protection under section 10(2) of the TMA than section 10(1), particularly where it can be argued that the mark has a distinctive character and a reputation (however either of those may be proved[31]). Let us take the example of Avnet discussed above. It is not in issue that the sign used by Isoact was identical to the trade mark. What of the distinctive character and reputation of the mark? Avnet is a made-up word with a distinctive character—and if registration was accepted without evidence of use, this will already have been accepted. In addition, it will have been used in the course of trade for a while, so will have some reputation. Looking to the services provided by the two companies it would not be difficult to argue that they are similar—both relate to advertising services. This may then give rise to a likelihood of confusion and therefore infringement under section 10(2) of the TMA. That is, unless it is accepted that the confusion arises only when the search engines turn in hits, rather than when the web pages are actually accessed, and it becomes clear to the surfer that they have arrived at the wrong site. Avnet might therefore have won its case had it been pled under section 10(2).

With this shift in emphasis by the ECJ, we also see a potential shift in domain name disputes, from the position where trade mark protection is accorded to the underlying goods and services for which there is a registration, to the position where trade mark protection is accorded to the domain name itself. Although the discussion in *Canon* was over the width of protection accorded to the underlying goods and services, the effect is that the broader the protection for these goods and services the stronger the protection for the mark itself—the domain name.

its recent judgment in *Sabel* v. *Puma* [1998] 1 CMLR 445 the question was whether the words 'likelihood of association' found in s. 10(2) were a subset of the test 'likelihood of confusion' or an independent test. If independent, so the breadth of the monopoly conferred on the registered mark would be enhanced. If a subset, so the monopoly is kept in check. The ECJ found that the test of likelihood of association was a subset. With *Canon* we are now seeing a fairly significant expansion of the monopoly conferred on a registered mark.

[31] In the USA in *Data Concepts Inc* v. *Digital Consulting Inc.*, 6th Cir No 97–5802 8/5/98, it was said that a mark that has been registered and uncontested for five years, as Digital's was, is entitled to a presumption that it is a strong mark. *Wynn Oil Co.* v. *American Way Serv. Corp.*, 943 F 2d 595, 600 (6th Cir. 1991). However, a mark is weakened outside the context in which it is used if there is third-party use of the mark.

British Telecommunications and Others v. One in a Million and Others[32]
(*One in a Million*)

Trade Marks Act 1994, section 10(3)

The judgment in *Canon* moves questions of infringement brought under section 10(2) of the TMA much closer to the considerations necessary for infringement under section 10(3), and starts to blur the distinction between the two. As mentioned, section 10(3)[33] of the TMA focuses on questions of dilution of trade marks. It is similar to provisions mainly used in the USA to deal with problems of cybersquatters.[34]

Section 10(3) was considered, albeit very briefly, in *One in a Million*.[35] In this case a number of domain names including marksandspencer.com, bt.org, britishtelecommunication.net were registered by, among others, One in a Million. The case was decided primarily by looking to the law of passing off, and by some extension of existing principles, the court determined that by registering the domain names the defendants had created instruments of deception. Thus the domain names had to be handed back to the trade mark and brand owners. The judgment has been criticised.[36] It is said that the bounds of the tort of passing off were extended—by implication possibly too far; and that it is not at all clear that even if a case of passing off is made out, that would necessarily provide the remedy required. In dealing with section 10(3), Aldous LJ seems to have considered that the domain name itself was the trade mark, observing that the domain names were registered to take advantage of the distinctive character and reputation of the marks, which was both unfair and detrimental. Section 10(3) was therefore infringed. The court made clear its dislike of these practices. But the cursory examination of trade mark law has left a number of questions unanswered.

First, it begs the question what is a mark with a reputation, and therefore one that would fall under this provision; and secondly, what is meant by taking advantage of the distinctive character or repute of a mark, more commonly known as dilution? The questions are important because there seems to be a body of judicial decisions developing which concern these marks, and which, when looking at Internet disputes, accords them 'special protection'. The wider this special protection gives to these marks, the more problematic it is for an individual or small business on the Internet to use any version of these marks for what may be legitimate business or personal reasons, without fear of being

---

[32] [1999] 4 All ER 476, [1999] RPC 1.
[33] See comment at n. 000.
[34] US Lanham Act s. 43© (known as the Federal Trademark Dilution Act 1995).
[35] [1999] 4 All ER 476, [1999] RPC 1.
[36] See, e.g., Thorne and Bennett, 'Domain Names—Internet Warehousing: Has Protection of Well-known Names on the Internet Gone too Far?' [1998] *EIPR* 468.

challenged by the mark owner. The marks are often owned by large businesses which will police any 'unauthorised' use aggressively.

What is a Well-known or Famous Mark or One with a Reputation?

There appears to be only patchy international consensus on what a famous or well-known mark is. In addition, terminology is used inconsistently, and comes with notions of 'reputation' and 'distinctiveness'. The Paris Convention, Article 6*bis* refers to 'well known marks'[37] as does section 56 of the TMA: section 10(3) of the TMA refers to marks with a 'reputation'. The court in *Canon* referred to 'distinctive' marks with a 'reputation'. Certain cases in the USA dealing with question of dilution in the context of trade marks and domain names have referred to 'famous' marks.[38]

It appears that *famous* marks are those well known marks that are so famous that protection is accorded in respect of dissimilar goods and services. This is usually subject to certain conditions. For instance the use of the infringing sign would indicate a connection in the course of trade between the owner of the mark and the goods and services belonging to the third party, and that the interests of the owner of the famous mark are likely to be damaged by such use. *Well-known* marks on the other hand are those which require protection against use in connection with the same or similar goods or services for which the well known mark is registered.[39] Often these terms are used almost synonymously— but it would help if they were separated.

Then there is the term *reputation* used in the Trade Marks Directive[40] and in the TMA,[41] and which indeed was used in *Canon*. Mostert[42] argues that a lower evidentiary threshold is required to establish that a mark has a reputation, merely that proof that the necessary reputation or secondary meaning has been acquired, 'in the sense of being exclusively associated with the owner's goods or

---

[37] Mostert (Mostert, *Famous and Well Known Marks* (Butterworths, London, 1997) argues that the concept of 'well known' flows from the Paris Convention where the intention was to provide the owners of marks which were not registered some protection so owners of foreign rights were protected against 'pirates' who launched a pre-emptive strike, and so covers reputation without use.

[38] e.g. *Intermatic Inc v. Toeppen*, 947 F Supp.

[39] Art. 6*bis* of the Paris Convention gives protection to well-known marks used in respect of identical or similar goods (not services). The TRIPS agreement extended the provisions of Art. 6*bis* to services (Art. 16.2) Further, Art. 16.3 of TRIPs extended Art. 6*bis* of the Paris Convention to goods or services which are not similar to those in respect of which a trade mark is registered where the use would indicate a connection between the goods and services and the owner of the registered trade mark, and provided the interests of the owner of the registered trade mark are likely to be damaged by such use. In other words, it extended the protection for famous marks.

[40] First Council Dir. 89/104 of 21 Dec. 1988 to approximate the laws of the Member States relating to trade marks. Art. 5(2). The term 'reputation' was considered by the ECJ in the C–375/97 *Chevy* case. The ECJ considered that the degree of knowledge required by the condition that the mark must have 'a reputation in the Member State' is attained when the earlier mark is known by a significant part of the public concerned with the products or services. Reputation in a substantial part of the territory will suffice.

[41] Trade Marks Act 1994, s. 10(3).

[42] Mostert, *supra* n.37, 23.

services'.[43] So protection may be extended to marks which are neither famous, nor well-known.

Many jurisdictions have developed guidelines[44] on what constitutes a famous or well-known mark. It has been one of the tasks facing the World Intellectual Property Organisation (WIPO) for several years now, and indeed in March 1999, the Standing Committee on the Law of Trademarks, Industrial Design and Geographical Indications (the WIPO SCT) adopted a list of factors as the recommended non-exhaustive criteria to be considered in determining whether a mark is well known.[45]

Although one can try to identify the various marks that would fall into the category of being famous or well-known, actually compiling lists of those included when one would be looking at least at all Paris Convention countries, is a mind boggling task. However, it is not one that should be ignored. After all, if these marks are to get special protection, then there should be something very special that distinguishes them from others. A starting point for Internet purposes might be that as the Internet is accessible globally, then only those marks that are known globally should be included, which may only be a very very small number. But keeping the numbers very low, at least for Internet disputes, would ensure that not too many are taken out of circulation for legitimate use by third parties.

What is Dilution?

Well known or *famous* marks, or marks with a *reputation* are in a particular category of trade mark law in that they can be infringed by 'dilution'. This can occur in two main ways, either by *blurring* or by *tarnishment* of the reputation. When blurring occurs there is an erosion or watering down of the distinctive quality of the mark, and therefore the ability to use that mark to call in mind the

---

[43] *Ibid.*

[44] Federal Trademark Dilution Act 1995. Guidelines were laid down in the UK in *Audi-Med Trade Mark* [1998] RPC 863.

[45] The recommendations state:

'In determining whether a mark is a well-known mark, the competent authority shall take into account any circumstances from which it may be inferred that the mark is well known.

In particular, the competent authority shall consider information submitted to it with respect to factors from which it may be inferred that the mark is, or is not, well known, including, but not limited to, information concerning the following:

1. The degree of knowledge or recognition of the mark in the relevant sector of the public;
2. The duration, extent and geographical area of any use of the mark;
3. The duration, extent and geographical area of any promotion of the mark, including advertising or publicity and the presentation, at fairs or exhibitions, of the goods and/or services to which the mark applies
4. The duration and geographical area of any registrations, and/or any applications for registration, of the mark, to the extent that they reflect use or recognition of the mark;
5. The record of successful enforcement of rights in the mark, in particular, the extent to which the mark was recognised as well known by courts or other competent authorities; and
6. The value associated with the mark.'

product. So if the mark 'Kodak' becomes well known in connection with cameras and films, and then is used on a wide variety of dissimilar products, its ability to call in mind films and cameras decreases. By contrast, using a trade mark in an offensive or unsavoury context could tarnish the ability of the mark to call into mind positive associations with the goods or services. For example the German Federal Supreme court prohibited use of the mark 4711 which was well known in Germany in respect of perfume, from being used on the side of a van belonging to a sewer company, despite the fact that the mark comprised the phone number of the sewer company.

However, there are a growing number of cases where dilution is pled and there is neither blurring nor tarnishment. Nevertheless the courts will find that a well-known or famous mark is infringed. In these cases the proprietary overtones of a trade mark are emphasised and the trade mark perceived as being protectible as a thing in itself[46] rather than fulfilling the function of an indication of origin. For instance in Germany, the term 'Rolls Royce' was not capable of being used for high-class whisky, a non competing product, even where there was no evidence of blurring or tarnishment. What there was however was an attempt to trade upon the reputation of the famous 'Rolls Royce' mark, and the courts were willing to protect this commercial magnetism attaching to the mark. By contrast in the US the mark 'Dom Perignon', which was registered for champagne, was held not to be diluted by the use of the words Dom Popignon for popcorn sold in a champagne shaped bottle, because the court was not satisfied that either blurring or tarnishment of the mark had occurred.[47]

In the UK, the courts have been struggling with the concept of dilution, particularly as confusion is not required for infringement. Some interesting comments have been made in the context of registration of marks under section 5(3) of the TMA.[48] *Oasis Stores Ltd's Trade Mark Application*[49] concerned an application to register the mark 'Eveready' for contraceptives and condoms. The application was opposed by Ever Ready plc, the owner of numerous 'Ever Ready' words and device marks for *inter alia* batteries, torches, plugs and smoke alarms. Ever Ready plc claimed that registration of the mark would be contrary to section 5(3) .

In giving its judgment, the court said that simply being reminded of a similar trade mark with a reputation for dissimilar goods did not necessarily amount to taking an unfair advantage of the repute of that trade mark. Section 5(3) was clearly not intended to have the sweeping effect of preventing the registration of any mark which was the same as, or similar to, a trade mark with a reputation.

---

[46]   Mostert, *supra* n.37, 65.

[47]   *Schieffelin & Co v. The Jack Co*9, 850 F Supp 232 (SDNY 1994). However, infringement was found on the basis rather of consumer survey results showing evidence of consumer confusion.

[48]   The wording of this s. is very similar to that of s. 10(3) TMA but focusing rather on registrability than infringement. Broadly a sign that is similar to a registered mark may itself not be registered for dissimilar goods and services where the registered mark has a reputation and the registration of the sign would take advantage of or be detrimental to the mark without due cause.

[49]   [1998] RPC 631.

In addition, when considering detriment it was appropriate to take into account the inherent distinctiveness of the earlier trade mark, the extent of the reputation which it enjoyed, the range of goods and services for which it enjoyed a reputation, the uniqueness or otherwise of the mark in the market place, whether the respective goods/services, although dissimilar, were in some way related, or were likely to be sold through the same outlets, and whether the earlier trade mark would be any less distinctive for the goods/services for which it had a reputation than it was before.

These guidelines take us back closer again to the considerations under section 10(2) originally identified by Jacob J in *British Sugar*. If they were applied in domain name disputes, the focus would remain on the underlying goods and services for which the mark was registered, and not on the domain name itself as a trade mark. In addition, it would allow many more applicants to have domain names that were similar to marks that were well known within the meaning of section 10(3).[50]

However, judging by *One in a Million* it would appear that these terrestrial guidelines are not being applied in domain name cases. For some of the marks in *One in a Million*, there was no registered trade mark in issue, and the question was one of passing off. However, for a few of the marks in question, the TMA was relevant. But there was only cursory analysis of section 10(3). Rather than getting into the depths of questions about well-known and famous marks, and notions of dilution, the courts are rather seizing on their dislike of cyber-squatting and developing the view that where it appears there may have been some nefarious practice, the cybersquatter is charged with creating an instrument of deception. This may present a number of problems if (and when) more difficult questions come before the courts. For instance, one wonders what the outcome would have been in the *Oasis* case, had the battle been over the domain name eveready.com[51] and if Oasis Stores Ltd had actually been the first to register the domain name evercady.com, and used it to sell its wares. In addition, as we will argue, there are a number of legitimate ways in which these famous and well-known marks could be used as domain names by traders who do not own the marks. A brusque analysis characterising registration of domain names

---

[50] A similar result was achieved in *Audi-Med Trade Mark* [1998] RPC 863 where an application to register AUDI-MED in respect of hearing aids, etc., was opposed under s. 5(3) having regard to the registration of, and the reputation in, the trade mark AUDI in respect of motor cars, parts and fittings, financial service relating to motor cars, etc. The court found *inter alia* that the extent of use of the opponents' mark, supported by evidence of national advertising, was sufficient to establish its reputation in motor cars, parts and fittings, and their repair and maintenance; that nothing was said to change the decision which was given in *Oasis Stores Ltd v. Ever Ready Plc* [1998] RPC 631; that it was possible for the damage referred to in s. 5(3) to occur without the likelihood of confusion. However, when the following were considered: similarity of marks; inherent distinctiveness of earlier mark; reputation of earlier mark and its range of use; uniqueness of earlier mark; channels of trade; whether the earlier mark would be less distinctive because of the later; there was nothing to support the case that the applicants' mark would be detrimental to the opponents.

[51] Eveready.com is, in fact, the home page of Ever Ready plc and the information relates to *inter alia* batteries.

consisting of famous or well-known marks as instruments of deception in all circumstances, may well ignore some of the legitimate defences that might be available in trade mark law.[52]

What is the Relevance for Internet Domain Names?

The danger in taking this wide approach to notions of dilution is that the focus of protection given shifts from the underlying goods and services to the domain name itself; and it is only a short leap from taking that view to taking the same view when dealing with infringement under section 10(2) and (1). The domain name itself is then protected. It suggests that, given time, so long as you have a trade mark bearing the name you wish to protect, you will have a right to the domain name. This is what, in essence, had been the subject of such fierce criticism in the NSI dispute resolution policy (discussed in more detail below[53]), where preference for domain names was given to traders who held a registered trade mark for a word, thus ignoring both unregistered rights and concurrent right holders.

It has to be said that there is some acceptance that a domain name can become a trade mark if it is used as a trade mark.[54] However, when a domain name is used only to indicate an address on the Internet and not to identify the source of specific goods and services, the name is not functioning as a trade mark.[55] It is imperative that the distinction between the two is maintained.

The seeming divergence when trade mark law is applied to domain name disputes as compared with terrestrial disputes, arguably leads to the conclusion that, for well-known or famous marks at the very least, there should be some sort of special Internet-related protection or body of rules which would deal with disputes concerning domain names. This was one of the proposals that was made by the World Intellectual Property Organisation (WIPO) which, although not currently implemented, may emerge at some point in the future. This will be discussed in more detail below.[56]

Technical solutions to the domain name disputes are imaginable, but there seems no great enthusiasm to pursue them. With all the brilliant minds focused on the workings of the Internet, one would have thought that just technical fixes

---

[52] See the discussion in part 3 below.

[53] See the discussion in part 4 below.

[54] The question is sometimes asked: 'Is a domain name a trademark?' The correct answer is: 'A domain name can become a trademark if it is used as a trademark': McCarthy, *Trademarks and Unfair Competition* (4th edn. 1998) § 7:17.1.

[55] See *Lockheed Martin Corp.* v. *Network Solutions, Inc.*, 985 F supp. 949, 956 (CD Cal. 1997). McCarthy, *supra* n.54, § 7:176.1, at 7–24. Courts and other commentators have generally recognised that an Internet domain name can be used for both trade mark and non-trade mark purposes. See, e.g., Gilson and Samuels, *Trademark Protection and Practice* (1997) §§ 5.11[3] & 5.11[5]; McCarthy, § 7:17.1, domain names, like telephone numbers, street addresses, and radio station call letters, which permit one to locate and communicate with a place or a person, do not, without more, function as trade marks.

[56] See Part 5 below.

would be found. In addition, arguably, the most severe problems are faced by the owners of famous and well known names—just the interest group that might have the resources to invest in finding solutions.[57] However, perhaps the last people who actually want the domain name system dismantled are the same well-known and famous mark owners. The domain name gives them an excellent advertising tool; an intuitive way to find their home pages on the Internet.[58] These mark owners want domain names and not some anonymous numbers or topic searches in search engines which might lead to sites belonging to competitors.

However, under trade mark law there are a number of defences to actions of trade mark infringement which do not yet appear to have been considered in the UK, and which may be relevant to cases of domain name envy and to the practice of cybersquatting. A number of US cases have looked at possible defences, and in many instances we have similar provisions in our legislation. We thus turn to the US jurisprudence in this area.

DEFENCES TO DEMANDS FOR THE RETURN OF A DOMAIN NAME

Trade mark holders—particularly those of famous or well-known trade marks—are extremely vigilant at protecting their trade mark rights on the Internet. To an extent this is justified. If they do not look after their marks, the danger is that they become generic and thus lost to the public domain. But there are many cases where the use of a mark by a third party, which is the same as a registered trade mark, is perfectly legitimate. Unfortunately either these uses are often not appreciated by the trade mark owners, or they contest that any such use is legitimate. This has resulted in a number of cases of *reverse domain name hijacking*, where the trade mark owner will take action, regardless of the merits of the case. It is most often the small business or individual who suffers as a result. However, the holder of a domain name should not be too quick to give it up in the face of pressure. The use may be quite legitimate.

'Use in the Course of Trade'

One of the first defences that was pled in the USA, in particular by cybersquatters, was that the domain name was not being used in the course of trade. The mere registration of the domain name, without more, was not sufficient to satisfy this test, or so it was argued. Thus there was no infringement. Much

---

[57] See Part 6 below for an indication of the numbers of domain names registered incorporating the word 'Porsche'.

[58] Some generic domain names have a very high value. The *L.A. Times*, 1 Dec. 1999, C–1, listed a half-dozen (mostly generic) domain names being offered for sale for over a million dollars each. These included Business.com and Websites.com.

academic ink has been spilt in trying to determine the question. Suffice it to say that the issue has not been one that has overly troubled the courts, in particular when the question is one of cybersquatting. The courts have been happy to find that mere registration, with a hint of the possibility of selling the domain name either to the owner of the famous mark or to a third party,[59] sufficient to satisfy this test, particularly where the action has been brought against the domain name holder.[60] In other cases, where it has been NSI that has been sued for infringement for actually registering the domain name, the courts have been willing to say that the mere act of registering a domain name is not a commercial use of a mark,[61] but that would seem rather to be a decision taken that it is not the registry that should be sued but rather the registrant. The distinction seems without difference, particularly if the intent is difficult to show. However, it reinforces the view that courts do not like cybersquatting and are willing to grant remedies, even if they involve creative use of trade mark law.

Non-commercial Use: Free Speech

A defence of non-commercial speech and of free speech has surfaced several times in the USA. In *Jews for Jesus* v. *Brodsky*,[62] Brodsky registered the domain name JewsforJesus.com. He used the Web site to make disparaging comments about the organisation 'Jews for Jesus' who had a registration for that phrase. When challenged, Brodsky pled non-commercial speech and free speech as defences; arguing that he was just using the domain name as an identifier to makes comments about an organisation whose policies and teachings he disagreed with. However, the court said that he had done more than just register the name; rather, the site was a conduit to another organisation that sold merchandise. Importantly the court also noted that Brodsky's actions were in bad faith. The judgment was based on similar reasoning to that in *Planned Parenthood Federation of America Inc.* v. *Bucci*[63] which involved a Web site set up by Bucci, using the domain name plannedparenthood.com. Bucci used the Web site to make anti-abortion statements and promote sale of an anti-abortion book. Free speech was argued as a defence. The court said that the information was not protected free speech because it was not part of a communicative message. The use of the domain name was more akin to use as a source identifier.

What becomes clear from an analysis of these cases is that if there is an element of bad faith by those registering the domain names in the use of the Web

---

[59] *Panavision* v. *Toeppen*, 945 F Supp. 1296, 2 ECLR 789 (DC Calif. 1996) In the UK the argument that One in a Million was not using the domain names in the course of trade was given short shrift by Aldous LJ who found that mere registration with the intent to sell the names back to the owners was sufficient for use in the course of trade.

[60] *Panavision* v. *Toeppen*, 945 F Supp. 1296, 2 ECLR 789 (DC Calif. 1996).

[61] *Lockheed Martin Corp* v. *Network Solutions Inc*, 2 ECLR 1244 (DC Calif. 1997).

[62] DC NJ Civil Action No. 98–274 (AJL) 3/6/98.

[63] 97 CIV–0629 (KMW) (3/19/97), 2 ECLR 370.

site, then any reliance on free speech will not be accepted. Rather the court will find, by whatever route, some tarnishment, commercial use or other overriding criterion that will trump the non-commercial and free speech arguments.

Do we have similar provisions, or indeed protections in our legislation? The requirement that a trade mark be used 'in a trade mark sense' for infringement is no longer relevant under the TMA.[64] If the question is one of dilution of a famous mark, the question may be whether the use was without due cause. It is likely that, if the facts were similar to those in the US cases, the courts would be willing to find some sort of tarnishment and therefore infringement. The question of free speech may, of course, also be raised as a result of the forthcoming UK incorporation of the European Convention on Human Rights into domestic law. Although it does not appear that free speech has been pled directly as a defence in a trade mark case to date in the UK, it has surfaced in a copyright case[65] and, given its potential but as yet untested breadth, it is likely that it will arise in consideration of these issues probably in the not too distant future.

Parodies

The defence of parody is another that has cropped up several times in the USA. Parodies of trade marks are accepted under certain circumstances. So, in a non-Internet case, a wild boar was called Spa'am in a Muppet Treasure Island Film. This was held not to dilute the mark 'Spam' which had been registered for pork and ham luncheon meat[66] because it was said the public identification of the mark with the owner would be increased: 'the joke magnifies the mark because it increases the fame'. Thus there was no blurring. Likewise, the mark was not tarnished because the character was likeable and positive.[67] It is certainly heartening to see that judges have a sense of humour. Would the same result be achieved on the Internet in relation to domain names? There certainly are parodies of well-known names: thus there is DrudgeRetort.com—a parody of the well-known Internet journalist Matt Drudge; and there was a Peta.org, the domain name for a Web site set up by a group calling themselves 'People Eating Tasty Animals', a parody of the organisation 'People for the Ethical Treatment of Animals'.[68] Sadly, this last one was the victim of NSI's dispute resolution policy which allowed no defence of parody .

[64] *British Sugar* v. *James Robertson* [1996] RPC 281. Compare *Bravado Merchandising Services Ltd* v. *Mainstream Publishing (Edinburgh Ltd)*, 1996 SLT 597, 1996 SCLR 1.

[65] In *Newspaper Licensing Agency* v. *Marks & Spencer plc*, *The Times*, 26 Jan. 1999, *Independent*, 28 Jan. 1999, mention was made of the proper balance between the rights of a creative author and the wider public interest—'of which free speech is a very important ingredient'. Free speech has been pled in a case under the ICANN dispute resolution policy: see the discussion in 'Natwestsucks.com' at http://arbiter.wipo.int/domains/deuxons/html/d2000-0636.html.

[66] *Hormel Goods Corp* v. *Jim Henson Productions*, 73 F 3d 497 (2d Cir 1996).

[67] Mostert, *supra* n.37, 454.

[68] Under this case the people for the ethical treatment of animals won because NSI dispute resolution policy allowed no defence of parody. People Eating Tasty Animals could not afford to defend the action.

Identifying Goods and Services

Another acceptable use of a trade mark is to use it to identify the goods and services belonging to the trade mark owner.[69] Thus, subject to certain parameters, a garage selling parts for Volkswagen cars will be able to use the term 'Volkswagen' in connection with its trade.[70] One particular way in which this issue has arisen in the USA, is where a trade mark was used within the file directory path of the Internet address, only to the right of the Top Level Domain.

In *Patmont Motor Works Inc.* v. *Gateway Marine Inc*,[71] Gateway used the URL www.gateway.com/goped for a Web page giving information about 'Gopeds' they distributed. Patamont complained that this was infringement of its trade mark 'Go-Ped'. The court said that this was not a trade mark and domain name dispute, and that the use of a trade mark in the part of the address listing directory information and file names does not suggest that the trade mark owner sponsors or endorses the site. The use was thus protected by the US fair use defence.[72]

In the UK, apart from the express provisions in the TMA which could be interpreted to include this type of use of a registered mark,[73] we have also had an interesting ruling from the ECJ. In *Dior* v. *Evora*[74] a dispute arose between Dior France and Evora, a drugstore in the Netherlands. Dior France objected to the way in which Evora presented advertisements in its promotional material advertising the Dior products. Dior argued that such use in a downmarket store harmed the image and reputation of its mark. The question was whether there were any 'legitimate reasons' within the meaning of Article 7(2)[75] of the Trade

---

[69] Trade Marks Act 1994 ss. 10(6), 11(2)(b).

[70] Apparently Volkswagen has wrestled the domain 'vw.net' away from Virtual Works Inc. in a federal court decision. Virtual Works claims it will appeal the ruling, characterising the case as a reverse hijacking: http://www.it.fairfax.com.au/breaking/20000229/A46143-2000Feb29.html.

[71] DC NCalif. No C 96–2703 THE 12/18/97.

[72] Lanham Act s. 43 c (4) The fair use defence has three elements:

a. the product or service must not be easily identifiable without the use of the trade mark
b. only so much of the mark may be used as is reasonably necessary to identify the goods or service in question
c. the user must do nothing that would suggest sponsorship or endorsement by the trade mark holder

These were satisfied in this case. See also *New Kids on the Block* v. *News America Publishing*, 971 F 2d 302 (CA 9 1991).

[73] Trade Marks Act 1994, s. 11(2) provides that a registered mark is not infringed by the use of indications concerning the kind, quality, quantity, etc. of goods or services. Nor is a registered trade mark infringed where its use is necessary to indicate the intended purpose of a product or services, provided always that such use is in accordance with honest practices in industrial or commercial matters.

[74] Case C–337/95, *Parfums Christian Dior SA & Parfums Christian Dior BV* v. *Evora BV* [1997] ECR I–6013, [1998] RPC 166, [1998] 1 CMLR 737.

[75] Art. 7(2) of the Trade Marks Dir. (First Council Dir. 89/104 of 21 Dec. 1988 to approximate the laws of member states relating to trade marks) states: the trade mark shall not entitle the proprietor of the mark to prohibit its use in relation to goods which have been put on the market in the community under that trade mark by the proprietor or with his consent. Para. 1 shall not apply

Mark Directive to argue that the allure attaching to high-quality goods could be impaired by the use of the mark in certain ways. Broadly, the ECJ said that damage done to the reputation of the trade mark might in principle be a legitimate reason for arguing such 'tarnishment'. Therefore the reseller must not act unfairly in relation to the legitimate interest of the trade mark owner, and must advertise goods in a way that would not damage the reputation of the trade mark owner. By analogy, there would be limits on the ability to use a registered trade mark within a URL of a Web site; however, used fairly, there appears to be no reason why resellers of products should not do the same as Gateway. The implications may be that so long as the use is fair, why should a reseller not use the registered trade mark as part of, or as, the second level domain name?

Use of Personal Names

There are a number of significant differences in various jurisdictions in relation to the use of personal names, both as trade marks and as domain names. In the UK, one of the specific exceptions to infringement in the TMA is the use by a person of his own name or address.[76] Hence, when there was much angst in Scotland recently over McDonald's, the fast food chain, asserting its rights to the name McDonald,[77] it was possible to reassure those Scots (and others) with the surname McDonald, that they would in no way be prevented in using it in (almost) any way that they wished. This would, or most certainly should, include use as a domain name. However, in Germany, there has been a recent dispute over the name Krupp.[78] A certain Herr Krupp registered the domain name Krupp.de in 1995. He was operating an on-line agency and offered Internet related services to the public. This was challenged by the German steel company bearing that name which wanted the domain name. The court held that a company with an outstanding reputation can prohibit the use of its usual name as a domain name by others. However, the court was only able to prevent the use of the name by Mr Krupp, not to order transfer to the steel company.[79]

The case is rather concerning as all Member States are now working from the same Directive, albeit that it may be implemented rather differently in national laws. One can imagine the outcry in Scotland should Mr McDonald McDonald from Aberdeen have registered the domain name McDonalds.com being

where there exists legitimate reasons for the proprietor to oppose further commercialisation of the goods, especially where the condition of the goods is changed or impaired after they have been put on the market. Trade Marks Act 1994, s. 12 implements this provision of the Dir.

[76] Trade Marks Act 1994, s. 11(2)(a).

[77] Often surfers spell a name incorrectly when looking for a Web site. No doubt, many searching for a burger may type in www.macdonalds.com. It appears that an entrepreneur has quickly cottoned on to this possibility. The reader is invited to try.

[78] *Re Krupp*, Regional Court of Appeal of Hamm, 13 Jan. 1998 noted in [1999] EIPR N–24.

[79] It appears there may have been another case involving the domain name shell.de registered by a Herr Shell. Again, apparently the court has ordered that Herr Shell cease use of this domain name. It appears that there may have been attempts to sell it to the multinational oil company, Shell.

ordered to stop using it on account of the reputation of 'McDonald' of golden arches fame. Another interesting name case is now coming to light. In an effort perhaps to comply with the rules on the use of personal names, a Doc Seagle who registered the domain name oxforduniversity.com, has changed his name to Mr Oxford University. The matter is apparently in the hands of the University lawyers.[80]

Generally, celebrity names are not registrable as trade marks in the UK.[81] However, it does appear that personal names are registrable as Community trade marks under the Community Trade Mark Regulation.[82] The name 'Dodi Fayed' was registered by Harrods Limited.[83] Dodialfayed.com was registered as a domain name by a Robert Boyd. An Administrative Panel Decision by WIPO[84] ordered this to be handed back to Harrods Ltd.[85] In the USA, a new Act called the Anticybersquatting Consumer Protection Act[86] broadly provides for protection against cybersquatting for domain names where those domain names consist of personal names that have been registered as trade marks.

These differing approaches to both registration of personal names as trade marks, and the use of personal names as domain names has already caused quite some conflict: one can imagine that there is a lot more to come.

THE NSI APPROACH TO RESOLUTION OF TRADE MARK AND DOMAIN NAME DISPUTES—THE OLD APPROACH

Historically, a number of the disputes that arose in relation to trade marks and domain names were, at least in part, fuelled by NSI's domain name allocation policy and dispute resolution procedures.[87] What is clear is that in at least some cases of dispute, there were defences to what appeared to be an infringement of a trade mark. Yet it was not clear that these were given full weight in the NSI dispute resolution process.

Without going into in detail, NSI's dispute policy broadly stated that domain names were registered on a first-come, first-served basis.[88] In the event that the

---

[80] For details see 'Oxford University in cybersquatter row', http://news2.thls.bbc.co.uk/hi/english/education/newsi.../694871.st 29 Mar. 2000. After completing this article, the case was heard under the ICANN dispute resolution procedure. Doc Seagle (Mr Oxford University) lost: http://arbiter.wipo.int/domains/decisions/html/d2000-0308.html. A number of other personal names have been considered under this procedure. These include Julia Roberts and Madonna.

[81] *Elvis Presley Enterprises Inc.* v. *Sid Shaw Elvisly Yours, The Times*, 22 Mar. 1999.

[82] Council Reg. 40/94 of 20 Dec. 1993 on the Community Trade Mark.

[83] EU Trade Mark Registration No 648444.

[84] For a discussion on the Arbitration procedures under the ICANN dispute policy see part 5 below.

[85] WIPO Case No D2000–0060.

[86] 106th Congress, 1st Session, S. 1948, Title III Trademark Cyberpiracy Prevention, Sec 3001. For further discussion on this Act see section 6 below.

[87] htp://www.internic.net/domain-info/internic-domain-6.html The latest revision became effective on 28 Feb. 1998.

[88] S. 9 of NSI's policy.

holder of a registered trade mark appeared claiming a 'right' to the domain name (the complainant), NSI would take a number of steps.

1. NSI would determine the domain name registration date.
2. If this date preceded the date of the trade mark registration (of which NSI required a copy), then NSI would take no further steps.
3. If however it was after the date of the trade mark registration, NSI requested evidence of the domain name owners trade mark. The date of registration of the trade mark had to be prior to the date on which the dispute began. If the domain name owner produced this, then no further action was taken.
4. If the creation of the domain name was after the date of the registration of the trade mark owned by the complainant, and the domain name holder had no trade mark pre-dating the complaint, then the domain name holder had to choose within 30 days, one of the following options:
   a. to provide the certified trade mark dated prior to the complaint;
   b. to relinquish the domain name to the complainant;
   c. to register a new and different domain name;
   d. to file a civil action.

If the owner did none of these, then the domain name was put on hold where it would stay until the parties resolved the dispute, or a court determined who was entitled to the domain name or the complainant requested that it not be put on hold.

This dispute resolution policy was rightly criticised for providing far too much ammunition to registered trade mark holders, and taking no cognisance of other intellectual property rights. Thus, the owner of the registered trade mark 'Fellowes' for stationery might be able to wrest the domain name fellowes.com from the garden centre called Fellowes which had registered the domain name first, but which had no registered trade mark right on which to base the name. Many examples of 'stronger' parties using the resolution procedures to their advantage exist.

Two cases which reached court in the USA were *Data Concepts Inc.* v. *Digital Consulting Inc.*[89] over the domain name DCI.com[90] and *CD Solutions Inc.* v. *CDS Networks Inc.*[91] over the domain name cds.com. In both of these cases, a small entity found itself having to take court action in order to preserve a domain name over which there should have been no question but that the right of the first to register should have been preserved. It was the dispute resolution policy, which would have meant that the domain name would have been put on hold, unusable by the first to register, that forced the smaller party into litigation. In the first case over the domain name dci.com, the court found there to be

[89] 6th Cir. No 97–5802, 8/5/98.

[90] It was said in the course of judgment that '[w]hen a domain name is used only to indicate an address on the Internet and not to identify the source of specific goods and services the name is not functioning as a trade mark'.

[91] D Or. Civil No 97–793–HA, 4/22/98.

no confusion, and in the second case over the domain name cds.com, the court found the combination of letters to be generic.[92]

There are many other unreported semi-anecdotal tales of strong-arm tactics used to try to obtain coveted domain names using the NSI dispute resolution policy as a basis. Thus for example, the domain name 'pokey.org' was used by an individual for his Web site because it was the family nickname for him. A toy company challenged this as infringement[93] of one of their registered marks. Again the dispute was fuelled by the provisions of the NSI dispute resolution policy. Other domain names may represent parodies: for example, the domain name mentioned above, peta.org. The animal rights organisation contested the registration under the NSI dispute policy and won because the policy allows no parody defence. The group 'People Eating Tasty Animals' did not have the resources to take court action.

Finally, domain names may have been registered for legitimate commercial use by small businesses who also lacked the resources to defend themselves against an attack by a large company. For example the school supply company that was forced to hand over its 'Pony.com' domain name when confronted by the athletic shoe manufacturer Pony International.

But time has moved on, and in the last year there have been significant changes to both the regulation of domain names, and the dispute resolution procedures.

REGULATION OF DOMAIN NAMES AND TRADE MARK AND DOMAIN NAME DISPUTES—THE NEW GTLD APPROACH

Over the last two years there have been changes to both the management of domain names and the resolution of disputes in the open generic Top Level Domains (gTLDs).[94] NSI, up to September 1998, had sole responsibility for allocation of domain names in the gTLDs, under a contract with the National Science Foundation. This contract expired at the end of September 1998. Prior to that date, there was much discussion about the future regulation of the Internet, not only of allocation domain names under the gTLDs, but in relation to monitoring and promotion of other standards used by the Internet community. One of the first moves was the formation of the International Ad Hoc Committee (IAHC)[95] 'at the initiative of the Internet Society and at the request

---

[92] It was said in the course of judgment that 'CDS cannot now expand their trade mark rights to generic descriptions existing in our everyday language'.

[93] The toy company clearly did not win the battle over the Web site pokey.org as any visitor will see. It is also fascinating to note the extent of technical expertise of a child in the area of web programming—and yet one who cannot spell 'submissions' Follow the links and you will see that the surfer is promised a full account of the battle with the toy company 'coming soon!' (or in web terms, 'under construction').

[94] For full details see http://www.icann.org.

[95] The IAHC was dissolved on 1 May 1997.

of the Internet Assigned Numbers Authority' with a view to trying to resolve the problems created by the domain name system. It proposed that a further seven gTLDs be created, and that multiple competing registrars be set up to administer the system. A memorandum of understanding (MoU)[96] was drafted which provided for, among other things, a council of registrars, a policy advisory board and a policy oversight committee.

Not all were happy. The USA was concerned about the involvement in the IAHC of the International Telecommunication Union, and unclear about the role of other organisations such as WIPO.[97] The US Government expressed the view that reforms should be driven by the private sector, and so initiated a consultation process inviting comments on future regulation of the domain name process. A report was produced.[98] Initially this was viewed with some scepticism by the EU,[99] but eventually agreement attained. From this rather *ad hoc*, self regulatory, state encouraged (controlled?) international mish-mash of events, the Internet Corporation for Assigned Names and Numbers (ICANN) emerged. ICANN is a non-profit corporation which has taken over 'responsibility for the IP address space allocation, protocol parameter assignment, domain name system management, and root server system management functions now performed under US Government contract by IANA and other entities'.[100]

One of the events that occurred during this process was that WIPO was invited to prepare a report on three particular aspects of the domain name process: first, to develop recommendations on how domain name disputes involving cybersquatting could be resolved; secondly to recommend a process for protecting famous marks in the gTLDs; and thirdly to make recommendations for the introduction for new gTLDs.[101] In this role WIPO undertook a number of virtual and physical consultations around the world to achieve the

---

[96] For a full listing of the documents in the discussion and negotiation process see http://www.ntia.doc.gov/ntiahome/domainname.

[97] 'A proposal to improve technical management of Internet names and addresses—discussion draft', 30 Jan. 1998, at http://www.ntia.doc.gov/ntiahome/domainname.

[98] http//www.uspto.gov/web/offices/com/doc/ipnii/index.html.

[99] Replies of the European Community and its Member States to the US Green Paper, http://www.ntia.doc.gov/ntiahome/domainname.

[100] http://www.icann.org.

[101] http://www.ntia.doc.gov/ntiahome/domainname. The invitation was included in the 5 June 1998 Statement of Policy on 'Management of Internet Names and Addresses' (Docket Number 980212036–8146–02) by the Department of Commerce of the United States of America ('the USG White Paper'): 'The U.S. Government will seek international support to call upon the World Intellectual Property Organisation (WIPO) to initiate a balanced and transparent process, which includes the participation of trademark holders and members of the Internet community who are not trademark holders, to (1) develop recommendations for a uniform approach to resolving trademark/domain name disputes involving cyberpiracy (as opposed to conflicts between trademark holders with legitimate competing rights), (2) recommend a process for protecting famous trademarks in the generic top level domains, and (3) evaluate the effects, based on studies conducted by independent organisations, such as the National Research Council of the National Academy of Sciences, of adding new gTLDs and related dispute resolution procedures on trademark and intellectual property holders. These findings and recommendations could be submitted to the board of the new corporation for its consideration in conjunction with its development of registry and registrar policy and the creation and introduction of new gTLDs.'

goals set out in the invitation.[102] In the course of this process WIPO produced an Interim Report[103] which contained some interesting, but highly controversial proposals. Broadly WIPO proposed a scheme for alternative dispute resolution (ADR) of all intellectual property disputes that involved domain names.[104] The suggestion was that, in the event of a dispute, arbitration by WIPO would be compulsory in the first instance, but allow appeal to the court thereafter. As far as choice of law was concerned, WIPO suggested that the Arbitrator should make reference to the particular laws that the circumstances of the case dictated, and to choose from principles established in domain name disputes in national courts, having regard to the interests of the trade mark holder and the registrant.

The proposals were the subject of fierce criticism from a number of quarters.[105] It was argued that the ADR process would invariably favour the holder of the registered trade mark. It was also said that the proposals were far too wide. WIPO (in the invitation to become involved) was only charged with proposing resolution of disputes involving cybersquatting. The proposals in the Interim Report by contrast sought to solve every domain name dispute imaginable. Finally, it was argued that the proposal that different principles of law from various jurisdictions should be applied depending on the dispute and the interests of the litigants, would result in uncertainty and unpredictability in giving advice in future disputes. There is no doubt that these were valid criticisms. WIPO, after a further period of reflection and consultation produced its Final Report[106] which changed quite significantly from the Interim Report. There were three significant recommendations: first, the proposal that ICANN should adopt a dispute resolution policy, under which a uniform administrative dispute resolution procedure be made mandatory for domain name disputes in all gTLDs. In contrast to the proposal in the Interim Report, the suggestion in the Final Report was that the scope of this administrative procedure be limited to *abusive domain name registration*.[107] It was not, however, to be limited to famous or well-known marks (cybersquatting), but to cover all those domain names where they are identical or confusingly similar to a trade mark or service mark in which another party (the complainant) has rights, although registration

---

[102] See generally http://ecommerce.wipo.int/domains/process/eng/processhome.html.

[103] http://wipo2.wipo.int/process/eng/processhome.html.

[104] WIPO Interim Report, para. 115: 'any dispute concerning a domain name could go before its administrative panels'.

[105] A particularly perceptive critique was produced by Professor Michael Froomkin, University of Miami which is well worth reading. See http://www.law.miami.edu/~amf.

[106] http://wipo2.wipo.int/process/eng/processhome.html.

[107] The problem of deciding exactly what is a famous mark remains. Interestingly, in its Final Report WIPO make reference to 'a very popular web site associated with the sale of books' and if that brings a particular name to mind, that may well qualify as a famous mark. But even here, we are on rocky territory as it transpires that Amazon.com was sued by a feminist bookstore in Minnesota called Amazon Bookstore Inc. claiming that amazon.com is causing confusion among its customers about its affiliation (or non-affiliation) with amazon.com. http://www.bizreport. com/news/1999/04/990416–3.htm. Amazon book store has never officially registered Amazon as a trade mark, but nonetheless has used it since 1970. Amazon.com opened its web doors in July 1995. It is understood that the action has now settled, although details do not appear to be available.

of the mark is not necessary. The second proposal in the Final Report[108] was that there should be various exclusions put into operation for holders of well-known and famous marks in the open gTLDs.[109] A panel of experts would be set up who would decide[110] whether a mark was sufficiently famous or well known enough to qualify for an exclusion. If exclusion were granted, then the registries would not register a domain name consisting of the trade mark for anyone but the trade mark holder. For similar domain names, a presumption would operate whereby the holder of the exclusion relating to the mark, who wanted to challenge a domain name registered by an unrelated party, would be required to show that the domain name was confusingly similar to the mark which was the subject of the exclusion, and that the domain name was being used in a way that was likely to damage the interests of the owner of the mark. On showing this, the burden of proof in the procedure would shift to the domain name registrant to justify that its registration of the domain made was in good faith, and to show why that registration should not be cancelled.[111] The third proposal concerned the introduction of new gTLDs. WIPO recommended that new gTLDs should only be introduced when improved registration practices were introduced, together with the dispute resolution procedures and exclusions suggested in the WIPO report.

These proposals were submitted to ICANN for consideration. ICANN has its own procedures whereby proposals are considered by one or other of its working parties.[112] Members of the public at large can become involved through discussion lists.[113] Of the three recommendations made by WIPO, to date only an amended form of the dispute resolution procedure has been implemented. The ICANN Domain Names Supporting Organisation (DNSO) is currently working on formulating recommendations on whether new gTLDs should be introduced, and if so how many, and what, if any, limitations on registration should apply. The DNSO has invited comments to be submitted by 20 April 2000.[114]

---

[108] ICANN 'provisionally endorsed' the proposals from WIPO which were passed on to DNSO (Domain Name Supporting Organisation), one of ICANN's supporting organisations, for further consideration: http://www.nytimes.com/library/tech/99/05/cyber/articles/28domain.html. For the DNSO Web site see http://www.dnso.org.

[109] It was proposed that new gTLDs should only be introduced as and when the measures in the WIPO report have been adopted and been shown to work.

[110] The criteria to be used would be those adopted by WIPO SCT plus the following criterion: evidence of the mark is the subject of attempts by non-authorised third parties to register the same or misleadingly similar names as domain names.

[111] WIPO Final Report, para. 289.

[112] http://www.dnso.org.

[113] http://www.icann.org.

[114] http://www.icann.org/dnso/new-gtlds-01apr00.htm. Since the time of writing, it has been argued that new gTLDs will be introduced. It is not yet known how many or what they will be. Interestingly, it would appear that, in an effort to get new domains in advance, the US Patent Office has been inundated with applications for trademarks for yet to be created domains, e.g. sex.web, http://www.wired.com/news/politics/0,1283,38824,00.html.

The Dispute Resolution Procedure

On 24 October 1999 ICANN adopted a dispute resolution policy, based partly on the proposals submitted by WIPO, but amended to reflect concerns that had been raised, in particular that some aspects of the policy did not adequately meet individual and non-commercial uses of trade marks, free speech defences, the right to court review of a decision, and the iniquities of *reverse domain-name hijacking*.[115]

In general, ICANN's dispute resolution policy provides that registrars receiving complaints concerning the impact of domain names they have registered on trade marks or service marks will take no action until they receive instructions from the domain name holder or an order of a court, arbitrator, or other neutral decision-maker deciding the parties' dispute. In cases of abusive domain name registration, the complaining party (the complainant) can invoke a special administrative procedure to resolve the dispute. Under this procedure, the dispute will be decided by neutral persons selected from panels established for that purpose. The procedure will be handled in large part online, and is designed to take less than 45 days. Parties to such disputes are also able to go to court to resolve their disputes or to contest the outcome of the procedure.[116]

The important parts of the dispute resolution policy state (where 'you' have registered the domain name that is contested by the Complainant):

4 a. Applicable Disputes. You are required to submit to a mandatory administrative proceeding in the event that a third party (a 'complainant') asserts to the applicable Provider, in compliance with the Rules of Procedure, that

(i) your domain name is identical or confusingly similar to a trademark or service mark in which the complainant has rights; and
(ii) you have no rights or legitimate interests in respect of the domain name; and
(iii) your domain name has been registered and is being used in bad faith.

In the administrative proceeding, the complainant must prove that each of these three elements are present.

b. Evidence of Registration and Use in Bad Faith. For the purposes of Paragraph 4(a)(iii), the following circumstances, in particular but without limitation, if found by the Panel to be present, shall be evidence of the registration and use of a domain name in bad faith:

(i) circumstances indicating that you have registered or you have acquired the domain name primarily for the purpose of selling, renting, or otherwise transferring the domain name registration to the complainant who is the owner of the trademark or service mark or to a competitor of that complainant, for valuable consideration in excess of your documented out-of-pocket costs directly related to the domain name; or

---

[115] http://www.icann.org.
[116] *Ibid.*

(ii) you have registered the domain name in order to prevent the owner of the trademark or service mark from reflecting the mark in a corresponding domain name, provided that you have engaged in a pattern of such conduct; or

(iii) you have registered the domain name primarily for the purpose of disrupting the business of a competitor; or

(iv) by using the domain name, you have intentionally attempted to attract, for commercial gain, Internet users to your web site or other on-line location, by creating a likelihood of confusion with the complainant's mark as to the source, sponsorship, affiliation, or endorsement of your web site or location or of a product or service on your web site or location.[117]

Each of the competing registrars authorised to register names in the .com, .org and .net gTLDs,[118] must sign up to this dispute resolution process.[119] Those who register domain names then agree to be bound when registering a domain name. So the policy is (or will be[120]) uniform in these gTLDs. So far, three[121] providers have been accredited as recognised to hear disputes arising under this dispute resolution process.[122] WIPO, the National Arbitration Forum, and the Disputes.org/cResolution.ca Consortium (eResolution).[123]

A Sample of Disputes Heard under the Dispute Resolution Policy

To date (6 April 2000), 260 cases have been filed with WIPO,[124] 288 cases with the National Arbitration Forum,[125] and 38 with eResolution.[126] WIPO has made decisions in 66 of the cases, of which 52 domain names have been ordered to be handed back to the complainant, and 14 remain with the person registering the domain name (the respondent). The National Arbitration forum has so far ordered 46 domain names to be handed back to the complainant, and allowed nine to remain with the respondent. eResolution has decided seven cases, and ordered five to be transferred to the complainant, while two have stayed with the respondent.

---

[117] http://www.icann.org/udrp/udrp-policy-24oct99.htm.

[118] For details see http://www.icann.org/registrars/accredited-list.html.

[119] A full list of these registries can be found at http://www.icann.org.

[120] Originally, NSI was given some leeway in the deadline for implementation of the policy because of the large number of people in its existing database it would have to contact: http://www.icann.org.

[121] A fourth was approved in May. CPR Institute for Dispute Resolution will begin accepting complaints on 22 May.

[122] http://www.icann.org.

[123] Information about the providers can be found at http://www.icann.org. Recently a fourth provider has been approved, CPR Dispute Resolution.

[124] http://arbiter.wipo.int/domains. By 20 Sept. 2000 well over 1000 cases had been filed with WIPO. A similar, although not quite so dramatic, increase is evident at the other dispute resolution providers. This gives some indication of the success of the procedure, at least for complainants.

[125] http://www.arbforum.com/domains.

[126] http://www.eresolution.ca.

Whose Law Applies when Arbitrators Decide a Dispute?

The rules under the ICANN policy give to the Panel deciding the case the authority to take into account the ICANN rules and 'any rules and principles of law that it deems applicable'.[127]

The first decision was made by WIPO in *World Wrestling Federation Inc* v. *Michael Bosman*.[128] The dispute was over the domain name worldwrestling federation.com which had been registered with MelbourneIT in Australia, but both the complainant and the respondent were domiciled in the US. The ICANN dispute resolution policy requires a complainant to show that the domain name has been registered and *used* in bad faith to prove abusive registration. It did appear in this case that the thorny issues over 'use' might prove to present the same sorts of problems that they have for the terrestrial courts. In order to determine what was meant by 'use' the Arbitrator looked to two US cases, *Panavision International LP* v. *Dennis Toeppen*[129]and *Intermatic Inc* v. *Toeppen*.[130] No cases from any other jurisdiction were considered. The arbitrator found that the act of registering the domain name and offering it for sale to the Wrestling Federation was sufficient to constitute use. As far as any legitimate use that Michael Bosman might have been making of the domain name, the arbitrator noted that he had not developed a Web site, nor was it his nickname, nor the name of a member of his family, the name of a household pet, nor or in any other way identified with or related to any legitimate interest that he had. Thus the domain name was ordered to be transferred to the complainant.

The second case decided by WIPO, *Robert Ellenbogen* v. *Mike Pearson*[131] concerned the domain name musicweb.com. US law was again referred to for guidance. The arbitrator pointed to the ICANN rules and to the WIPO Final Report which stated 'if the parties to the procedure were resident in one country, the domain was registered through a registrant in that country and the evidence of bad faith registration and use of the domain name related to actively in the same country, it would be appropriate for the decision-maker to refer to the law of the country concerned'.[132] In this case, the complainant, respondent and the registrar were all domiciled in the USA. *Intermatic Inc.* v. *Toeppen* was again referred to for clarification of the word 'use' with the result that the domain name was ordered to be transferred to the complainant.

---

[127] ICANN Rules for Uniform Domain Name Dispute Resolution Policy. Policy adopted: 26 Aug. 1999; implementation documents approved: 24 Oct. 1999. Rule 15. Panel Decisions: (a) A Panel shall decide a complaint on the basis of the statements and documents submitted and in accordance with the Policy, these Rules and any rules and principles of law that it deems applicable: http://www.icann.org/udrp/udrp-rules-24oct99.htm.

[128] WIPO Case no D99–0001 http://arbiter.wipo.int/domains/index.html.

[129] 141 F 3d 1316 (9th Cir 1998).

[130] 947 F Supp. 1227 (ND Ill. 1996).

[131] WIPO Case No D00–0001.

[132] http://ecommerce.wipo.int/domains/process/eng/processhome.html.

By contrast, the focus of the arbitrators from the National Arbitration Forum would appear to have been on paragraph 4(a) of the ICANN dispute resolution policy (reproduced above) rather than on the law of any particular jurisdiction. An arbitrator from eResolution on the other hand quoted both the US Anticybersquatting Consumer Protection Act and a recent US case[133] in a decision where the complainant and respondent were based in California.[134] Other, more recent cases from each of the providers seem to lay more stress on Article 4 of the dispute resolution policy, emphasising the need for the complainant to prove that she has rights in the name, that the respondent has no legitimate interests, and that the name has been registered and used in bad faith.

What Constitutes Bad Faith?

A very important part of the dispute policy requires the complainant to show that the respondent has registered and used the domain name that is being contested in 'bad faith'. A number of factors are emerging which are clarifying the meaning of 'bad faith'. Thus, efforts by the respondent to sell a domain name tend to weigh in favour of finding bad faith,[135] but are not necessarily fatal.[136] In common with well-established principles of trade mark law, intentionally creating a likelihood of confusion for consumers will count against the respondent.[137] In addition, failure to use a domain name,[138] as well as failure to defend against allegations of abusive registration, can count against the respondent, as can a pattern of registering domain names incorporating various names unrelated to the business of the respondent.[139]

However, the mere fact that the complainant has a registered trade mark covering the domain name does not give automatic rights in the domain name. In addition, if the respondent registers a domain name that incorporates the

[133] *Sporty's Farm LLC* v. *Sportsman's Market Inc*, 2000 US App Lexis 1246 53 USPQ 2D (BNA) 1570.

[134] *Beverages and More Inc* v. *Glenn Sobel Mgt*, eResolution Case No AF–0092 beveragesandmore.com.

[135] *Robert Ellenbogen* v. *Mike Pearson*, WIPO Case No D00–0001 musicweb.com; *Mary-Lynn Mondich and American Vintage Wine Biscuits Inc* v. *Shane Brown, t/a Big Daddy's Antiques*, WIPO Case No D00–0004 americanvintage.com; *Mr Walter Latham* v. *Mr Todd Shurn*, National Arbitration Forum File No FA0002000094184 kingsofcomedy.com; *Marriot International Inc* v. *Café au Lait*, File No FA0002000093670, National Arbitration Forum marriott-hotel.com.

[136] *Storage Technology Corporation* v. *Network Systems GA Inc*, National Arbitration Forum File No FA0002000094188 networksystems.com.

[137] *Alcoholics Anonymous World Services Inc* v. *Lauren Raymond*, WIPO Case No D2000–007, alcoholicsanonymous.com; *Hollywood Casino Corporation* v. *Global Interactive*, National Arbitration Forum File No FA0002000094107: Hollywood-casino.com and hollywood-casino.net to be transferred to complainant and hollywoodgoldcasino.com and hollywoodgoldcasino.net to be cancelled.

[138] *Entercolor Technologies Corporation* v. *Gigantor Software Development Inc*, National Arbitration Forum File No FA0002000093635 gigantor.com.

[139] *America Online Inc* v. *iDomainNames.com*, National Arbitration Forum File No FA0002000093766 go2aol.com.

complainant's trade mark, and offers to sell that domain name, that may not of itself amount to abusive registration. Rather, the burden of proof is on the complainant to show that all elements of the dispute resolution policy are fulfilled. In *Car Toys Inc* v. *Informa Unlimited Inc.,*[140] Informa registered the domain name cartoys.net. Car Toys Inc., the owner of the trade mark 'Car Toys', demanded that this be relinquished to it. Informa refused. The Arbitrator found the fact that Car Toys Inc. had a trade mark in the words was irrelevant. What was more, Informa was in the business of buying and developing descriptive domain names for sale, but that activity of itself did not constitute abusive registration. Car Toys Inc. had therefore not proven that Informa had no legitimate interest in respect of the domain name in dispute, and the domain name could stay with Informa. This case is particularly interesting because it tends to suggest that the practice of buying and selling descriptive domain names is perfectly acceptable, so long as it is not done in bad faith.[141] This seems to be particularly so where the name is generic.[142]

Free Speech

Questions of free speech in connection with domain names have surfaced and been considered under the ICANN dispute resolution procedure. Prior to the introduction of this policy, US courts had already grappled with such domain names as 'ballysucks.com' and verizonreallysucks.com [142a]. In a decision under the ICANN rules concerning the name natwestsucks.com, the arbitrator said:

> "Those who have genuine grievances against others or wish to express criticisms of them—whether they are against commercial or financial institutions, against governments, against charitable, sporting or cultural institutions, or whatever—must be at liberty, within the confines set by the laws of relevant jurisdictions, to express their views. If today they use a website or an email address for the purpose they are entitled to select a domain name which leads others easily to them, if the name is still available".[142b]

In this case, the respondent had to hand the domain name to the complainant. But that was because the respondent said it had been registered in order to prevent unscrupulous third parties obtaining the domain name to make criticisms of the institution. The respondent had offered it for sale to the complainant. The case does however suggest that there will be circumstances in which the respondent will be able to hold on to a similar name if the purpose is to make legitimate criticism.

---

[140] National Arbitration Forum File No FA 0002000093682.
[141] See also *Shirmax Retail Ltd* v. *CES Marketing Group Inc*, eResolution AF-0104 thyme.com.
[142] *Ibid.*
[142a] Apparently also registered is VerizonShouldSpendMoreTimeFixingItsNetworkAndLess MoneyOnLawyers.com, http://www.2600.com/news/2000/0508.html
[142b] http://arbiter.wipo.int/domains/decisions/html/d2000-0636.html

Comment

The number of cases being filed with the accredited dispute providers is increasing quickly. To date, and after a rather slow start, it appears that the arbitrators are coming to grips with some of the nuances of the dispute resolution policy, with the result that we are seeing some very interesting decisions. No longer does a registration of a trade mark give an automatic right to a domain name, a feature that was the subject of much criticism under the NSI policy, although we have yet to see what the dispute providers will decide if the respondent argues parody, or any one of the other possible defences discussed above.

With the numbers of disputes being referred to the accredited dispute providers it appears that complainants at least are in favour of the new procedure.[143] This may become all the more evident when new gTLDs are introduced in due course. However, it should be remembered that the dispute policy is limited to abusive registration cases, and to disputes in the gTLDs.[144] It remains to be seen what will happen if a complainant raises a case before one of the ICANN dispute resolution providers, loses the case, but then proceeds before a national court.[145] This is a procedure that is possible in terms of the ICANN dispute policy. The dispute policy is described as mandatory, but only meaning that a respondent agrees to submit himself to the dispute process. Merely because a dispute is referred to one of the accredited dispute providers under the dispute resolution policy does not preclude recourse to a national court for determination of the dispute either before the ICANN dispute procedure is instigated, or after the proceedings under the process are concluded.[146] Whereas this facility has had wide support,[147] it does mean that national policy bias may override attempts at global solutions, thus fragmenting attempts at global dispute resolution.

---

[143] Some commentators are in favour of the new procedure. Oborne, 'The ICANN Decisions—What Have we Learned?, *Computers and Law* Vol 11 Issue 1 April/May 2000, 32. Other commentators are, however, much more circumspect, pointing out that the majority of decisions are made in favour of trade mark holders, and questioning whether arbitrators are following the narrow parameters established by the board for reassigning domain names. http://www.qlinks.net/items/qlitem7428.htm.

[144] For discussion on the dispute resolution policy in the .uk ccTLD see Black, ch. 8 in this vol. Some countries are now also using the procedure. See http://arbiter.wipo.int/domains/cctld/index.html.

[145] Apparently a US court has recently discussed the effect of the ICANN domain name dispute resolution process on its right to rule. The court found that it is not bound by an ICANN decision but it declined to state what degree of deference, if any, it would give to an ICANN decision. The case stems from parallel proceedings launched in a US court and under the ICANN dispute resolution process. The case can be found in LEXIS as *Armitage Hardware* v. *Weber-Stephen Products*. The ICANN decision on the disputed names was still pending at the time of writing.

[146] Uniform Domain Name Dispute Resolution Policy, para. 4.k.

[147] WIPO Final Report http://wipo2.wipo.int para. 139.

The USA has already passed domestic legislation aimed at the practice of cyber-squatting. The Anticybersquatting Consumer Protection Act provides that a person can be found liable for actual or statutory damages[148] where the intent, with bad faith[149] is to profit from the goodwill of another's trade mark, by registering or using a domain name that is identical with, confusingly similar to, or which dilutes a trade mark, without regard to the goods or services of the parties.[150]

In rem Jurisdiction

One particular aspect that is of some concern in the Anticybersquatting Consumer Protection Act is the facilitation of an *in rem* action. An *in rem* action is one where action is taken against property, rather than against a person. For domain name disputes, the property against which action is taken is the registration certificate of the domain name kept at the registry where the domain name has been registered. Prior to the passing of the Anticybersquatting

[148] In civil actions against cybersquatters, the plaintiff is authorised to recover actual damages and profits, or may elect before final judgment to award of statutory damages of not less than $1,000 and not more than $100,000 per domain name, as the court considers just. The court is directed to remit statutory damages in any case where the infringer reasonably believed that use of the domain name was a fair or otherwise lawful use.

[149] The legislation outlines the following non-exclusive list of eight factors for courts to consider in determining whether such bad-faith intent to profit is proven:
(i)   the trademark rights of the domain name registrant in the domain name;
(ii)   whether the domain name is the legal or nickname of the registrant;
(iii)   the prior use by the registrant of the domain name in connection with the bona fide offering of any goods or services;
(iv)   the registrant's legitimate noncommercial or fair use of the mark at the site under the domain name;
(v)   the registrant's intent to divert consumers from the mark's owner's online location in a manner that could harm the mark's goodwill, either for commercial gain or with the intent to tarnish or disparage the mark, by creating a likelihood of confusion as to the source, sponsorship, affiliation or endorsement of the site;
(vi)   the registrant's offer to sell the domain name for substantial consideration without having or having an intent to use the domain name in the bona fide offering of goods or services;
(vii)   the registrant's intentional provision of material false and misleading contact information when applying for the registration of the domain name;
and
(viii) the registrant's registration of multiple domain names that are identical or similar to or dilutive of another's trademark.

[150] A number of claims have already been filed using this new law: one concerning the National Football League over the domains nfltoday.org, nfltoday.com, and nfltoday.net; http://www.mercurycenter.com/svtech/news/breaking/internet/docs/116821513.htm; once concerning Harvard University against a man who owns 65 domains with the word 'Harvard': http://www.boston.com/dailyglobe2/342/metro/Harvard_seeks_rights_to_own_name_in_cyber_suit+.shtml; and one concerning New Zealand's America's Cup team in relation to the domain name americascup.com: http://www.nytimes.com/library/tech/99/12/biztech/articles/09net.html.

Consumer Protection Act, Porsche[151] had commenced an action by filing an *in rem* complaint against a number of domain names that incorporated the name 'Porsche'. Just some of these domain names are reproduced below giving something of a flavour of the problem faced by Porsche.

porschecar.com porschagirls.com 928porsche.com accessories4porsche.com allporsche.com beverlyhillsporsche.com buyaporsche.com calporsche.com e-porsche.com everythingporschie.com formulaporsche.com ianporsche.com idoporsche.com laporsche.com myporsche.com newporsche.com parts4porsche.com passion-porsche.com porsche.net porsche-911.com porsche-944.com porsche-autos.com porsche-books.com porsche-carrera.com porsche-cars.com porsche-classic.com porsche-net.com porsche-nl.com porsche-online.com porsche-rs.com porsche-sales.com porsche-service.com porsche-supercup.com porsche-web.com porsche356.com porsche4me.com porsche4sale.com porsche911.com porsche911.net porsche911.org porsche911parts.com porscheag.com porscheaudiparts.com porschebooks.com porschecars.com porschecarsales.com porschecasino.com porschechat.com porschedealer.com

These domain names had all been registered by different individuals or entities, many of whom had given false information in the application procedure with NSI. By commencing an *in rem* action Porsche was trying to avoid the issues of having to locate and establish personal jurisdiction over the holders of all the domain names. Porsche thus requested the domain name registration certificates located at the offices of NSI (in Virginia) to be transferred to Porsche, or forfeited, because they diluted its trade marks. On 8 June 1999 the action was dismissed on the ground that the US Trade Mark Dilution Act, under which the action was taken, did not allow *in rem* proceedings in these circumstances. The court said that it did not consider that Congress intended that the Trade Mark Dilution Act be operated in such a way as to 'ignore traditional notions of fair play and substantial justice'.[152]

However, just this type of action has been re-introduced in the USA in the Anticybersquatting Consumer Protection Act. This Act provides that the owner of a mark may file an *in rem* civil action against a domain name in the district in which the domain name authority which registered the domain name is located, if they cannot locate or obtain *in personam* jurisdiction over the person or entity who registered the domain name.[153] This procedure has now been considered in

---

[151] *Porsche Cars North America Inc. v. Porsche.com*, ED Va No 99–0006–A, complaint filed 1/6/99. The case was subsequently vacated and remanded by the 4th Circuit Court of Appeal in June since the District Court did not consider the effect of the Anticybersquatting Consumer Protection Act 2000 US App. LEXIS 12843

[152] For full details see http://www.mama-tech.com/pc.html.

[153] Anticybercysquatting Consumer Protection Act 1999 s. 3002 amending s. 43 of the Trademark Act of 1946 (15 USC 1125).

Caesars World, Inc v. *Caesars-Palace.Com, et al.*[154] and found not to violate the Due Process clause of the US Constitution. In effect, the result is that the court in Virginia has claimed jurisdiction over all domain names which have been registered with NSI. Presumably the US courts would give the same answer should an action be brought in any of the other jurisdictions in the USA where the competing registries are now located. Anyone considering registering in one of the open gTLDs, and wishing to avoid the possibility of being subject to this action, might be well advised to register with one of the registries not located in the USA, and therefore not subject to the provisions of the Anticybersquatting Consumer Protection Act.[155]

The question arises whether the UK should be considering domestic legislation to deal with trade mark and domain name disputes. As we have seen, UK courts are able to deal adequately with cases under existing law where it is not pled that a famous or well-known mark is in question. It is only when these issues arise that problems occur in taking cognisance of possible legitimate defences to actions of trade mark infringement. In many ways it may be preferable for the time being to wait and see how the ICANN dispute resolution procedure develops. Although the procedure concerns only the gTLDs, and thus many disputes in the ccTLDs will still come before national courts (if litigated). Nonetheless, if workable and balanced solutions are developed at this level, then perhaps similar provisions could be considered for domestic disputes. A rush to implement national solutions may have the effect of fragmenting the rather fragile framework that is emerging.[156] Indeed, this is one of the dangers faced as a result of the US initiatives. When the Anticybersquatting Consumer Protection Act was introduced,[157] it was said:

> [These proposals] are not intended in any way to frustrate these global efforts already underway to develop inexpensive and expeditious procedures for resolving domain name disputes that avoid costly and time-consuming litigation in the court systems either here or abroad. In fact, the bill and amendment expressly provide liability limitations for domain name registrars, registries or other domain name registration authorities when they take actions pursuant to a reasonable policy prohibiting the registration of domain names that are identical, confusingly similar to or dilutive of another's trademark. The ICANN and WIPO consideration of these issues will inform the development by domain name registrars and registries of such reasonable policies.

Whether the ICANN and new US provisions can live happily side by side will only be determined once we are able to assess what US courts will decide if a

---

[154] Civil Action No. 99–550–A (EDVa., 3 Mar. 2000). In a subsequent case, *Heathmount AE Corp* v. *Technodrome* 2000 US Dist LEXIS 10591, the court found that it did not have personal jurisdiction based on registration of the domain name in Virginia, but allowed the *in rem* action to proceed.

[155] The ICANN website http://www.icann.org contains full details of the competing registries, including where they are located.

[156] It is debatable whether national initiatives would tip the balance in favour of respondants. See fn 144 above.

[157] For a view from the USA as to why the Act is a bad idea see http://www.nandotimes.com/technology/story/0,1643,500059069-500097375-500389377-0,00.html.

complainant who loses under the administrative procedure takes a case to a US court. If, in these cases, and given the favourable provisions of the Anticybersquatting Consumer Protection Act for mark holders, the complainant consistently wins cases,[158] then the credibility of the ICANN procedure will be undermined. If the UK introduces its own domestic measures, the danger is that a pattern of regulatory competition will emerge, and other jurisdictions may also take protectionery measures.

FINAL THOUGHTS

As can be concluded from the above discussion, a great deal is happening in domain name terms at the moment, and will no doubt continue to happen over the coming weeks, months and years. Particular areas to watch for developments include the decisions made under the ICANN dispute resolution procedure and the patterns emerging: decisions about when new gTLDs will be introduced and what they will be, and whether the exclusions suggested by WIPO will be introduced in the gTLDs for famous and well-known marks. If this last proposal is taken further, all the difficult questions over the definition of famous and well-known marks will resurface. WIPO has recently commenced a further round of consultations on questions of domain names. They aim to produce a report during 2000 making suggestions in relation to bad faith, abusive domain name registrations which violate *inter alia*:

— intellectual property rights aside from trademarks, including geographical indications (such as wine producing regions) and personality rights (such as the names of celebrities);
— the names and acronyms of international and governmental organisations (such as the United Nations);
— unfair competition law and the rights established under International Treaties.

---

[158] One US case which came in for much criticism from the International Internet community was fought over the domain name, etoy.com. A group of artists in Europe registered the domain name etoy.com in 1995. They used the Web site to mimic activities carried out by large organisations. Etoys.com, the toy retailer, sued etoy for the domain name after it had been contacted by members of the public complaining that children had accessed the etoy.com site by mistake, and found some inappropriate material. EToys did not go on-line until 1997 and sells toys. On 29 Nov. 1999 a Los Angeles Superior Court judge issued a preliminary injunction against etoy, threatening the artists with fines of as much as $10,000 a day unless they stopped using the etoy.com address. In response etoy went into hiding. However, the 'Internet Community' joined forces behind etoy, and a number of e-mail messages in favour of etoy were sent to eToys, and various Web sites were set up discussing the pros and cons of the case. In response, eToys dropped the case against etoy on 29 Dec. 1999 and agreed to pay their legal fees. Information can be found at http://news.cnet.com/news/0–1007–200–1531854.html; http://www.wired.com/news/politics/0,1283,33907,00.html; and http://www.nytimes.com/library/tech/00/01/cyber/articles/26etoy.html. The dispute, and its resolution, is a very interesting example of Internet self-regulation.

These negotiations are well worth following and indeed commenting on, online.[159]

It was said at the outset that if the domain name problems were not solved, the end of the Internet was nigh. That has, happily, not happened, and neither will it happen because there is just too much at stake. Governments around the world are doing what they can to promote the use of the Internet for e-commerce, and use is growing exponentially.[160] The disputes over trade marks and domain names represent just one of the tangled legal problems that arise with this burgeoning use. Over the years, progress has been made in devising ways to resolve these disputes, but in the drive to commercialisation of the Internet, sight should not be lost of the fact that there are many millions of ordinary and small commercial users of the Internet whose legitimate interests should not be ignored.

[159] http://wipo2.wipo.int/process2/index.html. WIPO have also considered trademark use on the internet in general See: 'Standing committee on the law of trademarks, industrial designs and geographical indications', Fourth Session, Geneva, 27–31 Mar. 2000. 'Draft provisions concerning protection of trademarks and other distinctive signs on the Internet' available at http://www.wipo.int/eng/main.htm.

[160] For the UK position see 'A Performance and Innovation Unit Report', *The Cabinet Office*, Sept. 1999.

8

Forthcoming Internet Trade Mark Disputes?

CHARLOTTE WAELDE

The purpose of this brief chapter is to take a light hearted look at some of the trade mark disputes that have arisen on the Internet which do not involve domain names. The reader will not find any in-depth comment, merely a brief look at the US to see what is currently happening there.

It has always somewhat surprised this writer that these types of disputes have not featured more prominently in litigation in the courts in this country, and that to date, the focus of the reported litigation has been squarely on the trade mark and domain name disputes.[1] However, we are now seeing more reported cases and anecdotal tales from around the world, and in particular from the US (where else!), which may just give a foretaste of what we might face in the UK.

The focus will be on the disputes concerning registered trade marks, although in a number of cases unregistered marks have been in issue and therefore pertinent for the laws of unfair competition. Although we have no tradition of unfair competition in this country, our law of passing off may be relevant, to at least some of the disputes.

TRADE MARKS WITHIN A WEB SITE

Trade marks, both registered and unregistered, have been appearing within web sites compiled by a person who is not the trade mark owner, and who is not associated with the trade mark owner. There are a variety of ways in which this has occurred: for instance the trade mark may appear in the body of some text on the web site, or on a menu bar or in a repeating watermark (an image in the back ground of web pages) throughout the web site. Such is the imagination of Internet users that they have popped up in surprising ways.

The courts have, in most cases to date, been applying terrestrial trade mark law without any hesitation and, subject to the novel technical issues that have arisen because of the technical nature of the Internet, without any problem. In *Richards v Cable News Network Inc.*[2] the issue concerned the phrase 'World

---

[1] For in depth comment see Waelde Chapter 7.
[2] E D Pa No 98–3165 7/28/98.

Beat' which had been registered in US by Richards for pre-recorded audio cassettes, phonograph records and compact discs. CNN (the news programme)
launched a feature news programme and web site called 'World Beat'. They
used the term World Beat within the web site for the news programme. CNN
did not, however, sell music on its web site. Richards alleged trade mark
infringement and sought preliminary injunction preventing CNN from using
the name World Beat in connection with the web site. The court applied the traditional likelihood of confusion test, as to the similarity of goods and services,
and found that the record label owned by Richards related to a distinctive style
of music. By contrast, CNN's program covered news from around the world.
Accordingly there was no likelihood of confusion between the goods and services covered by the registration, and the way in which the phrase was used by
CNN. In making judgement the court noted that Richards was trying to extend
the protections for his trademark beyond pre-recorded music into the more general category of news and entertainment.

Another case concerning the use of a trade mark within a web site was *Bally
Total Fitness Holding Corp* v *Faber*.[3] Bally operates a fitness club, and Faber
had obviously at some point used the facilities provided by Bally but was not
impressed. He produced a web site, and on one page he used the term 'bally
sucks' in his criticism of the health club. Bally asserted that this use diluted and
infringed their trade mark. The court said that the dilution argument failed
because Faber was not using the mark in commerce. Rather what Faber was
doing was reviewing the service provided by Bally, and in so doing he could use
the mark to identify the service he was complaining about. There was no likelihood of consumer confusion either. The services provided by Faber—web site
design services—were not likely to be confused with those provided by Bally—
health and fitness. Accordingly, no consumer would consider that Faber's site
was affiliated to connected with or sponsored by Bally. Interestingly, the court
also said that if he had used the term 'Ballysucks.com' there would still be no
consumer confusion, as it would not be likely that anyone would be confused.[4]

A third case where trade marks have been used within a web site is *Mattel Inc.*
v *Jcom Inc.*[5] Jcom operated a web site which offered for sale adult entertainment services. The site played a video which featured an actress by the name of
Barbie. The words 'Barbie's Playhouse' were on the site in a font and colour
scheme similar to those associated with Mattel's doll. Mattel brought an action
for trade mark dilution. The court found that the 'Barbie' mark is famous, and
the use of Barbie's playhouse in the font and colouring most associated with
Barbie, and the use of a doll like figure similar to the form of a Barbie doll,
diluted Mattel's 'Barbie' trade mark. Therefore the trade marks were infringed.
This case is most interesting as the focus was not really on the name—although

[3] *Bally Total Fitness Holding Corp* v *Faber* CD Calif No CV 98–1278 DDP (MANx) 12/21/98/.
[4] For a discussion on 'sucks' domains and free speech Waelde Ch. 7 in this vol.
[5] SDNY No 97 Civ 7191 (SS) 9/10/98.

it was relevant—but it also concerned other signs which can operate as trade marks. Given our relaxed regime in the UK for what will now qualify as a trade mark[6] and some of the most interesting registrations that have been accepted, we might be looking forward to some equally interesting trade mark infringement actions!

USING A TRADE MARK TO LINK TO THE SITE OF ANOTHER

The Internet works by creating a seamless web of hypertext links from one site to another allowing the surfer to glide effortlessly from one body of information to another. But in creating these links, often the name of the company, or the registered trade mark, is used by the site on which the link is created. This may be as part of the Uniform Resource Locator (URL), or may be the actual registered logo of a particular business.[7] Often there is no problem and certainly no infringement for trade mark law. Admittedly the owner of the registered trade mark will want to 'police' the use of the mark to ensure that the use does not become generic, but when the link is used purely as a link, then there is no question of confusion of dilution, nor indeed taking advantage of the repute of the registered mark. However, disputes have occurred where the link is made to a page deep within the receiving web site rather than to the home page. There are a number of reasons why the receiving web site may not want links to deep within the site. In some cases it may be that the home page, which carries the all important advertising paid for by third parties, is bypassed. This, in turn, threatens the revenue stream from the advertisers. We have already seen this issue implicit in the case of *Shetland Times* v *Wills*[8] in Scotland, which was challenged using the law of copyright rather than trade mark law.[9] *Ticketmaster v Microsoft*[10] in the US considered the same issues but using the law of trade marks. Ticketmaster sued Microsoft over Microsoft's use of hyperlinks that connected web users from Microsoft's page, directly to the ticket sales portions of Ticketmasters' site. Thus Ticketmaster's home page was bypassed, and so surfers did not see the advertisements. Ticketmaster alleged unfair trade practices and trade mark dilution. This case has now settled[11] sadly leaving us without court guidance as to whether such practices will be frowned upon or

---

[6] Trade Marks Act 1994 Section 1. All manner of signs have now been registered as trade marks. For example, the mini car; the Toblerone Bar; the Prit Stick glue container; the colour violet for chocolate. Also a number of sounds have been registered. The sound of a dog barking; the 'Direct Line' telephone jingle.

[7] See for example http://www.butterworths.co.uk/homepage.htm.

[8] 1997 SC 316; 1997 SLT 669; 1997 SCLR 160; [1997] FSR 604; [1997] EMLR 277.

[9] See MacQueen, *Law and the Internet: Regulating Cyberspace* in Edwards and Waelde (eds) (Oxford: Hart, 1997).

[10] CV 97–3055 RAP (CD Cal filed April 28 1997).

[11] The amended complaint can be found at http://www.ljx.com/LJXfiles/ticketmaster. Bob Tedeschi. *Ticketmaster and Microsoft Settle Linking Dispute*, February 15, 1999, Cybertimes at http://www.nytimes.com/library/tech/99/02/cyber/articles.

permitted. As part of the settlement Microsoft has agreed not to link from its city guides to pages deep within the Ticketmaster site. Rather visitors will be pointed to the Ticketmaster home page.

As with the Shetland Times case,[12] the Ticketmaster/Microsoft litigation prompted a number of comments as to how it was going to be the end of the Internet if the practice of linking were found unlawful. However, as far as registered trade mark law is concerned, it is hard to see how matters of confusion or dilution could actually be directly relevant. Unfair competition however, is perhaps another matter.[13]

META TAGS

There has been a flurry of activity concerning trade marks and meta tags, to which the courts have responded with fairly scathing judgments. A meta tag is hidden information within a web site that broadly contains a synopsis of the information contained in the web site, either in the form of single words, or as sentences. As an example, the meta tags for the Edinburgh University SCRIPT[14] web site look like this:

META name="keywords" content="Script SCRIPT, script, copyright, intellectual, property, technology, Scots, Scottish, Scotland, Edinburgh, University, Faculty, system, law, Law, legal, links, lawschool, school, index, UK, english, national, best, principal, launch, biotechnology, patent, patents, genome, design, publication, international, Europe, European, firms, internet, computer, computers, research, cyber, cyberspace, attorney, colloquia, trademark, trade, mark, conference, seminar, lecture">

As you see, the metatags contain all the important words that might be used to search for the page itself.

The information in meta tags is used mainly by search engines to rate how highly a search for a particular term matches the content in the page. The search engines work by sending out spiders to crawl over information in the web and index web pages. A database is then created which consists of a list of words and information on where the words are to be found. The hits are usually rated with the highest scoring hits displayed at the top of the list of hits found by the search engine. If a term is found in the meta tags it is likely to be rated by the

---

[12] *supra* n 8.

[13] Another dispute which is pending in the US is *Ticketmaster Corp., et al.* v *Tickets.Com, Inc.* U.S. District Court, Central District of California March 27, 2000. Tickets.com deep linked into Ticketmaster pages. Ticketmaster alleged infringement on a number of grounds including breach of contract, misappropriation, trespass, unjust enrichment, copyright infringement, federal unfair competition and reverse passing off, false advertising, state unfair business practices and interference with business advantage. Ticket.com were given ten days to submit an amended motion to dismiss the claims on the first four claims.

[14] http://www.law.ed.ac.uk/script/home.htm.

search engine as more relevant and so displayed more prominently in the search result.[15]

Businesses have been using trade marks both registered and unregistered belonging to others in their meta tags in order to generate business. In one of the first cases, *Oppedahl & Larson v Advanced Concepts*,[16] the defendants who were in the business of *inter alia* registering domain names, used the terms 'Oppedahl and Larson' in their meta tags several times.[17] Oppedahl and Larson are a US law firm who have specialised in Internet law. Mr Oppedahl has written a number of oft quoted articles on a variety of Internet subjects, mainly concerning various aspects of e-commerce. Oppedahl and Larson alleged unfair competition and violation of common law trade marks. The case completed with injunctions being issued against the defendants, and the removal of the offending terms from the meta tags. However, a number of questions, certainly as regards trade mark law, remain. Trade mark law is primarily geared to ensuring that a consumer is not confused. Using marks in meta tags may confuse the search engines: but would such practice confuse the consumer, especially once she has opened the web page?[18] Such use in meta tags may frustrate the surfer (horribly) but again may not confuse. The meta tags are invisible to the surfer, the all important consumer for trade mark law. Unfair competition may be apt, but it is more difficult to see where registered trade mark law might be relevant.[19]

How can you find out if a competitor is using your registered or unregistered mark in their meta tags? One way is to enter your trade mark as a search term in one of the search engines. Then note the web sites upon which the mark does not visibly appear. Once you have accessed one of these pages, you can view the HTML version of those pages (using the Netscape navigator browser by clicking on 'view' and then 'document source'). This will show the terms included in the meta tag.

One case in the US concerning meta tags, and where harmful and deceptive business practices was pleaded successfully, was *Niton Corp v Radiation Monitoring Devices Inc*.[20] Radiation put in its meta tags '*The Home Page of Niton Corporation, makers of the finest lead, radon and multi-element detectors*' which, fairly understandably, upset Niton Corp when they discovered what was going on. Niton and Radiation were not in competition in the

---

[15] Typing the word 'Disney' into Altavista on 21/06/99 returned 1,210,590 hits. Typing 'Pamela Anderson' in returned 73,658 hits.

[16] *Oppedahl & Larson v Advanced Concepts* (Civil Action No 97–Z–1592).

[17] David Loundy *Hidden Code Sparks High-Profile Lawsuit* Chicago Daily Law Bulletin September 11, 1997, p6 available at http://www.loundy.com/CDLB/Meta_Tags.html.

[18] See Waelde, Chapter 7.

[19] Another case that has looked at meta tag infringement (among other things) is *Playboy Enterprises Inc. v Calvin Designer Label* (Civil Action No. C–97–3204 (ND Cal Sep 8 1997) http://www.patents.com/ac/playord.sht where the defendant was accused of having incorporated Playboy's trade marks into meta tags and Internet domain names including www.playboyxxx.com, www.playmatelive.com, and on its home page. Under a temporary restraining order the court ordered the defendant to cease using Playboy's marks in any manner including in meta tags, on its home page and in the web site.

[20] D Mass No 98–11629–REK 11/18/98.

terrestrial world, but became so once they started to trade on the Internet. In giving judgment the court said that '*a company which uses references to a competitor in meta tags to lure customers to its site is likely to mislead users about the relationship between the companies*'.

A case has now been heard in the UK concerning meta tags. Apparently a company called Mandata (a reseller) was ordered to pay £15,000 in damages after including trademarks belonging to a rival, Road Tech Computer Systems, in its meta tags.[21]

PLAYBOY LITIGATION[21a]

It may not be totally in keeping with the headings in this summary to group a number of cases under the one head 'Playboy litigation'. However, this writer cannot resist grouping just to consider the extent to which our Internet trade mark law is being shaped by pornography.[22] As one honours student recently mused, given that pornography is immoral, surely it is not protected by intellectual property rights? Someone forgot to tell Playboy!

PLAYBOY WIN

In Playboy Enterprises Inc. v *Universal Tel-A-Talk Inc.*[23] the defendant ran a web site selling hard core porn via a subscription service called 'Playboy's Private Collection'. They also used (liberally) the words 'Playboy' and 'Bunny' on each web page, in the URL[24] and on the navigational bar on the home page. The court found (unsurprisingly) that consumers were likely to be confused, and the defendant liable for trademark infringement, dilution and counterfeiting.

---

[21] http://www.glinks.net/items/glitem7525.htm.

[21a] *Playboy Enterprises, Inc.* v *Frena*, 839 F. Supp. 1552 (M.D. Fla. 1993). *Playboy Enterprises, Inc.* v *Russ Hardenburgh, Inc.*, 982 F. Supp. 503 (N.D. Ohio 1997). *Playboy Enterprises, Inc.* v *Webbworld, Inc.*, 968 F. Supp. 1171 (N.D. Tex.), *injunction granted*, 991 F. Supp. 543 (1997). *Playboy Enterprises, Inc.* v *Calvin Designer Label*, 985 F. Supp. 1218 (N.D. Cal. 1997) (temporary restraining order) *injsunction granted*, 985 F. Supp. 1220 (1997). *Playboy Enterprises, Inc.* v *AsiaFocus International* (E.D. Va. Apr. 22 1998). *Playboy Enterprises, Inc.* v *Calvin Designer Label*, 985 F. Supp. 1218 (N.D. Cal. 1997) (temporary restraining order), *injunction granted*, 985 F. Supp. 1220 (1997). *Playboy Enterprises, Inc.* v *Welles* No. 98–CV–0413–K (JFS) (S.D. Cal. Apr. 21, 1998). *Playboy Enterprises, Inc.* v *Chuckleberry Publishing, Inc.*, 939 F. Supp. 1032 (S.D.N.Y.) *motion for reconsideration denied*, 939 F. Supp. 1041 (1996).

[22] Copyright law on the Internet is equally being shaped (influenced?) by the church of Scientology. See MacQueen *Copyright and the Internet* Ch. 9 in this vol.

[23] ED Pa No 96–6961 11/4/98.

[24] The URL included the paths URL adult-sex.com/playboy/members/pictures. If we compare this with *Patmont Motor Works Inc.* v *Gateway Marine Inc.* DC Ncalif No C 96–2703 THE 12/18/97 where the question was in relation to the use of the mark 'goped' in the path of the URL, the court found that there was no infringement where the web site had been established by a reseller of gopeds. See Waelde Chapter 7.

PLAYBOY WIN AGAIN

Playboy's arm has a very long reach when its interests are at stake. Consequently, the stakes can be very high for those who tangle with them. In *Playboy Enterprises Inc.* v *AsiaFocus Inc*[25] AsiaFocus were based in Hong Kong. They provided adult oriented Web sites at the Internet addresses asian-playmates.com and playmates-asian.com. They used the term 'Playmate' in their e-mail address. The web pages associated with their domain names included Playboy's marks, and their meta tags included the words 'Playboy' and 'Playmate'. They promoted goods including playing cards, calendars, watches and key chains, all items in classes for which Playboy holds registrations. They also offered access to adult pictures.

The court in Virginia found they had jurisdiction based on the Virginia long arm Statute,[26] which provides for jurisdiction over foreign residents if they regularly do business or engage in a persistent course of conduct in Virginia. Unsurprisingly, AsiaFocus were found liable for trade mark dilution because the distinctiveness of Playboy's marks was blurred, in particular by their inclusion in the meta tags. The use of the domain name was likely to cause confusion; the marks were used for the same goods and services as covered by Playboy's registration. The infringements were wilful and amounted to the use of counterfeit marks. Damages were awarded of $3 million. Whether or not Playboy actually receives the damages will, of course, depend on whether they have assets, and Playboy can get their judgement recognised and enforced in Hong Kong. But it is a timely warning. There are a lot of large commercial organisations out there with huge financial resources, and who are more than willing to police, quite aggressively, their intellectual property rights.

PLAYBOY—THE INNOCENT PARTY FIGHTS BACK

Playboy are, however, not having it all their own way, and a case in which Playboy are intimately interested is currently wending its way through the US courts. Indeed, it has been said that trade mark owners are quite concerned at the potential outcome should Playboy lose. On the other hand, it would appear from the facts of the case, that they perhaps should. The case concerns Terri Welles who was the Playboy Playmate of the Year in 1981. She set up a web site in order to inform the world of this fact, and used the words 'Playmate of the Year' as the heading to some of her pages. She also used the words 'Playboy' and 'Playmate' in her meta tags, and PMOY81 as a repeating watermark in the

---

[25] ED Va Civil Action No 97–734–A 4/28/98.
[26] Virginia Code 8.01.328.1(A). The court also cited *Zippo Manufacturing Co* v *Zippo Dot Com Inc*. 952 F. Supp. 1119 (WD Pa 1997) (2 ECLR 202 2/14/97) and *Maritz* v *Cybergold Inc*. 947 F. SUpp. 1328 (ED Mo 1996) (1 ECLR 587 9/27/96).

background of her site. Terri did not, however, use Playboy's marks in her domain name, nor did she use the Bunny logo. Ms Welles inserted notices disclaiming any connection between the site and Playboy. When challenged by Playboy, the court found that Ms Welles used the title 'Playmate of the Year' and the mark 'PMOY 81' in good faith to describe herself. The use of the term 'Playboy' in the meta tags referenced both her identity and legitimate editorial use of the term. Given that she *was* Playmate of the Year 1981, there was no other way that she could identify or describe herself and her services without venturing into absurd descriptive phrases,[27] such as '*The person that appeared nude on the centre pages of a well known men's magazine connected to a Rabbit*'. The mark was not being used to compete with Playboy, nor to trick customers into thinking that Playboy endorsed her site. The marks are not only trade marks, but also titles bestowed on models appearing in the magazine. Her use of these terms was therefore fair use.[28]

Needless to say Playboy is most upset at the success so far that Ms Welles has had in the courts. It is reported that Playboy were exerting much pressure on Ms Welles to settle, and amended their complaint to sue for trade mark counterfeiting which, if they win, could result in high statutory damages. If Ms Welles wins her battle, the question is as to how far others may then go in using trade marks in meta tags and other elements of a web site. For instance if a hard core porn site writes a story about Hugh Heffner and Playboy and includes it on their site, can they then bury these names in the meta tags? Can a travel agent bury the term Disney in theirs? The answer, as far as trade mark law is concerned, may well be yes.

USING TRADE MARKS IN E-MAIL MESSAGES

Spam, or unauthorised junk e-mail is something that irritates computer users regularly.[29] But it is not only the recipients of this mail that get annoyed. In two reported cases in the US, the sender's e-mail address has been tampered with to suggest that it has been sent from a certain ISP, when in fact it has not. In

---

[27] *Playboy Enterprises Inc.* v *Welles* SD Cal Case No 98–CV–0413–K (JFS) 4/22/98.

[28] US traditional fair use doctrine broadly states: '*That the use of the name, term, or device charged to be an infringement is a use otherwise than as a mark, of the party's individual name in his own business, or of the individual name of anyone in privity with such a party, or of a term or device which is descriptive of and used fairly and in good faith only to describe the goods or services of such a party, or their geographic origin.* 15 USC SS1115(b)(4). *New Kids on the Block* v *News America Publishing* 971 F.2d 302 (9th Cir. 1991) developed a three step test: The product or service must bet be readily describable without using the trade mark: only that portion of the trade mark necessary to identify the product or service must be used: nothing in the use of the trade mark must suggest connection or endorsement by the trade mark holder. Terri Welles again defeated Playboy in court as a federal court judge in San Diego has ruled that the use of the Playboy name on the site and in the meta-tags simply described the site and was done in good faith. http://www.signon-sandiego.com/news/computing/991204–0010_7m4playboy.html.

[29] See Edwards Chapter 13 in this vol.

Hotmail v *Van$ Money Pie Inc.*[30] Van$ sent out spam e-mails, and in so doing they altered the return addresses to falsely indicate that the mail emanated from Hotmail. Hotmail received numerous complaints. The court found that the fraudulent use of 'hotmail' in the return address was likely to confuse members of the public into thinking that the mail had been sent from a 'hotmail' account, and thus Hotmail was involved in sending them unwanted e-mail, when in fact they were not. Thus their trade mark was infringed. The court came to a similar conclusion in *America OnLine Inc. v IMS*[31] when unauthorised spam bulk e-mail advertisements containing the letters 'aol.com' in their header went sent to millions of America Online Inc. subscribers, quite upsetting AOL.[32]

A BUNDLE OF INTELLECTUAL PROPERTY RIGHTS

A new operating system, Linux, is currently being developed by the Internet community. Dr Linus Torvalds is the original author of the system. He placed the system 'in the public domain', renounced all copyright fees for copying and distribution of the system, and required that copies be freely distributable, and accompanied by the source code. Linux has subsequently been further developed by the author in co-operation with other Internet professionals from around the world, all operating *pro bono*. However, although the copyright rights were covered to ensure it remained free, trade mark issues were not considered. In 1994 a Mr Della Croce filed a US application for the trade mark Linux in the class pertaining to '*computer operating system software to facilitate computer use and operation*'. He then asked for a 10% royalty on the distribution of the Linux operating system in the US. The case was settled by an assignation of the trade mark to Dr Torvalds and repayment of registration fees to Mr Croce.[33] The moral? Beware of compartmentalising intellectual property rights![34]

SEARCH ENGINES SELLING TRADE MARKS

One of the latest rounds in the trade mark challenge on the Internet relates to the way in which search engines work and display advertisements.[35] Currently, when you type a word into a search engine, banner ads automatically appear on

---

[30] 47 USPQ 2d 1020 (ND Cal 1998) (3 ECLR 586 5/6/98).

[31] 48 USPQ 2d 1857 (ED Va 1998) (3 ECLR 1329 11/18/98).

[32] See further Edwards Chapter 13 in this vol.

[33] http://www.iplawyers.com.

[34] MP3 has apparently been registered as a trade mark in Germany. The company who registered the mark '*now awaits any observations from interested parties under the EU trademark rules*'. See http://www.theregister.co.uk/000322–000024.html.

[35] Carl Kaplan *Lawsuits Challenge Search Engines' Practice of 'Selling' Trade Marks* at http://www.nytimes.com/library/tech/99/02/cyber/cyberlaw/12law.html.

the site, sometimes advertising a competitor's products. The search engine site makes advertising revenue from this; effectively they 'sell' certain search terms to the highest bidder. So when you type in 'Playboy' (yes, Playboy again) an ad may appear advertising a competitor's site that has nothing to do with 'Playboy'. Playboy has taken exception to this and challenged it on the basis of trade mark infringement, arguing that it hijacks and usurps Playboy's reputation. The essence of the argument is that a banner ad appearing with the results of a search for one of its famous trade mark terms might confuse web users into making them think that Playboy is a sponsor of, or connected to the banner as buyer. Are consumers likely to be confused? Is it not more akin to walking past a shop window and seeing all the competing products lined up in the window even if you are looking for a particular product? The case has now been heard with the court finding in favour of the search engine. Broadly, the court held that the words 'playboy' and 'playmate' were not used in an unlawful manner, it was rather a 'non-trademark use of a mark'. Needless to say, Playboy is said to be appealing the decision.[35a]

A similar suit was filed by Estee Lauder Companies Inc. against Excite (the search engine) and The Fragrance Counter Inc. who sells cosmetics and fragrances on line. Estee Lauder claimed that when 'Estee Lauder' was typed as keywords, a misleading Fragrance counter banner ad appears that featured the Estee Lauder name. Estee Lauder argued that The Fragrance Counter was not an authorised retailer of its products. These ads no longer carry the name 'Estee Lauder' although the case appears to be churning on in the US. Estee Lauder filed a similar suite against Excite and iBeauty in Germany. The German court has recently ruled that the practice violates German unfair competition law.[36]

SUMMARY

These are but a few brief examples the types of disputes that have been troubling trade mark holders and the courts in the US over the last months and years. As e-commerce expands in Europe, and players become more aggressive as they battle to be noticed by consumers, it is possible that we will see more of these aggressive marketing tactics and 'unfair competition' practices arriving here as well. It will be a challenge for our courts to see what parameters can be placed on trademark law.

[35a] For the story see http://www.nytimes.com/2000/09/15/technology/ISCYBERLAW.html.
[36] See http://interactive.wsj.com/articles/SB952566860153204842.htm.

9

Copyright and the Internet

HECTOR L MacQUEEN[1]

INTRODUCTION

A major issue for copyright lawyers at the present time is how to deal with the rapid development of the Internet and the prospect of the 'information super-highway', world-wide telecommunications systems which permit the rapid, indeed virtually instantaneous, transmission around the world, at times chosen as much by individual recipients as by transmitters of information and enter-tainment in all media—print, pictures still and moving, sound, and combina-tions thereof. The issues are manifold. Is the ease of perfect reproduction and manipulation of material in the digital form used by our communications sys-tems the death-knell of the whole basis of copyright? Are we at least going to have to reconsider such fundamentals of copyright law as what constitutes pub lication, copying and public performance, or the old distinctions between cate-gories of work such as literary, artistic, sound recording and film? What rights should users enjoy? Are the rights accorded them in the analogue world so ill-defined that they will undermine the utility of copyright as a source of income for digital authors and their publishers? Will we see the emergence of a genuine market-place in which producer and user bargain about the price for individual transfers of information and cultural goods, rather than requiring intermedi-aries such as publishers? Given the ready flow of material across national frontiers, does the international harmonisation of copyright laws need intensification, and should the classic rules of private international law on juris-diction and choice of law be adapted to enable a party confronted with infringe-ments in another country to sue effectively in his own country and have judgments recognised abroad?

This chapter considers the main rules of British copyright relevant to the Internet against a comparative background, in order to demonstrate some of the difficulties with which the law is now confronted, and concludes with some of

[1] LLB (Hons), PhD, FRSE, Professor of Private Law, University of Edinburgh, email hector.mac-queen@ed.ac.uk. This is a substantially revised, updated and rewritten version of the chapter which appeared under the same title in L Edwards and C Waelde (eds), *Law and the Internet: Regulating Cyberspace* (1997). I am grateful to those who commented upon that earlier version, to those who sent me information about developments on the Internet (especially Dr Athol Murray), and to the editors once again for their help, guidance and patience over a prolonged period.

the international and, in particular, the European proposals to develop the law and to meet these problems.

A few preliminaries may be helpful, however. Copyright first developed in the early modern period as a response to the growth of the printing technology which facilitated the rapid multiplication and distribution of copies of written works. Change in the law has continued to be driven by technological advance in the means by which works can be presented to the public at large, and protection has been extended and adapted to cover photography, cinematography, sound recording, broadcasting, cable transmissions and computer programs. So there is no reason to suppose that, if the Internet does in fact present new problems for copyright, the law cannot be adapted to deal with them.[2] The practical benefit of working within the copyright mould is the continued applicability of the international regime under the Berne Convention and other treaties which ensure potentially world-wide protection for rightholders (a vitally important point in relation to the global Internet).

A second preliminary point concerns the functions of copyright. Two major conceptualisations of this can be identified in the world's legal systems. The Anglo-American or Common Law tradition emphasises the economic role of copyright. Protection of copyright subject-matter against unauthorised acts of exploitation enables right-holders either to go to market themselves with a product based on the material, or to grant others, by outright transfer or, more typically, by licence, the right to do so for whatever seems an appropriate price. In the absence of copyright, which would enable free-riding by would-be users, it is unlikely that producers of the material would earn any return for their work, and without that incentive production would dry up or slacken significantly. Copyright is thus essentially a response to market failure, a means by which socially beneficial activities can be made financially worthwhile. It rests ultimately upon the general or public interest.[3]

In contrast, the Continental or Civil Law tradition sees copyright as springing from the personality rights of the individual creator of the subject matter. Companies and organisations as such cannot be creators. This perception is reflected in the name 'author-law' given to the topic by the various Continental systems—*droit d'auteur*, *urheberrecht*, and so on. Protection is given out of respect for the individual's creative act of production, and extends beyond the merely economic to the so-called 'moral rights': the right to be identified as the creator of a work, the right to have the integrity of a work preserved, and others. Copyright is thus rooted in protection of the individual personality and interests of the author as expressed in her work.

---

[2] Contra the views of, e.g., John Perry Barlow: see his 'Selling wine without bottles: the economy of mind on the global Net', in P Bernt Hugenholtz (ed), *The Future of Copyright in a Digital Environment* (1996), 169–187. See further L Bently and B Sherman, *The Making of Modern Intellectual Property Law* (1999), and Computer Science and Telecommunications Board and National Research Council, *The Digital Dilemma: Intellectual Property in the Information Age* (2000), henceforth *Digital Dilemma*.

[3] See further G Davies, *Copyright and the Public Interest* (1994).

The distinction between the two conceptualisations is sometimes summarised by saying that the Anglo-American tradition is centred on the entrepreneur, the Continental one on the author. It is reflected in various rules: for example, where the Anglo-American tradition gives copyright protection to media works such as sound recordings and broadcasts, the Continental tradition uses a separate group of 'neighbouring rights' for these non-author works. Again, where the Anglo-American tradition vests first ownership of copyright in the employer of an author making a work in the course of employment, the Continental tradition always gives it to the author. In the present context, a significant aspect of the distinctness of the two traditions is their stances in relation to what may be called 'user rights'; that is, those activities in which members of the public may engage with regard to copyright works without any authorisation from the rightholders concerned. The Anglo-American tradition allows 'fair dealing' or 'fair use' for free in areas where it is thought that the public interest in the dissemination of information and ideas outweighs the interest of the rightholder in earning reward from the exploitation of the work and the public interest in encouraging the author's activities. In contrast, although the Continental traditions typically permit private copying, the author still receives remuneration by way of levies imposed upon the sale of the equipment that enables the copying to take place.[4]

But it is important not to over-emphasise the significance of such distinctions. Continental copyright laws are also a basis for market operations, while the author plays a fundamental role in Anglo-American copyright laws, where moral rights are now also developing.[5] Membership of the Berne Convention, which has been the basis of international copyright since 1886 and sets minimum standards for national copyright legislation, has embraced countries from both traditions for most of its history, and since 1989 has included the USA. The convergence promoted by the Convention's minimum standards has been further advanced by the 1994 Agreement on Trade-Related Aspects of Intellectual Property Rights (TRIPS). During the 1990s, even more fundamental steps towards convergence were taken within the European Union, by a policy of harmonisation of copyright law in its Member States through a series of directives, now including a draft dealing with the problems posed by the Internet. The global effects of these problems mean that purely national responses are inadequate, and that a convergent approach is required; but nonetheless the deep-seated differences in basic concepts have an effect upon international discussions, the outcome of which may sometimes reflect a somewhat uneasy compromise between the competing schools of thought.

The immediate relevance of noting copyright's economic functions, however, is that its deployment to protect material on the Internet is an important element

---

[4] See further below, 204.
[5] In the UK see Copyright Designs and Patents Act (CDPA) 1988, ss 77–89. The USA has not enacted moral rights as such but other rights granted in US law have been accepted as satisfying the requirements of the Berne Convention on this matter.

in enabling the medium to realise its commercial potential. It has to be recognised at once that a large amount of material is placed on the Internet by its originators so that it can be accessed and used freely by others. Governments, commercial and other organisations, and individuals want to draw the attention of others to themselves and their products, and to provide information and material without specific charge, in fulfilment of their perceived functions in society or for other reasons. The existence or otherwise of copyright in what is placed on the Internet by such parties will be of no or very limited relevance to them. The Internet publication will either contain express permission to access, use and reproduce, or that can be implied from the circumstances in which the material is made available.

But what is true of some will not hold good for all those who publish on the Internet. For many, the Internet is the latest means by which information and entertainment products created at substantial cost may be made available to the world at a price reflecting that cost plus the crucial element of profit, without which business loses its *raison d'être*. But the ease of high quality reproduction, onward distribution and dissemination of digital material poses as much of a threat as an opportunity to such entrepreneurs. Copyright protection therefore helps to make a market that would otherwise be limited to those who were unaware of their right (or ability) to copy, and is, in other words, a vital strand in the creation of a legal environment appropriate for electronic commerce, just as it has always been for those whose business is the creation and publication of entertainment and information products in analogue form, such as books, records and films; but perhaps even more so.

A third preliminary is to observe that the legal system that has so far thrown up most of the actual cases about Internet copyright is that of the USA. These cases are of course immensely valuable in showing the kinds of question likely to arise elsewhere. But it is necessary to be somewhat cautious in assuming that courts in other countries would necessarily reach the same conclusions on their facts. US copyright law is characterised by its express basis in the American Constitution, which empowers Congress "to promote the progress of science and useful arts, by securing for limited times to authors and inventors the exclusive right to their respective writings and discoveries".[6] The actual law is found in the Copyright Act 1976 with various additions and amendments thereto. The constitutional basis and the general American legal tradition encourages the courts to take a much more overtly policy-oriented approach to copyright questions than would be possible for a British or (even more so) another European court. In any event, as Jacob J once observed when several American cases were cited to him in a case about software copyright, the language of the American statute is not at all the same as that of the British one, and one must therefore be careful of reasoning which may be dependent ultimately on the legislative wording.[7]

---

[6] US Constitution, Article I, section 8.
[7] *Ibcos Computers Ltd v Barclays Mercantile Highland Finance Ltd* [1994] FSR 275 at 292.

Lastly, this chapter is a much compressed treatment of a very large subject, and space prohibits anything other than fairly abbreviated discussion of some of the major issues. In particular, the problems of international private law have been left to another contributor.[8]

SOME EXAMPLES

It is always helpful to have good examples with which to illustrate discussion of a complex matter. For Internet copyright in Scotland, fortunately, a particularly useful one is readily to hand in the case of *Shetland Times* v *Wills*.[9] The *Shetland Times* published by the pursuers is an originally hard copy only newspaper, the owner of which (Mr Robert Wishart) established an Internet website or home page (*http://www.shetland-times.co.uk*). The opening or front page of the site used headlines from the newspaper upon which users clicked to gain access to the stories as printed under these headlines in the newspaper. Dr Jonathan Wills, who was once well-known as a student Rector of Edinburgh University and was also at one time editor of the *Shetland Times*, began in November 1995 to publish *The Shetland News* only on the Internet after falling out with Mr Wishart. Dr Wills used news headlines as the means of access to the stories in his publication (*http://www.shetland-news.co.uk*). From about 14 October 1996 the *Shetland News* page included *Shetland Times* headlines as hypertext links, and by clicking on these access could be gained to the relative stories on the *Shetland Times* website, bypassing the front page of that site altogether. The *Shetland Times* alleged infringement of copyright and sought interim interdict in the Court of Session. The practical reason underlying the action was that the *Shetland Times* hoped to sell advertising space on its website front page, and this commercial benefit would be lost if readers could access the news stories directly and bypass the front page.[10] The *Shetland Times* obtained an interim interdict before Lord Hamilton in October 1996. A full hearing on the petition for permanent interdict was scheduled to take place on 11–14 November 1997, but the action was settled in the door of the court[11] on the basis that the *Shetland News* would be able to link to stories on the *Shetland Times* website by means of headlines. But each such link was to be acknowledged by the legend 'A *Shetland Times* story' appearing under each headline; closely adjacent would be a button showing legibly the *Shetland Times* masthead logo; legends and buttons could also be hypertext links to the *Shetland Times* online headline page. Neither party would be liable for the other's expenses.[12]

---

[8] See however J J Fawcett and P Torremans, *Intellectual Property and Private International Law* (1998), 158–161, 248–249; and further Torremans' contribution to this volume, 225–48.

[9] 1997 SC 316; 1997 SLT 669; 1997 SCLR 160; [1997] FSR 604; [1997] EMLR 277.

[10] It is perhaps worthy of note here that at the height of the dispute the *Shetland News* site seemed to have been much more successful in attracting advertisers than the *Shetland Times* counterpart.

[11] Appropriately enough, on Armistice Day.

[12] I am grateful to Dr Wills for sending me details of the settlement.

The case is not untypical of the copyright issues arising on the Internet so far. A parallel litigation in the USA, also eventually settled, involved an organisation called Total News, from whose website a reader could link on to the web pages of other news organisations such as the *Washington Post*. Again the real issue appears to have been advertising on the respective sites, inasmuch as even after a link had been made to another site from the Total News one, the display was still 'framed' with Total News advertisements. The settlement allowed linking but not framing.[13] Other decided American cases have in general held linking not to be infringement of copyright, and there have been similar decisions in Swedish, German and Dutch courts.[14]

Another type of case involves the creator of a website who puts other persons' copyright material on to his pages. In one of a number of French cases, for example, Raymond Queneau's "Cente Mille Milliards de Poemes" was placed on two different websites without the authorisation of the owners of the copyright in the work.[15] In August 1997 the BBC obtained the removal from nineteen private websites of unauthorised copies of pictures and texts from *Teletubbies*, the popular children's TV programme.[16] A well-known American case of this type is *Religious Technology Center v Netcom On-Line Communication Serv*,[17] in which Denis Ehrlich, acting without authority, posted to an electronic bulletin board both published and unpublished works by L Ron Hubbard, founder of the Church of Scientology. The case raised the additional issue of whether the bulletin board operator and the service provider with which the board was based could be liable for infringement of copyright along with the person who made the initial copy.[18]

More recent American litigation has concerned the liability of those who provide, not hyperlinks, but information about, and the technological means of accessing and exploiting, copyright material found on the Internet, in particular

---

[13] For details of the settlement dated 6 June 1997, see http://www.bna.com/e-law/cases/totalset.html. Note also the *Ticket Master v Microsoft* settlement discussed in Waelde chapter 8, in which it seems to have been accepted that linking to within another's site, as opposed to its home page, was wrong. For another interesting case involving the Ticketmaster website, see *Ticketmaster Corp v Tickets.Com, Inc*, S. District Court, Central District of California, 27 Mar 2000.

[14] See in the USA *Bernstein v J C Penney Inc*, Central District of California, 22 Sept 1999, http://eon.law.Harvard.edu/property/metatags/linking1.html; in Sweden the *Tommy Olsson* case, Dec 1999, Göta Hovrätt, http://www.juridicum.su.se/iri/karc/linking.htm; in Germany, OLG Düsseldorf, decision of 29 June 1999 that linking within frame not infringement; and for a Dutch decision see *Financial Times*, 23 Aug. 2000.

[15] (1997) 11 *World Intellectual Property Reporter* 266. Raymond Queneau (1903-1976) was a surrealist and experimental author. The poem in question is a collection of words which the reader is invited to assemble in any order to form his or her own version.

[16] *The Scotsman*, 15 Aug 1997.

[17] 907 F Supp 1361 (ND Cal, 1995). See also *Religious Technology Center v Lerma*, US District Court for the Eastern District of Virginia, 4 Oct 1996 (http://www.bna.com/e-law/cases/lerma.html), and E Cameron, (1997) 11 *International Review of Law Computers and Technology* 155–165.

[18] See for other recent examples *Playboy Enterprises Inc v Webbworld Inc*, US District Court, North District of Texas, 11 Dec 1997, [1998] EIPR N-100 (infringement by providing others' pictures to subscribers); *Cee Dee Empire v IFPI*, Eastern Division, High Court, Denmark, 8 Dec 1997, [1998] EIPR N-203 (providing 30–40 second clips of CDs available for sale from the website owner).

music. The arrival of MP3 software, which enabled the conversion of material recorded on CD (in particular music) into highly compressed computer files postable on and downloadable from the Internet, has been particularly important here.[19] Thus there was an unsuccessful challenge in 1999 to the lawfulness of the portable device known as the Rio MPMan player, to which people could copy an MP3 file of music downloaded initially from the Internet to a personal computer, thus enabling the file to be playable wherever the user wished.[20] However, in April 2000 Judge Rakoff of the District Court for the Southern District of New York found infringement of copyright in the service offered by a company called MP3.com. The company had purchased thousands of music CDs and made them available in MP3 format on the Internet to users who, after inserting their own copies of the CD in question into their personal computers while linked to MP3.com's 'My.MP3.com' website (*http://www.mp3.com*), could then, and again thereafter as often as wished, request a copy of the relative MP3 file held on the MP3.com servers to be transmitted to them.[21] Since the decision that these activities constituted infringement of copyright, MP3.com has entered a number of licensing agreements with recording companies such as Time Warner, Bertelsmann and EMI.[22]

The latest American litigation is concerned with the activities of Napster Inc, a company which makes available for downloading from the Internet its proprietary MusicShare software. This uploads to the Napster servers a list of all MP3 files on the hard disk of the user's computer, while that person is enabled to search the servers, which contain master indices of the locations of music files on the hard disks of all users of the service. Using these indices, users may then freely download to their own computers copies of the files they want, directly from the hard disks of other users. In early July 2000 there were said to be eight million users of Napster's services in the USA, each one exchanging on average about 20 songs per month, while in the UK the number of users had increased from 217,800 in May 2000 to 464,300 in June.[23] Although Napster itself does not make any copies of the files, it has been held liable for infringement of the copyrights involved, although at the time of writing (August 2000) the Ninth Circuit Court of Appeals in San Francisco had temporarily stayed an injunction granted

[19] On MP3 software (named from layer three of the Motion Pictures Experts Group's compression standard), see, e.g., *Guardian*, 20 Nov 1998, 22 Apr 1999; *The Times*, Interface supplement 4 Aug 1999. *The Scotsman*, 2 Dec 1999, reported that 'MP3' had overtaken 'sex' as the most popular search term on the Internet. See further *Digital Dilemma*, ch 2, for the impact of MP3 on the music industry.

[20] *Recording Industry Association of America Inc v Diamond Multimedia Systems Inc*, 180 F.3rd 10772 (9th Circuit Court of Appeals, 15 June 1999), http://laws.findlaw.com/9th/9856727.html.

[21] *UMG Recordings Inc and others v MP3.com Inc*, US District Court, SDNY (Rakoff J), 4 May 2000, http://www.nysd.uscourts.gov/courtweb/pdf/00-04756.pdf. On 7 Sept. 2000 MP3.com was ordered to pay at least $118m damages: *Times*, 9 Sept. 2000.

[22] See *The Times* 29 July 2000 for details of the EMI settlement.

[23] *The Times*, Interface supplement, 7 Aug 2000. The Napster website is at http://www.napster.com .

by US District Judge Marilyn Hall Patel on 27 July 2000, pending a full trial of the case expected in the autumn of 2000.[24]

Finally, there are the cases about those who access and download material from the Internet. Assuming that the material has copyright—as a literary, artistic or musical work, or as a computer program, sound recording or film—is such accession or downloading an infringement of copyright? An issue of this kind arose in *Sega Enterprises Inc v Maphia*,[25] where however the ultimate question was again the liability of the bulletin board operator who provided the service through which not only downloading, but also initial unauthorised uploading of copyright material (computer games), took place.

COPYRIGHT SUBJECT MATTER

The governing copyright statute in the UK is the Copyright Designs and Patents Act 1988, now several times amended. Under its provisions, the following subject-matter is protected[26]:

- original literary, dramatic, musical and artistic works (literary work including computer programs and compilations other than databases);
- films;
- databases;
- the typographical arrangement of published editions of literary, dramatic or musical works;
- sound recordings;
- broadcasts;
- cable programmes.

For convenience, literary, dramatic, musical and artistic works and films will be collectively referred to as 'author works' in the remainder of this chapter, and the other categories (apart from databases, which for reasons discussed below form a sub-category on their own) will be grouped as 'media works'. The distinction rests on a number of points, of which the most important conceptually is the idea that the second group relies essentially on the operation of machinery and technology where the first depends upon an individual as creator. As a consequence, there are differences in the rules applying to the two groups. The first

---

[24] *A & M Records Inc v Napster Inc*, US District Court for the Northern District of California, 5 May 2000; *Recording Industry Association of America Inc v Napster Inc*, injunction granted by Patel J 27 July 2000; stayed 29 July 2000. See *The Times* and *The Scotsman* of 28 July 2000, and the *Sunday Telegraph*, 30 July 2000. Other organisations offering services similar to those of Napster, such as Gnutella and Freenet, are thought to be less vulnerable to legal challenge for the practical reason that they do not operate on permanently located servers.

[25] 857 F Supp 679 (ND Cal, 1994); US District Court for the Northern District of California, 16 Dec 1996 (http://www.bna.com/e-law/cases/sega2.html).

[26] CDPA 1988, ss 1–8.

owner of the copyright in an author work is generally the author,[27] whereas in the media work it is the person by whose investment the work was produced. Only author works need be original to be protected,[28] meaning that they must be independent forms of expression achieved through their author's judgement, skill and labour.[29] Author works alone attract moral rights.[30] Copyright in an author work lasts for the lifetime of the author plus seventy years, while for sound recordings, the period is fifty years from the end of the year of manufacture or release, and for broadcasts and cable programmes it is fifty years from the end of the year of transmission.

To what extent are website contents capable of being brought within these categories of protected work? Several of the categories are clearly applicable to all or part of website contents in so far as they consist of text (literary), images still (artistic) and moving (film), and sounds (audio recordings). As Laddie J has observed, 'different copyrights can protect simultaneously a particular product and an author can produce more than one copyright work during the course of a single episode of creative effort, for example a competent musician may write the words and the music for a song at the same time'.[31] In general, websites and webpages will be covered by several different copyrights: protection will be cumulative. The difficulty is the multi-media nature of the site or page viewed as a whole; is there a category appropriate to protect the totality from misappropriation by another?[32] The digital medium in which all works on the Internet are expressed has enabled the drawing together in what for the author and the user is a single work, regardless of the character of its components in the hard copy or analogue world, and categorisations based on these previously

---

[27] In the case of films in the UK, joint authorship is attributed to the principal director and the producer (CDPA, s 9(2)(ab)). For a recent case on joint authorship, see *Robin Ray* v *Classic FM* [1998] FSR 622. The concept may be increasingly significant in the digital world; see J Ginsburg, 'Putting cars on the 'information superhighway': authors, exploiters and copyright in cyberspace', in Hugenholtz (ed), *Future of Copyright*, 189–219 at 192–197, and W R Cornish, *Intellectual Property: Patents, Copyright, Trade Marks and Allied Rights*, 4th edn (1999), para 13.65. Note also (1) the British concept of a computer-generated work where there is no human author (CDPA 1988, ss 9(3), 178); and (2) that copyright in a work produced in the course of employment falls to the employer unless otherwise agreed (CDPA 1988, s 11(2)). Employment should be distinguished from a commission, where the copyright would remain with the author unless otherwise agreed.

[28] There is no express requirement that a film be original (see CDPA s 1(1)(b)).

[29] *The Laws of Scotland: Stair Memorial Encyclopaedia*, vol 18, paras 941–948; H Laddie, P Prescott and M Vitoria, *The Modern Law of Copyright and Designs*, 2nd edn (1995), 46–79, 210–244; K Garnett, J R James and G Davies (eds), *Copinger & Skone James on Copyright*, 14th edn (1999), 105-119.

[30] Apart from computer programs (CDPA, s 79(2)(a)).

[31] *Electronic Techniques (Anglia) Ltd* v *Critchley Components Ltd* [1997] FSR 401 at 413. Laddie J continues: '. . . it is quite another thing to say that a single piece of work by an author gives rise to two or more copyrights in respect of the same creative effort.' In the case he decided that circuit diagrams containing both literary and artistic material was an artistic work. Contrast *Anacon Corporation Ltd* v *Environmental Research Technology* [1994] FSR 659 (Jacob J), followed in *Sandman v Panasonic* [1998] FSR 651; and see Cornish, *Intellectual Property*, para 10.04.

[32] This issue also arises with multi-media CD-Roms. See further Cornish, *Intellectual Property*, paras 13.60–13.67. A very full analysis of the issues is provided in I Stamatoudi, 'Multi-Media Products as Copyright Works', University of Leicester PhD, 1999.

established forms are therefore hard to apply.[33] For example, while films can include sounds as well as moving images under the 1988 Act,[34] meaning that computer games can be protected under that head,[35] it is very doubtful whether images consisting purely of written text and/or still pictures can ever be treated as film, even if the reader is able to move the material around on her screen by use of scroll bars, cursors and other control mechanisms.[36]

The likeliest avenue for copyright protection of a whole website may now be through categorising it as a database. In UK law until recently, databases were thought to be protected as 'compilations'; but from 1 January 1998 the position was changed as a result of the implementation of the Database Directive 1996.[37] 'Compilation' now expressly does not include databases,[38] which are defined as collections of independent works, data or other materials arranged in a systematic or methodical way and individually accessible by electronic or other means. This definition means that, unlike traditional compilations, database protection is not confined to collections the basic form of which is written as distinct from other forms of expression (e.g. graphic), and can therefore more readily extend to multi-media material.

Further, to attract copyright, the database must be the author's own intellectual creation by reason of the selection or arrangement of its contents.[39] From this, it follows that the protection is offered to the selection and arrangement of the database, rather than to its contents as such, although the latter may attract copyright —or several copyrights—in their own right. The use of the phrase 'intellectual creation' also indicates that the selection and arrangement must show more than the traditional skill and labour which make compilations original. It is derived from the Continental tradition, which has always set a slightly higher standard of creativity for the admission of works to copyright protection. In the USA, the Supreme Court has departed from the American version of the requirement of skill and labour, the 'sweat of the brow' test, and added a need for a spark of creativity, denying copyright protection to a telephone directory as a compila-

---

[33] See further A Christie, 'Reconceptualising copyright in the digital era', [1995] 11 EIPR 522–530.

[34] CDPA 1988, s 5B(2) and (5). This does not prevent the sound recording element having copyright in its own right.

[35] See *Sega Enterprises Ltd* v *Galaxy Electronics Pty Ltd* (1997) 145 ALR 21 (Fed Ct of Australia); *Golden China TV Game Centre* v *Nintendo Co Ltd* 1997 (1) SA 405 (A); Cornish, *Intellectual Property*, para 10.25, pointing out that the incorporated computer program will also have its own copyright as a literary work.

[36] Cf *WGN Continental Broadcasting Co* v *United Video Inc* 693 F.2d 622 (7th Circuit, 1982), where teletext accompanying a TV programme but broadcast from a different channel was held to be an audiovisual work.

[37] Parliament and Council Directive 96/9/EC, article 3(1), implemented in the UK by the Copyright and Rights in Databases Regulations 1997 (SI 1997/3032).

[38] CDPA 1988, s 3(1)(a).

[39] CDPA 1988, s 3A. See also for use of this formulation Council Directive on the legal protection of computer programs 91/250/EEC, art 1(3); but in the implementation of this the UK did not see fit to use the phrase.

tion.[40] The 'intellectual creation' requirement seems likely to have a similar effect in excluding some compilations from protection as databases: thus the Dutch Supreme Court has held that the selection of words for a dictionary has no copyright unless it reflects a personal selection of the compiler.[41]

The definition of a database as a systematically arranged collection of independent works none the less seems very apt to include websites. Individual pages as well as material embodied therein could easily be seen as independent works in their own right, because each element is intended to be and is indeed used on its own; there is no *necessary* interaction between them.[42] These works are individually accessible to the user through the electronic means provided by her computer link to the Internet. The website's author has undoubtedly 'selected and arranged' its contents, unless it is simply a random storehouse of materials over which no control or personal selection has been exerted (as, perhaps with the entire Internet itself[43]), or where the method of control used has been a standard or common one. The author of such a collection could however seek protection from the additional, *sui generis* database right also introduced under the Database Directive. While the database must still be organised in a systematic or methodical way, the system or method need not be a personal intellectual creation;[44] the principal substantive ground for protection is a substantial investment in obtaining, verifying or preserving the contents of the database, and it is immaterial whether or not the database is also a copyright work, i.e. is an intellectual creation of the compiler in its selection or arrangement.[45] Database right prohibits unauthorised extraction[46] from or re-utilisation[47] of all or a substantial part of the database, lasting for fifteen years from its making.

Another avenue of approach to the problem of protecting websites was suggested in the *Shetland Times* case, which focused on the applicability of the concept of a cable programme, in which the copyright is owned by the service provider.[48] The 1988 Act defines a cable programme as any item included in a

---

[40] *Feist Publications Inc* v *Rural Telephone Service Co*, 499 US 340; 111 S Ct 1282 (1991). See also *Tele-Direct Publications* v *American Business Information* (1997) 76 CPR (3d) 296 (Canadian Supreme Court).

[41] See *Van Dale* v *Romme* [1991] Ned Jur 608, [1994] Ned Jur 58, as cited by Cornish, *Intellectual Property*, para 10.10 n 44.

[42] Contrast films, which are not databases because there *is* interaction between script, music, sound recordings and the moving images: see J Holyoak and P Torremans, *Intellectual Property Law*, 2nd edn (1998), 173-4, 506.

[43] Holyoak and Torremans, *Intellectual Property Law*, 507.

[44] So e.g. an arrangement of surnames in alphabetical order would attract database right.

[45] Copyright and Rights in Databases Regulations 1997, reg 13.

[46] This means 'in relation to any contents of a database, . . . the permanent or temporary transfer of those contents to another medium by any means or in any form' (Copyright and Rights in Databases Regulations 1997, reg 12(1)).

[47] This means 'in relation to any contents of a database, . . . making those contents available to the public by any means' (Copyright and Rights in Databases Regulations 1997, reg 12(1)).

[48] CDPA 1988, ss 7 and 9(2)(c). Cable is to be distinguished from broadcasting, defined in the copyright legislation as 'transmission by wireless telegraphy'. Since the Internet is for the moment dependent on the wires of the telecommunications system, transmission on the Internet is not broadcasting, and copyright protection is unavailable through this medium.

cable programme service, which in turn is defined as a service consisting wholly or mainly in *sending* information by means of a telecommunication system, otherwise than by wireless telegraphy, for reception (a) at two or more places (whether or not simultaneously), *or* for presentation to members of the public. Excluded from this definition are two-way or inter-active communication systems, of which a very simple example is a telephone system.[49]

In the *Shetland Times* case, two main arguments were presented against the website being a cable programme service. One was that it did not involve *sending* information but rather allowed information to be accessed by members of the public. The other argument was that the service was two-way or inter-active, in as much as members of the public could communicate information to the site as well as receive it, and so fell outwith the definition of a cable programme service. Lord Hamilton rejected both these arguments, while noting that little technical information was available to him at this interim interdict stage. His rejection of a narrow approach to the word 'sending' used in the 1988 Act seems reasonable since, at the very least, a website operator enables the material to be sent. The interactivity point is more difficult. It is necessary to quote the statutory exclusion in full:

> "The following are excepted from the definition of 'cable programme service'—
> (a) a service or part of a service of which it is an essential feature that while visual images, sounds or other information are being conveyed by the person providing the service there will or may be sent from each place of reception, by means of the same system or (as the case may be) the same part of it, information (other than signals sent for the operation or control of the service) for reception by the person providing the service or other persons receiving it."

The possibility of interaction between the *Shetland Times* website and its readers arose because the webpage included a note inviting comments or suggestions to be sent in by electronic mail. Indeed this note was itself a hypertext link moving the reader into an already addressed email template. It was argued that this facility entailed the possibility of communication going beyond 'the operation and control of the service' by the users. Lord Hamilton thought, however, that this was not an essential part of the service provided, or that it was at any rate a severable part of the service, and hence the exception did not apply. But, although the subsection does talk about a need to show that interactivity is an essential feature of the service, it only requires that *part* of the service be inter-active, perhaps eliminating the notion of severability as a way of evading the exception. The subsection is also quite clear that only *potential* for interactivity is necessary—information *"will or may be* sent from the place of reception ... for reception by the person providing the service or other persons receiving it." This analysis suggests that the really crucial word in the subsection is 'essential', and it is on the meaning to be given to this word that Lord Hamilton's opinion will probably stand or fall in future. On the *Shetland Times* facts, it is

---

[49] CDPA 1988, s 7.

submitted, the interactivity was additional rather than essential to the service, and accordingly the site was capable of being a cable programme service.

A point which was not raised before Lord Hamilton, however, is whether anything on the website was a cable programme, even if the site was a cable programme service. The 1988 Act provides the rather inert definition of 'programme' as an item.[50] But it can be argued that in the context of broadcasting and cable transmission a 'programme' is an item with a content the sequence and length of which are determined by the provider, and that therefore, at least "in the case of data bases or other interactive information services . . . as a result of the severed tie between a single component and its predefined position in a sequential order, these services no longer constitute 'programmes' in the traditional sense."[51]

However these arguments are eventually resolved, it may not often be necessary to characterise the whole of a website or a webpage in this way. Although the different categories of work are protected for different lengths of time under the copyright legislation, the periods are uniformly long (at least fifty years from production) and are unlikely to have much practical impact in the fast-moving world of multi-media and the Internet. Again, there are various kinds of infringement, but they generally apply in more or less the same way to each of the categories of work.[52] In other words, for practical purposes a cumulative approach will generally suffice.

There are some further points to be made about the copyright possibilities with regard to certain key elements of websites. A literary work must be "'intended to afford either information and instruction or pleasure in the form of literary enjoyment".[53] This has been taken to mean that in general a single word, or the title of a work, does not have copyright; similarly with advertising slogans consisting of stock phrases or commonplace sentences.[54] An Australian court has held that there is no copyright in the names of computer program commands, since they are merely 'triggers' for a set of instructions to be given effect by the computer.[55] This well-settled part of copyright law suggests that the phrases or key words used for hypertext links will not be protected in their own right. This was in issue in the *Shetland Times* case, where the *Times* home page

---

[50] See also the definition of a programme as an 'item' for the purposes of broadcasting in CDPA 1988, s 6(3).

[51] T Dreier, 'The cable and satellite analogy', in Hugenholtz (ed), *Future of Copyright*, 57–65 at 58.

[52] A noteworthy exception to this has traditionally existed with infringement of literary and artistic copyright: with the latter, a two-dimensional work may be infringed by a three-dimensional one, whereas the former cannot be infringed by making an object in accordance with the work. No copyright is therefore infringed by making a nuclear bomb following website (or any other written) instructions on how to do so. See Cornish, *Intellectual Property*, para 11.24.

[53] *Exxon Corporation v Exxon Insurance Consultants International Ltd* [1982] Ch 119.

[54] *Stair Memorial Encyclopaedia*, vol 18, para 951, gives the authorities.

[55] *Powerflex Services Pty Ltd* v *Data Access Corporation*, (1996) 137 ALR 498 (Fed Ct of Australia); affirmed by the High Court of Australia 30 Sept 1999 ([2000] EIPR N-1, [2000] 14(1) WIPR 3).

used the newspaper headlines as links to the material deeper within the site, and the headline texts were then taken up by *The Shetland News* to act as the links on to the *Times* stories. But, surprisingly, Lord Hamilton held that the headline texts had copyright, so that the actions of the *News* in copying them for reproduction on its own website was an infringement. In defence of Lord Hamilton's view, the creation of a headline does involve skill and labour, in that the reader's attention has to be attracted, information about the relevant item conveyed, and (at least in the case of the tabloid press, which much favours punning and jokey headlines) entertainment provided. But the protection of such a work, if any, must be very 'thin', given the necessarily limited scope of the genre,[56] and it is unlikely to extend to the typical hypertext link. More difficult might be the question of slightly more elaborate texts, such as notes on what will be found through using a link, or material on help menus and the like.

OWNERSHIP RIGHTS

The discussion so far has established that the creator of a website is very likely to enjoy copyright protection in some aspect or other should she wish to use it. In this section we turn to examine what rights the owner of the website copyrights has as a result; or, putting it another way, what acts are prohibited to a user unless authorised, expressly or impliedly, by the copyright owner or by law through the exceptions to copyright. However, it is also useful to consider the position if the creator of the website has infringed someone else's copyright in assembling the site.

Under the Copyright Designs and Patents Act 1988 as amended there are now six major exclusive rights arising from ownership of the copyright in any protected work. The restricted acts for which a licence must be sought if they are to be lawfully carried out by a person other than the copyright owner may be listed as follows[57]:

- copying;
- issuing copies of the work to the public;
- renting or lending the work to the public;
- performing, showing or playing the work in public;
- broadcasting the work or including it in a cable programme service;
- making an adaptation of the work.

In addition, a person who without right to do so authorises another to do any of the above acts is himself an infringer as well.[58] Acts of infringement may be in relation to the whole of the work or to any substantial part of it; and mea-

---

[56] By 'thin', I mean that not very much variation from the first work would be required to evade a charge of infringement.

[57] CDPA 1988 s 16(1).

[58] CDPA 1988 s 16(2).

suring the substance of what has been taken "depends much more on the qual-ity than on the quantity of what he has taken."[59] It follows, of course, that if the act can be shown to have been in relation to an insubstantial part of a work there is no infringement, and the act was one which the actor had a perfect right to do.

What effect do these various forms of exclusive owner rights have in relation to activities on the Internet? An important point of which we need to remind ourselves is that in practical terms copyright is useless to its owner unless others want to perform the various restricted acts, whereupon it becomes the basis upon which a bargain may be struck between the two sides. It may be that the owner has no wish to bargain, and expressly or impliedly gives *carte blanche* to users; but for the reasons already discussed in the introduction, this will not always be the case. It certainly cannot be assumed that by the very act of putting material on the Internet the owner has yielded up all claims made possible by copyright. Comment here is restricted to those owner rights which appear par-ticularly pertinent to the Internet.

Copying

Only the author and her licensees and successors in title can make copies of her work. The 1988 Act tells us that copying in relation to literary, dramatic, musi-cal and artistic works means reproduction of the work in any material form, and includes storage of the work in any medium by electronic means.[60] It is also pro-vided that copying in relation to any category of work (i.e. this time extending to the media copyright works) includes the making of copies that are transient or incidental to some other use of the work.[61] This is generally accepted as cov-ering the loading of software into a computer's RAM and can therefore be read-ily extended to the browser on the Internet who calls up a webpage on her computer screen. Theoretically it also covers the reproduction which occurs on the various computers and servers through which the webpage travels as it threads its way across the networks to the user's machine, although if this is not allowed it has the remarkable result that the technical basis of the operation of the Internet itself is illegal.

The concept of transient reproduction also embraces activities such as proxy server caching, where by deploying appropriate software technology Internet service providers, librarians, archivists and others make and store on their own servers temporary and regularly updated copies of materials contained on other servers with the purpose of making the information more readily available to

[59] CDPA 1988 s 16(3)(a); *Ladbroke (Football) Ltd* v *William Hill (Football) Ltd* [1964] 1 WLR 273 at 276, HL, per Lord Reid.
[60] CDPA 1988 s 17(2).
[61] CDPA 1988 s 17(6).

their own clients by avoiding congestion at the 'live' site.[62] Such operations may also amount to the infringing act of storage by electronic means.

There seems to be no doubt, therefore, that under the present UK law browsing and caching are infringements of copyright unless either there is some form of licence for that act, or they can be brought under one of the statutory permitted acts.[63] It has been said in relation to browsing that this is akin to making it infringement of copyright to read a book,[64] but it appears to be also the law in the USA (at least in relation to the maintenance of software), although apparently not clearly so in some of the countries of Continental Europe.[65] In consequence, the Software and Database Directives both contained explicit statements that transient reproduction infringed the copyright in their respective subject matters.[66]

Since downloading material from a website leads to the production of a fixed and not transient copy, whether in digital form to one's own computer or floppy disk, or as hard copy by way of a printout, it is more readily recognised in most legal systems as an infringing reproduction. Further, recalling the *Shetland Times* decision that a website item can be a cable programme, copying in relation to such a work includes making a photograph of the whole or any substantial part of any image forming part of the programme.[67] Photographs are widely defined in the UK Act,[68] and a downloaded image, whether printed or electronically stored, would be caught.

Issuing copies of the work to the public

Section 18 of the 1988 Act in effect defines issuing to the public as putting copies into circulation for the first time.[69] It is sometimes described as the right of first sale or of distribution. Only the copyright owner or his licensee can put a new reproduction of the work on the market. The right is exhausted by the initial

---

[62] For a useful note on caching by the Global Internet Project, see http://www.gip.org/caching.htm. See also C Barlas, P B Hugenholtz and A E Burke, *The Digital Intellectual Property Practice Economics Report (The Dipper Report)* (Esprit Project No 29238, 2000).

[63] A licence may of course be readily implied in the case of the browser, given that material placed on the Internet is presumably there to be accessed; *sed quaere* caching and mirroring. On implied licences and statutory exemptions, see further below, 202–3.

[64] See e.g. J Litman, "The exclusive right to read", (1994) 13 *Cardozo Arts & Entertainment Law Journal* 29 (also available at http://www.msen.com/~litman/read.htm).

[65] See *Mai Systems Corporation v Peak Computer Inc* 991 F 2d 511 (9th Cir 1993), cert dismissed, 114 S Ct 671 (1994) and Title III of the Digital Millennium Copyright Act 1998 for the USA; and for comment on the lack of clarity in Europe see P Bernt Hugenholtz, 'Adapting copyright to the information superhighway', in idem, *Future of Copyright*, 81–102 at 88–89.

[66] Software Directive, art 4(a); Database Directive, art 5(a).

[67] CDPA 1988 s 17(4).

[68] CDPA 1988, s 4(2): 'a recording of light or other radiation on any medium on which an image is produced or from which an image may by any means be produced, and which is not part of a film.'

[69] CDPA 1988 s 18.

sale, however; the second-hand bookseller does not require copyright licences in order to carry on business.

The 'on demand' transmission characteristic of the Internet does not look much like the issue of copies to the public, although it might be seen as a form of 'circulation'. This is because section 18, unlike section 17 which deals with copying, makes no reference to the notion of a 'transient copy'; the copies required for the purposes of section 18 may therefore be limited to those which are non-transient, which would go beyond mere 'on demand' transmission. If so, it would then follow that the user who accesses material and passes it on to another is not guilty of infringement under this section so long as the transmission is electronic. But if these difficulties can be overcome, and initial accession be described as the issue of a copy to a member of the public, the question still arises whether the principle of exhaustion applies so that what a party accessing a website does subsequently by way of further electronic transmission is within her rights just as she would be free to sell on the second-hand market a book which she had been the first to acquire from the publisher.[70]

Rental or lending of a work to the public

Rental is making a copy of a work available for use, on terms that it will or may be returned, for direct or indirect economic or commercial advantage.[71] The familiar example is the video or computer game rental, but following the Rental Right Directive of 1992[72] most forms of copyright work are now subject to this right. Lending right, an innovation of the Directive, is similarly defined, save that the restricted act is one performed otherwise than for direct or indirect economic or commercial advantage, and is carried out through an establishment which is accessible to the public.[73] Thus a public library's lending activities now require a copyright licence unless the book lent is within the Public Lending Right scheme set up in 1979.[74] Rental and lending do not cover making copies available for the purpose of performance, showing, playing or exhibiting in public, or for the purpose of on-the-spot reference use.[75] Are rental and lending rights applicable to Internet activities?[76] There are again difficulties with the concept of a copy, which is what must be made available, and this is underlined by the need for an expectation that the copy will be returned. This is difficult to square with the ordinary usages of the Internet. For rental some sort of

---

[70] See further Hugenholtz, 'Adapting copyright', 95–98.

[71] CDPA 1988 s 18A(2)(a).

[72] Council Directive 92/100/EEC.

[73] CDPA 1988 s 18A(2)(b).

[74] CDPA 1988, s 40A. Note however that the library of an educational establishment is generally exempted from lending right: CDPA 1988 s 36A.

[75] CDPA 1988 s 18A(3).

[76] For discussion see J Reinbothe and S von Lewinski, *The EC Directive on Rental and Lending Rights and on Piracy* (1993), 41–42. Cf Hugenholtz, 'Adapting copyright', 90.

economic or commercial advantage is necessary, while for lending there must be an establishment accessible to the public. It is less difficult, but still not easy, to see these in normal Internet services. Finally the browser or surfer on the Internet may be making 'on-the-spot reference use' of the service, which would mean that the provider was not engaging in rental or lending activities.

Public performance, showing or playing

The public performance right is restricted to literary, dramatic and musical works, and is particularly important for the exploitation of music and drama for obvious reasons. There is no reason why the script or score of a dramatic or musical work should not appear on a website, but more typically a webpage will incorporate a purely literary work. For the purposes of the 1988 Act, a performance covers any mode of visual or acoustic presentation, including by means of a cable programme.[77] There is nothing in this language to prevent an unauthorised display on a computer screen of the text of a literary work being a 'performance' of that work, provided that it takes place 'in public'.[78] In the case of sound recordings, films, broadcasts and cable programmes, the equivalent form of infringement is playing or showing the work in public.[79]

What will prevent this form of infringement being of much relevance to the Internet, at least in its present pattern of usage, is the fact that most displays of material do not take place in public. But it is important to be aware that the definition of 'public' for this particular copyright purpose is quite wide. "To be in public a performance does not have to be to a paying audience or by paid performers."[80] There has to be an audience for the performance, and the critical question is the relation between the copyright owner and that audience, "emphasising the primacy of the owner's entitlement to an economic return from his proprietary rights".[81] Traditionally the audience has been grouped together in some place where members of the public may gather, such as a theatre, a club, a shop or a place of work. But it is no longer clear that a gathering in one place is a necessary condition for performance in public. Thus in recent times, it has been held in Australia that playing recorded music 'on hold' to users of mobile telephones was 'in public' even though the distribution of the material was not necessarily, or even very often, simultaneous for each member of the audience.[82] The Spanish Supreme Court has also held that non-simultaneous transmissions of copyright material to different persons in individual hotel bed-

---

[77] CDPA 1988, s 19(2)(b).
[78] As might also occur with an overhead projector which displays documents laid on its glass paten.
[79] CDPA 1988, s 19(3).
[80] Cornish, *Intellectual Property*, para 11.33.
[81] Ibid.
[82] *Telstra Corporation Ltd* v *Australasian Performing Right Association Ltd* (1997) 191 CLR 140 (High Ct of Australia).

rooms require copyright licences.[83] The impact of decisions like these is most likely to be felt, not by the individual user accessing a website from a personal computer, but by the website operator who has incorporated other people's copyright material on his site, and could therefore be seen as performing or playing or showing that material. The fact that the members of the audience would be quite unaware of each other, and joining and leaving the audience at various times, would not seem to be relevant. There does appear to be a statutory defence if needed for Internet service providers and website owners in section 19(4), however:

> "Where copyright in a work is infringed by its being performed, played or shown in public by means of apparatus for receiving visual images or sounds conveyed by electronic means [*computer on modem or network?*], the person by whom the visual images or sounds are sent … shall not be regarded as responsible for the infringement."

Broadcasting or inclusion in a cable programme service

Neither accessing a website nor incorporation of other people's copyright material thereon can constitute broadcasting, since as already noted broadcasting is a wireless technology.[84] But "inclusion in a cable programme service", was the second basis for the interim interdict in the *Shetland Times* case. A question which may be asked, however, is whether enabling a user of one website to link to another site means that the second is 'included' within the other, or whether there are simply two connected but otherwise independent sites, the appropriate analogy being perhaps with footnotes or bibliographies or 'further reading' lists in a printed text. It has been suggested that the concept of inclusion is apt to catch the situation where one website is linked to another but the first continues in view on screen by way of a 'frame' around the image from the second site.[85]

Authorisation: Internet service provider liability

Authorisation of another to infringe is itself infringement.[86] The courts have defined authorisation as meaning sanctioning, approving or countenancing,

---

[83] *SGAE* v *Hotel Blanco DonJ.SA*, 11 Mar 1996, [1997] 1 EIPR D-21. Interestingly Spain was one of the few countries prior to the implementation of the Database Directive with express provision that 'public *access* to computer databases by means of telecommunication' is infringement where the database incorporates or constitutes a protected work. Cf *AKM* v *X*, Supreme Court of Austria, 16 June 1998, [1999] EIPR N-1, holding that a hotel's distribution of satellite TV programmes by a collective antenna system was not an infringing broadcast or public performance.

[84] See above, n 48.

[85] Holyoak and Torremans, *Intellectual Property Law*, 515; and see above, 186.

[86] CDPA 1988 s 16(2).

at their request (hosting), so long as the provider does not know of the illegal activity, is unaware of facts and circumstances from which illegal activity is apparent, and acts expeditiously to remove or disable access upon learning or becoming aware of the activity.[102] There is explicitly no obligation actively to screen or monitor third party content.[103]

Technological measures of protection

One of the ways in which rightholders have sought to deal with the problems posed by the ease of copying digital material has been the deployment of anti-copying technology within the material: for example, copy protection, encryption and digital 'watermarking'.[104] In the context of the Internet and e-commerce, such technical barriers have an even greater importance as the means by which the user or customer may be compelled to pay in order to gain unfettered access to the work. The Copyright Designs and Patents Act 1988 supports the use of such protective measures by making it equivalent to infringement of copyright for a person to manufacture or deal in a device "specifically designed or adopted to circumvent" copy-protection, provided that he knows or has reason to believe that the device will be used to make infringing copies.[105]

USER RIGHTS

Implied licence

Copyright creates a regime in which certain acts may be carried out only with the permission—licence—of the rightholder. There is no requirement in UK copyright legislation that non-exclusive licences should be in writing.[106] "Express consent [of the copyright owner] is not necessary and a licence may be implied from the dealings between the parties."[107] Given the nature of the Internet, it seems highly probable that a person who puts material on a website without technological protection is consenting to its being accessed by users of the system, so nullifying the infringement by transient reproduction which would otherwise arise under UK law.[108] But it is much less clear that caching of one's site by another can be treated as impliedly licensed by merely putting it on the Internet, and there are also questions about whether access by means of hypertext links, as in the *Shetland Times* case, or through the use of search

---

[102] See Art 14 (hosting); Art 13 (caching) is dealt with more fully below, 213–5.
[103] Art 15.
[104] See *Digital Dilemma*, ch 5, for discussion.
[105] CDPA 1988, s 296.
[106] For exclusive licences, which do require writing, see CDPA 1988, s 92.
[107] Laddie, Prescott and Vitoria, para 14.12.
[108] See above, 195.

engines, can be legitimised in this way.[109] In particular, does the creator of a website impliedly license the producers of search engine databases to add her site to that database, thus making it easier for users to access with their implied licence? In *British Leyland* v *Armstrong Patents Co Ltd*,[110] the issue was the right of the defendants to mass-produce and supply spare parts for cars, the design of which was (as the law then stood) the copyright of the plaintiff car manufacturers. When the case began, owners of cars and other goods were thought to have an implied licence to infringe this copyright for the purpose of repairing their property. The defendants argued that this licence extended to their activities, to enable owners to exercise their rights efficiently. The argument that the implied licence could stretch to third parties was rejected both at first instance and in the Court of Appeal,[111] because the defendants manufactured the parts before receiving any particular commission from customers. Such reasoning seems clearly applicable also to the work of the creators of the search engine as providers of a service to third parties; on the other hand, the creation of a website which was not accessible through search engines would limit its effectiveness drastically.

Returning to the user's implied licence, can it go beyond access to cover other otherwise infringing acts, such as printing out or downloading material? This is more debatable, although again well-established practice might mean that, in the absence of express prohibition or security measures by the website operator, such activities should normally be treated as authorised. An Australian case, *Trumpet Software Pty Ltd* v *OzEmail Pty Ltd*,[112] shows how far a court may be prepared to go with the concept of an implied licence. The defendants were held entitled to bundle the plaintiffs' software with their own and distribute it commercially over the Internet against the plaintiffs' wishes, because the software had been originally marketed as 'shareware', that is, as available for free use and reproduction. This has obvious significance for the Internet because so many of those putting material up believe it to be a community rather than an area of sharply defined and fenced property rights. But the Australian court did draw limitations upon the implied licence, holding that the redistribution was only to be of the entire software, without any adjustment to the original product. It seems plausible to suppose in the light of this that, while a website may well be subject to an implied licence for private access, downloading and printing, this will not extend to dissemination of the material in another form (e.g. hard copy publication), especially for commercial gain or advantage. Nor should it extend to the obtaining of copyright material without express licence by way of, although not from, a website, as in the MP3.com and Napster cases.

---

[109] Note however that in its decision of 29 June 1999 the OLG Düsseldorf (above, n 14) held that publishing a website in general implied consent to linking from other sites.

[110] [1986] RPC 279.

[111] The House of Lords criticised the use of the concept of implied licence to justify repair by the owner, and took repair to be a right which needed no licence of any kind from the copyright owner.

[112] [1996] 18(12) EIPR 69.

Fair dealing

The Copyright Designs and Patents Act 1988 makes extensive and detailed provision by which various specified acts which would otherwise fall within the scope of the infringement rules are made lawful.[113] Such acts therefore do not require any licence from the copyright owner. In this there is a contrast with US law, which provides a general 'fair use' defence covering purposes 'such as' criticism, comment, teaching, scholarship and research, and indicating that factors to be taken into account 'include' such matters as whether the use is of a commercial nature or for non-profit educational purposes, the amount and substantiality of the portion used in relation to the whole work, and the effect of the use upon the market or value of the copyright work.[114] There is also, as already noted,[115] a contrast with Continental laws, which tend to exclude private copying from the scope of copyright, although a concomitant in many of these systems is levies on blank audio cassettes and reprography, the proceeds from which are routed back ultimately to copyright owners via their collecting societies.[116]

There has been little discussion in Britain to compare with the US debate on whether fair dealing rules merely provide defences to claims of infringement or are free-standing user or public rights. As observed in a recent US report:

> "The difference matters, for both theoretical and pragmatic reasons. If fair use is an affirmative right, for instance, then it ought to be acceptable to take positive actions, such as circumventing content protection mechanisms (e.g. decoding an encrypted file), in order to exercise fair use. But taking such positive actions may well be illegal under the regime of fair use as a defense."[117]

There has also been little British discussion of whether the fair dealing provisions to be discussed below prevail over contrary contractual provision, contained for example in a copyright licence. Cornish remarks that "it has generally been assumed in British and other copyright systems that exceptions [to copyright] do have this character".[118] Following the case of *ProCD* v *Zeidenberg*[119] and the passage in 1999 of what is now the Uniform Computer Information Transactions Act, however, the matter has become controversial in the USA,[120]

---

[113] CDPA 1988, ss 28-76.

[114] Copyright Act 1976, §107.

[115] See above, 183.

[116] See e.g. the French Intellectual Property Code of 1 July 1992, L122-5, L211-3, L212-10, and L311; and German Copyright Act 1965, §§ 53, 54 and 54a–h.

[117] See *Digital Dilemma*, 5. For further discussion of fair use see ibid, ch 4, and conclusions at 213–5.

[118] Cornish, *Intellectual Property*, para 13.86.

[119] 86 F.3d 1447 (7th Cir, 1996).

[120] See P Samuelson and K Opsdahl, "The tensions between intellectual property and contracts in the information age: an American perspective", in F W Grosheide and K Boele-Woelki (eds), *Molengrafica: Europees Privaatrecht 1998* (1999).

leading inevitably to discussion, as yet inconclusive, on the other side of the Atlantic.[121]

(a) Research and private study

Probably the most obviously significant permitted act for users of websites under the 1988 Act is fair dealing with a literary, dramatic, musical or artistic work (but not computer programs or media works), which is for the purposes of research or private study. The exemption would appear clearly applicable to the user of a website making hard or electronic copies of the material she finds there; but how much can be taken? Parliament has resisted publishing lobbies seeking a quantifiable measure of how much of a work may be copied or used under this exemption, and it remains arguable that in some circumstances the whole of a work may be taken. Can the operator of a website use the research and private study exemption to justify putting up on her site the copyright works of others? In the French cases about the unauthorised inclusion of the poetry of Raymond Queneau on websites, it was held that a website unprotected by security devices and open to any visitor was in the public domain and that the copying involved in its creation could not be justified by the general exemption in French law for private reproduction.[122] UK law has no general saving for private use, and it seems likely that a British court would reach the same conclusion as the French one, albeit by the route that the private study exemption applies only to one's own study and not to making private study possible for third parties.[123] Admittedly, in the British cases the copier was supplying the copied material in the course of business, while a website producer might well not be earning any financial return from her activities; but the court would likely be concerned about the probable damage to the earnings of the copyright owner and so deem the activity unfair. The rule that the exemption does not apply to one whose copying makes private study and research possible for others seems to eliminate any possibility that this exception could be used by those who provide materials by way of proxy server caches, and British courts would also probably agree with the New York decision that it was not fair use for MP3.com to copy CDs into MP3 format to enable them to be accessed by Internet customers who were lawful users of the CDs.[124]

---

[121] See L Guibault, "Pre-emption issues in the digital environment: can copyright limitations be overridden by contractual agreements under European law?", in ibid, and further, below, 222.

[122] French Intellectual Property Code of 1 July 1992, L122-5; above 186.

[123] *University of London Press Ltd v University Tutorial Press Ltd* [1916] 2 Ch 601; *Sillitoe v McGraw-Hill Book Co (UK) Ltd* [1983] FSR 545.

[124] *UMG Recordings Inc and others v MP3.com Inc*, US District Court, SDNY (Rakoff J), 4 May 2000, http://www.nysd.uscourts.gov/courtweb/pdf/00-04756.pdf. The logic would also seem applicable to the activities of Napster.

(b) Criticism or review

Fair dealing for purposes of criticism or review also exempts from charges of copyright infringement.[125] In an American case about posting the published and unpublished works of L Ron Hubbard on a bulletin board, the party who made the posting was held unentitled to a fair use defence although he had added to the texts some criticisms of Hubbard's doctrines, in consequence of the very small amount of commentary compared to the quantity of copied text.[126] There is a parallel case in the UK, also involving the unauthorised publication (although in a traditional rather than an electronic medium) of Hubbard's works with some critical commentary thereupon. But the Court of Appeal found that the criticism made the taking of substantial extracts of the copyright material fair dealing.[127] In *Pro Sieben Media AG v Carlton UK Television Ltd*[128] the Court of Appeal held that the extent of use was relevant in considering fair dealing, but that relevance would depend on the circumstances of each case. Most important was the degree of competition, if any, between the two works in question. The mental element of the user was of little importance, so that a sincere belief that one was being critical in one's handling of the previous work would not be enough to make out the defence. However, the court emphasised that the phrase 'criticism or review' was of wide and indefinite scope and should be interpreted liberally.

(c) Reporting current events

The Court of Appeal in *Pro Sieben* also directed its last comment above at the third form of fair dealing, namely, reporting current events. *Hyde Park Residence Ltd v Yelland*[129] was concerned with the unauthorised publication by the *Sun* in September 1998 of CCTV photographs of Princess Diana and Dodi al-Fayed, taken on the day of their deaths on 31 August 1997 at the former mansion of the Duchess of Windsor. Jacob J held that the one-year gap in time did not prevent these events continuing to be 'current', given the continuing publicity about the visit arising from statements made two days before the publication in question by Mohammed al-Fayed, tenant of the mansion and, through a security company which he controlled, owner of the copyright in the pho-

---

[125] CDPA 1988 s 30.

[126] *Religious Technology Center v Lerma*, US District Court for the Eastern District of Virginia, 4 Oct 1996 (http://www.bna.com/e-law/cases/lerma.html). In similar circumstances in *Religious Technology Center v Netcom On-Line Communication Service* 907 F Supp 1361 (ND Cal, 1995), however, the court held that Netcom, a service provider, might have a valid fair use defence.

[127] *Hubbard v Vosper* [1972] 2 QB 84 (CA). I fell into error in describing the outcome of this case in the previous version of this chapter.

[128] [1999] FSR 610 (CA).

[129] [1999] RPC 655 (Jacob J); [2000] TLR 104 (CA). A full transcript of the judgments can be found on the Smith Bernal Casetrack website: see in particular paras 32, 40 (Aldous LJ, with whom Stuart-Smith LJ agreed), and 77–78 (Mance LJ).

tographs. This 'liberal' approach to the definition of current events was accepted by the Court of Appeal, even although the *Sun's* actual use of the photographs was held not to be fair dealing because the falsity of Mr al-Fayed's statements was already public knowledge and the spread given to material itself dishonestly obtained and hitherto unpublished was excessive. In another case having some significance for those who gather and store information from the Internet, such as librarians and archivists, it was held that a company which ran a daily programme of circulating and distributing amongst its executives copies of newspaper cuttings provided by a licensed cuttings agency could maintain that this was fair dealing for the purpose of reporting current events.[130]

Education, libraries and archives

The limited scope of the permitted acts bears particularly harshly upon activities within educational establishments.[131] Sir Ron Dearing's 1997 report on the future of higher education in the UK argued strongly for greatly expanding the use of information technology in the sector, commenting that "there must be provision for the free and immediate use by teachers and researchers of copyright digital information,"[132] and recommending a review of copyright legislation to facilitate this. Such a sweeping exemption would run counter to the British tradition in this area (and indeed the Government has taken no action on the recommendation); but it would find some support in, for example, US and German legislation.[133]

The 1988 Act also contains very detailed provisions exempting certain activities of libraries and archives from the scope of copyright infringement. Speaking very broadly, these provisions enable libraries and archives prescribed by the Secretary of State to supply readers with a single copy of published literary, dramatic or musical material for the purposes of private study or research, provided that the reader pays a sum not less than the cost attributable to producing the copy.[134] The exemption is undoubtedly geared to a world of hard rather than electronic copies, and would not seem readily applicable to making

---

[130] *Newspaper Licensing Agency* v *Marks and Spencer plc* (CA), *The Times* 15 June 2000, rev'g [1999] TLR 60 (Lightman J). The Court of Appeal held that in any event there had been no infringement by the defendants, since what was copied was not a substantial part of the original copyright work (the typographical arrangement of the *whole* newspaper, as distinct from the articles copied).

[131] See apart from sections already cited CDPA 1988 ss 32-36; Cornish, *Intellectual Property*, paras 13.09–13.23.

[132] National Committee of Inquiry into Higher Education (Chairman Sir Ron Dearing), *Higher Education in the Learning Society* (1997), para 13.34; and see Recommendation 43.

[133] See US Copyright Act § 107 ('nonprofit educational purposes'); German Copyright Act 1965 § 53.

[134] CDPA ss 37-44; Copyright (Librarians and Archivists) (Copying of Copyright Material) Regulations 1989, SI 1989/1212.

Internet material available, or storing it in advance of a specific demand, via a proxy cache on the computers or servers in the library or archive.[135]

Shifting in time and space?

If it is right that a website is a cable programme service and a webpage a cable programme as an item within the service, as held in the *Shetland Times* case, then there may be room to plead the 'time-shifting' exemption which is specifically allowed under the 1988 Act for private recording of broadcast or cable material to enable it to be viewed at a more convenient time.[136] But since a user can access Internet material at any time, such an argument may be hard to sustain.[137] There seems to be no room, however, for an argument under British law such as that advanced, unsuccessfully, in the MP3.com case in the USA: that since the company's activities allowed users to listen to the music, not only at the time but also in the place most convenient to them ('space- or place-shifting'), a fair use defence was available.[138] Thus, copying a computer program from one's PC to a laptop, or a CD onto tape to play on one's car audio system, seem not to fall within the scope of any current copyright exception.

Public policy and public interest; no derogation from grant

Going beyond the strict confines of the copyright legislation, at least three, closely-linked, limitations upon copyright have been discussed in the cases.[139] One is the public policy concept that certain types of work—pornography or material published in breach of a lifelong obligation of secrecy, for example— are undeserving of the protection of copyright.[140] This could obviously cover much material on the Internet. A second limitation is one which allows otherwise infringing acts on the grounds that they are in the public interest.[141] The scope and, indeed, existence of this defence remain uncertain, although in twice affirming it in 1999 Jacob J formulated the test as being one of reasonable certainty that no right-thinking member of society would quarrel with the validity of the defence in the circumstances.[142] The public interest defence in the law of

---

[135] See H Brett and B Goodger, 'Libraries in the Internet and the electronic age', [1997] 13 EIPR 38–41; T Hoeren and U Decker, 'Electronic archives and the press: copyright problems of mass media in the digital age', [1998] 14 EIPR 256–266.

[136] CDPA 1988, s 70.

[137] Holyoak and Torremans, *Intellectual Property Law*, 518.

[138] *UMG Recordings Inc and others v MP3.com Inc*, US District Court, SDNY (Rakoff J), 4 May 2000, http://www.nysd.uscourts.gov/courtweb/pdf/00-04756.pdf.

[139] These exceptions are preserved by CDPA 1988, s 171(3).

[140] See e.g. *Glyn v Weston Feature Film Co* [1916] 1 Ch 261; *Attorney-General v Guardian Newspapers Ltd (No 2)* [1990] 1 AC 109.

[141] *Beloff v Pressdram* [1973] RPC 765.

[142] *Hyde Park Residence Ltd v Yelland* [1999] RPC 655; *Mars UK Ltd v Teknowledge Ltd* [2000] FSR 138.

confidential information has been applied in relation to the unauthorised publication of information and material generated but kept secret by public authorities. If the authority's motivation in preventing publication is improper—for example, to conceal the failings of its officials—then an unauthorised publication, including one on the Internet, may be justified.[143] In the *Hyde Park Residence* case,[144] described earlier, Jacob J took a similar approach to copyright, holding that the public interest defence was applicable against a private individual (Mohammed al-Fayed), enabling the defendant to counter misleading public statements about how much time Diana and Dodi had spent at the 'House of Windsor' on the day of their deaths. But this was overturned by the Court of Appeal,[145] the majority (Aldous LJ and Stuart-Smith LJ) holding that (1) there was no public interest defence separate from that of public policy; (2) the circumstances in which copyright would not be enforced must derive from the work itself (i.e. its immoral character or deleterious effects) rather than from the conduct of the owner of copyright; and (3) the considerations arising in breach of confidence cases, where the courts balanced the public interest in maintaining confidentiality against the public interest in knowledge of the truth and freedom of expression, were different from copyright ones, where property rights were involved and the legislation already provided fair dealing defences in the public interest. It should not be possible for public interest to uphold as legitimate an act that had been found, as in this case, not to be fair dealing.[146] While generally agreeing with this approach, the third member of the Court, Mance LJ, indicated that there might be cases where a public interest dimension did arise from the ownership of the work, although this was not such a case.[147]

Finally, in the *British Leyland* case[148] mentioned in a previous section, the House of Lords declared that a copyright owner could be deprived of his rights where their exercise was in 'derogation from grant'. The context, as already noted, was the manufacture and supply to consumers of spare parts for cars, to which the car manufacturers took objection by means of copyright. The House found that car owners had a right to repair their vehicles, and that the car manufacturers could not exercise their copyright so as to prevent third parties enabling the owners to exercise their rights as cheaply as possible. This was founded on the general legal principle of 'no derogation from grant', established in the context of leases, sales of goodwill and easements or servitudes. It had never been previously applied to copyright, and the reasoning of the House on

---

[143] See in particular the breach of confidence case, *Lion Laboratories Ltd* v *Evans* [1985] QB 526, in support of this broad formulation; but see comments on the case by the Court of Appeal in *Hyde Park Residence Ltd* v *Yelland* [2000] TLR 104. For a possible example involving the use of mirror sites on the Internet see Y Akdeniz, 'Copyright and the Internet', (1997) 147 *New Law Journal* 965.

[144] [1999] RPC 655.

[145] [2000] TLR 104.

[146] See paras 55, 58, 64–67; and above, 206–7, on the fair dealing issue.

[147] Paras 79-83.

[148] [1986] AC 577 gives the House of Lords' speeches only.

the point is unsatisfactory.[149] The Privy Council has since indicated that the principle should be interpreted very narrowly in copyright law, and that it is really based on public policy.[150] Nonetheless, it is therefore still applicable,[151] and may find some application in the context of the Internet, perhaps in relation to the questions about activities such as downloading and the construction and deployment of search engines mentioned above in the comments on implied licences.[152]

INTERNATIONAL REFORM: THE EUROPEAN DIRECTIVE

The foregoing survey of the application of UK copyright to the Internet has shown some of the difficulties with which the law is now faced, and the occasional comparative reference has shown that they are also confronted in other legal systems. Given the global reach of the Internet, and its social and commercial significance as the network matures into the information superhighway, it has seemed necessary to take international action to enable copyright law to respond and adapt in a reasonably uniform and harmonised way around the world. The USA took the initiative with a report in 1995 by its Information Infrastructure Task Force entitled *Intellectual Property and the National Information Infrastructure*. The European Union, concerned to harmonise the diverse copyright laws of its Member States, followed suit with Green Papers in 1995 and 1996.[153] The latter year also saw the completion, under the auspices of the World Intellectual Property Organisation, of a Copyright Treaty additional to the Berne Convention, and specifically aimed at some of the most troublesome issues.[154] Many of these initiatives are now bearing fruit in local legislation, actual and potential, around the world: for example, the Digital Millennium Copyright Act 1998 in the USA and the Copyright Amendment (Digital Agenda) Act 2000 in Australia. In the European Union, a draft Directive on Copyright and the Information Society was first published late in 1997.[155] It has since been making its way slowly through the Union's co-decision legislative procedures, involving complex interaction between the European Commission, the Council of Ministers and the European Parliament which was not complete at the time of writing (August 2000). If the text can be agreed, it will become a European Parliament and Council Directive for implementation

---

[149] See H L MacQueen, *Copyright, Competition and Industrial Design*, 2nd edn, 3(2) Hume Papers on Public Policy (1995), 45–47.

[150] *Canon Kabushiki Kaisha* v *Green Cartridge Co (Hong Kong) Ltd* [1997] AC 728.

[151] See in particular *Mars UK Ltd* v *Teknowledge Ltd* [2000] FSR 138 (Jacob J), a case about reverse engineering of computer programs and databases. The defence was rejected, however.

[152] See above, 202–3.

[153] *Copyright and Related Rights in the Information Society*, COM (95) 382 final; *Follow-Up to the Green Paper on Copyright and Related Rights in the Information Society*, COM (96) 568 final.

[154] For a general comment see T C Vinje, 'The new WIPO Copyright Treaty: a happy result in Geneva', [1997] 5 EIPR 230–236.

[155] Brussels, 10.12.1997, COM(97) 628 final; OJ 1998, C108/6.

in the Member States.[156] Now through the legislative process is a directive on electronic commerce, which has already been referred to in the context of on-line service provider liability, and which contains significant provisions on the problem of caching.[157]

The WIPO Treaty 1996

It is best to begin with the WIPO Treaty of 1996, which contains a number of provisions designed to address the copyright problems of the Internet, and to which the draft Copyright Directive is designed to give effect and, indeed, to go beyond. The Treaty is significant for its silence on certain subjects, reflecting a failure of the parties at the time to agree upon the appropriate way forward. So there was a proposal for an Article stating explicitly that the right of reproduction included temporary or transient reproduction, as is already the position in the UK, but this was dropped after much controversy, although it was agreed that the present Berne Convention provision (Article 9(1)) does not cover such reproduction.[158] As will be discussed further below, however, the draft directive does tackle this issue head-on.

Turning back for the moment to what the WIPO Treaty does say, Article 8 provides for a new 'right of communication to the public' by wire or wireless means. This right includes (and so is not confined to) making work available to the public in such a way that members of the public may access these works from a place and at a time individually chosen by them; i.e. by way of transmission on the Internet. This will certainly be the most immediately important aspect of the public communication right. The real significance of the right is that it removes the need for a physical copy to exist before the rightholder can control the distribution of a work. Further, Article 10 of the 1996 Treaty succeeds in setting the scene for a more restrictive approach to user rights or limitations on the scope of copyright. Article 9(2) of the Berne Convention states the 'three-step' test for user rights: reproduction may be allowed "in certain special cases, provided that such exploitation does not conflict with a normal exploitation of the work and does not unreasonably prejudice the legitimate interests of

---

[156] At the time of writing the current version of the draft Directive was that on which the Council of Ministers reached political agreement on 8 June 2000. I have relied upon a text obtained from the Brussels office of the Law Society of Scotland (to which my thanks), and bearing to have been approved by COREPER Brussels 16 June 2000. This text replaces that published by the Commission on 21 May 1999 (COM(1999) 250 final), OJ 1999, C180/6). The Commission proposal took account of amendments put forward by the European Parliament in January and February 1999. The progress of the Directive can be followed on the website of the Internal Market DG (http://europa.eu.int/comm/internal_market).

[157] European Parliament and Council Directive on certain legal aspects of Information Society services, in particular electronic commerce in the Internal Market, Directive 2000/31/EC, 8 June 2000. Note recital 50 of the Directive, stating that 'it is important' that the copyright and the E-Commerce Directives 'come into force within a similar timescale'.

[158] See Vinje, 'The new WIPO Copyright Treaty', 230–4.

the author."[159] For some reason, Article 10 of the WIPO Treaty repeats this formula no less than twice, but, significantly, where Berne talks of 'permitting' such acts, the Article speaks of 'confining' them. The scene is thereby set for the elimination or whittling down of user rights and the assertion of greater producer control over the use of the Internet. This is also apparent in other Articles, which require Contracting Parties to provide a legal framework to protect technological means of control over use such as copy protection and encryption against circumvention by third parties (Articles 11 and 12), and do not allow any reservations to the Treaty (Article 22).

The draft Copyright Directive

The draft Copyright Directive follows the basic approach of enhancing the position of the copyright owner and narrowing down the rights of the user.[160] Its underlying policies emerge clearly enough from the recitals, which, while paying lip service to the importance of user rights in the pursuit of ideals of freedom of expression and dissemination of information, ideas and culture (recitals 10ter, 14bis), emphasise still more strongly the need for a high level of intellectual property protection to "foster substantial investment in creativity and innovation, including network infrastructure" (recital 3) and to ensure the availability of reward and satisfactory returns on investment in creative work and the products by which that work is brought to its public (recitals 8-10, 14bis). The protection therefore has more of an entrepreneurial than a moral right justification, although there are glancing references to the maintenance and development of creativity and the independence and dignity of artistic creators

---

[159] The 'three steps' are: (1) special case; (2) no conflict with normal exploitation; (3) no unreasonable prejudice to author's legitimate interests. See also the Agreement on Trade-Related Aspects of Intellectual Property Rights (TRIPS Agreement) 1994, Art 13.

[160] Space prohibits consideration of Art 4, which will harmonise the distribution right. As the original Explanatory Memorandum makes clear, this right refers 'exclusively to fixed copies that can be put into circulation as tangible objects' (COM(1997) 628 final, 27 (para 1)). See also recital 18 of the amended proposal, which talks of 'the exclusive right to control distribution of the work incorporated in a tangible article'. The Agreed Statements concerning the WIPO Copyright Treaty provisions on distribution and rental right (Arts 6 and 7) also state that they apply 'exclusively to fixed copies that can be put into circulation as tangible objects'. The limitation of exhaustion of rights to the European Community, and implicit rejection of a principle of international exhaustion, in Art 4 of the Copyright Directive is interesting in light of the debate about this topic in trade mark law sparked by Case C-355/96, *Silhouette International Scmied GmbH & Co KG v Hartlauer Handelsgesellschaft* [1998] ECR I-3457; Case C-173/98, *Sebago Inc and Ancienne Maison Dubois et Fils SA* v *GB-Unic SA* [1999] ECR I-4103; and the contrasting judgments of Laddie J in *Zino Davidoff SA v A & G Imports Ltd* [1999] 3 All ER 711 and Lord Kingarth in *Zino Davidoff SA v M & S Toiletries; Joop! GmbH v M & S Toiletries* 2000 SLT 683. In Declaration 4 of the Annex to the COREPER text of the draft Directive the Commission confirms that Art 4 is intended to continue the present position on international exhaustion, while undertaking to keep a watching brief on developments. In Declaration 9, the Danish, Irish, Luxembourg, Dutch, Finnish and Swedish delegations state that they favour international exhaustion and call for reconsideration of the issue.

and performers (recitals 8, 9bis). The Directive is to be a basis for making the Internet commercial.

The specific provisions by which this goal is to be achieved are (i) harmonisation of the reproduction right to include temporary reproduction by any means and in any form (Article 2); (ii) the establishment of a public communication right for authors as set out in the WIPO Treaty, that is, communication "including the making available to the public of . . . works in such a way that members of the public may access them from a place and at a time individually chosen by them" (Article 3); and (iii) the restriction of user rights, at least so far as these may apply in a digital context (Article 5). While the first of these provisions is already essentially the law in the UK, the public communication right will, from the copyright owner's point of view, eliminate the gaps in protection left in the electronic and digital world of the Internet by the present rules on distribution (i.e. the limitation to first sale, rental and commercial lending of hard copies), public performance (i.e. the need for the infringing activity to be in public and a performance for an audience), and broad- and cable-casting (i.e. too technology-specific).[161]

The real controversy during the passage of the Directive to date, however, has been over whether these extended rights for owners have been sufficiently balanced by the provisions for users—the exceptions to the restricted acts of reproduction and public communication—set out in Article 5. The original proposals of the European Commission in this area were substantially modified at the behest of the European Parliament, which had been successfully lobbied by rightholder interests; it remains to be seen whether the responses of the Commission and the Council, by no means wholly accepting of the Parliament's views, will satisfy either that body or the vociferous opposing lobbies striving to affect the final text. The importance of the debate is that, at least with regard to reproduction and public communication rights in the digital context, these exceptions will entirely replace existing national rules on the subject,[162] including, therefore, the British provisions on fair dealing discussed earlier in this chapter.[163] However, at present all but one of the exceptions listed in Article 5 is permissive—that is, the Member States may (and therefore need not) introduce them.

Proposed mandatory exception to reproduction right

The only mandatory exception is to reproduction right, and is in respect of :

---

[161] Could it be applied to stop linking, which is a means of making works available to the public at a place and time individually chosen by them?

[162] COM(1997) 628 final, 28 (para 2); see also recital 22 and art 5(3)(p), the latter of which permits Member States to provide for 'use in certain other cases of minor importance where exceptions already exist under national law, *provided that they only concern analogue uses* [emphasis supplied] and do not affect the free circulation of goods and services within the Community'.

[163] See above, 204–7.

> "temporary acts of reproduction . . . which are transient and incidental, which are an integral and essential part of a technological process, whose sole purpose is to enable
> (a) a transmission in a network between third parties by an intermediary or
> (b) a lawful use,
> of a work or other subject matter to be made, and which have no independent economic significance . . ." [164]

The obvious example falling within this exception is the reproduction which occurs on computers and servers as material makes its way across the Internet from the supplier site to the recipient who has called it up. The European Parliament sought to prevent the exception also extending to proxy server caching, but such a limitation was rejected by the Commission on the ground that if right-owners' authorisation was required for cache copies, the effective operation of the Internet would be seriously hindered.[165] Caching may also be saved by the exception for temporary reproductions enabling 'lawful use'; as we will see below, such lawful uses include research and illustration for teaching,[166] and recital 23 comments that "this exception should include acts which enable browsing as well as acts of caching to take place, including those which enable transmission systems to function efficiently"—that is, those which prevent undue congestion at 'live' sites.[167]

The favouring of caching also emerges in the E-Commerce Directive, Article 13 of which is headed 'Caching' and which exempts Internet service providers from liability:

> "for the automatic, intermediate and temporary storage of that information, performed for the sole purpose of making more efficient the information's onward transmission to other recipients of the service upon their request."

The service provider must comply with a number of conditions, notably obligations not to modify the information and to comply with any requirements about access or updating of the material. Nor must it interfere with lawful uses of accepted technology to obtain data on the use of information at its site. Further, if the service provider obtains actual knowledge that either the information at the original source has been removed from the network or access to it has been barred or a competent authority has ordered such removal or barring, it must act expeditiously to remove or bar access itself, or else the exemption will be lost. Finally, national courts and administrative authorities are enabled to require the service provider to terminate or prevent infringements taking

---

[164] Art 5(1).

[165] See COM(1999) 250 final, para 4(1).

[166] See below, 221–2.

[167] In Declaration 1 in the Annex to the COREPER text of the draft Directive, the Council and Commission declare that they are of the view that the wording in recital 23, 'provided that the intermediary does not modify the information and does not interfere with the lawful use of technology, widely recognised and used by industry, to obtain data on the use of the information', does not exclude proxy server caching by an intermediary from being exempted under art 5(1), if such caching meets the conditions of the article.

place. Overall, this is broadly the approach already adopted in the USA under the Digital Millennium Copyright Act,[168] and it therefore appears likely to become the global rule in future,[169] although service providers remain profoundly concerned that it places an unrealistic burden upon them to respond to complaints of infringement from all and sundry.

Proposed non-mandatory exceptions

Of greater concern now are the non-mandatory exceptions provided for at some length in the remainder of Article 5 of the Directive. An obvious initial point is that the permissive regime certainly does not serve the basic goal of European harmonisation, and there still seems present the danger referred to in the Explanatory Memorandum to the Commission's initial proposal:

> "Without adequate harmonization of these exceptions, as well as of the conditions of their application, Member States might continue to apply a large number of rather different limitations and exceptions to these rights and, consequently, apply these rights in different forms."[170]

Indeed, France, Italy and Spain have expressly indicated their lack of satisfaction with the position and their intention to ensure that the optional exceptions are interpreted strictly in order to prevent the risk of substantial disparities between Member States.[171] On the other hand, Luxembourg believes that the closed list of exceptions is too restrictive "and introduces an imbalance in favour of rightholders at the expense of users, who run the risk of being deprived of the advantages offered by the new digital environment."[172] Recital 22 of the Directive notes that the list of exceptions;

> "takes due account of the different legal traditions in Member States, while, at the same time, aiming to ensure a functioning Internal Market. It is desirable that Member States should arrive at a *coherent application* [emphasis supplied] of these exceptions, which will be assessed when reviewing implementing legislation in the future."

Space does not allow for a detailed treatment of the provisions, not all of which are equally relevant to the Internet. Throughout, a balance or compromise has had to be struck between the different traditions of Continental and British copyright law, the former favouring private use provided the rightholder

---

[168] 17 USC Title II.
[169] Similar provisions are found in the Australian Copyright Amendment (Digital Agenda) Act 2000.
[170] COM(1997) 628 final, 28 (para 1). On the other hand, Cornish, *Intellectual Property*, paras 13.70 and 13.84, questions the constitutional power of the EU to confine national authority over copyright in these matters.
[171] See Addendum 13 to the Annex to the COREPER text of the draft Directive.
[172] Ibid, Addendum 12.

receives fair compensation,[173] the latter free use in a number of specified areas extending beyond the purely private domain. The key issues may be summarised as follows.

(i) Reprography

An initial proposal was to permit reprography (i.e. photocopying), within the scope of the 'three steps' of Article 9(2) of the Berne Convention (i.e. special cases of exploitation not conflicting with normal exploitation, and without unreasonable prejudice to the author's legitimate interests). This has been amended in the interests of the publishing industry, first, to exclude sheet music altogether from the scope of the exception, and, second, to say that reprography is only permitted if the right holder receives fair compensation (as to which see further below).[174] Reprography is defined as reproduction on paper or any similar medium, effected by the use of any kind of photographic technique or similar process; therefore it does not cover bringing material from a website onto a computer screen, downloading that material to disk, or printing it. It may therefore be of only very limited relevance to Internet copyright.

(ii) Private copies

Much more significant was a further initial proposal to allow natural persons to make private copies of audio, visual and audio-visual material, again subject to Berne Article 9(2). The supporting argument was that, in general, prevention of private copying was not possible; the relevance to the Internet was the fact that so much user activity was at least arguably of a private nature. But complex amendments were made in the European Parliament at the urgent and clamorous behest of the film, music and recording industries, already deeply concerned by piratical activities generally, and further alarmed by the Internet possibilities of MP3 software. In all cases, conditions that the rightholders receive fair compensation and that the copy be for 'strictly personal use' were added. In addition, a distinction was drawn between analogue and digital material: with the latter, the exception was to be "without prejudice to operational, reliable and effective technical means capable of protecting the interests of rightholders". The special concern with digital material was the ease and speed of perfect and multiple reproductions, especially by way of the Internet, which could make far deeper inroads upon the structures of the recording industries than was ever possible in the past with analogue copying.[175] On the other hand, digital technology itself may eventually provide the means to bar private

---

[173] France, Italy and Spain have indicated their intention to be 'particularly vigilant in ensuring . . . that, in all cases where this is provided for in the Directive, use of works is accompanied by fair compensation' (Addendum 13 to the COREPER text of the Annex to the draft Directive).

[174] Art 5(2)(a).

[175] COM(1997) 628 final, 30-31 (para 6). Consider the activities of MP3.com and Napster.

copying, and the draft thus left open this route to the rightholder's protection, reinforced by provisions in Article 6 making illegal the circumvention of such technological measures of protection.[176]

However, Article 5 has been further amended in the Council of Ministers, which has restored the generality of the exception favouring private use by a natural person for non-commercial ends, extended it to all copyright works, and dropped any distinction between the analogue and the digital. The potential impact for users of the Internet seems large. True to the Continental pattern, however, rightholders must receive 'fair compensation'; moreover, this must take into account "the application or non-application of technological measures referred to in Article 6 to the work or subject matter concerned".[177] How will these requirements affect the Internet?

(iii) Fair compensation

First, it will be apparent that the exemptions of reprography and private use look set to be dependent upon 'fair compensation' of the rightholders to be effective. So, directly or indirectly, these uses will not be free to the user. In other words, so far as the UK is concerned, and despite its now long-sustained opposition to such a move,[178] there will almost certainly have to be a falling into line with those other Member States which provide for levies upon the equipment, material and (perhaps) institutions which enable reprography or private copying of copyright works to take place, along with a machinery to ensure the collection of licence fees and the fair distribution of the proceeds amongst rightholders; functions in which the collecting societies and the Copyright Tribunal will probably have the major roles. The recitals to the draft Directive state that a 'valuable' criterion for measuring the amount of compensation "would be the possible harm to the rightholders resulting from the act in question. . . . In certain situations where the prejudice to the rightholder would be minimal, no obligation for payment may arise."[179] Further, "in cases where rightholders have already received payment in some other form, for instance as part of a licence fee, no specific or separate payment may be due."[180] This may be particularly relevant where the rightholder is using technological measures of protection against access to and copying of his material (see further (iv) below).

(iv) Technological measures of protection and copyright exceptions

The initial draft rules in Article 6 made unlawful any circumvention 'without authority' of effective technological measures designed to protect copyrights or

---

[176] See (iv) below for Art 6.

[177] Art 5(2)(b). See further (6) below for Art 6.

[178] Cornish, *Intellectual Property*, para 13–17.

[179] Recital 24bis. The Commission gives as an example copying for purposes of 'time-shifting' of broadcasts (see Declaration 2 of the Annex to the COREPER text of the draft Directive).

[180] Ibid.

related rights.[181] Technological measures were defined as "any technology, device or component that, in the normal course of its operation, is designed to prevent or inhibit" infringement of copyright or related rights; these were to be deemed effective "where the access to or use of a protected work or other subject matter is controlled through application of an access code or any other type of protection process which achieves the protection objective in an operational and reliable manner with the authority of the rightholders." Examples included "decryption, descrambling or other transformation of the work."[182] Thus, should the technology evolve to the point of complete effectiveness, the Internet user's right to make a private copy from a website, even for strictly personal use, would have been nullified, it seemed; unless the private use exception itself could be treated as an 'authority' justifying circumvention.

This last proposition was fiercely debated, and further amendments to clarify the relationship between Articles 5 and 6 were made in the Council of Ministers. They may be summarised as follows:

(1) Member States are now to provide 'adequate legal protection' against circumvention of any effective technological measures designed to prevent or restrict acts not authorised by the rightholder (i.e. by licence, express or implied) or by the law of copyright (i.e. through fair dealing and equivalent exceptions of the kind under discussion). Article 6(3) defines technological measures as "any technology, device or component that, in the normal course of its operation, is designed to prevent or restrict acts, in respect of works or other subject matter, which are not authorised by the rightholder"; these are deemed effective "where the use of a protected work or other subject matter is controlled by the rightholders through application of an access control or protection process, such as encryption, scrambling or other transformation of the work or other subject matter or a copy control mechanism, which achieves the protection objective."[183]

(2) However, with regard to the reprography exception,[184] "in the absence of voluntary measures by rightholders" (which can include agreements between the rightholders and other parties concerned), Member States are to take appropriate measures "to ensure that rightholders make available to the beneficiary ... the means of benefiting from that exception or limitation, to the extent necessary to benefit from that exception or limitation and where that beneficiary has legal access to the protected work or other subject matter concerned."[185]

---

[181] Art 6. See also Art 7 on the protection of rights-management information.
[182] See Art 6(3), first and second paras of May 1999 text.
[183] Art 6(3), only para of COREPER text of the draft Directive.
[184] Also the exceptions for libraries and similar establishments, and for teaching and research (discussed below) and the exceptions under Arts 5(2)(d) and (e) and (3)(b) and (e), not discussed in the text of this chapter.
[185] Art 6(4), first para of the COREPER text of the draft Directive.

(3) There is a similar obligation upon Member States with regard to the exception for private use, unless such reproduction has already been made possible by the rightholder to the extent necessary to benefit from the exception in accordance with its provisions and the 'three-step' test of Berne Article 9(2). But rightholders may adopt measures regarding the number of reproductions made under the exception:[186] for example, devices to ensure that no more than one reproduction is made by any user (as in the latest version of Microsoft Office, which allows only one copy to be made from a DVD onto a personal computer).

(4) None of the foregoing applies, however, to works made available to the public on agreed contractual terms in such a way that members of the public may access them from a place and at a time individually chosen by them.[187]

The basic position intended by these extremely complex and opaque provisions seems at first blush to be that Member States of the EU are to ensure that rightholders make available to the public the means of benefiting from the reprography and private use exceptions. But closer scrutiny suggests that at best this is so only to a very limited degree, in particular in the digital context. As already noted, the exception for reprography is likely to be of only limited importance for users of the Internet, so that it is the private use exception which is of greatest significance here. In general, the actions of rightholders are to be awaited before Member States can take steps to ensure that users can benefit from the exceptions; what actions by rightholders will suffice to prevent such steps? Do these actions have to go as far as the exceptions would do? How long must a Member State wait for such voluntary actions by rightholders? What steps can a Member State take if appropriate actions are not forthcoming? Since it is likely that the practice of rightholders will vary, it may be possible to take action only in individual cases rather than through generally applicable legislation. It is apparent that the existence and enforcement of copyright are the paramount considerations; the exceptions are not overriding user *rights*, but mere *defences* against claims of infringement, apt to be set aside in the face of countervailing interests.

Even more importantly, what is the scope of the provision in the fourth paragraph of Article 6(4), giving pre-eminence to contractual terms over the exceptions where works are made available in such a way that they may be accessed from places and at times individually chosen by users? Since this condition applies to everything found on the Internet, the provision seems to have the potential to eliminate the exceptions to copyright altogether in that context. Such apocalyptic conclusions need to be modified, however, because such elimination should only occur if a contract to that effect is previously in place between rightholder and user. On the other hand, this reinforces the position of

---

[186] Ibid, second para.
[187] Ibid, fourth para.

the rightholder barring access in order to create an opportunity to establish a contractual nexus under which the user pays for his use; and it is really only against the rightholder who wishes to deny access in order to be paid for the privilege that user rights giving access regardless of the rightholder's wishes are of any significance.

Contract, in other words, is to prevail over exceptions, at any rate in the digital environment. One wonders further what balance may be struck in the case where the rightholder, in addition to personal contractual rights against individual users, is also already benefiting from a scheme providing fair compensation for private use and administered by a rights management organisation of which it is a member. Recital 29bis states that the non-mandatory exceptions "must not .. prevent the definition of contractual relations designed to ensure fair compensation for the rightholders insofar as permitted by national law," while, as already noted,[188] the draft provision on private use states that fair compensation scheme should take account of the application or non-application of technological measures of protection. Perhaps the converse of the latter proposition should also be included, although it is at least hinted at in the other recital (24bis) quoted in the earlier discussion of the quantum of fair compensation,[189] stating that account should be taken of other income, already received by the rightholder in respect of the user's activity, when assessing the appropriate sum.

The provision disabling exceptions to copyright where works are made available to the public on the Internet under contractual terms also applies to the next two exceptions to be discussed, those in favour of public libraries and similar types of establishment, and those permitting research and illustration for teaching purposes.

(v) Public libraries, educational establishments, museums and archives

A rather vague initial proposal enabling reproductions by establishments accessible to the public which were not for direct or indirect economic or commercial advantage has now become an exemption in respect of "specific acts of reproduction" made by "publicly accessible libraries, educational establishments or museums, or by archives which are not for direct or indirect economic or commercial advantage."[190] So framed, the exemption certainly looks as though it will be useful to organisations who for archival or conservation purposes wish to digitise material previously held in other media. But the exemption says nothing about the institutions mentioned having a right to make available to others, whether for research or otherwise, *copies* of the material they hold (as distinct from the originals themselves), for example, in a cache. Could this activity therefore be caught as infringement by communication to the public by wireless

---

[188] See above, 217.
[189] Ibid.
[190] Art 5(2)(c).

means? It may however be saved by new exceptions, introduced in the Council of Ministers and applying to both reproduction and public communication rights. The first permits "communication to the public or making available of published articles on current economic, political or religious topics, of broad-cast works, or other subject matter of the same character, in cases where such use is not expressly reserved, and as long as the source, including the author's name, is indicated."[191] The second, also applicable to both reproduction and public communication right, allows "use by communication or making avail-able, for the purpose of research or private study, to individual members of the public by dedicated terminals on the premises of [libraries, educational estab-lishments, museums and archives] of works or other subject matter not subject to purchase or licensing terms which are contained in their collections".[192] However, the permission to cache Internet material, which will be available to service providers under Article 13 of the E-Commerce Directive, may not help librarians, who typically do not provide such services at a distance from the user and do not charge for them – both prerequisites in the definition of a service provider for the purposes of that Directive.[193]

(vi) Teaching, research and private study

The classic exemptions covered under the head of fair dealing in the UK—research, news reporting and criticism or review—are also optional extras under the draft Directive.[194] These exemptions extend to both the reproduction and the public communication rights.[195] If the UK decides to take up the options, there will have to be some amendment to the 1988 Act. Thus, for exam-ple, 'illustration for teaching', not 'private study',[196] is mentioned alongside 'research', which itself is qualified by the word 'scientific' (meaning 'academic' or 'in the pursuit of knowledge', rather than being confined to science[197]). But, most significantly of all, reproduction or communication for teaching and research will not require fair compensation for the rightholder: here the Anglo-American tradition of free use prevails and, at least so far as the UK is

---

[191] Art 5(3)(c).

[192] Art 5(3)(o). Note again the priority accorded to contrast terms.

[193] See recital 17 and Art 2 of the E-Commerce Directive (above, n 100).

[194] See generally Art 5(3), much extended in the amendments made in the Council of Ministers. For research, news reporting and criticism or review, see ibid, (a), (c) and (d).

[195] Apart from those mentioned, Art 5 as amended and much extended in the Council of Ministers also provides exemptions in relation to reproduction and public communication right for the disabled, for the purposes of public security and the proper performance or reporting of an administrative, parliamentary or judicial procedure, for use of political speeches and extracts of public lectures, for use during religious or official celebrations organised by a public authority, for use of works located in public places, for incidental inclusion in other material, for advertising pub-lic exhibitions and sales of artistic works, for caricature, parody or pastiche, for use in demonstra-tion or repair of equipment on commercial premises, and for reconstruction of buildings.

[196] Reproduction for private study will presumably now fall within the exception for reproduc-tion for the private use of a natural person for non-commercial ends (Art 5(2)(b)).

[197] The ambiguity in ordinary English usage is unfortunate.

concerned, and if it decides to take up the option of having this exception, is extended.

(vii) Pre-emption issues

Are there any means by which the proposed new rules might themselves be subject to regulation under other rules of law? All the exemptions in Article 5 are to be subject expressly to the 'three-step test' of Berne Article 9(2)[198]; but there is no forum in which their consistency with that Article can be tested,[199] nor is it easy to see how they might be deployed in the interpretation of either the Directive or subsequent implementing national legislation. But it may be a point of more than academic interest, given that the Human Rights Act 1998 came into force in the UK on 2 October 2000, whether some of the potential limitations upon exceptions to copyright in the digital environment infringe the European Convention on Human Rights, notably Articles 8 (protection of privacy) and 10 (freedom of expression).[200] In the 'Schoolbook' case in 1971 the Federal Constitutional Court in Germany concluded that the public interest in access to cultural objects could override a copyright requirement of the author's consent,[201] while French law contains provisions, consistent with its general abuse of rights doctrine, against manifest abuse of copyright.[202] Following the *Magill* decision of the European Court of Justice in 1995,[203] the use of competition law to control abuse of copyright should also be kept in mind as a factor giving some protection to user interests.

CONCLUSION

It is evident that the scope and reach of copyright protection are on the brink of significant extension in both the Internet and the 'real' world. For many, this will be a matter of regret. The aim is clearly to establish as strong a regime of protection as possible for authors, providing a situation where publication on the Internet can realise its full economic potential, while at the same time the damage which it might inflict upon the established copyright industries (publishing, sound recording, film and broadcasting) is so far as possible removed. In some sense the divergent Anglo-American and Continental approaches to

---

[198]   Art 5(4). See above, 211, for Berne Art 9(2).

[199]   Except perhaps the European Court of Justice, the authority of which to provide a definitive ruling on Berne may be doubted.

[200]   See Guibault, 'Pre-emption issues in the digital environment', at 249–251. For a general survey of the impact of the 1998 Act, see H L MacQueen, 'Human rights, private law and the private sphere', in A Loux (ed), *Human Rights in Scots Law*, forthcoming.

[201]   1 BvR 765/66 (1971).

[202]   French Intellectual Property Code of 1 July 1992, L 122–9. On abuse of rights, see E Reid, 'Abuse of rights in Scots law', (1998) 2 *Edinburgh Law Review* 129–157.

[203]   Joined Cases C-241-2/91, *Raidio Telefís Eireann v Commission* [1995] ECR I–808.

copyright are drawing together to ensure that the author and the industries which bring her material to the public gain recognition and reward on the Internet as elsewhere. But as a result, copyright is moving ever further from controlling the existence of copies to controlling the use made of material, and in this lurks a danger of overlooking the public interest in the dissemination of ideas, information, instruction and entertainment without undue burden, and in the rights of free expression and privacy. Yet the uneasy may take some comfort. Laws can be written in the most draconian terms, but the critical question is whether or not they can be enforced. It is all very well being able to say that the author has a copyright in the UK or the EU, but what good is that against an infringement in Eastern Europe or Asia? – or indeed against at least the private infringer in the EU? The problem of enforcement of rights is what should be taking up the attention of reformers who want to realise and maximise the commercial potential of the Internet. The new laws are being strongly expressed to act as a symbol of deterrence, an approach which may in fact reflect the real underlying weakness of the position in which commercial interests particularly now find themselves. The technological measures of protection to which such legal force is given by the Directive will always be vulnerable to technological circumvention, legitimate or illegitimate. Much depends on how the technology develops, but one possibility is clearly that the old problem with which copyright was originally designed to deal—market failure to make the production of ideas and information worthwhile—could begin to disappear. The technology which creates the Internet may soon mean that an author can make her material available while at the same time ensuring that every user is recorded and makes payment directly to her for the privilege, the whole transaction being triggered automatically in the system by the user's accession of the material. Contract, in other words, could replace copyright, with the main legal issue being the wrongfulness or otherwise of acts circumventing the technology requiring the would-be user to contract in the first place. The possibilities are already apparent in on-line publications by best-selling authors such as Stephen King, deploying the traditional technique of serialisation as well as technological devices in order to hook a paying readership, and the bypassing of recording companies by musical artistes making use of MP3 technology to reach out directly to their audiences via the Internet. But this will in turn raise questions about monitoring the standard form contracts which would be used in this world, whether the user might have rights which could not be overridden contractually, and whether there are other public interests outweighing the right of authors and publishers to earn a return from their work. Further, the probable role of collecting societies in a world where contract replaced copyright might in turn raise doubts about the real benefit to the individual author.[204] The future

---

[204] See generally the contributions to Part II of Grosheide and Boele-Woerki, *Molengrafica: Europees Privaatrecht 1998*, discussing what was then the draft Article 2B of the Uniform Commercial Code in the USA and is now the Uniform Computer Information Transactions Act 1999. On payment mechanisms on the Internet, see chapter 4 in this vol. Miller Cf. on the

should therefore be interesting, and the draft Copyright Directive only a first step towards it.

role of collecting societies A Firth, 'Copyright in the digital world' in A J Kinahan (ed), *Now and Then: a celebration of Sweet & Maxwell's bicentenary 1999* (1999), 69–79.

10

Private International Law Aspects of IP—Internet Disputes

PAUL TORREMANS*

INTRODUCTION

The interaction between intellectual property rights and private international law gives rises to many problems. The same can be said about the interaction between intellectual property rights and the Internet phenomenon. The interface between these two forms of interaction shows a high degree of complexity and the legal analysis of the issues involved is still in an early stage of development.[1] This chapter should be seen as a contribution to that development, rather than as an overview of all aspects of both the two forms of interaction and the interface between them. I refer the reader to my book on *Intellectual Property and Private International Law*[2] for further details concerning the first form of interaction. The analysis contained in that book applies fully to the Internet-related issues. Suffice it to say that the second interface between the internet and intellectual property rights does not render the latter superfluous, whilst nevertheless requiring a re-definition or a sharpening of the definition of some concepts, such as for example what exactly amounts to the act of copying a copyright work.[3]

In this chapter I will primarily turn my attention to issues of jurisdiction and choice of law. These issues will be discussed in the context of the use of copyright works and trade marks on the Internet. Other interesting topics, such as the definitional issues that arise in relation to qualification for copyright protection under the Berne Convention for works that are first published on the

---

* Senior Lecturer in Law and Sub-Dean for Graduate Studies, Faculty of Law, University of Leicester.

[1] See in general Boele-Woelki and Kessedjian (eds.), *Internet: Which Court Decides? Which Law Applies?* (Kluwer Law International, Deventer, 1998) and Lehmann, *Internet- und Multimediarecht (Cyberlaw)* (Schäfer-Poeschel, Stuttgart, 1997).

[2] Fawcett and Torremans, *Intellectual Property and Private International Law* (Clarendon Press, Oxford, 1998).

[3] See e.g. Torremans and Holyoak, *Holyoak and Torremans Intellectual Property Law* (2nd edn., Butterworths, London, 1998), at 512–19.

internet[4] and the whole issue of the recognition and enforcement of foreign judgments,[5] must unfortunately be left untouched, due to constraints of time and space. My analysis will take the legal provisions that are in place in the United Kingdom as a starting point, but US material will also be used.

JURISDICTIONAL ISSUES

Copyright works are distributed over or are published on the Internet. Works that are available on the net are downloaded, forwarded or copied. Existing trade marks are used on Internet sites or they are registered as domain names. All these situations may potentially involve an infringement of the intellectual property rights concerned. These rights may be held in different countries. The global nature of the internet and the technical way in which it functions mean that the straightforward solution under which only one national court can deal with the infringement claim has to be ruled out. Potentially many courts could have jurisdiction.

Two vital issues arise here. First, when will a court in the UK have jurisdiction? Secondly, the applicant wants to bring a single action that covers the infringement on the Internet. Due to the global nature of the Net such an action necessarily involves the infringement of copyright or trade mark rights that have been granted under more than one national law. Can a UK court deal with the infringement of foreign rights, especially if that infringement took place in a foreign jurisdiction? These issues involve an examination of the jurisdiction of the English or Scottish court. Both the traditional jurisdictional rules and the Brussels Convention rules will form the object of that analysis.

The Brussels Convention

The Scope of the Convention

The Brussels Convention 1968 has been incorporated into English law by the Civil Jurisdiction and Judgments Act 1982. It forms an autonomous system of jurisdictional rule.[6] The scope of these rules is limited to civil and commercial cases and the rules apply whenever the defendant is domiciled in a Member-State. There are a few exceptions to the latter rule.[7] The most important one for

---

[4] See Ginsburg, *Private International Law Aspects of the Protection of Works and Objects of Related Rights Transmitted through Digital Networks*, WIPO paper, Nov. 1998 (available as GCPIC/2 paper on the WIPO Web site).

[5] See Fawcett and Torremans, *supra* n.2, chap. 14.

[6] *Pearce* v. *Ove Arup Partnership Ltd and Others* [1997] 3 All ER 31, [1997] 2 WLR 779, at 783, *per* Lloyd J.

[7] See Cheshire and North, *Private International Law* (12th edn., Butterworths, London, 1992), at 291–2.

our current purposes is found in Article 16(4) of the Convention. Article 16 is concerned with grounds of exclusive jurisdiction and its paragraph 4 deals with intellectual property. It contains the rule that: '[t]he following courts shall have exclusive jurisdiction, regardless of domicile: . . . In proceedings concerned with the registration or validity of patents, trade marks, designs, or other similar rights required to be deposited or registered, the courts of the Contracting State in which the deposit or registration has been applied for, has taken place or is under the terms of an international Convention deemed to have taken place.' It is also relevant to note that Article 16 contains a separate and different rule on exclusive jurisdiction 'in proceedings which have as their object rights in rem in immovable property or tenancies of immovable property'. In these cases 'the courts of the Contracting State in which the property is situated' will have exclusive jurisdiction. One does not even have to decide whether or not intellectual property rights should be classified as immovable property for this purpose or not, since an action in a trade mark or copyright infringement case 'is not one which has as its object rights in rem to the copyright'[8] and the same can be said in relation to trade marks. That excludes the potential applicability of Article 16(1) straightforwardly.

An action for breach of copyright or for trade mark infringement comes clearly within the scope of the Convention, which is defined by Article 1 as embracing all civil and commercial matters. That any infringement action in relation to an intellectual property right is a civil and commercial matter has been confirmed by Lloyd J in *Pearce v. Ove Arup Partnership Ltd and Others.*[9] Moreover, the Court of Appeal in *Fort Dodge Animal Health Ltd and Others v. Akzo Nobel NV and Another*[10] has held that Article 5(3) applies in infringement cases,[11] which confirms that infringement actions come within the scope of the Convention.[12] Article 16(4) does not affect copyright, because copyright does not require any registration or any deposit for its creation. Trade mark infringement is also not affected by Article 16(4) because these proceedings are not concerned with validity or registration issues. The provisions of the Convention will therefore apply to cases of copyright and trade mark infringement if the defendant is domiciled in a Contracting State. In these cases the provisions of the Convention also exclude the applicability of any of the traditional rules on jurisdiction, which will be analysed below.

---

[8] Per Lloyd J in *Pearce v. Ove Arup Partnership Ltd and Others* [1997] 3 All ER 31, [1997] 2 WLR 779, at 785.

[9] [1997] 3 All ER 31, [1997] 2 WLR 779, at 784, *per* Lloyd J.

[10] [1998] FSR 222.

[11] See also *Mölnlycke AB and Another v. Procter & Gamble Ltd and Others* [1992] 1 WLR 1112, at 1117, *per* Dillon LJ.

[12] See now also explicitly the Court of Appeal's judgment in *Pearce v. Ove Arup Partnership Ltd and others* [1999] 1 All ER 769.

Articles 2 and 5(3)

The main jurisdictional rule of the Convention is contained in Article 2. According to this rule the defendant can be sued in the courts of the country in which he is domiciled. This rule applies to all cases. In an Internet context this rule works well in those cases where a single unauthorised copy of a copyright work is made or downloaded over the net. Unfortunately, copyright owners are mainly concerned about another scenario. In this scenario their copyright work is uploaded and made available on the Internet without their consent. Copies are then made globally. Article 2 is an ideal weapon to take action in such a scenario. A single action can be brought against the uploader in his or her domicile. However, the defendant must be domiciled in a Contracting State. That means that a determined infringer can easily relocate its operation to a non-Contracting State and effectively escape the clutches of Article 2. Often the non-Contracting State involved will also be a copyright haven with very lax or non-existent copyright laws. In a trade mark case the trade mark is either used on a website in an unauthorised way, or is used in the same way as an Internet domain name. Similar relocation problems arise in these cases in case the alleged infringer is not domiciled in a Contracting State. This is a rather important problem, because the Internet's nature makes it easy for an infringer to relocate itself. When Article 2 and the Brussels Convention as a whole do not apply the applicant will have to turn to the traditional rules on jurisdiction to bring the defendant to trial in England or Scotland. Another issue that creates problems is who can be sued. Is the service provider liable or is liability restricted to the content provider? A full discussion of this issue unfortunately has to remain outside the scope of this chapter.

The Convention also offers alternative fora for certain categories of actions.[13] For this purpose we have to classify the action for breach of copyright and the action for trade mark infringement. It can be said that the infringement of an intellectual property right amounts to a tort. Lloyd J had no hesitation in classifying an action for compensation for the infringement of copyright as a matter relating to tort, delict, or quasi-delict.[14] This must be the correct approach,[15] which also applies to trade mark cases, and it means that Article 5(3) of the Convention offers one or more alternative fora. In tort or delict-related cases Article 5(3) makes it possible to bring the case before the courts of the country in which the harmful event occurred. The Court of Justice (ECJ) had held that this could mean the place where the damage occurred, as well as the place where the act that gave rise to the damage took place.[16] This means that in a copyright

---

[13] As long as the defendant is domiciled in a Contracting State.

[14] *Pearce* v. *Ove Arup Partnership Ltd and Others* [1997] 3 All ER 31, [1997] 2 WLR 779, at 784, *per* Lloyd J.

[15] See also the Court of Appeal's judgment in *Fort Dodge Animal Health Ltd and Others* v. *Akzo Nobel NV and Another* [1998] FSR 222.

[16] Case 21/76, *Handelskwekerij GJ Bier* v. *Mines de Potasse d'Alsace* [1976] ECR 1735.

or trade mark infringement case the defendant can also be sued in the country where the infringing act took place,[17] as well as in the country where the damage that resulted directly[18] from the infringement was felt.

Often the two overlap each other in intellectual property cases, but the issue where copying takes place in an Internet context remains disputed. We have argued elsewhere that the process of downloading a work from the net into the RAM memory of a computer involves the making of a copy.[19] Sending a work over the net means that a copy is made and sent and that the original is retained in the memory of the sending computer.[20] A copy is made wherever the work is received, even temporarily, in the memory of a computer.[21] Article 5(3) therefore opens up the possibility of suing the defendant wherever such a copy is made. This approach works well if the damage occurs in a single jurisdiction, but the *Shevill* case[22] makes it clear that restrictions apply if that is not the case. If infringement occurs in more than one country, and the case is not brought in the domicile of the defendant, the court will only have jurisdiction to deal with the infringement that took place in the country of the court in which the action is brought.[23] For example, if a work is illegally uploaded in the Netherlands by a Dutch defendant and multiple copies have been downloaded in France, the UK and Italy, the French courts will only be able to deal with the damage that resulted from the downloading in France and the infringing copies that resulted from that activity.[24] This will lead to the fragmentation of internet related claims, and whilst Article 2 provides a neat solution to avoid such fragmentation in those cases where the defendant is domiciled in a Contracting State, the ease for a determined infringer to relocate his internet activity to a copyright haven means that in many cases 'there will be no point in litigating in the one forum that is competent to hear the entire claim'.[25] Article 5(3) only works well

---

[17] This must be the place of the event giving rise to the damage. See *Pearce* v. *Ove Arup Partnership Ltd and Others* [1997] 3 All ER 31, [1997] 2 WLR 779; *Ideal Clima SpA and Others* v. *SA Ideal Standard*, [1982] Gaz Pal, Somm, 378; D Series I-5,3-B13 (Cour d'Appel de Paris).

[18] See Case C-220/88, *Dumez France* v. *Hessische Landesbank (Helaba)* [1990] ECR I-49.

[19] Torremans and Holyoak, *Holyoak and Torremans Intellectual Property Law* (2nd edn., Butterworths, London, 1998), at 512–19.

[20] Some US judgments have held that making a work available on a Web site outside the jurisdiction for customers to download it from their own computers in the jurisdiction amounts also to 'distribution of copies' in the jurisdiction. It is submitted that this concept cannot be transposed to a UK context, as it falls outside the CDPA's concept of copying. The Web site owner has therefore not committed the act of copying in the jurisdiction which is necessary to trigger the application of Art. 5(3). See *Playboy* v. *Hardenburgh*, 982 F Supp. 503 (ND Ohio 1997); *Playboy* v. *Webworld*, 991 F Supp. 543 (ND Texas 1997); *Marobie Fla.* v. *NAFED*, 983 F Supp. 1167 (ND Illinois 1997).

[21] See *MAI Sys Corp* v. *Peak Computer, Inc*, 991 F 2d 511, 517 (9th Cir. 1993) and see also Ginsburg, *Private International Law Aspects of the Protection of Works and Objects of Related Rights Transmitted through Digital Networks*, WIPO paper, Nov. 1998 (available as GCPIC/2 paper on the WIPO website), at 14.

[22] Case C–68/93, *Fiona Shevill* v. *Presse Alliance* [1995] ECR I–415.

[23] See also Case C–364/93, *Marinari* v. *Lloyds Bank plc and another* [1996] 2 WLR 159.

[24] See French Cour de Cassation, first civil chamber, Judgment dated 16 July 1997 [1997] JCP IV No. 1993 and [1998] J Dr. Int. 136 (annotated by A. Huet).

[25] Ginsburg, *supra* n.21, at 19.

in those cases where there is a lot of damage in one or two Contracting States that are particularly targeted by the alleged infringer. A successful action in one of those Contracting States would mean that it is no longer worthwhile continuing the infringing activity for the infringer. Trade mark infringement cases are very similar to copyright infringement cases. Article 5(3) allows a case to be brought in any jurisdiction where the availability of the Web site carrying the mark allegedly infringes an existing trade mark. The restriction to local damage applies.

Article 6(1)

Up to now we have assumed that there is a single defendant. Many Internet cases will effectively be brought against multiple defendants, with domicile in more than one State. The applicant has an interest in being able to bring a single case in a single jurisdiction against all defendants, for example against the person who made the infringing copy available in Germany for his business partner to upload it onto its website in Italy. Article 6(1) of the Convention is vital in this respect. This Article allows the applicant to sue a defendant that is domiciled in a Contracting State in the court of the place where one of his co-defendants is domiciled, in case there is more than one defendant. This makes it possible to bring a single case against all defendants in a single court. This provision allowed the applicant in *Pearce* v. *Arup* to sue all defendants in the UK for breach of his United Kingdom and his Dutch copyright in respect of architectural plans for a building, even though only the first defendant was domiciled in that Contracting State.[26] All other defendants were domiciled in the Netherlands, another Contracting State. The actions that are brought against the various defendants must be related. It must be expedient to hear them together to avoid irreconcilable judgments.[27] Article 6(1) is also useful in cases involving a declaration of non-infringement. It was used successfully in *Chiron Corporation* v. *Evans Medical Ltd and others*,[28] where a worldwide exclusive licensee under a patent was held to be a proper party to an action for a declaration of non-infringement brought against the proprietor of a patent. In an internet context a Web site owner may use this technique to make sure that his use of a mark does not infringe the rights owned by a trade mark owner and its licensees in other jurisdictions. Instead of using Article 6(1) on its own, a plaintiff will often argue in the alternative, that the forum has jurisdiction by virtue of Article 5(3) and/or Article 6(1).

---

[26] Approved on appeal, see *Pearce* v. *Ove Arup Partnership Ltd and others* [1999] 1 All ER 769.
[27] There is a close relationship between Arts. 6(1) and 22: see Case 189/87, *Kalfelis* v. *Bankhaus Schröder, Munchmeyer-Hengst & Co* [1988] ECR 5565, at 5583–4.
[28] [1996] FSR 863.

Admissibility/Justiciability

It could, of course, be argued that the applicability of the Convention still does not oblige an English court to deal with the infringement of a foreign copyright or trade mark. This argument is based on the distinction between jurisdiction and the conditions governing the admissibility of the action.[29] The Convention would only deal with the first point, whilst the latter point would be left to the national law of the each forum. The obvious point that would arise under English law is the applicability of the *Mocambique* rule,[30] that bars English courts from dealing with actions in relation to title to foreign land. Because of the analogy with actions in relation to foreign land, that rule should lead the court to rule that an action for the infringement of a foreign copyright or trade mark is not admissible. The result of such an approach would be disastrous for internet-related cases as a separate case, dealing with local damage only, would have to be brought in each jurisdiction if it were to obtain any redress. I have always submitted[31] that such an approach must be wrong and the Court of Appeal has confirmed this in the *Pearce* case.[32] The whole analogy with land should be rejected and intellectual property rights cannot be classified as immovable, but in the context of the Brussels Convention these points are not even needed to rebut the argument. One reason for this is that the ECJ has made it clear that national procedural rules, including those on admissibility, may not impair the effectiveness of the Convention. Conditions of admissibility that are laid down by national law and that would have the effect of restricting the application of the rules of jurisdiction laid down in the Convention cannot be applied by the courts.[33] If this is read in combination with the fact that the Convention not only entitles Member-States' courts to exercise jurisdiction under its provisions, but also obliges them to do so, the application of the *Mocambique* rule must be rejected.[34] The aim of the Convention is to harmonise the rules on jurisdiction and to designate the court that will have jurisdiction. That court is not given a discretion to decline jurisdiction, since that would undermine the legal certainty that should surround the harmonisation process.[35] The applicant should in no case be left without a forum in which to sue. The application of the *Mocambique* rule would frustrate the operation of the basic rule in Article 2 of the Convention and is therefore overridden by the Convention.[36] The Court of Appeal has now expressly confirmed this view.[37]

[29] See Case C–365/88, *Kongress Agentur Hagen GmbH* v. *Zeehage BV* [1990] ECR I–1845, para. 17, at 1865.

[30] Established in *British South Africa Co.* v. *Companhia de Mocambique* [1893] AC 602 (HL).

[31] Fawcett and Torremans, *supra* n.2, at 280–93.

[32] *Pearce* v. *Ove Arup Partnership and Others* [1999] 1 All ER 769.

[33] See Case 288/82, *Duijnstee* v. *Goderbauer* [1983] ECR 3663.

[34] Although it was decided on different grounds, the outcome in *James Burrough Distillers Plc* v. *Speymalt Distributors Ltd* [1991] RPC 130 would now be a different one as a result of this.

[35] See Case C–383/95, *Rutten* v. *Cross Medical Ltd* [1997] All ER (EC) 121, para. 13, at 131.

[36] *Pearce* v. *Ove Arup Partnership and Others* [1995] 2 WLR 779, at 790.

[37] *Pearce* v. *Ove Arup Partnership and Others* [1999] 1 All ER 769, at 793.

the exercise of jurisdiction must be reasonable'.[45] 'Jurisdiction is proper . . . where contacts from actions by the defendant himself create a "substantial connection" with the forum state'.[46] In an Internet context the real issue is whether making available a Web site in the forum (and in the rest of the world) suffices to establish specific jurisdiction over a defendant. The *Zippo* court applied this rule to the Internet context and found that its review of the available cases 'reveal[ed] that the likelihood that personal jurisdiction can be constitutionally exercised is directly proportionate to the nature and quality of commercial activity that an entity conducts over the Internet'.[47] A passive Web site that does little more than make information available to those who are interested in it is not a ground for the exercise of personal jurisdiction.[48] This was for example the case when a jazz club operated a Web site that contained information about the venue and forthcoming events, but that did not offer the visitor the opportunity to send e-mails or to make bookings.[49] Things change when the site invites visitors to add their addresses to a mailing list. This was held to amount to a substantial connection because the conduct amounted to active solicitations and because every visitor received a reply.[50] It suffices that the visitors of the site can contact the siteowner from the forum to establish a substantial connection.[51] That shows that the defendant has taken deliberate action[52] towards the forum. A defendant that reaches intentionally beyond its boundaries to conduct business with foreign residents is subject to the exercise of specific jurisdiction. This was for example the case when Mr Patterson, a Texas resident, deliberately dealt with Compuserve in Ohio to upload his shareware software.[53] In the *Zippo* case Zippo Dot Com had contacted 3,000 individuals and seven Internet access providers in the Pennsylvania forum. This was sufficient in terms of contact to warrant the exercise of specific jurisdiction. The court pointed out though that 'the test has always focused on the "nature and quality" of the contacts with the forum and not the quantity of those contacts'.[54]

A substantial connection can also be shown by means of the effects doctrine in tort cases if the defendant's conduct is aimed at or has an effect in the forum. It has been held that 'simply registering someone else's trade mark as a domain name and posting a web site on the Internet is not sufficient to subject a party

[45] *Zippo Manufacturing Company* v. *Zippo Dot Com, Inc*, 952 F Supp. 1119, 42 USPQ 2D 1062 (DC WD Pa.).

[46] *Burger King Corp.* v. *Rudzewicz*, 471 US at 475, 105 S Ct. 2174 (1985).

[47] *Zippo Manufacturing Company* v. *Zippo Dot Com, Inc*, 952 F Supp. 1119, 42 USPQ 2D 1062.

[48] *Cybersell, Inc* v. *Cybersell, Inc, Webhorizons Inc, Websolvers, Inc and others*, 130 F 3d 414 (9th Cir. 1997).

[49] *Bensusan Restaurant Corp* v. *King*, 937 F Supp. 295 (SDNY 1996).

[50] *Marits, Inc Cybergold*, 947 F Supp. 1328 (E.D. Mo. 1996).

[51] *Inset Systems, Inc* v. *Instruction Set*, 967 F Supp. 161 (D Conn. 1996), see Ginsburg, *supra* n.4, at 13.

[52] *Ballard* v. *Savage*, 65 F 3d 1495, 1498 (9th Cir. 1995).

[53] *Compuserve, Inc* v. *Patterson*, 89 F 3d 1257 (6th Cir. 1996).

[54] *Zippo Manufacturing Company* v. *Zippo Dot Com, Inc*, 952 F Supp. 1119, 42 USPQ 2D 1062.

domiciled in one state to jurisdiction in another'.[55] But that changes if such action is taken to cause injury to the trade mark owner and an attempt is made to extract money from the trade mark owner.[56]

All these cases were concerned with allegations of trade mark infringement through use of the mark on a Web site. It is submitted that the purely passive scenario where the defendant escapes specific jurisdiction is not applicable in copyright cases. 'When an out-of-state website operator makes a work available for downloading from the website, the operator is not only informing forum residents about the work's availability; he is making it possible for forum residents to receive the work in the forum. . . . [T]hose who view or download copyrighted works from out-of-state websites receive the copy or display at home, as if the works were physically located in the forum'.[57] Most of these cases are transposable to a UK Order 11 context, because the event constituting the tort would occur in the jurisdiction when the website confronts the consumer with the trade mark. Nevertheless, it is more difficult to see how the Web site owner who makes copyright works available to users in the jurisdiction can be said to perform the events constituting the tort in the jurisdiction.

A Single Case Dealing with Infringements in Several Jurisdictions

All these cases dealt solely with infringement located in the forum. The problem that remains though is that many Internet-related cases would show alleged infringement by the same defendant of intellectual property rights in more than one jurisdiction. In an ideal scenario a single case against the defendant should be the solution. It seems that that solution requires the defendant to be present in the jurisdiction though (resident in US-speak), since the Order 11 cases and the specific jurisdiction cases in the USA only allow the court to deal with events that took place in the forum.[58] It has therefore been suggested that the fact that a safe haven relocation is easily achieved in an Internet context warrants the introduction of a new jurisdiction role that would allow the plaintiff to sue in its country of domicile for the global infringement of its rights. Such a rule may in the end be inevitable to preserve the right holders' rights in the Internet age, even if it presents a radical departure from existing private international law principles.[59] It is submitted that the plaintiff should be allowed to rely upon this rule only if it can demonstrate to the court that it is not feasible to sue the defendant in its domicile due to the lack in that domicile of intellectual property laws that meet the minimum public international law standard that has been established by the TRIPs Agreement.

---

[55] *Cybersell, Inc* v. *Cybersell, Inc, Webhorizons Inc, Websolvers, Inc and others*, 130 F 3d 414 (9th Cir. 1997).

[56] *Panavision International* v. *Dennis Toeppen and Network Solutions, Inc*, 141 F 3d 1316 (9th Cir. 1998).

[57] Ginsburg, *supra* n.4, at 13.

[58] *Ibid.*, at 15.

[59] *Ibid.*, at 22 and French Conseil d'Etat, *Internet et les Réseaux Numériques* (Paris, 1998), at 151.

In the past very few cases involving the infringement of foreign copyright, or any other intellectual property right, have been brought in England. I will discuss the problems surrounding jurisdiction in the next paragraphs, but it is important to mention the influence of the old double actionability choice of law rule as a preliminary point. In the context of territorially organised intellectual property rights, i.e. one right per country, it seemed obvious that any foreign infringement case would fall foul of the double actionability rule. From an academic point of view this conclusion may have been unsound, but it seemed clear that the courts would nevertheless arrive at it. In those circumstances many practitioners will have advised clients not to bring foreign infringement cases, as they would fail, even if they might have managed to clear the jurisdiction hurdle.

It must be wrong to suggest that double actionability plays a role in relation to jurisdiction. The rule has now been repealed by section 10 of the Private International Law (Miscellaneous Provisions) Act 1995, at least for facts that occurred after 1 May 1996, and in any case even in the past it was a choice of law rule and not a jurisdiction rule. Just how unsound and how unreal the perceived double actionability problem was became clear when the Court of Appeal pointed out in the *Pearce* case that a case involving the infringement abroad of a foreign intellectual property right would have passed the double actionability test, if in similar circumstances the English court would have given a remedy if the facts had occurred in England.[60] The exception established under *Chaplin* v. *Boys* and *Red Sea Insurance* would in such a case have applied to the first limb of the double actionability test.[61] The hurdle which remains, though, is the fact that an action for the infringement of a foreign copyright is considered to be a local action, and, therefore, not actionable as a result of the *Mocambique* rule.[62]

It is submitted that this classification as a local action is no longer sustainable. The historical starting point for it is the *Mocambique* case. This case was solely concerned with actions in relation to foreign land. It does, therefore, not have binding authority in relation to intellectual property rights. It has been used in relation to intellectual property rights by analogy, but the nature of intellectual property rights is very different from that of land. Any analogy with immovable property does not apply[63] and it will also be demonstrated that actions in relation to the infringement of foreign copyrights are not local in nature. It is therefore submitted that the traditional limitation on jurisdiction in relation to foreign intellectual property rights is not only unsound in a Brussels Convention context, as discussed above, but its foundations are also unsound in general. It should no longer apply, not even in the context of the English traditional rules

---

[60] We had already advocated such a solution in Fawcett and Torremans, *supra* n.2, at 611.

[61] *Pearce* v. *Ove Arup Partnership Ltd and Oth*ers [1999] 1 All ER 769, at 802–4.

[62] *British South Africa Co.* v. *Companhia de Mocambique* [1893] AC 602 (HL).

[63] See the comments by Lloyd J in *Pearce* v. *Ove Arup Partnership Ltd and Others* [1997] 3 All ER 31, [1997] 2 WLR 779, at 782–3 and those by Laddie J in *Coin Controls* v. *Suzo International* [1997] 3 All ER 45.

on jurisdiction. The following paragraph will analyse this issue in more detail. Apart from this point the application of the normal traditional rules on jurisdiction does not lead to exceptional problems.

The Nature of Intellectual Property Rights

When one needs to determine the nature of intellectual property rights the easy answer is to say that they are intangible. Intangible rights could be seen as a *sui generis* category which falls outside the traditional divide between moveable and immovable rights. Movable or immovable rights all have a *situs* which can be determined, while intangible rights have no *situs* as it is impossible to locate them precisely. While this neat theoretical solution which would result in the creation of a third category of rights may have its attraction, it does not work in practice.

Let us first of all turn to the intellectual property statutes. Unfortunately, they do not provide a conclusive answer. What is common ground is that patents, copyright and trade marks are personal property.[64] The Patents Act 1977 adds that this is so without a patent being a thing in action.[65] As the category of movable goods is normally divided into tangible things in possession and intangible things in action when one does not accept the existence of a *sui generis* third category, this could mean that patents should be treated by means of a legal fiction as things in possession. Or one could rely on the fact that patents are not really tangible rights and conclude that they must thus be immovable in nature. The Copyright, Designs and Patents Act 1988 contains a slightly different provision in relation to copyright. It is described as a personal right which can be transferred as a movable right.[66] Section 90(1) does not declare copyright to be movable though; it only refers by analogy to movable rights when discussing the transmissibility of copyright. The Trade Marks Act 1994 describes a registered trade mark as personal property, but significantly adds that in Scotland this means incorporeal movable property.[67] One cannot find any good reason why the nature of a patent would be different from that of copyright or a trade mark. All intangible intellectual property rights must reasonably be expected to have the same nature.[68] What conclusion can we arrive at on the basis of these statutory provisions then? It is hardly acceptable to assume that a trade mark which is valid for the whole of the United Kingdom changes in nature when crossing the Anglo-Scottish border. As a fundamental aspect of the right, its nature must be the same. This would lead us to the point of view that intellectual property

---

[64] Patents Act 1977, s. 30(1), Copyright, Designs and Patents Act 1988, s. 90(1) and Trade Marks Act 1994, s. 22.

[65] Patents Act 1977, s. 30(1).

[66] Copyright, Designs and Patents Act 1988, s. 90(1).

[67] Trade Marks Act 1994, s. 22.

[68] Cf. *Tyburn Productions Ltd* v. *Conan Doyle* [1990] 3 WLR 174.

The second stage of the test leads the law of the country where the thing is situate (the *lex situs*) to determine whether the thing is movable or immovable.[78] In *Tyburn* v. *Conan Doyle* a US copyright was at issue. The *lex situs* must have been US law, whose provisions would have to provide an indication whether copyright is movable or immovable. As no evidence regarding these provisions was brought before the court, the judge assumed that US law was identical to English law in this respect. That leads us to the English rule in this respect. Vinelott J relied on the Australian case *Potter* v. *Broken Hill Proprietary Co Ltd*[79] which classified patents as immovable, and he saw no reason not to follow this decision. It is submitted that this approach is wrong. *Dicey and Morris*, while agreeing that intangible things such as intellectual property rights do not really fit in with the distinction between movables and immovables,[80] clearly arrive at the following distinction in English law. Movables can be tangible or intangible, but the special category of immovables can only be tangible. They clearly classify intangible rights as movables, especially as they discuss the assignment of intangibles in the chapter concerned with the transfer of movables.[81] Intellectual property rights must be movable, unless there are other reasons to deviate from this conclusion.

Looking at *Potter* v. *Broken Hill* one can discern an argument for putting intellectual property rights on a land footing. Land is linked to sovereignty and the sovereign territory of states. Courts clearly do not want to interfere with titles to foreign land. That area is reserved for the courts of the nation in whose territory the land is situated. Originally, patents, being the ultimate example of intellectual property rights, were granted as a Royal Privilege. One can easily distinguish the same link with sovereignty and the exercise of the executive power of a state. And an English court would not want to interfere with the sovereignty and the exercise of the executive power of another state. This policy argument, which underlies the *Mocambique* rule, may have been valid in relation to intellectual property rights until the beginning of the twentieth century, but clearly modern intellectual property rights can no longer be seen as Royal Privileges or even exercises of the executive power of a state. They are, in the words of the statutes, personal rights, which can be dealt with commercially. They are tools of business and commercial policy. The interference of several government agencies in economic life is not exceptional at all and the normal legal rules apply to their activities. There is no reason to treat intellectual property differently in this respect. Even the argument that intellectual property rights institute monopolies and that competition policy is an area each state

---

[78] *Dicey and Morris* (11th edn, London, Sweet & Maxwell, 1987) Rule 114.

[79] (1906) 3 CLR 479; see also *Norbert Steinhardt & Son Ltd* v. *Meth* (1961) 105 CLR 440.

[80] Something which cannot be touched cannot be moved logically speaking and moveability is the primary criterion to distinguish between moveable and immoveable things. This supports the creation of a separate category for intangibles apart from the category of tangible things which are either moveable or immoveable (2 sub-categories), but, as stated earlier, the conflict of laws system only operates a moveable-immoveable distinction.

[81] Collins, Hartley, McClean and Morse, *supra* n.75, Rule 113; *supra* n.78, Vol 2 at 902–903.

deals with independently does not convince.[82] This may be true when intellectual property statutes are drafted. We do determine which rules we need to implement our views on competition and the scope of monopolies. But things are different when it comes to applying these rules in individual patent, trade mark or copyright cases. The sovereignty rule might apply when rules are drafted, but it clearly does not apply when these rules are not changed but simply applied to the individual case before the court. At least it does not seem to matter in other competition law related issues in commercial conflict of law cases where it is never argued that the English court should not have subject matter jurisdiction.

Arguments concerning the difficulty of applying foreign intellectual property laws and working with texts in foreign languages have also been advanced. Applying the *Mocambique* rule to intellectual property would avoid all these difficulties. This argument simply cannot be accepted.[83] It would lead to the abolition of private international law and courts would always simply apply the *lex fori*, while refusing to hear cases where they might have to deal with foreign law. The courts do not seem concerned about applying foreign law in other equally complex and technical areas, so why single out intellectual property rights? Besides foreign courts have been applying foreign intellectual property laws for years, apparently without finding it unduly difficult or without making disturbing mistakes.[84]

One could also look at the territorial scope of intellectual property rights and derive their immovable nature on the basis of their link to the territory of a state. This is artificial.[85] The norm is that Acts of Parliament apply only within the territory of the state, which means that any rights, such as intellectual property rights, which are granted by statute are only valid within the territory of a state. Other states may recognise these rights, but Parliament has no powers or influence on this point. One cannot imagine that all these rights should therefore be treated as immovable rights.[86] Both points are in reality unrelated.

Up to now we have not considered whether the Brussels Convention has any influence in those cases that come within its scope. It is submitted that it does. Article 16 deals with exclusive jurisdiction and it contains special rules for immovables in paragraph (1) and rules on registered intellectual property rights in paragraph (4). Clearly the drafters of the Convention would have incorporated

---

[82] Contra: e.g. Arnold, 'Can One Sue in England for Infringement of Foreign Intellectual Property Rights?', [1990] 7 EIPR 254 at 258.

[83] Contra: *ibid.*

[84] See e.g. Landgericht Düsseldorf, 27 Oct. 1966, (case 4 O 127/63), [1968] GRUR Int. 101; Hof van Beroep (Court of Appeal) Amsterdam [1984] Nederlandse Jurisprudentie 713 and *Baars Kaas and De Vijfheerenlanden BV* v. *Westland Kaas Export BV*, Gerechtshof Amsterdam, 4 Apr. 1984, [1986] BIE 77.

[85] The link between the territorial character of the right and its allegedly immoveable nature was not accepted in *Norbert Steinhardt & Sons Ltd* v. *Meth* (1961) 105 CLR 440 at 443 (High Court of Australia).

[86] See Jooris, 'Infringement of Foreign Copyright and the Jurisdiction of English Courts', [1996] 3 EIPR 127 at 138.

nationality of the author-creator of the work.[95] Historically this was explained as a link between the author and his work on the one hand and the country under the aegis of which the work was born[96] on the other hand, but that explanation no longer has the same significance in the Internet age where the place of uploading-first publication can almost be picked at random and where that choice is not even necessarily made by the author.[97] Now the practical considerations described above have taken over and provide a justification for the rule. It is interesting to note that the first appellate decision that addressed this point to emerge from the courts in the USA reached the same conclusion. The law of the country of origin was applied by the second Circuit in *Itar-Tass Russian News Agency* v. *Russian Kurier, Inc.*[98] despite the fact that the court labelled it the law of the country with the 'most significant relationship' to the work.

Infringement

De lege lata the situation is fairly straightforward. In the patchwork of parallel national copyrights each national legislation determines as a matter related to public policy how much of a restriction to competition can be granted by an exclusive right such as copyright. The obvious choice of law implication, already hinted at in Article 5(2) of the Berne Convention, is that the law of the country for which protection is sought should apply to infringement issues. In internet terms that means that the law of the country where the unauthorised uploading of the work, which technically speaking necessarily involves an act of copying, takes place or the law of the country where the work is accessed or downloaded without prior authorisation from the right holder is the applicable law. In many cases that will mean that the judge will have to apply the law of many different countries to different bits of the infringement that he or she is dealing with. This must be undesirable as a lasting situation in the internet age.

It is therefore submitted that *de lege ferenda* an alternative solution should be introduced. Such an alternative solution would lead to the application of a single law to all acts of infringement. Whilst it may at first sight seem harsh to apply a non-domestic law to activities that have taken place domestically, it should be pointed out that the TRIPs harmonisation has resulted in the same minimum standards being upheld in virtually every law. Surely it is not that unfair to apply this harmonised standard, albeit in the form it has taken in one jurisdiction. To make it work this uniform solution should be introduced by

---

[95] The *lex contractus* and Ginsburg, *supra* n.4, at 27.

[96] French Cour de Cassation, *Société Lancio* v. *Société Editrice Fotoromanzi Internazionali*, Judgment of 29 Apr. 1970, [1971] Revue Critique de Droit International Privé 270 (annotated by H. Batiffol).

[97] Compare Lucas, *Aspects de Droit International Privé de la Protection d'Oeuvres et d'Objets de Droits Connexes Transmis par Réseaux Numériques Mondiaux*, WIPO paper, Nov. 1998 (available as GCPIC/1 paper on the WIPO website).

[98] 153 F 3d 82, 47 USPQ2D 1810.

way of an international treaty, the provisions of which are subsequently copied into the various national laws.[99]

How do we choose the one applicable law though? It is submitted that the Satellite Directive[100] can provide inspiration.[101] That would led us to the law of the country of uploading or the law of the country where the server that hosts the allegedly infringing content is located. It has correctly been pointed out that the similarities with the Satellite Directive overlook the fact that the main feature of the Intenet is interactivity rather than passive one-way transmission,[102] but a choice for the country of receipt or a combination of the country of receipt with the country of uploading[103] would once again lead to the application of more than one law in most cases. That would destroy the desired effect. It is therefore submitted that the following alternative points of attachment should be introduced:

—The normal rule should be that any infringement issue is governed by the law of the country in which the server that hosts the allegedly infringing content is located.
—If the law that is applicable under the normal rule does not meet the minimum standards that have been laid down in the Berne Convention and the TRIPs Agreement (and eventually the WCT) that law should be replaced with the law of the country in which the operator of the website that contains the allegedly infringing material has its residence or its principal place of business.
—If the latter law too does not meet the minimum standards that have been laid down in the Berne Convention and the TRIPs Agreement (and eventually the WCT) the law of the forum will be the applicable law if the law of the forum meets the minimum standards that have been laid down in the Berne Convention and the TRIPs Agreement (and eventually the WCT).[104]

The latter points are there to counter the impact of the save haven relocation of the server, a tactic that can easily be applied in the Internet age.

---

[99] It has been suggested that this result could be achieved by means of a creative interpretation of the exisiting Art. 5(2) of the Berne Convention. (see the description in Ginsburg, *supra* n.4) It is submitted that such an interpretation is too creative to be safe and to be relied upon.

[100] Council Dir. 93/83/EEC on the co-ordination of certain rules concerning copyright and rights related to copyright aplicable to satellite broadcasting and cable retransmission [1993] OJ L248/15.

[101] Lucas, 'Les questions épineuses: responsabilité, compétence, loi applicable' in Janssens (ed.), *Intellectual Property Rights in the Information Society* (Bruylant, Brussels, 1998), 247.

[102] Lucas, *supra* n.97.

[103] See Gautier, 'Du droit applicable dans le "village planétaire" au titre de l'usage immatériel des oeuvres' [1996] D 131 and P. Schønning, 'Applicable Law in Transfrontier On-Line Transmissions' (1996) 170 *RIDA* 21.

[104] This is also the approached suggested by Ginsburg, *supra* n.4, at 45–6 (my view differs slightly on the application of the law of the forum).

Public Policy

It should be added by way of warning that the choice of law rules that are described above remain subject to the overruling operation of the mandatory rules and the public policy of the forum.[105]

CONCLUSION

The technical developments in relation to the Internet are unfolding under our eyes at an ever increasing speed. One could easily start wondering whether the law will ever be able to follow that speed and catch up with these developments. There is probably no easy answer to this question, but in the area of private international law things are after all not that bad. As we have seen above, the existing provisions on private international law are fairly adequate, especially in the light of the recent change of heart by the judiciary. It can confidently be predicted that the changes that have been advocated in this contribution to the legal Internet debate will take time to be implemented and that in the meantime the Internet industry and the holders of intellectual property rights will come up with further often conflicting demands, but adequate provisions are now within reach.

---

[105] See Fawcett and Torremans, *supra* n.2, chaps. 10–12.

PART 3

Content Liability

11

Defamation and the Internet

LILIAN EDWARDS*

The topic of Internet defamation was one of the earliest areas of controversy to emerge in the new discipline of Internet law. As such, it has played a more significant role than might be expected in shaping the legal debate around liability for illegal, indecent or offensive content on the Internet. Some of the first Internet legal disputes were fought on, and legislation specifically tailored for the Internet drafted to deal with, libel or defamation. The possible reasons are worth considering. As discussed in detail below, parties communicating via the Internet are rather more likely than ordinary citizens to publish libels which come to the attention of their target. Early Internet users (who were predominantly American, and conscious of their First Amendment rights) placed considerable emphasis on their rights of freedom of expression, regarding protection of the reputation of others as perhaps a minor concern by comparison. Furthermore the Internet provides a global audience at almost zero cost. No one needs a town cryer or a speaker's corner, a television studio or a radio mike, when they have access to the net; an obsolete PC or street cybercafe will do. Finally, and perhaps most relevantly to the commercial Internet which has developed since the mid-1990s, Internet libel enticingly offers to victims not one but two possible people to sue: obviously, the original author of the allegedly defamatory comments (the 'content provider') may be vulnerable, but so also may be the intermediary who conveys the defamatory words to the world. Such intermediaries which provide access to the net are commonly known as Internet Service Providers or ISPs; they include, to name a random few well known names, AOL, CompuServe, Demon, Virgin and Freeserve, and they are often seen as a potentially lucrative alternative defender or 'deep pocket' worth attacking. As we shall see, the wider issue of ISP liability for all types of content disseminated via the Internet is a matter which is currently engendering serious debate in the UK, European Union, United States and elsewhere, as all nations scurry to provide a healthy Internet environment in which electronic commerce can flourish.

* Senior Lecturer, The School of Law, University of Edinburgh; email L.Edwards@ed.ac.uk.
This is a revised and updated edition of the chapter which appeared in Edwards and Waelde, *Law and the Internet: Regulating Cyberspace* (Hart Publishing, Oxford, 1997).

As one of the first topics to attract the attention of lawyers, the early impact of the Internet on libel law has been well documented.[1] This chapter will not attempt a comprehensive survey of world developments[2] but will focus on three crucial points.

(i)   why users of the Internet are more likely than ordinary citizens to libel others;

(ii) what problems (or, looking at it from the other side of the fence, opportunities) arise if those who are libelled on the Internet attempt to take legal action; and arising therefrom,

(iii) what particular issues, in both law and policy, surround the liability of ISPs for libellous content they transmit, distribute or host. As we shall see, this issue is of concern in relation to all types of illegal or offensive Internet content.

One point is worth over-emphasising at the start: Internet libel is a transnational phenomenon. In pre-Internet days, international publication would, for economic reasons, have been almost exclusively the preserve of a traditional publisher, such as a newspaper, TV station or book publishing house, who would be likely to have both the resources to take legal advice, and the foresight to have a system of prior checking in place to head off legal risk. The position is very different now that the Web is ubiquitous. Individuals sitting in their own front rooms with no more help than a mouse, a PC and a cup of coffee, set up Web sites, contribute to news-groups, send e-mails and make friends in chat-rooms, without any knowledge of their potential liability under libel law and with as few defensive strategies to protect against it as one would expect in the circumstances. Some even become ISPs—the ISP industry is far less concentrated in the hands of a few giant corporations than any other sector of the media—without stopping to think about legal risk: a situation unimaginable in any other public medium.

The legal problems faced by such unprepared Internet users do not stop at libel law pure and simple. Because Internet communications cross national borders, the rules of private international law may also need consideration in any potential dispute. Questions such as what country (or countries) will have jurisdiction to hear any action for damages raised; what country's law should gov-

---

[1] See for only a small selection, Cutrera, 'Computer Networks: Libel and the First Amendment' (1992) 11 *Computer Law Journal* 557; Naughton, 'Is Cyberspace a Public Forum? Computer Bulletin Boards, Free Speech and State Action' (1992) 81 *Georgetown Law Journal* 409; Arnold-Moore, 'Legal Pitfalls in Cyberspace: Defamation on Computer Networks' (1994) 5 *Journal of Law and Information Science* 165; Braithwaite, 'The Internet and Bulletin Board Defamations' (1995) 145 *New Law Journal* 1216; Auburn, 'Usenet News and the Law' (1995) 1 *Web LJ*; Pearson, 'Liability of Bulletin Board Operators' [1995] 2 *CTLR* 54; Dooley, 'Specific Risks on the Internet: Defamation' *Computers and Law*, Oct./Nov. 1995, 10; Howarth, *Textbook on Tort* (Butterworth, London, 1995) 563–5; Waelde and Edwards, 'Defamation and the Internet: A Case Study of Anomalies and Difficulties in the Information Age' (1996) 2 *Int. Rev. of Law, Computers and Technology* 263; Vick, Macpherson and Cooper, 'Universities, Defamation and the Internet' (1999) 62 *MLR* 58.

[2] For such a survey, see Waelde and Edwards, *supra* n. 1.

ern the action (the choice of law question); and if a decree is obtained, how can it be enforced if the defender lives outwith the jurisdiction of the court, may all arise. To add insult to confusion, all these issues will probably have been totally invisible to the individual concerned until legal liability reared its head, since the Web as a medium is explicitly designed to operate transparently no matter where Web pages are physically located, or indeed where the person browsing the page is. A person writing comments to a Web forum on Aston Villa FC, for example, is unlikely to stop to consider where the server is physically located (even if they can find out, which may not be easy) or what the legal risks attached to that jurisdiction are. It may be in England; it may equally well be in Germany or China. A country code ending will not always give the game away (.com for example is used all over the globe). Potential Internet libel defenders will be dismayed in the extreme to find that they are open to suit in the courts of multiple countries to which they have little or no connection, where the law applied is foreign to them and where legal aid may be impossible to get. Hardened libel lawyers will say there is nothing very new here, which is, form-ally, true—but the problems of traditional publishing and defamation are so multiplied when applied to a forum as large, as accessible, as cheap and global as the Internet, that it is not hard to see why there is a perception that the law of libel has been transformed therein.

SITES OF DEFAMATION ON THE INTERNET

In considering why the Internet is a dangerously risky place for defamation, it is worth separating out at least four distinct sites where defamation may occur.

One to One E-mail Messages

As anyone who has used e-mail will know, it is remarkably quick and easy to use. Comments can be typed in haste and sent at the press of a button. Compared to conventional written correspondence, where there is typically time to draft the statement, print or type it out, re-read, re-draft, and then *think* before signing, putting the message in an envelope, attaching a stamp and putting in the post, transmission of e-mail is virtually instantaneous and usually, once sent, is irrevocable. As a result, e-mail correspondence is often in substance more like spoken conversation than written interaction for habitual users—hasty, ungrammatical and rash—and tends to lead parties to say things they would not only not normally commit to writing, let alone widely published writing, but would in fact often also not say in face-to-face interaction with the other party. Psychologically, electronic interaction combines a sort of deceptive distance—one is after all sitting safe behind a terminal in one's own office when writing—with a kind of equally deceptive intimacy. Studies and anecdotal evidence show that there is a lack of body language, eye contact or spoken cues, as there would be in conversation or on the phone, to prevent the making of inappropriate statements.[3] All this means that those sending e-mail are dangerously prone to making remarks that turn out to be legally actionable.

To add insult to injury, it is very easy to repeat or forward the defamatory comments of *others* via e-mail, and in the libel law of many countries a re-publisher is just as liable as the original publisher (bar the possibility of innocent dissemination defences, discussed below).[4] For example, party A receives an e-mail concerning the foul practices of a competitor and forwards it with a few keystrokes to parties C and D who later send it on to E and F.[5] Only later is it discovered that the message is not true; subsequently the competitor discovers the re-publication and sues party A rather than or as well as the original author who may be (say) without funds. In this way, actionable e-mail statements can be re-published far and wide with the speed of transmission of any other computer virus.

Sending an e-mail containing defamatory statements from person A to person B will in some legal systems not be regarded as 'publication' for the purposes of libel law, since there is no communication to the public but only to the specified recipient. This is true, for example, of English law,[6] but not apparently, of Scots law.[7] However, as is true with Internet publication generally, e-mails can be, and often are, sent across national boundaries e.g. from Scotland to England, or to France or the USA. This may mean that the law governing any potential action may not be that of the defender's residence or domicile. Thus the risk will not go away just because the e-mail sender (or their ISP) is resident in England.

Mailing Lists

The format of an electronic mailing list is that various parties subscribe by e-mail to the list, which is administered by some central host. The subject of discussion of the list may be anything from Internet law to real ale to homosexual fantasies. Usually the list is set up so that, by default, any e-mail message sent by any one subscriber to the list is 'bounced' or 'exploded out' to every other subscriber (many of whom will, as the parlance goes, 'lurk' and never be known to exist to the person commenting). Mailing lists combine all the general problems

---

[3] See Cutrera, *supra* n.1, at 559–60.

[4] In Scots law, e.g., any repetition of a defamatory statement is actionable: (see *Hayford v. Forrester-Paton*, 1927 SC 740).

[5] These were very much the facts of the Western Provident case, discussed below at p. 254.

[6] *Pullman v. Hill* [1891] 1 QB 524. It is possible however that e-mails might be regarded as inherently insecure and so as akin to postcards, which may be read by anyone in transit, in which case communication to a third party is not essential for publication even in English law: *Sadgrove v. Hole* [1901] 1 KB 1 and see Napier, 'Logging on to Libel Laws' (1995) 92 *Law Society Gazette* 21).

[7] See McK Norrie, *Defamation and Related Actions in Scots Law* (Butterworths, Edinburgh, 1995), 28.

of e-mail discussed above, with some extra difficulties of their own. It is very easy for the slightly careless or inexperienced user of such a list to think they are replying *only* to the maker of a particular comment—but *actually* send their reply to every member of the list. The embarrassment factor can be considerable, particularly where the members of the list form a small professional community within which the professional reputation of the person defamed can be severely damaged. It is not a coincidence that one of the very few cases across the globe on Internet libel not settled out of court, *Rindos v. Hardwick*,[8] revolved around comments made on a mailing list for academic anthropologists in which comments were made implying that Rindos, the Australian plaintiff, had been denied tenure because he was not a properly ethical researcher and was academically incompetent.

Newsgroups, the USENET and Discussion Fora

Newsgroups are discussion fora which are made up of comments from their subscribers, sorted by subject matter. All it takes to subscribe and post comments to a newsgroup is rudimentary software, obtainable for free as shareware, and an Internet connection. Collectively, the newsgroups available to Internet users are sometimes known as the 'Usenet'. There are something like 80,000 Usenet newsgroups nowadays, subscribed to *en masse* by millions of subscribers, located in every country where there is Internet access. As a result, any comment posted to a Usenet newsgroup is virtually guaranteed to be published, and read, within days if not hours, in many hundreds of national jurisdictions. As can be imagined, the volume of material published in these fora is enormous—millions of postings per day, some of which are not text and therefore not straightforwardly readable,[9] are available at any particular time. Although the Web has become by far the more ubiquitous face of the Internet to most people, the volume of newsgroup traffic has still tripled in the last two years.

Apart from the sheer amount of material they contain, newsgroups are even more problematic from the defamation point of view than the rest of the Internet because of what may be described as traditional 'Internet culture'. When the Internet was in its early, pre-commercial stage of development-roughly, until the early to mid-1990s—the Internet was largely the domain of technophiles, students, academics and workers in the computer industry, principally in the USA. These users largely accessed the Internet for free and for non-business purposes. There was a strong collective sentiment towards anarchy,

---

[8] Unreported, Supreme Court of Western Australia, 31 Mar. 1994. See comment in Auburn, *supra* n. 1.

[9] This full count of newsgroups amounts to around 90 Gigabytes of traffic per day. In fact this is considerably greater than the maximum storage of most servers, which is currently usually around 36 Gigabytes, so most take a curtailed service, for example, not taking the many newsgroups which distribute binary non text files (such as MP3 files, or digitised images).

libertarianism and free speech rights—and a strong corresponding dislike of corporate, governmental or legal authority or control. In this culture, full, frank and unfettered discussion known as 'flaming', which in the off-line world might seem indistinguishable from rudeness and abuse, was not only tolerated, but by and large encouraged as part of the learning experience of joining the Internet community. Although many flames were no doubt libellous, the usual remedy for being flamed was not to post a writ, but extra-legal self-help—in other words, flame back. It was and is not uncommon for newsgroups to degenerate into 'flame wars'—torrents of abusive comments which destroy all sensible discussion in the group. This was all very well, perhaps, when most Internet users shared a similar cultural background. But in recent years the Internet has ceased to be the domain of 'netizens' and become extensively used by individuals and families, including children, who pay for Internet access and expect it to respect the same standards of decency and courtesy as other media. Even more importantly, corporate use has expanded enormously, as e-commerce has become the inescapable buzzword of the moment. For these newer users, flaming and abuse are not acceptable, nor are self-help remedies, and preservation of corporate reputation is paramount. Corporate culture collided resoundingly with the Internet in the UK in July 1997, when the first corporate e-mail libel case to be publicly settled in the UK received extensive publicity. This case was brought by Western Provident Association which sued Norwich Union Healthcare for spreading untrue rumours on its internal e-mail system about Western's financial stability.[10] A settlement was reached under which Western Provident paid out the not insubstantial sum of £450,000.[11]

Another problem with newsgroups is that a comment posted to a newsgroup is a moving target. Suppose person A posts a comment libelling person B via their ISP, which is (let us say) OzEmail in Australia. The effect of this posting is that the comment is not just made public by OzEmail to its subscribers but is also sent out as part of the 'news feed' and is propagated via the Internet to all other networks and servers giving newsgroup access, depending on what news group the comment is posted to, and whether the system administrator of each particular network or server chooses to take that particular newsgroup.[12] In the infamous case of Lawrence Godfrey, discussed below, an anonymous comment was posted to a newsgroup which allegedly defamed and was damaging to the

[10] *Scotsman*, 18 July 1997.

[11] The asserted clash between 'traditional' Internet culture and 'new' corporate Internet culture can be seen in many other areas under discussion in this volume. In the field of trade marks and domain names, for example (see further Waelde, Ch. 7) there have been running clashes between cybersquatters, who have poached the domain names normally associated with famous corporate brand names such as Marks and Spencers and Harrods, and the corporations in question, which have turned to conventional legal remedies such as trade mark protection to rectify what they perceive as interference with their business interests. See also the discussions in this volume on encryption and pornography.

[12] Newsgroups might not be taken because they are not geographically relevant, e.g. scot.news for a French network; or because they are seen as undesirable, eg alt.sex, which has historically been unavailable via the UK university hierarchy.

professional reputation of Godfrey, a British physicist. Since the comment was anonymous, there was no content originator available to sue. Godfrey was instead chose to sue a variety of ISPs (to date in Australia, New Zealand, Canada and the UK) in his crusade to suppress the comment, as the message had effectively been re-published across the globe by countless different hands.

The World Wide Web

The Web is now so large, and increasing in size so fast that it is increasingly meaningless even to attempt estimates of its size. In September 1996, there were 30 million Web pages, located on 275,000 servers, indexed by the Alta Vista search engine. At around the same date, it was estimated that the Web doubled in size every 45 days.[13] More recent estimates suggest that there are now around 5 million Web sites[14] but effectively it now makes sense simply to acknowledge the Web as a global medium. This no longer needs to be proven by figures any more than we normally stop to consider how many people across the world have a TV in their homessss, or how many channels they can access. Since the Web is now by far the most visible zone of the Internet, it is probable that most Internet libel cases will arise here in the future. Surprisingly few Web-based cases have arisen thus far, but one interesting unreported UK case concerned the Poetry Society, which, in February 1996, was sued for publishing a Web page which contained comments that a vanity publishing company was 'preying on poets who could not otherwise get their poems published'.[15] The matter appears to have been subsequently settled out of court. Interestingly, although the Poetry Society's Web site at the time was itself physically hosted by the BBC server, there was no apparent attempt made to involve the BBC as co-defenders possibly because the aim was removal of the offending statement rather than financial compensation.

Like newsgroups, Web sites can be accessed and read in multiple jurisdictions, and they therefore share many of the problems—or advantages—of transnational publication discussed above. In the first reported Australian case on Internet libel, *Macquarie Bank* v. *Berg*,[16] a disgruntled employee of an Australian bank put up a Web site, 'macquarieontrial.com', stating his grievances against the bank to the world, from the perceived safety of a server located in the USA, where rules forbidding libel are relatively trammelled by First Amendment rights of expression. Clearly this site had rather more global impact than the old-fashioned approach of writing a letter to *The Times* (or in this case, perhaps the *Sydney Morning Herald*). It is interesting to note that despite the possible damage that could be done by such a Web site, the New South Wales court in *Macquarie Bank*, asked

---

[13] *Scotland on Sunday*, 26 May 1996.
[14] See Terrett, *supra* n. 3, ch. 1, p. 2.
[15] *Forward Press* v. *Poetry Society*, reported in the *Guardian*, 16 Mar. 1998.
[16] [1999] NSWSC 526, 2 June 1999, available at http:\\www.austlii.edu.au.

to grant interim interdict to restrain publication, declined not only to provide this remedy but even to accept jurisdiction. Its reasoning was that not only would any remedy granted be in all probability ineffective, as the server lay outside the territorial jurisdiction of the NSW court, but also interdict *should* not be granted as to do so would be effectively to superimpose the NSW law on libel to the rest of the world; the successful imposition of interdict by the NSW court would stop the Web site being accessed in countries like 'the Bahamas, Tazhakistan [*sic*], or Mongolia' where the rules about, and defences to, libel might be completely different. These problems, inherent in the fact that Web publication is invariably global publication even where it is targeted at one or more specific jurisdictions, are discussed further in the next section.

PROBLEMS AND OPPORTUNITIES FOR INTERNET LIBEL PURSUERS AND DEFENDERS

Jurisdiction, Choice of Law and Enforcement

Since Internet libel or defamation is almost invariably transmitted across national boundaries, disputes may allow the victim of libel a useful chance to pick a forum and governing law perceived as favourable to his or her side. For example, if we take a random scenario :

> *An individual resident and domiciled in Scotland posts a defamatory comment about a person also resident and domiciled in Scotland, but having a national reputation throughout the UK, to a Usenet newsgroup. The group is read by subscribers in many countries, including England. The defamed party wishes to sue.*

The rules of jurisdiction in domestic disputes between Scottish domiciliaries are the rules of the 1968 Brussels Convention on Jurisdictions and Judgments, as implemented in Schedule 8 of the Civil Jurisdiction and Judgments Act 1982. The obvious court in which to sue is the Court of Session (or the appropriate sheriff court) in Scotland. But under the 1982 Act, Schedule 8, Articles 1 and 5(3), there can be jurisdiction *either* in the court of the defender's domicile— Scotland (this being the pre-eminent rule of the Brussels Convention)—*or* in the place where the delict is committed (a 'special jurisdiction'). Where, then, is a delict such as defamation committed? There are two obvious interpretations— first, the place where the remark was originally made (the 'source' of the delict); and secondly the place where the remark is 'published' i.e. where it is made public and has an impact on the reputation of the person defamed (the 'target' of the delict). Case law from the European Court of Justice interpreting the Brussels Convention—notably the recent reference to the ECJ from the House of Lords in the case of *Shevill* v. *Presse Alliance SA*[17]—seems clearly to establish that

---

[17] Case C–68/93 [1995] 2 WLR 499, and see comment by Forsyth at [1995] *CLJ* 515. Note that *Shevill* is an authoritative interpretation of the place of the delict for the purpose of fixing jurisdiction only, not of choice of law.

either interpretation is a valid alternative for the purposes of fixing jurisdiction. Thus in the scenario above, notwithstanding the fact that both the pursuer and defender are Scots, jurisdiction can be founded in both Scotland and England. A smart lawyer will at this point begin to think seriously about suing in England (assuming the pursuer has a reputation there to be affected, which is the case in our example) since an English damages award will almost certainly be higher than a Scottish one. There is one important caveat to ponder before embarking on this kind of forum-shopping though; another matter clarified in *Shevill* is that if the action is raised in England on this kind of basis, damages can only be sought in respect of damage caused to the reputation *in that jurisdiction*. To sue for damages caused by the defamatory statement in *every* jurisdiction where it was published—which could be every country where the newspaper was read in the case of a global celebrity with a matching reputation—the action must be raised in the courts of the domicile of the defender (in this example, Scotland).

Although good news for our Scottish pursuer, this is a rather unsatisfactory result for the defender. He will have to find funds and expertise to defend the case in a foreign jurisdiction, where, arguably, he did not expect to find himself in court. One of the basic aims of the Brussels Convention is to prevent this kind of forum-shopping, on the ground that there should be a 'level playing field' for those involved in legal actions across Europe, so as to avoid distortions to the single market. The Convention has as its basic rule Article 1, which provides that jurisdiction is founded in the court of the defender's domicile, because it is contrary to natural justice if a defender can be sued in any country the plaintiff cares to pick, which may be foreign culturally, linguistically or in other ways likely to impede a fair hearing for the defender. Yet this kind of forum-shopping is exactly what is encouraged in Europe in relation to Internet-related torts or delicts, as seen by the example above. Are the rules of the Brussels Convention, then, really appropriate to such actions? As we have just seen, the whole nature of Internet causes is that they are not really substantially linked to one geographical place or domestic legal system. The defamatory remarks in *Macquarie* were physically located in the USA but were in actuality available everywhere. The only single jurisdiction they could truly be said to inhabit is cyberspace, which sadly has no system of courts.[18]

What if a court thinks, as one might try to persuade the English court in the example above, that it is *not* the appropriate forum in which the matter should be decided? In *Macquarie*, as discussed above, the New South Wales court refused to accept jurisdiction, partly on the grounds that if it did it might be faced with granting a remedy which it would be impossible for it to enforce. In the USA, state courts have developed a flexible doctrine as to when they will choose to accept what is known as personal jurisdiction in Internet-related

---

[18] Although there are increasingly moves to set up effective virtual tribunals or other forms of alternative dispute resolution (ADR) for cyberspace disputes. See *infra* n. 68.

actions.[19] The courts will look to see whether the defender's 'electronic contacts' with the forum state reach a certain minimum level of interaction, and arise as a result of deliberate activity targeted at that forum by the defender, not merely an accidental result of the global nature of Internet publishing. In the courts of Scotland and England however, *forum non conveniens* is available only as a possible plea in actions where the dispute is between parties both of whom are domiciled in the UK.[20] Where the dispute is between parties from different states which are both parties to the Brussels Convention, e.g. a dispute between a Scot and a Spaniard, the first court seised of any action must hear it.[21] It may be questioned whether European states would not be better served by a more flexible approach to taking jurisdiction, such as is available in the USA or Australia. However it should be noted that the more rigid European rules potentially provide a greater degree of certainty, the lack of which may deter Internet litigation and increase costs for both plaintiff and defender.

But in England, site of the potential *forum non conveniens* argument in our hypothetical example above, the courts are unlikely to be sympathetic to the hapless Web publisher. The general attitude of the English courts in cases where the domestic rules of English jurisdiction not the Brussels rules apply (i.e. wholly domestic cases between two English litigants, or international cases involving parties who are not from a Brussels Convention contracting state) is that they need strong persuasion not to accept jurisdiction in cases where a *prima facie* case has been made and the plaintiff has connections to the forum in terms of reputation or property. As England is already well known to be an attractive site for libel plaintiffs in terms of its substantive law and jury system, it has been said this will conspire to make England a 'libel magnet' for Internet-related actions. The recent House of Lords case of *Berezovsky* v. *Forbes*[22] provides an illustration. In this case, an American magazine, *Forbes*, was sued in the English courts in respect of an allegedly defamatory article describing two prominent Russian businessmen as 'criminals on an outrageous scale'. The case was brought within the English jurisdiction on the grounds that the businessmen had a reputation to suffer in England, and around 2,000 copies of the magazine issue in question had circulated in England (as opposed to nearly 800,000 in the USA and only 13 copies in Russia). It was acknowledged that, in principle, jurisdiction could be founded in England under the normal rules, but it was suggested that jurisdiction should be declined as England was not the most appropriate forum. The House of Lords rejected this proposition by three to two. On the authority of *The Spiliada*,[23] their Lordships found that the correct approach was to refuse to

---

[19] See e.g. *Zippo Manufacturing Co* v. *Zippo Dot Com*, 952 F Supp. 1119 and *Barrett* v. *Catacombs Press*, Civil No 99–736, 12 Apr. 1999, at http://paed.uscourts.gov/opinions/99DO282p.htm.

[20] See *Cumming* v. *Scottish Daily Record and Sunday Mail and others* [1995] EMLR 538.

[21] Art. 21 of the Brussels Convention. There is a small exception in Art. 22 on related actions.

[22] [2000] 1 WLR 104 (HL), available at http://www.parliament.the-stationery-office.co.uk/pa/ld199900/ldjudgmt/jd000511/bere-1.htm.

[23] [1987] AC 460.

decline jurisdiction, even though it was likely the case in question had more connection to the USA than to any other single state. If unfortunate for the defendants, this was not an unexpected result. One matter the House of Lords specifically refused to comment on, however, was the fact that the article in question had not only circulated in hard copy but had also been made available globally on the *Forbes* Web site, forbes.com. It would have been interesting to hear if it regarded the 'Internet factor' as making any difference. Logically, the English courts, by embracing *The Spiliada* so inflexibly, are effectively saying they are prepared to exercise jurisdiction over every Internet published libel in the world, no matter if an English person is not involved, so long as the plaintiff can establish that he or she has some reputation in or other significant connection to England—not difficult in an era of rapid communications and globalised media. As one of the lawyers for Forbes put it, 'this is a shot in the arm for libel tourism'.[24]

Returning to the scenario above, if we accept that jurisdiction can be and is established in England, the logical next question is to determine what law the English court will apply to govern the action (the question of 'choice of law'). Actions for defamation brought in both Scotland and England are still subject to the common law requirement of 'double actionability', i.e. the requirement that there must be a successful cause of action under both the *lex loci delicti* (the law of the place of the delict) and the *lex fori* (the law of the forum) before the action can be succeed.[25] In the example chosen, both the *lex fori* and the *lex loci delicti* are English law—so double actionability is not a problem for the plaintiff. (This is on the assumption—as seems likely but is not wholly clear—that for the purposes of choice of law, the place of the delict is also the place where damage is caused to the reputation of the victim, i.e. the 'target' jurisdiction.)[26] But the rule of double actionability *can* have invidious effects where two legal systems are involved, and the law differs between them. Let us vary our scenario a little.

> The person defamed is a public figure, e.g. a media celebrity, originally an American national, but who has established his principal home in Scotland. Both pursuer and defender are resident and domiciled in Scotland. The defamatory comment, as before, is published in a Usenet newsgroup readable

---

[24] See David Hooper of Biddles, Solicitors, quoted at http://news2.thls.bbc.co.uk/hi/english/world/europe/newsid_746000/746780.stm.

[25] This restrictive requirement has recently been abolished in both Scottish and English law for most transnational delict or tort actions under the Private Law (Miscellaneous Provisions) Act 1995, but was specifically retained for actions for libel and defamation.

[26] See *Bata* v. *Bata* [1948] WN 366 (CA). Scots law seems to have reached a similar conclusion in *Longworth* v. *Hope and Cook* (1865) 3 M 1049 and *Evans* v. *Stein* (1904) 7 F 65. An unresolved problem however is the fact that in this scenario there are at least two jurisdictions where there is publication and loss to reputation, while for the purposes of choice of law (unlike jurisdiction) there can only be one 'place of the delict'. Can the courts deal with triple or n-multiple actionability? In reality the matter is likely to be simplified by the fact that at least in UK law, foreign law can only be taken into account if pled by a party and proven as a fact by expert witnesses.

in many countries including Scotland, England and the United States. The principal harm done to the pursuer's reputation is in the United States.

Will the action by the celebrity succeed if raised in Scotland? There is jurisdiction to sue in the place of the defender's domicile—Scotland—for the whole damage caused to the pursuer's reputation in all countries. In order to sue for damages in respect of the damage to the reputation in the USA, there must however be a successful cause of action under both Scots and US law.[27] In the USA, it is a defence to an action for libel that the pursuer or plaintiff is a 'public figure'.[28] In such cases, the burden is put on the *pursuer* to show by clear and convincing evidence that the defender made the comments with actual malice. In Scots law, by contrast, such malice is presumed. It is quite possible, then, that although the action would *succeed* under Scots law, the pursuer may fail as a result of the double delict rule—an example of US law controlling the result of an action between two Scots domiciliaries. The only possible line of attack for the pursuer in this example lies in the approach taken in the cases of *Boys* v. *Chaplin*[29] and *Red Sea Insurance Co Ltd* v. *Bouyges SA & Others*[30] in which the House of Lords and the Court of Appeal, respectively, chose to approve the possibility that in appropriate circumstances the double actionability rule might be displaced in favour of a 'proper law' approach. In a case of the kind above, there might conceivably be a conclusion that the 'centre of gravity' of the action was in Scotland and that Scots law should be the proper law. Again we have the problem that traditional rules for establishing choice of law, which have been established over time and on the whole work fairly when a wrongful act clearly occurs in a specific physical place, work haphazardly when applied to Internet events which can be seen as occurring either *in* cyberspace or *across* national boundaries.

Finally it is important to remember that winning the action is only half the battle. Where the defender in an Internet libel case lives abroad, the judgment will still need to be recognised and enforced by the courts of the defender's residence (unless he has left assets in the pursuer's country of residence). Many countries may choose not so to recognise, either because they have no clear mechanisms in place for recognition of foreign decrees, or because the legal basis of the judgment runs against principles of their own legal system, e.g. an overriding constitutional preference for freedom of expression. Such problems have arisen in respect of judgments for libel obtained in the English courts where enforcement was then sought against a US defender.[31]

---

[27] The example is simplified. In reality the relevant law would be of a particular US state.

[28] See *New York Times Co* v. *Sullivan*, 376 US 254, 11 L Ed. 2d 686, 84 S Ct. 710 (1964).

[29] [1971] AC 356.

[30] [1994] 3 All ER 749.

[31] See *Matusevitch* v. *Telnikoff*, 877 F Supp.; Civil Action no. 94-1151 RMU (see comment at 23 *Media L.Rep.* 1367).

Liability of Internet Service Providers

As was noted above, no-one can publish or distribute material on the Net without the aid of an intermediary. In the UK, as in the USA and many other jurisdictions, in principle any person who publishes or re-publishes the defamatory statement of another is as liable for the loss caused to the victim of the libel as the original maker of the statement. Therefore it will often be more attractive for someone who claims to have been defamed to sue the ISP as publisher—since it is likely to be locatable, with a registered place of business, and probably significant liquid assets—rather than to sue the original defamer, who may have vanished, acted under the cover anonymity or pseudonymity,[32] be living in another country where judgments for damages are difficult or impossible to get recognised and enforced, or simply have no attachable assets. As a result, ISPs by virtue of their role as gatekeepers to the Internet, have long felt themselves to be sitting on a liability time-bomb.[33]

This would be unfortunate enough without going on to consider the nature and quantity of the content which ISPs distribute. A commercial ISP typically allows its subscribers access both to read and write to newsgroups or local forums, chatrooms, mailing lists and the millions of Web home pages. This is simply far too much material to be manually checked and supervised for potentially defamatory comment. In comparison a newspaper editor (or the newspaper's lawyer) can generally check over the entire paper each day. Furthermore the content which ISPs handle is in the main supplied by persons out of the control of the ISP, whereas a conventional publisher such as a newspaper can limit its risk by, for example, issuing acceptability guidelines to its employees, or putting indemnity clauses into contracts with the freelancers who contribute columns. Software filtering technologies, which usually depend on searching for and blocking certain notorious sites by their address, or sites containing certain keywords or images, can be helpful to ISPs which seek to block access to criminal content such as child pornography images, or particularly offensive words,[34] but are of no use at all in relation to libel where legal risk may arise as much from a discussion of poetry publishing as a discussion forum on sex or paedophilia.

Since the early 1990s therefore, in the USA, the UK, and elsewhere, ISPs have tried to claim that they should be exempted from liability on the basis of some kind of innocent dissemination defence—essentially claiming that they have no effective control over the material they redistribute, and thus should not be held

---

[32] This is true of many well-known Internet libel cases. See e.g. *Godfrey*, discussed below, and *Zeran* v. *AOL*, 1997 US Dist Lexis 3429 (ED Va., 21 Mar. 1997).

[33] The best known case which has provided grounds for such fears is the *Felix Somm* case in the Bavarian courts, Germany, where Somm in his capacity as chief executive of CompuServe Europe was sentenced to a jail sentence for distributing obscene material in Bavaria in the form of newsgroups handled routinely by CompuServe. After criticism in both Germany and abroad, the conviction was reversed on appeal on 17 Nov. 1999.

[34] See further Edwards, p. 297.

legally liable in respect of it as publishers. To some extent this argument rest on whether ISPs are seen as more akin to conventional hard-copy publishers, or TV and radio broadcasters—who have control over what they publish, and a corresponding duty to check that the material they publish is *not* defamatory—or whether they should be seen as more like 'common carriers' such as the phone company, who are seen as 'mere passive conduits' for information, with no effective control over it, and who are thus usually not held liable for whatever material they carry. Somewhere between the two a third analogy can be drawn, to news-stands or bookstores—persons who are responsible for distributing large quantities of potentially defamatory material and have some chance to examine it, but who cannot reasonably be expected to check it all in detail if they are to stay in business.[35]

Two early, widely discussed US cases failed to settle for US law the issue of whether ISPs should have the benefit of an innocent dissemination defence.[36] In *Cubby* v. *CompuServe*,[37] CompuServe was sued in respect of a message appearing in a local forum hosted by it, called 'Rumorville USA'. CompuServe had employed a third party specifically to edit and control the content of this forum. The third party posted the information on the Internet once it was edited, with no intervening opportunity for CompuServe to review the material prior to publication. CompuServe argued it was were merely a distributor of the information, not a publisher, and should therefore not be held liable. The New York District Court agreed, holding that CompuServe was here acting in a way akin to a news-stand, bookstore or public library, and that to hold it to a higher standard of liability than these distributors would place undue restrictions on the free flow of electronic information.

But in *Stratton Oakmont Inc* v. *Prodigy Services*,[38] the decision went the opposite way. On similar facts, Prodigy was sued in respect of comments posted to a local discussion forum it hosted. Again, Prodigy had employed persons known as 'board leaders' to monitor and edit the content of the forum and had empowered these board leaders to remove material, although only after it was posted. The crucial difference from the CompuServe case (such as there was) was that Prodigy had explicitly marketed itself as 'a family oriented computer network', which as part of its 'value added' services, would control and prevent the publication of inappropriate messages. This seems to have been enough to lead the court to regard Prodigy as the publisher of the libels in question, rather than as a mere distributor, and accordingly it was held liable.[39]

---

[35] While this three-category analysis is commonly accepted in US law and has by extension penetrated global Internet law, it should be noted that it has been rejected in English law, albeit in the context of hard copy magazine publishing: see *Goldsmith* v. *Sperrings* [1977] 1 WLR 478.

[36] But see now *Zeran* v. *AOL*, discussed *supra* at n. 44.

[37] 766 F Supp 135 (SD NY 1991).

[38] 1995 NY Misc., 23 Media L. Rep. 1794.

[39] *Prodigy* was in fact overruled by the US Sup. Ct. in a subsequent case, *Lunney* v. *Prodigy Services Co*, 2000 US LEXIS 3037 (available at http://www.courts.state.ny.us/ctapps/decisions/164opn. htm). However by that time, as discussed below, the force of the decision had been overtaken by the

The most unfortunate aspect of the *Prodigy* and *CompuServe* decisions was that the ratio that could most easily be extracted from the two contrasting results was that to avoid liability, an ISP should do as little as possible to monitor and edit the content of the messages or other material it carries. This, it was argued, would make it seem more like a newsstand, and less like a publisher. But such a strategy (which can be labelled the 'put your head in the sand' approach) has unfortunate results both for ISPs and the public interest in the development of the Internet.

For ISPs, the *Prodigy* principle equates any attempt to exercise control over even some of the content the ISP carries with risk. Yet commercial ISPs, and other sites which double as intermediaries, increasingly *wish* to provide large amounts of local edited content as a key part of their business strategy. So-called 'portal sites' such as Yahoo!, Netscape, Alta Vista, and so forth now make some of their money from subscriptions, but increasingly revenue is derived from sponsorship, advertising and a cut from the business acquired via the ISP by e-commerce sites like Amazon.com. These revenues depend on hit rates and other audience indices, and audiences are gathered partly by providing unique local editorial content; but also by providing easier, faster, more convenient or more sanitised access to key information which is ubiquitously available (such as weather, comment, horoscopes, financial information and so forth). However if ISPs *do* decide to exercise editorial control over *some* content, they will then, following the Prodigy reasoning, perhaps enter the class of publishers rather than distributors, and find themselves liable for *all* illegal or actionable material they 'publish', no matter who originated it and however little actual control the ISP has over it. The ISP industry complains, with good reason, that if it is made to take responsibility for checking every item of content it carries, it will be unable to fulfil this duty due to the volume of traffic,[40] and faced with unquantifiable risk, will either have to go out of business, leave the jurisdiction for one with more helpful laws, or pass the potential insurance costs on to the consumer, thus raising the costs of Internet access.

What about the public and the state? The public's interest is complex. First, as noted above, ISPs are seen as the natural gatekeepers to the Internet and are unarguably in the best position to filter out and stop the distribution of illegal and offensive content throughout the Internet. Both the UK government and the EC are currently strongly interested in ISPs taking up this role, not just in the interests of public morality and decency and the protection of vulnerable groups such as children, but also so as to allow Europe to catch up with the USA in development e-commerce. To date Europe has lagged considerably behind the

immunity provisions for ISPs introduced in the Communications Decency Act 1996. The case does however confirm that in US law an ISP is now officially regarded as not a publisher at common law.

[40] British Telecom's ISP branch has estimated that it would have to employ another 1,500 employees working around the clock just to monitor the traffic it handles in news-groups alone. See *WIPO Workshop on Service Provider Liability*, Geneva, 9–10 Dec. 1999, paper prepared by Janet Henderson, Rights Strategy Manager, BT Internet.

USA in developing a lucrative e-commerce market[41] and one of the reasons most often cited is lack of public confidence that the Internet is a safe, secure and respectable medium for commercial transactions. Cleaning up the Net is thus not a matter of mere squeamishness, but a business priority. However public access to the Internet, both for private and public, commercial and democratic purposes, is predicated on a healthy and competitive ISP market, which placing unreasonable or impossible to fulfil burdens on ISPs will not foster (especially as, compared to most industries, it is not that difficult for ISPs physically to move to a more supportive legal environment).

So the question is how best to encourage ISPs to take up an active role in the control of Internet content without reducing their business efficiency. There is a general consensus now that market forces—the desire to gain and retain market share in a competitive market for Internet services—will lead ISPs, left to their own devices, naturally to take on an editorial and filtering role. Thus the task of legislatures, it seems, is to *protect* ISPs from liability as content hosts or transmitters, so that they can fulfil their role as editors and monitors to the extent they find commercially enticing—a self-regulatory strategy. In particular, legislatures should refrain from imposing impossible demands on ISPs that they monitor all traffic they carry.

In the USA, the question of ISP liability was first tackled head-on in the Communications Decency Act 1996 (CDA). This Act attempted to prohibit the publication of obscene or indecent speech in cyberspace wherever it might be known to be accessible by a minor child (i.e. everywhere). The state took the view that the Act would only be enforceable if in return for their co-operation in monitoring and filtering content, ISPs were granted the *quid pro quo* of absolute immunity as publishers, in respect of civil, criminal and statutory liability for all content originated by a third party.[42] Although the main provisions of the CDA were later struck down by the US Supreme Court as being unreasonably in breach of the constitutional rights of freedom of speech of adults,[43] this portion of the Act remains in force, and in fact has operated, as was held in the case of *Zeran* v. *AOL*,[44] wholly to suspend actions in common law (including actions for defamation) against ISPs for publishing material originated by another content provider. In *Zeran*, the Eastern Virginia District Court found that the existence of the CDA pre-empted the right of the court to hear an action for libel and negligent mis-statement brought against AOL.[45] Imposition of common law liability on AOL would have frustrated the objective of section

---

[41] e.g. in 1998 7,000 US companies were conducting business on-line compared to only 2,000 in the EU.

[42] See s. 230 (c). See further judicial interpretation in *Zeran* v. *America On-Line*, 1997 US Dist. Lexis 3429 (ED Va. 21 Mar. 1997); *Blumenthal* v. *Drudge* 1998 BNA EC&L 561.

[43] Sup. Ct. decision in *Reno* v. *ACLU* (1997) 2 BNA EPLR 664, available at http://www.aclu.org/court/renovacludec.html.

[44] 1997 US Dist Lexis 3429 (ED Va. 21 Mar. 1997).

[45] See also *Doe* v. *America Online Inc*, Fla Cir.Ct, Palm Beach Cty, No.CL 97–631 AE, 13 June 1997.

230(c), which was to encourage ISPs to put in place monitoring and blocking controls so as to restrict circulation on the Internet of offensive material. Accordingly the action was struck out.

The UK approach to ISP liability was heavily influenced by the pre-CDA US experience, and the decision was taken that statutory reform in the field of defamation to protect ISPs was justified. Unfortunately however when the Defamation Act 1996 was introduced in September 1996, with the intention *inter alia* of clarifying the defence of innocent dissemination for ISPs in both England and Scotland[46] many commentators thought that it had inadvertently transplanted into UK law the most unhelpful aspects of the *Prodigy* decision.

Section 1(1) of the Defamation Act 1996 provides that:

In defamation proceedings a person has a defence if he shows that—
    (a) he was not the author, editor or publisher of the statement complained of,
    (b) he took reasonable care in relation to its publication, and
    (c) he did not know, and had no reason to believe, that what he did caused or contributed to the publication of a defamatory statement.

Although this section was an improvement over the vagueness of the pre-existing common law on innocent dissemination, its phrasing still left much to be desired from the viewpoint of ISP liability. The defence of proving 'reasonable care' provided by section 1(1)(b) is only available to persons who are not 'publishers' or 'editors' according to section 1(1)(a). A 'publisher' is defined in section 1(2) as a commercial publisher, i.e. a person whose business is issuing material to the public. This certainly seems to exclude non-commercial hosts such as universities, but to embrace commercial ISPs. Meanwhile an 'editor' is defined as including any person 'having editorial or equivalent responsibility for the content of the statement or the decision to publish it'. Again this might well cover most ISPs. However section 1(3) goes on to state that:

A person shall *not* be considered the author, editor or publisher of a statement if he is *only* involved . . .

    (c) in . . . operating or providing any equipment, system or service by means of which the statement is retrieved, copied, distributed or made available in electronic form;. . .[or]
    (e) as the operator of or provider of access to a communications system by means of which the statement is transmitted, or made available, by a person over whom he has no effective control.' [parts omitted and emphasis added]

It is clear that section 1(3)(e) was intended by Parliament to be the umbrella under which ISPs could shelter themselves from liability.[47] But this sub-section is problematic in that it seems on literal interpretation to require, in a style

---

[46] See Chap. 2 of the Lord Chancellor's Consultation Document on the draft Defamation Bill, *Reforming Defamation Law and Procedure*, July 1995.

[47] See Hansard, HL vol 571, col 605. The wording of this section was changed from its original form following criticism of the Draft Bill in, *inter alia*, Charlesworth, 'Legal Issues of Electronic Publishing on the World Wide Web' (1995) 26 *Law Librarian* 524.

rather reminiscent of the *Prodigy* decision, that to get the benefit of the section 1(1) defence, the ISP must *only* provide Internet access, and not do anything else—not, for example, exercise editorial control or filter content—for if it does, it seems it will be exercising 'effective control' over the maker of the defamatory statement. Yet a more purposive interpretation would note not only that section 1 was clearly intended to protect electronic 'bulletin boards'(as they were then known) but also that it was unlikely that an ISP which neither monitored nor edited the content it hosted or transmitted could succeed in proving, as section 1(1)(b) requires, that it had taken 'reasonable care' to prevent the publication of the defamatory statement. There is thus an inherent catch 22 if the literal interpretation is adopted.

One possible escape might lie in claiming that an ISP which edits content is only exercising effective control over the defamatory *statement*, not the person who makes the statement. Another approach might be to seek exemption from publisher/editor status under section 1(2)(c) rather than section 1(2)(e), which, although less obviously aimed at describing ISPs, does not contain any 'hands off' requirement.

If either of these arguments is accepted, what must an ISP do to be seen to exercise reasonable care? Section 1(5) provides that a court should have regard to the nature or circumstances of the publication, and in particular to the 'extent of the responsibility of the defender for the content of the statement'. In relation to a Usenet newsgroup, for example, where very large amounts of material arrive by the hour from all over the globe, and the system operator has almost no control except to censor the entire newsgroup, this would, one hopes, be very little responsibility at all. It is noteworthy that both the CompuServe and Prodigy cases involved local rather than Usenet discussion fora, where the ISPs had at least a reasonable chance of keeping an eye on the material complained of.

The first case on section 1, *Godfrey* v. *Demon Internet*,[48] has now gone some way to clarifying matters. The case involved allegations by a British physicist, Lawrence Godfrey, that an anonymous hoax message posted in a newsgroup, soc.culture.thai, in 1997, was libellous and damaging to his reputation. Godfrey asked the ISP Demon, which carried the newsgroup in question, to remove the offensive posting. When Demon did not comply, Godfrey raised an action against them for publishing a libel. Demon claimed the benefit of the section 1 defence.

The ensuing judgment had both good and bad news for ISPs. The good news was that the judge wasted no time in finding that Demon was *not* a publisher under section 1(2) and (3), despite the fact that Demon *does* provide extra content, filter incoming email for spam, etc, and does not *only* 'operate equipment'.[49] The bad news however, was that because Demon had been notified of the allegedly libellous posting and not removed it, the judge held it fell foul of section 1(1)(c) ('did not know and had no reason to believe what they did con-

---

[48] [1999] 4 All ER 342.
[49] Unfortunately he did not indicate whether this was by virtue of the s. 1(3) or (e) exception—both were quoted in the opinion.

tributed to the publication of a defamatory statement') and thus could not take advantage of the section 1 defence.[50]

This judgment does not, as has been suggested,[51] put ISPs back in the financially ruinous position of having to check every item of traffic they carry for legality for fear of being sued—only those items to which specific objection has been raised need be examined, a rather more feasible task. What it does perhaps mean however is that ISPs, in the interest of avoiding litigation, are likely to remove any item which is brought to their notice without too much fuss, however unfounded or trivial the objection seems to be. Cyber-liberty groups have protested that this has serious implications for freedom of expression, since in effect any crank caller or pressure group can censor text posted on the Internet simply by complaining that it is illegal to the ISP. ISPs may thus be forced into acting as private censors even though they do not have the authority or legal knowledge of a court. There is a further possible difficulty in that, if an ISP does take down a Web site for fear of possible liability, the ISP might conceivably suffer a breach of contract claim from the subscriber whose material was taken down.[52] (A whole site might be removed for example when only a single page contained illicit material.) In this worst case scenario, an ISP might consider itself damned if it does take down and damned if it doesn't.

However arguably there is no reason why ISPs, if they really wish to remain defenders of freedom of speech (as Demon claimed they did), or if they want to protect themselves against possible breach of contract suits, cannot protect themselves against pressure to take down without question, simply by retaining legal advice or taking out liability insurance, as other commercial operations do when specific legal challenges about their activities are brought to their attention. Furthermore ISPs can insert into contracts with their own subscribers clauses which require such subscribers to indemnify them if they subsequently incur legal liability as a result of content originated by that subscribers.[53] Admittedly however such an indemnity strategy will be ineffective in respect of content originated by a non-subscriber, and even in the former case, the indemnity might fall foul of unfair contract clauses legislation designed to protect consumers.[54] However it is true that 'notice and take down' procedures, already

---

[50] The case was subsequently settled. Demon originally publicly stated its intention to appeal on the s. 1 defence point, but later dropped the appeal, ostensibly because it was anticipating legislative change, but probably because of the adverse publicity it received at the time of a takeover battle.

[51] See Demon press release, 26 Mar. 1999, at http://www.dispatches.demon,net/pr/1999/pr1999-03-26a.html.

[52] If a site *does* contain illegal material, then presumably the hosting contract between the owner of the site and the ISP is one for an illegal purpose, and thus a breach of contract by the ISP who takes down will not be actionable by the site owner (at least in UK law). However there is still a possible booby trap where the take down notice is issued in respect of illicit material placed on an 'innocent' site by a third party : if the site owner had no knowledge of illegality it is possible they would still be entitled to sue for breach.

[53] Interestingly, Demon's standard-form contract with its subscribers (as posted on their Web site) contained no indemnity clause at the time of the *Godfrey* judgment.

[54] See for UK law, the Unfair Contract Terms Act 1977, especially s. 18, and the EC Dir. on unfair terms in consumer contracts.

common practice, will become an even more appealing and cheap (though not wholly risk-free) option after *Godfrey*.

The issues raised by the *Godfrey* case are especially relevant given the general approach to ISP liability espoused by the EC in its Draft Electronic Commerce Directive.[55] This legislation is broadly intended to provide a framework for facilitating e-commerce within the EU by legislating in a number of areas including such matters as the requirements for electronic contracts, and the control of unsolicited commercial communications (spam) as well as ISP liability. National laws are clearly ineffective when trying to provide favourable conditions for Internet transactions and publications which cross state boundaries at will. Demon at least had the opportunity to cite section 1 of the 1996 Act when sued in London by Godfrey, but it would have been of no help to them if they had been sued in Paris under French law in respect of the same news-group item. The Draft Directive is thus intended to provide a minimum harmonisation of important aspects of the law in all EC Member States.

The EC Directive takes a horizontal approach to ISP liability—in other words it deals with *all* kinds of content issues—intellectual property, criminal obscenity, libel, *et al.*—rather than focusing as the 1996 Act does on a single area. Furthermore, rather than giving a blanket immunity to ISPs in *all* circumstances where the content is provided by a third party other than the ISP, as the US CDA section 230(c) does, which can unfairly protect ISPs to the detriment of victims of libel, it takes a more subtle approach[56] in which the various activities of ISPs are addressed separately. Where ISPs act as a 'mere conduit'—i.e. as a relay station transmitting content originated and received by other parties—the Directive regards them as basically absolved from all liability. This is very much in line with the position as to liability for 'common carriers' such as the post office and the phone company.[57] The Directive also makes it clear[58] that ISPs

[55] This legislation was introduced in draft in Nov. 1998. The Directive came into force on 17 July 2000. Member States have 18 months to implement it in national laws, i.e., by 17 Jan. 2002, see App. I.

[56] Consider e.g. the American, post-CDA case of *Blumenthal* v. *Drudge*, 1998 BNA EC&L 561, in which the libellous remarks in question were made in an on-line gossip column supplied to AOL by Matt Drudge, a well-known political columnist, for $36,000 a year. Although AOL clearly benefited from the content Drudge supplied in terms of audience capture, since the content was provided by a third party, it was held immune from liability under s. 230(c) of the CDA. By contrast under the Draft Dir., Art. 14(2) Drudge would be acting 'under the authority or control of' AOL and AOL's immunity would be lost. Since AOL gained profit from Drudge's willingness recklessly to defame others, it is suggested this is the fairer result.

[57] Art. 12. Transmission includes automatic, intermediate, and transient storage, and the ISP must not modify the information contained in the transmission. Presumably 'information' excludes header information which ISPs routinely and automatically add to through traffic they forward. Such header information is vital to the routing of packets through the Internet to their destination, but does not form part of the message information actually read by the recipient.

[58] In Art. 13. Worries that the European Parliament had introduced provisions incompatible with Art. 13 into another draft EC Dir., on copyright and related rights, have now been allayed by the European Commission—see App.

will not be held liable simply because they *cache* material.[59] Caching is a common practice whereby ISPs store a local copy of a Web page that has been retrieved from a remote server at a user's request, so that any future requests for that page can be met more quickly. The effect of caching is to speed up the Web for all users since traffic is reduced. It is therefore important that caching not be legally discouraged lest the Internet slow to a crawl.

The most controversial part of the liability provisions, is however, Article 14, which deals with circumstances where ISPs host or store more than transiently content originated by third parties. This would, e.g., cover the typical situation where an ISP physically finds space on its server for Web sites for each of its subscribers as part of their contractual package. Under Article 14, ISPs are declared exempt from *criminal* liability in respect of such material so long as they have no 'actual knowledge' of illegal content, and from *civil* liability as long as they have no such actual knowledge *and* have no awareness of facts and circumstances from which such illegality would be apparent. It is made very clear that ISPs do not have to go out and actively *seek* this awareness in Article 15, which provides that EC states are not to impose any general monitoring requirement on ISPs (except in special circumstances, e.g. for national security). But what if an ISP is told, for example, by a member of the public, that a Web site it hosts contains illegal material? Does it become liable immediately since it now has 'knowledge' or 'awareness' that the content may be illegal? This is very similar to the issue raised in *Godfrey* above. Article 14 in response provides specifically that so long as the ISP 'acts expeditiously to remove or to disable access to' the information in question, it will retain its protection from liability. This wording may deal better with the freedom of expression/'privatised censorship' issue than section 1 does, since it appears to leave the ISP an interval of opportunity to consult a lawyer. If a lawyer then advises the ISP that in his or her professional opinion the material is not illegal, then that ISP can validly claim to have no actual knowledge or awareness of *illegality*—even if the material *is* subsequently found by a court (or perhaps a perverse jury) to be (say) defamatory. On the other hand, if the ISP seeks no legal advice but simply refuses to remove the material (or does not respond at all, as appears to have been the case in *Godfrey*) it seems fair for it to be denied immunity if the material is subsequently adjudged illegal or actionable, since it has actively been reckless as to its dissemination on the Net.

Articles 12–15 are not a complete panacea for the question of intermediary liability. One important point raised earlier that is not covered by the EC Directive is the catch 22 situation ISPs may face on a request for take down: the fact that they may be found liable as publishers or some other kind of contributory if they do not comply with the request, but may be found liable for breach

---

[59] Immunity for caching is obviously most relevant to content copied by an ISP *prima facie* in breach of copyright. However it is conceivable that a cached copy of a page containing a libel might be deemed to be 'published' by an ISP since it can be retrieved by other subscribers to that ISP seeking that particular page.

12

Pornography and the Internet

LILIAN EDWARDS[1]

INTRODUCTION[2]

Even in these days of relentless coverage of e-commerce in the media, the most prominent feature of the Internet in the average person's perception is perhaps still as a repository of pornography. The Internet has been anecdotally described as "the biggest dirty bookshop in history" and as an "Internet Babylon".[3] Reports appear daily in the press that "every day thousands of paedophilic photographs showing adults abusing small children are posted on the Web."[4] Such news stories have been ubiquitous in the UK ever since *The Times* and *Sunday Times* reported in 1996 on the problem of hard core porn and paedophilia appearing on Internet news-groups, and appeared even earlier in the USA : the *Time* magazine cover story on "Cyberporn" of 3 July 1995 has been suggested as the trigger which lead to the US Communication Decency Act 1996, a failed attempt to make the Internet safe for children, discussed further below.[5] Pornography on the Internet has to some extent become a "new moral panic"[6] and the paedophile who uses the Internet to meet his needs has become the folk devil of the shadowy hinterland that lies behind the gleamingly clean information superhighway. As a result, it is unsurprising that state control by criminal sanctions of obscene and pornographic text and pictures has become an area of major concern for would-be users and exploiters alike of the Internet. The problem of illegal, harmful, distasteful or offensive content on the Internet is of course not restricted to pornography. Internet content exists which contravenes

---

[1] Senior Lecturer, the School of Law, University of Edinburgh: email L.Edwards@ed.ac.uk.

[2] Parts of this chapter appeared in substantially different form in L Edwards "Regulation of Freedom of Expression on the Internet: The Roles of Law and of the State." in Pare and Desbarats eds. *Freedom of Expression and New Communications Technologies* (IQ/Orbicom, 1998). My thanks to Joachim Genge for research assistance.

[3] Anne Wells Branscomb "Internet Babylon? Does the Carnegie Mellon study of pornography on the Information Superhighway reveal a threat to the stability of society?" (1995) 83 *Georgetown Law* Journal 1935.

[4] This example is from *The Observer*, 19 March 2000.

[5] See W.Grossman, "Unsafe Sex in the Red Page District", chapter 9 of *Net.Wars* (NYUP, 1997), at p. 120.

[6] See for a critique of the mythology around the net and pornography, A Hamilton "The Net Out of Control: A New Moral Panic: Cansorship and Sexuality" in Liberty (ed) *Liberating Cyberspace* (Pluto Press, 1999).

the rules enacted to prevent the making of anti-religious statements (the law of blasphemy), the making of racist or inflammatory statements (incitement to racial hatred or "hate speech" rules) and the making of politically subversive or seditious statements. These categories in no way mop up all the potentially worrying content on the Internet. In both the UK and the USA for example, considerable moral panic has been whipped up recently over the availability of "bomb-making" recipes on the Web.[7]

Rules dealing with illegal or harmful content tend to vary a great deal from country to country depending on their social, ethical, legal and religious history. For example in Germany, strict rules exist forbidding the publication of material which denies the occurrence of the Holocaust; in the UK, material can only be blasphemous where it offends those who practice the Christian religion;[8] in China and other Far Eastern countries rules restricting political speech exist which tend to be regarded as unduly restrictive by Western standards. The fact that standards concerning what material is criminally offensive vary so much from jurisdiction to jurisdiction complicates still further the issue of control of Internet content, given the fact that it is inherent to the nature of the Internet that content is freely distributed across physical national boundaries. In this chapter we will mainly be concerned with obscene or pornographic content, especially child pornography, since this is the most central and universal focus of concern. Many of the issues discussed below have significance however for other types of illegal, offensive or harmful content.

Some of the basic issues in this area which this chapter will try to address are:[9]

- What laws regulating the media and freedom of speech already exist which can be applied to regulate content communicated or accessed via the Internet?
- Has the Internet created novel problems which can *not* be adequately regulated by the existing legal and regulatory framework?
- Can existing laws be *enforced* successfully in the environment of the Internet and if not, what steps can be taken?

---

[7] For example, the BBC reported on 30 June 2000 that Copeland, the notorious nail bomber of a gay pub in London, had discovered how to make bombs from the Internet. See http://news6.thdo. bbc.co.uk/hi/english/uk/newsid%5F808000/808745.stm .

[8] See *R v. Bow St Magistrates ex parte Choudhury* [1991] 1 All ER 306 (the "Satanic Verses" case).

[9] For a good general critique of how free speech is regulated and restricted globally on the Internet, see V Mayer-Schoenberger and T E Foster "A Regulatory Web: Free Speech and the Global Information Infrastructure" in Kahin and Nesson (eds) *Borders in Cyberspace* (MIT Press, 1997). Up to date information on the whole area of cyber-space and freedom of expression can best be gathered from websites: in the UK, Cyber-Rights and Cyber-Liberties run by Yaman Akdeniz is the most comprehensive source at http://www.cyber-rights.org/; in the USA, numerous good sites exist including the Electronic Frontier Foundation and its associated Blue Ribbon Online Free Speech campaign (http:://www.eff.org/blueribbon.html); and the Campaign for Internet Freedom (http://www.netfreedom.org); in Australia the main site is Electronic Frontiers Australia at http://www.efa.org.au/. See also Godwin M *Cyber Rights: Defending Free Speech in the Digital Age* (Times Books, 1998).

One important factor to realise in this area is that there are few neutral speakers or statements in the debate on the Internet, pornography and freedom of speech. The debate both on- and off-line is significantly polarised between "cyber-libertarians",[10] who tend to view any attempt by the state (or other agencies)to regulate Internet content as potential or overt censorship; and those who might be called "cyber-paternalists" or "protectionists", usually representing state or conservative concerns, who take the view that the new medium offers special and extensive risks which justify special restrictions, legal or extra-legal. In order to protect the interests of parties such as children, women, minority races, and religious groups, therefore, as well as the general moral fibre of society, a certain degree of regulation is justified. As we will see below, this attitude is taken to a greater or lesser extent by many Western governments. It is currently of particular concern to many regulators including, notably, the European Union, that a high profile of sleaze on the Internet inhibits user trust of the medium and is thus an impediment to the growth of a vibrant and competitive e-commerce market.[11]

The following quote is representative of a moderate cyber-libertarian attitude:

"Cyberspace is probably the richest source of creative, diverse, empowering and democratizing communication ever to connect people across the globe. It is perhaps the world's first true "mass media" because it allow anyone with a few simple tools to communicate ideas to thousands of persons at once. It inspires tolerance and promotes mutual understanding by connecting people of all ilk around the world. It is a tool for community organising and citizen involvement.

But all the innovation and citizen empowerment inspired by online communications will be lost if your free speech and privacy rights don't apply in cyberspace.

An unprecedented wave of censorship and overzealous law enforcement is sweeping through the online world. State and federal legislators have proposed and passed legislation to criminalise online speech. Police have raided community bulletin boards and seized entire systems—with evidence that a miniscule portion of the files might be legally obscene. And the privacy rights of online users have been threatened by indiscriminate snooping and interference by government and industry in private email."[12]

A more blood-curling account of state censorship on line comes from the American Civil Liberties Union, commenting on the promotion of the use of filtering software programs which block certain types of speech:[13]

"In his chilling (and prescient) novel about censorship, Fahrenheit 451, author Ray Bradbury describes a futuristic society where books are outlawed. "Fahrenheit 451" is, of course, the temperature at which books burn. In Bradbury's novel—and in the

---

[10] Disparate cyber-libertarian and cyber-rights organisations have founded a Global Internet Liberty Campaign, at http://www.gilc.org .

[11] Similar concerns were examined in relation to the control of defamation and spam on the Internet: see Edwards, Chapters 11 and 13.

[12] A Beeson "Top Ten Threats to Civil Liberties in Cyberspace", 1996 (Spring) *Human Rights* 10.

[13] See further below, 297.

physical world—people censor the printed word by burning books. But in the virtual world, one can just as easily censor controversial speech by banishing it to the farthest corners of cyberspace using rating and blocking programs."[14]

Contrast the measured tones of the European Parliament in its influential Communication of 16 October 1996 *on Illegal and Harmful Content on the Internet*:

"The vast majority of Internet content is for purposes of information for totally legitimate (and often highly productive) business or private usage. However like any other communications technology, particularly in the initial stages of their development, the Internet carries an amount of potentially harmful or illegal content or can be misused as a vehicle for criminal activities. . . . As in any other sector of activities, the Internet may be used for legitimate purposes or misused by some elements of society. The framework for the Internet should, therefore, *foster economic development*, while taking account of *justified social and societal concerns*. Consumers and businesses must be reassured that the Internet is a safe and secure place to work, learn and play."[15]

The UK government have similarly made a number of recent policy statements emphasising the need for protection of the public from illegal and harmful material,[16] both for ordinary reasons of public policy and, increasingly, as a foundation stone to creating the conditions of trust necessary for e-commerce to flourish: for example from the recent UK government policy document *e.commerce@its.best.uk* we find:

"Internet users are concerned about protecting children and vulnerable people from illegal or immoral material. A May 1999 survey of US parents showed that 78 per cent have concerns about the content of Internet material to which their children have access. [footnote deleted] In the UK the IWF handled 2,407 reported cases of illegal content in 1998, compared with 898 in 1997 . . . Control of content for consumers is thus a serious and growing issue and a problem that must be solved."[17]

Finally, a last important question to consider in this area is, if restrictions are to be placed on the availability of certain types of content on the Internet, who is to enforce these restrictions or to pay the penalty if these restrictions are breached? As we have noted throughout this book, to obtain a connection to the Internet usually requires the service of an Internet Service Provider (ISP)—who may take the form of a commercial operator such as CompuServe, America On

---

[14] ACLU White Paper, *Fahrenheit 451.2: Is Cyberspace Burning? How Rating and Blocking Proposals May Torch Free Speech on the Internet*, available at http://www.aclu.org/issues/cyber/burning.html#Free.

[15] COM (1996) 487. Available at http://www.ispo.cec.be/legal/en/internet/internet.html.

[16] Such arguments have also been used extensively to justify the passing of the Regulation of Investigatory Powers Act 2000 which broadly allows state authorities under certain conditions to intercept and de-encrypt communications sent via the Internet. The Act is discussed more fully in Hogg, chapter 3. See also discussion in *Building Confidence in Electronic Commerce* (DTI Consultation Document URN 99/642), especially pp. 20–2.

[17] *e-commerce @its.best.uk*, Performance and Innovation Unit Report, September 1999, para 10.13.

Line or VirginNet to give just a few examples; or may be a non-commercial host such as a university or employer's server. The ISP may find that in its role as a "carrier" or "publisher" or "distributor" of Internet content, they may be held liable in respect of content which runs foul of the law (such as a racist statement or pornographic picture) rather than, or as well as, the original content provider. ISP liability in relation to content is thus a controversial area in terms of freedom of expression since ISPs act effectively as the gatekeepers to the Internet. If they are placed in a position where they can be sued or prosecuted in respect of speech originated by others but distributed via the ISP, then their natural response will be to limit their risk and close the gates to that material even though it may not actually be illegal, merely distasteful to some.[18] Cyberlibertarians tend to characterise this as undemocratic censorship, or less, politely, "gagging the Internet".[19] It is useful to consider whether it is "better" or more efficient, in terms of maintaining the balance between free speech and protection of the public and industry, for the state to turn its efforts towards those who *originate* potentially harmful content (authors); those who *read or access* it (Internet users); or those who participate in *publishing and distributing* it (mainly ISPs). We shall discuss modes of control of content by users as well as ISPs and other bodies such as schools and libraries under the head of "self-regulation" below.

In this chapter we will make specific reference to the laws of the United Kingdom (which differ significantly in criminal matters between England and Scotland) but will also take account of developments in the USA, Australia and Europe. One important distinction to note right from the start is that two types of pornography are under discussion herein. First, there is pornography aimed at adults which is illegal for adults to read or view according to the rules of a particular legal system. The material most universally accepted as falling into this category is child pornography, ie, material featuring actual or simulated sex acts involving children. Secondly, there is pornography or other sexual material which is not illegal for adults to access, but may be considered harmful or upsetting for *children* to see. As we shall see, on the Internet it is not easy to set aside separate zones where adults can indulge in adult erotica without fear of child access, and this issue cannot be addressed, as it is in the non-virtual world, by criminalising the sale of pornography where children can buy it, or its display where they can can see or gain entry to it. The issues raised by the two types of pornography are separable but overlapping. Should attempts to control Internet porn concentrate only on what is incontrovertibly illegal for all—as cyberlibertarians generally seem to advocate— or also attempt to facilitate parents who are concerned about what their children may see, and adults who wish not to be barraged with material they find offensive? As we shall see, these different goals point in different directions; the first towards direct enforcement of

---

[18] See further discussion in Edwards, Chapter 11, pp. 263ff.

[19] See G Wilson, "Gagging the Net in 3 easy steps" on the BBC News homepage, 13 April 2000 at http://news.bbc.co.uk/hi/english/newsid_711000/711782.stm .

national criminal laws, the second towards the empowerment of Internet *users* to make choices about what content they receive.

CONTROL OF INTERNET CONTENT: NATIONAL CRIMINAL LAWS

There is more anecdotal evidence than hard statistics concerning the nature and prevalence of Internet pornography. The only comprehensive survey is the much cited Carnegie-Mellon study of 1995[20] but even it has been repeatedly attacked on grounds of methodological flaw.[21] Pornography can undoubtedly be found on many thousands of sites on the Web, and even more frequently in Usenet news-groups, and may take the form of text, pictures, video or animation. What most informed commentators seem to agree on is that the percentage of Internet content which is pornographic or obscene (what ever that, of course, means) is miniscule[22] compared to the content on the Internet as a whole; however that small percentage of material is disproportionately accessed compared to, say, Internet content about badgers (one easy way to substantiate this is to look at the search terms most often entered into search engines, especially at certain hours); however relatively little of such content is available for free (since pornographers, like everyone else, want to make a living, and so tend to protect their saleable goods behind protection such as passwords.) As we shall see below, this point that, contrary to popular myth, it is difficult for casual browsers (such as children) simply to stumble upon serious pornography, was taken up as significant by the US Supreme Court in its judgment declaring unconstitutional the Communications Decency Act 1996.

The lack of a base line for the exact amount and whereabouts of pornographic material on the Net makes it difficult to assess in any empirical way how effective, if at all, national laws are in controlling illegal or offensive Internet content. Nonetheless it would undoubtedly be politically unsound in most nations to dismiss the belief that existing laws encompass the threat to public security and morals posed by Internet pornography, or at least could do so with a little tinkering. As noted above, pornography on the Net is a tempting target for media propagandists and has a remarkable ability to conceal or divert attention from the more positive aspects of Net culture.[23] Some would say that the controversy over pornography on the Internet is nothing new and that indeed, on the other hand, exactly the same problems arose from the dramatic extension of possible dissemination of illicit content when the printing press was intro-

---

[20] Reported in M Rimm "Marketing Pornography on the Information Superhighway" (1995) 83 *Georgetown Law Journal* 1849.

[21] See Grossman, n. 5 above, p. 120.

[22] Hamilton (see n. 6 above) asserts that only 0.002% of newgroups contain sexual images but does not give a source for this data.

[23] See for example the storm of press coverage around the former rock star Gary Glitter's conviction for possession of child pornography obtained from the Internet in November 1999; for example "Fury as Glitter gets only 4 months", *The Sun*, 13 November 1999.

duced to Europe in the 1600s.[24] Jeffrey Shallit, a US academic and "cyber-libertarian", has usefully coined Three Laws of New Media:

Rule 1 Every new medium of expression will be used for sex.

Rule 2 Every new medium of expression will come under attack, usually because of Shallit's First Law.

Rule 3 Protection afforded for democratic rights and freedoms in traditional media will rarely be understood to apply to new media.[25]

As a general principle of Western legal systems, state jurisdiction in criminal matters is territorial. Thus in theory at least, there is no legal vacuum in relation to criminal activities on-line. Each state's laws on pornography, hate speech, blasphemy, etc, apply within their own territory, and will apply to criminal acts perpetrated there, and Internet users and ISPs situated there, just as they do in respect of communications distributed via more conventional media such as books, magazines etc. Most states already have in place rules of criminal law extensively prohibiting the distribution, publication, import and use of child pornography; many have also criminalised racist or hate speech, the other type of offensive content on the Internet which is beginning to command serious attention.[26] Why then is it that effective regulation and proscription of pornography and hate speech on the Internet appears so problematic for states? Or, to look at the other side of the fence, why do cyber-libertarians like Shallit and Beeson[27] feel that rights of free expression which are acknowledged as protected in the non-virtual world, are likely to be abrogated on the "electronic frontier" unless actively defended? We will examine these questions after briefly surveying the relevant UK law in the area of pornography and obscenity.

UK law

At first sight, there is already a considerable amount of overlapping legal regulation of obscene material within the UK. In England, the main pieces of general obscenity legislation are the Obscene Publications Acts 1959 and 1964, which make it an offence to publish an obscene article, or to have an obscene article for publication for gain.[28] These Acts, it should be noted, did not criminalise the

---

[24] See Hudson "Online Pornography: Balancing Freedom of Expression and Community Values in Practice" in Pare and Desbarats, n. 1 above.

[25] Taken from J Shallit "Public Networks and Censorship" in Ludlow (ed) *High Noon on the Electronic Frontier: Conceptual Issues in Cyberspace* (MIT Press, 1996).

[26] See for comprehensive coverage of global developments in this area, Hatewatch (http://www. hatewatch.org/) and the Simon Wiesenthal Centre (http://www.wiesenthal.com/index. html). In the UK, the Jewish Policy Centre takes a watching brief in this area (79 Wimpole St, London W1M 7DD): see their report *The governance of cyberspace: racism on the Internet* (July 1996); also the EMAIN project reported at J Craven "Extremism on the Internet" (1998) 1 *JILT* at http://elj.war wick.ac.uk/jilt/wip/98_1crav/

[27] Quoted on p. 277.

[28] 1959 Act, section 2(1) and 1964 Act, s 1(2).

mere private *possession* of obscene material. An "article" is defined to include matter which may be looked at as well as read, as well as sound records and any film or other record of a picture or pictures.[29] An article is "obscene" if its effect is "such as to tend to deprave and corrupt persons who are likely . . . to read, see or hear" it.[30] In practice, ever since the Williams Committee[31] reported on the operation of the Acts in 1976 following the unsuccessful prosecution of the paperback *Inside Linda Lovelace*, the 1959 Act has not been used to prosecute books for which any claim of literary merit could be made. Its substantial use is to restrain the circulation of obscene pictures, films and videos rather than the written word and, more particularly, the circulation of hard-core pornography.[32] In terms of computer pornography, the 1959 Act has been amended so that an "article" includes a computer disc, and "publication" clearly includes the electronic transmission of material from one computer to another.[33] Thus the downloading of porn from the Internet to, say, a laptop, without any physical medium as intermediary, such as a disc or a printout, is clearly caught. In Scotland, similar prosecutions can be brought under the Civic Government (Sc) Act 1982, section 51, which broadly covers the publication, sale or distribution of "obscene material", which is defined to include *inter alia* a computer disc and any kind of recording of a visual image.[34] Prosecutions can be and are also brought in Scotland under common law, which is discussed below at p 285.

The traditional liberal approach embodied in both the Scottish and English legislation is that it is acceptable to possess obscene material in private so long as there is no attempt to publish, distribute or show it to others, particularly for gain. However in the case of child pornography, which in its nature features the sexual abuse of children, Parliament has taken the view that the phenomenon is so heinous that possession as well as circulation should be criminalised.[35] The primary Acts here are the Protection of Children Act 1978 (which does not apply in Scotland or Northern Ireland) and, more recently, the Criminal Justice Act 1988 (which in various provisions has effect throughout the UK[36]), the latter of which makes it an offence for a person to have any indecent photograph of a child in his *possession*[37], on top of the pre-existing offences of taking, distributing, showing or publishing such a photograph.[38] A child is defined as a person

---

[29] 1959 Act, s 1(2).
[30] 1959 Act, s 1(1).
[31] Committee on Obscenity and Film Censorship, HMSO, 1979, Cmnd 7772.
[32] See Robertson and Nicol *Media Law* (3rd edn, 1992), Chapter 3.
[33] See Criminal Justice and Public Order Act 1994, Sched 9, para 3.
[34] 1982 Act, s 51(8).
[35] Robertson and Nicol (n 29 above) note that this may be contrary to the European Convention on Human Rights' guarantee of respect for private life, which is incorporated into UK law within the Human Rights Act 1998 from October 2000.
[36] In Scotland, the Criminal Justice Act 1988 inserted a s 52A into the Civic Government (Sc) Act 1982 which provides the simple possession offence for Scotland in s 52A (1). Other offences relating to child pornography are found in s 52 of the 1982 Act.
[37] 1988 Act, s 160 (England) and 161 (Scotland).
[38] Protection of Children Act 1984 , s 1.

under 16. In 1995, the UK police used these new possession offences to organise their first major crackdown on international Internet paedophile rings, in an operation known as Operation Starburst. Nine UK men were arrested (other arrests being made abroad of foreign nationals) and at least two convicted of possession offences under section 160 of the 1988 Act.[39] Subsequent operations have followed, such as Operation Cathedral in 1998, which resulted in nine people being charged with various offences.[40]

Finally an increasing worry in recent years for law enforcement agencies has been "cyber-solicitation": the use of Internet chat-rooms by paedophiles to lure children into meetings, sometimes across state boundaries, and also their use to orchestrate the sexual abuse of children and arrange "sex tourism" trips. The anonymity of the Internet lends itself to paedophiles disguising their identity, age and sex in order to entice children to sexual encounters. Partially to meet these concerns, the Sexual Offences (Conspiracy and Incitement) Act was introduced in 1996 to make it an offence to incite another person to commit sexual acts against children abroad.

PROBLEMS WITH APPLYING NATIONAL CRIMINAL LAWS TO INTERNET PORNOGRAPHY

Adaptability of existing legislation to the Internet

In theory therefore, UK authorities seeking to regulate Internet pornography appear to have adequate existing legislation and case law to apply. Question has arisen however whether these existing rules are sufficiently flexible when applied to the novel environment of the Internet and electronic publishing. This tends to be more of a problem for common law legal systems such as English law, where legislation is seen as an encroachment on the common law and is usually both drafted and interpreted in a narrow, technical way, than it is for Continental style legal systems where legislative codes are drafted widely and interpretation tends to be teleological. A good recent example of the problems that can arise can be taken from English case law relating to the Protection of Children Act 1978. As noted above, this Act makes it an offence *inter alia* for any person to take, distribute or show indecent photographs of children, or to have such photographs in one's possession with a view to their being distributed or shown by oneself or others. In the case of *R v Fellows and Arnold*[41] the Court of Appeal had to consider whether the Act applied in a case involving the use of

---

[39] See further Y Akdeniz "Governance of Pornography and Child Pornography on the Internet" in L Edwards and C Waelde (eds) *Law and the Internet: Regulating Cyberspace* (Hart Publishing, 1997), pp. 229–30.

[40] See NCIS report *Project Trawler: Crime on the Information Highways*, June 1999, pp. 16–17. Contact details can be found at http://www.ncis.co.uk .

[41] [1997] 2 All ER 548. See also Cobley "Child pornography on the Internet", 1997 2 *Communications Law* 30.

a computer by two paedophiles. Images of child pornography were maintained on an electronic database and access was allowed to other paedophiles by issue of a password which allowed the images to be viewed and downloaded. The main issue for the court was whether the images stored in the computer memory could be defined as "photographs" in terms of the Act. At the time of the alleged offences, the Act merely defined a photograph as including an indecent film, a copy of an indecent photograph or film and an indecent photograph comprised in a film.[42] The photographs in this case had never been printed out by the accused but merely stored on the computer hard disc and shown on the monitor screen, and similarly made available to others. Taking a purposive approach to the statute, the court found that a visual image stored electronically on disc was not a photograph itself, but *was* a "copy of a photograph" which fell within the definition quoted above. Furthermore, the court went on to find that knowingly holding such images on computer disc where they could be found and accessed by others had elements of active participation such that the offence of distributing or showing such photographs to others could be held to have been committed by the maintainers of the database.

The 1978 Act was in fact amended subsequent to the events of the *Fellows* case by the Criminal Justice and Public Order Act 1994, which extended the definition of a "photograph" to include "pseudo-photographs" which are defined as any "image, whether made by computer graphics or otherwise howsoever, which appears to be a photograph".[43] This amendment was not however applicable at the time of the case itself. The case is interesting in that, first, the courts managed to adapt the legislation to secure the policy goal even without the benefit of statutory amendment ; but also, significantly, the legal amendment made by the 1994 Act not only deals with the problem highlighted in *Fellows* (of non-hard copy Internet porn) but arguably goes further and restricts freedom of expression more severely than might be strictly necessary to meet the social goals of the original legislation. Akdeniz, commenting on the 1994 Act, has noted that "pseudo-photographs" as now defined, might include child pornographic images created by digitally doctoring perfectly respectable pictures of children (or adults).[44] Such images might be created without necessarily involving the abuse of any living child in which case, arguably, criminal sanction might not be appropriate—indeed, perhaps such images should be encouraged as non harmful alternatives for those psychologically addicted to child pornography. On the other hand, the argument remains that all such pictures should be criminalised, because they feed and encourage the existence of a paedophilia market which will inevitably lead to abuse of or harm to actual children.

---

[42] See 1978 Act, s 7(2).
[43] 1994 Act, s 84(7). The 1994 Act also amended the definition of a photograph in the Civic Government (Sc) Act ss 52 and 52A (see n. 36 above) .
[44] See further Akdeniz , n. 39 above, at p. 228.

In Scotland, unusually among the nations of Europe, criminal law is mainly founded in common law rather than in statute. For example, offences related to distribution of obscene or offensive matter are often tried as the common law crime of "shamelessly indecent conduct".[45] In one unreported Scottish case, a scheme whereby photographs of partially naked children were held on disc and linked up to "sexual curriculum vitae" which had been constructed from questions put to children in computer questionnaires, was successfully prosecuted under this head.[46] On one view, this may be seen as a victory for the powers of adaptation and flexibility of the Scottish criminal legal system. Cyber-libertarians however might well feel that it is best for emerging new areas of criminal behaviour to be governed by clearly laid down and publicly available codes, not by uncertain common law and judicial interpretation which will be retrospective in effect.

Creative judicial activism to adapt existing law will always be an attractive option in Internet related areas, given the speed of technological progress and the relative slowness of making new laws. But judicial activism does not always have to work in favour of increased censorship of new media, contrary to Shallitt's third law. In *Atkins v DPP; Goodland v DPP*[47] the Queen's Bench Division found themselves asked to consider two interesting questions relating to Internet pornography. First, did having indecent photographs stored on the *cache* of a computer system belonging to a certain person constitute "possession" by that person for the purpose of section 160(1) of the Criminal Justice Act 1988?; and secondly, did the downloading (saving) of indecent photographs to a particular *drive* on that computer system, from the Internet, constitute the separate offence of the "making"[48] of an indecent photograph under section 1(1) of the Protection of Children Act?

At first instance, the magistrate's court had found the answer to the first question to be yes, even though an image browsed on a Web page can be (and, in fact, usually is) saved to a computer's cache without either the knowledge or intent of the browser. Possession in the magistrate's view was an offence of strict liability, and so, since the image was there, the offence had been committed (unless one of the specific statutory defences was proved). On the other hand, the magistrate took the view that simply saving existing digital images to a particular drive on a computer was not *"making"* a new photo. This was storage,

---

[45] See further G Gordon *Criminal Law*, 2nd edn, and Second Supplement to 2nd edn, 1992, Chapter 36. Shameless indecency has been revived and used in Scotland to control the selling and distribution of obscene articles—see *Robertson* v. *Smith* 1980 JC 1. By contrast, the last reported common law conviction for obscenity in Scotland was in 1843.

[46] *HMA* v. *Chambers*, Stornoway Sheriff Court, 1996, reported in Cullen "Computer Crime" in Edwards and Waelde (eds), n. 39 above.

[47] [2000] All ER 425.

[48] The offence of "making" an indecent photograph was added both to the 1978 Act and the equivalent Scottish legislation by the Criminal Justice and Public Order Act 1994, at the same time that the concept of a "pseudo-photograph" was also introduced to the legislation. The argument that the offence of "making" was thus referrable *only* to "pseudo-photographs" and not to other types of indecent photographs was however explicitly rejected in *Atkins* .

reservation, or some concept of that kind; there was no creative, new act of manufacture, which he felt to be a requisite.

The Queen's Bench however reversed the magistrate on both points. Possession was not an offence of strict liability; rather it did involve the need for some kind of knowledge of the existence and effect of the cache. An analogy was suggested with the case of *R v Steele*[49] where a man charged with the offence of possession of a firearm was held guilty despite his plea that he did not know that what he had in a hold-all of which he had possession was a firearm. However the correct analogy here, the court held, was of the cache to the hold-all, not the firearm. Thus a person who knows that computers can be set up automatically to cache images browsed may reasonably expect consequences if he looks at indecent photos on the Net; whereas a person who knows nothing of caches or that his computer has one will not. Accordingly the possession offence was struck down. In contrast however, the Queen's Bench found that the accused *had* "made" indecent photos by saving images *deliberately* to a computer hard disc. The natural and ordinary meaning of the word "to make" was "to cause to exist; to produce by action, to bring about"; so this was sufficient to include both the saving and the printing off of an image from the Internet. However, the court emphasised that if an image was automatically and inadvertently saved to a cache, this would not be "making" , since it, along with other offences under section 1(1) of the 1978 Act such as taking or permitting to be taken an indecent photo of a child, were serious offences which could not be committed unintentionally.

The interesting result of the case is that both the "possession" and the "making" offences discussed above end up with judicially supplied requirements of intention, rather than being interpreted as offences of strict liability. This is not the conservative response to the policy goal of restricting the ownership and transmission of child pornography that might have been anticipated by cyber-cynics.

Does the novel environment of the Internet justify new and/or more intensive regulation of content?

We noted above that both the UK and EU have been sensitive to the view that illegal or harmful content on the Internet presents novel risks not found in other media. While the *content* of Internet pornography may be identical to that circulated via other media, undoubtedly the *environment* in which it circulates is significantly different in a number of ways. Electronic porn can be indefinitely copied at marginal cost; the quality of the image does not degrade on multiple copying; material is childishly easy to circulate, both within states and across national boundaries; material is hard for law enforcement authorities to detect

---

[49]   [1993] Crim LR 298.

because of the infinite size of cyberspace and the availability of encryption ; even if Internet porn is located, "seizure" is not a major restricting expense as it is with stocks of (for example) glossy hardcore magazines; it is easy to "restock" with electronic porn, or to copy the material from one site or one country to another.

The most vociferous arguments that Internet porn is a "new horror" however have been made in relation to the ease of access by children.[50] As access to computers and the Net has become commonplace not just at work but in schools and the home, so has the ability of children to get on to the Net without adult supervision grown. It is the stuff of anecdote that in many households children are more adept at surfing the Web than their parents (and at disguising their tracks, eg by deleting History files); and access to the Internet is increasingly cheap, especially in the USA where calls made to local nodes of ISPs at local telephone rates are free. Flat rate and free Internet access in the UK and Europe is also expanding, which is likely to lead to more unsupervised access by children to the Net. Public awareness of the diversity of content available to children on the Web, combined with the fact that it is always available, not limited to a "post watershed" time period, and is unregulated by a state or industry governing body or censor (unlike radio, TV, film and video) led to a moral panic in both the USA and UK in the early to mid 1990s.[51] Demands were made across the world that children be protected by a clamp down on Internet content generally.

In the USA, this led to the passing of the Communications Decency Act 1996, an Act which broadly attempted to impose criminal sanctions on anyone who placed "obscene or indecent" content on the Internet, knowing that it might be read or seen by a person under 18. Since it is generally impossible without overt technical measures such as credit card checking (and perhaps even then) to know if a child is "lurking" in a newsgroup, or reading a website, effectively this criminalised such content even in respect of inter-adult communication throughout the Internet. The Act was attacked moreover because it affected not just matter such as child pornography, which was already, uncontroversially, illegal, whether found in hard copy or on the Internet; but also "indecent" material, which in traditional media had been acknowledged in the USA as having some degree of First Amendment protection. At a more symbolic level, the Act was seen as a declaration of war on the "traditional" free-speechers of the Internet, and as demonstrating flagrant disregard for the right of freedom of expression on-line.[52]

The legality of the CDA was challenged by a variety of civil liberties groups and to the great delight of much of the long-standing Internet community, the

---

[50] Phrase taken from the UK House of Commons Home Affairs Committee First Report on Computer Pornography, HC 126.

[51] See T Gibbons "Computer Generated Pornography" in (1995) 9 *International Yearbook of Law, Computers and Technology* 83.

[52] See most famously, John Perry Barlow's "A Cyberspace Independence Declaration", issued on the Web the day after the CDA was signed into operation and archived at http://www.eff.org/~barlow.

Supreme Court quashed the offending provisions on 25 June 1997.[53] Their argument was effectively that the CDA would turn the whole of the Internet into a medium pitched at the level of a children's reading room. Since it was not yet possible technically to guarantee that adult speech would only be accessed by adults, no "zoning" was possible as it was with, for example, adult films and sex shops. The rationale that the CDA was a necessary infringement on the freedom of speech of adults to protect the interests of children was robustly rejected. Forty years earlier in the *Butler v Michigan*[54] case, the Supreme Court had overturned a state law banning the sale of books unfit for children on the oft-quoted grounds that such legislation burns down the house to roast the pig. In *Reno v ACLU*,[55] the Court now re-asserted that while protection of children was an important goal, it could not be legitimately achieved by interfering with the constitutional rights of adults to speak. The Internet was not as invasive a medium as radio or TV: pornographic websites for example were usually well signposted and often password protected and were unlikely to be stumbled upon by accident. Accordingly censorship of the Internet to bring its content down to the "lowest common denominator" that should be exposed to children would be even less acceptable in relation to the Internet than broadcast media. In attempting to turn the Internet into a child-safe forum, the CDA "cast a far darker shadow over free speech" and "threaten[ed] to torch a large segment of the Internet community." While it was true that sites could make efforts to restrict access by children to adult-oriented material by putting in place requirements for adult verification passwords such as AdultCheck,[56] or credit card details, these would present a formidable financial overhead to small website operators, some of whom might be providing socially useful information such as help on sexual abuse, homosexuality or AIDS. Some would cease to publish this information as a result, or close down altogether. The restrictions on these sites were not justifiable given the impact on the free speech rights of adults. The CDA was accordingly overturned.[57]

In the aftermath of the *Reno* decision, Congress enacted the Child Online Protection Act (COPA). Section 1403(a) of this Act provides that any *commercial* Web publisher who knowingly makes available to minors material that is "harmful to minors" is to be subject to penalties of up to six months imprisonment or a $50,000 fine. COPA was tailored to be more robust under constitutional inspection than the CDA in that it (i) applied only to commercial websites (ii) gave a fuller definition of what material was "harmful to minors" (but which

---

[53] *Reno* v. *ACLU,* 521 US 844 (1997) at http://www.aclu.org/court/renovacludec.html

[54] 353 US 380, 97 S Ct 524 (1957).

[55] Cited at n. 50.

[56] AdultCheck (http://www.adultcheck.com/) is currently the most popular adult verification site. Clients give the site information including credit card details and it provides an AdultCheck ID which can then be used to gain access to "adult" sites. AdultCheck (according to its own publicity) is currently used on around 125,000 adult sites.

[57] See a detailed analysis of the judgment in J Wallace "Extinguishing the CDA fire" (1997) 3 *JILT* at http://elj.warwick.ac.uk/jilt/cases/97_3cda/. Some parts of the CDA relating to ISP immunity remained in force: see further chapter 11.

still included material not illegal for adults to access, such as some types of adult pornography) and (iii) gave more evidence about the possible harm to children of Internet content. These distinctions have, so far, been not enough to save it from meeting the same fate as the CDA. The statute has been overturned as unconstitutional first by the District Court[58] and subsequently by the US Court of Appeals.[59] Interestingly, the latest decision places emphasis on the point relatively subsidiary in relation to the CDA that no reliable technical means as yet exist to enable blocking of Web traffic to or from certain locations. Since COPA defined material "harmful to minors" in accordance with the community standards of the place where the material was accessed, this would mean that Web communications, which are effectively accessible globally, would have to meet "the most restrictive and conservative state's community standards in order to avoid criminal liability". This leaves a chink of possibility that when or if technical "zoning" does become available, a US anti-Internet porn Bill may yet be allowed to come into action.[60]

Although these courtroom victories have been celebrated world-wide by "netizens" and cyber-libertarians, it must be remembered that the kind of judicial scrutiny that was applied in *Reno v ACLU* is only possible in states such as the USA which allow constitutional overturn of legislation. In the UK, for example, even despite the incorporation of the European Convention of Human Rights[61] (which includes rights to freedom of expression), the doctrine that courts cannot declare statutes invalid is to be preserved (although a fast track procedure for the government to amend defective statutes will be available). Clearly, constitutional arguments as utilised in the CDA case can be marshalled by free speech activists world-wide but may have to be fed in at the level of policy and law creation in the UK and other states without Bills of Rights rather than in direct court challenges. It is noticeable however that the European Union's ongoing attempts to formulate policy and action relating to Internet content have taken cognisance of the US CDA debacle, and explicitly seek to avoid any assertion that adult rights must suffer to protect the interests of children, or that in general the state should directly censor material on the Internet which goes beyond the category of illegal, to merely harmful or undesirable content.[62]

---

[58] *ACLU* v. *Reno II* 31 F Supp. 2d 473 (E.D.Pa.1999)

[59] *ACLU* v. *Reno II*, June 22 2000, US Court of Appeal for the 3rd Circuit, available at http://www.epic.org/free_speech/copa/3d_cir_opinion.html.

[60] COPA has thus far never come into operation; its existence was challenged and its operation suspended one day after it was passed by Congress by ACLU.

[61] By the Human Rights Act 1998.

[62] See European Parliament Communication of 16 October 1996 on *Illegal and Harmful Content on the Internet* (op cit n 13) at chapter 3: "In terms of illegal and harmful content it is crucial to differentiate betwen content which is illegal and other harmful content. *These different categories of content pose radically different issues of principle, and call for very different legal and technological responses.* It would be dangerous to amalgamate *separate issues such as children accessing pornographic content for adults, and adults accessing pornography about children.* Priorities should be clearly set and resources mobilised to tackle the most important issues, that is the fight against criminal content."

As we shall see in more detail below, both the USA and EU, in the wake of the CDA and COPA debacles, have indeed turned away from direct state enforcement of specialised on-line content rules, towards "self regulation" strategies—a much employed term loosely used to cover control of access to Internet content by users, ISPs and other non-governmental bodies such as schools and libraries—as a more fruitful, more effective and hopefully more constitutionally sound, way forward. In particular, recent US policy statements[63] lay emphasis on three principles: first, that regulation of Internet conduct should be based on general policy principles, be technology neutral and be no more restrictive to on-line than off-line content; secondly, that legal restrictions placed on the Internet should be enforceable, taking into account issues such as transnational enforcement, jurisdictional problems and resources; and thirdly, that measures should be pursued which actively involve, empower and educate the private Internet industry, and Internet users. In Australia, by contrast, mainly as a result of political bargains struck with conservative elements to shore up a minority government, new rules were introduced as of January 2000 which at first glance appear to be far more in keeping with legislation such as the CDA in directly applying state censorship to the Internet, ISPs and "Internet content hosts," and out of pace with the world wide trend towards self regulation. However as we shall see below,[64] this difference has in the end turned out to be less significant than expected, and possibly illusory.

Can national laws criminalising Internet content be enforced?

One of the many reasons for the "traditional" Internet community's hostile response to the CDA was that it felt it amounted to an attempt to impose American cultural standards of what was acceptable speech on the Internet throughout the world. Since Internet publication is by default global, in theory any person anywhere in the world who made an "indecent" statement in (say) a news-group might find him or herself technically subject to criminal penalties in the US. Of course in practice prosecutions would generally only be possible where the maker of the statement was within the territory of the USA and therefore subject to the power of its law enforcement authorities. It is for this practical reason of enforcement that states usually only apply their criminal laws to events occurring, or persons within, their own territory (territorial jurisdiction).[65]

---

[63] See *The Electronic Frontier: the Challenge of Unlawful Conduct involving the Use of the Internet*, Report of the President's Working Group, March 2000 at http://www.usdoj.gov/criminal/cybercrime/unlawful.htm .

[64] See p. 301.

[65] Note however that states may sometimes assert jurisdiction over extraterritorial events if those events are initiated in or affect their territory. See discussion in McCall-Smith and Sheldon *Scots Criminal Law* (2nd edn) pp. 13–16. Statutes (such as, in the UK, the Computer Misuse Act 1990) may also include extraterritorial jurisdiction clauses, although of course they may be externally viewed as infringing the jurisdiction of other nations.

The problem with enforcement of national pornography laws of course is that Internet pornography is a global phenomenon. Porn is as likely to be accessed by a UK citizen sitting at a terminal in Edinburgh from a server or website physically located in Denmark, or Japan, or the US, as from one within UK criminal jurisdiction. Indeed this can in fact be proven to be the case: in the UK, according to reports of complaints about Internet content made over a six-month period to a hot line run by the Internet Watch Foundation (IWF),[66] only four per cent of the pornographic items complained about originated from sites physically located in the UK.[67]

It is usually both practical and legally possible (although much may depend on the exact wording of the criminal laws in question) for the national authorities to prosecute and punish the *recipient* of pornographic material even if the material itself is hosted on a foreign server,[68] and also to punish parties who store illicit material on foreign located servers, or supply it by download from such servers, so long as *they themselves* are personally located within the jurisdiction. In the UK, the first such successful prosecution was concluded in 1998 in respect of a student living in Lancaster who stored more than 5,000 indecent photographs of children on a website physically located in the USA.[69] More recently, in *R* v. *Waddon*, a businessman running a large Internet porn operation in the UK from websites physically located in the US, was found guilty of publishing obscene articles in the UK under the Obscene Publications Act 1959; the court held that "publication" took place both when the defendant transmitted the data constituting the images to the US websites and continued when the material was received in the UK by a client of those websites (using a site password).[70]

Although the rather liberal interpretation adopted in *Waddon* allows state authorities not only to prosecute individual recipients of porn from abroad, but also to close down British porn distributors using foreign websites, where pornography is stored on foreign sites, and distributed by foreign pornographers not resident in the UK, international co-operation will be necessary to facilitate extraterritorial law enforcement. In some cases, pornographic websites will operate from abroad specifically to avoid criminal investigation in the UK and other countries where they make money. But it must also be taken into account that countries have very different attitudes as to what is legal in relation to indecent and pornographic content and that content held on foreign websites may be quite legal in that country although not in others where it is made

---

[66] The Internet Watch Foundation is a private non-governmental body, established by representatives of the ISP industry to meet law enforcement concerns about Internet pornography in September 1996. See further below, pp. 295.

[67] See 3rd Annual Report of the IWF (1999) at http://www.iwf.org.uk/about/stats/stats.html#origin . The overwhelmingly most common apparent origin of the items complained about in 1999 was the USA.

[68] See for example the discussion of "making" in *Atkins*, n. 47 above.

[69] "Student given eight month sentence over porn site", *Scotsman*, 1 April 1998.

[70] See report at http://www.cyber-rights.org/documents/rvgraham.htm .

available. Japan, for example has historically had a more liberal cultural attitude towards child sex than Europe, while the USA has stronger First Amendment protection for free speech than the UK. This is germane to the problem of control of electronic porn as it means that international co-operation will not always be easy to secure. As Cyber-Rights (UK) suggest,[71] there is never going to be popular support in any country for stamping out content which is legal there, simply because it is forbidden abroad.

One way to improve the chances for international co-operation would be by seeking harmonisation of global rules on criminal content, although this is a somewhat ambitious project given the enormous cultural and legal differences in this area.[72] Some efforts along these lines are beginning to emerge however with the publication in April 2000 of a draft International Convention on Crime in Cyberspace by the Council of Europe, which includes a requirement that all signatories enact measures criminalising the possession, distribution, transmission or production of child pornography via the Internet.[73] Although this is not that radical a step, given the already near universality of prohibitions on child pornography, the Convention also includes harmonising provisions on jurisdiction, search and seizure of computer data, extradition and mutual assistance. These procedural matters may in the end do far more to expedite international co-operative policing than agreement on substantive law.

One form of international co-operation which does seem to have some potential is the growing use of whistle-blowing "hot lines", discussed further in the next section. These enable members of the public to complain about objectionable content which they discover on the Internet. In the hot line system pioneered in Holland, complaints are made to the Dutch police, but where the material turns out to come from abroad, rather than giving up (or prosecuting the Dutch ISP) the police notify their opposite numbers in the country in question, whose responsibility it then is to take action. A similar hot line now operates in the UK run by the International Watch Foundation[74] but more emphasis is placed there on the UK ISPs agreeing to remove from their servers illicit material originating from foreign sites, than in co-operation with foreign law enforcement authorities to remove the material at source. Neither approach fully meets the difficulties of differences between foreign laws, nor addresses the fact that even if UK ISPs remove, say, a foreign originated indecent photograph posted in a news-group, that item can quite likely still be obtained from other servers

---

[71] See "Who Watches the Watchmen: Internet Content Rating Systems and Privatised Censorship", November 1997, at http://www.cyber-rights.org/watchmen.htm.

[72] Mayer-Schoenberger and Foster (n 1 above) suggest that if international norms as to unacceptable speech were identified then these types of speech might be regarded as illegal under international law using the concept of *ius cogens*. This avoids the need for an international treaty but does not seem a wholly practical solution.

[73] See Title 3, Article 9 of the Convention, draft text issued on 27 April 2000 at http://conven tions.coe.int/treaty/en/projets/cybercrime.htm. The Convention is expected to be finalised by December 2000.

[74] See further p. 295 below.

abroad. The EU is currently encouraging the development of, and co-operation between, European hot line providers[75] as part of the European Action Plan, described on p 303.

"SELF REGULATION": CONTROL OF CONTENT BY ISPS

If direct regulation of illegal content by the state is difficult or impossible—as we seem to have established—how else can the problem be addressed? As we noted above, because ISPs effectively act as gatekeepers regulating access to Internet content, it is always going to be tempting for state authorities to deem them to be "importers" or similar of foreign originated illicit material, and therefore responsible for preventing its "entry" or circulation within that state. In one of the most infamous incidents in Internet legal history, in May 1998, a court in Bavaria, Germany, found Felix Somm, the Chief Executive Officer of CompuServe Europe, guilty of distributing child pornography and other adult content.[76] This rested on the fact that CompuServe, as most ISPs do as a normal part of their business, had circulated Usenet news-groups within Bavaria, including some which were deemed to contain illegal content under Bavarian law. Pleas that CompuServe had neither originated this content nor could effectively monitor it, or control it (news-group feeds taken by ISPs usually run to millions of individual news items[77]) failed to prevent the original prosecution succeeding; however an appeal in November 1999 (after Germany had enacted new legislation in the area) did eventually reverse the decision, to somewhat less publicity.[78]

The EC has attempted to address the understandable fears of the ISP community subsequent to the *Somm* affair by introducing as part of the Electronic Commerce Directive[79] provisions relating generally to ISP liability in relation to all kinds of illegal and actionable content. These are discussed in some detail in Chapter 11 in relation to defamation, and also in Chapter 9 in relation to copyright. Broadly, ISPs are absolved from liability where they act as a "mere conduit"—akin to the idea of a common carrier—that is, where they merely transmit and do not in any way alter material provided by, and intended for, a third party.[80] Similarly, an ISP is not liable for the "automatic, intermediary or

---

[75] See for example the INHOPE (Internet Hotline Providers in Europe Forum) scheme at http://www.childnet-int.org/hotlines/index.html .

[76] Local Court, Munich, May 12 1998. An English language version of the case is available at http://www.cyber-rights.org/isps/somm-dec.htm . See also Bender "Bavaria v Felix Somm: the Pornography Conviction of the Former CompuServe Manager" (1998) IJCLP Web-Doc 14-1-1998 at http://www.digital-law.net/papers/index.html .

[77] See Chapter 11, especially n. 40.

[78] See "Germany clears Net chief of child porn charges" *The Independent*, 18 November 1999.

[79] The Directive came into force on July 17 2000 and must be implemented by EU member states by January 17, 2002. See Appendix I.

[80] Electronic Commerce Directive, Directive 2000/31/EC, OJ L178, 8 June 2000, available at http://www.europa.eu.int/eur-lex/en/dat/2000/l_178/l_17820000717en00010016.pdf .

temporary storage" of content provided by a third party where that storage is done for the sole purpose of speeding up the transmission of Internet content. This refers to the practice of caching, which is generally implemented automatically so that calls for the same piece of content by other users can be fulfilled without the need to retrieve that content again from the original site. This speeds up the Internet for all parties. The most important provisions for ISPs and illegal content are in Article 14 of the Directive on Hosting, which deals with where ISPs host or store content more than transiently. Article 14(1)(a) provides that ISPs are exempt from *criminal* liability so long as they do not have "actual knowledge" of illegal activity or information; and are exempt from *civil* liability so long as they do not have actual knowledge *and* are not "aware of facts and circumstances from which the illegal activity or information is apparent." The ISP is not required to actively seek this knowledge or awareness, nor can a general obligation to monitor all material hosted or transmitted be placed on the ISP.[81] However if an ISP does obtain such knowledge or awareness—for example, if the police or a member of the public notifies it that it is hosting an illegal photo as an item in a news-group it carries—then under Article 14(1)(b), it becomes liable again if it does not remove that item "expeditiously".

While there has to date been no case in the UK in which an ISP has been prosecuted for distributing or publishing pornography, as we have seen, laws such as the Protection of Children Act 1978 could probably in theory be invoked against them as possessors, publishers or distributors of pornography, although some statutory defences might also be available.[82] ISPs usually have a physical base of operations within the jurisdiction and, unlike most pornographers, are therefore locatable, respectable and susceptible to pressure and sanctions imposed by the state. So, for example, in 1996 the London Metropolitan Police, following the lead provided by the then Science and Technology Minister, threatened to prosecute a number of UK ISPs for distributing around 130 Usenet news-groups to their subscribers which had been found in the past to contain illegal pornography or other types of sexual material, unless the ISPs moved towards "self-regulation"[83] i.e. took steps themselves to remove these news-groups from the service they provided to their subscribers.[84] This action led

---

[81] Ibid, article 15.

[82] For example, the Protection of Children Act 1978, s 1 (4), provides that it shall be a defense to an offense under s 1(1)((b) or (c) (distribution or possession offences) that the defender had not himself seen the indecent photographs and did not know, nor had any cause to suspect them to be, indecent." See G Leong "Computer Child Pornography—the Liability of Distributors" [1998] *Crim LR, Special Edition on Crime, Criminal Justice and the Internet* 19 and Palfrey T "Pornography and the possible criminal liability of Internet Service Providers under the Obscene Publication(s) and Protection of Children Act" (1997) 6 *Information and Communications Technology Law* 187.

[83] Akdeniz quotes Mike Hoskins, Commander of the Metropolitan Police Clubs and Vice Unit in 1996 as saying to ISPs at a public meeting "either the industry takes it upon itself to clean up the Net or the police intervene." See Akdeniz "The Regulation of Pornography and Child Pornography on the Internet" (1997) 1 *JILT*, http://elj.warwick.ac.uk/internet/97_1akdz/ .

[84] It has been suggested that one of the purposes of this exercise was to put UK ISPs "on notice" of what content they were carrying so that the defence outlined in n 82 below would not be available to them in any subsequent prosecution.

directly to the creation of the quasi-industry body, the Internet Watch Foundation (IWF)[85] (originally "Safety-Net") which has become the "quasi-public face of Internet regulation in the United Kingdom".[86]

The IWF's main role is to provide a free hot-line channel so that the public can report by phone, email or fax offensive material they encounter on the Internet. The IWF then vets these reports of objectionable content and takes action if appropriate, which can consist of some combination of making a report to the UK police (if the item appears to have originated within the UK), reporting to the National Crime Intelligence Service (NCIS) (which organises liaison with foreign police forces in the case of foreign content), or recommending removal of the item from the servers of UK ISPs (which may be the only way to deny access in the UK where the item is of foreign origin). Advice to remove an item is given by the IWF to UK ISPs, whose decision it then is whether to comply. Over 99 per cent of reports which are actioned by the IWF are about child pornography.[87] Material actioned overwhelmingly appears to be of foreign origin, the proportion originating in the UK having declined from 6 per cent in 1998 to 4 per cent in 1999. In 1999, the IWF notified UK ISPs of nearly 10,200 potentially illegal items with advice to remove them. In terms of the total number of items reported by the public, the figure in 1999 was nearly 5,000 reports comprising nearly 20,000 items, a volume which was nearly double the reports received in 1998, which itself was more than 2½ times the number received in 1997, the first year of operation.[88] It is probable however that this reflects more of a growth in public access to and awareness of the Internet than in the quantity of illegal material itself.[89]

The Internet Watch Foundation has been strenuously attacked by organisations such as Cyber Rights & Cyber Liberties UK for performing a quasi-judicial function—assessing whether material reported by the public is illegal—when it is not a court; and performing a public function—deciding if material should be censored—when it is a private and self-appointed body. Akdeniz, the Director of Cyber Rights UK, encapsulates these criticisms by asserting that "the formation of the IWF sets a dangerous precedent for privatised censorship".[90] The IWF has partially attempted to meet these criticisms by reconstituting its executive board to embrace a wider representation of interested parties[91] but it

---

[85] The original Board of the IWF was composed exclusively of representatives from ISPs. The current Board has a wider representation comprising an independent chair, 4 members selected from ISPs, and 8 non-industry members selected from eg charities concerned with child welfare, the National Union of Students and the Campaign against Censorship of the Internet in Britain. See http://www.iwf.org.uk/press/archives/p140400.html .

[86] See D Wall "Policing and the Regulation of the Internet" [1998] *Crim LR, Special Edition on Crime, Criminal Justice and the Internet* 79.

[87] 11,412 items of child pornography were reported in 1999 compared to 75 items of other types.

[88] Information and statistics available at http://www.iwf.org.uk .

[89] See ibid, 3rd Annual Report of the Board of the IWF.

[90] See Akdeniz, *op cit supra* n. 83, at p. 235.

[91] See n. 85 above.

is still basically true that it is far more an industry body than it is a public one, and that it is not accountable to the public through any kind of parliamentary or other scrutiny (although it does publish both annual reports and minutes of meetings). On the other hand it is also true that, as Wall notes, if "the IWF [were] to canvass public opinion over the issues such as child pornography, then such public support would be considerable."[92] Furthermore when, as at present, the IWF's vetting is confined almost exclusively to child pornography, this presents relatively little difficulty in identification or legal nuance. If, on the other hand, it expands its hot-line duties to deal with other forms of Internet content such as hate speech, as has been floated, the board may find more difficulties in coping with the legal ramifications of what IWF Chair David Kerr himself has admitted is a far more "fuzzy area". [93]

ISPs themselves have a strong interest in using the IWF as a shield against threat of prosecution and will continue to have even when the E-Commerce Directive comes into operation on or before January 2002. If ISPs are notified of illegal content and do not take steps to remove it, then according to Article 14 (1)(b), as discussed above, they will still remain liable in respect of it according to the relevant national laws. Indeed, ISPs need a good working "notify and take down" framework in place sufficient to take down "expeditiously" or they will find themselves potentially in trouble. This may be difficult to achieve for both very large and very small ISPs. By mediating, and providing a central hotline for, complaints about Internet content, the IWF effectively protects ISPs from having to deal with public complaints as part of daily business, and from being distracted by frivolous or unfounded ones. It may even, although this is not a popular sentiment with cyber-rights groups, actually act in defence of free speech, since the IWF will (one hopes) throw out complaints about entirely legal Internet content, which a small ISP, lacking legal advice and resources for a court battle, might simply give in to and remove the item in question.[94]

Finally the "considerable public support" which Wall cites for the suppression of child pornography will also tend to favour the relatively quick and effective (and cheap) disposal of "if it looks like an elephant, then it's an elephant" cases that the IWF is able to provide. Criminal prosecutions of those who provide pornography at source may be judged more politically correct by libertarians than going after ISPs, but in practice will probably take longer, be more expensive and potentially be less effective in actually suppressing the distribution of child pornography than the kind of notify and take down procedure the IWF offers.

Providing a hot-line and responding to IWF notices of content to be removed is one way in which ISPs can "self-regulate" or, more cynically, attempt to cover their backs, or divert police attention from themselves towards the actual orig-

---

[92] See Wall, n. 86 above, at 86.
[93] See *Wired*, 26 Jan 2000, at http://www.wired.com/news/politics/0,1283,33906,00.html.
[94] See further the discussion around *Godfrey v Demon Internet* [1999] 4 All ER 342 in ch. 11.

inators of the illegal content. Another approach ISPs can take is to use filtering software to sift out potentially objectionable content before it is made available to their customers; or to provide such software to their subscribers. Filtering has become a major avenue of attack in the "self-regulatory" approach to controlling illegal content; for cyber-libertarians it has also become a source of considerable anxiety.

"SELF-REGULATION" BY USERS AND ISPS: FILTERING AND RATING SYSTEMS

Filtering systems are software programs which stop certain types of Internet content or certain sites from being accessed by the end user. Filtering systems can be applied by the users themselves, to filter out material they do not want to have inflicted on them; by users to protect or restrict others, such as their employees, or children; or by ISPs, to provide their clientele with a filtered service. (Such filtered feeds are often regarded as a "premium service" to customers who want, for example, a "family friendly" service, or one with a high information to noise ratio, and as such are often made available at special rates.) Filtering systems may work by picking out keywords such as "sex" or "xxx"; or may contain black-lists of the addresses of sites or newsgroups which are known, or thought to be known, to contain undesirable content (such lists are usually updated fairly frequently so as to remain relevant).

Rating systems can be used in conjunction with filtering software to provide more sophisticated systems than those described above. The scheme espoused by the European Union as a potential global industry standard is that of PICS (the Platform for Internet Content Selection).[95] PICS works on a principle known as "neutral labelling". PICS allows sites to be tagged with labels which contain different types of information—for example, a tag may reveal that a site does, does not or to a certain degree contains bad language, nudity, depictions of violence and racial intolerance. Users such as parents can then adjust the filtering software loaded on their computer[96] so that only sites with appropriate PICS tags can be viewed by those using that computer. Sites which do not have PICS tags are usually blocked as a default as are sites with inappropriate tags. A user may rate sites, sites may rate themselves, or users may ask a third party to rate sites for them. Users can thus at least in theory select the rating system that tells their computers if a particular site is bad, good or indifferent from a marketplace of suppliers who reflect a spectrum of moral or cultural attitudes.

---

[95] See European Parliament Communication of 16 October 1996 on *Illegal and Harmful Content on the Internet* (n. 13 above), Chapter 5; EU Internet Action Plan, adopted 25 January 1999, Decision No 276/1999/EC available at http://www.qlinks.net/iap/IAP_Decision_en.pdf. PICS was developed by the World Wide Web Consortium (W3C).

[96] PICS now comes as standard with recent versions of Netscape Navigator and Microsoft Internet Explorer, the two most commonly used Web browsers.

While the user control embodied in filtering systems is welcomed by most parties to this debate, there are a number of aspects to them which are unsettling to cyber-libertarians.[97] PICS, for example, claims to be "value neutral", but the ratings schemes it uses to block content are clearly not. They necessarily reflect a set of values by means of which decisions on what content is offensive are made. In a PICS scheme, websites may rate themselves with the appropriate PICS tags, or may be rated by third parties. Self rating is clearly unreliable and will be patchy, but third party rating may be inaccurate, or accurate but oppressive in terms of freedom of information ; for example, a Roman Catholic Church third party rating body might tag all pro-abortion or pro-homosexuality websites as unsuitable for view, thereby denying families who bought that software the chance to seek guidance from those sites, even though such material would not be criminal in any way. Depending on what ratings scheme is purchased or packaged with PICS, its values are then embedded in the user's software. A rating system devised by the American Civil Liberties Union will not be the same as one devised by (say) the Roman Catholic Church.

This would not be so worrying if filtering systems worked perfectly; after all, in the example above, the user at least knows what kind of slant the ratings scheme he or she is using has. But there is considerable anecdotal evidence that, in general, filtering and rating systems, in attempting to exclude certain unacceptable types of material, exclude a wider penumbra of sites than is necessary[98], while letting slip by some sites which should have been excluded.[99] Representations were made as early as the first *Reno* v. *ACLU* case in 1997 that filtering, if widely adopted, was likely to cut off access to sites which served useful social purposes, such as sites about AIDS, safe sex, child abuse, etc. Perhaps most worryingly, many filtering systems are not transparent about what sites they are excluding, or what criteria they are using for exclusion. For example, in 1996, a journalist and programmer together deconstructed the database of the filtering software Cybersitter and discovered that it was blocking such non-pornographic material as the website of the National Organisation for Women and the server of the respectable on-line community, the WELL.[100] The hacking needed to find such facts out may often be both difficult and a potential breach

[97] See Lessig L. "Tyranny in the Infrastructure", *Wired* 5.07, at http://www.wired.com/wired/5.07/cyber_rights.html; "Who Watches the Watchmen?" n. 68 above; ACLU White Paper, *Fahrenheit 451.2: Is Cyberspace Burning?* n. 12 above.

[98] A report from Peaceware, an anti-"censorware" site, asserts that one AI-based software filtering product, BAIR , for which claims had been made that it could discern and block pornographic images, was tested on this claim, and the result was that BAIR could indeed block 2/3 of randomly selected pornographic images, but also blocked 2/3 of randomly selected pictures of people's faces as well. See http://peacefire.org/censorware/BAIR/second-report.7-19-2000.html .

[99] See the UK Consumer Association/Which? survey of filtering tools in the UK, reported May 2000 (see http://www.which.net) which concludes that filtering tools often let through "porn, drugs and bomb making sites" and suggests that parents should not rely on them.

[100] See Grossman, n. 5 above, p. 125. Another report claims that filtering software installed in public schools in some US states blocked sites about Serbia and sex education while letting through more than 40 hard core porn sites (see Yeomans "The World's Wide Web: the rating game," *The Standard,* 30 September 1999, at http://www.thestandard.com/article/display/0,1151,6705,00.html .

of the copyright of the software manufacturer; in the Cybersitter case, litigation was threatened over the "reverse engineering" that had taken place.[101]

PICS, as noted above, has at least the potential to avoid accusations of non-transparency since users can choose a particular rating system—or "cultural filtering template"[102]—to subscribe to.[103] In practice however, at the moment PICS is still most commonly used in conjunction with RSACi, a ratings system which was originally developed in the USA to rate computer games, and which is not conspicuously suitable for rating wider categories of material, since, while it is capable of grading the violence, nudity, sex and bad language content of a site, it contains no assessment of the *quality* of the information contained, such as its usefulness (consider safe sex information sites), source, authorship, etc.[104]

Filtering and rating systems such as PICS can be seen as a neat solution for states and conservative interests because they avoid accusations of state censorship[105] but potentially allow questionable sites to be collectively excluded by the users themselves. They also to some extent meet the demands of ISPs to be exculpated from liability: since if illegal material does make its way to the user, they can claim it was the user's own fault for not properly using the filtering software, and not that of the ISP.[106] But for cyber-libertarians, PICS may be said to replace state censorship with "privatised censorship" which is applied covertly by the collaboration of the state and the inventors of the ratings schemes popularly in use.[107] Whether the state overtly censors or covertly

---

[101] In a more recent case, Microsystems Software Inc. (owned by Mattel) filed a lawsuit against two programmers who had published a program allowing users to circumvent the Cyber Patrol filtering software and examine its blocked sites list. See http://www.openpgp.net/censorship/index2.html . Mattel claimed breach of the copyright in the source code of Cyber Patrol, which they owned. On 28 March 2000, the programmers were enjoined from publishing the software source code and binaries known as "CP4break.zip" or "cphack.exe". See n. 105 below.

[102] See Yeomans, n. 100 above.

[103] Another alternative for such users is to subscribe to an ISP which overtly filters the service supplies its users; ISPs already exist catering to Roman Catholic, evangelical Christian and Jewish sensibilities. See "Filtered Internet Services Reach More Religious Groups," *New York Times*, 20 October 1999.

[104] See Hudson, n. 24 above, pp. 151 2, who describes a more effective system known as the Dublin Core developed by the World Wide Web Consortium (W3C). The IWF in their report *Rating and Filtering Internet Content: a UK perspective* broadly back PICS/RSaCi, but suggest that there should be additional categories added eg to cover sites which expose financial details, or demand financial commitments. They also suggest that users should be able to choose to over-ride their selected limits when the site is about factual news or contains documentary, scientific or artistic content. See http://www.iwf.org.uk/rating/rating_r.html .

[105] See note issued when permanent injunction granted in *Microsystems and Mattel* v *Scandinavia Online et al*, Civil Action No 00-10488-EFH, US District Court of Massachusetts (see n 98 supra): "Under our Constitution, all have the right to disseminate even evil ideas and such ideas cannot by law be suppressed by the government. On the other hand, parents, in the exercise of their parental obligation to educate their young children, have the equal right to screen and thus, prevent noxious and insidious ideas from corrupting their children's fertile and imaginative minds."

[106] It is more germane to avoiding liability, however, if the ISP has itself installed filtering systems to regulate the access provided to subscribers—since this may be seen in many legal systems as taking "reasonable care" to prevent the distribution of illegal content.

[107] See Akdeniz, n. 83 above, who cites *Living Marxism Online* as stating that "PICS is just the modern face of censorship."

encourages the use of blocking software, they claim, the result is the same: certain sites, whose content is not illegal but merely offensive to some, find that their words are blocked from reaching an audience. On the other hand, many might say that this is no different or more objectionable than the right of any members of the public to choose not to borrow books they find offensive from the library, or not to buy magazines they find disgusting.

Where PICS and associated rating schemes become more obviously problematic, however, is where they are adopted by ISPs or other institutions "upstream" from the end user (such as schools, universities or libraries), who have the chance to filter what that user reads, without that user necessarily knowing that certain content is being withheld from them. Lessig, in his influential book *Code and Other Laws of Cyberspace*, notes that "[i]n principle . . ., content could be filtered by a PICS filter somewhere upstream and you would not necessarily know this was happening" and then goes on to ask whether even this is really anything to worry about, given that everyone would like to have certain aspects of the world around them filtered out all the time, e,g., by not having to confront the reality of homeless people living on the street. He concludes that since PICS has the potential to provide both perfect and non-transparent "upstream filtering" it should be resisted. "We should not design for the most efficient system of censoring. . . . Nor should we opt for perfect filtering so long as the tendency worldwide is to over-filter speech. If there is speech the government has an interest in controlling, then let that control be obvious to the users. Only when regulation is transparent is a political response possible."[108] The logical extension of these fears is that national censorship could be achieved by a government requiring all ISPs and telecoms companies providing Internet access in that state to filter out certain types of material.

In the USA, attempts have been and are currently being made at both state and federal level compulsorily to impose filtering on schools and libraries, where the argument to protect children is most pressing.[109] Constitutional freedom of speech arguments as well as political pressure have been advanced to resist them, with some degree of success. At present official Presidential policy appears to be that the federal government should *not* mandate any particular type of technology, such as filtering or blocking software, for schools or libraries, but should encourage "acceptable use" policies by all public institutions offering access to on-line resources[110]—essentially another self regulatory solution.

---

[108] *Code and Other Laws of Cyberspace*, (1999, Basic Books) pp 179-181. See also Lessig, n 97 above, in which he suggested that PICS imposes "the most effective global censorship technology ever designed".

[109] For example, Senator John McCain who has been prominent in this field, re-introduced on 8 June 2000 the Children's Internet Protection Act, a measure which would tie receipt of federal funding by a school or library to its use of filtering or blocking software. A rival proposal, the Neighbourhood Children's Internet Protection Act, introduced to Congress on 5 August 1999, would allow schools to decide how best themselves to protect children from access to "inappropriate" matter.

[110] See "The Role of Public Education and Empowerment" chapter IV of *The Electronic Frontier*, n 63 above.

The new Australian Broadcasting Services Amendment (On-Line Services) Act 1999,[111] noted above, provides an interesting side-note to this discussion of the merits of overt censorship versus covert filtering. The controversial legal regime ushered in by this Act has largely been seen as a political gesture indicating the government's commitment to cleaning up the Net rather than a practical attempt actually to succeed in this aim. The Act attempts to regulate both Internet content hosted and physically held in Australia, and content physically held abroad but accessible in Australia via Australian ISPs. When originally introduced, the shape of the scheme was broadly that Australian ISPs were required either to *remove* "prohibited content"[112] if they physically hosted the offending material within Australia (by order of a "take-down" notice) ; or to *block access* to it if it was physically held abroad (by order of an "access-prevention" notice). The sanctions for failing to do so were draconian: a scale fine of A\$27,5000 per day was imposed for failure to meet these duties, accumulating on a daily basis.

Appalled reaction met this scheme both from the Australian ISP industry and the global cyber rights community. The main practical complaint was that it was simply not possible effectively to block access to foreign content. Blocking could be evaded if the foreign site changed its URL, or merely changed its underlying IP address (which would not require a change of URL and hence not confuse existing customers). Foreign proscribed sites could also still be accessed through Australian ISPs by using a foreign proxy server site as an anonymiser. A change to the wording of the then Bill which allowed ISPs only to take steps which were "technically and commercially feasible" did not assuage the flood of complaints. Furthermore if access-prevention was impossible, it was said, then take-down of domestic content was also largely futile. Internet content is extremely portable, and any domestic site served with a take-down notice could fairly easily transfer itself to a foreign site simply by signing on with a foreign ISP; which would then still be accessible by the Australian public using the modes discussed above.

Faced with a potentially very embarrassing situation, the Australian government appears to have retreated to a compromise solution. A late draft of the Bill had introduced the concept that some ISPs which agreed to comply with a Code of Practice formulated by agreement between the Australian Broadcasting Authority (ABA) and an ISP industry body might be exempted from access-prevention notices. This had first been thought of as an exceptional provision,

[111] See at http://scaleplus.law.gov.au/html/comact/10/6005/0/CM000060.htm. The Australian scheme is a complex one and is described in rather condensed style here. A more detailed description can be found in L Edwards "The Liability of ISPs for Internet Content: global problems, local solutions", forthcoming [2000] *JILT*; also in C Kendall "Australia's New Internet Censorship Regime : Is This Progress?" (1999) 1 *Digital Technology Law Journal*, at http://wwwlaw.murdoch.edu.au/dtlj/articles/vol1_3/kendallDTLJ1_3.html .

[112] "Prohibited content" is that classified as Refused Classification (RC) or X by the National Classification Board, or R when not in a restricted access system. See further Kendall, *supra,* paras 37–45.

to exempt only ISPs which already provided a high standard of content filtering (for example ISPs providing Internet access to schools), and thus had no need of being served with access-prevention notices as well. By the time the Bill was finally passed however, compliance with a Code, if one were accepted by the ABA, had entirely replaced the issue of access-prevention notices.[113] When the Internet Industry of Australia's (IIA) Code of Practice was finally rubber-stamped by the ABA, however, it required only that ISPs undertake to make software filtering tools from an approved list *available* to their subscribers (and at the expense of the subscriber).[114] As a result, the IIA's own *Guide for Internet Users* in December 1999 shortly before the coming into force of the Act pronounced that:

> "We anticipate that industry developed code alternatives will entirely circumvent ABA action in respect of internationally sourced content."[115]

In other words, a legal regime aimed at exerting direct censorship over ISPs has decayed almost without notice to a regime which is in essence totally self regulatory (at least in relation to foreign content). In future, in all cases where foreign content is classified as "prohibited" according to Australian law, what will happen is not that a public access-prevention notice will be served—which would potentially arouse court challenge, global publicity and international concern— but that the URL of the offending site will be passed to the makers of the approved software filtering tools so these can be updated to block those sites.[116] Essentially the Australian system has moved from one of overt censorship imposed by publicly debated legislation, to covert filtering implemented with the co-operation of private industry interests, the first scheme attracting vociferous criticism, the second being regarded as an acceptably moderate self regulatory regime.

Yet is this a positive step for any aim other than PR and appeasing the ISP industry? On the side of protectionism/paternalism, it is unlikely this regime is doing very much to stop the Australian public being confronted with Internet smut, domestic or foreign. In the first three months of the Act coming into operation, out of 45 foreign sites which were deemed "prohibited content", 17 were originally Australian hosted.[117] Domestic Australian content coming under fire is thus, it seems, merely relocating abroad as was predicted. More subtly, on the Lessig analysis, the new regime, far from being more conducive to free speech,

---

[113] See s 40(1)(b) of the 1999 Act.

[114] See Internet Industry Code of Practice, draft 6.0, December 1999, para 6.2, at http://www.iia.net.au/code6.html. Note that ISPs were in no way required to *ensure* that subscribers either obtained or used the filtering tools.

[115] See http://www.iia.net.au/guide.html.

[116] See the ABA report, *Internet content complaints scheme—the first 3 months* at http://www.aba.gov.au/about/public_relations/newrel_2000/27nr2000.htm, which reveals that in the first 3 months of operation, take down was ordered in respect of 31 items of Australian-hosted content, 45 items of content hosted outside Australia were referred to the makers of filtering software products and 7 items of content were referred to lsaw enforcement agencies.

[117] *Ibid,* Table 2. See also "Down Under Smut Goes Up and Over" *Wired*, 2 February 2000, at http://www.wired.com/news/politics/0,1283,34043,00.html, which describes the move of www.teenager.com.au (an Australian teen sex site) to a US server (without change of URL) after a take down notice was issued.

may actually be more subtly insidious in enabling blocking of content that users never knew existed. However, although Australian ISPs must make available approved filtering software to their subscribers, they are not as yet required to ensure that they *use* it (and the evidence, as we shall see below, is that they will not). Public inertia may in the end be the best defence of civil liberties in the Australian regime.

THE EUROPEAN ACTION PLAN

In the EU, the current political consensus is that the way forward to promote the safe use of the Internet is by a mixture of the strategies we have surveyed above, including self regulation, use of technical tools, international co-operation, and public education.[118] This model, known as the European Action Plan[119], draws a clear division between *illegal* content which is already proscribed by state law; and *harmful* content, which while offensive to some is not banned but should possibly be restricted in its precise circulation eg not for children.[120] In the EU Action Plan, as a primary policy aim, *illegal* content is to be removed from the net, possibly by co-operation with ISPs undertaking self regulation by code of conduct. ISPs however are not to be scapegoated where the providers of original content prove difficult to find or prosecute.[121] *Harmful* content on the other hand is a matter for the personal choice of users who would wish to avoid it. Such users should be empowered to block access to such material for themselves and their children by the provision of appropriate filtering and rating software, tailored to the cultural and linguistic diversity of Europe's heterogeneous population. This is intended to avoid the threat of US based ratings systems imposing US cultural sensibilities on European users. Finally the EU plan looks to the future with a plan to raise awareness among parents and children of the opportunities and risks of the Internet by public education schemes.

Considerable sums of money (25 million Euros) are being invested by the EU in furthering this plan, which is due to last until 31 December 2002.[122] Following the Call for Proposals launched in 1999, there are now ten projects underway with more to come. The projects so far cover a variety of activities across the Action Plan including three addressing the creation of a European network of

[118] Useful analyses of the European approach to controlling illegal and harmful content can be found in P Campbell and E Machet, "European Policy on Regulation of Content on the Internet" in Liberty (ed), n. 6 above; and Hudson, n. 24 above.

[119] N. 95 above.

[120] This approach was developed in the earlier EC *Communication on Illegal and Harmful Content*, n. 13 above, the subsequent Green Paper COM (1997) 582 of the same name, and the Council Recommendation 98/560/EC of September 1998, both available at http://www.ispo.cec.be/legal/en/internet/internet.html .

[121] As we have seen, this part of the Plan is achieved legally by Arts 12–15 of the E-Commerce Directive.

[122] The progress of the Action Plan and new Calls for Proposals can be followed at http://www.qlinks.net/iap/.

hotlines; five working on development of rating and filtering systems for Internet content; and two dealing with preparatory awareness activity.

FINAL THOUGHTS

As the above discussion has made plain, adopting a regime for regulating Internet content is fraught with difficulty. On the one hand, cyber-libertarians resist any attempts to apply special restraints to Internet access on the apparently reasonable grounds that freedom of expression applies as strongly in the new media as in traditional media. On the other hand, a variety of other interests including corporations, parents, ISPs and governments recognise that a number of factors make the Internet a place where special risks arise which have no parallel in traditional media. These circumstances include the anarchic and forthright nature of "traditional" Internet culture; the difficulty of applying existing law to an environment in a constant state of change ; the ease and cheapness both of access to, and publication on, the Internet; and the difficulty of enforcement of existing national criminal laws given the trans-jurisdictional nature of the net. These are all real problems. However the "self regulatory" solutions currently being promoted by conservative interests in countries like the USA and Australia, whether they are labelled "privatised censorship" or not, do have an inherent risk of curtailing freedom of expression without adequate transparency or accountability, and are rather blunt instruments with which to protect children and other vulnerable groups (eg racial minorities) given the current state of filtering technology.

    The debate is a problematic one to bring to any kind of conclusion. No reasonable person, it seems, could argue that, in what has been called the most perfect medium for communication ever devised, freedom of expression should not be defended and not be compromised simply to facilitate matters such as e-commerce. On the other hand, the genuine concerns of ordinary people to protect their children and their own feelings from attack by those whose views and material they find offensive should also not be jeopardised to appease what sometimes seems like a relatively few "electronic freedom" fanatics throughout the world. The debate is, as I noted in the introduction, a very polarised one; and this chapter has to a large extent been structured by this polarisation in being informed by a desire to present a middle-ground, objective academic view. It seems odd to this writer, however, that so little attention has been paid to interest groups involved in this arena other than libertarians and protectionists. These notably include women, whom jurisdictions such as Canada[123] have explicitly recognised as suffering harm and discrimination from the dissemination of the subservient model of women portrayed in most adult pornography; and to some extent, children, who are usually cited by conservatives as the class

[123] See *R v. Butler* [1992] 1 SCR 452.

most intrinsically in need of protection on the Net and therefore the justification for control/"censorship" of Internet content which is harmful rather than illegal for all.

Vast amounts of literature, both popular and academic, have been written round the subject of pornography, particularly from the various feminist schools. Given this, surprisingly little has been written from the point of view of the interaction between pornography, women and the Internet. From this perspective, the debate on pornography that has filled this chapter is remarkably hermetic and unavoidably partial.[124] The reason for this need not be at all sinister—it may merely be that at present the number of people who feel confident about all three of cyberspace, law and pornography/feminist politics is relatively small; unsurprising, given that the first two domains can both still be seen as male dominated and the third of predominantly female interest.[125] One interesting article that is worth noting is by Laura Miller (a non-lawyer), written in 1995 when the Internet was at the beginning of its commercial expansion.[126]

Miller notes the prevalence of the metaphor of the Internet as the "lawless frontier" or an electronic "Wild West." In Western mythos, civilisation—and its regulation by law, not force—became necessary only when the arrival of women and children demanded it. Women and children were at the time seen as peculiarly vulnerable, and thought to live under constant threat of kidnap, abuse and rape without the protection of civilised norms. Thus on the modern "electronic frontier", demands that the Internet should be regulated by various interest groups have similarly been justified, Miller notes, by the claim that on-line women need these kinds of controls to be put in place if they are not to be seen off by the anti-social, sexist and intimidatory conduct of on-line men. And indeed, in the mid 1990s, there was a plethora of news stories and folk anecdotes describing the ways in which women felt alienated and threatened when, for example, men downloaded pornography in front of them in public microlabs, or made indiscriminate sexual advances towards anyone who used a female name in newsgroups or bulletin boards.[127] Such stories have become far less

---

[124] There are of course a significant number of commentators who have written on the interaction of gender with cyberspace; to name but a few, Sherry Turkle, Alison Adam, Donna Haraway and Dale Spender. However none of these commentators has a substantive legal background. One notable protagonist in the feminist wars over law and the regulation of pornography who has applied her mind to cyberspace is Catherine Mackinnon: see C Mackinnon, "Vindication and Resistance: A Response to the Carnegie Mellon Study of Pornography in Cyberspace," (1995) 83 *Georgetown Law Journal* 1959. See also Kendall, *op cit supra* n. 111.

[125] It is interesting that one of the few academic articles which takes an explicit MacKinnon/ Dworkin approach to critiquing recent laws relating to Internet pornography (here, the Australian regime described at pp XX) is by a man—see Kendall, n. 111 above.

[126] Miller "Women and Children First: Gender and the Settling of the Electronic Frontier" in J Brook and I Boal, *Resisting the Virtual Life: The Culture and Politics of Information* (City Lights, San Francisco, 1995)

[127] See discussion in D Spender, "Male Menace on the Superhighway" in *Nattering on the Net* (Spinifex Press, 1995). See also the publicity surrounding the case of *US* v. *Baker* 890 F Supp 1375 involving a University of Michigan student Jake Baker, who was charged with making threats on-line for writing stories on the newsgroup alt.sex.stories which were violently anti-women. The charges were later dismissed on freedom of speech grounds.

common these days; cyberspace is simply now so widely accessible to persons of both genders that it is hard to sustain a mythos of women on the Internet as an endangered minority.[128] Miller's most interesting and indeed prophetic point is, however this: "[i]f on-line women successfully contest these attempts to depict them as the beleaguered prey of brutish men, expect the paedophile to assume a larger profile in arguments that the Net is out of control." This may well be just what is happening. Can the possibly disproportionate attention that almost all states are currently giving to the "folk menace" of the on-line (as opposed to off-line)[129] paedophile be rooted in its convenience as a means for justifying control of the Internet? (Or, as Grossman puts it, "For would be regulators, focusing on the bogeymen—terrorists, drug dealers, spies and paedophiles—is a clever strategy, because it puts those who would defend freedom of speech on the Net in a position where it looks like they're defending those crimes."[130]) Is the opposition of some cyber-libertarians to even seemingly reasonable attempts to control pornography such as allowing users access to filtering software understandable as a (perhaps unconscious) perception that this is the back door route to greater state regulation of the Internet as a general phenomenon?

Looking at children as a group with an interest in this area also raises some new issues that have had relatively little exposure in the debate so far. In general, perhaps one of the few things cyber-libertarians and cyber-paternalists have in common is the belief that it is parents who should have the right to control what a child sees or does on the Internet.[131] This is all very well except what about the rights of *children,* especially of children who are approaching adolescence? Legislation dealing with parental rights, obscenity and child related offences tends to define a child as someone under 18, or possibly 16.[132] Yet it is well known that children under this kind of age are often extremely practised and sophisticated Internet users, increasingly so as Internet access becomes a central part of the school curriculum. Is it right to regard such net-savvy children as wholly spectators in this debate, objects rather than subjects? In the non-Internet off-line world, modern thinking in child related law is that children go through a process of maturing before they reach the full age of capacity or majority and thus the age of 16 or 18 cannot be regarded as a sudden cut off

---

[128] Interestingly, an American study by Media Matrix/Jupiter Communications claimed that in May 2000 for the first time the number of women on the Web in America had surpassed the number of men (50.4%) (*Times* August 14 2000, *Interface* section).

[129] It is not in any way being claimed here that the law should not seek to stop the circulation of paedophile material. The point being made is that paedophile activities on-line are only part of the larger issue of paedophilic activities in the real world (and indeed that part of the larger phenomenon of domestic child abuse within families).

[130] Grossman, n. 5 above, at p. 200.

[131] See for example the quote from *Microsystems and Mattel* v. *Scandinavia Online et al* at n. 102 above; Akdeniz, n. 83 above, at para 5.6, "By using [filtering] technology it will be up to the parents to decide what is good for their children and what is not, and this would also save the Internet's content becoming ultimately suitable only for children."

[132] 16–18 is a frequent penumbra of uncertainty for the law as to whether a person is a "child" or a "young person." In Scotland, for example, a person does not reach the age of majority till 18, but has legal capacity to perform most juridical acts at 16.

point at which parents relinquish all responsibility, and children go from having zero to full adult civil rights. Instead in the UK and many other countries a concept has developed that individual children may acquire rights as they become sufficiently mature to understand the risks and consequences of a particular course of action.[133] These rights include rights of free expression; both under domestic law and international human rights conventions such as the European Convention on Human Rights. One place where these rights have, unusually, been drawn in as relevant in the Internet porn debate is in the first judgement striking down the Child Online Protection Act as an unconstitutional breach of the First Amendment:

"Despite the Court's personal regret that this preliminary injunction will delay once again the careful protection of our children, I without hesitation acknowledge the duty imposed on the Court and the greater good such duty serves. Indeed perhaps we do the minors of this country harm if First Amendment protections, which they will with age inherit fully, are chipped away in the name of their protection."[134]

Beyond a simple knee-jerk fetishism as to "rights" (ideology-based responses based on children's rights in this area may be as inflexible or inappropriate as those based on cyber-libertarianism), thinking about children as actors with rights rather than merely as objects to be protected may give a usefully different perspective on the debate. Turkle for example, reports that children of 12 upwards playing virtual sex or relationship games on-line found them a useful way to learn about or foreshadow relationships in the off-line world.[135] Perhaps these benefits should be weighed against the unquantified but much publicised risks to children of being preyed on by paedophiles in Internet chat-rooms.

Of course, the idea of children as right-holders with emerging capacity is not incompatible with the idea that parents have a responsibility and right to supervise what children do or see on the Net. Responsible parents, it can be argued, will adjust their views as to what their children can and cannot do as those children mature, and will allow increasing access to "risky" Internet content. In fact, however, it seems doubtful that many parents have a sophisticated enough knowledge both of their children and their filtering software to do this.[136] The most dominant parental behaviour in relation to controlling where their children go on the Net seems at the moment to be to do nothing, though it is unclear

---

[133] In the UK, this concept of the "mature minor" was most famously developed in a case involving the rights of girls under 16 to go on the Pill without telling, or seeking the consent of, their parents (*see Gillick* v. *W Norfolk and Wisbech Area Health Authority* [1986] 1 AC 112.)

[134] See n. 59 above.

[135] S Turkle *Life on the Screen: Identity in the Age of the Internet* (1995, Phoenix, Orion Books) at pp 226-228.

[136] See IDATE *Review of European third party filtering and rating software and services*, December 1999, at http://www.ispo.cec.be/iap/IDATEexec.html . This project was funded by the European Action Plan. More than 95% of 95 users surveyed by IDATE had never used filtering tools before. When they were asked to install the tools and use them, more than half (52%) reported "profound disappointment" with them and only 45% were satisfied. More than 50% did not exploit the full functionality of the tools, eg, did not set up personal user profiles.

whether this is inspired by apathy, ignorance, confusion or a belief that it is not worth undertaking the task; several recent reports on filtering software projects have bemoaned the lack of uptake by, parents of the tagging facilities provided by PICS, although this is usually (and apparently, without empirical justification) linked to the lack of a critical mass of websites as yet self-labelling.[137]

In the end one wonders if the whole debate surrounding control of harmful (as opposed to illegal) content may simply wither away through the inertia of both parents and content-providing sites, and the silent acquiescence of government and the ISP industry. Control of harmful content will on current trends focus mostly on self–regulatory solutions such as hot-lines and filtering. Yet, on current showing, hot-lines, even co-operative European hot-lines, are ineffective outside of a few areas such as child pornography which are almost universally illegal, since most content complained about comes from states outside the EU (notably the USA) where it is legally protected speech. Meanwhile, parents are less well equipped to use filtering tools than their children are to disable them; and content providers tend to see self-rating or labelling as yet another costly, time consuming and pointless bureaucratic burden. The situation is a feedback one rather like that which operated in the war over the VHS as opposed to Betamax video standard. Most sites must self rate before parents will find filtering tools effective and useful; yet sites have no competitive incentive to self rate till most parents demand it. In the meantime the mere availability of filtering and rating systems to parents and ISPs (and, ultimately, governments) will continue to make some cyber-libertarians feel threatened. This seems a rather pyrrhic defeat for all parties in this debate. On the other hand, these may be gloomy prognostications and it is possible that parents do merely need a certain critical mass of websites to start self-rating themselves with PICS tags,[138] before they will think it fruitful to start working out how to use their copy of Net Nanny or Cyber Patrol. In Europe, the EC Action Plan's remit to produce Euro-centric filtering and rating products, as well as to raise awareness of Internet risks and opportunities with both children and parents, may eventually lead to greater take up of these products. For the moment, however, the jury is still out.

[137] See Internet Content Rating for Europe (INCORE—also one of the projects funded by the European Action Plan) Final Report, April 2000 (available at http://www.ispo.cec.be/iap/INCORE exec.html): para 1.2. ". . . Existing systems do not however fulfill the promise of such systems. The main problem is limited access to content because insufficient sites are labelled. European consumers naturally look for sites in their own languages and very few non-English language sites are labelled. What is more surprising is that the same problem affects English consumers. The number of English sites that are rated still fall short of the "*critical mass*" required to persuade consumers to use the existing systems." See also Report of ICRA (Internet Content Rating Association) Advisory Board 2000 (at http://www.icra.org/adreport.htm) para 5 : "We were very challenged during our deliberations by two fundamental questions. . . *Why did RSACi not attract a much higher proportion of content publishers to label their sites? and why did more users not avail [themselves] of this free parental control system?*"

[138] See reports cited above. The ICRA Report stresses the need for "very effective marketing to ensure it [Rsaci] is broadly used."(para 7).

13

Canning the Spam: Is There a Case for Legal Control of Junk Electronic Mail?

LILIAN EDWARDS*

Few Internet users will not at some point have received an e-mail message of the following kind:

> Subject: Fantastic opportunity!!!
> From: makemoney@yahoo.com
>   MAKE MONEY THE EASY WAY!!!!
> Your skills and experience can make you $$$$$$$ in only a few months. Send $50 dollars to Make Money Promotions to set yourself up in easy street for life.
> Go to http://www.makemoney.com/getajob/index.html for further details!!!

Such unsolicited or 'junk' e-mails are colloquially known as spam.[1] They are usually sent out to thousands if not millions of electronic mailboxes simultaneously, most often for dubious commercial purposes, though some are also sent by private individuals, for example to spread racist or homophobic hate speech. Spam can usually be spotted quickly by its use of multiple exclamation marks and capital letters (the Internet equivalent of shouting), or by enticing subject lines such as 'get rich quick' or 'hot sex here'. Although most often found in the context of e-mail, Usenet newgroups can also be spammed, and for this reason LINX, the London Internet Exchange, has suggested a better description would be 'unsolicited bulk material' or UBM. The presenting features of spam are that they advertise goods or services the recipient has not actively sought (typical examples being pornography, get rich quick schemes, pyramid selling schemes, dating agencies or software with which to become a spammer yourself), they are often misleading or outright fraudulent, very often offensive in content, and often arrive more than once to the same recipient. One problem may to be to

---

* Senior Lecturer, The School of Law, Edinburgh University. E-mail: L.Edwards@ed.ac.uk. My grateful thanks to John Dallman, who provided useful information in relation to technical fixes for spam, and also to Mark Lemley and Geraint Howells for their helpful comments and advice.

[1] The name 'spam' is, as a matter of Internet urban myth, supposed to derive from a well known Monty Python TV comedy sketch involving the chanting of 'spam, spam, spam' over and over again.

separate 'legitimate' bulk mailing from spam: is it simply a matter of volume or must these other criteria be brought into play? As we shall see below much of the harm caused by spam is simply a result of its bulk rather than its actual content. Organisations such as clubs and universities do send out mass e-mailing to eg their students, alumni, staff or sponsors—should such bulk mailings be classified as spam?

Almost all spam originates in the US currently, though this may change as UK entrepeneurs become more aware of the almost cost free opportunities of direct marketing by bulk e-mail. While spam has been very much in evidence ever since the Internet moved on from its earlier, quieter non-commercial incarnation (ie, roughly since the mid 1990s)[2] and has been the subject of much Internet user complaint and disgruntlement, there has until very recently been very little *legal* debate on how spam could, or should, be controlled in this country. By contrast there have for some time been active running battles in the US courts between spammers and those who would seek to stamp out the practice—notably Internet Service Providers (ISPs)—as well as a flood of proposed and in some cases, implemented state and Federal legislation intended to 'can the spam'.[3] UK interest is however now increasing[4] as spam is increasingly seen not just as a local annoyance to users but as a disincentive to the development of consumer confidence in the Internet as a commercial medium, and both the UK and the EC are now actively considering solutions to the problem of spam and whether existing or new legislation can be an effective tool to control it.[5]

WHY SHOULD SPAM BE SUBJECT TO REGULATION?

The historic response to spam has been to regard it as a nuisance, and perhaps to take self help measures such as 'flaming' (sending abusive e-mails to the spammers) but not as a fit subject for legal (or extra-legal) regulation. However a number of factors have conspired to make it a subject that is worth taking seriously.

---

[2] An interesting non legal account of the genesis of spam can be found in 'Make.Money.Fast' in W.Grossman *Net.Wars* (NYUP, 1997).

[3] This is the informal title of a US Bill introduced into the House of Representatives by Congressman Miller on 10 June 1999.

[4] Tentative but growing legal interest in the UK can be seen taking visible shape in the form of a number of short articles and industry reports, nearly all of which seem to be entitled 'A Spammer in the Works'; cf. Onwusah (1998) 148 *NLJ* 1718; Drew (1998) 9 *Computers and Law* 13; Mackay, 4 May 1999, *Scotsman* Interactive section; Novell report commissioned from Benchmark Solutions on impact of spam on UK industry, reported in *Scotsman*, 29 April 1998. This author has resisted the temptation to continue in this grand tradition. An industry based pressure group, associated with the US body CAUCE, the Coalition against Unsolicited Commercial Email, has recently been formed in Europe to resist spam : The European Coalition Against Unsolicited Commercial Email, web site at http://www.euro.cauce.org/en/index.html. The UK pages are to be found at http://www.euro.cauce.org/en/countries/c_uk.html. CAUCE's web site can be found at http://www.cause.org. Another useful US anti-spam site is Junkbusters at http://www.junkbusters.com.

[5] See further below, pp 322 ff.

Most obviously, spam is annoying and in some cases, offensive, to its recipients. Worse still, traditional direct marketing is usually only directed at solvent adults, while spammers will indiscriminately spam children and other vulnerable groups so long as they have an e-mail address.[6] From a legal perspective, spam is an invasion of the privacy of the individual whether the mail box is situated at home or work. Spam has been described as combining the worst aspects of junk mail, telephone solicitation ('cold calling') and junk faxes.[7] In this aspect, spam is not dissimilar to traditional, non electronic direct marketing, although it is significant that the costs of marketing by spam are shifted almost wholly from the spammer, to the recipient who pays his ISP for downloading time.[8]

'Spamming' however has serious consequences other than irritation for the recipients of the message, and also has economic implications for persons *other* than the recipient. It is the financial detriment spam potentially causes which has arguably created the most compelling public interest in the prevention of spam. In the EC especially, the main current concern in this area is that spamming fundamentally impedes consumer confidence in the Internet as a safe and serious commercial medium, rather than one full of sharks, wide boys and fraudsters.[9] In this respect the European debate around spam is similar to that around the regulation of encryption and pornography[10]: in both cases, the public interest in protection from offensive content, or protection of privacy rights, carries less weight than the economic argument that unless the Internet is cleaned up and made secure for consumers and businesses, electronic commerce cannot thrive.[11] Furthermore, because so much spam fails to meet fair trading and honesty standards,[12] 'legitimate' adverts from reputable advertisers are almost always ignored or deleted, or attempts are made to filter it out by the system

---

[6] Dallman and Dowling note 'The British Government is shortly due for a nasty shock due to their policy of connecting all schools to the Internet. Imagine the reaction when the tabloid press discovers that schoolchildren are being sent advertisements for pornography via the email accounts that the government has provided.' *Towards Useable Email*, p 2 at http://www.davros.org/legal/dmaspam.html.

[7] See Byrne 'Squeezing Spam Off the Net : Federal Regulation of Unsolicited Commercial Email' (1998) 2 *W.Va. JL and Tech* 4.

[8] Although this is a less serious issue in the USA where local calls are free, and, increasingly, is also diminishing in significance in the UK as freeserves and flat rate schemes such as that provided by NTL have become available.

[9] See especially the EC Electronic Commerce Directive, Arts 6 and 7, originally proposed on 18 November 1998, and finalised as of 17 July 2000, (see appendix). The Dir. must be implemented by EC Member States by 17 January 2002.

[10] See further Edwards, Ch. 12; Hogg, Ch. 3.

[11] Dickie has described this as a 'market' rather than a 'welfarist' focus in regard to regulation of the Internet: see *Internet and Electronic Commerce Law in the European Union* (1999, Hart Publishing), p 101.

[12] The Report to the Federal Trade Commission of the Ad Hoc Working Group on Unsolicited Commercial Email (http://www.cdt.org/spam) estimated that around a half of unsolicited commercial email messages contained fraudulent or deceptive content, and of the other half, much contained inaccurate email header information ie, misleading subject lines or sender.

administrator. Effectively, the result is that the Internet cannot be used sensibly for legitimate direct marketing currently.

Certain particular groups suffer direct economic losses as a result of spam. Some well known ISPs with a large client base whose e-mail addresses can be easily 'harvested' by acquiring a temporary guest account, tend to be heavily spammed, e.g. AOL and CompuServe, and this causes them to lose custom as users become annoyed with receiving spam and leave and subscribe to another ISP (it should be remembered that the ISP market is a highly competitive one where users tend to show little brand loyalty). Users waste on-line time, which despite the growth of free ISP services in the UK, is still often charged on an hourly basis (plus local call costs), downloading, reading and deleting spam. Employers also suffer additional costs, as spam wastes employee time, both in examining and deleting spam, or by becoming frustrated and replying to it. A report commissioned by Novell in April 1998 concluded that junk e-mail was costing UK industry £5 billion per year.[13]

Finally and perhaps most importantly, spam threatens the efficiency and speed of the Internet for all users. The sheer bulk of traffic sent out by spammers—who use special spamming software to sometimes send tens of millions of messages at one go—congests the Internet, using up bandwidth and slowing down, not just e-mail, but also other services such as the Web. Servers from which spam is sent, or to which or through which it is transmitted, may crash, not just as a result of the initial volume of mail sent out but because of 'mail undeliverable' messages returned from inaccurate e-mail addresses. ISPs tend to buy only as much bandwidth as they need to support the estimated traffic of their subscribers and massive surges of use caused by spammers will either crash the server or require the ISP to waste money buying excess bandwidth as preventative strategy. This again represents a major problem to ISPs and their system administrators who to retain customer confidence need to provide 24 hour access and keep networked workplaces going.[14] In one recent US case,[15] the court estimated that the real costs to an ISP of dealing with each spam message were 0 .078 cents per message. Since in that case 130 million junk e-mails were sent, the court awarded US$400,000 dollars against the spammer (including a punitive triple multiplier on the estimated damages). In another case it was estimated that handling spam had so degraded the performance of the server afflicted by spamming that e-mails that should have been delivered in minutes were taking three days to arrive.[16]

---

[13] Report commissioned from Benchmark Solutions by Novell on impact of spam on UK industry, reported in *Scotsman*, 29 April 1998

[14] Compare the international furor caused, when Microsoft were forced by hackers to shut down the free web based email system Hotmail for a few hours as a result of its compromise by hackers. See http://news2.thls.bbc.co.uk/hi/english/sci/tech/newsid%5F434000/434120.stm.

[15] *AOL* v. *Prime Data Systems Inc* ED Va No 97-1652-A, 12/10/98.

[16] *Compuserve Inc* v. *Cyber Promotions Inc* No C2-96-1070 (SD Ohio 24/10/96).

WAYS TO STOP SPAMMERS

Having perhaps established that spam is a problem worthy of regulatory concern, how , if at all, how can it be stopped? The naïve or perhaps the optimistic among us might think that the simplest thing in the world to do would be to ask the spammer to simply stop annoying us. Spam messsages, like all e-mails, carry a return address. Indeed, most spam messages do include a line to the effect of 'If you wish to receive no more mail from this address, please reply to nospam@spam-domain.com'. The many users who take this up as a genuine offer tend to discover however that the return or reply-to address is nearly always fake,[17] resulting in an undeliverable mail message. This has three advantages for the spammer; one, he is not deluged by a flood of complaints from the spammed population; two, he is effectively untraceable so that he can avoid having legal writs served on him; three, the spammer can use your reply to the 'nospam' address to ascertain that the e-mail address spammed is indeed valid (which sometimes, to add insult to injury, may result in the address so validated being offered for sale to other spammers or direct marketers). So if asking for direct removal from a spammer's list is unlikely to work, then other solutions—legal or extra-legal—must be explored. Below are canvassed some suggestions for ways in which both law and technology can be harnessed to help prevent spam.

As was noted above there are a number of persons who may suffer from spamming—individuals who receive it, ISPs who handle it, and the general public who absorb the costs and ill will it creates. Legal action by victims of spamming will generally have one or both of two goals: one, to stop the spammer by closing down the ISP account the spammer is using; and two, to recover damages. An underlying goal for ISPs especially, is publicity: to make it plain that spamming is not something they will tolerate in the best interests of their customers. The public interest in removal of spam may also be sufficient to justify invoking the criminal law.

CAN CIVIL LIABILITY BE IMPOSED ON SPAMMERS?

(i) Contractual claims

For a spammer to go about their work, they must have access to the Internet. This will require the formation of a contract for the ongoing or temporary services of an ISP. Many ISPs insert as standard provisions in their subscriber contracts that spamming is regarded as a fundamental breach allowing the contract

---

[17] Most email programs have a simple command which allows a 'reply-to' address to be set which has no relation to the actual address of sender. Ironically, such tactics are sometimes used by spam-avoiders to avoid giving a true reply address out to the world which spammers can then harvest.

to be terminated unilaterally by the ISP at any time[18] and even where there is no express anti-spam clause, it is possible that the courts would be prepared to accept it as a term implied by the common practice of the business of providing Internet access.[19]

In many US ISP contracts, furthermore, a system of rising penalties is also put in place for repeated spamming, which may be imposed as well as or instead of, termination of the contract. The problem with provisions of the latter type is that in both Scotland and England, such might be struck down as illegal penalty clauses, rather than as true liquidated damage clauses.[20] There might also be some difficulty if either termination or penalty clauses were to be contested as unfair; as ISPs invariably only offer standard form contracts to subscribers, terms imposed by such would be subject to scrutiny both under the Unfair Contract Terms Act 1977 (UCTA77) and the Unfair Terms in Consumer Contracts Regulations 1994. A challenge however might be mounted to the applicability of the 1994 Regulations on the basis that a spammer signing up for an ISP account is not a 'consumer', but someone acting in the course of business.[21] In any case, the question is often academic, as spammers tend to gain access to the Internet by using free and transient guest memberships, often giving false identifying details, and then moving on speedily to the next account. In such circumstances, contractual remedies tend to be of little avail. However it is noteworthy that the first UK writ served against a spammer, one Adrian Paris, was raised by Virgin under two grounds one of which was breach of contract.[22] (The case was settled in June 1999 for £5,000.[23]) The case was however unusual in that Paris (remarkably) had subscribed to Virgin under his true identity.[24]

As we saw above, it is not always the ISP with which the spammer has a contractual relationship which alone suffers financial loss. Where can we find reme-

---

[18] In a brief survey of contracts of six leading ISPs in the UK market, four (Demon, Virgin, Freeserve and Sharkhunt) imposed anti-spam clauses in their subscriber contracts. Interestingly, the ISP Association, a UK industry body, has adopted a voluntary Code of Practice as of 25 January 1999 which requires ISP members to follow best industry practice in using anti spamming software so that customers can elect to minimise the amount of spam they receive, but does not require an anti-spam termination clause (para 7.1.6).

[19] In a recent Canadian case, *127623 Ontario Inc* v. *Nexx Online Inc*, Court File No C20546/99, (Ontario Superior Court of Justice, June 14 1999), an ISP had no explicit anti-spam clause in the hosting agreement, but did have a clause requiring compliance with 'generally accepted netiquette'. The court held this entitled the ISP to terminate the agreement when it discovered its client was an active spammer.

[20] Although as seen above there is a reasonable body of knowledge about how costs of spam can be pre-estimated. See further *Stair Memorial Encyclopaedia*, Vol 15, pp 510ff, and *Dunlop Pneumatic Tyre Co* v. *New Garage & Motor Co* [1915] AC 79.

[21] See r 2(1) and 3(1) of the Regulations. Under UCTA77, however, terms in a standard form contract are subject to review by the court if they allow one party to offer a performance substantially different from that which the other party reasonably expected under the contract, *even if* the contract is made business to business (1977 Act, 17(1)(b)).

[22] See further 'Virgin Sues Spam Man', BBC News, at http://news2.thls.bbc.co.uk/hi/english/sci/tech/newsid%5F323000/323817.stm.

[23] See *E-Commerce Law and Policy*, June 1999, Vol 1, issue 5.

[24] Although he subsequently set up three more accounts with Virgin under false names.

dies for those affected economically by spamming activity who either do not have a contractual relationship or cannot rely on an appropriate contractual term?

(ii) Claims in tort or delict

The US courts have several times allowed claims in tort against spammers by ISPs whose service to their client base is degraded by spam e-mails. The basis of such actions is usually the tort of trespass, which under the US Restatement can be established where intentional damage is done to the moveable property of the service provider.[25] One successful US trespass case was *CompuServe Inc* v. *Cyber Promotions*,[26] the case cited above, in which CompuServe's server's performance was so degraded that e-mail took three days to deliver which would normally have taken minutes. In that case, the US District Court of Eastern Ohio had little difficulty in finding that damage caused by electronic signals could be sufficiently tangible to found the tort; that the damage caused to the plaintiff's property did not need to be permanent so long as it had resulted in actual impairment of its quality or value; and that CompuServe had not given permission to any use at all the spammers made of the Internet access they offered simply by forming a contract for ISP services with that person.

It is difficult, unfortunately, to see how these US cases could be applied directly to Scots law though there may be a possibility of such an approach succeeding in England, where the law on trespass to moveables is not dissimilar to that in the US Restatement.[27] In the English *Virgin* case cited above,[28] the second head of action was trespass. In Scotland, however, the law of trespass is considerably narrower than in England, and the delict of trespass relates almost exclusively to use without permission of heritage (land and buildings). It seems that trespass can only be an actionable delict in relation to moveables such as cars or ships, which can be occupied.[29] The tort of conversion is also unknown in Scots law. A general action for interference with moveable property on the grounds of *culpa* would seem possible, as *culpa* is sometimes seen as covering both intentional and unintentional conduct so long as loss is caused to another—but the difficulty then arises that the loss to an ISP may well be wholly purely economic, for which the courts are generally reluctant to allow recovery.[30] As we have seen, even

---

[25] A notable recent success story using this approach is *Earthlink Networks* v. *Cyber Promotions*, No BC 167502 (Cal.Super. Ct.LA County, March 30 1998) where the ISP achieved a $2m settlement against the spammer. See also *AOL Inc* v. *IMS* 1998 US Dist LEXIS 17437 (ED Va. October 29 1998).

[26] *Supra* n. 16.

[27] See *Winfield and Jolowicz on Tort* (London, Sweet & Maxwell,1998,15th edn) pp583–588.

[28] *Supra* n. 22.

[29] See Thomson *Delictual Liability* (London, Butterworths, 1994) p 21 citing *Leitch* v *Leydon* 1931 SC (HL) 1; *Walker on Delict*, Vol II (Edinburgh, W.Green & Co, 1966) pp. 938ff.

[30] See further *Thomson, supra* n 29, pp 1 and 22ff on the use of culpa to cover intentional and unintentional wrongs. However it is clear that historically Scots law used *culpa* only for negligent acts and *dolus* for intentional wrongs cf A. T. Glegg, *A Practical Treatise on the Law of Reparation* (1st edn, 1892) 8, 12, 34–5.

servers put out of commission by spam recover without any permanent damage, and losses based on client dissatisfaction are clearly purely economic.

A more workable possibility might be to seek damages on the basis of what are known as economic torts or delicts: eg that the spammer has interfered with the ISP's performance of its contract with its clients to provide them Internet access,[31] or, more broadly still, that the spammer has wrongfully interfered with the ISP's business.[32] The law relating to such economic delicts in both Scotland and England is however not at all clear on a number of points, e.g. does the spammer have to have *intended* to interfere with the ISP's contractual performance or business, or will his recklessness about this likely consequence do? Does the spammer's interfering act, ie, sending spam, itself have to be an unlawful act even before it interferes with the ISPs activities? Can the restraint of one party's business activities be justified merely because it interferes with another party's business—or is it legitimate competition, even though spammers and ISPs have quite different trades? A court appraised of how damaging spam can be, is perhaps unlikely to be sympathetic to the spammer in these regards but the uncertainty may still impede legal claims. Even if a claim was allowed in principle, uncertainty persists about what heads of damages would be accepted by a UK court as sufficiently proximate (direct losses suffered due to server shutdown, general loss of goodwill, loss of reputation, customers switching ISPs, slowdown in ISP performance?).

(iii) Trademark infringement

Where well known brands are spoofed within the main text of the messages sent by spammers, or, more interestingly, a well known ISP name is given as part of a fake or 'spoofed' reply-to address, then claims for trademark infringement or passing off may arise (as may a common law action for fraud). The argument in the latter situation is that recipients will be confused into believing the messages were sent out with the complicity of the spoofed ISP when they were not, and so their trademark is infringed.[33] In the US case of *AOL v Prime Data Systems*,[34] spammers sent out 130 million junk e-mails all of which gave their reply-to address, fraudulently, as from the domain *aol.com*. The court found that there was wilful trademark infringement and awarded US$400,000 damages. American ISPs have found this a particularly attractive remedy in that it sends a

---

[31] See *Torquay Hotel* v. *Cousins* [1969] 2 Ch 106.

[32] See *Lonhro plc* v. *Fayed* [1990] QB 490 and Thomson,supra n. 29, pp. 38–39; *Stair Memorial Encyclopaedia*, Vol 15, pp. 380ff; *Winfield and Jolowicz*, supra n. 27, Chapter 18.

[33] See further Waelde, p. 178.

[34] *Supra* n 16. See also *Hotmail Corp* v. *Van$ Money Pie Inc* 47 USPQ 2d 1020 (ND Cal 1998) (also at (1998) 3 BNA ECLR 586); *AOL* v. *IMS* 1998 US Dist Lexis 17437 (ED Va. October 29, 1998).

signal out to the public, spammers, and subscribers alike, that 'attempts to pig-gyback off [the ISP's] name'[35] will be vigorously repelled.

(i) The Computer Misuse Act 1990

The Computer Misuse Act 1990 (CMA) was introduced primarily to deal with the perceived vice of computer hacking.[36] It was never anticipated during its drafting that it might be used to deal with junk e-mail. However in one infor-mally reported case,[37] an ISP known as Colloquium had its system brought down by an overload of spam causing downtime, loss and interference with its business—some 300,000 messages per hour were sent out by the spammer using its server. Unusually, the spammer was not only resident in UK but was an ex-customer of the ISP and had given it his correct name and phone number. Strathclyde Police investigated and the possibility was raised of charges under the CMA, although it is not clear under what provisions, or indeed if any pro-secution subsequently transpired.

Does the CMA provide a means, as the operator of Colloquium suggested, to 'make a junk mailer think twice'? The problem with this approach is that the sanctions provided by the CMA are not really tailored to deal with a legitimate user who then abuses Internet access provided, but rather with an unauthorised or intrusive user. Use of an account with an ISP to send spam, where the con-tract expressly or impliedly states that spamming is forbidden, may, taking a common sense approach, appear to be 'unauthorised' access under s 1 of the Act and thus criminal. However *DPP* v. *Bignell*[38] makes it clear that so long as the *access* to the server has been authorised—which it will have been if the spam-mer has lawfully acquired some kind of legitimate ongoing or guest account—then a s 1 offence is not committed whatever *purpose* the access is then used to secure. In *Bignell* itself, a policeman was given legitimate access to the Police National Computer—but then used this access not for the proper purposes of his job, but for an unauthorised purpose, namely finding out personal details about his estranged wife. It was held that no s 1 offence had been committed. This result is a particularly unfortunate one since a s 1 offence must be estab-lished as a prerequisite to prosecution for more serious offences, with heavier sentences, under s 2 of the Act.

Section 2 is known as the 'ulterior intent' section and provides that an offence is committed where anyone commits the s 1 offence with the intent to commit

---

[35] Yahoo!, commenting on their successful suit for trademark infringement against spammers in *Yahoo! Inc* v. *World Wide Network Marketing* ND Calif No C-99-20234 (14 April 1999), reported at (1999) 4 BNA ECLR 384.

[36] See further Law Commission Report No 186 *Computer Misuse* Cm 819.

[37] See *Scotsman, Interactive* section, 1998.

[38] [1998] Masons *CLR*, Rep 141.

or facilitate the commission of another offence to which the section applies. So for example, if (as is often the case) the spam itself contained statements that were criminally fraudulent, s 2 would allow for a penalty of up to 5 years' imprisonment or a fine to the statutory maximum to be imposed so long as 'unauthorised' access under s 1 could be established. *Bignell* however currently blocks this approach (although straightforward prosecution for fraud would still be available).

A final possible ground of prosecution under the CMA may be found in s 3, which provides that an offence is committed if anyone with deliberate intent[39] causes an 'unauthorised modification of the contents of any computer'. Section 17(7) defines such a modification as taking place if *either* any program or data held on the computer concerned is altered or erased, *or* any program or data is added to the contents of the computer. The modification must *then* be intended to (a) impair the operation of the computer; or (b) to prevent or hinder access to any program or data held on any computer; or (c) to impair the operation of any such program or the reliability of any such data (s 3(2)).

Again, we have the problem that these provisions were clearly drafted to catch the disseminators of computer viruses or logic bombs, not direct marketers. To fit the facts of spamming into s 3 requires extremely convoluted interpretation. In the Colloquium case, it appears that the server crash mainly occurred because 'mail undeliverable' messages, returned due to inaccurate e-mail addresses being used by the spammers, were 'added' to the ISP's server. Can s 3 apply? Three problems arise. First, are return e-mail messages 'data'? They are certainly not programs.[40] No definition of data is given in the Act (deliberately), so, perhaps.[41] Secondly, even if adding e-mail messages to the server is seen as a 'modification', again we have the *Bignell* problem of whether it is an 'unauthorised' modification if the spammer had legitimate access to the e-mail program provided by the ISP (and to storage space on the server).[42] Again, there is some possibility *Bignell* might be distinguished in this context, since the issue here is whether the *modification* was unauthorised, rather than the *access*.[43] But the main stumbling block is that the spammer clearly did not *intend* to create any of the impairments described in s 3(2). He merely intended to send out spam. It seems unlikely that his mere recklessness as to other possible results, including server crashes, or even interference with services ('pro-

---

[39] See further s 3(1)(b) and (3) of CMA, and below. The intent need not be directed at any particular computer or any particular program or at securing any particular modification.

[40] Although they can contain programs e.g. attached .exe files.

[41] *The Concise Oxford Dictionary*, 7th edn, defines data as the plural of datum, and that, inter alia, as 'facts or information, especially as basis for inference; quantities or characters operated on by computers etc and stored or transmitted on punched cards, etc.'

[42] There is also an interesting reductio ad absurdam result to this argument in that entirely legitimate Internet users who are not subscribed to an ISP but send email to users who are clients of that ISP are as likely as spammers to be guilty of an 'unauthorised modification'—hence sending email would in principle be potentially criminal under s 3!

[43] To secure a s 3 conviction, the spammer must also *know* their modification was unauthorised—s 3(2) and (4).

grams') provided to ISP clients, while he carried out this primary intention, would be enough to found criminal liability.

Although this result is unfortunate from a spam point of view, it makes perfect sense given the intention of the legislators. Any forced interpretation which allowed spammers to be caught might also allow, say, any innocent user who sent an e-mail or used a program in some way which inadvertently caused a system crash to be tried under s 3. Every local area network user knows that modern computer systems are, unfortunately, still very fragile. Given the debate about whether even intentional computer virus creation and dissemination is a serious enough issue to deserve criminal penalties, it seems unlikely a court would bend over backwards merely to criminalise the activities of unscrupulous direct marketers without taking cognisance of possible side effects.

(ii) Alternative criminal remedies

As we have already mentioned, some (though not all) spam may be criminally fraudulent under English statute[44] or Scottish common law. In addition, the Telecommunications Act 1984, s 43 makes it a criminal offence to use a public telecommunications network to send 'grossly offensive, threatening or obscene' material, and a 'public telecommunications network' is widely defined enough to cover Internet traffic which goes through phone lines or other cables. Thus we have a partial remedy for at least that portion of spam which is criminally offensive or deceptive. The outstanding problem however, from the Scottish or English perspective, is that most spam currently comes from the US and thus, criminal jurisdiction being territorial, the spammers will probably fall outside the jurisdictional and enforcement capabilities of the UK authorities. We shall return to the difficulties of enforcement below.

REMEDIES FOR THE *RECIPIENTS* OF SPAM?

Data protection law

Given this, and the apparent inadequacy of the civil and criminal remedies canvassed so far, perhaps it is better to try another approach. So far we have mainly focused on

(i) sanctioning the person who *sends* the spam, and (usually simultaneously)
(ii) providing financial compensation for ISPs who are economically hurt by their activities.

---

[44] See the Thefts Act 1968 and *Smith and Hogan on Criminal Law* (London, Butterworths, 8th edn, 1996).

We now turn however to seeking to protect the members of the public who are spammed. As noted above, apart from the question of offence and alarm, the main impact on the public of spam is that of annoyance, invasion of privacy, and generally of loss of confidence in the Internet as a lawful and honest medium. The response to ordinary direct marketing as a nuisance factor in the EU has mainly been to look at protection of personal data, an idea which springs fundamentally from the European Convention on Human Rights' protection of the individual's right to privacy.[45] (In the US by contrast it has been accepted, albeit with some reluctance that direct marketing is a form of speech and as such protected by First Amendment rights, although the protection given is less than that which would be accorded non-commercial speech.[46]) European protection originates in the activities of the Council of Europe, who in 1981 passed a Convention on Automatic Processing of Personal Data which was incorporated into UK law by the Data Protection Act 1984, one of whose main purposes was to control the unauthorised transfer of personal data held on computers for the purposes of direct marketing. More recently the EU has passed a Data Protection Directive of 1995[47] which required all member states of the EU to implement it in national law by 24 October 1998 (although in many states, including the UK, that deadline has not been met). In the UK, the revised data protection law is now to be found in its entirety in the Data Protection Act 1998.[48] Does the 1998 Act put in place a regulatory scheme adequate to provide remedies to members of the public concerned about spam, as it attempts to do for the victims of traditional direct marketing?

The first question is whether spammers come within the remit of the 1998 Act at all. The Act is less than crystal clear in its drafting,[49] but speaks of 'data controllers', who are under a statutory duty (i) to comply with the Data Protection Principles[50] and (ii) to register with the Data Protection Commissioner ('notify' within the 1998 Act terminology) as persons who are processing personal data.[51] If these duties are breached, then the data controller may be liable to compensate any individual adversely affected, even if the Commissioner does not serve an enforcement notice,[52] and criminal liability may also be incurred.[53]

The first question then is whether spammers are 'data controllers'. A data controller is 'a person who . . . determines the purposes for which and the manner in which personal data are, or are to be, processed'.[54] This begs the question, do spammers process 'personal data'? Typically, spammers harvest from news-

[45] In Art 8.
[46] *Virginia State Board of Pharmacy* v. *Virginia Citizen's Consumer Council Inc* 425 US 748.
[47] 95/46/EC, OJ 1995 L281/31.
[48] See further, Charlesworth, Ch. 5.
[49] A useful concise analysis of how the 1998 Act relates to the Internet can be found in Millard 'Data Protection and the Internet' (1999) 9 *Computers & Law* 29.
[50] 1998 Act, s 4(4).
[51] *Ibid*, s 17(1).
[52] *Ibid*, s 13.
[53] *Ibid*, s 21.
[54] *Ibid*, s 1(1)).

groups, web sites or ISP mail programs, buy, or otherwise obtain, long lists of personal e-mail addresses, to which a spam e-mail is then sent by special software. Under s 1(1)of the 1998 Act, 'Processing' includes '. . . carrying out any operation on the information or data', which seems to fit these activities satisfactorily. However the meaning of 'personal data' itself may be more problematic. Section 1(1) defines personal data as 'data which relates to a living individual who can be identified (a) from those data, or (b) from those data and other information which is in the possession of, or likely to come into the possession of, the data controller'. Does an e-mail address, without any other added information, identify an individual, in the same way that a name and physical address would? Some may seem to, others may not. This writer, for example, maintains e-mail addresses both as *Lilian.Edwards@ed.ac.uk* and *eusl01@law. srv0.ed.ac.uk*. At first blush, one might think the first address might be 'personal data' since it reveals a person of female sex who probably works or studies at Edinburgh University, and the second not—an absurd result in itself—but the matter is complicated still further by the additional qualifier that data may be 'personal' if it allows identification of an individual when combined with *other* information which is '*likely* to come into the possession of the data controller' (italics added). On the Internet, identifying information about many persons is easily obtainable simply by putting their e-mail address into one of the many search engines available. However, Gringras[55] points out that simply because such additional information is *easy* to obtain, does not mean that it is *likely* a spammer would obtain it, as his principle aim will be to send out spam, not to research the character of its recipients[56]. The point remains however that given the use of search engines and other Web based aids, an e-mail address makes an Internet user 'identifiable' and nothing in the Act requires that 'personal data' must provide the actual *name* of the individual or 'data subject' to which it pertains.

If the 1998 Act does apply to spammers, it is clear that on most occasions, they will be *prima facie* in breach of the 1998 Act in multiple ways. For example, spammers typically fail to register with the Data Commissioner as required, and also usually fail to meet the requirement of the First Data Protection Principle, that the consent of data subjects to the processing of their data must be obtained. Admittedly, such consent is not required if one of the other exemptions in Schedule 2 is applicable, but the only one that seems relevant to spam is that the processing is 'necessary for the purposes of legitimate interests pursued by the data controller' which interests must be balanced against the data subject's rights, especially to privacy.[57] If the processing is detrimental to the

---

[55] *Laws of the Internet* (London, Butterworths, 1997), p. 253.

[56] Although this might not always hold true : if e.g. the spammer was seeking to send spam concerning pornography only to males between 18 and 50. The economics of spamming however—ie its cheapness, however many are spammed—tend to make selection amongst those targetted for particular groups unlikely.

[57] 1998 Act, Sched 2, para 6(1).

interests of the data subject, as it arguably will be in the case of spam, then Carey[58] suggests the exemption is unlikely to exculpate the data controller. Spammers also typically fail to comply with the right of the data subject under s 11 to demand to cease receiving direct marketing[59] from the data controller in that they usually provide a spurious reply-to address for such requests(see above).

However all of the above is interesting but of little avail, given that the Data Protection Act only operates in the UK, and the 1995 Directive within the European Economic Area (EEA), when overwhelmingly, spam emanates from the US. (These remedies may of course become more useful once the local marketers do jump on board.) Although the jurisdictional provisions of the 1998 Act do perhaps extend to cover data controllers established outside the EEA who use 'equipment' in the UK for 'processing' the data[60] (are the servers and networks through which e-mail is routed 'equipment'? Does the spammer use them for 'processing'?) the problem still remains that enforcement of the data protection principles by EC nations effectively ends outwith the EEA.[61] Spam is inherently a global problem not just (or even mainly) an EC one.

It is also worth noting that the scheme of data protection is inherently regulatory, rather than designed to provide remedies to individuals. As noted above, individuals can pursue civil claims against those who break the 1998 Act rules, and criminal prosecutions may in some cases be brought. But the main enforcement apparatus of the 1998 Act is the enforcement notice,[62] which is served as a 'last chance warning' on a malfeasant by the Data Protection Commissioner, with the intention of securing, if at all possible, compliance without criminal proceedings. In other words, data protection law is better seen as a way of creating a commercially cleaner Internet for the public to enjoy, than as a means of getting private remedy or revenge.

CONSUMER RIGHTS

Similar problems attach to other consumer remedies which may be relevant to protection from spam, and which will or may become available under the general umbrella of EU consumer protection. One of the more promising provisions is that EC consumers are to be guaranteed the right under the EC Distance Selling Directive[63] (which was to have been implemented in the UK by 4 June

---

[58] Carey *Blackstone's Guide to the Data Protection Act 1998* (London, Blackstones, 1998).

[59] 'Direct marketing' is defined for these purposes as 'the communication (by whatever means) of any advertising or marketing material which is directed to particular individuals' (s 11(3) and so includes spam as well as traditional junk mail.

[60] 1998 Act, s 5(1).

[61] Although to some extent these extra-EU enforcement problems are being addressed, if slowly, in relation to trans-border data flows to the USA (see Charlesworth, ch. 5).

[62] 1998 Act, s 40.

[63] Directive 97/7/EC, OJ No L 144/19.

2000[64]) not to receive unsolicited communications relating to distance selling where there is a clear objection from the consumer.[65] The Directive is clearly intended to cover communications sent via the Internet as well as conventional mail and phone communications.[66] Although the UK government is still considering the exact form of the regulations which will implement the scheme,[67] what was first envisaged was that a register, printed or electronic, would be held under the supervision of OFTEL, which would record the names of individuals who positively asked *not* to receive distance selling communications: in other words an 'opt-out' regime. Direct marketers were to be compelled to search this register in order to remove any such opting-out consumers from their lists before sending out communications. The more recent consultation paper issued by the DTI in November 1999 however took a more ambiguous line, with draft regulations being supplied which contained alternate opt-out and opt-in schemes.[68] An 'opt-in' scheme would mean that consumers would actually have to express a preference to receive unsolicited communications from the business in question before it would be legal for them to be sent such communications. Such an approach is generally seen as more effective at controlling spam (see further below). The Distance Selling Directive is however limited in relation to curtailing spam in that financial services are excluded from the Directive (and much spam involves financial scams[69]) as are business to business communications (which may cover almost all spam if commercial spamming is accepted as a business).

Another analogous source of remedies may be the Telecomunications (Data Protection and Privacy) (Direct Marketing) Regulations 1998,[70] which implement in the UK the direct marketing provisions of the 1997 Telecommunications Data Protection Directive.[71] Currently, Art 12 of this Directive deals with unsolicited telephone calls and is aimed at cutting down on such 'cold calling' against the wishes of consumers. Although the Directive gave states discretion to implement the Directive using either an 'opt-in' or 'opt-out' system, the DTI chose after consultation to opt for the latter, so that those who wish *not* to receive unsolicited calls will have to register to this effect. Breach of the Regulations is to be enforceable in the same way as breach of the Data Protection Act 1998, discussed above.

---

[64] However as no regulations had been implemented by this deadline in the UK. See now the Consumer Protection (Distance selling) Regulations 2000, which came into force on 31 October 2000.

[65] Art 10(1).

[66] See Art 2 and Annex 1, which specifically refers to 'electronic mail'.

[67] See the November 1999 DTI consultative document *Distance Selling Directive— Implementation in the UK* and attached draft regulations at http://www.dti.gov.uk/cacp/ca/distance/dist.htm.

[68] *Ibid.*

[69] However the draft EC Directive on Distance Marketing of Financial Services (COM (1998) 468) will fill this gap.

[70] SI 1998 No 3170.

[71] 97/66/EC. The Regulations came into force on 1 May 1999.

The DTI made it clear during the consultation period that the Regulations, and in particular, the word 'calls', are not intended to extend to e-mail solicitations.[72] However more recently, while consulting generally on issues surrounding electronic commerce,[73] the DTI have suggested that one way forward on the problem of spam might be to extend these Regulations expressly to cover e-mail.

There are two clear problems, however, with both the existing Distance Selling protection and the possible extension of the Telecoms Regulations. First, the difficulties of enforcing EU rules against predominantly American spammers are as compelling here as they were in relation to the Data Protection Act. Secondly, even if there were some kind of practical co-operation from the US in enforcing these rules, an 'opt-out' regime—which both sets of rules envisage— is of very little practical help. Human nature is such that even faced with a constant source of annoyance, very few people are equipped to find out that a regulatory scheme exists which may help them, and even fewer will then make the effort to register their veto on spam. Most independent (ie not connected with the direct marketing industry) commentators agree that an opt-in scheme for spam would be more appropriate, under which consumers would have to indicate (bizarrely) their actual *desire* to receive spam. This is particularly so given that the Distance Selling Directive already prescribes a mandatory 'opt-in' regime for junk faxes and automated calling machines,[74] which repetitively contact certain telephone numbers and then either play a pre recorded message or connect the consumer to a human salesperson when the call is answered. The reason why these means of selling are distinguished from ordinary distance selling is, in the case of faxes, because the costs of marketing are transferred from seller to recipient, and in the case of automated calling machines, because of the extreme aggravation they cause. Both reasons apply to spam, and therefore it seems remarkable that the DTI has not so far taken the opportunity given to unambiguously prescribe an opt-in regime for spam.[75] At the moment however (September 2000) they are resolutely sitting on the fence.

It should also be noted that 'opt-in' is rather easier to achieve in relation to business-to-consumer (B2C) e-commerce than traditional distance selling. Any consumer who buys something from a web site can be offered a box to click if they want to 'receive further information'. This would do as 'opt-in'; there is no need for it be done via a central register as with 'opt-out', so for small busi-

---

[72] See *Telecoms Data Protection Directive Implementation In the UK—Draft Regulations*, para 2.3 at http://www.dti.gov/CII/tdpd/condoc2.ytm.

[73] See *Building Confidence in Electronic Commerce*, 5 March 1999, para s 28–31, at http://www.dti.gov.uk/CII/elec/elec/elec_com.html.

[74] See Art 12(1). It is noteworthy that even in the US, the home of free speech, automated calling machines are banned (although enforcement of this is patchy) and this ban has been upheld as constitutional (see *Moser* v. *Federal Communications Commission* 46 F.3d 970 (9th Cir. 1995).

[75] The November 1999 consultation on implementation of the Distance Selling Directive (supra) does seem to move closer towards a view that spam should be classed as more invasive and annoying than ordinary hard copy unsolicited communications, and therefore more appropriately controlled by an opt-in regime.

nesses, 'opt-in' may actually be a cheaper regime under which to operate than 'opt-out' where search fees will be a significant overhead. A final problem with 'opt-out' regimes is that spammers in the US (who have already shown they are generally undaunted by law in the UK or EU in relation to data protection) may well just see a list of customers who have 'opted out' as a list of particularly tempting targets—to put it bluntly, since these people presumably tend not to receive traditional junk mail or EC based spam, they will be fresh meat for US based spam.[76] No doubt any list of consumers opting out from spam will in theory be held securely, but since it will have to be made available to spammers to fulfil its purpose—so that they can strike opt-outs from their mailing lists— how long can it be before it is circulating the Net or publicly available on a web site?

Finally there are some rather toothless proposals relating to commercial communications in the EC Electronic Commerce Directive, Arts 6 and 7, which has recently made its way through the co-decision procedure of the European Parliament and was finalised on 8 June 2000.[77] First, commercial communications must be 'transparent' in the sense that certain information must be compulsorily available which identifies the sender, adequately discloses the nature and conditions of promotional offers made by the communication, etc.[78] Secondly, *unsolicited* commercial communications must be 'clearly and unambiguously' identifiable as such as soon as they arrive. The obvious way to implement such labelling in the case of spam at least is by requiring a word such as 'advertising' to appear on the subject line of any spam e-mail. It is dubious how useful such a provision is, and when the DTI suggested it as one of the options for dealing with spam in its consultation document on promoting electronic commerce[79] there was little enthusiasm for it from respondents.[80] Labelling may spare the sensibilities of recipients who are spared the experience of opening a message labelled (say) 'Advertising: red hot porn', but will do little for the more economic problems caused by spam discussed above, eg, the on-line time they waste being downloaded and deleted, and the clogging up of Internet bandwidth. Labelling *will* give email filtering systems a tag to act upon, but may also interfere with users forwarding spam to ISP postmasters and other spam 'vigilantes' so that they can be 'blacklisted' (see below) as they are currently encouraged to do. And as for the general transparency requirements, why again would spammers, especially those from outwith the EC, comply, when they have generally failed to follow any other rules or business etiquette? Enforcement will certainly require, even within the EC, a considerable budget

---

[76] This point is made by Clive Feather of Demon Internet in his response to the DTI consultation document, supra, no 61. See http://www.davros.org/legal/ecommsub.html.

[77] *Supra*, n 9. .

[78] The Draft Directive suggests that such information might satisfactorily be provided by a hyper link in the case of a web page making a commercial communication; such a link could also be placed in an email.

[79] *Supra*, n. 61.

[80] See http://www.dti.gov.uk/CII/elec/conrep.htm at para 24.

for investigation, given the ease of falsifying one's origins on the Internet, something which is exacerbated further by the current growth in Europe of free ISP accounts. What is most noticeable in Arts 6 and 7 is the absence of any decision by the Commission and Parliament to enforce the implementation of 'opt-in' regimes. Art 7 provides merely that states must 'respect the opt-out registers'; although since the E Commerce Directive is a minimum harmonisation this still leaves it open to individual states to implement more stringent regimes if they so wish.

THE FUTURE?

So far we have surveyed a rather gloomy terrain upon which legal solutions to the problem of spam present themselves, and then, like ghosts, fade away when confronted with the spectre of enforceability. We seem to be at the stage where everyone knows there is a problem, but no one knows what to do. As noted above, the DTI made tentative efforts in March 1999 to suggest a number of solutions to spam in its consultation document on promoting electronic commerce, but reached the dispiriting conclusion that the problem should be left at the moment for industry to resolve, although the government would retain a watching brief and might be required to muster a legal response to deal with persistent offenders.[81] The EC Commission and Parliament are also well appraised of the problem, but so far have done little more to address it than subsume the problem into the general issues of consumer protection and regulation of commercial communications, despite some last minute efforts by MEPs during the Parliament reading of the Draft E-Commerce Directive to add an amendment which would have banned unsolicited spam altogether.[82] These interventions have in the end resulted only in the provision of Art. 7(2) noted above which enjoins member states to take measures to ensure that *'service providers'* provide means by which consumers can register their desire to opt out from unsolicited commercial communications. 'Service providers' are defined in Art 2 of the Directive as natural or legal persons providing an 'Information Society service', which essentially means any service provided commercially at a distance via electronic equipment or networks, at the individual request of a customer. In other words, *states* are not being enjoined themselves to provide an opt out scheme; instead responsibility is being passed, it seems, to spammers and to ISPs to 'self regulate' the spamming industry. This is a predictable response, given the EC's current action plan in relation to unwelcome Internet content control generally[83] but is again of dubious utility. How exactly are ISPs to know with-

---

[81] *Ibid.*, in 'Notes on responses to specific questions'.

[82] The Committee on Culture, Youth, Education and the Media also recommended an amendment to the Directive which would have required prior consent from consumers to unsolicited commercial communications; however this was not adopted.

[83] See Edwards, p. 303.

out constant monitoring (specifically not required by Art 15 of the Directive) whether spammers using the ISP are respecting any opt-out register, however collected? How are non-European spammers to be cajoled into respecting opt-out registers at all, as discussed above? And in any case, the objections raised generally to opt-out as opposed to opt-in schemes above apply *passim*.

As Dickie notes,[84] although the EC does have a longstanding commitment to consumer protection, at the moment in terms of *Internet* regulation, the dominant focus seems to be liberalisation of the market, inspired by fears that over-regulation will impede European industry in its drive to catch up with the US in the development of e-commerce. Similar trends can be seen in the UK[85] in the DTI's approach to Internet regulation. All this, combined with the globalised nature of the spam problem, seems to have conspired to leave both consumers and ISPs as disempowered victims of spam.

This lies in odd contrast to developments in the US, which has also in recent years leant towards light-handed regulation of the Internet industry. Despite this liberal tendency, there has been a flood in recent years of US state legislation specially tailored to deal with the spam problem and a number of federal proposed statutes are also working their way through the legislative process.[86] At least 18 states have enacted anti-spam legislation to date. The best known state statute is probably that passed by Washington State in March 1998[87] which not only makes it an offence to send unsolicited e mail and to provide a false reply to or origin address, but also provides civil remedies of damages for actual harm caused to an ISP or recipient.[88] The Californian Internet Consumer Protection Act, which came into force in January 1999, has in addition the interesting approach of pointedly giving teeth to anti-spam clauses imposed in ISP contracts by authorising ISPs to sue violators for damages for $50 per message, to a maximum of $25,000 per day.[89] It is possible that the US has taken the route of statutory control of spam, not least because there is at least a fighting chance of being able to find and sue or prosecute the spammers there. Many state spam statutes have provisions exerting jurisdiction over persons outwith the state who send unsolicited e-mail to residents within the state, and clearly a Federal statute would be able to provide country-wide sanctions. But the US is also disadvantaged in terms of legislating for spam in that statutes have to be tailored narrowly to withstand the challenge that the government is restricting the First

---

[84] *Supra*, n. 11.

[85] Some European states, notably Germany and Austria, have however passed legislation which explicitly makes it illegal to send unsolicited email.

[86] A full list of US state legislation in this area can be found at http://www.jmls.edu/cyber/statutes/email/state.html.

[87] House Bill 2752, subsequently amended by HB 1037.

[88] The Washington State anti-spam law was however declared invalid on 10 March 2000 as violating the interstate commerce clause of the US Constitution by being 'unduly restrictive and burdensome', the claim upheld being that the law restricted legitimate business more than it aided consumers. An appeal is in progress.

[89] However this statute was also ruled unconstitutional on 19 June 2000 by a San Francisco state court (*Ferguson* v. *Friendfinder*.)

Amendment and Commerce Clause rights of spammers,[90] while the EU in this area is only largely impeded in its competence by the issue of freedom of movement of commercial communications within the single market.[91] In fact both of the US statutes mentioned above have been declared invalid as contrary to the First Amendment (subject to possible appeals) during the course of writing this chapter, a fascinating example of a legal system divided schizophrenically on how to regulate the Internet.[92]

Within the knowledgeable Internet community itself, there is a fair degree of consensus that the best results will come not from legal regulation at all, but from 'self regulation' by technical strategies or fixes.[93] There are a number of less or more successful approaches. The first line of defence is that ISPs, local network managers, and individual users can use filtering software to remove e-mails sent from the addresses of known spammers. This however is only ever partially effective as the addresses of spammers change constantly (using guest, free or anonymous accounts), and are in any case usually disguised. There is some degree of co-operative 'blacklisting' of sites and ISPs known to harbour spammers : one such blacklist often consulted by system administrators is known as the Real Time Black Hole List and is available on the Web.[94] Traffic coming from a blacklisted site will not be transmitted on via other networks or ISPs where administrators have consulted the blacklist, with the effect that the black-listed site becomes isolated from the rest of the Internet. However no such system is foolproof, and a site which is being made use of by spammers against its own policies, or one which is sending out multiple copies of an e-mail for a valid reason (eg an alumni e-mailing from a university) may find itself black-listed alongside the 'guilty' sites.[95] It has been suggested that mistaken placing of a site on the list might be seen as libellous, which also provides a disincentive to co-operate in providing information to the organisers.

Another simple mode of protection which is becoming commoner with the advent of more sophisticated e-mail programs[96] is to restrict the number of people who can receive a copy of a single message. Again however this can be counter-productive when there are legitimate reasons to mail a large number of people at once. Sophisticated e-mail servers can also be configured to notice any difference

[90] See further Byrne, *supra* n 7, and Goldstone 'A Funny Thing Happened on the Way To The Cyber Forum: Public v. Private in Cyberspace Speech' (1998) 69 *U of Colorado Law Rev* 1. It has been held that it is *not* an unconstitutional infringement of the right of free speech for an ISP to take steps to filter out or prevent spam arriving in mailboxes: this is because an ISP is a private actor, not an organ of the state, See *Cyber Promotions Inc* v. *AOL* CA No 96-2486, November 4 1996.

[91] Arts 28 and 49 of the EC Treaty.

[92] See ns 88 and 89 above.

[93] See Dallman and Dowling, *supra* n. 6.

[94] Run by the Mail Abuse Protection System (MAPS). See further http://maps.vix.com.

[95] Both Harvard University and Virgin Net have at one time been listed on the Real Time Black Hole List.

[96] For example, Pegasus Mail, a mail program used extensively in universities, affixes information to the header of any email mesage sent to more than 50 recipients, indicating if it is 'moderate', 'bulk' or 'mass' distribution. Systems administrators on receiving networks can then use their filtering tools to reject any message sent to more than a certain number of recipients.

between the true origin of an e-mail message and a fake 'repy-to' address in the message header. It is not then difficult to filter out all mail with fake reply addresses on the basis that it is almost certainly spam.[97] Finally both ISPs[98] and networks increasingly have 'acceptable use' policies which prohibit spamming. For example, JANET, the UK academic network, has a policy that its network cannot be used for the transmission of unsolicited commercial or advertising material.[99] Such policies, like laws, are difficult to enforce against determined spammers (every UK academic, it has to be said, still receives spam), but they well be a useful disincentive to spammers of a more amateur variety and will open the door to sanctions of a local nature such as suspension of user accounts.

This article began by asking if there was a case for legal regulation of junk electronic mail. In this concluding paragraph, it seems that although a case can be established, the legal solutions currently available may be at best only moderately effective and at worst either ineffective or actively counter productive. Although technical solutions may offer the best current hope of a practical solution, this should not be seen as a blanket excuse for governments in Europe to opt out of their responsibility to help clean up the Internet for both private users and businesses. Nor can they expect the problem to go away simply by packaging it off to be dealt with by ineffective self regulatory codes negotiated with the direct marketing industry or ISPs. Both European governments and the EU must actively seek American support and co-operation, in this area as in the field of data protection, if what is effectively an American vice is not to be exported without impediment to the rest of the world.[100] However the recent protracted and halting status of negotiations between the EU and the US on trans-border data flows and 'safe harbour' provisions does not inspire great sanguinity that this approach will bear fruit in a hurry.[101] In the end it may be that as with other vices currently afflicting the Internet such as child pornography, the way forward for the EU nations is some kind of concerted Action Plan by virtue of which hard cash is put on the table, not only to improve technical fixes, but also to provide public education as to what opt-out (and one hopes, in future, opt-in) schemes are available to empower consumers to avoid unsolicited commercial communications of all kinds, and to support ISPs, such as America Online in the States, who are prepared to go to court to protect their client base and reputation from the tinge of spam. This has merely been a progress report on the long road to stamping out spam.

---

[97] Unfortunately the commonest email server software, Microsoft Exchange, is currently not configurable to reject falsified addresses.

[98] For the ISP Association's approach, see *supra* n. 18.

[99] See http://www.ja.net/documents/use.html.

[100] It is worth noting however that a determined victim of spamming can take the fight to the US courts. The UK Internet company Bibiliotech sued spammer Sam Khuri in the US and in March 2000 were awarded undisclosed damages plus a ruling that Khuri would have to pay $1000 dollars to any future person spammed. This is the first case involving a European company brought against a spammer in the US courts.

[101] See further Charlesworth, Ch. 5.

14

Legal Regulation of Telecommunications: The Impact on Internet Services

PAUL CARLYLE*

There has been considerable discussion in legal journals in recent years on the liability of Internet Service Providers (ISPs) for content made available via their service. A body of jurisprudence is developing which tends to address the issues from the content perspective. Much has been said about liability for defamation on the internet and the recent case of *Godfrey* v. *Demon Internet*[1] has brought this question to the fore once more. However, one area of law that has a major commercial impact on all Internet businesses (and in particular ISPs), and which is often overlooked in legal commentaries, is regulation of telecommunications. The impact of telecommunications regulation on Internet businesses can easily be dismissed as a purely economic issue but is actually very much a legal issue, and is increasingly critical for ISPs as it becomes more and more a driver for both their revenue stream and relations with other businesses. Publicity throughout the year 2000 surrounding local loop unbundling and high-speed internet access has only served to emphasise this point.

One critical area of the Internet that tends to receive less attention is the operation of the telecommunications links to and within the Internet. The general approach is to complain about the speed of connection and otherwise forget about this area of the Internet which permits the whole thing to work. This chapter will seek to explore to some extent the role that telecommunications regulation plays in the development of the Internet and the impact that this has on the economics of Internet service provision. Two particular regulatory issues which have aroused recent debate will be considered and then, finally, the role of telecommunications regulation in the future of the Internet revolution will be considered.

---

* Paul Carlyle of Shepherd & Wedderburn, is a solicitor specialising in telecommunications, information technology and intellectual property law with Shepherd & Wedderburn and a member of both the firm's Competition and Regulation Group and Intellectual Property and Technology Group. Email: <Paul.Carlyle@shepwedd.co.uk>.

[1] *Godfrey* v. *Demon Internet Limited* [1999] ITCLR 282.

ROLE OF THE REGULATOR

As other chapters have explained, the myth of the Internet as an unregulated anarchic community is largely false. When one looks away from content issues and into the hardware and infrastructure issues it becomes clear that operation of the Internet in the UK relies very heavily on the regulatory structure which surrounds the operation of telecommunications in the UK.

The history of telecommunications regulation in the UK dates from the privatisation of public telecommunications provision in 1984. At this point British Telecommunications plc was created, having almost a monopoly in the telecommunications sector.[2] To restrict the extent to which BT could abuse the power given to it by its market position and to encourage other operators into the market the Telecommunications Act 1984—which created the deregulated market in communications in the UK—created the role of the Director General of Telecommunications. The Director's administration—OFTEL—is the more commonly known manifestation of this role, but the Act places the obligation of regulation squarely on the shoulders of the individual appointed as Director from time to time.[3]

Telecoms regulation operates at two levels in the UK. First, the Telecommunications Act 1984 requires all telecoms operators to be licensed under the Act[4] and the Director, as regulator, administers the operation and compliance of operators with licences.

Secondly, competition law has a very important role in controlling the operations of telecommunications operators. At present each licence contains a 'Fair Trading' condition[5] which effectively contains the standard competition law tests derived from Articles 81 and 82 of the Treaty of Rome, and which is enforced by OFTEL. Historically this has given OFTEL the power to enforce European competition law directly in the absence of equivalent UK legislation. Under the Competition Act 1998, however, the prohibitions in Chapter 1 and Chapter 2 will effectively replicate Articles 81 and 82, and will give the Director General of Telecommunications a specific role to enforce these in the telecommunications sphere, all of which will remove the need for the Fair Trading

---

[2] The creation of Mercury Communications was intended to create some form of competition although Mercury was very much the junior player in this market at that time.

[3] At the time of writing the current Director General is David Edmonds although the role is perhaps most commonly associated with his predecessor, Don Cruikshank.

[4] UK Licences are issued in terms of s.7 of the Telecommunications Act 1984. The UK government has recently completed the process of amending all Telecommunications Act licences to comply with the requirements of Dir. 97/13/EC (of the European Parliament and Council on a common framework for general authorisations and individual licences in the field of Telecommunications services). This process has brought all licences into a common form and new licences were issued to all operators during Sept. 1999.

[5] Condition 31 of both the current British Telecommunications Licence and the standard form Fixed PTO Licence is the Fair Trading Condition.

Condition.[6] Other competition law powers are also exercised by OFTEL[7] and will continue to be under the 1998 Act. This level of regulation has a significant impact on the operation of the various telecommunications links which make Internet communication possible. Although ISPs are not directly regulated, they have a significant interest in the regulatory approach to telecommunications.

The Internet itself is a very robust network which operates largely on a packet switched basis. Thus failures in one line of the web do not have a significant impact on functionality as data can be routed another way. However, access to customers or users is the key to success for Internet businesses and the weak link, from both a technical and economic perspective, is the connection between the user and the ISP, and in particular the local connection from user to the local exchange.

Any Internet 'session' requires a real-time telecommunications link between the user and his ISP which normally involves the following operations (see Figure 1 below):

1. A dial-up (or ISDN or leased line) connection from the users PC via the copper telephone line to the local exchange (the 'local loop'[8]);
2. conveyance of the call by the originating operator (usually BT) via the 'trunk' network using digitally managed switch units 'DMSU' to a point of interconnect with another telecommunications operator's network;
3. translation of the '0845' or similar number to a geographical number (e.g. 0131) representing the site of the ISP so that the call can be routed to the correct location (Number Translation Services 'NTS'); and
4. conveyance of the call by the interconnecting operator to the ISP's premises where it connects to their modem/server infrastructure.

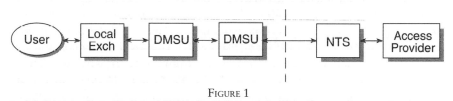

FIGURE 1

---

[6] It should be noted that the Fair Trading Condition is drafted in current licences as coming to an end on 31 July 2001, or earlier if legislation is introduced to give the Director General powers to enforce prohibitions similar to the Fair Trading Condition (e.g. The Competition Act 1998).

[7] Certain powers of the Director General of Fair Trading under the Fair Trading Act 1973 and the Competition Act 1980 were transferred to the Director General of Telecommunications in terms of the Telecommunications Act 1984 in respect of telecommunications services and apparatus. The Competition Act 1998 specifically empowers the Director General of Telecommunications in relation to the Chapter 1 and Chapter 2 prohibition in respect of telecommunications matters. OFTEL has published guidelines on how the 1998 Act will apply to telecommunications which can be found at www.oftel.gov.uk/competition/cact0100.htm. The position is the same for other utility regulators.

[8] Local loop is the term used to describe the lines which connect buildings and customers to the fibre optic cable network. It is often referred to as 'the last half-mile' of cabling. BT's historical position as a nationalised telecommunications operator has resulted in the privatised company owning the majority of the local loop in the UK.

All the operations in Figure 1 above give rise to a call charge to the user (at local rates) for every minute that they are connected. A proportion of the revenue charged to the user by the operator who originates the call is passed to the interconnecting operator, who in turn passes a proportion to the ISP. In the debate over the relative merits of free and subscription ISPs this charge for Internet usage is often lost sight of. In actual fact this charge represents a very significant proportion of the income for an ISP.[9] Why does this interconnection charge arise?

British Telecom, as the former nationalised telecommunications operator, controls over 85 per cent of the local loop link to domestic and small business customers in the UK.[10] Consequently BT has significant market power giving it effective control over the link used to access ISPs, creating what has become known as a 'bottleneck service'. To overcome this, and similar situations where BT has such market dominance, BT has been forced by the regulator to permit interconnection to its network by other operators so that it can access customers through its local loop network.[11]

INTERCONNECTION CHARGES FOR NUMBER TRANSLATION SERVICES

However, notwithstanding that BT is required to provide access to the local loop it can still control the bottleneck service by pricing for such access in such a way that other operators and ISPs cannot economically access the local loop.

Internet access using '0845' numbers at local rate is one of a range of telecommunication services which have become known as Number Translation Services ('NTS'). This definition includes free rate calls (0800 or 0500), and premium rate calls (0891 etc.). Common to all of these services is a requirement to translate the number from the general 'non-geographic' number to the relevant geographic number (e.g. 0207, 0161 or 0141), which is known as number translation. Also common to these services is a requirement for revenue sharing between the originating operator (e.g. BT) and the terminating operator.[12] The principle of revenue sharing arises from the fact that the telecommunications network provides the only 'channel to market' for the services offered[13] and also because the availability of such services creates use of the network and thus rev-

---

[9] OFTEL estimates that for subscription ISPs revenue is divided 60/40 between subscription revenue and interconnection revenue.

[10] OFTEL Consultation document—*Access to Bandwidth: Proposals for Action* (July 1999), Section 1.2, which can be found at www.oftel.gov.uk/competition/llu0799.htm.

[11] The Telecommunications (Interconnection) Regs. 1998, see also Dir. 97/33/EC on interconnection in telecommunications with regard to ensuring universal service and interoperability through application of the principles of open network provision.

[12] The terminating operator is the operator who hosts the service (such as Internet access) at the other end of the call.

[13] The type of services offered include premium and national rate information services for a very wide range of interests from football scores to weather forecasts, free calls to other information services (e.g. helpdesks) and, of course Internet access.

enue for the operator. In this way a mixture of competition law and commerciality promotes revenue-sharing between the originating operator and the service provider (via the terminating operator).

In 1996, OFTEL took a direct role in relation to the distribution of revenue for such services, imposing a formula to calculate such distribution (the 'NTS Formula'). The formula sets out the amount of the revenue from customers which is retained by the originating operator. This formula is consequently a very important issue for Internet Service Providers as it controls approximately 40 per cent of their revenue on average. It is probable that the recent explosion in subscription-free Internet service providers[14] is directly related to the existence of this formula as it provides a reliable source of income. This is a point very much recognised by OFTEL.[15] The increase in Internet users which the success of free services has created has caused a massive increase in the use of the Internet.[16]

In 1998 British Telecom reported that for the first year ever it carried more minutes of data traffic than voice and the average length of each telephone call has increased over the last 10 years by nearly 20 minutes, which is largely due to Internet access. This is a huge increase in the demands being made on the telecommunications infrastructure and BT is concerned that its responsibility for a significant proportion of the local loop means that the demand for investment to maintain the level of service is equally increasing. This is particularly the case as more complex Internet applications demand more and more bandwidth, of which see more below.

Balanced against this is the fact that BT's income (or retention) from NTS services is limited by the NTS Formula. Consequently, the NTS Formula has been the source of significant debate over the course of 1998 and 1999. BT and other originating operators (principally cable companies) have sought a greater share of the revenue in order to meet the additional requirements for investment, while at the same time the terminating operators want a larger share of the division as the ISPs arguably provide the innovative services which are creating the increase in demand for call minutes.

Initially, OFTEL accepted that the NTS Formula was not designed specifically with the current high level of Internet use in mind and sought to encourage the operators to reach agreement between themselves, but when a solution could not be reached by the end of 1998, OFTEL stepped in. In March 1999, OFTEL produced a consultation paper[17] in which it considered in detail the arguments for alteration of the NTS Formula on both sides. Ultimately, OFTEL

---

[14] The initial Dixons Freeserve offering was quickly joined by other free Internet offerings from *inter alia* Tesco, BT (BT ClickFree), and America On-line.

[15] OFTEL Consultation Paper on *The Relationship between Retail Prices and Interconnection Charges for Number Translation Services* (Mar. 1999), Section 1.8.

[16] In 1998 there were 80,000 new Internet users every day—Department of Trade and Industry White Paper, *Our Competitive Future: Building the Knowledge Driven Economy* (Cm 4176, The Stationery Office, London) at section 1.3 of the Digital Economy chapter.

[17] OFTEL *supra* n.15.

proposed that the principles of the NTS Formula should remain in place until August 2001 on the basis that the current price control position imposed on BT is to be reviewed at this point anyway by OFTEL in consultation with the other operators and BT.

Although the position remains largely as it was, the extremely fast development of the telecommunications and Internet industries will doubtless ensure that by 2001 the technical drivers for these economic decisions will have moved on again. The Internet service provision industry in the UK depends on these regulatory decisions for survival, and will be carefully following the development of the argument over the next two years. The development of unmetered services where flat rates are charged for unlimited Internet connection time will in time reduce the impact of the NTS formula on the economics of the Internet in the UK although this solution is already attracting significant regulatory and competition attention.[18] In the end, in the time taken to resolve the NTS issue, the debate has moved on to unmetered services.

BANDWIDTH ACCESS: COMBATING THE WORLD WIDE WAIT

The second example of an area where regulation of telecommunications impacts on the development of the Internet is that of access to bandwidth.

The development of more efficient browser software and better Web site design, together with the investment by Internet service providers in more and faster modems, has meant that references to the 'world wide wait' rather than 'world wide web' have become more infrequent in recent years.[19] However, the telecoms 'buzz-word' for some years has been 'convergence'. This refers to convergence and concentration between telecommunications, entertainment, Internet content provision and broadcasting. Radio and certain video items can be accessed already via the Internet and the development of Internet protocol voice telephony and Internet video conferencing among other Internet applications are all driving the ever increasing demand for faster Internet connection.

Current high bandwidth solutions such as ISDN or broadband fibre access are expensive and largely out of reach of domestic users and small businesses. This is an issue of general functionality and also a barrier to the development of e-commerce on the Internet. Only once the full capabilities of Internet technology are available to a substantial proportion of potential customers will full exploitation of electronic commerce and the interactive possibilities of the Internet be possible. However, new technology will permit the copper lines of the local loop to be used to provide high speed Internet access. Currently the

---

[18] See OFTEL's 26 May 2000 determination of a dispute between BT and MCI Worldcom concerning the provision of a Flat Rate Internet Access Call Origination product (FRIACO), www.oftel.gov.uk/competition/fria0500.htm.

[19] Although the demise of the online retailer Boo.com in May 2000 was attributed to some extent to the site being slow and difficult to use for customers.

most talked about of these technologies is Asynchronous Digital Subscriber Loop or ADSL technology.[20]

The key to rolling out such services is the use of the existing local loop which avoids the laying of new lines into the premises of customers, and again the dominant market position of British Telecommunications is proving to be an obstacle to progress. Unless BT is willing to roll out this technology across all of its local loop, the increased speed of Internet access will not be available to the majority of UK Internet users. Alternatives such as high bandwidth cable networks are only available to very few users.[21]

In order to justify regulatory intervention, OFTEL has reviewed the position and stated that the regulator considers that there are barriers to competition arising and that customers (particularly small businesses) are not being provided with the high bandwidth services they wish to purchase, when the relevant technology to provide such services is in theory available. Consequently, OFTEL has concluded that there is a case for regulatory intervention.[22]

In December 1998, OFTEL started the debate by consulting on five options for creating competition in ADSL provision and promoting the supply of high bandwidth services.[23] Each of these options involved upgrading the local loop to make ADSL available as a wholesale offering. Some involved BT implementing the upgrade and making this available to other operators permitting them to provide high bandwidth services to users over the BT upgraded local loop. Others took the more radical approach of permitting competing operators to have access to BT's local exchanges for the purpose of implementing new technology themselves, leasing the local loop connection from BT. From a wider telecommunications view this involves the much discussed 'unbundling' of the local loop.[24]

This consultation produced responses concentrating on two of the five options and OFTEL produced a further consultation paper in July 1999 identifying these two options (known as Option 2 and Option 4) and expressing a preference for Option 2.[25] OFTEL's preferred option involved permitting competing operators access to the BT local loop so that they can upgrade the connections from the local exchange to end users and provide high-speed services. BT has clearly expressed a preference for Option 4 which would involve BT

---

[20] In simple terms this involves routing traffic over the local loop and then directly over the Internet protocol backbone to the relevant Internet service provider.

[21] OFTEL estimates that cable networks currently only pass around 50% of UK homes and that only 16% of homes actually take cable services capable of providing high speed Internet access at present—*Access to Bandwidth: Proposals for Action* (July 1999) at section 3.4; see www.oftel.gov.uk/competition/llu0799.htm.

[22] *Ibid*, at section 3.2 .

[23] *Access to Bandwidth: Bringing Higher Bandwidth Services to the Consumer* (Dec. 1998).

[24] As noted above the local loop owned by the privatised telecoms company has a significant impact on the operation of deregulated telecoms services. In 1999 the Netherlands implemented a significant unbundling process and the European Commission announced in May 2000 that it would require all Member States to implement unbundling of the local loop.

[25] *Access to Bandwidth: Proposals for Action*, *supra* n 21.

itself carrying out these upgrades and making the upgraded service available as a wholesale service to competing operators on a non-discriminatory basis to permit them to provide high-speed services over the upgraded local loop to end users.

BT's preferred option would leave the timing and implementation of ADSL technology up to BT which, although OFTEL may consider regulatory controls on roll out, would again create the barrier to progress of high bandwidth access across the UK. BT's priorities for the geographic areas to start this roll out and the overall timing may not reflect the market's requirements, nor those of the competing operators. It would also leave the choice of the relevant technology to BT. OFTEL's option would avoid this problem but would involve a number of other issues such as the terms on which operators would be provided with access to local exchanges. There are also a number of technical matters to be resolved. Both options create difficulty in the regulation of the charges which BT can make for the use of its facilities.

The OFTEL proposal would represent a small but very significant change in the regulatory approach to telecommunications in the UK and is a matter which is likely to cause BT substantial concern. Providing competing operators with access to BT's network infrastructure will impact severely on the value to BT of its major asset in defending its position in the market. The consultation period for this second consultation ended on 30 September 1999.

In early August 1999 BT announced a very substantial investment in rolling out ADSL technology to a large amount of its local network. Commentators at the time suggested that this was part of an effort by BT to ensure that by the end of the consultation period the arguments against Option 4 (BT's preferred option) would be weaker as ADSL technology will soon be available to much of the country in any event, without requiring competitors to be given access to the local loop and local exchanges.

However, OFTEL responded by welcoming this development but noting that this still did not overcome its concerns that competing operators required to be able to take their own decisions on when, where and how to roll out this technology. In November 1999, an OFTEL statement confirmed that a new clause was to be introduced into BT's licence under the Telecommunications Act to implement OFTEL's Option 2. As a result, provision of unbundled loops is to be introduced by July 2001.[26]

Consultation on the licence condition was undertaken in April 2000 and consultation is ongoing as to the pricing proposals between BT, the regulator and other operators. In addition, BT has declared that, notwithstanding the Option 2 approach which OFTEL has forced it to follow, it will also offer Option 4 unbundling as a wholesale offering to other telecoms operators. The new condition in BT's licence was inserted on 8 August 2000 with OFTEL expressing the hope that this will permit other operators to bring forward a wide range of new telecoms offerings.

[26] *Access to Bandwidth: Delivering Competition for the Information Age* (Nov. 1999), available at www.oftel.gov.uk/competition/a2b1199.htm.

The outcome of this debate has had, and will continue to have, a significant impact, in the short term, on the services which Internet service providers can offer, and the design of e-commerce solutions. In the longer term new technologies may however make this debate less important, if not entirely irrelevant.

NEW TECHNOLOGY

Both these debates result from the control which BT currently exerts over the local loop, which is a historical position arising from BT's former position as a nationalised utility. Consequently, BT has 'Significant Market Power' which is the telecommunications legislation equivalent of having a 'Dominant Position' in terms of Article 82 of the Treaty of Rome (as amended). BT's operation of a bottleneck service gives rise to regulatory intervention to control BT's operations and promote competition in a market where competitors are at a historical disadvantage.

However, new technologies are coming to the fore. At the time of writing the government has just awarded five UMTS[27] licences through a very lucrative auction procedure. These licences will permit the licensee to develop a network for the next generation of mobile communication technology, which is designed to provide high speed data access as well as the current voice capability.[28] The roll out of Fixed Radio Access ('FRA')[29] services as an alternative to BT's local loop continues to grow and the recently commissioned Iridium network of low-level satellites has the potential to offer high-speed data communications without relying on existing local loop technology.[30] In the short term WAP protocol mobile telephones are providing a limited type of Internet access. This technology will in time remove the reliance on the local loop for access to the Internet which gives rise to the NTS formula and unmetered call debates, and will provide high speed alternatives to ADSL for bandwidth access.

The availability of alternatives to the BT local loop will create competition in the market for the ' last half mile' connection between the trunk network and the customer. ISPs will no longer be reliant on BT to provide connectivity to

[27] Universal Mobile Telecommunications System. This is the third generation of mobile telephone technology which will operate in conjunction with the current second generation (GSM) protocols to provide data transfer service at high speeds using mobile technology.

[28] However, the mobile operators who were successful in the auction required to pay vast sums to win the licences (in some cases in excess of £20bn) and the recovery of these costs (together with the costs of building the UMTS networks) may in the short term restrict UMTS services from competing on a price basis with the local loop for data access.

[29] A radio-based telecommunications system which replaces the copper local loop with radio access directly between an aerial at the user's premises and a base station connected to the operator's network. FRA Licences are controlled by the Radio Communications Authority.

[30] Although at the time of writing the Iridium project was filing for bankruptcy protection in the US with debts of $1.45 billion. The company has begun talks on restructuring seeking to convert $1.45 billion of debt into equity and to extend bank loans. Investors may have no alternative as many of Iridium's assets are in orbit.

customers and the need for regulatory input will inevitably fall away. Already the creation of US-style unmetered call Internet offerings such as BT's 'SurfTime' can in some way be attributed to this competitive threat.

In fact, the position of ISPs will radically alter. Providers of network infrastructure will look to find ways of attracting users to their network and the provision of Internet services will be one weapon in the battle for minutes. ISPs with significant customer bases will become even more attractive partners for network providers.[31]

Once there are realistic alternatives to local loop technology the rationale behind regulatory and competition law action against BT and other formerly nationalised telecommunications operators will be less prevalent. Essentially, technology may provide its own competition to the local loop, without regulators creating artificial competitive structures.

However, these are developing technologies which may take some time to gain market share against the existing operators. In the meantime the trend is towards more regulation of Internet related activities rather than less.

THE FUTURE OF REGULATION FOR THE INTERNET

Regulation is not a precise tool, the requirement for consultation often hindering the process of licence modification with substantial delays.[32] This must be contrasted with the speed of development of Internet technology which can often leave legal debates behind. However, the current position where Internet businesses have to date largely escaped the operation of direct regulation is almost inevitably to change.

The debates over the NTS Formula and access to bandwidth demonstrate how the economics and technology of Internet businesses can be very much subject to regulatory decisions and the telecommunications regime. These are only two examples of how current telecommunications regulation can apply to the Internet. The battles between operators over unmetered flat rate access are only just beginning.[33] The next challenge for the Internet is that of convergence between Internet, telecommunications and broadcasting services. This will cause changes both in the services provided by Internet businesses and in the regulatory structures which exist to control these services.

Internet protocol telephony presents a good example of such a new service. Technology now allows Internet users to communicate by voice using the packet switched protocol of the Internet. The main attraction of this is that

---

[31] AOL and BT are already offering subscription services which involve freephone access to the internet. The revenue stream for this service is in fact the internet monthly subscription. Freeserve is offering free calls to their internet service but only to Energis customers, thus attracting users to the Energis service for other purposes.

[32] Although it should be noted that Part III of the Electronic Communications Act 2000 contains provisions for streamlining the procedure for modifying Telecommunications Act licences.

[33] See *supra* n. 19.

long-distance connections can be achieved at local call rates (or within whatever Internet access offering is being used). Traditionally, voice telephony has been the most heavily regulated service in terms of UK and European legislation and the specific offering of this service is likely to be a regulated service in the near future.[34] An example of both a new service and a new regulatory structure is to be found in the Electronic Communications Act 2000 which provides for Cryptography Service Providers to be approved under a voluntary mechanism operated under delegated authority from the Secretary of State.[35] The Act does not specify a particular body to which this authority will be delegated, although it was proposed in the government's consultation paper in April 1999 that the Director General of Telecommunications would be given this responsibility, being the first occasion that Internet services providers would fall under direct regulation by OFTEL.[36]

In recent times a number of ISPs have been acquired by telecommunications operators.[37] Largely this is driven by a desire to concentrate interconnection revenues but it also brings Internet service provision under the wing of directly regulated businesses.

In conclusion, there are a number of reasons in the short term for the current telecommunications regulatory regime to apply in certain areas of Internet operation. In the longer term these reasons may have less weight. At the same time convergence of telecommunications, Internet and broadcasting services continues to bring Internet service provision within the realms of both the telecommunications and broadcasting regulatory regimes and as time goes on it is safe to predict that Internet service provision will be caught up in the ongoing changes which will serve to combine the two regimes.[38]

The question of regulation of Internet services is a difficult one. At present, existing regulation mainly affects the infrastructure issues and is aimed at ensuring competition in the market in areas where there is a risk of one or more operators having too much economic power. As set out above, it is likely that the justifications for this type of regulation will fall away. However, by contrast,

---

[34] The European Commission issued a statement in Jan. 1998 to the effect that internet protocol telephony is not currently within the definition of 'voice telephony' for the purposes of European legislation on liberalisation of telecommunications. However, it made it clear that as the technology improves such that internet telephony become more reliable then it is likely that it will be included within that definition. See 'Status of Voice Communications on Internet under Community Law and, in particular, under Directive 90/388/EC' [1998] OJ C6/4.

[35] Electronic Communications Act 2000, Part I.

[36] *Building Confidence in Electronic Commerce* (Mar. 1999). Responses to this paper from the industry were not in favour of appointing OFTEL here, and this has been a constant theme throughout the consultation process on the Bill. At the time of writing this Part of the Act is not yet in force and the final resolution on who will be delegated this role has yet to become clear.

[37] Energis has acquired the ISP Planet On-Line, MCI Worldcom took over the French ISP Internet Way and Demon Internet is a division of Thus plc.

[38] See the Government Green Paper, *Regulating Communications: Approaching Convergence in the Information Age* (1999), the follow up paper, *Results of the Consultation on the Convergence Green Paper* (1999) and Long, 'Whether and How to Regulate Convergence' [1999] *CTLR* 1 for further information on regulation of converging services.

regulatory activity on the Internet is likely to increase in relation to the content that is transmitted and accessed using Internet services, as the number of people able to gain such access increases. However, as with the early years of broadcasting, there is a fine line between content regulation and censorship and any form of regulation will be viewed as contrary to the spirit of the Internet.[39] This is the challenge for regulators and all Internet based industries as the new century develops.

This chapter is not intended to provide a complete overview of the application of telecommunications regulation to Internet businesses, but rather to look at some examples of the significant economic impact which such regulation can have, and to underscore that this area of law has a major role in the future of the Internet. At this point in the development of the telecommunications industry both the industry and its regulators are changing very quickly. While it is possible to predict firmly that there will continue to be change over the coming years, and to predict (less firmly) that regulation will continue to play a growing role in the Internet, it is impossible to predict with certainty the final outcome of the battle between the Internet and those who would seek to regulate it. However, what is clear is that for current Internet businesses issues affecting their revenue stream, such as licensing, bandwidth and hardware regulation, are of equal or greater importance to issues affecting of legal liability for the content they carry, even though the latter may attain a higher public profile.

ADDENDUM

By way of a postscript, and a recognition of the speed of development in this area, it is perhaps worthy of note that in the period between submission of this chapter and proofreading the unmetered call debate has continued to rage with operators withdrawing flat rate offerings as they cannot economically support them at the rates charged by BT for the wholesale service. In addition, BT's pedestrian approach on local loop unbundling has caused OFTEL to be criticised from Europe for failing to sufficiently regulate. With calls being made for the resignation of the Director General over this issue it is clear that in a short period of time we have moved from telecoms regulation being a very substantial driver for the development of the Internet, to the Internet being a substantial driver in the development of telecommunications regulation.

---

[39] The issues of content regulation and censorship are discussed further in Edwards, Chapters 12.

Appendix I

I

(Acts whose publication is obligatory)

DIRECTIVE 2000/31/EC OF THE EUROPEAN PARLIAMENT AND OF THE COUNCIL
of 8 June 2000

on certain legal aspects of information society services, in particular electronic commerce, in the Internal market (Directive on electronic commerce)

THE EUROPEAN PARLIAMENT AND THE COUNCIL OF THE EUROPEAN UNION

Having regard to the Treaty establishing the European Community, and in particular Articles 47(2), 55 and 95 thereof,

Having regard to the proposal from the Commission,[1]

Having regard to the opinion of the Economic and Social Committee,[2]

Acting in accordance with the procedure laid down in Article 251 of the Treaty,[3]

Whereas:

(1) The European Union is seeking to forge ever closer links between the States and peoples of Europe, to ensure economic and social progress; in accordance with Article 14(2) of the Treaty, the internal market comprises an area without internal frontiers in which the free movements of goods, services and the freedom of establishment are ensured; the development of information society services within the area without internal frontiers is vital to eliminating the barriers which divide the European peoples.

(2) The development of electronic commerce within the information society offers significant employment opportunities in the Community, particularly in small and medium-sized enterprises, and will stimulate economic growth and investment in

---

[1] OJ C 30, 5.2.1999, p. 4.
[2] OJ C 169, 16.6.1999, p. 36.
[3] Opinion of the European Parliament of 6 May 1999 (OJ C 279, 1.10.1999, p. 389), Council common position of 28 February 2000 (OJ C 128, 8.5.2000, p. 32) and Decision of the European Parliament of 4 May 2000 (not yet published in the Official Journal).

innovation by European companies, and can also enhance the competitiveness of European industry, provided that everyone has access to the Internet.

(3)   Community law and the characteristics of the Community legal order are a vital asset to enable European citizens and operators to take full advantage, without consideration of borders, of the opportunities afforded by electronic commerce; this Directive therefore has the purpose of ensuring a high level of Community legal integration in order to establish a real area without internal borders for information society services.

(4)   It is important to ensure that electronic commerce could fully benefit from the internal market and therefore that, as with Council Directive 89/552/EEC of 3 October 1989 on the coordination of certain provisions laid down by law, regulation or administrative action in Member States concerning the pursuit of television broadcasting activities,[4] a high level of Community integration is achieved.

(5)   The development of information society services within the Community is hampered by a number of legal obstacles to the proper functioning of the internal market which make less attractive the exercise of the freedom of establishment and the freedom to provide services; these obstacles arise from divergences in legislation and from the legal uncertainty as to which national rules apply to such services; in the absence of coordination and adjustment of legislation in the relevant areas, obstacles might be justified in the light of the case-law of the Court of Justice of the European Communities; legal uncertainty exists with regard to the extent to which Member States may control services originating from another Member State.

(6)   In the light of Community objectives, of Articles 43 and 49 of the Treaty and of secondary Community law, these obstacles should be eliminated by coordinating certain national laws and by clarifying certain legal concepts at Community level to the extent necessary for the proper functioning of the internal market; by dealing only with certain specific matters which give rise to problems for the internal market, this Directive is fully consistent with the need to respect the principle of subsidiarity as set out in article 5 of the Treaty.

(7)   In order to ensure legal certainty and consumer confidence, this Directive must lay down a clear and general framework to cover certain legal aspects of electronic commerce in the internal market.

(8)   The objective of this Directive is to create a legal framework to ensure the free movement of information society services between Member States and not to harmonise the field of criminal law as such.

(9)   The free movement of information society services can in many cases be a specific reflection in Community law of a more general principle, namely freedom of expression as enshrined in Article 10(1) of the Convention for the Protection of Human Rights and Fundamental Freedoms, which has been ratified by all the Member States; for this reason, directives covering the supply of information society services must ensure that this activity may be engaged in freely in the light of that Article, subject only to the restrictions laid down in paragraph 2 of that Article and in

---

[4] OJ L 298, 17.10.1989, p. 23. Directive as amended by Directive 97/36/EC of the European Parliament and of the Council (OJ L 202, 30.7.1997, p. 60).

Article 46(1) of the Treaty; this Directive is not intended to affect national fundamental rules and principles relating to freedom of expression.

(10) In accordance with the principle of proportionality, the measures provided for in this Directive are strictly limited to the minimum needed to achieve the objective of the proper functioning of the internal market; where action at Community level is necessary, and in order to guarantee an area which is truly without internal frontiers as far as electronic commerce is concerned, the Directive must ensure a high level of protection of objectives of general interest, in particular the protection of minors and human dignity, consumer protection and the protection of public health; according to Article 152 of the Treaty, the protection of public health is an essential component of other Community policies.

(11) This Directive is without prejudice to the level of protection for, in particular, public health and consumer interests, as established by Community acts; amongst others, Council Directive 93/13/EEC of 5 April 1993 on unfair terms in consumer contracts[5] and Directive 97/7/EC of the European Parliament and of the Council of 20 May 1997 on the protection of consumers in respect of distance contracts[6] form a vital element for protecting consumers in contractual matters; those Directives also apply in their entirety to information society services; that same Community acquis, which is fully applicable to information society services, also embraces in particular Council Directive 84/450/EEC of 10 September 1984 concerning misleading and comparative advertising,[7] Council Directive 87/102/EEC of 22 December 1986 for the approximation of the laws, regulations and administrative provisions of the Member States concerning consumer credit,[8] Council Directive 93/22/EEC of 10 May 1993 on investment services in the securities field,[9] Council Directive 90/314/EEC of 13 June 1990 on package travel, package holidays and package tours,[10] Directive 98/6/EC of the European Parliament and of the Council of 16 February 1998 on consumer protection in the indication of prices of products offered to consumers,[11] Council Directive 92/59/EEC of 29 June 1992 on general product safety,[12] Directive 94/4/EC of the European Parliament and of the Council of 26 October 1994 on the protection of purchasers in respect of certain aspects of contracts relating to the purchase of the right to use immovable properties on a timeshare basis,[13] Directive 98/27/EC of the European Parliament and of the Council of 19 May 1998 on injunctions for the protection of consumers' interests,[14] Council Directive 85/374/EEC of 25 July 1985 on the approximation of the laws,

[5] OJ L 95, 21.4.1993, p. 29.

[6] OJ L 144, 4.6.1999, p. 19.

[7] OJ L 250, 19.9.1984, p. 17. Directive as amended by Directive 97/55/EC of the European Parliament and of the Council (OJ L 290, 23.10.1997, p. 18).

[8] OJ L 42, 12.2.1987, p. 48. Directive as last amended by Directive 98/7/EC of the European Parliament and of the Council (OJ L 101, 1.4.1998, p. 17).

[9] OJ L 141, 11.6.1993, p. 27. Directive as last amended by Directive 97/9/EC of the European Parliament and of the Council (OJ L 84, 26.3.1997, p. 22).

[10] OJ L 158, 23.6.1990, p. 59.

[11] OJ L 80, 18.3.1998, p. 27.

[12] OJ L 228, 11.8.1992, p. 24.

[13] OJ L 280, 29.10.1994, p. 83.

[14] OJ L 166, 11.6.1998, p. 51. Directive as amended by Directive 1999/44/EC (OJ L 171, 7.7.1999, p. 23).

regulations and administrative provisions concerning liability for defective products,[15] Directive 1999/44/EC of the European Parliament and of the Council of 25 May 1999 on certain aspects of the sale of consumer goods and associated guarantees,[16] the future Directive of the European Parliament and of the Council concerning the distance marketing of consumer financial services and Council Directive 92/28/EEC of 31 March 1992 on the advertising of medicinal products;[17] this Directive should be without prejudice to Directive 98/43/EC of the European Parliament and of the Council of 6 July 1998 on the approximation of the laws, regulations and administrative provisions of the Member States relating to the advertising and sponsorship of tobacco products[18] adopted within the framework of the internal market, or to directives on the protection of public health; this Directive complements information requirements established by the abovementioned Directives and in particular Directive 97/7/EC.

(12) It is necessary to exclude certain activities from the scope of this Directive, on the grounds that the freedom to provide services in these fields cannot, at this stage, be guaranteed under the Treaty or existing secondary legislation; excluding these activities does not preclude any instruments which might prove necessary for the proper functioning of the internal market; taxation, particularly value added tax imposed on a large number of the services covered by this Directive, must be excluded from the scope of this Directive.

(13) This Directive does not aim to establish rules on fiscal obligations nor does it preempt the drawing up of Community instruments concerning fiscal aspects of electronic commerce.

(14) The protection of individuals with regard to the processing of personal data is solely governed by Directive 95/46/EC of the European Parliament and of the Council of 24 October 1995 on the protection of individuals with regard to the processing of personal data and on the free movement of such data[19] and Directive 97/66/EC of the European Parliament and of the Council of 15 December 1997 concerning the processing of personal data and the protection of privacy in the telecommunications sector[20] which are fully applicable to information society services; these Directives already establish a Community legal framework in the field of personal data and therefore it is not necessary to cover this issue in this Directive in order to ensure the smooth functioning of the internal market, in particular the free movement of personal data between Member States; the implementation and application of this Directive should be made in full compliance with the principles relating to the protection of personal data, in particular as regards unsolicited commercial communication and the liability of intermediaries; this Directive cannot prevent the anonymous use of open networks such as the Internet.

---

[15] OJ L 210, 7.8.1985, p. 29. Directive as amended by Directive 1999/34/EC (OJ L 141, 4.6.1999, p. 20).
[16] OJ L 171, 7.7.1999, p. 12.
[17] OJ L 113, 30.4.1992, p. 13.
[18] OJ L 213, 30.7.1998, p. 9.
[19] OJ L 281, 23.11.1995, p. 31.
[20] OJ L 24, 30.1.1998, p. 1.

(15) The confidentiality of communications is guaranteed by Article 5 Directive 97/66/EC; in accordance with that Directive, Member States must prohibit any kind of interception or surveillance of such communications by others than the senders and receivers, except when legally authorised.

(16) The exclusion of gambling activities from the scope of application of this Directive covers only games of chance, lotteries and betting transactions, which involve wagering a stake with monetary value; this does not cover promotional competitions or games where the purpose is to encourage the sale of goods or services and where payments, if they arise, serve only to acquire the promoted goods or services.

(17) The definition of information society services already exists in Community law in Directive 98/34/EC of the European Parliament and of the Council of 22 June 1998 laying down a procedure for the provision of information in the field of technical standards and regulations and of rules on information society services[21] and in Directive 98/84/EC of the European Parliament and of the Council of 20 November 1998 on the legal protection of services based on, or consisting of, conditional access;[22] this definition covers any service normally provided for remuneration, at a distance, by means of electronic equipment for the processing (including digital compression) and storage of data, and at the individual request of a recipient of a service; those services referred to in the indicative list in Annex V to Directive 98/34/EC which do not imply data processing and storage are not covered by this definition.

(18) Information society services span a wide range of economic activities which take place on-line; these activities can, in particular, consist of selling goods on-line; activities such as the delivery of goods as such or the provision of services off-line are not covered; information society services are not solely restricted to services giving rise to on-line contracting but also, in so far as they represent an economic activity, extend to services which are not remunerated by those who receive them, such as those offering on-line information or commercial communications, or those providing tools allowing for search, access and retrieval of data; information society services also include services consisting of the transmission of information via a commercial network, in providing access to a communication network or in hosting information provided by a recipient of the service; television broadcasting within the meaning of Directive EEC/89/552 and radio broadcasting are not information society services because they are not provided at individual request; by contrast, services which are transmitted point to point, such as video-on-demand or the provision of commercial communications by electronic mail are information society services; the use of electronic mail or equivalent individual communications for instance by natural persons acting outside their trade, business or profession including their use for the conclusion of contracts between such persons is not an information society service; the contractual relationship between an employee and his employer is not an information society service; activities which by their very nature cannot be carried out at a distance and by electronic means, such as the statutory

---

[21] OJ L 204, 21.7.1998, p. 37. Directive as amended by Directive 98/48/EC (OJ L 217, 5.8.1998, p. 18).
[22] OJ L 320, 28.11.1998, p. 54.

auditing of company accounts or medical advice requiring the physical examination of a patient are not information society services.

(19) The place at which a service provider is established should be determined in conformity with the case-law of the Court of Justice according to which the concept of establishment involves the actual pursuit of an economic activity through a fixed establishment for an indefinite period; this requirement is also fulfilled where a company is constituted for a given period; the place of establishment of a company providing services via an Internet website is not the place at which the technology supporting its website is located or the place at which its website is accessible but the place where it pursues its economic activity; in cases where a provider has several places of establishment it is important to determine from which place of establishment the service concerned is provided; in cases where it is difficult to determine from which of several places of establishment a given service is provided, this is the place where the provider has the centre of his activities relating to this particular service.

(20) The definition of 'recipient of a service' covers all types of usage of information society services, both by persons who provide information on open networks such as the Internet and by persons who seek information on the Internet for private or professional reasons.

(21) The scope of the coordinated field is without prejudice to future Community harmonisation relating to information society services and to future legislation adopted at national level in accordance with Community law; the coordinated field covers only requirements relating to on-line activities such as on-line information, on-line advertising, on-line shopping, on-line contracting and does not concern Member States' legal requirements relating to goods such as safety standards, labelling obligations, or liability for goods, or Member States' requirements relating to the delivery or the transport of goods, including the distribution of medicinal products; the coordinated field does not cover the exercise of rights of pre-emption by public authorities concerning certain goods such as works of art.

(22) Information society services should be supervised at the source of the activity, in order to ensure an effective protection of public interest objectives; to that end, it is necessary to ensure that the competent authority provides such protection not only for the citizens of its own country but for all Community citizens; in order to improve mutual trust between Member States, it is essential to state clearly this responsibility on the part of the Member State where the services originate; moreover, in order to effectively guarantee freedom to provide services and legal certainty for suppliers and recipients of services, such information society services should in principle be subject to the law of the Member State in which the service provider is established.

(23) This Directive neither aims to establish additional rules on private international law relating to conflicts of law nor does it deal with the jurisdiction of Courts; provisions of the applicable law designated by rules of private international law must not restrict the freedom to provide information society services as established in this Directive.

(24) In the context of this Directive, notwithstanding the rule on the control at source of information society services, it is legitimate under the conditions established in this

Directive for Member States to take measures to restrict the free movement of information society services.

(25) National courts, including civil courts, dealing with private law disputes can take measures to derogate from the freedom to provide information society services in conformity with conditions established in this Directive.

(26) Member States, in conformity with conditions established in this Directive, may apply their national rules on criminal law and criminal proceedings with a view to taking all investigative and other measures necessary for the detection and prosecution of criminal offences, without there being a need to notify such measures to the Commission.

(27) This Directive, together with the future Directive of the European Parliament and of the Council concerning the distance marketing of consumer financial services, contributes to the creating of a legal framework for the on-line provision of financial services; this Directive does not pre-empt future initiatives in the area of financial services in particular with regard to the harmonisation of rules of conduct in this field; the possibility for Member States, established in this Directive, under certain circumstances of restricting the freedom to provide information society services in order to protect consumers also covers measures in the area of financial services in particular measures aiming at protecting investors.

(28) The Member States' obligation not to subject access to the activity of an information society service provider to prior authorisation does not concern postal services covered by Directive 97/67/EC of the European Parliament and of the Council of 15 December 1997 on common rules for the development of the internal market of Community postal services and the improvement of quality of service[23] consisting of the physical delivery of a printed electronic mail message and does not affect voluntary accreditation systems, in particular for providers of electronic signature certification service.

(29) Commercial communications are essential for the financing of information society services and for developing a wide variety of new, charge-free services; in the interests of consumer protection and fair trading, commercial communications, including discounts, promotional offers and promotional competitions or games, must meet a number of transparency requirements; these requirements are without prejudice to Directive 97/7/EC; this Directive should not affect existing Directives on commercial communications, in particular Directive 98/43/EC.

(30) The sending of unsolicited commercial communications by electronic mail may be undesirable for consumers and information society service providers and may disrupt the smooth functioning of interactive networks; the question of consent by recipient of certain forms of unsolicited commercial communications is not addressed by this Directive, but has already been addressed, in particular, by Directive 97/7/EC and by Directive 97/66/EC; in Member States which authorise unsolicited commercial communications by electronic mail, the setting up of appropriate industry filtering initiatives should be encouraged and facilitated; in addition it is necessary that in any event unsolicited commercial communications are clearly

[23] OJ L 15, 21.1.1998, p. 14.

identifiable as such in order to improve transparency and to facilitate the functioning of such industry initiatives; unsolicited commercial communications by electronic mail should not result in additional communication costs for the recipient.

(31) Member States which allow the sending of unsolicited commercial communications by electronic mail without prior consent of the recipient by service providers established in their territory have to ensure that the service providers consult regularly and respect the opt-out registers in which natural persons not wishing to receive such commercial communications can register themselves.

(32) In order to remove barriers to the development of cross-border services within the Community which members of the regulated professions might offer on the Internet, it is necessary that compliance be guaranteed at Community level with professional rules aiming, in particular, to protect consumers or public health; codes of conduct at Community level would be the best means of determining the rules on professional ethics applicable to commercial communication; the drawing-up or, where appropriate, the adaptation of such rules should be encouraged without prejudice to the autonomy of professional bodies and associations.

(33) This Directive complements Community law and national law relating to regulated professions maintaining a coherent set of applicable rules in this field.

(34) Each Member State is to amend its legislation containing requirements, and in particular requirements as to form, which are likely to curb the use of contracts by electronic means; the examination of the legislation requiring such adjustment should be systematic and should cover all the necessary stages and acts of the contractual profess, including the filing of the contract; the result of this amendment should be to make contracts concluded electronically workable; the legal effect of electronic signatures is dealt with by Directive 1999/93/EC of the European Parliament and of the Council of 13 December 1999 on a Community framework for electronic signatures;[24] the acknowledgement of receipt by a service provider may take the form of the on-line provision of the service paid for.

(35) This Directive does not affect Member States' possibility of maintaining or establishing general or specific legal requirements for contracts which can be fulfilled by electronic means, in particular requirements concerning secure electronic signatures.

(36) Member States may maintain restrictions for the use of electronic contracts with regard to contracts requiring by law the involvement of courts, public authorities, or professions exercising public authority; this possibility also covers contracts which require the involvement of courts, public authorities, or professions exercising public authority in order to have an effect with regard to third parties as well as contracts requiring by law certification or attestation by a notary.

(37) Member States' obligation to remove obstacles to the use of electronic contracts concerns only obstacles resulting from legal requirements and not practical obstacles resulting from the impossibility of using electronic means in certain cases.

---

[24] OJ L 13, 19.1.2000, p. 12.

(38) Member States' obligation to remove obstacles to the use of electronic contracts is to be implemented in conformity with legal requirements for contracts enshrined in Community law.

(39) The exceptions to the provisions concerning the contracts concluded exclusively by electronic mail or by equivalent individual communications provided for by this Directive, in relation to information to be provided and the placing of orders, should not enable, as a result, the by-passing or those provisions by providers of information society services.

(40) Both existing and emerging disparities in Member States' legislation and case-law concerning liability of service providers acting as intermediaries prevent the smooth functioning of the internal market, in particular by impairing the development of cross-border services and producing distortions of competition; service providers have a duty to act, under certain circumstances, with a view to preventing or stopping illegal activities; this Directive should constitute the appropriate basis for the development of rapid and reliable procedures for removing and disabling access to illegal information; such mechanisms could be developed on the basis of voluntary agreements between all parties concerned and should be encouraged by Member States; it is in the interest of all parties involved in the provision of information society services to adopt and implement such procedures; the provisions of this Directive relating to liability should not preclude the development and effective operation, by the different interested parties, of technical systems of protection and identification and of technical surveillance instruments made possible by digital technology within the limits laid down by Directives 95/46/EC and 97/66/EC.

(41) This Directive strikes a balance between the different interests at stake and establishes principles upon which industry agreements and standards can be based.

(42) The exemptions from liability established in this Directive cover only cases where the activity of the information society service provider is limited to the technical process of operating and giving access to a communication network over which information made available by third parties is transmitted or temporarily stored, for the sole purpose of making the transmission more efficient; this activity is of a mere technical, automatic and passive nature, which implies that the information society service provides has neither knowledge of nor control over the information which is transmitted or stores.

(43) A service provides can benefit from the exemptions for 'mere conduit' and for 'caching' when he is in no way involved with the information transmitted; this requires among other things that he does not modify the information that he transmits; this requirement does not cover manipulations of a technical nature which take place in the course of the transmission as they do not alter the integrity of the information contained in the transmission.

(44) A service provider who deliberately collaborates with one of the recipients of his service in order to undertake illegal acts goes beyond the activities of 'mere conduit' or 'caching' and as a result cannot benefit from the liability exemptions established for these activities.

(45) The limitations of the liability of intermediary service providers established in this Directive do not affect the possibility of injunctions of different kinds; such

injunctions can in particular consist of orders by courts or administrative authorities requiring the termination or prevention of any infringement, including the removal of illegal information or the disabling of access to it.

(46) In order to benefit from a limitation of liability, the provider of an information society service, consisting of the storage of information, upon obtaining actual knowledge or awareness of illegal activities has to act expeditiously to remove or to disable access to the information concerned; the removal or disabling of access has to be undertaken in the observance of the principle of freedom of expression and of procedures established for this purpose at national level; this Directive does not affect Member States' possibility of establishing specific requirements which must be fulfilled expeditiously prior to the removal or disabling of information.

(47) Member States are prevented from imposing a monitoring obligation on service providers only with respect to obligations of a general nature; this does not concern monitoring obligations in a specific case and, in particular, does not affect orders by national authorities in accordance with national legislation.

(48) This Directive does not affect the possibility for Member States of requiring service providers, who host information provided by recipients of their service, to apply duties of care, which can reasonably be expected from them and which are specified by national law, in order to detect and prevent certain types of illegal activities.

(49) Member States and the Commission are to encourage the drawing-up of codes of conduct; this is not to impair the voluntary nature of such codes and the possibility for interested parties of deciding freely whether to adhere to such codes.

(50) It is important that the proposed directive on the harmonisation of certain aspects of copyright and related rights in the information society and this Directive come into force within a similar time scale with a view to establishing a clear framework of rules relevant to the issue of liability of intermediaries for copyright and relating rights infringements at Community level.

(51) Each Member State should be required, where necessary, to amend any legislation which is liable to hamper the use of schemes for the out-of-court settlement of disputes through electronic channels; the result of this amendment must be to make the functioning of such schemes genuinely and effectively possible in law and in practice, even across borders.

(52) The effective exercise of the freedoms of the internal market makes it necessary to guarantee victims effective access to means of settling disputes; damage which may arise in connection with information society services is characterised both by its rapidity and by its geographical extent; in view of this specific character and the need to ensure that national authorities do not endanger the mutual confidence which they should have in one another, this Directive requests Member States to ensure that appropriate court actions are available; Member States should examine the need to provide access to judicial procedures by appropriate electronic means.

(53) Directive 98/27/EC, which is applicable to information society services, provides a mechanism relating to actions for an injunction aimed at the protection of the collective interests of consumers; this mechanism will contribute to the free movement of information society services by ensuring a high level of consumer protection.

(54) The sanctions provided for under this Directive are without prejudice to any other sanction or remedy provided under national law; Member States are not obliged to provide criminal sanctions for infringement of national provisions adopted pursuant to this Directive.

(55) This Directive does not affect the law applicable to contractual obligations relating to consumer contracts; accordingly, this Directive cannot have the result of depriving the consumer of the protection afforded to him by the mandatory rules relating to contractual obligations of the law of the Member State in which he has his habitual residence.

(56) As regards the derogation contained in this Directive regarding contractual obligations concerning contracts concluded by consumers, those obligations should be interpreted as including information on the essential elements of the content of the contract, including consumer rights, which have a determining influence on the decision to contract.

(57) The Court of Justice has consistently held that a Member State retains the right to take measures against a service provider that is established in another Member State but directs all or most of his activity to the territory of the first Member State if the choice of establishment was made with a view to evading the legislation that would have applied to the provider had he been established on the territory of the first Member State.

(58) The Directive shall not apply to services supplied by service providers established in a third country; in view of the global dimension of electronic commerce, it is, however, appropriate to ensure that the Community rules are consistent with international rules; this Directive is without prejudice to the results of discussions within international organisations (amongst others WTO, OECD, Uncitral) on legal issues.

(59) Despite the global nature of electronic communications, coordination of national regulatory measures at European Union level is necessary in order to avoid fragmentation of the internal market, and for the establishment of an appropriate European regulatory framework; such coordination should also contribute to the establishment of a common and strong negotiating position in international forums.

(60) In order to allow the unhampered development of electronic commerce, the legal framework must be clear and simple, predictable and consistent with the rules applicable at international level so that it does not adversely affect the competitiveness of European industry or impede innovation in that sector.

(61) If the market is actually to operate by electronic means in the context of globalisation, the European Union and the major non-European areas need to consult each other with a view to making laws and procedures compatible.

(62) Cooperation with third countries should be strengthened in the area of electronic commerce, in particular with applicant countries, the developing countries and the European Union's other trading partners.

(63) The adoption of this Directive will not prevent the Member States from taking into account the various social, societal and cultural implications which are inherent in

the advent of the information society; in particular it should not hinder measures which Member States might adopt in conformity with Community law to achieve social, cultural and democratic goals taking into account their linguistic diversity, national and regional specificities as well as their cultural heritage, and to ensure and maintain public access to the widest possible range of information society services; in any case, the development of the information society is to ensure that Community citizens can have access to the cultural European heritage provided in the digital environment.

(64) Electronic communication offers the Member States an excellent means of providing public services in the cultural, educational and linguistic fields.

(65) The Council, in its resolution of 19 January 1999 on the consumer dimension of the information society,[25] stressed that the protection of consumers deserved special attention in this field; the Commission will examine the degree to which existing consumer protection rules provide insufficient protection in the context of the information society and will identify, where necessary, the deficiencies of this legislation and those issues which could require additional measures; if need be, the Commission should make specific additional proposals to resolve such deficiencies that will thereby have been identified,

HAVE ADOPTED THIS DIRECTIVE:

CHAPTER I

GENERAL PROVISIONS

Article 1

Objective and scope

1.   This Directive seeks to contribute to the proper functioning of the internal market by ensuring the free movement of information society services between the Member States.

2.   This Directive approximates, to the extent necessary for the achievement of the objective set out in paragraph 1, certain national provisions on information society services relating to the internal market, the establishment of service providers, commercial communications, electronic contracts, the liability of intermediaries, codes of conduct, out-of-court dispute settlements, court actions and cooperation between Member States.

3.   This Directive complements Community law applicable to information society services without prejudice to the level of protection for, in particular, public health and consumer interests, as established by Community acts and national legislation implementing them in so far as this does not restrict the freedom to provide information society services.

---

[25] OJ C 23, 28.1.1999, p. 1.

4. This Directive does not establish additional rules on private international law nor does it deal with the jurisdiction of Courts.

5. The Directive shall not apply to:

(a) the field of taxation;
(b) questions relating to information society services covered by Directives 95/46/EC and 97/66/EC;
(c) questions relating to agreements or practices governed by cartel law:
(d) the following activities of information society services:
— the activities of notaries or equivalent professions to the extent that they involve a direct and specific connection with the exercise of public authority,
— the representation of a client and defence of his interests before the courts,
— gambling activities which involve wagering a stake with monetary value in games of chance, including lotteries and betting transactions.

6. This Directive does not affect measures taken at Community or national level, in the respect of Community law, in order to promote cultural and linguistic diversity and to ensure the defence of pluralism.

Article 2

Definitions

For the purpose of this Directive, the following terms shall bear the following meanings:

(a) 'information society services': services within the meaning of Article 1(2) of Directive 98/34/EC as amended by Directive 98/48/EC;
(b) 'service provider': any natural or legal person providing an information society service;
(c) 'established service provider': a service provider who effectively pursues an economic activity using a fixed establishment for an indefinite period. The presence and use of the technical means and technologies required to provide the service do not, in themselves, constitute an establishment of the provider;
(d) 'recipient of the service': any natural or legal person who, for professional ends or otherwise, uses an information society service, in particular for the purposes of seeking information or making it accessible;
(e) 'consumer': any natural person who is acting for purposes which are outside his or her trade, business or profession;
(f) 'commercial communication': any form of communication designed to promote, directly or indirectly, the goods, services or image of a company, organisation or person pursuing a commercial, industrial or craft activity or exercising a regulated profession. The following do not in themselves constitute commercial communications:
— information allowing direct access to the activity of the company, organisation or person, in particular a domain name or an electronic-mail address,
— communications relating to the goods, services or image of the company, organisation or person compiled in an independent manner, particularly when this is without financial consideration;
(g) 'regulated profession': any profession within the meaning of either Article 1(d) of Council Directive 89/48/EEC of 21 December 1988 on a general system for the

recognition of higher-education diplomas awarded on completion of professional education and training of at least three-years' duration[26] or of Article 1(f) of Council Directive 92/51/EEC of 18 June 1992 on a second general system for the recognition of professional education and training to supplement Directive 89/48/EEC;[27]

(h) 'coordinated field': requirements laid down in Member States' legal systems applicable to information society service providers or information society services, regardless of whether they are of a general nature or specifically designed for them.

  (i) The coordinated field concerns requirements with which the service provider has to comply in respect of:
    — the taking up of the activity of an information society service, such as requirements concerning qualifications, authorisation or notification,
    — the pursuit of the activity of an information society service, such as requirements concerning the behaviour of the service provider, requirements regarding the quality or content of the service including those applicable to advertising and contracts, or requirements concerning the liability of the service provider.

  (ii) The coordinated field does not cover requirements such as:
    — requirements applicable to goods as such,
    — requirements applicable to the delivery of goods,
    — requirements applicable to services not provided by electronic means.

Article 3

Internal market

1. Each Member State shall ensure that the information society services provided by a service provider established on its territory comply with the national provisions applicable in the Member State in question which fall within the coordinated field.

2. Member States may not, for reasons falling within the coordinated field, restrict the freedom to provide information society services from another Member State.

3. Paragraphs 1 and 2 shall not apply to the fields referred to in the Annex.

4. Member States may take measures to derogate from paragraph 2 in respect of a given information society service if the following conditions are fulfilled:

(a) the measures shall be:
  (i) necessary for one of the following reasons:
    — public policy, in particular the prevention, investigation, detection and prosecution of criminal offences, including the protection of minors and the fight against any incitement to hatred on grounds of race, sex, religion or nationality, and violations of human dignity concerning individual persons,
    — the protection of public health,
    — public security, including the safeguarding of national security and defence,
    — the protection of consumers, including investors;

---

[26] OJ L 19, 24.1.1989, p. 16.
[27] OJ L 209, 24.7.1992, p. 25. Directive as last amended by Commission Directive 97/38/EC (OJ L 184, 12.7.1997, p. 31).

(ii) taken against a given information society service which prejudices the objectives referred to in point (i) or which presents a serious and grave risk of prejudice to those objectives;

(iii) proportionate to those objectives;

(b) before taking the measures in question and without prejudice to court proceedings, including preliminary proceedings and acts carried out in the framework of a criminal investigation, the Member State has:

— asked the Member State referred to in paragraph 1 to take measures and the latter did not take such measures, or they were inadequate,

— notified the Commission and the Member State referred to in paragraph 1 of its intention to take such measures.

5.   Member States may, in the case of urgency, derogate from the conditions stipulated in paragraph 4(b). Where this is the case, the measures shall be notified in the shortest possible time to the Commission and to the Member State referred to in paragraph 1, indicating the reasons for which the Member State considers that there is urgency.

6.   Without prejudice to the Member State's possibility of proceeding with the measures in question, the Commission shall examine the compatibility of the notified measures with Community law in the shortest possible time; where it comes to the conclusion that the measure is incompatible with Community law, the Commission shall ask the Member State in question to refrain from taking any proposed measures or urgently to put an end to the measures in question.

CHAPTER II

PRINCIPLES

Section 1: Establishment and information requirements

Article 4

Principle excluding prior authorisation

1.   Member States shall ensure that the taking up and pursuit of the activity of an information society service provider may not be made subject to prior authorisation or any other requirement having equivalent effect.

2.   Paragraph 1 shall be without prejudice to authorisation schemes which are not specifically and exclusively targeted at information society services, or which are covered by Directive 97/13/EC of the European Parliament and of the Council of 10 April 1997 on a common framework for general authorisations and individual licences in the field of telecommunications services.[28]

Article 5

General information to be provided

1.   In addition to other information requirements established by Community law, Member States shall ensure that the service provider shall render easily, directly and

[28] OJ L 117, 7.5.1997, p. 15.

permanently accessible to the recipients of the service and competent authorities, at least the following information:

(a) the name of the service provider;
(b) the geographic address at which the service provider is established;
(c) the details of the service provider, including his electronic mail address, which allow him to be contacted rapidly and communicated with in a direct and effective manner;
(d) where the service provider is registered in a trade or similar public register, the trade register in which the service provider is entered and his registration number, or equivalent means of identification in that register;
(e) where the activity is subject to an authorisation scheme, the particulars of the relevant supervisory authority;
(f) as concerns the regulated professions:
     — any professional body or similar institution with which the service provider is registered,
     — the professional title and the Member State where it has been granted,
     — a reference to the applicable professional rules in the Member State of establishment and the means to access them:
(g) where the service provider undertakes an activity that is subject to VAT, the identification number referred to in Article 22(1) of the sixth Council Directive 77/388/EEC of 17 May 1977 on the harmonisation of the laws of the Member States relating to turnover taxes—Common system of value added tax: uniform basis of assessment.[29]

2.   In addition to other information requirements established by Community law, Member States shall at least ensure that, where information society services refer to prices, these are to be indicated clearly and unambiguously and, in particular, must indicate whether they are inclusive of tax and delivery costs.

Section 2: Commercial communications

Article 6

Information to be provided

In addition to other information requirements established by Community law, Member States shall ensure that commercial communications which are part of, or constitute, an information society service comply at least with the following conditions:

(a) the commercial communication shall be clearly identifiable as such;
(b) the natural or legal person on whose behalf the commercial communication is made shall be clearly identifiable;
(c) promotional offers, such as discounts, premiums and gifts, where permitted in the Member State where the service provider is established, shall be clearly identifiable as such, and the conditions which are to be met to qualify for them shall be easily accessible and be presented clearly and unambiguously;

---

[29] OJ L 145, 13.6.1997, p. 1. Directive as last amended by Directive 1999/85/EC (OJ L 277, 28.10.1999, p. 34).

(d) promotional competitions or games, where permitted in the Member State where the service provider is established, shall be clearly identifiable as such, and the conditions for participation shall be easily accessible and be presented clearly and unambiguously.

Article 7

Unsolicited commercial communication

1. In addition to other requirements established by Community law, Member States which permit unsolicited commercial communication by electronic mail shall ensure that such commercial communication by a service provider established in their territory shall be identifiable clearly and unambiguously as such as soon as it is received by the recipient.

2. Without prejudice to Directive 97/7/EC and Directive 97/66/EC Member States shall take measures to ensure that service providers undertaking unsolicited commercial communications by electronic mail consult regularly and respect the opt-out registers in which natural persons not wishing to receive such commercial communications can register themselves.

Article 8

Regulated professions

1. Member States shall ensure that the use of commercial communications which are part of, or constitute, an information society service provided by a member of a regulated profession is permitted subject to compliance with the professional rules regarding, in particular, the independence, dignity and honour of the profession, professional secrecy and fairness towards clients and other members of the profession.

2. Without prejudice to the autonomy of professional bodies and associations, Member States and the Commission shall encourage professional associations and bodies to establish codes of conduct at Community level in order to determine the types of information that can be given for the purposes of commercial communication in conformity with the rules referred to in paragraph 1.

3. When drawing up proposals for Community initiatives which may become necessary to ensure the proper functioning of the Internal Market with regard to the information referred to in paragraph 2, the Commission shall take due account of codes of conduct applicable at Community level and shall act in close cooperation with the relevant professional associations and bodies.

4. The Directive shall apply in addition to Community Directives concerning access to, and the exercise of, activities of the regulated professions.

Section 3: Contracts concluded by electronic means

Article 9

Treatment of contracts

1.   Member States shall ensure that their legal system allows contracts to be concluded by electronic means. Member States shall in particular ensure that the legal requirements applicable to the contractual process neither create obstacles for the use of electronic contracts nor result in such contracts being deprived of legal effectiveness and validity on account of their having been made by electronic means.

2.   Member States may lay down that paragraph 1 shall not apply to all or certain contracts falling into one of the following categories:

(a)   contracts that create or transfer rights in real estate, except for rental rights;
(b)   contracts requiring by law the involvement of courts, public authorities or professions exercising public authority;
(c)   contracts of suretyship granted and on collateral securities furnished by persons acting for purposes outside their trade, business or profession;
(c)   contracts governed by family law or by the law or succession.

3.   Member States shall indicate to the Commission the categories referred to in paragraph 2 to which they do not apply paragraph 1. Member States shall submit to the Commission every five years a report on the application of paragraph 2 explaining the reasons why they consider it necessary to maintain the category referred to in paragraph 2(b) to which they do not apply paragraph 1.

Article 10

Information to be provided

1.   In addition to other information requirements established by Community law, Member States shall ensure, except when otherwise agreed by parties who are not consumers, that at least the following information is given by the service provider clearly, comprehensibly and unambiguously and prior to the order being placed by the recipient of the service:

(a)   the different technical steps to follow to conclude the contract;
(b)   whether or not the concluded contract will be filed by the service provider and whether it will be accessible;
(c)   the technical means for identifying and correcting input errors prior to the placing of the order;
(d)   the languages offered for the conclusion of the contract.

2.   Member States shall ensure that, except when otherwise agreed by parties who are not consumers, the service provider indicates any relevant codes of conduct to which he subscribes and information on how those codes can be consulted electronically.

3.   Contract terms and general conditions provided to the recipient must be made available in a way that allows him to store and reproduce them.

4. Paragraphs 1 and 2 shall not apply to contracts concluded exclusively by exchange of electronic mail or by equivalent individual communications.

Article 11

Placing of the order

1. Member States shall ensure, except when otherwise agreed by parties who are not consumers, that in cases where the recipient of the service places his order through technological means, the following principles apply:
— the service provider has to acknowledge the receipt of the recipient's order without undue delay and by electronic means,
— the order and the acknowledgement of receipt are deemed to be received when the parties to whom they are addressed are able to access them.

2. Member States shall ensure that, except when otherwise agreed by parties who are not consumers, the service provider makes available to the recipient of the service appropriate, effective and accessible technical means allowing him to identify and correct input errors, prior to the placing of the order.

3. Paragraph 1, first indent, and paragraph 2 shall not apply to contracts concluded exclusively by exchange of electronic mail or by equivalent individual communications.

Section 4: Liability of intermediary service providers

Article 12

'Mere conduit'

1. Where an information society service is provided that consists of the transmission in a communication network of information provided by a recipient of the service, or the provision of access to a communication network, Member States shall ensure that the service provider is not liable for the information transmitted, on condition that the provider:
(a) does not initiate the transmission;
(b) does not select the receiver of the transmission; and
(c) does not select or modify the information contained in the transmission.

2. The acts of transmission and of provision of access referred to in paragraph 1 include the automatic, intermediate and transient storage of the information transmitted in so far as this takes place for the sole purpose of carrying out the transmission in the communication network, and provided that the information is not stored for any period longer than is reasonably necessary for the transmission.

3. This Article shall not affect the possibility for a court of administrative authority, in accordance with Member States' legal systems, of requiring the service provider to terminate or prevent an infringement.

Article 13

'Caching'

1. Where an information society service is provided that consists of the transmission in a communication network of information provided by a recipient of the service, member States shall ensure that the service provider is not liable for the automatic, intermediate and temporary storage of that information, performed for the sole purpose of making more efficient the information's onward transmission to other recipients of the service upon their request, on condition that:

(a) the provider does not modify the information;
(b) the provider complies with conditions on access to the information;
(c) the provides complies with rules regarding the updating of the information, specified in a manner widely recognised and used by industry;
(d) the provides does not interfere with the lawful use of technology, widely recognised and used by industry, to obtain data on the use of the information; and
(e) the provider acts expeditiously to remove or to disable access to the information it has stored upon obtaining actual knowledge of the fact that the information at the initial source of the transmission has been removed from the network, or access to it has been disabled, or that a court or an administrative authority has ordered such removal or disablement.

2. This Article shall not affect the possibility for a court or administrative authority, in accordance with Member States' legal systems, of requiring the service provider to terminate or prevent an infringement.

Article 14

Hosting

1. Where an information society service is provided that consists of the storage of information provided by a recipient of the service, Member States shall ensure that the service provider is not liable for the information stored at the request of a recipient of the service, on condition that:

(a) the provider does not have actual knowledge of illegal activity or information and, as regards claims for damages, is not aware of facts or circumstances from which the illegal activity or information is apparent; or
(b) the provider, upon obtaining such knowledge or awareness, acts expeditiously to remove or to disable access to the information.

2. Paragraph 1 shall not apply when the recipient of the service is acting under the authority or the control of the provider.

3. This Article shall not affect the possibility for a court or administrative authority, in accordance with Member States' legal systems, of requiring the service provider to terminate or prevent an infringement, nor does it affect the possibility for Member States of establishing procedures governing the removal or disabling of access to information.

Article 15

No general obligation to monitor

1.   Member States shall not impose a general obligation on providers, when providing the services covered by Articles 12, 13 and 14, to monitor the information which they transmit or store, nor a general obligation actively to seek facts or circumstances indicating illegal activity.

2.   Member States may establish obligations for information society service providers promptly to inform the competent public authorities of alleged illegal activities undertaken or information provided by recipients of their service or obligations to communicate to the competent authorities, at their request, information enabling the identification of recipients of their service with whom they have storage agreements.

CHAPTER III

IMPLEMENTATION

Article 16

Codes of conduct

1.   Member States and the Commission shall encourage:

(a) the drawing up of codes of conduct at Community level, by trade, professional and consumer associations or organisations, designed to contribute to the proper implementation of Articles 5 to 15;

(b) the voluntary transmission of draft codes of conduct at national or Community level to the Commission;

(c) the accessibility of these codes of conduct in the Community languages by electronic means;

(d) the communication to the Member States and the Commission, by trade, professional and consumer associations or organisations, of their assessment of the application of their codes of conduct and their impact upon practices, habits or customs relating to electronic commerce;

(e) the drawing up of codes of conduct regarding the protection of minors and human dignity.

2.   Member States and the Commission shall encourage the involvement of associations or organisations representing consumers in the drafting and implementation of codes of conduct affecting their interests and drawn up in accordance with paragraph 1(a). Where appropriate, to take account of their specific needs, associations representing the visually impaired and disabled should be consulted.

Article 17

Out-of-court dispute settlement

1.   Member States shall ensure that, in the event of disagreement between an information society service provider and the recipient of the service, their legislation does not

hamper the use of out-of-court schemes, available under national law, for dispute settlement, including appropriate electronic means.

2.   Member States shall encourage bodies responsible for the out-of-court settlement of, in particular, consumer disputes to operate in a way which provides adequate procedural guarantees for the parties concerned.

3.   Member States shall encourage bodies responsible for out-of-court dispute settlement to inform the Commission of the significant decisions they take regarding information society services and to transmit any other information on the practices, usages or customs relating to electronic commerce.

Article 18

Court actions

1.   Member States shall ensure that court actions available under national law concerning information society services' activities allow for the rapid adoption of measures, designed to terminate any alleged infringement and to prevent any further impairment of the interests involved.

2.   The Annex to Directive 98/27/EC shall be supplemented as follows:

   '11.   Directive 2000/31/EC of the European Parliament and of the Council of 8 June 2000 on certain legal aspects on information society services, in particular electronic commerce, in the internal market (Directive on electronic commerce) (OJ L 178, 17.7.2000, p. 1).'

Article 19

Cooperation

1.   Member States shall have adequate means of supervision and investigation necessary to implement this Directive effectively and shall ensure that service providers supply them with the requisite information.

2.   Member States shall cooperate with other Member States; they shall, to that end, appoint one or several contact points, whose details they shall communicate to the other Member States and to the Commission.

3.   Member States shall, as quickly as possible, and in conformity with national law, provide the assistance and information requested by other Member State or by the Commission, including by appropriate electronic means.

4.   Member States shall establish contact points which shall be accessible at least by electronic means and from which recipients and service providers may:

(a)   obtain general information on contractual rights and obligations as well as on the complaint and redress mechanisms available in the event of disputes, including practical aspects involved in the use of such mechanisms;

(b)   obtain the details of authorities, associations or organisations from which they may obtain further information or practice assistance.

5.   Member States shall encourage the communication to the Commission of any significant administrative or judicial decisions taken in their territory regarding disputes relating to information society services and practices, usages and customs relating to electronic commerce. The Commission shall communicate these decisions to the other Member States.

Article 20

Sanctions

Member States shall determine the sanctions applicable to infringements of national provisions adopted pursuant to this Directive and shall take all measures necessary to ensure that they are enforced. The sanctions they provide for shall be effective, proportionate and dissuasive.

CHAPTER IV

FINAL PROVISIONS

Article 21

Re-examination

1.   Before 17 July 2003, and thereafter every two years, the Commission shall submit to the European Parliament, the Council and the Economic and Social Committee a report on the application of this Directive, accompanied, where necessary, by proposals for adapting it to legal, technical and economic developments in the field of information society services, in particular with respect to crime prevention, the protection of minors, consumer protection and to the proper functioning of the internal market.

2.   In examining the need for an adaptation of this Directive, the report shall in particular analyse the need for proposals concerning the liability of providers of hyperlinks and location tool services, 'notice and take down' procedures and the attribution of liability following the taking down of content. The report shall also analyse the need for additional conditions for the exemption from liability, provided for in Articles 12 and 13, in the light of technical developments, and the possibility of applying the internal market principles to unsolicited commercial communications by electronic mail.

Article 22

Transposition

1.   Member States shall bring into force the laws, regulations and administrative provisions necessary to comply with this Directive before 17 January 2002. They shall forthwith inform the Commission thereof.

2.   When Member States adopt the measures referred to in paragraph 1, these shall contain a reference to this Directive or shall be accompanied by such reference at the time of their official publication. The methods of making such reference shall be laid down by Member States.

Article 23

Entry into force

This Directive shall enter into force on the day of its publication in the *Official Journal of the European Communities*.

Article 24

Addresses

This Directive is addressed to the Member States.

Done at Luxemburg, 8 June 2000.

For the European Parliament	*For the Council*
The President	*The President*
N. FONTAINE	G. d'OLIVEIRA MARTINS

ANNEX

DEROGATIONS FROM ARTICLE 3

As provided for in Article 3(3), Article 3(1) and (2) do not apply to:
— copyright, neighbouring rights, rights referred to in Directive 87/54/EEC[1] and Directive 96/9/EC[2] as well as industrial property rights,
— the emission of electronic money by institutions in respect of which Member States have applied one of the derogations provided for in Article 8(1) of Directive 2000/46/EC,[3]
— Article 44(2) of Directive 85/61/EEC,[4]
— Article 30 and Title IV of Directive 92/49/EEC,[5] Title IV of Directive 92/96/EEC,[6] Articles 7 and 9 of Directive 88/357/EEC[7] and Article 4 of Directive 90/619/EEC,[8]
— the freedom of the parties to choose the law applicable to their contract,
— contractual obligations concerning consumer contacts,
— formal validity of contracts creating or transferring rights in real estate where such contracts are subject to mandatory formal requirements of the law of the Member State where the real estate is situated,
— the permissibility of unsolicited commercial communications by electronic mail.

---

[1] OJ L 24, 27.1.1987, p. 36.
[2] OJ L 77, 27.3.1996, p. 20.
[3] Not yet published in the Official Journal.
[4] OJ L 375, 31.12.1983, p. 3. Directive as last amended by Directive 95/26/EC (OJ L 168, 18.7.1995, p. 7).
[5] OJ L 228, 11.8.1992, p. 1. Directive as last amended by Directive 95/26/EC.
[6] OJ L 360, 9.12.1992, p. 2. Directive as last amended by Directive 95.26/EC.
[7] OJ L 172, 4.7.1988, p. 1. Directive as last amended by Directive 92/49/EC.
[8] OJ L 330, 29.11.1990, p. 50. Directive as last amended by Directive 92/96/EC.

Appendix II

EUROPEAN PARLIAMENT AND COUNCIL DIRECTIVE

SN/2696/00 (PI)

of 8 June 2000

on certain harmonisation of certain aspects of copyright and related rights in
the Information Society

THE EUROPEAN PARLIAMENT AND THE COUNCIL OF THE EUROPEAN UNION

Having regard to the Treaty establishing the European Community, and in particular Articles 47(2), 55 and 95 thereof,

Having regard to the proposal from the Commission,[1]

Having regard to the opinion of the Economic and Social Committee,[2]

Acting in accordance with the procedure laid down in Article 251 of the Treaty,[3]

Whereas:

(1) The Treaty provides for the establishment of an Internal Market, the removal of barriers to the free movement of goods, the freedom to provide services and the right of establishment and the institution of a system ensuring that competition in the Internal Market is not distorted. Harmonisation of the laws of the Member States on copyright and related rights contributes to the achievement of these objectives;

(2) The European Council, meeting at Corfu on 24 and 25 June 1994, stressed the need to create a general and flexible legal framework at Community level in order to foster the development of the Information Society in Europe. This requires, inter alia, the existence of an Internal Market for new products and services. Important Community legislation to ensure such a regulatory framework is already in place or is well under way. Copyright and related rights play an important role in this context as they protect and stimulate the development and marketing of new products and services and the creation and exploitation of their creative content;

(2bis) The proposed harmonisation will help to implement the four freedoms of the internal market and relates to compliance with the fundamental principles of law and especially of property—including intellectual property—freedom of expression and the public interest;

---

[1] COM(97)628 final of 10.12.1997, OJ C 108, 7.4.1998, p. 6 and COM(1999) 250 final of 25.5.1999, OJ C 180, 25.6.1999, p. 6.

[2] OJ C 407, 28.12.1998, p. 30.

[3] Opinion of the European Parliament of 10.2.1999, OJ C 150, 28.5.1999, p. 171.

(3)   A harmonised legal framework on copyright and related rights, through increased legal certainty and while providing for a high level of protection of intellectual property, will foster substantial investment in creativity and innovation, including network infrastructure, and lead in turn to growth and increased competitiveness of European industry, both in the area of content provision and information technology and more generally across a wide range of industrial and cultural sectors. This will safeguard employment and encourage new job creation;

(4)   Technological development has multiplied and diversified the vectors for creation, production and exploitation. While no new concepts for the protection of intellectual property are needed, the current law on copyright and related rights will have to be adapted and supplemented to respond adequately to economic realities such as new forms of exploitation;

(5)   Without harmonisation at Community level, legislative activities at national level which have already been initiated in a number of Member States in order to respond to the technological challenges might result in significant differences in protection and thereby in restrictions on the free movement of services and products incorporating, or based on, intellectual property, leading to a refragmentation of the Internal market and legislative inconsistency. The impact of such legislative differences and uncertainties will become more significant with the further development of the Information Society, which has already greatly increased transborder exploitation of intellectual property. This development will and should further increase. Significant legal differences and uncertainties in protection may hinder economies of scale for new products and services containing copyright and related rights;

(6)   The Community legal framework for the legal protection of copyright and related rights must, therefore, also be adapted and supplemented as far as is necessary for the smooth functioning of the Internal Market. To that end, those national provisions on copyright and related rights which vary considerably from one Member State to another or which cause legal uncertainties hindering the smooth functioning of the Internal Market and the proper development of the Information Society in Europe should be adjusted, and inconsistent national responses to the technological developments should be avoided, whilst differences not adversely affecting the functioning of the Internal market need not be removed or prevented;

(7)   The various social, societal and cultural implications of the Information Society require that account be taken of the specific features of the content of products and services;

(8)   Any harmonisation of copyright and related rights must take as a basis a high level of protection, since such rights are crucial to intellectual creation. Their protection helps to ensure the maintenance and development of creativity in the interests of authors, performers, producers, consumers, culture, industry and the public at large. Intellectual property has therefore been recognised as an integral part of property;

(9)   If authors or performers are to continue their creative and artistic work, they have to receive an appropriate reward for the use of their work, as must producers in order to be able to finance this creative work. The investment required to product

products such as phonograms, films or multimedia products, and services such as 'on-demand' services, is considerable. Adequate legal protection of intellectual property rights is necessary in order to guarantee the availability of such a reward and provide the opportunity for satisfactory returns on this investment;

(9bis) A rigorous, effective system for the protection of copyright and related rights is one of the main ways of ensuring that European cultural creativity and production receive the necessary resources and of safeguarding the independence and dignity of artistic creators and performers;

(10) Adequate protection of copyright works and subject matter of related rights is also of great importance from a cultural standpoint. Article 151 of the Treaty requires the Community to take cultural aspects into account in its action;

(10bis) A common search for, and consistent application at European level of, technical measures to protect works and to provide the necessary information on rights are essential insofar as the ultimate aim of these measures is to give effect to the principles and guarantees laid down in law;

(10ter) This Directive must seek to promote learning and culture by protecting creative and artistic works while permitting exceptions in the public interest for the purpose of education and teaching;

(11) The Diplomatic Conference held under the auspices of the World Intellectual Property Organisation (WIPO) in December 1996 led to the adoption of two new Treaties, the 'WIPO Copyright Treaty' and the 'WIPO Performances and Phonograms Treaty', dealing respectively with the protection of authors and the protection of performers and phonogram producers. Those Treaties update the international protection for copyright and related rights significantly, not least with regard to the so-called 'digital agenda', and improve the means to fight piracy world-wide. The Community and a majority of Member States have already signed the Treaties and the process of making arrangements for the ratification of the Treaties by the Community and the Member States is under way. This Directive also serves to implement a number of the new international obligations;

(12) Liability for activities in the network environment concerns not only copyright and related rights but also other areas, such as defamation, misleading advertising, or infringement of trademarks, and will be addressed horizontally in European Parliament and Council Directive 000/000/EC on certain legal aspects of information society services, in particular electronic commerce, in the internal market ('Directive on electronic commerce'),[4] which clarifies and harmonises various legal issues relating to Information Society services including electronic commerce. The provisions relating to liability in the context of electronic commerce should come into force within a timescale similar to that of this Directive, since they should provide a harmonised framework of principles and provisions relevant to *inter alia* important parts of this Directive. This Directive is without prejudice to provisions relating to liability in that Directive;

---

[4] Council common position adopted 28 February 2000, OJ C 128, 8.5.2000, p. 32.

(12bis) Especially in the light of the requirements arising out of the digital environment, it is necessary to ensure that collecting societies achieve a higher level of rationalisation and transparency with regard to compliance and competition rules;

(12ter) This Directive is without prejudice to modalities, in the Member States, of management of rights, such as extended collective licences;

(12quater) The moral rights of rightholders should be exercised according to the legislation of the Member States and the provisions of the Berne Convention for the Protection of Literary and Artistic Works, of the WIPO Copyright Treaty and of the WIPO Performances and Phonograms Treaty. Such moral rights remain outside the scope of this Directive;

(13) This Directive is based on principles and rules already laid down in the Directives currently in force in this area, in particular Nos. 91/250/EEC of 14 May 1991, 92/100/EEC of 19 November 1992, 93/83/EEC of 27 September 1993, 93/98/EEC of 29 October 1993 and 96/9/EC of 11 March 1996,[5] and it develops those principles and rules and places them in the context of the Information Society. The provisions of this Directive should be without prejudice to the provisions of those Directives, unless otherwise provided in this Directive;

(14) This Directive should define the scope of the acts covered by the reproduction right with regard to the different beneficiaries. This should be done in conformity with the *acquis communautaire*. A broad definition of these acts is needed to ensure legal certainty within the Internal Market.

(15) This Directive should harmonise further the author's right applicable to the communication to the public of works. This right should be understood in a broad sense covering all communication to the public not present at the place where the communication originates. This right covers any such transmission or retransmission of a work to the public by wire or wireless means, including broadcasting. This right does not cover any other acts;

(15bis) The right of making available to the public of subject matter referred to in Article 3(2) should be understood as covering all acts of making available such subject matter to members of the public not present at the place where the act of making available originates, and as not covering any other acts;

(16) The legal uncertainty regarding the nature and level of protection of acts of on-demand transmission of copyright works and subject matter protected by related rights over networks should be overcome by providing for harmonised protection at Community level. It should be made clear that all rightholders recognised by the Directive have an exclusive right to make available to the public copyright works or

---

[5] Council Directive 91/250/EEC of 14 May 1991 on the legal protection of computer programs (OJ L 122, 17.5.1991, p. 42), Council Directive 92/100/EEC of 19 November 1992 on rental right and lending right and on certain rights related to copyright in the field of intellectual property (OJ L 346, 27.11.1992, p. 61), Council Directive 93/83/EEC of 27 September 1993 on the coordination of certain rules concerning copyright and rights related to copyright applicable to satellite broadcasting and cable retransmission (OJ L 248, 6.10.1993, p. 15), Council Directive 93/98/EEC of 29 October 1993 harmonising the term of protection of copyright and certain related rights (OJ L 290, 24.11.1993, p. 9) and Directive 96/9/EC of the European Parliament and of the Council of 11 March 1996 on the legal protection of databases (OJ L 77, 27.3.1996, p. 20).

any other subject matter by way of interactive on-demand transmissions. Such interactive on-demand transmissions are characterised by the fact that members of the public may access them from a place and at a time individually chosen by them;

(16bis) With regard to the making available in on-demand services by broadcasters of their radio or television productions incorporating music from commercial phonograms as an integral part thereof, collective licensing arrangements are to be encouraged in order to facilitate the clearance of the rights concerned;

(17) The mere provision of physical facilities for enabling or making a communication does not in itself amount to communication within the meaning of this Directive;

(18) Copyright protection under this Directive includes the exclusive right to control distribution of the work incorporated in a tangible article. The first sale in the Community of the original of a work or copies thereof by the rightholder or with his consent exhausts the right to control resale of that object in the Community. This right should not be exhausted in respect of the original or of copies thereof sold by the rightholder or with his consent outside the Community. The rights of rental and lending for authors have been established in Directive 92/100/EC. The distribution right provided for in this Directive is without prejudice to the provisions relating to the rental and lending rights contained in Chapter I of that Directive;

(19) The question of exhaustion does not arise in the case of services and on-line services in particular. This also applies with regard to a material copy of a work or other subject matter made by a user of such a service with the consent of the rightholder. Therefore, the same applies to rental and lending of the original and copies of works or other subject matter which are services by nature. Unlike CD-ROM or CD-I, where the intellectual property is incorporated in a material medium, namely an item of goods, every on-line service is in fact an act which will have to be subject to authorisation where the copyright or related right so provides;

(20) The rights referred to in this Directive may be transferred, assigned or subject to the granting of contractual licences, without prejudice to the relevant national legislation on copyright and related rights;

(21) A fair balance of rights and interests between the different categories of rightholders, as well as between the different categories of rightholders and users of protected subject matter must be safeguarded. The existing exceptions to the rights as set out by the Member States have to be reassessed in the light of the new electronic environment. Existing differences in the exceptions to certain restricted acts have direct negative effects on the functioning of the Internal Market of copyright and related rights. Such differences could well become more pronounced in view of the further development of transborder exploitation of works and cross-border activities. In order to ensure the proper functioning of the Internal market, such exceptions should be defined more harmoniously. The degree of their harmonisation should be based on their impact on the smooth functioning of the Internal Market;

(22) This Directive provides for an exhaustive enumeration of exceptions to the reproduction right and the right of communication to the public. Some exceptions only apply to the reproduction right, where appropriate. This list takes due account of the different legal traditions in Member States, while, at the same time, aiming to

ensure a functioning Internal market. It is desirable that Member States should arrive at a coherent application of these exceptions, which will be assessed when reviewing implementing legislation in the future.

(23) The exclusive right of reproduction should be subject to an exception to allow certain acts of temporary reproduction, which are transient or incidental reproductions, forming an integral and essential part of a technological process carried out for the sole purpose of enabling either efficient transmission in a network between third parties by an intermediary, or a lawful use of a work or other subject matter to be made. The acts of reproduction concerned should have no separate economic value on their own. To the extent that they meet these conditions, this exception should include acts which enable browsing as well as acts of caching to take place, including those which enable transmission systems to function efficiently, provided that the intermediary does not modify the information and does not interfere with the lawful use of technology, widely recognised and used by industry, to obtain data on the use of the information. A use should be considered lawful where it is authorised by the rightholder or not restricted by law.

(24) Member States should be given the option of providing for certain exceptions for cases such as educational and scientific purposes, for the benefit of public institutions such as libraries and archives, for purposes of news reporting, for quotations, for use by people with disabilities, for public security uses and for uses in administrative and judicial proceedings;

(24bis) In certain cases of exceptions, rightholders should receive fair compensation to compensate them adequately for the use made of their protected works or other subject matter. When determining the form, modalities and possible level of such fair compensation, account should be taken of the particular circumstances of each case. When evaluating these circumstances, a valuable criterion would be the possible harm to the rightholders resulting from the act in question. In cases where rightholders have already received payment in some other form, for instance as part of a licence fee, no specific or separate payment may be due. The level of fair compensation should take full account of the degree of use of technological protection measures referred to in this Directive. In certain situations where the prejudice to the rightholder would be minimal, no obligation for payment may arise;

(24ter) The Member States may provide for fair compensation for rightholders also when applying the optional provisions on exceptions which do not require such compensation;

(25) Existing national schemes on reprography, where they do exist, do not create major barriers to the Internal Market. Member States should be allowed to provide for an exception in respect of reprography;

(26) Member States should be allowed to provide for an exception to the reproduction right for certain types of reproduction of audio, visual and audio-visual material for private use, accompanied by fair compensation. This may include the introduction or continuation of remuneration schemes to compensate for the prejudice to rightholders. Although differences between those remuneration schemes affect the functioning of the Internal Market, those differences, with respect to analogue private reproduction, should not have a significant impact on the development of the

Information Society. Digital private copying is likely to be more widespread and have a greater economic impact. Due account should therefore be taken of the differences between digital and analogue private copying and a distinction should be made in certain respects between them;

(27) When applying the exception on private copying, Member States should take due account of technological and economic developments, in particular with respect to digital private copying and remuneration schemes, when effective technological protection measures are available. Such exceptions should not inhibit the use of technological measures or their enforcement against circumvention;

(28) Member States may provide for an exception for the benefit of certain non-profit making establishments, such as publicly accessible libraries and equivalent institutions, as well as archives. however, this should be limited to certain special cases covered by the reproduction right. Such an exception should not cover uses made in the context of on-line delivery of protected works or other subject matter. This Directive should be without prejudice to Member States' option to derogate from the exclusive public lending right in accordance with Article 5 of Council Directive 92/100/EEC of 19 November 1992 on rental right and lending right and on certain rights related to copyright in the field of intellectual property, as amended by Directive 93/98/EEC. Therefore, specific contracts or licences should be promoted which, without creating imbalances, favour such establishments and the disseminative purposes they serve.

(28a) When applying the exception in respect of ephemeral recordings made by broadcasting organisations it is understood that a broadcaster's own facilities include those of a person acting on behalf of and under the responsibility of the broadcasting organisation;

(28bis) When applying the exception for non-commercial educational and scientific research purposes, including distance learning, the non-commercial nature of the activity in question should be determined by that activity as such. The organisational structure and the means of funding of the establishment concerned are not the decisive factors in this respect;

(28ter) It is in any case important for the Member States to adopt all necessary measures to facilitate access to works by persons suffering from a disability which constitutes an obstacle to the use of the works themselves, and to pay particular attention to accessible formats;

(28quater) Deleted;

(29) When applying the exceptions provided for in this Directive, they should be exercised in accordance with international obligations. Such exceptions may not be applied in a way which prejudices the legitimate interests of the rightholder or which conflicts with the normal exploitation of his work or other subject matter. The provision of such exceptions by Member States should, in particular, duly reflect the increased economic impact that such exceptions may have in the context of the new electronic environment. Therefore, the scope of certain exceptions may have to be even more limited when it comes to certain new uses of copyright works and other subject matter;

(29bis) The exceptions referred to in Article 5(2) and (3) must not, however, prevent the definition of contractual relations designed to ensure fair compensation for the rightholders insofar as permitted by national law;

(29ter) Recourse to mediation could help users and rightholders to settle disputes. The Commission, in co-operation with the Member States within the Contact Committee, should undertake a study to consider new legal ways of settling disputes concerning copyright and related rights;

(30) Technological development will allow rightholders to make use of technological measures designed to restrict acts not authorized by the rightholders of any copyright, rights related to copyright or the *sui generis* right in databases. The danger, however, exists that illegal activities might be carried out in order to enable or facilitate the circumvention of the technical protection provided by these measures. In order to avoid fragmented legal approaches that could potentially hinder the functioning of the Internal market, there is a need to provide for harmonised legal protection against circumvention of effective technological measures and against provision of devices and products or services to this effect;

(30bis) Such a legal protection should be provided to technological measures that effectively restrict acts not authorized by the rightholders of any copyright, rights related to copyright or the *sui generis* right in databases without, however, preventing the normal operation of electronic equipment and its technological development. Such legal protection implies no obligation to design devices, products, components or services to correspond to technological measures, so long as such device, product, component or service does not otherwise fall under the prohibition of Article 6. Such legal protection should respect proportionality and should not prohibit those devices or activities which have a commercially significant purpose or use other than to circumvent the technical protection. In particular, this protection should not hinder research into cryptography;

(30ter) The legal protection of technological measures is without prejudice to the application of any national provisions which may prohibit the private possession of devices, products or components for the circumvention of technological measures;

(31) Such a harmonised legal protection does not affect the specific provisions of protection provided for by Council Directive 91/250/EEC of 14 May 1991 on the legal protection of computer programs, as amended by Directive 93/98/EEC. In particular, it should not apply to the protection of technological measures used in connection with computer programs, which is exclusively addressed in that Directive. It should not inhibit, nor prevent the development or use of any means of circumventing a technological measure that is necessary to enable acts undertaken in accordance with the terms of Article 5(3) or Article 6 of Directive 91/250/EEC. Articles 5 and 6 of that Directive exclusively determine exceptions to the exclusive rights applicable to computer programs;

(31bis) The legal protection of technological measures applies without prejudice to public policy, as reflected in Article 5, or public security. Member States should promote voluntary measures taken by rightholders, including the conclusion and implementation of agreements between rightholders and other parties concerned, to accommodate achieving the objectives of certain exceptions or limitations provided for in national law in accordance with this Directive. In the absence of such voluntary measures or agreements within a reasonable period of time, Member States should take appropriate measures to ensure that rightholders provide beneficiaries of such exceptions or limitations with appropriate means of benefiting from them, by modifying an implemented technological protection measure or by other means. However, in order to prevent abuse of such measures taken by rightholders, including in the framework of agreements, or taken by a Member State, any technological protection measures applied in implementation of such measures should enjoy legal protection;

(31ter) When implementing an exception or limitation for private copying in accordance with Article 5(2)(b), Member States should likewise promote the use of voluntary measures to accommodate achieving the objectives of such exception or limitation. If, within a reasonable period of time, no such voluntary measures to make reproduction for private use possible have been taken, Member States may take measures to enable beneficiaries of the exception or limitation concerned to benefit from it. Voluntary measures taken by rightholders, including agreements between rightholders and other parties concerned, as well as measures taken by Member States, do not prevent rightholders from using technological measures, which are consistent with the exceptions or limitations on private copying in national law in accordance with Article 5(2)(b), taking account of the condition of fair compensation under Article 5(2)(b), and the possible differentiation between various conditions of use in accordance with Article 5(4), such as controlling the number of reproductions. In order to prevent abuse of such measures, any technological measures applied in their implementation should enjoy legal protection;

(32) Important progress has been made in the international standardisation of technical systems of identification of works and protected subject matter in digital format. In an increasingly networked environment, differences between technological measures could lead to an incompatibility of systems within the Community. Compatibility and interoperability of the different systems should be encouraged. It would be highly desirable to encourage the development of global systems;

(33) Technological development will facilitate the distribution of works, notably on networks, and this will entail the need for rightholders to identify better the work or other subject matter, the author or any other rightholder, and to provide information about the terms and conditions of use of the work or other subject matter in order to render easier the management of rights attached to them. Rightholders should be encouraged to use markings indicating, in addition to the information referred to above, *inter alia* their authorisation when putting works or other subject matter on networks;

(33bis) There is, however, the danger that illegal activities might be carried out in order to remove or alter the electronic copyright-management information attached to it, or otherwise to distribute, import for distribution, broadcast, communicate to the public or make available to the public works or other protected subject matter from which such information has been removed without authority. In order to avoid fragmented legal approaches that could potentially hinder the functioning of the Internal Market, there is a need to provide for harmonised legal protection against any of these activities;

(34) Any such rights-management information systems referred to above may, depending on their design, at the same time process personal data about the consumption patterns of protected subject matter by individuals and allow for tracing of on-line behaviour. These technical means, in their technical functions, should incorporate privacy safeguards in accordance with European Parliament and Council Directive 95/46/EC of 24 October 1995 on the protection of individuals with regard to the processing of personal data and the free movement of such data;[6]

(35) Deleted—see Recital 36ter.

(36) Member States should provide for effective sanctions and remedies for infringements of rights and obligations as set out in this Directive. They should take all the measures necessary to ensure that those sanctions and remedies are applied. The sanctions thus provided for should be effective, proportionate and dissuasive and should include the possibility to seek damages and/or injunctive relief and, where appropriate, to apply for seizure of infringing material;

(36bis) In particular in the digital environment, the services of intermediaries may increasingly be used by third parties for infringing activities. In many cases such intermediaries are best placed to bring an end to such infringing activities. Therefore, without prejudice to any other sanctions and remedies available, rightholders should have the possibility of applying for an injunction against an intermediary who carries a third party's infringement of a protected work or other subject matter in a network. This possibility should be available even where the acts carried out by the intermediary are exempted under Article 5. The conditions and modalities relating to such injunctions should be left to the national law of the Member States;

(36ter) The protection provided under this Directive should be without prejudice to national or Community legal provisions in other areas, such as industrial property, data protection, conditional access, access to public documents, and the rule of media exploitation chronology, which may affect the protection of copyright or related rights;

(37) In order to comply with the WIPO Performances and Phonograms Treaty, Directives 92/100/EEC and 93/98/EEC should be amended;

(38) After a period of two years following the date of implementation of this Directive, the Commission should report on its application. This report should examine in particular whether the conditions set out in the Directive have resulted in ensuring a proper functioning of the Internal market, and should propose action if necessary;

(39) Deleted.

---

[6] OJ L 281, 23.11.1995, p. 31.

HAVE ADOPTED THIS DIRECTIVE:

CHAPTER I

OBJECTIVE AND SCOPE

Article 1

Scope

1.   This Directive concerns the legal protection of copyright and related rights in the framework of the Internal Market, with particular emphasis on the Information Society.

2.   Except in the cases referred to in Article 10, this Directive shall leave intact and shall in no way affect existing Community provisions relating to:

(a) the legal protection of computer programs;
(b) rental right, lending right and certain rights related to copyright in the field of intellectual property;
(c) copyright and related rights applicable to broadcasting of programmes by satellite and cable retransmission;
(d) the term of protection of copyright and certain related rights;
(e) the legal protection of databases.

CHAPTER II

RIGHTS AND EXCEPTIONS

Article 2

Reproduction right

Member States shall provide for the exclusive right to authorise or prohibit direct or indirect, temporary or permanent reproduction by any means and in any form, in whole or in part:

(a) for authors, of their works;
(b) for performers, of fixations of their performances;
(c) for phonogram producers, of their phonograms;
(d) for the producers of the first fixations of films, in respect of the original and copies of their films;
(e) for broadcasting organisations, of fixations of their broadcasts, whether those broadcasts are transmitted by wire or over the air, including by cable or satellite.

Article 3

Right of communication to the public of works and right of making available to the public of other subject matter

1.   Member States shall provide authors with the exclusive right to authorise or prohibit any communication to the public of their works, by wire or wireless means, including the

making available to the public of their works in such a way that members of the public may access them from a place and at a time individually chosen by them.

2.   Member States shall provide for the exclusive right to authorise or prohibit the making available to the public, by wire or wireless means, in such a way that members of the public may access them from a place and a a time individually chosen by them:

(a) for performers, of fixations of their performances;
(b) for phonogram producers, of their phonograms;
(c) for the producers of the first fixations of films, of the original and copies of their films;
(d) for broadcasting organisations, of fixations of their broadcasts, whether these broadcasts are transmitted by wire or over the air, including by cable or satellite.

3.   The rights referred to in paragraphs 1 and 2 shall not be exhausted by any act of communication to the public or making available to the public as set out in this Article.

4.   *Deleted.*

Article 4

Distribution right

1.   Member States shall provide for authors, in respect of the original of their works or of copies thereof, the exclusive right to authorise or prohibit any form of distribution to the public by sale or otherwise.

2.   The distribution right shall not be exhausted within the Community in respect of the original or copies of the work, except where the first sale or other transfer of ownership in the Community of that object is made by the rightholder or with his consent.

Article 5

Exceptions to the restricted acts set out in Articles 2, 3 and 4

1.   Temporary acts of reproduction referred to in Article 2, which are transient or incidental, which are an integral and essential part of a technological process, whose sole purpose is to enable

(a) a transmission in a network between third parties by an intermediary or
(b) a lawful use

of a work or other subject matter to be made, and which have no independent economic significance, shall be exempted from the right set out in Article 2.

2.   Member States may provide for exceptions to the exclusive right of reproduction provided for in Article 2 in the following cases:

(a) in respect of reproductions on paper or any similar medium, effected by the use of any kind of photographic technique or by some other process having similar effects, with the exception of sheet music, provided that the rightholders receive fair compensation;
(b) in respect of reproductions on any medium made for the private use of a natural person and for non-commercial ends, on condition that the rightholders receive fair

compensation which takes account of the application or non-application of techno-logical measures referred to in Article 6 to the work or subject matter concerned;

(b bis) *partially merged with (b).*

(c) in respect of specific acts of reproduction made by publicly accessible libraries, educational establishments or museums, or by archives, which are not for direct or indirect economic or commercial advantage;

(d) in respect of ephemeral recordings of works made by broadcasting organisations by means of their own facilities and for their own broadcasts; the preservation of these recordings in official archives may, on the ground of their exceptional documentary character, be permitted;

(e) in respect of reproductions of broadcasts made by social institutions pursuing non-commercial purposes, such as hospitals or prisons, on condition that the rightholders receive fair compensation.

3. Member States may provide for limitations to the rights referred to in Articles 2 and 3 in the following cases:

(a) use for the sole purpose of illustration for teaching or scientific research, as long as, whenever possible, the source, including the author's name, is indicated and to the extent justified by the non-commercial purpose to be achieved;

(b) uses, for the benefit of people with a disability, which are directly related to the disability and of a non-commercial nature, to the extent required by the specific disability;

(c) reproduction by the press, communication to the public or making available of published articles on current economic, political or religious topics or of broadcast works or other subject matter of the same character, in cases where such use is not expressly reserved, and as long as the source, including the author's name, is indicated, or use of works or other subject matter in connection with the reporting of current events, to the extent justified by the informatory purpose and as long as, whenever possible the source, including the author's name, is indicated;

(d) quotations for purposes such as criticism or review, provided that they relate to a work or other subject matter which has already been lawfully made available to the public, that, whenever possible, the source, including the author's name, is indicated, and that their use is in accordance with fair practice, and to the extent required by the specific purpose;

(e) use for the purposes of public security or to ensure the proper performance or reporting of administrative, parliamentary or judicial proceedings;

(f) use of political speeches as well as extracts of public lectures or similar works or subject matter to the extent justified by the informatory purpose and provided that, whenever possible, the source, including the author's name, is indicated;

(g) use during religious celebrations or official celebrations organised by a public authority;

(h) *replaced by Article 5(2)(e)*

(i) use of works, such as works of architecture or sculpture, made to be located permanently in public places;

(j) incidental inclusion of a work or other subject matter in other material;

(k) use for the purpose of advertising the public exhibition or sale of artistic works, to the extent necessary to promote the event;

(l) use for the purpose of caricature, parody or pastiche;

(m) use in connection with the demonstration or repair of equipment;

(n) use of an artistic work in the form of a building or a drawing or plan of a building for the purposes of reconstructing the building;

(o) use by communication or making available, for the purpose of research or private study, to individual members of the public by dedicated terminals on the premises of establishments referred to in paragraph 2(c) of works and other subject matter not subject to purchase or licensing terms which are contained in their collections;

(p) use in certain other cases of minor importance where exceptions already exist under national law, provided that they only concern analogue uses and do not affect the free circulation of goods and services within the Community, without prejudice to the other exceptions and limitations contained in this Article.

(3bis)   Where the Member States may provide for an exception to the right of reproduction pursuant to paragraphs 2 and 3 of this Article, they may provide similarly for an exception to the right of distribution as referred to in Article 4 to the extent justified by the purpose of the authorised act of reproduction.

4.   The exceptions and limitations provided for in paragraphs 1, 2, 3 and 3bis shall only be applied in certain special cases that do not conflict with a normal exploitation of the work or other subject matter and do not unreasonably prejudice the legitimate interests of the rightholder.

CHAPTER III

PROTECTION OF TECHNOLOGICAL MEASURES AND RIGHTS-MANAGEMENT INFORMATION

Article 6

Obligations as to technological measures

1.   Member States shall provide adequate legal protection against the circumvention of any effective technological measures, which the person concerned carries out in the knowledge, or with reasonable grounds to know, that he or she pursues that objective.

2.   Member States shall provide adequate legal protection against the manufacture, import, distribution, sale, rental, advertisement for sale or rental, or possession for commercial purposes of devices, products or components or the provision of services which:

(a) are promoted, advertised or marketed for the purpose of circumvention of, or

(b) have only a limited commercially significant purpose or use other than to circumvent, or

(c) are primarily designed, produced, adapted or performed for the purpose of enabling or facilitating the circumvention of,

any effective technological measures.

3.   The expression 'technological measures', as used in this Article, means any technology, device or component that, in the normal course of its operation, is designed to prevent or restrict acts, in respect of works or other subject matter, which are not authorized by the rightholder of any copyright or any right related to copyright as provided by law or the *sui generis* right provided for in Chapter III of European Parliament and Council

Directive 96/9/EC. Technological measures shall be deemed 'effective' where the use of a protected work or other subject matter is controlled by the rightholders through application of an access control or protection process, such as encryption, scrambling or other transformation of the work or other subject matter or a copy control mechanism, which achieves the protection objective.

4.   Notwithstanding the legal protection provided for in paragraph 1, in the absence of voluntary measures taken by rightholders, including agreements between rightholders and other parties concerned, Member States shall take appropriate measures to ensure that rightholders make available to the beneficiary of an exception or limitation provided for in national law in accordance with Article 5(2)(a), (2)(c), (2)(d), (2)(e), (3)(a), (3)(b) or (3)(e) the means of benefiting from that exception or limitation, to the extent necessary to benefit from that exception or limitation and where that beneficiary has legal access to the protected work or subject matter concerned.

A Member State may also take such measures in respect of a beneficiary of an exception provided for in accordance with Article 5(2)(b), unless reproduction for private use has already been made possible by rightholders to the extent necessary to benefit from the exception concerned and in accordance with the provisions of Article 5(2)(b) and (4), without preventing rightholders from adopting adequate measures regarding the number of reproductions in accordance with these provisions.

The technological protection measures applied voluntarily by rightholders, including those applied in implementation of voluntary agreements, or technological protection measures applied in implementation of the measures taken by Member States, enjoy the legal protection provided for in paragraph 1.

The provisions of the first and second subparagraphs shall not apply to works or other subject matter made available to the public on agreed contractual terms in such a way that members of the public may access them from a place and at a time individually chosen by them.

This paragraph shall apply *mutatis mutandis* to Council Directive 92/100/EEC of 19 November 1992 on rental right and lending right and on certain rights related to copyright in the field of intellectual property,[7] and to Directive 96/9/EC of the European Parliament and of the Council of 11 March 1996 on the legal protection of databases.[8]

Article 7

Obligations concerning rights-management information

1.   Member States shall provide for adequate legal protection against any person knowingly performing without authority any of the following acts:

(a) the removal or alteration of any electronic rights-management information;
(b) the distribution, importation for distribution, broadcasting, communication or making available to the public of works or other subject matter protected under this Directive or under Chapter III of Directive 96/6/EC from which electronic rights-management information has been removed or altered without authority,

---

[7] OJ L 346, 27.11.1992, p. 61.
[8] OJ L 77, 27.3.1996, p. 20.

if such person knows, or has reasonable grounds to know, that by so doing he is inducing, enabling, facilitating or concealing an infringement of any copyright or any rights related to copyright as provided by law, or of the *sui generis* right provided for in Chapter III of Directive 96/9/EC.

2.   The expression 'rights-management information', as used in this Article, means any information provided by rightholders which identifies the work or other subject matter referred to in this Directive or covered by the *sui generis* right provided for in Chapter III of Directive 96/9/EC, the author or any other rightholder, or information about the terms and conditions of use of the work or other subject matter, and any numbers or codes that represent such information.

The subparagraph shall apply when any of these items of information is associated with a copy of, or appears in connection with the communication to the public of, a work or other subject matter referred to in this Directive or covered by the *sui generis* right provided for in Chapter III of Directive 96/9/EC.

CHAPTER IV

COMMON PROVISIONS

Article 8

Sanctions and remedies

1.   Member States shall provide appropriate sanctions and remedies in respect of infringements of the rights and obligations set out in this Directive and shall take all the measures necessary to ensure that those sanctions and remedies are applied. The sanctions thus provided for shall be effective, proportionate and dissuasive and act as a deterrent to further infringement.

2.   Each Member State shall take the measures necessary to ensure that rightholders whose interests are affected by an infringing activity carried out in its territory can bring an action for damages and/or apply for an injunction and, where appropriate, for the seizure of infringing material as well as of devices, products or components referred to in Article 6(2).

3.   Member States shall ensure that rightholders are in a position to apply for an injunction against intermediaries whose services are used by a third party to infringe a copyright or related right.

Article 8 bis

Continued application of other legal provisions

This Directive shall be without prejudice to provisions concerning in particular patent rights, trade marks, design rights, utility models, topographies of semi-conductor products, type faces, conditional access, access to cable of broadcasting services, the protection of national treasures, legal deposit requirements, laws on restrictive practices and unfair competition, trade secrets, security, confidentiality, data protection and privacy, access to public documents, the law of contract.

Article 9

Application over time

1.   The provisions of this Directive shall apply in respect of all works and other subject matter referred to in this Directive which are, by the date referred to in Article 11(1), protected by the Member States' legislation in the field of copyright and related rights, or which meet the criteria for protection under the provisions of this Directive or the provisions referred to in Article 1(2).

2.   This Directive shall apply without prejudice to any acts concluded and rights acquired before the date referred to in Article 11(1).

3.   *Deleted.*

4.   *Deleted.*

Article 10

Technical adaptations

1.   Directive 92/100/EEC is hereby amended as follows:
(a)   Article 7 is deleted.
(b)   Article 10(3) is replaced by the following

'3.   The limitations may only be applied to certain special cases and may not be interpreted in such a way as to allow their application to be used in a manner which unreasonably prejudices the rightholders' legitimate interests or conflicts with normal exploitation of their subject matter.'

2.   Article 3(2) of Directive 93/98/EEC is replaced by the following:

'2.   The rights of producers of phonograms shall expire 50 years after the fixation is made. However, if the phonogram is lawfully published during this period, the rights shall expire 50 years from the date of the first such publication. If no lawful publication takes place during the period mentioned in the first sentence, and if the phonogram is lawfully communicated to the public during this period, the rights shall expire 50 years from the date of the first such communication to the public.'

If, however, through the expire of the term of protection which was granted under the previous wording of Article 3(2) of Directive 93/98/EEC, a phonogram is no longer protected, this Article shall not have the effect of protecting this phonogram anew.

Article 11

Final provisions

1.   Member States shall bring into force the laws, regulations and administrative provisions necessary to comply with this Directive not later than . . . (time two years following its publication in the *Official Journal of the European Communities*). They shall immediately inform the Commission thereof and shall also communicate to the

Commission the text of the provisions of domestic law which they adopt in the field governed by this Directive.

When Member States adopt these provisions, these shall contain a reference to this Directive or shall be accompanied by such reference at the time of their official publication. The procedure for such reference shall be adopted by Member States.

2.   Not later than at the end of the second year after the date referred to in paragraph 1 and every three years thereafter, the Commission shall submit to the European Parliament, the Council and the Economic and Social Committee a report on the application of this Directive, in which, *inter alia*, on the basis of specific information supplied by the Member States, it shall examine in particular the application of Articles 5, 6 and 8 in the light of the development of the digital market. In the case of Article 6, it shall examine in particular whether that Article confers a sufficient level of protection and whether acts which are permitted by law are being adversely affected by the use of effective technological measures. Where necessary, in particular to ensure the functioning of the Internal Market pursuant to Article 14 of the Treaty, it shall submit proposals for amendments to this Directive.

3.   Protection of rights related to copyright under this Directive shall leave intact and shall in no way affect the protection of copyright.

(4a)   A Contact Committee is hereby established. It shall be composed of representatives of the competent authorities of the Member States. I shall be chaired by a representative of the Commission and shall meet either on the initiative of the Chairman or at the request of the delegation of a Member State.

(4b)   The tasks of the Committee shall be as follows:
— to organise consultations on all questions deriving from application of the Directive;
— to facilitate the exchange of information on relevant developments in legislation and case-law, as well as relevant economic, social, cultural and technological developments;
— to act as a forum for the assessment of the digital market in works and other items, including private copying and the use of technological measures.

Article 12

Entry into force

This Directive shall enter into force on the twentieth day following its publication in the *Official Journal of the European Communities*.

Article 13

Addresses

This Directive is addressed to the Member States.

Done at . . . ,

For the European Parliament   *For the Council*
The President   *The President*

ANNEX

A. Declarations by the Council and/or the Commission

1. Council and Commission declaration concerning Recital 23:

    The Council and the Commission are of the view that the wording 'provided that the intermediary does not modify the information and does not interfere with the lawful use of technology, widely recognised and used by industry, to obtain data on the use of the information' does not exclude proxy caching by an intermediary from being exempted under Article 5(1), if such caching meets the conditions set out in that Article.

2. Commission declaration on Recital 24bis:

    The Commission is of the view that no obligation for payment may arise regarding certain single temporary acts of copying a broadcast work or other subject matter which are undertaken solely for the purpose of enabling it to be viewed and/or listened to at a more convenient time ('time-shifting'), provided that the conditions set out in Article 5(4) of this Directive are met.

3. Commission declaration on Recital 31bis:

    The Commission is of the view that Member States, when taking measures to ensure that rightholders accommodate achieving the objective of the exception for private copying provided for in Article 5(2)(b), may allow certain single temporary acts of copying a broadcast work or other protected subject matter which are undertaken solely for the purpose of enabling it to be viewed and/or listened to at a more convenient time ('time shifting'), provided that the conditions set out in Article 5(4) of this Directive are met.

4. Commission declaration on Article 4(2):

    The Commission confirms that the regime on exhaustion as enshrined in Article 4(2) of this Directive corresponds to that established in the existing Directives on copyright and related rights. Any future work on this issue will take account of, and take place against the background of, reflections on this issue in the wider area of intellectual and industrial property.

5. Commission declaration on the hierarchy of exceptions:

    The Commission is of the view that no hierarchy exists between the exceptions and limitations contained in Article 5 and, therefore, Member States may choose among them, notwithstanding the mandatory nature of Article 591).

6. Commission declaration on optional exceptions:

    The Commission considers that the optional exceptions regime in Article 5(2), (3) and (3bis) of the Directive should not create any imbalances either for rightholders or for any of the other parties concerned; if such imbalances were to arise, the

Commission, in the context of Article 11(2) of the Directive, would make appropriate proposals.

7. Council and Commission declaration on rights management:

The Council and the Commission confirm the need for adequate and transparent conditions for the exploitation and management of rights in the Internal Market, both with respect to individual and collective rights management, which reflect an appropriate balance between all rights and interests (in particular of users) involved. The Commission will study further the issue of management of rights, in the light of market developments with particular regard to digital technologies and will decide upon the appropriate follow-up.

8. Commission declaration on further adaptation of the existing Directives:

The Commission will closely survey technological and market developments relevant to the protection of copyright and neighbouring rights in the Internal Market and consider preparing, at an early stage, adaptations and consolidations of the existing Directives adopted in this area, where appropriate to safeguard continued coherence, based on the experience gained with the application of this Directive. In this context, it will pay particular attention to the need for an exception to the reproduction right for certain acts of copying as contained in Article 5(1) of this Directive to be applied to computer programs and databases and for the legal protection of technological measures as contained in Article 6 of this Directive to be applied to computer programs.

B. Unilateral declarations[9]

9. Declaration by the Danish, Irish, Luxembourg, Netherlands, Finnish and Swedish delegations on article 4(2):

Denmark, Ireland, Luxembourg, the Netherlands, Finland and Sweden are in favour of international exhaustion and would like to stress the need for a reconsideration of the issue of exhaustion within the field of copyright in the light of the general international development and the ongoing discussion on international exhaustion within the field of trade mark protection.

10. Declaration by the Netherlands delegation on Article 5(3)(c):

The Netherlands recalls that with respect to Article 5(3)(c), Member States remain free to further define in their legislation the notion of 'press'.

11. Declaration by the Swedish delegation on Article 8bis:

Sweden recalls that the wording 'legal deposit requirements' covers *inter alia* national systems under which the designated authorities may circumvent technological measures when downloading works or other subject matter from computer networks for national archiving purposes.

---

[9] Several delegations have indicated their intention of making additional declarations.

Index

Agency, *see* contract

Banks, *see* payment
Berne Convention, *see* copyright
Blasphemy, 276, 281
  see also pornography
Brussels Convention, *see* international private
  law; defamation

Cable service, *see* copyright
Cache, *see* copyright; trademarks; pornography
Cash, *see* payment
Checksum, 26
  see also contract
Choice of laws, authorship, 234
  contract and, 31–4
  defamation, 256, 259
  domain names and, 161, 165, 166
  infringement, 244
  international private law, 236
  ownership, 243
  policy, 246
  spam, 319
  see also copyright; international private law;
    trademarks
Click-wrap, *see* contract
Commerce:
  law, commercial, 5
  see also e-commerce
Conflict of laws, *see* international private law
Consumer protection:
  Rome Convention, 34
    see also Rome Convention
  spam, *see* spam
Content liability:
  defamation, 249
    see also defamation
  junk mail, 309
    see also spam
  pornography, 275
    see also pornography
  spam, 309
    see also spam
Contract:
  acceptance,
  checksum, 26
  click-wrap, by, 25
  email, 22
  generally, 17, 22–26, 29

agency, 24
breach, 61, 267, 269–70
checksum, 26
choice of laws, 31–4
click-wrap, by, 19, 25
consensus ad idem, 17, 21
copyright, 219
crime, 50
cross-border, 26
DTI recommendations, 20
digital cash, 67, 68
  see also payment
documents constituting, 29, 30
email, 18, 22
entering into, 17
European proposals, 26
express terms, 29, 70
form, 27, 32
implied terms, 31, 70
intention of parties, 71
invitation to treat, 21
ISPs, 267
  see also ISPs
lex loci contractus, 32
methods, 18
misrepresentation, 61
offer, 17, 21, 69
payment, 55, 57
  see also payment
third party rights, 68
claims against, 68
performance, 57, 60–2
principles, 18
privacy, 37, 88, 101
  see also cryptography; privacy
postal rule, 22–6
regulation, 19
remedy, without, 57
Rome Convention, 32
  see Rome Convention
secure order form, 25
spam, 313
  see also spam
statute, 20
terms
express, 29
generally, 28
implied, 31
unjustified enrichment, 70
validity, 32

virtual, 19
Contract (*cont.*):
    writing, 19, 20
Copyright:
    analogue, 181, 189, 216
    archives, 207, 220
    audience requirement, 198
    authorisation, 199, 214
    authorship, 182, 188, 195
    Berne Convention, 183, 210, 211, 216, 222,
        225, 226
    browsing, 196
    bulletin boards, 186, 201
    cable, 191, 198, 199
    caching, 195, 202, 214, 220
    commercial use, 184, 185
    compensation, 220
    competition, 206, 217
    compilations, 190
    continental tradition, 183
    contract, 219
    copying, 181
    criticism, 206
    Dearing Report, 207
    downloading, 189, 203, 228, 229
    Draft Directive, Appendix 2
    duration, 189, 191
    e-commerce, 184
    education, 207, 205, 205, 207, 220, 221
    employment, 183
    encryption, 202, 205
        see also cryptography
    entrepreneurs, 183, 184
    Europe, 182, 190, 191, 196, 197
    facilities, 200
    fairness, 183, 204, 205–6, 217
    foreign, 236
    frames, 186
    functions, 182
    harmonisation of laws, 183, 213
    history, 182
    Human Rights Act, 222
    infringement, 194
        authorisation, 199
        broadcast, 199
        cable service, 199
        contributory, 200
        copying, 195
        international private law, 231, 236
        loan, 197
        performance, 198
        protection against, 202
        rental, 197
    intellectual creation, 191
    interactive sites, 192
    international private law, 181, 184, 236
        see also international private law
    ISPs, 199, 214

    legislation, 184, 189, 193, 194, 200, 201, 237
    lex situs, 240
    libraries, 207, 220
    licence, 202
    limitations of, 208
    links, 186, 192, 193, 202
    media works, 188
    movables, 240
    MP3, 187, 205, 208, 216
    music, 187
    ownership, 194, 195
    parallel, 244
    performance, 181, 197, 198
    personality rights, 182
    piracy, 216
    pornography, 208
        see also pornography
    pre-emption issues, 222
    printing, 203
    private use, 216
    public policy, 208
    publication, 181
    reform, 210
    relevance, 184
    reporting, 206, 221
    reproduction, 195, 202, 211, 213
    review, 206
    rights, 194, 202, 222
    search engines, 202
    secrecy, 208
    software, 196
    storage, 196
    subject matter, 188
    technology and, 182
    third parties, 302
    time-shifting, 208
    TRIPS, 183
        archives, 207,
        education, 207
        fair dealing, 204
        licence, 202
        public interest, 207
        public policy, 207, 240
        watermark, 202
        WIPO treaty, 211
        writing, 202
    see also intellectual property; trademarks;
        domain names
Crime:
    forgery:
        cryptography, 38, 50
            see also cryptography
        fraud, 57, 58, 319
            see also fraud
        hacking, 317
        offensive material, 276
            see also pornography
        pornography, 280

see also pornography
sedition, 276
spam, 313, 317, 319
theft, 63
    see also payment
Cryptography:
    applications, 41
    approval, 47
    cash, 64, 73
    confidentiality, 38
    controls, 52–53
    copyright, 202, 2–5
    definition, 39, 41
    description, 2118
    encryption, 41
    European Union, 52
    forgery, 38
    forms, 39–40
    asymmetric, 40
    private key, 39
    public key, 39
    symmetric, 39
    generally, 37, 38–42
    international dimension, 51, 53
    key escrow, 47,48
    law enforcement agency access, 49
    laws on, 43
    law reform, 44, 53
    legislation, 37, 51
    payment mechanisms, 63
        see also payment
    pornography, of, 287
        see also pornography
    privacy, 37
        see also privacy
    register, 47,48
    service providers, 38, 47, 48
    signature, 38
    spam, 311
    supranational controls
    voluntary approvals regime, 47
    Wassenaar agreement, 51
        see also crime; human rights; payment
Cyber porn, see pornography
Cyber squatting, 136, 143, 147, 149, 154, 158,
    165, 166
Cyphertext, see cryptography

Data Encryption Standard, 39
    see also cryptography
Data privacy, see privacy
Data protection, see privacy
Defamation:
    author, 165
    Brussels Convention, 256, 271
    bulletin boards, 266
    caching, 269
        see also copyright

choice of laws, 256, 259
commerce, 254
content liability, 249, 264
    see also content liability
damages, 257, 261
defences, 265
discussion fora, 253
domicile, 260
e-commerce, 271
editorial control, 263
email, 251
enforcement, 256, 260
first amendment rights, 249, 255
forum, law of, 257, 258
freedom of expression, 249, 254, 258, 267
generally, 8
immunity, 264
indemnity, 267, 268
innocent dissemination, 261, 262, 265, 271
intermediaries, 249
ISPs, 249, 261
judgements, 260
jurisdiction, 255, 256, 258
legislation, 264–5
libel, 249
links, 270
    see also copyright; trademarks
mailing lists, 252, 261
pornography, 261, 275
    see also pornography
public interest, 263
publication, 252, 261, 263, 265
republication, 261
reputation, 257, 258, 270
sites of, 251
telecommunications, 331
    see also telecommunications
USENET, 253, 261, 266
world wide web, 255
Delict:
    defamation, see defamation
    economic, 315
    generally, 47
    international private law, 228, 256
    jus quaesitum tertio, 49
    negligence, 49
    passing off, see trademarks
    pure economic loss, 315
    spam, 315
    trespass, 315
    see also tort
Digital Cash, see payment
Digital Signatures:
    admissibility, 44
    circumstances, 46
    certification authority, 46
    context, 46
    encryption, 41

Digital Signatures (*cont.*):
  European directive, 53
  evidence, 42, 45
  generally, 7
  jurisdiction, 45
  law, 42
  requirement, 42–3
  secrecy, 37
  statute, 6
  time and place, 47
  validity, 44
  see also cryptography
Discussion fora, *see* defamation
Dispute resolution, *see* domain names
DNS, *see* domain names
Domain Names:
  arbitration, 162
  bad faith, 160, 163, 165
  choice of laws, 151, 165, 166
    see also choice of laws
  confusion, 163
  consistency, 128
  cyber envy, 135, 138
  cyber squatting, 136, 143
  deception, as instruments of, 143
  definition, 134
  dilution, 148, 166
  disputes, 130, 131, 133, 135, 142, 159,
    160, 162, 165
  DNS, 125
  fairness, 128
  free speech, 150
  generally, 7
  goodwill, 128, 160, 163
  hijacking of, 133, 136, 149, 160
  ICANN, 157
  IAHC, 156
  in rem action, 177
  integrity of, 126, 128
  international private law, 225
    see also international private law
  ISPs, 131
    see also ISPs
  jurisdiction, 166
  levels, 125, 126, 134, 152, 156
  management, 4
  mechanisms, 125
  mediation, 130
  national initiatives, 165
  nominet, 127
  NSI, 148, 154
  parodies, 151
  passing off, 131, 135
  payment, 127, 129
  personal names, 152
  privacy, 129
  property, action against, 166
  protection, 148

  protocol, 125
  publicity, 129
  regulation, 128, 129, 130, 150, 154, 156
  responsibility for, 128
  return of, 149
  sale of, 163
  surrender of, 129
  system of, 125
  top level, 126, 134, 152, 156
  trade, use in, 149
  trademarks and, 137, 148, 163
    see also trademarks
  transfer of, 129
  URLs, 125
  use, 150, 156

E-commerce:
  charge-back clauses, 59
  copyright, 184
  defamation, 268, 271
  DTI, 17
  European Directive, 6, 27, 268
  generally, 8–10, 15, Appendix 1
  Global Business Dialogue, 119
  Regulation, statutory, 5, 6
  payment, *see* payment
  pornography and, 278
  privacy, 104
    see also privacy
  sites, 88
  spam, 268, 324
    see also spam
  telecommunications, 336
  UNCITRAL model, 27
  value of, 17
Electronic payment, *see* payment
Electronic signatures, *see* digital signatures
Email:
  contract, 18
    see also contract
  defamation, 251
    see also defamation
  junk, 100
    see also spam
  privacy, 100
  services, 2
  trademarks, 178
    see also trademarks
Encryption, *see* cryptography
European Union:
  copyright, 182
    see also copyright
  cross-border transactions, 26
  cryptography, 52
  data protection, 82
  ECJ, 228
  e-commerce, 6, 27, 57
  fraud, 58

generally, 5–6
international private law, 228
payment, *see* payment
pornography, 278, 293, 297
privacy, 80n, 82, 84–90, 104, 107, 112
   see also privacy
spam, 311, 320
see also contract

Flaming, *see* libel
Forgery, *see* crime
Fraud:
   burden of, 75
   charge-back clauses, 59
   digital cash, 73–4
   forgery, 72
   international private law, 239, 240
   loss, 60, 61
   payment, 57, 58
   safeguards, 59
   trademarks, 179
      see also trademarks

Government:
   agencies, mistrust of, 97
   legislation, 5
      see also European Union

Hacking, 317
Hate speech, 276, 281, 296
   see also spam
Human Rights:
   privacy, 37
   see also privacy; cryptography

Insolvency:
   bank, 73
     lost, 73
     reclaiming, 73
   contract, originator, of, 72
Intellectual property:
   copyright, *see* copyright
   domain names, *see* domain names
      see also trademarks
   goodwill, 128
   limits, reasonable, 139
   passing off, 128, 131, 136
   privacy, 83
   rights, 83, 179, 242
   trademarks, *see* trademarks
      see also domain names
International Private Law
   admissibility, 231
   alternative fora, 228
   authorship, 243
   Berne Convention, 225, 226, 231, 253
      see also copyright
   Brussels Convention, 226, 227, 228

choice of law, 236, 256
choses in action, 239
competition, 240–1
conflict of laws, 241
contract, 27
copyright, 181, 227, 236
cryptography, 51
defamation, 252, 255, 256, 258
defender, multiple, 230
delict, 228
designs, 227
domain names, 225
   see also domain names
domicile, 226, 228, 235, 252, 256, 260
double actionability, 236, 259
ECJ, 228
EFTA, 232
European Community, 232
forum, 234, 235, 256, 257
forum non conveniens, 258
fraud, 239, 240
generally, 27
harmonisation of rules, 231
immovables, 238, 239, 241–2
infringement, 244
ISPs, 228
   see also ISPs
jurisdiction, 225, 227, 235, 236, 255, 256, 258
justiciability, 231, 232
language, 241
legislation, 226, 236, 238
lex fori, 259
lex loci delicti, 259
lex situs, 240
libel, 250
local actions, 236
Mareva injunctions, 242
movables, 238, 240, 242
ownership
   parallel, 244
patents, 227
policy, 240, 246
pornography, 290
   see also pornography
relocation, 228, 229, 245
rights, 237–8
rules, 233
Satellite Directive, 245
spam, 319
substantial connection, 234
territory, 241
tort, 228, 234
trademarks, 227, 235
TRIPS, 235, 244, 245
Wassenaar agreement, 51
see also choice of laws; jurisdiction; domicile
Internet:
   advertising, 1

Internet (*cont.*):
   see also webvertising
  communication tool, 18
  content liability, 247
   see also content liability
  cyber squatting, 136
  definition, 1–2
  education through, 1
  future, 11–13
  global nature, 135
  government, 3
  ISPs, 4
  infrastructure, physical, 7
  language of,
   generally, 12
   HTML, 12–13
   XML, 12–13
  law,
   interaction with, 7
   settled, 5
  liability
   internet relay chat, 2
  management, 4
  ownership, 3
  pornography, *see* pornography
  protocol, domain names, 125
  regulation, 340
   see also regulation
  services, 2, 7
  service providers, *see* ISPs
  structure, 7–11
  telecommunications, 333
   see also telecommunications
  trademarks, 135
   see also trademarks
ISPs:
  agent, 130
  codes of conduct, 301
  common carriers, 262, 279
  content control, 264, 331
  contract, 267, 269–70, 313
  copyright, 199, 214, 272
   see also copyright
  cryptography, 48
   see also cryptography
  defamation, 249, 261, 265, 267
  delict, 315
  domain names, 130
  domicile, 28
  editorial control, 263
  European Union, 293
  gatekeepers, 261, 263, 268, 293
  generally, 3–4
  immunity, 264
  innocent disseminators, 262
  intermediary, 268, 269, 293
  international private law, 228
   see also international private law

  jurisdiction of, 4
  liability, 8, 265, 269, 301
  libel, 250
  management, 4
  PICS, 300
  pornography, 279, 290, 293, 297, 301
  portal sites, 263
  relocation, 229
  self-regulation, 293
  spam, 310, 312, 313, 315, 326–7
   see also spam
  telecommunications, 341
  tort, 315

Junk email, *see* spam
Jurisdiction:
  choice of laws, 31–4
   see also choice of laws
  convergence, 82
  defamation, 258
  digital signatures, 45
  domain names, 166
  international private law, 236
  ISPs, 4
  pornography, 281, 290
   see also pornography
  privacy, 95
   see also privacy
  private enterprises, 81–2
  regulation, 82
  rules, 233
  spam, 319
  territorial, 281, 319
  see also international private law

Legislation:
  international co-operation, 6
  privacy, *see* privacy
  trends, 6
Libel:
  defamation, 249
  flaming, 254
  internet, issues, 250
  international private law, 250
  ISPs, 250
  see also defamation
Licence, *see* telecommunications

Marketplace:
  Europe, privacy, 85
  global, 96
  industry, 85
  internet, 5
   see also e-commerce
  privacy, 81
   see also privacy
  trade barriers, 86
Metatags, *see* trademarks

MP3:
  copyright, 187, 203, 208, 216

Network:
  definition, 2

Obscenity, *see* pornography
OECD, 6, 96
Ownership, *see* copyright

Passing off, *see* domain names; trademarks
Personal data, *see* privacy
Patents:
  international private law, 237
  legislation, 237
Payment:
  business-to-business, 56
  business-to-consumer, 57
  cash, digital,
    generally, 63–4, 71
    legal issues, 63, 65, 66
    mondex, 64
  consumer
  action against, 71
  confidence, 57
  position of, 70
  contract
    breach, 61
    claims under, 68–70
    misrepresentation, 61
  credit card, 58, 74–6
  debit card, 62–3, 74–6
  digital cash, 63–4, 65, 67, 69, 73, 74–6
  e-commerce, 56
  electronic, 55
  encryption, 58
    see also cryptography
  float, dissipation of, 72
  fraud, 57, 60, 72
  insolvency. *see* insolvency
  law, role of, 57
  legislation, 58–62, 66n
  loss, 60, 61
  mechanisms, 63
  merchandise, 56–7
  mondex, 64, 67, 69
  negotiable instrument, 74
  performance, 57, 60
  redemption, 69
  risks, 67
  smart cards, 64, 65
  see also contract
Photographs, *see* pornography
Piracy, *see* copyright
Police, 43
Pornography:
  authorship, 279
  availability, 287

cache, 285, 294
censorship, 278, 295, 299, 302
child
  protection of, 287, 294, 295, 299, 304–5,
    306–7
  subject of, 282, 283, 295, 296
commercial sites, 288
common law, 285
content, 286
control, 275, 279, 280
copyright, 208
cyber-
  libertarians, 277
  paternalists, 277
  solicitation, 283
definitions, 282
downloading, 285, 291
e-commerce, 278
encryption, 287
  see also cryptography
enforcement, 276, 278, 290, 304
environment, internet, in, 286
ECHR, 307
European Action Plan, 303
European Union, 276, 289, 292, 293, 297
extradition, 292
filtering, 297, 304
first amendment, 307
forms, 279, 280
free speech, 276, 287, 304
generally 8
global phenomenon, 291
harm, 278, 303, 308
harmonisation of laws, 292
hate speech, 296, 309
  see also hate speech; spam
intermediary, role of, 282
international co-operation, 291, 292, 303
internet watch foundation, 295
ISPs, 279, 290, 293, 297, 302
jurisdiction, 290, 291
  see also jurisdiction
legislation, 281
literary merit, 282
national laws, 280, 283, 290, 299, 304
new media, laws of, 281
origins, 295
penalties, 278
PICS, 297, 300
photographs, 284, 285–6
possession, 282, 285
prevalence, 280
protectionism, 277
rating , 297, 304
regulation, 286, 297, 303
rights, 301
seizure, 292
sex tourism, 283

Pornography (*cont.*):
  software, 278
  storage, 291
  types, 279, 280
  whistle-blowing, 292
  women, interests of, 304
  see also defamation
Portal sites, *see* ISPs
Postal rule, *see* contract
Privacy:
  access and, 109, 112, 116
  agencies, industrial, 105
  approaches, clash of, 94–106, 119
  arts, 95
  choice, 109, 115, 118
  commerce, 83, 95, 120
  compliance, 98, 110, 116
  consent, 111
  costs, 98
  credit card companies, 98
  credit reports, 100
  data, 79, 82, 121
    integrity, 109, 116
    processing, 81
  dissemination, 116
  domain names, 129
  e-commerce, 104
  economic construct, 82–3
  ECHR, 89
  ECJ, 89
  email, 100
  enforcement, 105, 110, 117
  Europe, 80n, 82, 84–90, 104, 107, 112
  financial services, 116
  generally, 79
  governments, 83–4, 92, 93, 97, 102, 121
  human rights, 85, 120
  individual, 120
  information, 109
  international approaches, 119
  jurisdiction, 95
  legislation, 88, 89, 93, 95, 98, 102, 106
  market, 81
  media, 80, 95
  model, 82–3
  notice, 109, 115, 118
  OECD, 96, 110, 119
  onward transfer and, 109, 115
  personal data,
    access, 112
    availability, 87
    definition, 87
    generally 81,
    holding, 102
    individual, 120
    processing, 87, 102
    supervisory agencies, 88
    use, 121

  politics, 79, 106
  profit, 99
  quartenary, 90
  regimes, 109
  remedies, 95
  rights, 37, 83, 89, 91, 99, 107
  rules, substantive, 88
  sanctions, 116
  secrecy, 208
  security, 109, 116
  safe harbor proposals, 106, 108, 109, 115
  self-regulation, 102, 105, 106, 110–11, 117,
      119, 120–1
  sourcebook, 92
  spam, 323
    see also spam
  technical infractions, 118
  technical solutions, 108
  tertiary, 90
  third parties, 92, 93, 109
  Trans-Atlantic Consumer Dialogue, 113
  TRUSTe, 104–5, 119
  US approach, 90–4, 107, 108
  World Trade Organisation, 108
  see also cryptography

Racism, 276
Regulation:
  bandwidth, 336
  contract, 19
    see also contract
  digital cash, 72
  domain names, 128, 129, 150, 154, 156
    see also domain names
  equivalence, by, 20
  pornography, *see* pornography
  privacy, *see* privacy
  self:
    generally, 8
    pornography, 293, 297, 303
    privacy, 102, 105, 106, 110–11, 117
  spam, of, 310, 326
  statutory:
    e-commerce, 5
    equivalence, 20
  telecommunications, 331, 336, 340
    see also telecommunications
  trademarks, 135, 139
Rights:
  freedom of expression, 249
  First Amendment, 249
  immovables, 237, 238
  international private law, 238, 242
    see also international private law
  movables, 237, 238
  ownership, 194
    see also copyright
  pornography, 301

see also pornography
statute, 222
user, 202
   see also copyright
Rome Convention:
consumer protection, 34
contract, 32
   see also contract
telecommunications, 332, 339

Satellite Directive, *see* international private law
Safe harbor proposals, *see* privacy
Secrecy, 37, 208
   see also cryptography; privacy
Signatures, *see* digital signatures; cryptography
Spam:
advertising, 311, 325
combating, 313
complaints over, 310
consumer rights, 322
contract, 313
costs, 312
criminal law, 313, 317
cryptography, 311
   see also cryptography
damages, 314, 317
data protection, 323
definition, 8
delict, 315
distance selling, 322–3, 324
e-commerce, 324, 326
economic implications
European Union, 311, 320, 322, 324, 325, 326
exculpation of spammer, 322
features, 309
filtering, 311–12
first amendment, 320, 328
   see also pornography
future, 326
hacking, 317
intention, 318
international law, 319
ISPs, 310, 312, 326–7
labeling, 325
legislation, 310, 320, 327
liability, 313
opt-in regime, 323, 324
opt-out regime, 323
penalties, 314
personal data, 321
privacy, invasion of, 311
regulation, 310, 313, 324, 326, 328, 329
remedies
   civil law, *see* delict, tort
   consumer, 319
   criminal law, *see* crime
   generally, 311
   privacy, 320

targets, 311
tort, 315
trademarks, 178, 316
   see also trademarks
ulterior intent, 317

Technology:
copyright, 202, 217
pornography and, 278
privacy, 108
Telecommunications:
bandwidth access, 336
competition, 333
content liability, 331, 341
defamation, 331
e-commerce, 336
infrastructure, 335
interconnection charges, 334
internet, 331, 333
ISPs, 331, 333, 341
licence, 38, 332, 339
links, 331
number translation, 334
OFTEL, 332, 334, 337
regulation, 331, 332, 333, 336, 340, 341
Rome Convention, 332, 339
   see also Rome Convention
voice telephony, 341
Tort:
defamation, *see* defamation
economic, 316
effects doctrine, 234
generally, 49
international private law, 228, 233
negligence, 49
passing off, *see* trademarks
pure economic loss, 315
spam, 315
trespass, 315
   see also delict
Trade, *see* e-commerce; market; payment
Trademarks:
advertisements, 179
   see also webvertising
confusion, 140, 146, 165, 172, 174, 176, 180
copyright, 173, 179
   see also copyright
counterfeiting, 176
cyber squatters, 143
defenses, 149
definition, 135
dilution, 137, 143, 145, 148, 151, 165, 172,
   176
disputes, 133, 135, 142, 171
distinctiveness, 142, 147
detriment, 147
domain names, 137, 163
   see also domain names

Trademarks (*cont.*):
  ECJ, 141–2
  email, 178
  European Directive, 152
  famous, 144, 159, 172
  fraud, 179
  generally, 7
  generic use, 173
  guidelines, 145, 147
  identity, 139, 140,
    goods, 152
    services, 152
  infringement, 137, 138, 140, 143, 146, 172,
    316
  international private law, 235
  legislation, 130, 138, 237
  links, 173
  logos, 139
  metatags, 174
  Paris Convention, 144, 145
  passing off, 136, 143, 147
  personal names, 153
  Playboy litigation, 156
  registration, 171
  regulation, 135, 136, 139
  reputation, 141, 142, 144, 145, 180
  sale, 179
  search engines, 179
  spam, 316
    see also spam
  special protection, 134
  terrestrial law, 171
  territoriality, 135
  unfair competition, 175

URLs, 173
watermark, 171, 177
website, within, 171
see also domain names
Transactions:
  international nature, 9–11
  virtual, 10
  see also e-commerce
TRUSTe, *see* privacy

United Nations, 6
Unjustified enrichment, *see* contract
Unfair competition, *see* trademarks
USENET, *see* defamation

Watermark, *see* trademarks; copyright
Web:
  definition, 2–3
  defamation, 255
  sites:
    permanent establishment, 6
    trademark in, 171
      see also trademarks
  size, 255
WIPO, *see* copyright
Writing:
  copyright, 202
    see also copyright
  requirement, 7, 19–20, 43, 46
  statute, 43, 46–7
    see also contract; digital signatures
Webvertising:
  generally, 21–2, 30, 34, 100, 179
  spam, 311